EUGENE ULRICH, Ph.D. (Harvard 1975) is O'Brien Professor emeritus of Hebrew Scriptures at the University of Notre Dame and Chief Editor of the Biblical Scrolls. Editor of six volumes of scrolls in the official series *Discoveries in the Judaean Desert*, he published *The Biblical Qumran Scrolls* in 2010.

The Dead Sea Scrolls and the Developmental Composition of the Bible

Supplements
to
Vetus Testamentum

The Text of the Bible at Qumran

VOLUME 169

The titles published in this series are listed at *brill.com/vts*

The Dead Sea Scrolls and the Developmental Composition of the Bible

By

Eugene Ulrich

BRILL

LEIDEN • BOSTON
2015

Library of Congress Control Number: 2015937222

ISSN 0083-5889
ISBN 978-90-04-27038-1 (hardback)
ISBN 978-90-04-29603-9 (e-book)

This book is printed on acid-free paper.

MIX
Paper from responsible sources
FSC
www.fsc.org
FSC® C004472

PRINTED BY DRUKKERIJ WILCO B.V. - AMERSFOORT, THE NETHERLANDS

Dedicated to mentors and friends
who showed me the path

Frank Moore Cross

Patrick W. Skehan

Joseph A. Fitzmyer, S.J.

Shemaryahu Talmon

My Qumran Friends and Colleagues

and to

The University of Notre Dame

The National Endowment for the Humanities

CONTENTS

Preface xi
Acknowledgements xiii
Abbreviations and Sigla xv
Bibliographical Abbreviations xix

Introduction
Chapter 1. The Developmental Composition of the Biblical Text 1
Chapter 2. Post-Qumran Thinking: A Paradigm Shift 15

The Scriptures Found at Qumran
Chapter 3. The Developmental Growth of the Pentateuch in the Second Temple Period 29
Chapter 4. Joshua's First Altar in the Promised Land 47
Chapter 5. A Shorter Text of Judges and a Longer Text of Kings 67
Chapter 6. The Samuel Scrolls 73
Chapter 7. The Great Isaiah Scroll: Light on Additions in the MT 109
Chapter 8. 1QIsaiah^{b} and the Masoretic Family 131
Chapter 9. Additions and Editions in Jeremiah 141
Chapter 10. The Septuagint Scrolls 151

Learnings from the Scrolls
Chapter 11. The Absence of "Sectarian Variants" in the Jewish Scriptural Scrolls Found at Qumran 169
Chapter 12. "Nonbiblical" Scrolls Now Recognized as Scriptural 187
Chapter 13. "Pre-Scripture," Scripture (Rewritten), and "Rewritten Scripture": The Borders of Scripture 201
Chapter 14. Rising Recognition of the Samaritan Pentateuch 215
Chapter 15. Insights into the Septuagint 229
Chapter 16. The Masada Scrolls 251

The Road Toward Canon: From Collection of Scrolls to Canon
Chapter 17. The Notion and Definition of Canon 265
Chapter 18. From Literature to Scripture: Reflections on the Growth of a Text's Authoritativeness 281
Chapter 19. The Scriptures at Qumran and the Road toward Canon 299

Conclusion 309

Acknowledgements and Permissions 317
Statistical Table of Scriptural Scrolls from the Judaean Desert 321
Index of Ancient Sources 323
Index of Authors 339
Index of Subjects 345

We must ask to what measure does the evident equanimity with which Qumran scribes viewed varying, even conflicting wordings, throw light on their very attitude towards the Bible qua Bible. What is needed is an investigation of what the Qumran finds can contribute to a clarification of the progressive evolution of what was to become the 'Hebrew Bible canon'; in other words, a clarification of the question 'How did the Bible grow?'

– SHEMARYAHU TALMON

[11QPs-a] termed a 'Psalms Scroll' may . . . turn out to be the beginning of a new stage. . . . a reformulation of existing theories. . . . [It] may be a representative of a different collection of psalms which was regarded as 'canonical' by some group somewhere at some time. In that case we are offered a unique opportunity to cast a glance into the workshop in which Biblical literature, as we know it, grew into a 'canon,' and the term 'Psalms Scroll' is appropriate. . . . At least typologically we are then carried back to a stage in the growth of the canon that we would have never dreamt of reaching.

– MOSHE GOSHEN-GOTTSTEIN

PREFACE

THIS VOLUME, a sequel to *The Biblical Qumran Scrolls*, has a single predominant purpose: to present an overview with my understanding of what the scriptural scrolls discovered at Qumran have taught us. Its aim is to paint for scholars, students, and the educated public the comprehensive picture that I have gradually gained over the past four decades of specific ways that major parts of the Hebrew Bible developed. The earlier volume, *The Biblical Qumran Scrolls*, presented the evidence—the transcriptions and textual variants of all the Hebrew biblical manuscripts from Qumran—and the present volume offers a synthesized view of the implications and significance of that evidence.

The Bible has not changed, but our knowledge of it certainly has changed, thanks to the Dead Sea Scrolls. These manuscripts, older by a millennium than our previous Hebrew manuscripts, have opened a window and shed light on a period in the history of the formation of the Hebrew Bible that had languished in darkness for two thousand years. Dating from the time that the Jerusalem Temple stood, they are our oldest, most authentic witnesses to the Scriptures in antiquity and are the types of texts that Hillel and Jesus would have known.

The scrolls offer a parade of surprises that greatly enhance our knowledge of how the sacred texts came to be. They provide sources that enable us to read and interpret more accurately the biblical text as it is found in the multiple witnesses that have survived over the past two millennia. In turn, what the scrolls teach us will serve as a basis for mining the treasures of the Samaritan Pentateuch and especially the Old Greek and Old Latin versions.

My view of the scrolls has been shaped by editing many of the scriptural scrolls and by working closely with the other editors of the scriptural scrolls. The secondary literature on the scrolls is vast and constantly expanding. Since I am offering a broad view and treating the larger scope of the Law and the Prophets, not just a single book or passage, it is not possible to address others' views of individual passages here. Where alternate possible interpretations are suggested, often the full contextual overview provides a helpful guide to better understanding.

I have no illusions that the views offered here will be the last word. Scholarship advances through the insights of one generation being made yet more accurate by the next. This volume will have accomplished its purpose if it provides a foundation for the next generation to build upon and envision the scriptural text more accurately.

EUGENE ULRICH
Chief Editor, Qumran Biblical Scrolls

University of Notre Dame
June 2014

ACKNOWLEDGEMENTS

I am indebted to many teachers, scholars, friends, students, and organizations that made this volume possible. For the education that prepared me for this study of the biblical scrolls I thank the rigorous *ratio studiorum* of the Jesuits, Harvard's Department of Near Eastern Languages and Civilizations, and specifically my mentors, Frank Moore Cross, Joseph Fitzmyer, S.J., Patrick W. Skehan, and Shemaryahu Talmon.

I am forever grateful to both Patrick Skehan and Frank Cross for entrusting me with the completion and publication of the Cave 4 biblical manuscripts assigned to them. Subsequently I thank the Associate Editors Cross and I enlisted to publish specific sets of scrolls — Sidnie White Crawford, James Davila, Julie Duncan, Peter Flint, Russel Fuller, Nathan Jastram, Sarianna Metso, Catherine Murphy, Curt Niccum, Donald Parry, Richard Saley, Judith Sanderson, Emanuel Tov, and Julio Trebolle Barrera. Their speed combined with accuracy in expeditious publication helped make the scrolls publication project move from "the academic scandal *par excellence*" (Geza Vermes) to a publication blitz that kept the Clarendon Press at Oxford very busy.

Notre Dame graduates and Ph.D. students, especially Kristin Palacios, Brandon Bruning, and Justus Ghormley, have earned my gratitude for proofreading these chapters, removing numerous errors as well as the more obscure and the less precise forms of earlier drafts. I, of course, remain responsible for the deficiencies that remain. Kristin especially deserves great thanks for undertaking the drudgery of compiling the indices.

It has been a continuing pleasure to know and work with Suzanne Mekking, Liesbeth Hugenholtz, and Mattie Kuiper, the highly competent and encouraging editors at Brill. They and series editor Christl Maier graciously allowed me the exception of preparing and publishing this volume in camera-ready form. I am grateful as well to the publishers listed in the appendices for allowing me to publish revised forms of some previous articles.

The National Endowment for the Humanities offered a fellowship yet again, and the University of Notre Dame provided a generous final research leave, providing the concentrated time necessary to start and complete this volume. I am enduringly grateful to both for their support. The work was also made possible in part by support from the Institute for Scholarship in the Liberal Arts, College of Arts and Letters, University of Notre Dame.

ABBREVIATIONS AND SIGLA

1QIsa^{a}	Cave 1 at Qumran, manuscript of Isaiah, the first (^{a}) in the series
4QpaleoExod^{m}	Cave 4 at Qumran, a Palaeo-Hebrew manuscript of Exodus, the twelfth in the series
7QpapLXXExod	Cave 7 at Qumran, papyrus Septuagint manuscript of Exodus
א א̇ א̊	certain letter, probable letter, possible letter
[ ]	missing letters, space between fragments, or surface of manuscript missing
{ }	in the text, indicates letters or words erased; in a reconstruction, indicates letters or words which the editor thinks should not be included
vacat	interval for paragraph division; the writing space is intentionally blank
ס	*setuma*, a closed section in MT or *BHS*; used to denote a new section of text beginning on the same line
פ	*petuḥa*, an open section in MT or *BHS*; used to denote a new section of text beginning on the line below the end of the previous section
+	additional word(s)
>	word(s) lacking
*	original or reconstructed form
2m, 3m	second, third scribal hand
corr	corrected reading
→	develops to; is followed dirctly by
∩	loss of text through homoiarchton or homoioteleuton
1°, 2°	first, second occurrence of a form
II 4–5	the second column of the manuscript, lines 4–5
frg. 10 ii 4–5	fragment 10, column 2 (where frg. 10 preserves two columns), lines 4–5
2:23^{init}, 2:23^{fin}	at the beginning, or end, of v 23
10:2a, 10:2b	first part, second part of verse 2 in chapter 10
10:2^{b}	additional part of a verse, usually in the Samaritan text, as numbered by von Gall
2:23[24]	differing verse numbering; the number in brackets is usually the Greek verse number

MT, $\mathfrak{m}$	the Masoretic Text (as in *BHS*)
MT^{A}, $\mathfrak{m}^{A}$	The Aleppo Codex
MT^{L}, $\mathfrak{m}^{L}$	Leningrad Codex, now St. Petersburg Codex
MT^{ed}, $\mathfrak{m}^{ed}$	the edition of the Masoretic Text (as in *BHS*)
MT^{Cairo}, $\mathfrak{m}^{\mathfrak{C}}$, $\mathfrak{C}$	fragments from the Cairo Geniza (cited from *BHS*)
MT$^{ms(s)}$, $\mathfrak{m}^{ms(s)}$	Masoretic manuscript(s)
MT^{q}, $\mathfrak{m}^{q}$	*qere* for the Masoretic Text, as opposed to the consonantal text of MT^{L} (= *ketiv*)
SP	the Samaritan Pentateuch, usually the von Gall edition

OG, 𝔊	the Old Greek (as in the text of the Göttingen editions, where possible)
OG*, 𝔊*	the original or reconstructed reading of the Old Greek
OG_2, $𝔊_2$	form(s) of the Old Greek with minor changes during the course of transmission
OG^{ed}, $𝔊^{ed}$	the reading in the Göttingen edition in contrast to an alternate reading considered to be the original Old Greek reading
OG^{ap}, $𝔊^{ap}$	a reading in the critical apparatus
LXX	The Septuagint
LXX^{Bmg}, $𝔊^{Bmg}$	a marginal reading in Codex Vaticanus
$LXX^{B\,93}$, $𝔊^{B\,93}$	Codex Vaticanus and manuscript 93
LXX^{A+}, $𝔊^{A+}$	Codex Alexandrinus and other manuscripts
LXX^{omn}, $𝔊^{omn}$	all Greek manuscripts
LXX^{L}, $𝔊^{L}$, *L*′	the Lucianic text
LXX^{O}, $𝔊^{O}$, *O*′	Origen's hexaplaric recension
LXX^{R}, $𝔊^{R}$	a Greek recensional text
OH	an Old Hebrew text
OL, La, 𝔏	an Old Latin text
Vulg, 𝔙	the Vulgate, ed. Monachi Sancti Benedicti
α′ σ′ θ′ ο′ π′	attestations to Aquila, Symmachus, Theodotion, the Seventy (ο′ = 70), all (πάντες)
εβρ′	the Hebrew text of Origen (in Greek transliteration)
Syh	the Syrohexapla

add	addition
ante	before
Ch.	chapter in this book
dbl	doublet
diff div	different division of text
ditt	dittography
err	error
euph	euphemism
gls	gloss
hab	the witness has the reading
hapl	haplography
homoi	homoiarchton or homoioteleuton
insrt	insertion
litt	*littera(e)*, letter(s)
metath	metathesis, inversion of letters
n.	note, usually in *BHS* apparatus
n, *n+1*, *n+2*	last edition prior to extant MSS, first extant edition of a book, second extant edition
olim	formerly
om totum comma	the entire verse is omitted

passim	occasionally throughout
pr	*praemittit*, *-unt*, placed before
rell	*reliqui*, the rest of the manuscripts
sfx	suffix
tr	*transpone(ndum) -it*, *-unt*, the letters or words are (to be) transposed
tt	translation technique
v(v)	verse(s)
vid	*ut videtur*, as it appears from the evidence available
vs.	versus

ABD	*Anchor Bible Dictionary*
BAR	*Biblical Archaeological Review*
BETL	Bibliotheca ephemeridum theologicarum lovaniensium
BIOSCS	*Bulletin of the Organization for Septuagint and Cognate Studies*
BQS	*The Biblical Qumran Scrolls*
FIOTL	Formation and Interpretation of Old Testament Literature
FRLANT	Forschungen zur Religion und Literatur des Alten und Neuen Testaments
HALOT	*The Hebrew and Aramaic Lexicon of the Old Testament*
JSCS	*Journal of Septuagint and Cognate Studies*
JSJS	Supplements to *Journal for the Study of Judaism*
LSJ	Liddell–Scott–Jones, *A Greek-English Lexicon*
NABRE	*The New American Bible: Revised Edition*
NIDB	*The New Interpreter's Dictionary of the Bible*
QTSJ	*The Qumran Text of Samuel and Josephus*
SBLEJL	SBL Early Judaism and Its Literature
SBLRBS	Resources for Biblical Study
STDJ	Studies on the Texts of the Desert of Judah
VTSup	Supplements to *Vetus Testamentum*

BIBLIOGRAPHICAL ABBREVIATIONS

DJD I: Discoveries in the Judaean Desert. Oxford: Clarendon Press.
Dominique Barthélemy and Jozef T. Milik. *Qumrân Cave 1*. 1955.

DJD II, IIa
Pierre Benoit, Jozef T. Milik, and Roland de Vaux. *Les grottes de Murabbaʿat*. 1961.

DJD III, IIIa
Maurice Baillet, Jozef T. Milik, and Roland de Vaux, *Les 'petites grottes' de Qumrân*. 1962.

DJD IV
James A. Sanders, *The Psalms Scroll of Qumrân Cave 11 (11QPs^a)*. 1965.

DJD V
John M. Allegro with Arnold A. Anderson, *Qumrân Cave 4.I (4Q158–4Q186)*. 1968.

DJD VIII
Emanuel Tov with the collaboration of Robert A. Kraft, *The Greek Minor Prophets Scroll from Naḥal Ḥever (8ḤevXIIgr) (The Seiyal Collection I)*. 1990, repr. 1995.

DJD IX
Patrick W. Skehan, Eugene Ulrich, and Judith E. Sanderson, *Qumran Cave 4.IV: Palaeo-Hebrew and Greek Biblical Manuscripts*. 1992.

DJD XII
Eugene Ulrich, Frank Moore Cross, et al., *Qumran Cave 4.VII: Genesis to Numbers*. 1994, repr. 1999.

DJD XIII
Harold W. Attridge et al. in consultation with James VanderKam, *Qumran Cave 4.VIII: Parabiblical Texts, Part 1*. 1994.

DJD XIV
Eugene Ulrich, Frank M. Cross, et al., *Qumran Cave 4.IX: Deuteronomy, Joshua, Judges, Kings*. 1995, repr. 1999.

DJD XV
Eugene Ulrich et al., *Qumran Cave 4.X: The Prophets*. 1997.

DJD XVI
Eugene Ulrich et al., *Qumran Cave 4.XI: Psalms to Chronicles*. 2000.

DJD XVII
Frank Moore Cross, Donald W. Parry, Richard J. Saley, and Eugene Ulrich, *Qumran Cave 4.XII: 1–2 Samuel*. 2005.

DJD XXIII
Florentino García Martínez, Eibert J. C. Tigchelaar, and Adam S. van der Woude, *Qumran Cave 11.II: 11Q2–18, 11Q20–30*. 1998.

DJD XXXII
Eugene Ulrich and Peter W. Flint, *Qumran Cave 1.II: The Isaiah Scrolls*. Parts 1 and 2. 2010.

After Qumran

Hans Ausloos, Bénédicte Lemmelijn, and Julio Trebolle Barrera, eds. *After Qumran: Old and Modern Editions of the Biblical Texts — The Historical Books*. Bibliotheca ephemeridum theologicarum lovaniensium 246; Leuven: Peeters, 2012.

ANET

James B. Pritchard, ed. *Ancient Near Eastern Texts Relating to the Old Testament*. 3d ed. Princeton: Princeton University Press, 1969.

The Bible as Book

Edward D. Herbert and Emanuel Tov, eds. *The Bible as Book: The Hebrew Bible and the Judaean Desert Discoveries*. London: The British Library and Oak Knoll Press, 2002.

The Biblical Canons

Jean-Marie Auwers and H. J. de Jonge, eds. *The Biblical Canons*. Colloquium Biblicum Lovaniense; Bibliotheca ephemeridum theologicarum lovaniensium 163. Leuven: Leuven University Press and Peeters, 2002.

The Biblical Qumran Scrolls [BQS]

Eugene Ulrich, ed. *The Biblical Qumran Scrolls: Transcriptions and Textual Variants*. Supplements to Vetus Testamentum 134. Leiden: Brill, 2010.

Bruning, "The Making of the Mishkan"

Brandon Bruning. "The Making of the Mishkan", (Ph.D. dissertation; University of Notre Dame, 2014.

The Canon Debate

Lee M. McDonald and James A. Sanders, eds. *The Canon Debate*. Peabody, Mass.: Hendrickson, 2002.

The Dead Sea Scrolls after Fifty Years

Peter W. Flint and James C. VanderKam, eds. *The Dead Sea Scrolls after Fifty Years: A Comprehensive Assessment*. 2 vols. Leiden: Brill, 1998, 1999.

The Dead Sea Scrolls Bible

Martin Abegg Jr., Peter Flint, and Eugene Ulrich. *The Dead Sea Scrolls Bible: The Oldest Known Bible Translated for the First Time into English*. San Francisco: HarperSanFrancisco, 1999.

Eerdmans Dictionary of Early Judaism

John J. Collins and Daniel C. Harlow, eds. *The Eerdmans Dictionary of Early Judaism*. Grand Rapids, Mich.: Eerdmans, 2010.

Encyclopedia of the Dead Sea Scrolls

Lawrence H. Schiffman and James C. VanderKam, eds. *The Encyclopedia of the Dead Sea Scrolls*. 2 vols. New York: Oxford University Press, 2000.

Fernández, *The Septuagint in Context*

Natalio Fernández Marcos. *The Septuagint in Context: Introduction to the Greek Versions of the Bible*. Translated by W. G. E. Watson. Leiden: Brill, 2000.

Harl, Dorival, and Munnich, *La Bible grecque des Septante*

Marguerite Harl, Gilles Dorival, and Olivier Munnich. *La Bible grecque des Septante: Du judaïsme hellénistique au christianisme ancien*. Paris: Cerf and C.N.R.S., 1988.

Qumran and the History

Frank Moore Cross and Shemaryahu Talmon, eds. *Qumran and the History of the Biblical Text*. Cambridge, Mass.: Harvard University Press, 1975.

Rediscovering the Scrolls

Maxine Grossman, ed. *Rediscovering the Dead Sea Scrolls: An Assessment of Old and New Approaches and Methods.* Grand Rapids, Mich.: Eerdmans, 2010.

Sanders, *Sacred Story*

James A. Sanders. *From Sacred Story to Sacred Text.* Philadelphia: Fortress, 1987.

Sanderson, *An Exodus Scroll*

Judith E. Sanderson. *An Exodus Scroll from Qumran: 4QpaleoExod ^{m} and the Samaritan Tradition.* Harvard Semitic Studies 30. Atlanta: Scholars Press, 1986.

Talmon, *Text and Canon*

Shemaryahu Talmon. *Text and Canon of the Hebrew Bible: Collected Studies.* Winona Lake, Ind.: Eisenbrauns, 2010.

van der Toorn, *Scribal Culture*

Karel van der Toorn. *Scribal Culture and the Making of the Hebrew Bible.* Cambridge, Mass.: Harvard University Press, 2007.

Tov, *The Greek and Hebrew Bible*

Emanuel Tov. *The Greek and Hebrew Bible: Collected Essays on the Septuagint.* Leiden: Brill, 1999.

Tov, *Hebrew Bible, Greek Bible, and Qumran*

Emanuel Tov. *Hebrew Bible, Greek Bible, and Qumran: Collected Essays.* Tübingen: Mohr Siebeck, 2008.

Tov, *Scribal Practices*

Emanuel Tov. *Scribal Practices and Approaches Reflected in the Texts Found in the Judean Desert.* STDJ 54; Leiden: Brill, 2004.

Tov, *Textual Criticism*

Emanuel Tov. *Textual Criticism of the Hebrew Bible.* 3d ed. Minneapolis: Fortress, 2012 (*Textual Criticism*, 2d ed., 2001).

Trebolle, *The Jewish Bible*

Julio Trebolle Barrera. *The Jewish Bible and the Christian Bible: An Introduction to the History of the Bible.* Leiden: Brill; Grand Rapids, Mich.: Eerdmans, 1998.

Ulrich, *The Qumran Text of Samuel [QTSJ]*

Eugene Ulrich. *The Qumran Text of Samuel and Josephus.* Harvard Semitic Monographs 19. Missoula, Mont.: Scholars Press, 1978.

Ulrich, *Scrolls and Origins*

Eugene Ulrich. *The Dead Sea Scrolls and the Origins of the Bible.* Grand Rapids, Mich.: Eerdmans; Leiden: Brill, 1999.

VanderKam, *Scrolls and the Bible*

James C. VanderKam. *The Dead Sea Scrolls and the Bible.* Grand Rapids, Mich.: Eerdmans, 2012.

VanderKam and Flint, *The Meaning of the Scrolls*

James C. VanderKam and Peter W. Flint. *The Meaning of the Dead Sea Scrolls: Their Significance for Understanding the Bible, Judaism, Jesus, and Christianity.* San Francisco: HarperSanFrancisco, 2002.

INTRODUCTION

CHAPTER 1

THE DEVELOPMENTAL COMPOSITION OF THE BIBLICAL TEXT

THE HEBREW BIBLE—Tanakh in Jewish tradition, the Old Testament in Christian tradition—has been transmitted to us in a complex array of variant forms. Most people encounter the text in the form of a single book with a clear text, but that apparent simplicity is the result of numerous editorial or religious decisions which have made repeated selections from among the myriad variant forms. Behind that clarity is a long and fascinating history of growth from innumerable sources into unified books, as well as an intriguing political-social-religious history of the selection process that determined which books were eventually to be included and which to be excluded.

There is no single existing text that exhibits what we seek. The text of the Hebrew Bible is an abstract entity: the ideal pure text to which our combined extant manuscripts witness. This chapter, building on the cumulative results of centuries of intense international and interconfessional biblical scholarship, anticipates the evidence presented in subsequent chapters. It will offer the reader a general map of the territory, a brief overview, sketching the main paths by which the text has been transmitted, from its earliest beginnings to the forms in which we encounter it.

The history of scholarship shows a classic contrast between theories proposing a single *Urtext* (the "original" form of the text) which spread to multiple forms, and theories proposing early texts already showing pluriformity which were eventually supplanted by a single standardized text. In order to achieve perspective on these views, to appreciate why scholars propose such contrasting explanations of the evidence, and to adjudicate this classic contrast, it is important to explore the full range of the origins and transmission of the text from its earliest visibility to its current forms.

THE FORMATION AND NATURE OF THE TEXT

The Hebrew Bible is an anthology of ancient Israel's faith literature. Thus, any description of its text and transmission must include the complexity occasioned by the diverse compositions and genres which constitute that anthology in its final form. Each of those diverse compositions, while giving the appearance of homogeneity in its final, collected form as the Bible, has its own trajectory of development from its origins to its final form. Since many of the books are themselves composite works, the origins of each become yet more difficult to sketch. In short, the seemingly unified Hebrew Bible, as its origins and composition are explored, appears more diverse the further back one goes. The text during its early centuries was not a single static object but a pluriform and organically developing entity. At least three factors help to explain this.

One of the principal reasons is the adaptability of the subject matter. It is partly because certain ancient texts, meaningful in their original context, could also be experienced as meaningful by new generations in new contexts that they were preserved, handed on, and eventually recognized as Sacred Scripture. Often, the wording of those older traditions was adapted to apply more specifically to the new context, thus creating variant forms of the text.

A second reason for the variation is that the Scriptures for the most part originated and developed as traditional literature in a largely oral culture and thus were community-created. That is, each book is the product not of a single author, such as Plato or Shakespeare, but of multiple, anonymous bards, sages, religious leaders, compilers, or tradents. Unlike much classical and modern literature, produced by a single, named individual at a single point in time, the biblical books are constituted by earlier traditions being repeated, augmented, and reshaped by later authors, editors, or tradents, over the course of many centuries. Thus the text of each of the books is organic and developmental, a composition-by-multiple-stages, sometimes described as a rolling corpus.

Thirdly, the path that stretches from the original "authors" to our earliest preserved manuscript evidence often spans several centuries and is tortuous indeed. Over and over, oral tradents and scribal copyists did their best to hand on the text as accurately as possible, but each was fallible and some were creative; so it is difficult to find any single text that does not have in it unintentional errors and synonymous variants, as well as intentional expansions and clarifications. Each of these factors complicates in its own way the search for "the original text."

An earlier view, still held by some today, saw a dichotomy between two virtually discrete periods: the period of the composition or formation of the text, which eventually became fixed, and the period of transmission, which attempted to hand down as faithfully as possible that fixed text. But the evidence from Qumran indicates that the two processes of textual formation and textual transmission repeatedly overlapped for extensive periods of time. Thus, the two must be studied together.

Oral Beginnings

Large parts of what end up as passages in the written books began as small oral units. Certain legal pronouncements, cultic prayers, or wisdom sayings, for example, secured an enduring existence by becoming part of a law code, a liturgy, or a collection of proverbs. Individual hymns, love songs, or dirges were transmitted across generations and immortalized in the Psalter, the Song of Songs, or narratives involving death. Myths, legends, and tales that taught and entertained successive generations became incorporated into the large narrative strands that constitute many of the biblical books.

Israelite culture, like most ancient cultures, was primarily an oral culture. Even when extended narratives, law codes, prophetic traditions, or wisdom collections were written down, they were nonetheless primarily recited and transmitted orally. Although oral transmission can preserve texts with great accuracy, it is quite likely that certain variations of synonymous words and phrases, as well as expansions by inclusion of related materials, characterized the handing down of the texts through the centuries.

Again, these oral units would normally have been recited and transmitted accurately, but they would also sometimes be logically adapted to the larger context or framework into which they were being placed. This process of incorporation into larger frameworks could happen several times. For example, an initial anonymous saying from antiquity could secondarily be attributed to Abraham in a certain story, then be included in a form of the larger pre-monarchic national epic, which would finally be incorporated into the major Pentateuchal strand which we now read in Genesis. So the search for "the original text" is blurred from the start, since any of the stages above could qualify as "the original."

Biblical scholars since the Enlightenment, in analyzing book after book, had identified both ancient oral and written sources which biblical authors employed, as well as later redactional layers through which the biblical authors organized those sources and finalized the editions of the texts as we receive them. Well-known examples of such hypotheses would be the J, E, D, and P sources of the Pentateuch; First-, Second-, and Third-Isaiah; and the Deuteronomistic History. The analytical work of those scholars was hypothetical, without manuscript evidence since there was none available; it was based on analysis of literary and historical clues embedded in the texts. Now the witness of the scriptural manuscripts from Qumran provides documentary evidence for that process of compositional development during its last phases and validates in general the theories of organic composition-by-stages of most biblical books in their early, formative phases.

Foreign Literature

One of the features that gives the Bible such broad appeal is its ability to speak across cultures, and one reason for that is that Israel drew on the rich religious and literary treasury of older, more established cultures among which it came to be and continued to live. Themes from universally appealing narratives, such as creation and flood stories, were derived from Mesopotamia. Elements of religious, lyrical, and wisdom traditions from Egypt, the major empire which controlled the Canaanite area at the time of Israel's origins, influenced various types of Israelite literature. Egypt's hymns to the Sun god are reflected in Psalm 104 and its *wasfs* in the love poetry of the Song of Songs.

Within the land itself, Canaan's worship of the fertility and storm god Baal provided a basis for Psalm 29. Israel mirrored certain Canaanite concepts, motifs, terminology, and divine titles, such as "Creator of Earth," "God Almighty," "God Most High," and "Eternal God" (see *ANET*, 654, as well as the blessing of Abraham by the Canaanite priest Melchizedek in Gen 14:19, 22). Some of the patriarchal stories probably have origins in the traditions of the Aramaeans or Canaanites, from which cultures some of Israel's ancestors emerged.

Additional wisdom traditions from neighboring peoples such as the Ahikar proverbs, the Sumerian "innocent sufferer," and a drama exploring suffering and the divine-human interrelationship probably influenced Proverbs and Job (*ANET*, 427–30; 589–604). While Israel drew liberally from the literary richness of its predecessors and neighbors, it adapted those sources to fit its cultural character and religious beliefs. In addition to the original Israelite adaptations, further theological changes may well have taken place as such foreign materials were assimilated into a monotheistic text, creating several variant forms of the texts, each of which could be considered "original," depending upon one's perspective.

Small Collections

As time passed, the various oral and perhaps written traditions of Israel were increasingly gathered into small collections, especially as the result of the transition to monarchy. Just as the formation of the Roman Empire occasioned the composition of Virgil's *Aeneid*, the formation of the Israelite monarchy very likely occasioned a collection of narrative themes, such as the promise of the land, the bondage in Egypt, the wilderness stories, and the gaining of the land. Further cycles of war stories, of hero stories such as the "Saviors" cycle in Judges, and of prophetic stories such as the Elijah-Elisha cycle were collected. Similarly, legal and administrative sources, such as early law codes and the boundary and city lists in Joshua 13–21 were collected. Disciples of prophets preserved collections of sayings such as those of Amos, Isaiah, and others. Priests gathered traditions of liturgical hymns and sacrificial rituals, and sages collected wisdom materials. Each of these early traditions undoubtedly underwent some development when incorporated into larger contexts and frameworks. Double uses of certain units allow us to see some of the variants that could occur: the Yahwistic vs. Elohistic psalms, the oracle found in both Isaiah 2:2-4 and Micah 4:1-3, and the psalm in both Psalm 18 and 2 Samuel 22.

Early Forms of the Biblical Books: National Literature

The long-established ancient Near Eastern cultures in the midst of which Israel came into being had developed a variety of genres: legal materials, royal annals, treaties, hymns, prayers, letters, wisdom texts, and others. These genres in general and certain specific literary traditions and themes influenced Israel's developing literature.

Just as the cultures that preceded and surrounded Israel had developed rich and varied treasuries of oral and written literature, so too Israel gradually built its own collections. Of these works of national literature, many very likely ended in obscurity, while some were preserved, transmitted, and collected in the Hebrew Bible, the Apocrypha or Deuterocanonical books, the Pseudepigrapha, or the Qumran manuscripts.

These works, somewhat parallel to the Homeric poems and other literature, served to articulate the spirit of the culture, to educate and entertain the people, to express proper religious beliefs, and to probe religious themes such as the nature of God and humanity's proper stance toward the divine. Referring to these works as national literature does not imply that they did not serve as religious literature, since there was no strong division between the religious and the secular spheres. But just as theological and spiritual writings produced today are not regarded as "Scripture," it is likely that neither was much of Israel's literature at the time of its composition (see Ch. 18).

As an example, it is perhaps easy to see that originally the Song of Songs was, and was considered to be, (merely) literature: a collection of poems celebrating human love. Thus, before it became an allegory of God's love for Israel, it was quite likely susceptible to changes, embellishment, and insertion of additional poems. In fact, the Qumran scrolls display different arrangements of the poems. Through their literature, and especially their religious literature, Israel's religious leaders or creative tradents appear to have been seeking in varying degrees to understand the nature of the unseen God and producing literature that probed this mystery. Indeed, the fact that the Song was found at Qumran probably indicates that at least some Jews had already come to view it as an allegory of God's love for Israel.

As the liberated Judean exiles returned from Babylon to Jerusalem and its environs, they gradually rebuilt the temple, the walls, and the city. Religious leaders also assumed the responsibility for reconstituting the literary heritage from the monarchic culture as well as producing new religious works which attempted to help the people refocus their understanding of their relationship with God after the disaster of exile.

In the early part of the Second Temple period, narrative complexes that had been formed presumably during the monarchic period about the patriarchs, the escape from Egypt, the wilderness wandering, and the gaining of the land were gathered and compiled into an epic-scale story of national origins now seen in the narrative portions of Genesis, Exodus, Numbers, and Joshua. Eventually, the principal legal corpora in Exodus, Leviticus, and Numbers were combined with that narrative of national origins. In addition, the main Deuteronomistic History, usually viewed as composed in the late seventh century, was later re-edited due to the Babylonian destruction of Jerusalem and the loss of the land. Again, we should remember that the texts, even though probably written down, lived in oral form.

Earlier small collections of prophetic sayings and stories were gathered into larger books which continued to develop. The collections of "the words of Amos," for example, which were originally warnings to the northern kingdom, were expanded and re-edited by the Deuteronomistic school after the northern kingdom had fallen, to apply those warnings to Judah. Similarly, the wisdom literature also continued to develop as, for example, the prose Prologue-Epilogue of Job was combined with the poetic Dialogue.

This literature served a variety of purposes: the early narrative strands of the Pentateuch and the Deuteronomistic History served as a national epic and national history; Leviticus and Psalms were used for cultic purposes; Jubilees, the Deuteronomistic History, Proverbs, Job, Qohelet, and Ben Sira contributed to religious, moral, and practical education; the Song of Songs, Tobit, and Ruth were models for human love and loyalty; and Daniel and Esther provided models for courage in perilous times. The literature grew as community literature, and countless tradents and copyists contributed to its dynamic development from its earliest origins as sayings, reports, songs, etc., into books sufficiently well known and treasured to assure that they would be transmitted as important for successive generations. Just as the community formed the literature, so too the literature formed the community as it moved through history.

Early Forms of the Biblical Books: Authoritative Scripture

Of the many works produced, some came to be regarded as Sacred Scripture; that is, they were regarded as in some sense having God as author and guarantor. There was a gradual set of shifts in the various communities' understanding as these books came to be seen no longer as merely religious literature but increasingly as divinely inspired Sacred Scripture. There is little evidence for reconstructing this important transition, but certain contributing factors can be proposed.

One factor is the explicitly stated conviction of the authors that God had spoken certain words. From the ancient Pentateuchal stories, it was common to hear that God spoke to Adam, Abraham, and Moses. Similarly, certain prophets claimed to be delivering "the word of the Lord," and many of those claims were endorsed by the ongoing community.

Thus, God was increasingly understood to be speaking through the texts to the people. For the Greeks the *Iliad* and the *Odyssey* held essential religious importance, but they were principally seen as national epics. Similarly, the early Hexateuchal narratives originally would likely have been perceived more as a national epic than as "Scripture." Just as the gods spoke in the Homeric poems, so too did God speak in Israel's texts. But once the priestly portions were incorporated, especially the legal materials listed as divinely spoken on Sinai, and insofar as the divine source was reinforced by the preaching of the Torah as articulating God's will, it is quite easy to understand how God came to be viewed as the author.

The divine authorship envisioned on Sinai was extended to material that had presumably been simply the priests' cultic directives for the various Temple sacrifices. It is quite plausible that editorial framing in the Second Temple period produced that transformation. The directives in Leviticus 1–7 may at an earlier point have begun with "When any of you bring an offering of livestock to the LORD, you shall. . ." (1:2b), then proceeded with the detailed sacrificial directives, and ended with "This is the ritual of the burnt offering, the grain offering, the sin offering, the guilt offering, the ordination offering, and the sacrifice of well-being" (7:37). The editorial framing of those priestly directives would then have introduced the section with "The LORD called Moses and spoke to him from the tent of meeting saying, 'Speak to the people of Israel and say to them'" (1:1-2a), and concluded it with "which the LORD commanded Moses on Mount Sinai, when he commanded the people of Israel to bring their offerings to the LORD, in the wilderness of Sinai" (7:38; cf. also 4:1-2a; 5:20; 27:1-2a, 34). According to this view, the priestly cultic directives were transformed into a divinely authored book.

Again, just as Moses relayed God's word in the Torah, certain prophets were seen to deliver God's message to the king and people. But eventually the entire prophetic book, including stories about the prophet and the full editorial framework, was considered sacred. With the passage of time a book containing God's word came to be considered a divinely inspired book.

Occasionally, textual variants in manuscripts also show secondary editorial introductions to or insertions into the earlier text which helped the books be seen as divinely inspired. For example, formulas such as נאם יהוה ("oracle of the LORD"), which are not in the earlier version of the text of Jeremiah witnessed by the LXX, were inserted into the secondary MT at 8:3; 9:2; 12:17; 31:14, etc. Editorial introductions to oracles, such as "The word of the LORD that came to Jeremiah, saying" (7:1), which were not in the earlier LXX, were also later inserted into the MT tradition. These introductions and formulas made explicit what had been implicit beliefs.

A number of other developing shifts also helped the community to see the books as Scripture. One was the increasing aura of authority due to the antiquity of the books of the Torah and the early prophets. Memory of the origins of the disparate, anonymous oral units was lost, and the entire books were now envisioned as produced by Moses or prophets. Isolated sayings understood as divine messages were collected into books, the entirety of which, including editorial prose, gained divine status.

Another shift involved the texts that served in liturgical and educational settings. This literature was proclaimed as speaking in the name of God, and the people increasingly regarded them as expressing God's will or commands.

Finally, the texts, which had held secondary rank relative to the Temple and its rituals as the central focus of the religion, rose to primary status and essential importance for the geographically dispersed communities after the destruction of the Second Temple.

Many of these shifts had taken place by the end of the Persian period or by the early Hellenistic period, as suggested by the Temple Scroll (third or early second century B.C.E.) and the book of Jubilees (second quarter of the second century B.C.E.). The Temple Scroll presumes the divine authorship of the Torah by reproducing large parts as direct first-person speech by God. And Jubilees' statement (Jub 2:1) that "The angel of the presence spoke to Moses according to the word of the LORD, saying: 'Write the complete history of the creation...'" shows that explicit Mosaic authorship had previously been extended to Genesis 1–11 and that the text was considered to have been divinely revealed.

It was religious leaders and pious individuals sincerely trying to understand and articulate the divine who produced the religious classics of Israel. As generation after generation pondered their religious traditions in light of their current historical, political, and social reality, they experienced the "resignification" or adaptability of the texts to their current community's ongoing life. They identified their situations with those in which God had interacted with their ancestors in the past. They heard God speaking to them through the texts. In a sense, the word about God became the word of God. The communities continued to hear it repeated as such, and eventually they recognized and described it explicitly as such.

These developments indicate that the texts were important not only for the educated and cultured, and spoke not only to the past; they were central to the ongoing life of the entire community and had to be applicable to the future situations which individuals and communities would encounter.

Early Translations: Aramaic and Greek

The first indication that the five books of the Torah and perhaps some of the prophetic books were virtually complete and considered as essential Scripture was that they were important enough to be translated. Because the texts were important for the liturgy and education and had to be applicable to the future situations and foreign surroundings in which the Jewish people would find themselves, the Scriptures were translated into Aramaic and Greek, the languages of the Jewish communities in Babylon and Alexandria, respectively, and increasingly of the Jews in Palestine.

It is likely, although evidence is lacking, that the Jewish community in Babylon had begun to translate the Torah, and possibly other books, into Aramaic by around the fourth or third century B.C.E. We do not know whether these may have been complete, written translations or rather oral, functional explanations of the Hebrew. The latter scene is mirrored in Nehemiah 8:8, narrated probably in the fourth century: accompanying a public reading from the Hebrew scroll, the Levites translated it and gave the sense, so that the people could understand. The earliest extant manuscripts are a Targum of Leviticus (4QtgLev) from the late second or early first century B.C.E. and two Targums of Job (4QtgJob, 11QtgJob) from the middle of the first century C.E. Apart from these Qumran texts, however, the witness of the remaining Targums for text-critical purposes is reduced, irrespective of the date when complete Targums of the Torah and other books were finally written down, since all preserved Targum texts have subsequently been revised to agree with the early rabbinic texts eventually received in the MT. It is difficult to have confidence that any specific readings in surviving manuscripts provide pre-Mishnaic evidence.

In Alexandria the picture is clearer than the nebulous situation regarding Aramaic translations. The probability is strong that the Jewish community there translated the Torah into Greek during the third century B.C.E. The legendary *Letter of Aristeas* elaborately narrates such an early translation, though it is generally believed to be written in support of a version making claims for hegemony about a century later. Nevertheless, plausible examples of quotations in the late third and the second century B.C.E., as well as manuscript evidence, make a third-century translation close to certain. Already in the late third century Demetrius the Hellenist quotes the Greek Genesis, and some suggest that in the mid-second century Eupolemos uses the Greek Chronicles, which would probably mean that the more important Prophets had already been translated as well. Moreover, in the last third of the second century Ben Sira's grandson translates his grandfather's work and only casually mentions the translation of the Torah and the Prophecies and other books, which suggests that those translations were not recent but had become widely known. Finally, the discovery of second-century manuscripts of Greek Pentateuchal books both in Egypt and in Palestine (already showing noticeable development) make a third-century translation probable. Again, this unprecedented fact of translation may be a strong indicator that the Torah had become regarded as authoritative Scripture.

In contrast, the hero Gilgamesh is featured in three different Sumerian compositions that find echoes in the later Akkadian epic, but the latter cannot be considered a translation. Similarly, the *Iliad* and the *Odyssey*, despite their central cultural importance when the Romans took over the Greek culture, were apparently never translated into Latin in antiquity. A summary of the *Iliad* is attributed to Baebius Italicus in Nero's time, but it is a brief (only 1070 hexameters) pedestrian version of the majestic original. By contrast with the Homeric poems which were not translated, the fact that the Torah was translated in subsequent centuries into languages that the people could understand reflects additional factors in the Jewish community's view beyond that of the Greeks. The texts concerned not only the past; they were in some way authoritative for guiding the people's life and thinking in the present and the future.

Early Manuscript Witnesses

The earliest extant manuscript evidence for the history of the scriptural text derives from the second half of the third century B.C.E. The more than two hundred scriptural manuscripts from Qumran and neighboring sites along the western side of the Dead Sea exhibit two principal features: mainly the accurate reproduction of each book and occasionally the creative revised edition of some books. For the most part the earliest scrolls show that the books were already in a form easily recognizable from the traditional *textus receptus*, though there are some notable surprises.

The evidence of the manuscripts first discovered as well as of most subsequent manuscripts shows that the text of the individual books exhibits a combination of an established large core of text as well as a measured pluriformity in the formulation and quantity of text. These two main features were observable already by 1955 with the publication of the photographs and transcriptions of 1QIsa^{a} and 1QIsa^{b}. These features will be displayed in the following chapters.

As the Qumran manuscripts were analyzed, scholarly appreciation of the accuracy and reliability of other available sources grew. Manuscripts such as 1QIsa^{b} showed the accuracy of the transmission of the MT. 4QpaleoExod^{m} and 4QNum^{b} demonstrated the legitimacy of the Samaritan Pentateuch (SP) as a text form produced within general Judaism and altered in only minor ways (textually) by the Samaritans. 4QDeut^{q}, 4QSam^{a,b}, and 4QJer^{b,d} showed that the OG translation was often a faithful reflection of an ancient Hebrew text, but simply of an alternate Hebrew form of the text which was different from the one transmitted in the MT and which existed equally validly alongside the MT.

These surprises from Qumran offered the possibility of seeing more clearly the dimly lit and insufficiently appreciated evidence that had long been available from other sources. For example, the OG for Exodus 35–40 revealed, not a confused text, but an earlier edition of those chapters than the edition in the MT. Analysis of the MT and LXX, especially Papyrus 967, of Ezekiel and Daniel also revealed variant editions of those books. Similarly, Chronicles was seen to be based on a version of Samuel similar to 4QSam^{a} that was different from and often textually superior to the MT Samuel; thus, the Masoretic Chronicles is non-Masoretic with respect to its source. Finally, the biblical narrative of Josephus was seen supporting major readings in 4QJosh^{a} and 4QSam^{a} as opposed to the MT.

As the following chapters unfold, the Qumran manuscripts will provide clear evidence for variant literary editions of at least five and possibly six books of the twenty-four in the traditional Hebrew Bible: Exodus, Numbers, Joshua, Jeremiah, Psalms, and possibly the Song of Songs. Renewed study of the SP and the LXX in light of the Qumran evidence will show variant literary editions for seven additional books or sections of books: Genesis, Samuel, Kings, Ezekiel, the Twelve Minor Prophets, Proverbs, and Daniel. Variant editions for Judges, Job, and Lamentations are possible, but the evidence is insufficient for certainty. Thus, variant literary editions for half or more of the twenty-four books of the Hebrew Bible existed in Jewish circles at the birth of Christianity and rabbinic Judaism.

The illumination of this previously dark and insufficiently understood period of the dynamic, developmental growth of the books of Scripture is a major contribution of the Qumran scriptural scrolls.

Uniform Hebrew Text

The collection of texts preserved by the ancient Rabbis and vocalized and transmitted with exceptional care by the medieval Masoretes came to be widely envisioned in the modern period as "the original text," and the assumption of an *Urtext* often accompanied that common view. As a result of the First Jewish Revolt (66–73) with the destruction of the Temple and the Second Revolt (132–135) with the banishment from Jerusalem, the Rabbis were seen as "standardizing" the text in its proto-MT form and suppressing or neglecting other text forms. Due to these convictions scholars were somewhat slow to adopt the new paradigm provided by the Qumran manuscripts.

But the text forms selected by the Rabbis for the individual books are not homogeneous; they are demonstrably not the best text to select for some books; and their character vacillates: sometimes they contain an earlier edition in comparison with other Jewish texts (e.g., the Qumran or LXX texts), and sometimes a later edition. These factors suggest a rather different scenario that requires a different description. In the wake of the destruction of the Temple and the dispersal of Jewish communities, it rather appears that certain Rabbis found themselves with a somewhat random collection of scrolls — one copy from the available forms of each book — and that copy became the text they used, guarded, and transmitted. There is no evidence that they closely compared entire texts and chose the proto-MT because of its textual superiority. After 70, the texts supplanted the Temple as the center of the religion, and as the new center, the texts now had to be more seriously guarded. Moreover, the use of the Scriptures to support the claims of Jewish followers of Jesus prompted a greater focus on the details of the text. And so, the phenomenon of a unified Hebrew text appears to be the result of the double threat of the Romans to political identity and the threat of the Christians to religious identity. Thus, in light of the developmental nature of the books from their very beginnings up to the Revolts, it may be more accurate to say, not that the texts of the various books were "standardized" after the Revolts, but that they were abruptly "frozen" in their development.

The Transmission of the Uniform Hebrew Text

The textual profile of the various books collected in the MT differs from book to book, just as the profile of the books in the LXX. But after the Second Revolt, all Hebrew witnesses (except those in the Samaritan community) and all translations made from the Hebrew attest to the sole consonantal text form for each book that is transmitted in the Masoretic family of manuscripts. The texts or fragments circulating under the rubrics or names of *kaige*, Aquila, Symmachus, Theodotion, and Origen's Hebrew column, as well as quotations in rabbinic sources, all show close agreement in general with an early precursor of the MT. There are sufficient individual variants, however, both to rule out the idea of a single Jewish *Urtext* and to show some subsequent minor development in the proto-MT tradition. But from the second century onward that Hebrew tradition, with only minor variants, was the only one transmitted within Judaism.

As was noted above, the Samaritans adopted a text that they and the Judeans held in common. That Judeo-Samarian text had already been re-edited and expanded, and the few changes the Samaritans made differed only in making explicit what they believed the text implicitly authorized: Mount Gerizim versus Jerusalem as the central Israelite sanctuary. The Targums and the Peshitta, whatever their origins, were revised in accordance with early precursors of the MT books, so that they seldom serve as major independent witnesses. Jerome's Vulgate also was translated primarily from a pre-MT tradition, although he used the LXX to a greater extent than he admits.

The Old Greek translation, insofar as it survived the challenges of the subsequent Greek recensions, was transmitted through Christian communities and continued to attest for some books an early, alternate Hebrew tradition. The Old Latin for the most part was translated from OG, and so, even where the OG was lost, one can at times work from the OL, back through the OG, to attain the Old Hebrew.

Thus, at the close of antiquity the MT tradition was the uniform text throughout the Jewish diaspora, and the Samaritan Pentateuchal text was preserved in that community. Especially in the eastern Roman world the LXX continued to serve as the Scriptures of Christianity, while further east the Syriac versions were used. In the West the Vulgate gradually replaced the LXX and the OL. Through the Middle Ages, this situation changed little, except for the detailed vocalization and cantillation of the Hebrew text by the Masoretes.

The Resurgence of the Hebrew for Christian Bibles

In the late Middle Ages, especially in Spain, there was a rich sharing of Jewish, Christian, and Muslim cultures, learning, and texts. Although the close of the fifteenth century saw an unfortunate end to that cultural communication, the Renaissance produced a different type of advance. The rediscovery of the Greek and Latin classics had as one by-product the desire in Christian scholarship to return to the original languages for studying their texts. This included a return to the Hebrew form of the Old Testament for closer understanding of the meaning than the Vulgate provided. But the desire to return to the original text only half succeeded. Since the MT was the only Hebrew text known, people commonly presumed that it was the original text, but they confused the original *language* with the original *text*. More accurately, the MT was *one* of the forms of the ancient text in the original language.

Appreciation of the ancient languages and the rewards of systematic textual comparison led to the Complutensian Polyglot, the first biblical polyglot, in 1514–1517 at the University of Alcalá. It included the Masoretic Hebrew, the LXX, a Targum, and the Vulgate. A century later Pietro della Valle traveled to the Near East and returned in 1616 enriched with a manuscript of the Samaritan Pentateuch, which was then included in the Paris Polyglot in 1632. The comparison of the SP with the MT highlighted some six thousand discrepancies; and when about one third of those showed agreement with the LXX, the reputation of the LXX as a faithful witness to an ancient Hebrew text climbed and that of the MT diminished. Through this period and for the next few centuries, however, the religious agenda of the researchers often clouded their textual conclusions. The SP-LXX agreement caused some to suggest that the MT had been secondarily revised by the Rabbis, and thus that the LXX preserved the divine word in purer form. But the Renaissance focus on the original language and the Reformation's concern for translation into the vernacular from the Hebrew rather than the Vulgate served as a counter-weight in favor of the MT.

Pre-Qumran Theories of the History of the Text

In the eighteenth century Benjamin Kennicott and Giovanni de Rossi each collected myriads of variants found in European Hebrew manuscripts, but the variants proved to be constricted to such a small and insignificant scope that the admirable preservation of even the minutiae of the MT proved the reliability of that text tradition. For example, toward the end of the eighteenth century, Ernst F. C. Rosenmüller surveyed the variants from Kennicott, de Rossi, and other sources and concluded that all variants within the Masoretic manuscripts are relatively late and witness to a single recension. That is, analysis of those assembled variants can lead us only to the early Masoretic tradition of each book, not to "the original text." This conclusion was subsequently reconfirmed by Moshe Goshen-Gottstein.

In 1815 Friedrich Wilhelm Gesenius studied the SP and showed that most of its variant readings displayed a secondary reworking of a base text like the MT. Others, such as Zacharias Frankel and Salomon Kohn, added to the devaluation of the SP as a textual witness, due to its obviously secondary nature as dependent on the MT, and thus its inability to penetrate behind the MT.

Paul de Lagarde, toward the end of the nineteenth century, took Rosenmüller's idea of a single recension and tightened it to a single manuscript behind the entire Masoretic tradition, though in his view that archetype was not a perfect replica of the original text but already contained scribal errors and changes. Others, such as J. G. Sommer, even claimed that the proto-MT archetype originated from the Jerusalem Temple. Turning his attention to the LXX, Lagarde theorized that all LXX manuscripts could be traced back to the three recensions of Origen, Hesychius, and Lucian, and that comparison of those three recensions could lead to the original Greek translation. That translation, even with any imperfections, would witness to a variant Hebrew text that antedated the archetype behind the MT.

Lagarde's theories were highly influential. His general view that a single Greek translation spread to the three recensions which lay behind all extant LXX manuscripts eventually inspired the Göttingen Septuaginta Unternehmen and its series of critical editions of the Greek books. It also proved at least functionally correct against P. E. Kahle's theory of multiple translations eventually standardized into one official text. Lagarde's view of a single Hebrew archetype, or *Urtext*, behind all MT manuscripts, was also widely accepted, though challenges again came from Kahle's evidence of Cairo Geniza manuscripts from the turn of the second millennium showing variant vocalization and different Masoretic systems. But the fact that those texts were medieval, not ancient, and that the variation was mainly in vocalization, not in the ancient consonantal text, prevented overthrow of Lagarde's *Urtext* theory. Debate also continued regarding whether that *Urtext* had been, as J. Olshausen argued, officially selected as a result of careful textual comparison or, as T. Noeldeke argued, simply adopted because it happened to be the only collection of texts available (for endorsement of Noeldeke's view see Ch. 2 "Coincidental Nature").

Conclusion

This chapter has summarized representative views regarding the nature and history of the biblical text prior to the discovery of the Dead Sea Scrolls and hinted at the revised view the Scrolls offer. With this larger map of the history of the biblical text as background we are now prepared to examine in detail the lenses that will help us see more clearly the Qumran manuscripts with all the rich evidence they provide. In the next chapter we will contrast clearer post-Qumran thinking with some current views inherited from, and not sufficiently reevaluated from, the pre-Qumran era.

Sources Used and Suggestions for Further Reading

Abegg, Martin, Jr., Peter Flint, and Eugene Ulrich. *The Dead Sea Scrolls Bible* (see "Bibliographical Abbreviations").

Auwers, Jean-Marie and H. J. de Jonge, eds. *The Biblical Canons*.

Bruning, Brandon. "The Making of the Mishkan."

Carr, David M. *The Formation of the Hebrew Bible: A New Reconstruction*. New York: Oxford University Press, 2011.

Cross, Frank Moore and Shemaryahu Talmon, eds. *Qumran and the History*.

Fernández Marcos, Natalio. *The Septuagint in Context*.

Flint, Peter W. and James C. VanderKam, eds. *The Dead Sea Scrolls after Fifty Years*.

Goshen-Gottstein, Moshe. "Hebrew Biblical Manuscripts: Their History and Their Place in the HUBP Edition." Pages 42–89 in F. M. Cross and S. Talmon, eds. *Qumran and the History*. Repr. from *Biblica* 48 (1967): 243–90.

Harl, Marguerite, Gilles Dorival, and Olivier Munnich. *La Bible grecque des Septante*.

Herbert, Edward D. and Emanuel Tov, eds. *The Bible as Book*.

McDonald, Lee M. and James A. Sanders, eds. *The Canon Debate*.

Menocal, María Rosa. *The Ornament of the World: How Muslims, Jews, and Christians Created a Culture of Tolerance in Medieval Spain*. New York: Little, Brown, 2002.

Niehoff, Maren R. *Jewish Exegesis and Homeric Scholarship in Alexandria*. Cambridge: Cambridge University Press, 2011.

Person, Raymond E. *The Deuteronomic History and the Book of Chronicles: Scribal Works in an Oral World*. Ancient Israel and Its Literature 6. Atlanta: Society of Biblical Literature, 2010.

Pritchard, James B., ed. *Ancient Near Eastern Texts Relating to the Old Testament* (*ANET*).

Rajak, Tessa. *Translation and Survival: The Greek Bible of the Ancient Jewish Diaspora*. Oxford: Oxford University Press, 2009.

Sanders, James A. *Sacred Story*.

Schiffman, Lawrence H. and James C. VanderKam, eds. *The Encyclopedia of the Dead Sea Scrolls*.

Talmon, Shemaryahu. "The Old Testament Text." Pages 1–41 in F. M. Cross and S. Talmon, eds., *Qumran and the History of the Biblical Text*. Repr. from pages 159–99 in Peter R. Ackroyd and Craig F. Evans, eds. *The Cambridge History of the Bible*, Vol. 1: *From the Beginnings to Jerome*. Cambridge: Cambridge University Press, 1970. The section above on "Pre-Qumran Theories" is largely summarized from this article.

Talmon, Shemaryahu. *Text and Canon*.

Toorn, Karel van der. *Scribal Culture*.

Tov, Emanuel. *The Greek and Hebrew Bible*.

Tov, Emanuel. *Hebrew Bible, Greek Bible, and Qumran.*

Tov, Emanuel. *Textual Criticism.*

Trebolle Barrera, Julio. *The Jewish Bible.*

Ulrich, Eugene. *Scrolls and Origins.*

Ulrich, Eugene. "The Old Testament Text and Its Transmission." Pages 83–104 in James Carleton Paget and Joachim Schaper, eds. *The New Cambridge History of the Bible,* Vol. 1: *From the Beginnings to 600.* Cambridge: Cambridge University Press, 2013. This essay forms the basis of the present Chapter 1.

Ulrich, Eugene. "The Text of the Hebrew Scriptures at the Time of Hillel and Jesus." Pages 85–108 in [IOSOT] *Congress Volume Basel 2001.* Edited by André Lemaire. Supplements to Vetus Testamentum 92. Leiden: Brill, 2002.

Ulrich, Eugene, ed. *The Biblical Qumran Scrolls.*

VanderKam, James C. *Scrolls and Bible.*

VanderKam, James C. and Peter W. Flint. *The Meaning of the Scrolls.*

CHAPTER 2

POST-QUMRAN THINKING: A PARADIGM SHIFT

THE PREVIOUS CHAPTER presented a general map of the landscape to help situate the more detailed areas that will be explored in the following chapters. This chapter offers another form of preparation for understanding the evidence better: accurate vision. If the lenses through which we view the new evidence are not properly calibrated—if we look at the new evidence with old categories and outdated concepts—we may lose much of what the discoveries can teach us.

Often since Socrates' strong denunciation of "the unexamined life," methodological reflection has enhanced not only personal life but also the practices of scientific inquiry. Methodological reflection, both on the setting of the Scriptures within general Judaism during the first centuries B.C.E. and C.E. and on modern scholars' attempts at evaluating the Qumran scriptural evidence, has already produced major advances and holds great promise for further advances.[1] Were earlier generations of scrolls scholars, and are we today, looking at, seeing, and interpreting with correct vision the nature of the Scriptures? Or might there be distortions in our vision that it would be good to correct? What can we learn from observing scholarly assessments of the evidence provided by the Qumran discoveries? The new evidence provided by the Scrolls, much older and much closer to the origins of Judaism and Christianity, requires a paradigm shift. We must start with our old categories and questions, but we must let the Scrolls correct our vision toward newly refined categories and more precise questions.

PRELIMINARY CONSIDERATIONS

It will be helpful to consider a few points before proceeding. First, the destruction of Qumran in 68 C.E., the Jerusalem Temple in 70, and Masada in 73 unfortunately marks the end of an era. Since it does not seem likely that anything in Jewish life was securely established or "standard" between 70 and the end of the first century, for simplicity's sake, we can designate the period under investigation as "the first centuries B.C.E. and C.E.,"[2] or (near) "the end of the Second Temple period," or (to use the late Shemaryahu Talmon's felicitous phrase) "before the Great Divide."[3]

---

[1] See Maxine Grossman, ed., *Rediscovering the Dead Sea Scrolls: An Assessment of Old and New Approaches and Methods* (Grand Rapids, Mich.: Eerdmans, 2010).

[2] The term "the first centuries" will be used to denote the first centuries B.C.E. and C.E., the time period on which this chapter is focused. The bulk of our manuscript scriptural evidence comes roughly from these two centuries, and they are crucial for understanding the emergence of Christianity and rabbinic Judaism.

[3] Talmon coined the term to refer to the watershed between "the waning of the biblical epoch," the older period when development in the Hebrew Scriptures was still practiced, and "the onset of the 'Age of the Sages,'" the later period when only the rabbinic collection of texts was transmitted with no further

Second, I understand the enterprise of historical inquiry as the science-and-art which aims at objective description of phenomena of the past. It aims at objective truth but is always conducted (a) by subjective minds which view a subjective selection of evidence, (b) by subjective minds which are conditioned by cultural presuppositions, partial knowledge, and limited categories as they view the evidence, and (c) by subjective minds which are even liable to faulty conclusions due to the equivalent of optical illusions—we look at one object but interpret it as something else because of our preconditioned categories. Our educational and religious training, the concepts we have learned, the theories we have developed, all shape the way we see the evidence.[4]

In the case of Qumran, we have only highly fragmentary evidence available. Of all the manuscripts from antiquity, probably less than five percent have survived. What is more, the scrolls that did survive seldom preserve even five percent of the original manuscript. This is representative of the broader reality that first-century evidence for Judaism in general is fragmentary and elusive. History is a science-and-art which deals in large measure with reconstruction. We scientifically analyze the data available, but the data must be interpreted, subjectively interpreted, and we must be aware that the process of interpretation is as much art as science. The data are a bunch of dots, and the significance assigned to the data is a product of intelligence, subjective intelligence—the art of properly connecting the dots which the data partially and mutely provide. History necessarily involves reconstruction, and, in the case of the Dead Sea Scrolls, a great deal of reconstruction.

Third, the chapters which follow attempt to offer an empirical search to find the relevant evidence, a neutral analysis and presentation, and precise vocabulary to describe it neutrally and accurately, as much as this is possible.

Just as the invention of the telescope and accurate observation of astronomical data allowed the Copernican solar system to eclipse the previously unquestioned Ptolemaic-medieval view of the earth as the center of creation, so too the discovery of the scriptural scrolls and accurate observation of the data they provide have, in the academic sphere, eclipsed the MT as the text-critical center of the Hebrew Bible (see *A "Standard Text"* below). Though the scriptural scrolls were early assumed to be sectarian, the more they are studied, the more it is obvious that there is nothing sectarian about them (see Ch. 11): they constitute the most ancient and authentic witness to what the texts of the Jewish Scriptures were like generally at the time of the origins of Christianity and rabbinic Judaism.

Thus, the question this study attempts to answer is: What was, in fact, the nature of the scriptural texts in antiquity?

---

alteration to the Hebrew texts. The date is not precisely known but "should probably be located in the late first or in the second century C.E." ("The Crystallization of the 'Canon of Hebrew Scriptures' in the Light of Biblical Scrolls from Qumran," in *The Bible as Book*, 14). For books cited without full bibliographic data, see "Bibliographical Abbreviations."

[4] On subjectivity see Bertil Albrektson, "Masoretic or Mixed: On Choosing a Textual Basis for a Translation of the Hebrew Bible," *Textus* 23 (2007): 33–49, esp. 35–38; and Emanuel Tov, *Textual Criticism*, 22.

Theoretical Issues

Among the first aspects to be discussed is the question of perspective, or coign of vantage. Where should our observation point be, and where should we aim our focus, when setting out to think and speak accurately about the scriptural scrolls? Should we start from the modern world, using modern concepts, categories, and terms? Or should we enter the world of the Second Temple, using concepts, categories, and terms that would have been appropriate in the first centuries, at the close of the Second Temple period? At the time of their discovery, the Dead Sea Scrolls represented a unique body of evidence for the history of scriptural development. It was only natural that scholars reverted to familiar categories to make sense of this new material. But when we encounter something radically new, in whole or even in part, that goes beyond our acquired knowledge, we are at risk of failing to interpret it correctly or adequately. Since the texts and the collection of Scriptures evidenced by the scrolls are distinctly different from the biblical text and canon of the twentieth and twenty-first century, it is possible that our interpretation and explanation of them could be less than adequate. If, instead of viewing them from the present, we attempt to immerse ourselves in the first centuries, observing and discussing as best we can the scriptural manuscripts according to the understanding the people had then and the reality they knew, we may achieve a clearer, more accurate understanding.

Epistemologically, we come to achieve new knowledge through a process of experience, understanding, and judgment. Through experience or sense perception we take in new data and then begin the work of understanding, conceptualizing, interpreting. Researchers have repeatedly shown that we do not take in data purely but that our a priori theories condition even how we perceive data. The conceptualization or interpretation takes place according to the categories we already know, categories well established and confirmed by our past experience of their repeated usefulness for absorbing and correctly classifying knowledge. When the data are complex, alternate interpretations are possible, and then it is the task of judgment to decide which of the interpretations is in fact the one that best explains the data.

Should our initial interpretation be our final, definitive one? Examination of the process exposes a possible pitfall in attaining a proper understanding of the new evidence. If our present categories are not adequate or not sufficiently refined for accurate interpretation of the new evidence, we may adopt a judgment regarding the evidence that, though perhaps partly accurate, may also be partly misleading. Thus, articulations of that judgment and future decisions could reinforce the misleading viewpoint.

There can be different methodologies according to which people proceed to understand the evidence for the biblical text. One model or method, often unexamined, is to start by presupposing that we know what the content, wording, and orthography of the biblical text is. We have known it all along, we know it well from the MT. That text has had an amazingly stable existence since the early second century C.E., and much of it is demonstrably based on one form of texts that go back at least to the second century B.C.E. When we discover new data that appear to be biblical or biblically related, we know how to understand the data because we know what the biblical text is supposed to look like. Our categories and well-learned criteria are determined by our present knowledge, and data from antiquity are interpreted according to these categories.

A second model or method, in contrast, acknowledges that conclusions should follow upon data and upon an adequate understanding of the data. We should operate according to the empirical principle that we must start our intellectual construct from the evidence, viewed in its context as neutrally as possible, not from preconceived notions of what historical reality must have been like. Every other source of evidence we have for the nature of the text of the Scriptures in the Second Temple period—the Qumran scrolls, the SP, the LXX, the NT, and Josephus—demonstrates that the text of Scripture was pluriform and dynamically growing, with variant literary editions for many of the books. According to the second model, the data are first understood on their own terms in their historical context.[5] If that picture clashes with our modern picture, we honestly ask whether our modern picture ought not be revised.

According to the first model, if a text does not look similar enough to the traditional MT, or even to the MT-SP-LXX, then it is classified as "nonbiblical," or "parabiblical," or "reworked Bible." But according to the second model, as we will see in Ch. 12, that same text could be classified as "biblical" if it fits the profile of what the scriptural text was really like in antiquity. Once seen correctly, it can help us better understand the history of the biblical text.

An illustration may help. When the Great Isaiah Scroll (1QIsa[a]) was first discovered, it was labeled a "vulgar" or even "worthless" manuscript.[6] It did not conform with the "biblical" text that scholars knew—the MT. They had their categories well learned and their criteria well formed, and because they knew what a biblical manuscript should look like, 1QIsa[a] did not make the grade. A number of other, analogous judgments were made, many of which have since been revised in the light of ongoing investigation.

Thus, a paradigm shift is needed, one element of which is the attempt to adopt an ancient, in contrast to a modern, perspective.

The Scriptures

A significant element in that paradigm shift is the revision of our view of the MT in comparison with other witnesses to the biblical text, and it is important to formulate questions correctly.

Formulating the Questions Correctly

One way of formulating an important question is: "Was there a standard biblical text" toward the end of the Second Temple period? Rumination, however, over the formulation of this question illuminates a presupposition which suggests that we ought to reformulate the question. The question "Was there a standard biblical text?" implies the

[5] Florentino García Martínez ("Light on the Joshua Books from the Dead Sea Scrolls," in *After Qumran: Old and Modern Editions of the Biblical Texts—The Historical Books* [ed. Hans Ausloos, Bénédicte Lemmelijn, and Julio Trebolle Barrera; BETL 246; Leuven: Peeters, 2012], 145–59) is of the same mind: "the only correct way to look at the evidence preserved in the collection is to try to understand it from the perspective and categories of the people who put the collection together, rather than with our own categories and perspectives" (159).

[6] Harry M. Orlinsky, "Studies in the St. Mark's Isaiah Scroll, IV," *JQR* 43 (1952–53): 329–40, esp. 340.

existence of a category of "standard text." First, though today we may have the category of "standard text," was there already in place in the period we are examining a category of "standard text"? If not, we risk seeing items that did exist in that period according to a category or concept that did not exist; we may have seen the evidence correctly but we have not understood it correctly.

Secondly, the term "a standard text" implies or even denotes a single text which is not only fixed, but is *acknowledged* to be "the text," as opposed to other forms of the text. Though it need not, it may even imply a critically selected text. One should also distinguish, when thinking of the MT as "the standard text," between "standard" in the sense of normative (the way the text ought to be, the text by which other texts are judged), and "standard" in the simpler sense of the common, practical, and traditional form that is routinely used (the only collection readily available for use, the only collection of texts fully preserved in the Hebrew language).

With the word "biblical" also slips in another presupposition, that "The Bible" already existed toward the end of the Second Temple period; and what the question asks is whether "The Bible" did or did not have a standard text. I do not think that "The Bible" in our modern sense (whether Jewish, Protestant, Catholic, or any other) existed as such in the Second Temple period, if by "Bible" we mean a complete and closed collection of books of Scripture. References to "the Scriptures" or "the Law and the Prophets" are numerous enough and sufficiently broadly attested to ensure that certainly there were books considered as Sacred Scriptures toward the close of the Second Temple period. But the point would have to be demonstrated that "The Bible" as such was an identifiable reality at the end of the Second Temple period. In order to filter out those aspects which might possibly constrain or skew our investigation, I suggest that the question be reformulated: *What were the texts of the Scriptures like near the end of the Second Temple period?*

A number of other questions must be posed and answered before we can arrive at a solution. What is the evidence available for determining the nature and characteristics of the scriptural texts in the first centuries B.C.E. and C.E.? Even if we have the proper evidence, are we looking at it through the correct interpretive lenses? Since the term "a standard biblical text" normally refers to the so-called proto-MT, what was the proto-MT? What would be an adequate description of it? Was there such a thing as "a/the standard text"? If so, was it in reality the proto-MT that was "the standard text"? Was there an identifiable group of leaders in the first centuries B.C.E. and C.E. that knew of the variety of texts, was concerned about the diversity of textual forms, therefore selected a single form, had the authority to declare a single form to be the "standard text," and succeeded in having that standard text acknowledged by a majority of Jews? Was there sufficient cohesion in Judaism in the late Second Temple period and sufficiently acknowledged leadership to make it conceivable that a majority of Jews recognized and used a "standard text"?

Thus, I return to the proposal that a preferable, more neutral formulation of the question would be: *What were the texts of the Scriptures like near the end of the Second Temple period?* Having attempted to pose the question correctly, so as not to color the way the answer is formulated, we should next ask whether we are looking at the evidence correctly.

A "Standard Text" in the First Centuries?

The common view of the text of the Hebrew Bible is that it is basically a "purified" MT. That is, the *textus receptus*, the single "standard text" form that the Rabbis and the Masoretes handed on, once the obvious errors are removed, is considered to present the "original text," or the closest one can come to it. Accordingly, most Bible translations translate "the MT except where there is a problem," at which point they look to the SP, the LXX, the versions, or emendation.[7] But the Qumran scrolls show that the textual form of the MT was not and is not the central text of the Hebrew Bible, but is simply one of several forms that existed in antiquity.

The common mentality of privileging the MT is usually formed from the very beginning of a reader's interest in the Bible. Normally, when one desires to pick up and read a Bible, the translation is basically from the MT. If one wishes to proceed further and learn the original language, the introductory Hebrew textbook presents the details of Tiberian Hebrew, the form solidified by the Masoretes. When one advances to reading the Hebrew text, one purchases *Biblia Hebraica Stuttgartensia* (*BHS*) or *Biblia Hebraica Quinta* (*BHQ*), both of which are transcriptions of Codex Leningradensis, the oldest complete Masoretic manuscript of the Hebrew Bible (1009 C.E.). Advanced problems are solved by Gesenius' grammar, which explains MT anomalies mainly within the Tiberian system. To be fair, since only one Hebrew text tradition has been transmitted after the second century C.E., it is difficult to do otherwise, and prior to the scrolls it was virtually impossible to do so. But we should now be aware of the situation and attempt to broaden the patterns.

As early as 1988 both Emanuel Tov and I had challenged the text-critical centrality of the MT. Tov correctly stated that the Qumran texts have "taught us no longer to posit MT at the center of our textual thinking."[8] Similarly, I discussed a series of variant editions of biblical books, several Qumran scrolls, and LXX readings which "prove to be superior in general to the MT" and which thus demonstrate "the decentralization of the MT as *the* text of the Hebrew Bible."[9] Based on the available evidence, which will be

---

[7] See, e.g., Bruce M. Metzger's preface "To the Reader" of the New Revised Standard Version: "For the Old Testament . . . *Biblia Hebraica Stuttgartensia* [is used]. . . . Departures from the consonantal text of the best [Masoretic] manuscripts have been made only where it seems clear that errors in copying had been made before the text was standardized"; and *The New Jerusalem Bible*, p. xii: "For the Old Testament the Massoretic Text is used, that is the text established in the eighth/ninth centuries AD by Jewish scholars who fixed its letters and vowel signs, the text reproduced by most manuscripts. Only when this text presents insuperable difficulties have emendations or the versions of other Hebrew manuscripts or the ancient versions (notably the LXX and Syriac) been used. . . ."

[8] Emanuel Tov, "Hebrew Biblical Manuscripts from the Judaean Desert: Their Contribution to Textual Criticism," *JJS* 39 (1988): 5–37, esp. 7. He also speaks (*Textual Criticism*, 365) of the "conceptual problem in the focusing of all editions on 𝔐." These "do not contain *the* Bible but merely one textual tradition. . . . However, the text of the Bible is found in a wide group of sources, from 𝔐, through the Judean Desert Scrolls, to 𝔊" (emphasis in the original).

[9] Eugene Ulrich, "Double Literary Editions of Biblical Narratives and Reflections on Determining the Form to be Translated," in *Perspectives on the Hebrew Bible: Essays in Honor of Walter J. Harrelson* (ed. James L. Crenshaw; Macon, Ga.: Mercer University Press, 1988), 101–16; repr. in *Scrolls and Origins*, 34–50, esp. 46–47; and idem, "The Biblical Scrolls from Qumran Cave 4: An Overview and a Progress Report on Their Publication," in *Biblical Texts* (vol.1 of *The Texts of Qumran and the History of the Community:*

supplied in the following chapters, one must conclude that there was no "standard text" in the Second Temple period.[10] Beginning from these observations, we must reassess how we approach the text of the Hebrew Bible.[11]

The Masoretic Text: The Single "Official Text" in the Jerusalem Temple?

A related problem concerning the perception of the MT is that it—as opposed to other forms of the texts as encountered in the Qumran scrolls, the SP, the LXX, or others—represents the single "correct" text preserved by the priests in the Jerusalem Temple and somehow transferred to the Pharisees, Rabbis, and Masoretes.[12] But is there any evidence that the texts preserved in the medieval MT transmit the single set of texts guarded by the priests in the Jerusalem Temple? Has a line of succession of the proto-MT—from Temple priests to Pharisees to Rabbis to Masoretes[13]—been convincingly demonstrated?

If any group outside the Temple had Temple texts that they preserved and copied, the Qumran group would seem to be a more likely candidate than the Pharisees. Their early leaders are thought to have been priests who separated themselves because they believed the Temple had been defiled. The texts taken to Qumran with all their pluriformity would most likely have been produced by the priests of the Jerusalem Temple. There does not seem to be any evidence that the Pharisees were conscious that their texts

---

Proceedings of the Groningen Congress on the Dead Sea Scrolls [20–23 August 1989]; ed. F. García Martínez; Paris: Gabalda, 1989) [= *RevQ* 14/2 No. 54–55 (1989)], 207–28, esp. 223 (emphasis in original).

10 Tov (*Textual Criticism*, 179) agrees: "there is no evidence for the assumption of a standard text or stabilization for the biblical text as a whole. . . ."

11 One new approach is *The Hebrew Bible: A Critical Edition* (formerly called *The Oxford Hebrew Bible*), under the leadership of Ronald Hendel, currently in preparation. It is the first effort since the discovery of the scrolls to produce a critically established text. For a description of the project plus individual samples, see Ronald Hendel, "The Oxford Hebrew Bible: Prologue to a New Critical Edition," *VT* 58 (2008): 324–51; and Sidnie White Crawford, Jan Joosten, and Eugene Ulrich, "Sample Editions of the Oxford Hebrew Bible: Deuteronomy 32:1-9, 1 Kings 11:1-8, and Jeremiah 27:1-10 [34 G]," ibid., 352–66. For views expressing reservations, see Hugh G. M. Williamson, "Do We Need a New Bible? Reflections on the Proposed Oxford Hebrew Bible," *Biblica* 90 (2009): 153–75; Emanuel Tov, "Hebrew Scripture Editions: Philosophy and Praxis," in *From 4QMMT to Resurrection—Mélanges qumraniens en hommage à Émile Puech* (ed. Florentino García Martínez et al.; STDJ 61; Leiden: Brill, 2006) 281–312 [rev. ed.: *Hebrew Bible, Greek Bible, and Qumran*, 247–70]; idem, *Textual Criticism*, 359–64.

12 See, e.g., Arie van der Kooij, "Preservation and Promulgation: The Dead Sea Scrolls and the Textual History of the Hebrew Bible," in *The Hebrew Bible in Light of the Dead Sea Scrolls* (ed. Nóra Dávid et al.; FRLANT 239; Göttingen: Vandenhoeck & Ruprecht, 2012), 29–40: "All in all, it is my thesis that the MT goes back to an official text kept in the Temple and preserved with great care by the appropriate Temple officials, the chief priests. . ." (p. 37).

See also Emanuel Tov, "Some Thoughts about the Diffusion of Biblical Manuscripts in Antiquity," in *The Dead Sea Scrolls: Transmission of Traditions and Production of Texts* (ed. Sarianna Metso, Hindy Najman, and Eileen Schuller; STDJ 92; Leiden: Brill, 2010), 151–72: "Current views on the development of the Scripture books allow for and actually require the assumption of a single copy in the Temple" (p. 167); and idem, "Scriptures: Texts," in *Encyclopedia of the Dead Sea Scrolls*, 2:834: ". . . the masoretic family, which probably was the only acceptable text in Temple circles. In a way this text should be considered an official text, and this assumption would explain the great number of copies of it found at Qumran, and that it was the only text found at Masada, Naḥal Ḥever and Wadi Murabbaʿat." See note 24.

13 See Tov, *Textual Criticism*, 36.

differed from other less valuable textual forms. Nor did they have the religious authority — acknowledged by other Jewish parties — to claim that their texts were standard and others were not.[14]

So it is important to ask: "Who Ran What?"[15] Who were the leaders within Judaism in the late Second Temple period? What group was "in charge" that might render a decision in an important matter such as the selection of "standard texts"? Leadership in general was always a mixture of political and religious leadership, but who decided how the religion functioned practically? When there were significant differences and debates, did most people know and care about them? Whom did most people follow? Was Judaism sufficiently unified to ground the concept of a single standard or authoritative text form?

In this period, leadership in Judaism was basically the same as it had been in the earlier period after the return from Babylon: "an aristocratic oligarchy, headed by the high priest whenever there was no king."[16] The Sadducees were "a key element in the Hasmonean aristocracy, supporting the priest-kings and joining with the Pharisees in the Gerousia"; they dominated that body "for most of the reign of John Hyrcanus and that of Alexander Janneus" (135/4–104 and 103–76 B.C.E.).[17] The Pharisees probably arose in early Hasmonaean times and "played a major role during the period from 135 to 63 B.C.E.; they could affect public events very substantially when everything was intra-Jewish."[18]

Upon the death of Alexander Jannaeus in 76 B.C.E., during the rule of his wife Salome Alexandra (76–67) and in accord with her wishes, the Pharisees wielded great power. But in 63 B.C.E., once Rome's power menaced Palestine, matters were increasingly no longer intra-Jewish. "For the most part, Roman authority was channeled through the high priest and his allies and friends — the chief priests and 'the powerful'. . . . The Pharisees on the whole were not in this category. . . . Rome's policy of ruling through the local aristocracy . . . excluded most of the Pharisees from positions of influence."[19]

Thus, the high priest, the chief priests, the Sadducees, and the powerful exercised the main leadership among Jews throughout most of the late Second Temple period. The Pharisees seem to have played a major (but not dominant) role from 135 to 76, and to have risen to leadership briefly, from 76 to 63 B.C.E., but then were eclipsed when the Romans invaded. Talmon states that "it was yet an open question which faction would ultimately win the day and come to be considered 'normative,' and which others would resultingly be relegated to the status of 'dissenters' or 'sects'. . . . One wonders whether

[14] Lawrence H. Schiffman, *From Text to Tradition: A History of Second Temple and Rabbinic Judaism* (Hoboken, N.J.: Ktav, 1991), 98 and 112.

[15] For this apt formulation I am obviously indebted to E. P. Sanders, who gave that title to Chapter 21 in his book, *Judaism: Practice and Belief 63 B.C.E. – 66 C.E.* (London: SCM; Philadelphia: Trinity Press International, 1992), 458.

[16] Sanders, *Judaism*, 383.

[17] Schiffman, *From Text to Tradition*, 111.

[18] Sanders, *Judaism*, 383.

[19] Sanders, *Judaism*, 388.

the model 'normative' vs. 'sectarian' is at all legitimately applicable to Judaism before the turn of the era."[20]

As Lawrence Schiffman notes, "the gradual transfer of influence and power from the priestly Sadducees to the learned Pharisees went hand in hand with the transition from Temple to Torah. . . ."[21] The question, then, is the date of this transition. But, if one is peering through the antique fog and shadows looking to find "the proto-MT," it is presumably in the hands of the Pharisees where one would expect to find it.[22] Now, if the text in the hands of the Pharisees for each book was consciously "the proto-MT," then it was either the same text as that in the hands of the Jerusalem priesthood, or it was their distinctive text choice. If it were the same as that of the priests, it would be meaningless to refer to it as the specifically proto-rabbinic text, and it should be the text attested by the majority of manuscripts or citations from Judaism in antiquity—which is demonstrably not the case, as the SP, the LXX, quotations in the NT, and Josephus show. If it were different from that of the Jerusalem Temple and priesthood, it would not (could not?) have been considered the dominant text, much less the "standard text," prior to the end of the Second Temple period. Schiffman helpfully points out that "Rabbinic tradition *claimed* [a dominant or normative] status for Pharisaic Judaism, but it is difficult to consider a minority, no matter how influential, to be a mainstream."[23]

For producing copies of the books of Scripture, the group that was most likely responsible was the priesthood.[24] Insofar as there might have been a conscious prioritizing of more "official" texts versus "vulgar" texts (were one to consider the distinction historically operative), again the Jerusalem (and perhaps Samari[t]an and Alexandrian)[25] priesthood would presumably have been the responsible producers of the more "official" or "authoritative" texts. But the question is: Was there one "official text" and was the proto-MT the "single copy in the Temple";[26] or was the pluriformity seen at Qumran also the situation in the Temple? Insofar as the Jerusalem priesthood had been the original milieu of the leaders of the Qumran movement, we should expect that the scriptural scrolls in the covenanters' possession would be texts in line with those of the Jerusalem priesthood and Temple, and clearly those texts are pluriform. Similarly, the translators of the Greek Pentateuch presumably used approved Hebrew texts as their basis (most of the LXX = MT), but its *Vorlage* was not consistently the MT (as the OG especially of Exodus 35–40 demonstrates).

---

[20] Shemaryahu Talmon, "Qumran Studies: Past, Present, and Future," *JQR* 85 (1994): 1–31, esp. 6.

[21] Schiffman, *From Text to Tradition*, 112.

[22] I suspect that at this early stage we cannot really focus sufficiently—analogous to the bottom line on the ophthalmologist's chart—to identify text types. But even if such precise focus were possible, it must be remembered that we would have to repeat the procedure for each individual book.

[23] Schiffman, *From Text to Tradition*, 98 (emphasis added).

[24] One can readily agree with van der Kooij ("Preservation and Promulgation," 35) that "the highest authorities, i.e., the chief priests, were in charge of the ancient books deposited and kept in the temple." The crux is whether there was only a single text form and whether the proto-MT can be identified as the single specific form of those books.

[25] See Gary N. Knoppers, *Jews and Samaritans: The Origins and History of Their Early Relations* (Oxford: Oxford University Press, 2013).

[26] Tov, "Some Thoughts about the Diffusion," 167.

As a condition for claiming that the MT or any single text form was to be considered the authoritative or dominant form, there would have to be several types of awareness required. There would have to be awareness not just vaguely that "some texts differ," or awareness of a few sporadic "hot-topic" variants, but awareness of variant textual editions or "text types" as such. This awareness would also have to encompass each individual book of the collection, because the MT, just as the LXX, is not a unified "text type" but varies from book to book through the collection. Demonstration—if possible—of these types of awareness in the Second Temple period would be a significant contribution to scholarship, but thus far seems lacking.

Moreover, in addition to (a) an *awareness* of different text forms for each book, there would have to be (b) *conscious concern* that one specific form ought to be preferred to others, (c) some *authoritative group* who decided one way or the other, and (d) the *acknowledgement* by a reasonably large percentage of Jews of that specific text form. That is: (a-b) if there were no awareness of different text forms and no conscious concern that one form be preferred to others, then the claim for a standard text (in the normative sense) could not be made; simple use does not constitute normativeness.[27] (c) If there were an awareness of different text forms and a conscious concern that one form be preferred to others, but there were no authoritative group which could command a decision one way or the other, then again the claim for a standard text cannot be made; there would simply be different text forms that people disagreed over, and the disagreement is the end of the story. (d) Similarly, if there were an authoritative group which did make a decision but there were no acknowledgement by a reasonably large percentage of Jews of that text form, the claim for a standard text cannot be made; that text form would not in fact have achieved the status of "the standard text."[28]

Finally, to claim that the assortment of forms of the books that became the MT collection was considered the authoritative text form, one would have to demonstrate for a significant number of individual books that the *edition* as well as the *specific sub-family* attested by the MT was *consciously preferred* to other known text editions, to demonstrate that the *main leadership group* who decided such matters *concurred* in this conscious selection, and to demonstrate that most influential religious *leaders and authors actually used* those specific texts when they wrote.

Nothing in my text-critical experience supports any of the notions above.

The Coincidental Nature of Text Selection

Was the selection of the specific texts that make up the MT collection a conscious and deliberate process, or did it happen rather by chance? Shemaryahu Talmon, Emanuel Tov, and Eugene Ulrich all concur now for various reasons on the coincidental or chance nature of the selection of the texts found in the MT collection. For example, Talmon states that "the combined evidence of Qumran and Rabbinic techniques proves the contention that variant readings in the Biblical textual traditions were viewed with

---

[27] Such a text form might be called "the standard text," but only in the authoritatively insignificant sense of the text that people happen to use.

[28] If all these conditions appear to be excessive, I would point to the quotation cited by Sanders (*Judaism*, p. vi) from Macaulay's *Machiavelli*: "Historians rarely descend to those details from which alone the real estate of a community can be collected."

relative equanimity by both groups."[29] Tov agrees: "This development [from pluriformity to uniformity] is often described as the 'stabilization' of MT, but in my view the survival of MT as the sole text rather than the preponderant one is merely a result of sociological developments";[30] the selection was "mere coincidence."[31]

No conclusive evidence has been produced to confirm or disprove that view, although all the available indications point toward a chance collection, whereas none indicates conscious comparison and deliberate selection from among the available text forms. Timothy Lim similarly concludes that "the sectarian scrolls do not exhibit any such preference for a particular text" and offers as an example that "4Q175 (4QTest) tolerates various textual forms."[32] That one-page text has four quotes: the first cites the SP against the MT; the second agrees with the MT; the third agrees with 4QDeut[h] and the LXX against the MT; and the fourth partly agrees with the LXX against the MT and partly quotes 4QApochryphon of Joshua[b] (see Ch. 11.IV.B).

Several phenomena argue against the notion of deliberate comparison and choice: the inferior condition of some MT books such as Samuel and Hosea, when better texts were available; the existence of pluriform text types for over a century at Scripture-focused Qumran with no indication that one was to be chosen rather than another; and the LXX translations, quotations in the NT and Talmud, and sources for Josephus, many of which are based on variant text forms.[33]

Classification of Qumran Scriptural Scrolls

The set of categories used most commonly for describing scriptural scrolls from Qumran proposes four classifications: "Masoretic-like texts," "pre-Samaritan texts," "texts close to the presumed Hebrew source of the Septuagint," and "non-aligned texts."[34] This system has the distinct pedagogical advantage, especially for students and non-specialists, of helping one understand and classify the textual situation of the new scrolls quickly.[35] For example, in an article on the canon James VanderKam uses these classifications as a

[29] Shemaryahu Talmon, "Aspects of the Textual Transmission of the Bible in the Light of Qumran Manuscripts," in *Qumran and the History*, 263; idem, "The Old Testament Text," in *Qumran and the History*, 21).

[30] "The Many Forms of Hebrew Scripture: Reflections in Light of the LXX and 4QReworked Pentateuch," in *From Qumran to Aleppo: A Discussion with Emanuel Tov about the Textual History of Jewish Scriptures in Honor of his 65th Birthday* (ed. Armin Lange, Matthias Weigold, and József Zsengellér; FRLANT 230; Göttingen: Vandenhoeck & Ruprecht, 2009), 11–28, esp. 13.

[31] Tov, *Textual Criticism*, 179; idem, "The Coincidental Textual Nature of the Collections of Ancient Scriptures," *Congress Volume Ljubljana 2007* (VTSup 133; Leiden: Brill, 2010), 153–69.

[32] Timothy H. Lim, *The Formation of the Jewish Canon* (New Haven: Yale University Press, 2013), 126.

[33] On the untrustworthiness of the Talmudic tradition of the three scrolls of the Temple Court (*y. Ta'an. 4.68a*), see John Van Seters, *The Edited Bible: The Curious History of the "Editor" in Biblical Criticism* (Winona Lake, Ind.: Eisenbrauns, 2006), 65–67; and Tov, *Textual Criticism*, 176–77.

[34] See Tov, *Textual Criticism* (3d ed., 2012), 107–9. These categories are refined from the earlier five classifications in the second edition (2d ed., 2001): "Proto-Masoretic texts," "Pre-Samaritan texts," "texts close to the Septuagint," "texts written in the Qumran Practice," and "Non-Aligned texts."

[35] Tov emphasizes this pedagogical aspect in "A Didactic Approach to the Biblical Dead Sea Scrolls," in *Celebrating the Dead Sea Scrolls: A Canadian Collection* (ed. Peter W. Flint, Jean Duhaime, and Kyung S. Baek; Early Judaism and Its Literature Series; Atlanta: SBL Press; Leiden: Brill, 2011), 173–98.

starting point, saying that they "give one extremely well informed scholar's [Tov's] overview of the situation."[36] But I suggest that one must quickly go further and redescribe the situation in terms appropriate to a Second Temple mentality for proper focus.

While those categories offer an initial pedagogical advantage, they also entail significant problems. The first is that they are anachronistic. People at that time would not have had conceptually available, and thus would not have used, textual categories such as "Masoretic" or "Masoretic-like," "Samaritan" or "pre-Samaritan." The term "proto-Masoretic text" prior to the Middle Ages, or even "proto-rabbinic," seems anachronistic, as does "pre-Samaritan." The term "Samaritan" would be used of the religion or of a person; but it would be used of a text only when describing the theologically variant texts with a Mount Gerizim perspective, and such are not found at Qumran. The category "texts close to the Septuagint" raises the anomalous situation that the MT of Genesis or Leviticus would be classified as Septuagintal, since the MT is largely identical with the LXX for those books.

Second, an additional complication is that the textual character of the MT changes from book to book, and so the criteria for labeling any text "Masoretic-like" change, depending on whether, for example, the text is Numbers or Jeremiah or Daniel. Third and importantly, the MT and the LXX are not "text types." The text of each of their books is simply the only one (for MT) or one of the few (for LXX) text forms preserved. They are, in varying degrees, simply *copies*—more accurate or less accurate copies—of whichever edition they happen to attest. Thus, the last category, "non-aligned," is also problematic, since the MT and the LXX do not constitute proper standards against which other manuscripts should be judged "aligned" or "non-aligned."

Biblical vs. Nonbiblical Distribution in the Discoveries in the Judaean Desert Series

Another area where modern terminology can confuse, because it does not adequately address the situation in the first centuries, is along the border between what are labeled "biblical" and "nonbiblical" scrolls. Understandably, before a full picture of the nature of the scriptural text in antiquity was achieved, the early editors of the DJD series classified the scrolls according to modern classifications and divided the "biblical" scrolls from the "nonbiblical" scrolls according to the contents of the MT. For consistent continuation of the series, Emanuel Tov and I decided to follow the established practice, classifying mechanically according to those same modern formal categories. Thus, those manuscripts, and only those, would be classified as "biblical" that correspond to books of the traditional Hebrew Bible. That practice does, however, involve the double anomaly that some books that were very likely considered Scripture at Qumran (such as 4Q["Reworked"] Pentateuch, 1 Enoch, and Jubilees) are classified as "nonbiblical," while some of the Ketuvim, for which there is little evidence that they were yet considered Scripture, are classified as "biblical." VanderKam correctly notes more broadly that "what are identified as 'biblical' manuscripts are often treated separately by scrolls scholars, with some focusing all or almost all of their scholarly labors on them. It

[36] James C. VanderKam, "Questions of Canon Viewed through the Dead Sea Scrolls," in *The Canon Debate*, 91–109, esp. 94.

seems to me that this segregation of texts is not a valid procedure in that it does not reflect what comes to expression in the ancient works found at Qumran."[37]

The Collection of the Scriptures

Throughout this chapter we have been discussing the textual character of individual texts. Applying similar scrutiny to the *collection* of texts that eventually would become the canon of Scripture will also produce valuable insight (see Chs. 17–19).

Conclusion

Methodological reflection on the ideas discussed above promises to yield continuingly greater precision in our understanding of the Scriptures. Careful analysis of methodological procedure in itself is always warranted in scientific endeavors. It is important that we reflect on how it is that we have come to know what we know, and on whether there might be flaws in our perception or our articulation of its significance. We should be aware that our store of knowledge and our ways of thinking are largely derived from the preceding generations; as grateful as we are for that, we should always ask whether current advances require revision of our ways of thinking.

Methodological rigor should also be applied to assessments and discussions of both individual texts and the process toward the canon. Just as clarifying advances have been made on texts such as 4QPentateuch and the Cave 11 Psalms scroll (see Ch. 12), and as the text-critical value of the SP and the LXX has been restored, other texts undoubtedly hold analogous promise.

---

[37] VanderKam, "Questions of Canon," 95.

THE SCRIPTURES FOUND AT QUMRAN

CHAPTER 3

THE DEVELOPMENTAL GROWTH OF THE PENTATEUCH IN THE SECOND TEMPLE PERIOD

MORE THAN ONE HUNDRED fragmentary manuscripts of the books of the Torah were found in the Qumran caves plus twenty-six more in the other caves near the Dead Sea, and they have greatly deepened knowledge of the growth of the Pentateuch during the Second Temple period. Previously, the Pentateuch was assumed to have been basically complete and static at the time of Ezra,[1] but the scrolls show that it was still developing in substantial ways in the late Second Temple period. Although most of the material evidence needed to construct the history of its development has perished through the centuries, the small amount of preserved evidence nonetheless affords valuable illumination: the text of the Pentateuch developed in a succession of gradually changing forms leading up to the forms encountered in the Bible today and even forms beyond them. These forms are genetically related, with the new form generated by adapting the old, due to new religious, historical, political, or social situations, or to scribal creativity.

It is important to stress at the beginning that there is no extant material evidence for the text of the Hebrew Bible prior to the middle of the third century B.C.E. But now the Qumran biblical manuscripts have opened a window onto a period in the history of the biblical text that lay mostly in darkness since the second century C.E. Since the Second Jewish Revolt in 132–135 C.E. no Hebrew text form (prescinding from the Samaritan Pentateuch) other than the Masoretic *textus receptus* was transmitted to posterity. This absence of evidence—which was too easily assumed to be evidence of absence—led to the notion of a single *Urtext* which had been transmitted most faithfully by the MT, and less so by the SP, the LXX, and other versions.

Literary critics since the Enlightenment, however, had theorized that the biblical books had grown in evolutionary stages from their beginnings as oral stories, laws, etc., to composite works at the hands of creative tradents and editors, eventually assuming forms recognizable as early editions of what we know as the biblical books.[2]

---

[1] See, e.g., Otto Eissfeldt, *The Old Testament: An Introduction* (trans. Peter R. Ackroyd; New York: Harper and Row, 1965), 562–71; and Jack P. Lewis, "Jamnia Revisited," in *The Canon Debate* (ed. Lee M. McDonald and James A. Sanders; Peabody, Mass.: Hendrickson, 2002), 146–62, esp. 148–51.

[2] Eissfeldt, *The Old Testament*, 158–66 and 9–127.

The Qumran manuscripts now give us documentary evidence—even for the Torah—to ground those literary theories: evidence that prior to the Jewish Revolts the text was pluriform and still developing by creative expansion techniques analogous to those envisioned by post-Enlightenment scholars for the earlier stages. This chapter will trace some of the stages of the growth of the Pentateuch witnessed by the scrolls[3] in comparison with the MT, the SP, and the LXX, in the hope of laying a foundation for understanding the early development of the text in the period before manuscript evidence becomes available.

I. 4QpaleoExod^{m}

It is important to begin with an examination of the evidence, starting with that from Qumran, since it is the most ancient and presents a clear picture. One of the more dramatic examples of the pluriformity of the text is 4QpaleoExod^{m}.

The elegant and carefully inscribed manuscript 4QpaleoExod^{m}, one of the most well-preserved scrolls, copied in approximately the late second or first century B.C.E., provides a lens through which we can begin to see the development of the biblical text in significantly better light and focus.[4]

The first fragment preserved from 4QpaleoExod^{m} offers a clear example of one of its characteristic features at Exod 7:18 (Frg.1, col. II, see Table 1). Lines 5–11 display a lengthy addition that is inserted into the scroll but is lacking in the MT.[5] On the basis of this one reading, it could be argued that 4QpaleoExod^{m} has the original text and that the MT has lost the passage through homoioteleuton, since the scribe's eye could have skipped from מים מן היאר ("water from the Nile") at the end of v. 18^{a} (in line 5) to the same phrase at the end of v. 18^{b} (in line 11). This hypothesis is strengthened when one notices that the SP also has the same passage, thus offering double attestation. An alternative explanation, however, would be that v. 18^{b} was added to record explicitly that Moses and Aaron actually carried out the Lord's command. The MT gives the command to speak to Pharaoh and turn the Nile water into blood; it then tacitly presumes, but does not narrate, the execution of that command. The scroll and the SP explicitly state that Moses and Aaron actually carried out the Lord's command.

Methodologically, one should consider the merits of both possibilities but withhold judgment for additional clues, if available. That the longer text is, in fact, a secondary insertion into the Exod^{m}-SP text type, rather than a haplographic loss, is made clear by the fact that such insertions form a pattern repeated often in the book (see Table 2). There are five instances partially preserved in the scroll of an insertion reporting the execution of a command which was presumed but not explicitly recorded in the MT: $7{:}18^{b}$, $7{:}29^{b}$[$8{:}4^{b}$𝔊], $8{:}19^{b}$[$8{:}23^{b}$𝔊], $9{:}5^{b}$, $9{:}19^{b}$.

---

[3] See Ch. 13; for further evidence from the SP and LXX see Chs. 14 and15.

[4] For the edition see Patrick W. Skehan, Eugene Ulrich, and Judith E. Sanderson, DJD 9:53–130, and Skehan's early preliminary report in "Exodus in the Samaritan Recension from Qumran," in *JBL* 74 (1955): 182–87. See also the analyses by Judith E. Sanderson, *An Exodus Scroll*, and James R. Davila, "Exodus, Book of," in *Encyclopedia of the Dead Sea Scrolls*, 1:277–79.

[5] Many of the scrolls' textual phenomena described in this and following chapters are translated and explained in *The Dead Sea Scrolls Bible*.

TABLE 1: *Exodus 7:18-19*

Witness	Text	Line
4QpaleoExod[m]	[18]והדגה אשר]	3
	בת[וך [הֹיאֹר תמות]ובאש היאר ונלאו מצריים לשתות]	4
	מיֹם מן היאֹר *va] cat* [18b]וילך משה ואהרן אל פרעה]	5
	וי]א[וֹמר אליו יה]וה אלהי העברים שלחנו אליך לאמור]	6
	שלח את עמי ויעבד[ני במדבר והנה לא שמעת עד כה]	7
	כה אֹמר יהוה בז[את תדע כי אני יהוה הנה אנכי]	8
	מֹ]כ[הֹ במטה אשר [בידי על המים ונהפכו לדם]	9
	ו]הד[גה אשר בת[וך היאר תמות ובאש היאר ונלאו]	10
	מֹ]צ[ריים לש[תות מים מן היאר [19]𐤅]	11
	י]או[מֹר יהו[ה . . .]	12
SP	[18]והדגה אשר	3
	ביאר תמות ובאש היאר ונלאו מצרים לשתות	4
	מים מן היאר [18b]וילך משה ואהרן אל פרעה	5
	ויאמרו אליו יהוה אלהי העברים שלחנו אליך לאמר	6
	שלח את עמי ויעבדני במדבר והנה לא שמעת עד כה	7
	כה אמר יהוה בזאת תדע כי אני יהוה הנה אנכי	8
	מכה במטה אשר בידי על המים אשר ביאר ונהפכו לדם	9
	והדגה אשר ביאר תמות ובאש היאר ונלאו	10
	מצרים לשתות מים מן היאר	11
	[19]ויאמר יהוה . . .	12
MT	[18]והדגה אשר	3
	ביאר תמות ובאש היאר ונלאו מצרים לשתות	4
	מים מן היאר ס	5
	[19]ויאמר יהוה . . .	12

[18] [. . . the Egyptians shall be unable to drink] water from the Nile.

[18b] [*So Moses and Aaron went to Pharaoh,*] *and he* [*s*]*aid to him, "The LO*[*RD, the God of the Hebrews has sent us to you to say,*] *'Let my people go, so that they may worship* [*me in the wilderness.' But until now you have not listened.*] *Thus says the Lord, 'By th*[*is you shall know that I am the LORD.' See,*] *with the staff that is* [*in my hand I will*] *st*[*rik*]*e* [*the water, and it shall be turned to blood. The fi*]*sh in the mid*[*st of the river shall die, the river shall stink, and*] *the E*[*gy*]*ptians* [*shall be unable*] *to dr*[*ink water from the Nile.'*]

[19]The LORD [s]aid . . .

single underline = orthography
double underline = individual textual variants
dotted underline = patterned sets of larger insertions which together form a new edition

TABLE 2: *Major expansions and variant sequences in SP–Exod^m, absent from MT*

SP	Exod^m as Extant	Reconstructed	Type of Expansion
Major Expansions			
6:9^b	—	?	[Harmonization, Exod 14:12]
7:18^b	II 6–11	II 5–11	Execution
7:29^b	III 2–4	II 31 – III 4	Execution
8:1^b	—	III 7–8	[Execution]
8:19^b	IV 4–9	IV 3–10	Execution
9:5^b	V 1–3	IV 30 – V 3	Execution
9:19^b	V 28–31	V 23–32	Execution
10:2^b	VI 27–29	VI 24–30	Anticipated Command
11:3^b (i)	—	VIII 11–16	[Anticipated Command]
11:3^b (ii)	—	VIII 19–20	[Anticipated Command]
18:25 SP	XIX 7–17	XIX 6–20 or 21	Harmonization, Deut 1:9-18
20:17^b	—	>	[absent]
20:19^a	XXI 21–28	XXI 21–29	Harmonization, Deut 5:24-27
20:21^b	—	XXI 33 – XXII 16	[Harmonization Deut 5 & 18]
24:1	XXVI 20	XXVI 19–20	Addition of Eleazar & Ithamar
24:9	XXVI 31	XXVI 31	Addition of Eleazar & Ithamar
27:19^b	XXXI 9	XXXI 9(–10)	Addition of garments
32:10	XXXVIII 1–2	XXXVIII 1–2	Harmonization, Deut 9:20
39:21^b	—	?	[Execution]
Major Variants in Order of Text			
30:1-10 after 26:35	XXX 12–13	XXX 2–13	Golden incense altar
29:21 after 29:28	[cf. XXXIV 6–7]	XXXIV 22–24	Sprinkling of garments

Yet another instance is probably to be reconstructed at 8:1^b[8:5^{b}𝔊].[6] Conversely, there is one instance (10:2^b) where the scroll inserts a lengthy command by the Lord which the MT does not include, though all texts report the execution of that command. The scroll anticipates Moses' speech to Pharaoh by first providing the Lord's precise wording for Moses to relay to Pharaoh. A similar instance of anticipated material is to be reconstructed according to the two insertions at the beginning and the end of SP 11:3, though the scroll is not extant at that point.[7]

A second type of intentional addition to the text of 4QpaleoExod^m can be seen at Exod 32:10 (see Table 3). 4QpaleoExod^m and the SP have a longer reading that the MT does not have. There is little or no reason to suppose that the MT accidentally skipped the reading. Rather, it is a virtually word-for-word insertion of a verse from Deut 9:20. Deuteronomy is, as the designation "deutero-nomos" would suggest, a book which repeats

[6] "Reconstruction" as used here is not highly speculative but is based on careful plotting of the spatial requirements of the scroll's format dictated by the preserved fragments.

[7] See the detailed explanation in DJD 9:84–85.

TABLE 3: *Exodus 32:10-11*

4QpaleoExod[m]	א[ו]תך] לגוי גדול [ובאהרן התאנף יה]וה מאד להשמידו[ ]	1
	ו[י]תפלל משה בעד א[הרן] [[11]ל] [ ]	2
	י[ח]ל משה את[פנ]י [יהוה אלהיו ויא]מר למ[ה]יהוה יחר א[פך]	3
	בעמך אשר הו[צ]את מארץ מצרים בכח גדול ו[בזרוע חזק]ה]	4
SP	אתך לגוי גדול ובאהרן התאנף יהוה מאד להשמידו	1
	ויתפלל משה בעד אהרן	2
	[11]ויחל משה את פני יהוה אלהיו ויאמר למה יהוה יחר אפך	3
	בעמך אשר הוצאת ממצרים בכח גדול ובזרוע נטויה	4
MT	אותך לגוי גדול:	1
		2
	[11]ויחל משה את פני יהוה אלהיו ויאמר למה יהוה יחרה אפך	3
	בעמך אשר הוצאת מארץ מצרים בכח גדול וביד חזקה:	4

[10] ". . . and of y[ou I will make] a great nation." [*The* LO]RD *was so* [*angry with Aaron*] *that he was ready to destroy him, but Moses* [*in*]*terceded on behalf of A*[*aron.*]

[11] Moses im[plo]red the [LORD his God, and sa]id, "O Lord, wh[y] does [your] wr[ath] burn hot against your people, whom you brou[ght out of the land of Egypt with great power and] with a stron[g] arm?"

much of the Book of Exodus, and so scribes inserted into this Exodus tradition pertinent parallel details narrated in Deuteronomy which had not been mentioned in the original Exodus narrative. In the passage in Deuteronomy 9 about the people making the golden calf while Moses is up on Mount Sinai, Moses intercedes for the people, and it is explicitly said that Moses intercedes for Aaron as well. In the parallel passage in Exodus 32, however, the earlier tradition as in the MT records that Moses intercedes for the people, but it does not mention Aaron. Thus, the tradition behind the scroll and SP imports from Deut 9:20 the detail that Moses intercedes for Aaron specifically. Again, there are two additional examples (plus one more reconstructed) of preserved harmonizations drawn from Deuteronomy that are inserted into the text of the scroll.[8] A similar lengthy borrowing from Deut 1:9-18 is inserted after Exod 18:24 in place of the brief report in 18:25 MT. A third harmonization from Deut 5:24-27[21-24 SP] is preserved at Exod 20:19^{a}, and a fourth, interrelated, harmonization from Deut 5:28-31 + 18:18-22 is to be reconstructed at 20:21^{b}.

[8] Whether 4QpaleoExod^{m} had or lacked the harmonization at 6:9^{b} and the report of execution in 39:21^{b} cannot be decided with any certainty, since they occur before and after the range of preserved fragments of the scroll. There is no reason, however, to doubt that they were present in the scroll: in fact, 39:21^{b} does occur in 4QExod-Lev^{f} (see below).

The scroll also exhibits smaller indications of thoughtful additions. In Exod 24:1 and 9 the names of Aaron's sons, Eleazar and Ithamar, though not in the MT, are added in the scroll and in the SP. The traditional MT mentions only Aaron's older sons, Nadab and Abihu. But since both were subsequently killed for offering unholy fire (Lev 10:1-7), it is quite likely that the two younger sons, one of whom would become high priest (cf. Num 3:22; 4:16), were included to be present at and favored to witness the theophany on Sinai.

In only a single instance does 4QpaleoExod^{m} appear not to contain a major expansion found in the SP: 20:17^{b}. The SP has three expansions in chapter 20: (a) 17^{b}, the commandment to build an altar on Mount Gerizim; (b) 19^{a}, the people request Moses as mediator at Sinai; and (c) 21^{b}, the Lord's response to that request. The amount of spacing for the text originally contained in the scroll can be calculated by the regular margins preserved for the columns before and after; there is too much space for the text of Exod 20:1–21:6 as in the MT, but too little space for the text as in the SP, which includes the three expansions. Of those three, only the second, 19^{a}, is partially preserved; it inserts the text from Deut 5:24-27[21-24 SP], narrating the people's request that Moses act as mediator. The close interrelationship between that request and the Lord's response to the request in 21^{b} makes it highly unlikely that a scroll which contained the first half of the exchange between the people and the Lord would lack the second. These two insertions fit the space allowed in 4QpaleoExod^{m}, and, since the space is too small for all three insertions, it is most reasonable to conclude that v. 17^{b} was not included.[9] The significance of its absence was quickly recognized by Patrick Skehan (see n. 15).

Note, moreover, that there are two transpositions of passages shared by the scroll and SP in common against the order of the MT. In the first, the passage about the gold incense altar, 30:1-10, is transposed to follow 26:35, and in the second, the sprinkling of the priestly garments in 29:21 is placed after 29:28 (see also Lev 8:22-30). In light of the other major indicators, it is probably best to assume that these two transpositions are due to the tradition behind the scroll.[10]

II. 4QExod-Lev^{f}

A second Exodus manuscript, only sparsely preserved, shows similar patterns. 4QExod-Lev^{f} is one of the oldest manuscripts from Qumran, from the second half of the third century B.C.E., and is a "witness to the textual family [of the] Proto-Samaritan. . . ."[11] It displays an interesting reading at Exod 39:21 (see Table 4): "He made the Urim and [the Thummim, just as the Lord had commanded] Moses." Frank Moore Cross, the editor of the manuscript, notes that this "reading in 4QExod-Lev^{f} and SP echoes Exod 28:30," and he judges that it "is best taken as original in the Hebrew text, lost . . . in other

9 For more detailed explanation see DJD 9:66 and 101–02.

10 For the physical evidence supporting these transpositions see DJD 9:112–13, 117–18. For discussion of the possible purpose regarding the order of the altar passage see Sanderson, *An Exodus Scroll*, 111–15.

11 Frank Moore Cross, "17. 4QExod-Lev^{f}," DJD 12:136. I thank Chelica Hiltunen for bringing this reading to my attention in her paper at the meeting of the Canadian Society of Biblical Studies, 29 May 2007.

TABLE 4: *Exodus 39:21*

4QExod-Lev^{f} 39:21	[21]וי]רכסו את החשן . .].	1
	ולא יזח החשן]מעל האפוד כאשר צוה יהוה את משה[	2
	ויעש את האורים ו]את התמים כאשר צוה יהוה את] משה	3
SP 39	[21]וירכסו את החשן . . .	1
	ולא יזח החשן מעל האפוד כאשר צוה יהוה את משה	2
	ויעשו את הארים ואת התמים כאשר צוה יהוה את משה	3
MT 39	[21]וירכסו את החשן . . .	1
	ולא יזח החשן מעל האפד כאשר צוה יהוה את משה:	2
	>	3

[21] They b[ound the breastpiece . . .] that the breastpiece should not come loose [from the ephod; as the Lord had commanded Moses.] *And he made the Urim and* [*the Thummim, just as the Lord had commanded*] *Moses.*

traditions."[12] That is quite possible (cf. Lev 8:8), although the alternative possibility deserves further examination in light of the increasing understanding of the SP tradition.

Exodus 39 relates the execution of the commands in chapter 28. In Exodus 28 in both the MT and the SP Moses is commanded to make the priestly vestments, and the order of the detailed commands for the vestments includes the Urim and Thummim. Exodus 39 in the MT then reports the making of the priestly vestments but does not include mention of the Urim and Thummim. 4QExod-Lev^{f} and SP, however, do include them. The order of the execution agrees with the order of the commands, with the one exception that in the MT the Urim and Thummim are not mentioned:

MT SP 28	[31]מעיל	[30]ונתת אל חשן המשפט את האורים ואת התמים	[15]חשן	האפד 28[6]
MT 39	[22]מעיל	>	[8]החשן	האפד 39[2]
4QExod-Lev^{f} SP 39	[22]מע]יל[	[21]ויעש את האורים ו]את התמים . . .[	[8]]החשן[	]האפוד[39[2]

Thus, rather than seeing the longer text of 39:21 with "the Urim and Thummim" as original but lost in other manuscripts, it rather appears to follow the general pattern of the expanded edition as transmitted in 4QpaleoExod^{m} and the SP. The scribe, remembering that the Lord had commanded Moses to put the Urim and Thummim in the breastpiece, adds in proper order a detail that was left unmentioned in the earlier text. He explicitly adds the execution of that command in the same manner that other executions of commands were explicitly added in the tradition behind 4QpaleoExod^{m} and the SP.

[12] Cross, "17. 4QExod-Lev^{f}," 139.

III. 4QNum^B

The Book of Exodus was by no means the only surprise among the scrolls of the Pentateuch. The largest Qumran manuscript of the Book of Numbers, 4QNum^{b}, from the latter half of the first century B.C.E., provided evidence analogous to that of 4QpaleoExod^{m}, as can be seen in the examples from Numbers 21:12-13 (see Table 5) and 27:23 (Table 6).[13]

There are thirteen major expansions in the SP of Numbers, and for five of those, 4QNum^{b} is partly extant and preserves them. For three more, careful reconstruction demonstrates that the scroll contained them as well. For the remaining five, there are no nearby fragments preserved to provide evidence, but there is no reason to suspect that 4QNum^{b} lacked those expansions. The five extant expansions are:

Num 20:13^{b} (= Deut 3:24-28)	Moses pleads to be able to enter the land
Num 21:12^{a} (= Deut 2:9)	Command not to fight Moab
Num 21:13^{a} (= Deut 2:17-19)	Command not to fight Ammon
Num 21:21^{a} (= Deut 2:24-25)	Promise of defeat of the Amorites
Num 27:23^{b} (= Deut 3:21-22)	Moses promises Joshua God's help

In Num 20:13^{b} the Lord tells Moses and Aaron that, because they did not trust him at Meribah, they will not lead the Israelites into the land. In the MT there is no reaction from Moses described, but in 4QNum^{b}, followed by the SP, Moses begs the Lord, "Please let me cross over and see the good land. . . ."

In the short, early MT text of Numbers 21, verse 12 has only five words. In 4QNum^{b} and the SP, however, that brief verse is preceded and followed by lengthy commands brought in from Deuteronomy (Table 5).[14] Israel is commanded not to engage the Moabites (Deut 2:9) and Ammonites (Deut 2:17-19) in battle, since the Lord has not given them those lands to inherit. They are, however, commanded to fight the Amorites (Num 21:21^{a} = Deut 2:24-25).

After Num 27:23 (Table 6), in which Moses appoints Joshua as his successor, 4QNum^{b} and the SP insert an encouraging saying of Moses recorded in the parallel at Deut 3:21-22: "Your own eyes have seen what the LORD has done to these two kings; so the LORD will do. . . ."

Thus, in the closing centuries of the Second Temple period at least two of the five books of the Torah were circulating within Judaism in variant editions. Since 4QExod-Lev^{f} (third-century B.C.E.) presumably pre-dated the Samaritan-Jewish split, since 4QpaleoExod^{m} apparently did not contain the Samaritan commandment to build an altar

---

[13] For the edition see Nathan Jastram, "27. 4QNum^{b}," DJD 12:205–67.

[14] The fragment concerned (frg. 18), though small, fits well with another large fragment (frg. 17i–ii) containing Numbers 21:1 in one column and Num 21:20-21 in the following, attached column.

TABLE 5: *Numbers 21:12[a]-13[a]*

4QNum[b]	]מזרח השמש *vacat* [12a]ו]יואמ[ר יהוה אל[	13
	]מושה אל תצור את מואב ואל תתגר בם מלחמה כיא]לוא אתן_מ[ארצו ירושה[	14
	]כיא לבני לוט נתתי את ער ירושה [12b]משם נסעו ויחנו]בנחל זר[ד *vacat* [	15
	[[13a]וידבר יהוה אל מושה לאמור אתה עובר היום את] גבול[ ]מ[ואב את[	16
	]ער וקרבתה מול בני עמון אל תצורם ואל תתגר בם]כיא ל[וא אתן מארץ[	17
SP	מזרח השמש [12a]ויאמר יהוה אל	13
	משה אל תצור את מואב ואל תתגר בם __ כי לא אתן לך מארצו ירשה	14
	כי לבני לוט נתתי את ער ירשה [12b]משם נסעו ויחנו בנחל זרד	15
	[13a]וידבר יהוה אל משה לאמר אתה עבר היום את גבול מואב את	16
	ער וקרבת מול בני עמון אל תצורם ואל תתגר בם כי לא אתן מארץ	17
MT Num 21	ממזרח השמש	13
		14
	[12b]משם נסעו ויחנו בנחל זרד	15
		16
		17
MT Deut 2	[9]ויאמר יהוה אלי	13
	___ אל תצר את מואב ואל תתגר בם מלחמה כי לא אתן לך מארצו ירשה	14
	כי לבני לוט נתתי את ער ירשה	15
	[17]וידבר יהוה אלי__ לאמר [18]אתה עבר היום את גבול מואב את	16
	ער [19]וקרבת מול בני עמון אל תצרם ואל תתגר בם כי לא אתן מארץ	17

[11][. . . toward the sunrise. [12a]*The* L*ORD*] *sai[d to Moses, "Do not harass Moab or engage them in battle, for] I will not give (you) any [of its land as a possession, since I have given Ar as a possession to the descendants of Lot."* [12b]From there they set out and camped] in the Wadi Zere[d. [13a]*The* L*ORD said to Moses, saying, "Today you are going to cross the] boundary of M[oab at Ar. When you approach the frontier of the Ammonites, do not harass them or engage them, for I will not give the land. . . .]*

on Mount Gerizim (Exod 20:17b),[15] and since 4QpaleoExod[m], 4QExod-Lev[f], and 4QNum[b] were in use[16] by the covenanters at Qumran (who would not have been recep-

[15] Already by 1959 Patrick W. Skehan ("Qumran and the Present State of Old Testament Text Studies: The Masoretic Text," *JBL* 78 [1959]: 21–25, esp. 22–23) had noted that "the paleohebrew Exodus is not a Samaritan sectarian document, though it does offer the type of text the Samaritans have preserved as their own." Unfortunately, none of the Qumran Pentateuchal scrolls attests an occurrence of either יבחר or בחר, often regarded as key indicators of Jewish or Samaritan affiliation, respectively. A possible exception is 4QpaleoDeut[r] at Deut 12:4, which contains חר[at the edge of frg. 16. The controlled spacing

TABLE 6: *Numbers 27:23[a]–28:1*

4QNum[b]	[[23a]ויסמו]ך את ידיו עליו ויצוהו כאשר דבר יהוה ביד מושה [[23b]ויואמר]	30
	[מוש]ה אליו עיניכה הרואות את אשר עשה יהוה לשני המ[לכים האלה כן יעשה]	31
	[יהוה לכול הממלכות אשר אתה עובר שמה . . .]	1
	[[28:1]וידבר . . .]	2
SP	[23a]ויסמך את ידו עליו ויצוהו כאשר דבר יהוה ביד משה [23b]ויאמר	30
	___ אליו עיניך הראות את אשר עשה יהוה לשני המלכים האלה כן יעשה	31
	יהוה לכל הממלכות אשר אתה עבר שמה . . .	1
	[28:1]וידבר . . .	2
MT	[23]ויסמך את ידיו עליו ויצוהו כאשר דבר יהוה ביד משה: פ	30
	[28:1]וידבר . . .	2

[23a][He lai]d his hands on him and commissioned him—as the LORD had directed through Moses. [23b]*[Mose]s[said] to him: "Your own eyes have seen what the Lord has done to these two k[ings; so the Lord will do to all the kingdoms into which you are about to cross. . . ."]*

receptive to Samaritan theology), these witnesses to the variant editions must be considered Jewish manuscripts, apparently regarded as no less sacrosanct than scrolls containing the editions later transmitted in the MT collection. Formerly, it was thought that the Samaritans had taken the shorter editions of the Torah books later transmitted by the Rabbis and made large-scale additions and changes. With the evidence, especially of 4QpaleoExod[m] and 4QNum[b], we can see more clearly that the Jewish Scriptures were still developing, that variant editions were circulating within and were used by different groups, and that the Samaritans simply took one of the available common Jewish editions that had (apart from the commandment after Exod 20:17 || Deut 5:21[5:18 SP]) at most only minor variants specifying Mount Gerizim.

of the adjacent frg. 15 suggests that the *yod* (a very wide letter in the Palaeo-Hebrew script) was necessarily included, thus אשר[יב]חר; see DJD 9, Plate XXXIV and pp. 134 and 139. Adrian Schenker argues that MT Neh 1:9 as well as several manuscripts of the LXX, the OL, and the Bohairic and Sahidic show that the perfect בחר was the earlier form of the tradition, and that the imperfect יבחר was the revised form; see "Le Seigneur choisira-t-il le lieu de son nom ou l'a-t-il choisi?: L'apport de la Bible grecque ancienne à l'histoire du texte samaritain et massorétique," in *Scripture in Transition: Essays . . . in Honour of Raija Sollamo* (ed. Anssi Voitila and Jutta Jokiranta; JSJS 126; Leiden: Brill, 2008), 339–51. I thank Gary Knoppers for alerting me to this article.

16 The 4QpaleoExod[m] fragments display corrections by a later hand and include a patch (see DJD 9, Plate XI and pp. 70 and 84–85) which was secondarily sewn onto a presumed hole in the leather and was inscribed by a different scribe. These features indicate that this variant edition of Exodus was indeed used, studied, and considered worthy of repair for reuse by the covenanters.

Two points may be noted here. First, analysis of the examples above from Exodus and Numbers shows different types of variation between the textual witnesses: at the levels of orthography (single underline in the Tables), individual textual variants (double underline), and patterned sets of larger insertions of new material (dotted underline) that constitute a new edition of a book. It should be noticed that the orthographic differences, the individual variants, and the major additions do not coordinate with or influence each other but appear to work on unrelated levels.

Secondly, the large insertions in 4QpaleoExod^{m} and 4QNum^{b} are similar in that they are basically the addition of "biblical text" to biblical text. That is, the insertion in Exod 7:18^{b} is simply the word-for-word repetition of the content of God's command in 7:15-18, now as a past-tense report of the carrying out of that command. The insertion in Exod 32:10^{b} is the word-for-word repetition of the comment at Deut 9:20 seen as pertinent to the narrative in Exodus 32. Num 21:12^{a}-13^{a} and 27:23^{b} are similarly the repetition of Deut 2:9, 17-19 and 3:21-22, respectively, at the pertinent parallels in the narrative of Numbers.

IV. 4QLev^{D} and 11QpaleoLev^{A}

Though the more dramatic examples of pluriformity in the Pentateuchal texts were found in Exodus and Numbers, smaller examples appear in Genesis, Leviticus, and Deuteronomy as well. One interesting reading shows a variant between two Qumran manuscripts of Leviticus, one of which is supported by the SP and the LXX, the other by the MT (see Table 7).[17]

This reading from Lev 17:4 is debated: from a mechanical point of view it seems that the reading in 4QLev^{d}-SP-LXX could be original, lost from the 11QpaleoLev^{a}-MT tradition through homoioteleuton (הביאו∩הביאו/יביאנו). Alternatively, it could be interpreted as an intentional addition inserted into the original short text, in order to clarify an otherwise ambiguous legal prescription: the law in 17:3-7 conflicts with Deut 12:15.[18]

If the 4QLev^{d}-SP-LXX reading is original, then the 11QpaleoLev^{a}-MT reading falls into the category of "simple error," that is, unintentional loss of text. If 11QpaleoLev^{a}-MT is original, however, then 4QLev^{d}-SP-LXX show an intentional scribal insertion. But however the factual case may be decided, it is here heuristically instructive to think about this as an intentional supplementary addition, since such additions do occur frequently in other biblical texts, especially in the prophetic texts (see Ch. 7).

[17] For the edition of 4QLev^{d} see Emanuel Tov, "26. 4QLev^{d}," DJD 12:193–95; for the edition of 11QpaleoLev^{a} see David Noel Freedman and Kenneth A. Mathews, *The Paleo-Hebrew Leviticus Scroll (11QpaleoLev)* (Winona Lake, Ind.: Eisenbrauns, 1985), revised in *The Biblical Qumran Scrolls*.

[18] This is the view of David Andrew Teeter in his dissertation, "Exegesis in the Transmission of Biblical Law in the Second Temple Period: Preliminary Studies" (Ph.D. dissertation, University of Notre Dame, 2008). He stresses the importance of the sacrificial context in judging this reading. Noting secondary linguistic, conceptual, and literary features of the plus, he adopts the position in agreement with A. Geiger ("Neuere Mittheilungen über die Samaritaner IV," *ZDMG* 19 [1864]: 601–15, esp. 606–7) that this is an attempt to assimilate the law of vv. 3-7 to that of vv. 8-9, thereby harmonizing the requirements of Leviticus 17 and Deuteronomy 12. See now his *Scribal Laws: Exegetical Variation in the Textual Transmission of Biblical Law in the Late Second Temple Period* (Tübingen: Mohr Siebeck: 2014), which arrived after this volume was sent to press. See also Jacob Milgrom, *Leviticus 17–22* (Anchor Bible 3A; New York: Doubleday, 2000), 1456.

TABLE 7: *Leviticus 17:4*

4QLev[d]	[ ] +ו[א]ל פת[ח אוהל מועד לוא הביאו]	3
	[לעשות אתו עלה]או שלמים ליהוה לרצונכם ל[ריח ניחח וישחטהו]	4
	[בחוץ ואל פתח אוהל מו]עד לוא יביאנו להקריבו ק[רבן ליהוה לפני משכן]	5
	[יהוה דם יחשב לאיש ה]הו[א] דם שפך ונכרת[האיש ההוא מקרב עמו]	6
SP	+ואל פתח אהל מועד לא הביאו	3
	לעשות אתו עלה או שלמים ליהוה לרצונכם לריח ניחח וישחטהו	4
	בחוץ ואל פתח אהל מועד לא הביאו להקריבו קרבן ליהוה לפני משכן	5
	יהוה דם יחשב לאיש ההוא דם שפך ונכרת האיש ההוא מקרב עמו	6
MT	+ואל פתח אהל מועד לא הביאו	3
		4
	להקריב קרבן ליהוה לפני משכן	5
	יהוה דם יחשב לאיש ההוא דם שפך ונכרת האיש ההוא מקרב עמו	6
11QpaleoLev[a]	+ואל פתח אהל מוע[ד ל]א הביאו	3
		4
	ל]הקריב קרבן ליהוה לפני מש[כן]	5
	יהוה דם יחשב לאי[ש ההוא דם שפך]ונכרת האיש ההוא מק[רב] עמו	6

+and [do not bring it to the] entr[ance of the tent of meeting, *to make it a burnt offering*] *or an offering of well-being to the Lord for acceptance on your behalf as* [*a pleasing aroma, but slaughter it outside and*] do not bring it [*to the entrance of the tent of mee*]*ting*, to present it as an off[fering to the LORD before the tabernacle of the LORD, he shall be held guilty of bloodshed;] he has shed blood, and he shall be cut off [from his people.]

V. FOUR CATEGORIES OF TEXTUAL VARIATION IN THE BIBLICAL TEXTS

This example from Lev 17:4, were it to be judged an addition, would exemplify yet a fourth type of variation commonly encountered between manuscripts: isolated insertions. Although it is a somewhat large insertion, it has more the character of an isolated supplement or isolated clarifying specification, unrelated to other insertions and thus not constituting part of a new edition. The chapters that follow will reveal numerous other such examples, so we may then list here four categories of variation detectable through comparison between the Scrolls and the traditional witnesses, the MT, SP, and OG:

1. patterned sets of similar substantial revisions or expansions forming new editions
2. isolated insertions of information, commentary, halakah, piety, etc.
3. individual textual variants
4. orthography

1. Variant Editions

There are numerous ways that the traditional texts were supplemented with additions of varying lengths. The resulting pluriformity, however is not chaos but shows patterns that can be clearly seen and intelligibly classified. The principal way that the biblical text developed in the Second Temple period was through successive revised and expanded editions of each book, with the process and the timing different for each book or set of books.

The many large expansions in 4QpaleoExod^{m} and the SP exhibit a definite, consistent, intentional pattern. Commands not matched by reports of the execution of those commands are repeatedly supplied with an expansion explicitly reporting the execution; and conversely, Moses' words to Pharaoh not anticipated with God's command to speak those words are repeatedly supplied with an expansion providing the wording of that command. In addition, details in the Deuteronomy narrative of the Moses story not mentioned in the traditional text of Exodus are inserted on four occasions. The consistent pattern of many intentional large expansions added to an earlier base text merits the designation "new revised edition" of the book of Exodus. Similarly, 4QNum^{b} and the SP exhibit the same pattern of frequently inserting material from Deuteronomy into the Numbers narrative, forming a revised edition of that book. The following chapters will present a number of other revised editions of certain books. Thus, the identifying criteria of variant or revised editions are a significant number of additions or changes to a base text that are intentional, repeated, and similar in themes or tendencies.

Source-critical examples such as the retheologizing of the older monarchic traditions in light of the destruction and exile (traditional P) help analogously to illustrate the phenomenon. The resulting Pentateuchal text was achieved not through displacement of the old but through supplementing the old with additional material.

The double or multiple literary editions illumined by the Scrolls are products of the latter stages of the compositional process of the Scriptures. The composition of the various books took place in numerous stages that were different for each book (consider the growth, e.g., of Isaiah, Jeremiah, the Twelve Prophets, Psalms, Proverbs) or set of books (e.g., the Tetrateuch, the Deuteronomistic History). Each new edition resulted from the creative efforts of some author/redactor/scribe/priest/teacher who took the current edition and intentionally revised it in light of the new opportunity or need of the time, whether religious, national, historical, social, or literary. The scholarly analysis of Israel's literary and redactional work that has accumulated since the Enlightenment richly charts this history for each of the books, from their hazy beginnings to their final form. But those analyses, while persuasive in varying degrees, did not have the benefit of manuscript evidence. The Qumran scrolls have now documented evidence for the latter stages of this dynamic process of the growth of the biblical books, and have enabled us to recognize the collateral evidence that the SP and the LXX furnish. If evidence were available from earlier centuries, it is not overly sanguine to expect that we would see variant editions of the other books as well.

It is important to reflect as well, first, on the diachronic aspect of the transmission and availability of successive variant editions, and second, on the limited time period for which evidence is preserved.

First, the lifespan of older and newer editions varies with each book or group of books and depends upon the point at which an editor produces a new edition and the time when the older edition ceases to be used. The individual books had their separate lives, and a new edition could arise at any given time. Both the old and the new editions could co-exist for a period, but usually one would continue to be transmitted and the other would eventually be forgotten (see Ch. 16,I. "MasEzek"). Since the OG texts had been translated in the third and second centuries B.C.E., they each witness to one, early variant edition of the Hebrew at the time. The rabbinic collection contains one of the available editions current at the time of the fall of the Temple, and thus their books often show later editions than those of the OG. The Qumran scrolls show the true historical state of affairs over time—multiple variant editions living side-by-side for a period, whereas the rabbinic-Masoretic editions show a cross-section at the time the texts ceased to develop because of external factors.

Second, the window of available evidence from Qumran is approximately only from 250 B.C.E. to 68 C.E., and even within that window, only a small percentage of the manuscript evidence survives. If an edition was produced prior to that period and no new edition is made within that period, then no variant editions will surface and all manuscripts will present that single edition, with the usual minor variants.

Thus, the Hebrew editions underlying the OG translation of the Pentateuch and those retained in the MT had already been completed. We can only speculate about the earlier forms that preceded our preserved manuscripts. Manuscripts with variant editions of both Exodus and Numbers are fortunately preserved, but only the single, then-available editions of Genesis, Leviticus, and Deuteronomy remain.[19] There were undoubtedly earlier versions of those books, but within the window of our evidence, only the single received edition is attested.

Nonetheless, our sparse surviving evidence clearly demonstrates the phenomenon of successive revised editions, and from that evidence—just as sections of the jawbone, skull, and skeleton of an extinct animal are sufficient for a rough but plausible reconstruction of the original—we can plausibly reconstruct some aspects of the early history of the texts. From their earliest, shadowy beginnings the texts developed and solidified by faithful repetition but also by occasional creative updated editions to form the books as we begin to see them when manuscript evidence becomes available. Usually, the newer edition eventually replaced the older one(s); but sometimes it did not, presumably because the newer one was not yet sufficiently established, or was known to be recent and not ancient, or conflicted with current beliefs (e.g., 4QpaleoExod^{m} and 4QNum^{b} with their affinities to the SP, or 11QPs^{a} and Jubilees advocating a 364-day solar calendar).

2. Isolated insertions

The Qumran biblical scrolls have brought into prominence a second category of variation in addition to variant literary editions. Learned scribes occasionally inserted into the text

---

[19] Thus, the fact that Pentateuchal fragments of only Genesis, Leviticus, and Deuteronomy, but not Exodus or Numbers, were found at Masada lessens the weight of views such as "the 𝔐-group remained internally stable" (Tov, *Textual Criticism*, 179). It is perhaps better to say, "As at Qumran, so at Masada, the single current editions of those Pentateuchal books are attested with minor variants, and they were retained by the Rabbis and eventually the MT" (see Ch. 16).

they were copying what they considered an appropriate piece of additional material. Comparisons between the Scrolls, the MT, the SP, and the LXX highlight insertions of one and up to eight verses now in one text, now in another.[20] Depending upon the genre of book being copied, the insertions were informational (2 Sam 5:4-5 in MT vs. 4QSam^{a}), offered instruction (Isa 2:22 in 1QIsa^{a} MT vs. LXX), solved nomistic inconsistencies (perhaps Lev 17:4 in 4QLev^{d} SP vs. 11QpaleoLev^{a} MT), stemmed from piety (Isa 2:9b in 4QIsa^{a} 4QIsa^{b} MT LXX vs. 1QIsa^{a}), added prophetic apparitions (Judg 6:7-10 in MT vs. 4QJudg^{a}), showed apocalyptic tendencies (Isa 2:10 in 4QIsa^{a} 4QIsa^{b} MT LXX vs. 1QIsa^{a}, plus many ביום ההוא passages in Isaiah), added details such as the Urim and Thummim (Exod 39:21 in 4QExod-Lev^{f} SP vs. MT), inserted notices as the religion developed about new festivals such as the wood offering (Neh 10:35[Eng. 34], 4QPent C [*olim* 4QRP^{c}] 4Q365 23 5–11, and 11QT^{a} 23:3–25:1), or simply added similar material (Isa 34:17b–35:2 in MT LXX vs. 1QIsa^{a}; Jer 7:30–8:3 in MT 4QJer$^{a\ 2m}$ vs. 4QJer^{a*}) or contrasting material (Jer 10:6-8, 10 in MT vs. 4QJer^{b} LXX).[21] The prophetic books especially are replete with such, and results of this activity have penetrated many texts. Indeed such isolated insertions seems to have been a widespread factor in the development of many the biblical books. As we now read the *textus receptus*, however, we see them not as insertions but as simply an embedded part of "the biblical text."

3. *Individual textual variants*

We have noticed a few individual textual variants in the examples presented, and many more will appear later, but they are so ubiquitous and so routine in older approaches to textual criticism that they need little mention here. The human difficulty in accurately copying large amounts of complicated text resulted in readings which differed from the parent text for virtually every ancient manuscript. Many variants were unintentional (e.g., numerous types of errors, inadvertent substitution of *lectiones faciliores*, loss of letters, loss of one or more words through inattention or homoioteleuton); others were intentional (clarifying insertions, scribal corrections [whether correct or not], additional information, linguistic smoothing, euphemistic substitutions, literary flourishes, theological ideas). The Qumran textual examples presented above, as well as other examples to follow, show that individual textual variants are random and not related to the major edition of the book in which they occur.

4. *Orthography*

During the almost six centuries that the Second Temple stood, the language, and especially the spelling practices developed noticeably. Since the consonantal text of the Scriptures was sometimes ambiguous, scribes used fuller spellings, inserting *matres lectionis*, to ensure the correct reading and preserve the correct understanding. This was an early

[20] See especially the large insertion in Jer 7:30–8:3 visible in 4QJer^{a}. For the text see Emanuel Tov, "70. 4QJer^{a}," DJD 15:145–70, esp. p. 155 and Plate 24; for two analyses see Tov, ibid., and Eugene Ulrich, "Qumran Witness to the Developmental Growth of the Prophetic Books," in *With Wisdom as a Robe: Qumran and Other Jewish Studies in Honour of Ida Fröhlich* (Hebrew Bible Monographs 21; ed. Károly D. Dobos and Miklós Kőszeghy; Sheffield: Sheffield Phoenix Press, 2008), 263–74.

[21] Most of these examples are discussed in the pages that follow.

form of the same urge that eventually produced the vocalization by the Masoretes. In the tendency toward fuller spelling, the *matres lectionis* were inserted sometimes inadvertently, sometimes intentionally, insofar as the source text may have had one spelling but the scribe nonetheless inadvertently or intentionally wrote the word as he customarily spelled it, regardless of the source text. In manuscript after manuscript it appears clear that, just as with individual textual variants, orthographic practice is unrelated to the text type involved.

Usually orthographic differences do not affect the meaning of the words but rather aid in pronunciation and interpretation of the correct form amid possibly ambiguous forms. On occasion, however, orthographic insertion of a *mater lectionis* was deemed quite necessary. For example, at Isa 19:3 both the original form of 1QIsa^{a} and the MT have האבות. This, of course, could be taken to mean "fathers" or "ancestors," as is correct in most cases. But in this case the scribe of 1QIsa^{a} inserted a supralinear *vav*, האובות, to help the reader know that the word meant "spirits of the dead," not "fathers." The Masoretes accomplished the same goal by adding the vowel point *holem*, הָאֹבוֹת, but the unvocalized form would have been ambiguous until the Masoretic pointing in the early Middle Ages. Again, in Isa 40:6 the ambiguous ואמר was interpreted in the MT as third person וְאָמַר ("he said"), whereas it was clarified in 1QIsa^{a} through the insertion of *vav* and final *he* as first person ואומרה ("I said").

The Masoretic tradition also introduced *matres lectionis*, correctly or incorrectly; for example, 1QIsa^{a} has the correct form טלים for "lambs" at 40:11, whereas the MT adds a *mater lectionis* for the pronunciation *telāʾim*. Similarly the MT incorrectly adds *alef* in מאזנים ("scales, balances") at 40:15, for מזנים (without *alef*) in 1QIsa^{a}.[22]

These four different types of variation within manuscripts are unrelated to each other; that is, the orthographic profile of a manuscript happens on a different stratum, not related to the individual textual variants, which in turn happen on a different stratum unrelated to the edition that is being copied.[23]

A number of additional factors more difficult to substantiate with preserved evidence were at work in the development of the Pentateuchal text. Oral tradition was still an important factor, since, even though there may have been written texts in the earlier part of the Second Temple period, the traditions were mainly held in oral memory, and this continued to influence phrase-by-phrase transmission. Conceptually there were also other factors such as the increasing sacralization of the traditions, from religious and national literature toward Sacred Scripture (see Ch. 18).

The four principal types of variation described above form, in descending order, the main ways that the text of the Pentateuch developed in the Second Temple period. All the text traditions of a given book are genetically related; that is, all surviving manuscripts can be envisioned simply as dots on a chart, but each is derived from some other earlier text by a direct line, and all texts as they are traced back are eventually shown to

---

[22] The roots for these two examples are (1) original טלי = טלה (cf. טלה in *HALOT*, p. 375 and טלה at MT 1 Sam 7:9), and (2) יזן *HALOT*, p. 404; see מאזנים, p. 539, and "IIאזן : denom[inative] from a wrongly supposed אֹזֶן in מאזנים," p. 27). For טלה see also Shalom M. Paul, *Isaiah 40–66: Translation and Commentary* (Grand Rapids: Eerdmans, 2012), 137.

[23] The unrelatedness of these levels will be demonstrated in more detail in subsequent chapters.

be interconnected.[24] Thus, for each book the full chart looks like a tree, with the earliest form of the book as the trunk, which then diverges into a series of branches. The early traditions had reached one pristine text form (oral or written, which we think of as "original," since we can detect no earlier) which lasted for a certain period (edition *n*, where *n* is the latest non-preserved edition). From that trunk, due to some historical, social, or religious change in the life of the people a new revised edition (edition *n + 1*) of that text was created. This process, different in details and timing for each book, was repeated a number of times (editions *n + 2*, *n + 3*, etc.) all through the developing life of the texts. For a while both the earlier and the new editions circulated in common, with each gathering more individual variants. Then eventually one edition (usually, but not always, the new one) supplanted the other and became the new accepted version. Again, we have preserved for Exodus a number of different stages of this process (see Ch. 13).

All the while these main developments in editions were taking place, random individual textual variants were populating all sections of the tree, and occasionally scribes inserted isolated comments or additional material. Meanwhile, the orthographic practice sometimes continued to mirror the older orthography of the source text, and sometimes it was updated with fuller spellings to aid or determine interpretation. These four types of variation, however, operated separately on different levels, independent of each other. They were the work of different scribes at different times in the transmission.

With regard to the editions, our surviving manuscripts—the Masoretic codices, the Samaritan and Greek manuscripts, the Qumran scrolls—are *copies* of their various editions. We should never presume that we are dealing with the archetype of that edition, but rather with simply one, somewhat-variant copy of the edition. The dots on the chart identifying these by-chance-preserved manuscripts, while eventually connected, are always to some extent removed from the main branches that represent the new editions themselves.

Conclusion

As a result of the few examples presented above and those in the chapters that follow, one can confidently state that the text of the Pentateuch developed in numerous types of ways during the Second Temple period. And although most of the evidence is lost, enough remains to give some detailed description of that development.

---

[24] Depending on the strength of the argument of this chapter, the idea of differing pristine texts cannot be sustained; see also Tov, *Textual Criticism*, 161–65.

CHAPTER 4

JOSHUA'S FIRST ALTAR IN THE PROMISED LAND

WHICH SACRED CENTER in ancient Israel's traditions had the privilege of being the place designated by Moses for the first altar to be built in the newly entered promised land? Some fragments of 4QJosh^a offer a surprising alternative to the traditional *textus receptus* and provide new illumination concerning the redactional history of the book. Frank Moore Cross identified the remnants of 4QJosh^a and classified its script as Hasmonaean, thus dating it probably in the second half of the second century or the first half of the first century B.C.E.[1] It is the oldest extant witness to the Book of Joshua in any language, and so its contents and textual character deserve careful attention. Indeed it teaches us new and eye-opening things about this fascinating book.[2] Insofar as the interpretation below is correct, the manuscript is significant in that it preserves a sequence of the narrative that is at variance with, and probably prior and preferable to, that found in the received text of Joshua: it narrates that the first altar built by Joshua in the newly entered land was built at Gilgal immediately after the crossing of the Jordan (after Joshua 4), not later on Mount Gerizim (as commanded at Deut 27:4 in the SP) or on Mount Ebal (as commanded at Deut 27:4 and carried out at Josh 8:30-35 in the MT, or as carried out in the LXX^B at 9:2a-f).[3]

The question of the locality of the first altar exposes an issue that may well have been polemically debated.[4] There now appear to be three different rivals for that honor.

---

[1] The edition of 4QJosh^a is in DJD 14:143–52. See the general confirmation by Carbon-14 dating of Cross's palaeographic system for dating the manuscripts from the Judean Desert: A.J. Timothy Jull et al., "Radiocarbon Dating of Scrolls and Linen Fragments from the Judean Desert," *Atiqot* 28 (1996): 85–91.

[2] See Leonard Greenspoon, "The Qumran Fragments of Joshua: Which Puzzle Are They Part of and Where Do They Fit?" in *Septuagint, Scrolls and Cognate Writings. Papers Presented to the International Symposium on the Septuagint and Its Relations to the Dead Sea Scrolls and Other Writings (Manchester, 1990)* (ed. George J. Brooke and Barnabas Lindars; SBLSCS 33; Atlanta: Scholars Press, 1992), 159–94.

[3] Ed Noort ("4QJosh^a and the History of Tradition in the Book of Joshua," *JNSL* 24/2 [1998], 127–44, esp. 129) endorses as "a generally accepted proposition" Trent Butler's statement (*Joshua*; WBC 7 [Waco, Tex.: Word Books, 1983], 94) that Josh 8:30-35 in the MT "does not fit the present geographical, chronological, or narrative context." Noort (p. 135) deserves kudos for perceiving, even before the publication of this scroll, that "There would be an ideal place for Joshua 8:30-35 for this going together of writing down and reciting the law: Joshua 5. There the stopping of the manna, keeping the Passover and the circumcision of the people describe an ideal people in an ideal land with an ideal beginning of a life *coram deo* in the promised land." He quotes from his *Een plek om te zijn: over de theologie van het land aan de hand von Jozua 8:30-35* (Kampen: Kok Pharos, 1993), 15.

[4] An additional incident to remember concerning altar polemics is the excessive defensiveness stirred by the building of the altar by the tribes of Reuben, Gad, and half of Manasseh in Joshua 22. Moreover, examining the Chronicler's work, Gary Knoppers ("Mt. Gerizim and Mt. Zion: A Study in the Early History of the Samaritans and Jews," *SR* 34 [2005]: 309–38, esp. p. 320) convincingly states that "the

Tantalizing bits of evidence from 4QJosh^{a}, the MT, a new scroll fragment (discussed below), the SP, the LXX, the OL, Josephus, Pseudo-Philo, and rabbinic sources weave an intriguing pattern of textual variants regarding that first altar. Some of the variants appear to be intentional, aimed at favoring or demoting one of the contenders. The pieces of the puzzle fit most cogently, in my view, according to the following three-stage schema, which I will sketch briefly and then attempt to demonstrate.[5]

At an early stage, the mixed and highly repetitious[6] set of commands concerning this altar in Deuteronomy 27 may not yet have mentioned a specific place for that first altar (see especially vv. 2-3a); Israel was simply to set up the stones and inscribe the law "on the day that you cross over the Jordan into the land" (v. 2), which would logically be immediately near Gilgal.[7] The report of the proclamation of the Torah at Gilgal and presumably the report of the prior building of the altar on which its words were written was narrated at the end of Joshua 4, after the crossing of the Jordan and before the circumcision and Passover passages in Joshua 5. These three religious observances serve to prepare for the military conquest that starts in Joshua 6.

Then at a second stage, some unknown person or group inserted "on Mount Gerizim" in the repetitious Deut 27:4. This is documented in the SP and other texts. The question is whether it originated in the specifically Samaritan or in the common Judean-Samarian (see Ch. 14) text. This reading arose either in conjunction with the insertions in the common text at Deut 11:29 and 27:11-13 regarding the blessing on Mount Gerizim and the curse on Mount Ebal, or, more likely, due to later northern concerns to promote Mount Gerizim. The passage about the altar (now in the MT at Josh 8:30-35 and in LXX^{B} at 9:2a-f) was transposed from after the crossing of the Jordan in Joshua 4 to after the destruction of Ai (8:29). That rearranged placement may have taken place in conjunction with the addition of "on Mount Gerizim" or "on Mount Ebal" in Deut 27:4.

Chronicler's allusions and appeal to institutions associated with Israel's national beginnings are best understood as reflecting a time in which there were multiple discrepant and competing claims to the nation's past."

[5] See Eugene Ulrich, "4QJoshua^{a} and Joshua's First Altar in the Promised Land," in *New Qumran Texts and Studies: Proceedings of the First Meeting of the International Organization for Qumran Studies, Paris 1992* (ed. George J. Brooke with Florentino García Martínez; STDJ 15; Leiden: Brill, 1994), 89–104 and Pls. 4–6; idem, "47. 4QJosh^{a}," in DJD 14:145–46. See also Heinz-Josef Fabry, "Der Altarbau der Samaritaner—Ein Produkt der Text- und Literaturgeschichte?" in *Die Textfunde vom Toten Meer und der Text der Hebräischen Bibel* (ed. Ulrich Dahmen et al.; Neukirchen-Vluyn: Neukirchener, 2000), 35–52, esp. 44.

[6] See Fabry, "Der Altarbau"; Kristin De Troyer, "Building the Altar and Reading the Law: The Journeys of Joshua 8:30-35," in *Reading the Present in the Qumran Library: The Perception of the Contemporary by Means of Scriptural Interpretations* (SBLSymS 30; ed. Kristin De Troyer and Armin Lange; Atlanta: SBL, 2005), 141–62; and Michael Fishbane, *Biblical Interpretation in Ancient Israel* (New York: Oxford University Press, 1985), 160–62.

[7] The temporal clause "on the day you cross over" need not be taken in its narrow literal sense (see Josh 6:10, where עד יום means not "day" but "time/moment"), but the literal sense does fit naturally here. The more general sense, "when you cross over," is equally likely and would also presumably indicate Gilgal. Noort ("4QJosh^{a} and the History of Tradition," 141) starts his analysis with Deut 27:4, 8, 5-7 as in the MT (including "Mount Ebal") as the earliest parts of the narrative and thus ends with four mountains and "a mystery for exegetes." But starting more logically with Deut 27:2, one discovers a plausible three-stage literary history regarding the first altar in the newly entered promised land (see II.C below).

Finally, at a third stage, "Mount Gerizim" in the common Judean-Samarian text at Deut 27:4 was replaced in the MT with the odd and problematic "Mount Ebal" (inserted also at Josh 8:30), which begs for a better explanation than simply as a hasty and ill-thought-out polemical reaction against Mount Gerizim. It is now imperative to examine the evidence that grounds this three-stage hypothesis.[8]

I. The Evidence from the Various Textual Traditions

A. The Textual Forms of 4QJosh^a, the MT, and the LXX

For perspective, it is necessary to consider the relationship between the textual character of the witnesses (4QJosh^a, MT, and LXX) and their editorial and redactional history. The topic is vastly beyond the scope of this chapter; entire books have been written on the subject,[9] and it still requires a serious monograph for satisfactory solution. Here we can but briefly mention that 4QJosh^a exhibits a short edition, the LXX often a more expanded edition, and the MT an even more expanded edition.[10] Note also variations in the localities: (a) Joshua and the tribes are camped in Gilgal until Josh 14:6 and then

---

[8] A reverse sequence is proposed by Kristin De Troyer, "Building the Altar and Reading the Law." She concludes that the OG is "the oldest stratum of the text of the book of Joshua"; the second stratum would have been the "(proto)-Masoretic text"; whereas 4QJosh^a is "an example of how the Qumranites read Scripture as a way of interpreting their present," (162 and 142). I agree with De Troyer concerning the general priority of the OG over the MT, but I do not agree that 4QJosh^a is a Qumranite interpretive revision. I respond in detail to her arguments in "The Old Latin, Mount Gerizim, and 4QJosh^a" (in *Textual Criticism and Dead Sea Scrolls Studies in Honour of Julio Trebolle Barrera: Florilegium Complutense* [ed. Andrés Piquer Otero and Pablo Torijano Morales; JSJS 157; Leiden: Brill, 2012], 361–75), but some main objections are: (1) 4QJosh^a contains no sectarian readings and there is no indication that it was edited or copied at Qumran, whereas the proposal works only if "4QJosh^a is an example of how the Qumranites [specifically] read scripture in order to interpret their present" (147); (2) it is difficult to attribute the relocation at Gilgal specifically to "the Qumranites," since Josephus and Pseudo-Philo (who clearly were not Qumranites) attest the altar at Gilgal; and (3) "[t]here are rabbinic traditions that reflect the same sequence of events as the Qumran text and probably reflect the same motivation to harmonize Joshua with Deuteronomy: *y. Soṭa* 7:3, *t. Soṭa* 8:7–8" (Nelson, *Joshua*, 117 n. 4). The multiple witness of Josephus, Pseudo-Philo, and rabbinic traditions seems sufficient to demonstrate a broader Judean-Samarian text tradition and to preclude a Qumranite revision. Another detailed and erudite analysis is offered by Michaël N. van der Meer, *Formation and Reformulation: The Redaction of the Book of Joshua in the Light of the Oldest Textual Witnesses* (VTSup 102; Leiden: Brill, 2004), though I find it also unpersuasive. Emanuel Tov ("Literary Development of the Book of Joshua as Reflected in the MT, the LXX, and 4QJosh^a," in *The Book of Joshua* [ed. Ed Noort; BETL 250; Leuven: Peeters, 2012], 65–85, esp. 82 and nn. 31 and 36) also has hesitations about this work, though he agrees with certain points (regarding some of which I would disagree with both).

[9] See the large amount of literature cited in Tov, "Midrash-Type Exegesis in the LXX of Joshua," *RB* 85 (1978): 50–61, especially Samuel Holmes, *Joshua: The Hebrew and Greek Texts* (Cambridge: Cambridge University Press, 1914). More recently, see Alexander Rofé, "The End of the Book of Joshua in the Septuagint," *Henoch* 4 (1982): 17–36; Lea Mazor, "The Septuagint Translation of the Book of Joshua: Its Contribution to the Understanding of the Textual Transmission of the Book and Its Literary and Ideological Development" (Ph.D. diss.; Hebrew with English summary; Hebrew University, 1994). More recent analyses are offered by Tov, "The Growth of the Book of Joshua in Light of the Evidence of the Septuagint," in *The Greek and Hebrew Bible*, 385–96, and "Literary Development."

[10] See Tov, "The Growth of the Book of Joshua" and "Literary Development," 3–6. Note also the secondary addition of place names in the MT at Josh 6:26; 8:17; 10:15, and 10:43.

appear to be centered in Shiloh in chapters 18–22.[11] (b) No place is designated in the MT or the LXX as the setting for Joshua's speech in chapter 23, though Shiloh may thus be presumed. (c) Finally, the LXX has the final speech in chapter 24 still set in Shiloh (24:1), though the MT places the setting in Shechem.

B. 4QJosh[a]

Since the conclusions regarding the altar partly hinge on correct placement of the fragments of 4QJosh[a], it is important to begin by distinguishing demonstrable data from uncertain reconstruction, though the latter is necessary and, hopefully, plausible. First, on a single fragment of 4QJosh[a] (frg. 1; see Table 1), the account of Joshua's reading of the Torah (8:34-35 in the MT, 9:2e-f in LXX[B]) is followed by a transitional temporal clause (about a line and a half not in the MT-LXX) and then by what appears to be the beginning of the account of the circumcision (5:2 in the MT-LXX). Secondly, frg. 15 displays a text shorter than that in the LXX, which in turn is shorter than that in the MT. Those are the certain, challenging data. Moreover, it is highly probable, though not absolutely certain, that frg. 3, with text of Josh 6:5-8, was originally connected directly to frg. 1. Both fragments clearly preserve the top margin and share the same shape in their pattern of deterioration. Even judging from the photographs it is safe to conjecture that frg. 3 joins neatly to the left of frg. 1. Study of the leather in the Rockefeller Museum in Jerusalem clinches this as virtually certain. Examination, on the recto and verso, of the edges of the torn fragments yields a perfect fit, including both the contours of the leather edges viewed from above and the diagonal angle of the torn skin viewed cross-sectionally. It is conceivable that another piece of the leather was originally here and torn in precisely the same fashion, but that is highly unlikely. Furthermore, an enhanced digital image of the two edges produced by Gregory Bearman and Bruce and Kenneth Zuckerman confirms that the two edges of these fragments align perfectly. Thus, we may proceed on the assumption that frg. 3 followed directly to the left of frg. 1, especially since the amount of text required to fill out the column is roughly 28 lines, the equivalent amount required for other, predictable columns.

There are two plausible, but not certain, elements of the reconstruction. First, lines 4–6 of frg. 1 are best read as Josh 5:2-4, though there is little unique text to prove conclusively that it was chapter 5 that followed the Torah-reading passage in chapter 4 (MT 8:34-35); however, frg. 2 has six lines that contain 5:4-7, and its first partly-preserved word fits perfectly with the last preserved letter on frg. 1. The different physical appearance of frg. 2 does not present a problem, since frg. 2 is taken from a different photograph from that of frgs. 1 and 3, and since this separated fragment underwent a different type of deterioration after being separated from frgs. 1 and 3.

Second, though the first two lines of frg. 1 correspond to Josh 8:34-35 (the reading of the Torah), it is not certain that 8:30-31 (the building of the altar) preceded, since that would occur at the bottom of the preceding column which is not preserved. The building of the altar, however, is closely linked with the reading of the Torah in both the MT and the LXX[B], despite the fact that the combined passage is placed at different points in those two texts. Furthermore, the two elements are linked in the earlier passage

---

[11] See Josh 18:1, 8, 9, 10; 19:51; 21:2; 22:9.

TABLE 1: *4QJosh*[a]

Frgs. 1–2: Josh 4[MT 8]:34-35; 5:X, 2-7 *(DJD 14:147; BQS 249)*

top margin

[בספר]התורה 35 לא היה דבר מכל צוה משה[את יה]ושוע אשר לא קרא יהשע נגד כל	1	
[העם אשר עברו]את הירד[ן]והנשים והטף והג[ר] ההולך בקרבם 5:X אחר אשר נתקו[ ]	2	
[העם מן הירדן ויקרא]ל[הם יהשע]את ספר התורה אחר כן [ע]לו נושאי הארו[ן וישמו]	3	
[את ספר התורה מצד הארון 5:2 בעת]ההיא אמר יהוה אליהש[ע ע]שה לך חרבות צרים]	4	
[ושוב מל את בני ישראל 5:3 ויעש]ל[ו י]השע ח[רבות צ]רים וימל את בני ישראל אל]	5	
[גבעת הערלות 4 וזה הדבר אשר מל יהושע כ]ל[ ]העם היצ[א ממצרים הזכרים כל]	6	f.2
[אנשי המלחמה מתו במדבר בדרך בצאתם]ממצרים 5 כי[מלים היו כל העם היצאים]	7	
[וכל העם הילדים במדבר בדרך בצ]אתם ממצ[רים לא מלו 6 כי ארבעים שנה הלכו]	8	
[בני ישראל במדבר עד תם כל הגוי]אנשי המלח[מה היצאים ממצרים אשר לא שמעו]	9	
[בקול יהוה אשר נשבע יהוה להם לב]לתי ראות את ה[ארץ אשר נשבע יהוה לאבותם]	10	
[לתת לנו ארץ זבת חלב ודבש 7 ואת בני]הם הק[ים]	11	

Frgs. 3–7: Josh 6:5-7 *(DJD 14:148; BQS 249)*

top margin

גדולה ונפלה חמת[ ]ועלה העם[א]יש [נ]גדו [6]	1	f.3-6
יהושע בן נון אל הכ[הנים ויאמ]ר אל[יהם] שאו א[ת]	2	
ושבעה כהנים ישא[ו יוב]לים לפני א[רון יהוה 7 ויאמר]	3	
יהושוע אל העם[והח]ל[וץ יעבר לפ]נ[י ארו]ן[יהוה]	4	f.7

(Deut 27:1-8) where Moses commands that this altar be built: all the words of the Torah are to be written on the altar.

Emanuel Tov, however, holds that the altar and the Torah reading can be separated. Though in the second edition of *Textual Criticism* (346) he apparently agreed with the view presented here, in the third edition (315) he offers an alternate interpretation. He concludes that "Col. I 1–3 describes the crossing of the Jordan" (thus chapter 4), but that "4:19–5:1 (seven verses) are lacking." That is, what corresponds to the reading of the Torah in MT 8:34-35 is severed from 8:30-33, so that the "reading of the Torah at the time of erecting the altar [is] reinterpreted as taking place in the context of crossing the Jordan...."

The argument seems to hinge on the infrequent word נתקו ("they withdrew") which indeed occurs in 4:18a. But the fragment has אחר אשר נתקו[ ], whereas 4:18 in MT does not have אחר אשר ("after"). So the question is: After *who* withdrew from the Jordan? Both Tov and I would admit that any reconstruction of lines 2–4 is subjective, but the reconstruction I tentatively suggest in Table 1 seems to fit the context and sequence of events more naturally. It seems unlikely that Joshua read out the Book of the Law while standing in the middle of the Jordan. That proposed interpretation would introduce an entirely new scene (reading the Book of the Law while standing in the Jordan), while at the same time losing essential elements of the story. The return of the normal flowing of the Jordan waters (4:18b), the people coming up out of the Jordan (4:19), and the setting up of the twelve stones (4:20) would all be missing, although Tov says that "All the lacking elements may be considered secondary in the context."[12]

It seems more likely that 4QJosh[a] contained something like: "After [the people] had withdrawn [from the Jordan, Joshua read] to [them] the book of the law. After that, the bearers of the ark [we]nt up and [put the book of the law beside the ark]." This last would be a fulfillment of the command in Deut 31:25-26: "Moses commanded the Levites, *the bearers of the ark* of the covenant of the Lord, saying, Take this *book of the law and put it beside the ark* of the covenant of the Lord your God; let it remain there...."[13] Moreover, that fulfillment of Moses' command would follow Joshua's fulfillment of his command to build the altar and read the Torah.

Ed Noort also considers it possible that the link between altar and Torah reading could be separated, because Josephus at Joshua 4–5 (*Ant.* 5.20) narrates the building of the altar but does not mention the Torah reading, whereas much later he "waits with the 'real' Joshua 8:30-35 till the whole country, south and north, has been conquered.... all the elements from Joshua 8:30-35 return here" (*Ant.* 5.69–70).[14] But that is an argument about silence, and note that Josephus is also entirely silent about the immediately following circumcision scene at Joshua 5, though clearly that was in his biblical text. Moreover, "all the elements" do not return here: the blessing and the curse are engraved on the altar, but not the ספר התורה, and, just as in the first passage, so too in this passage (*Ant.* 5.69–70), Josephus "does not mention the Torah reading." Josephus knows the two textual traditions about the altar and narrates them both in his own style in different places, this one at the same point as 4QJosh[a].

Since virtually all agree that 8:30-35 is out of place; since Noort had insightfully concluded even before seeing 4QJosh[a] that the end of chapter 4 is an ideal place for the misplaced Joshua 8:30-35; since it is more likely than not that the altar and the Torah reading should be linked; and since the loss of seven verses would be unusual and would entail the loss of essential elements of the story, the interpretation presented in this chapter seems more persuasive.

C. *The Masoretic Text*

The MT recounts the building of the first altar and the reading of the Torah at Josh 8:30-35, though it retains at 4:20-24 the memory of the significant stones taken out of the Jordan. The MT placement at the end of chapter 8 is odd (see nn. 3 and 18), but it is clearly linked with the command of Deut 27:4. But why wait to get to Mount Ebal, far

---

[12] Tov, "Literary Development of the Book of Joshua," 84; see also idem, *Textual Criticism*, 315. Tov's proposal lists only "4:19–5:1" as lacking, but the resumption of the flowing of the Jordan waters (4:18b), would also be missing, since the elements in "lines 2–3 and probably at the beginning of line 4 [which do not mention the resumption]... provide a rewritten version of Josh 4:18" (ibid.).

[13] The words of the command in italics mirror those of the fulfillment of that command in the reconstruction.

[14] Noort, "4QJosh[a] and the History of Tradition," 137–38. Observe in n. 3 above that Noort does link the two in this "ideal place for Joshua 8:30-35 for this going together of writing down and reciting the law."

to the north and center of the country?[15] Why carry the large stones (Deut 27:2) all the way to Shechem? Why march the entire population, including women and children (Josh 8:35) twenty miles through hostile land, build an altar, then immediately abandon it in enemy territory and march back to Gilgal (9:6)? And indeed, why place the altar on Mount Ebal, associated with the curse and otherwise insignificant?[16] In addition, it is important to observe both that the beginning of Josh 5:1 (ויהי כשמע כל מלכי, "when all the kings heard") is similar to that of 9:1, and that the narrative in 9:1 logically follows 8:29, not 8:35.[17] The narrative logic betrays that 8:30-35 is a secondary insertion.[18]

D. The Septuagint

Two general points should be kept in mind regarding the LXX. The OG translation probably represents its Hebrew *Vorlage* faithfully, and many of our later LXX manuscripts exhibit secondary correction toward a text like the MT.

With regard to the *order* of the narrative, the hexaplaric LXX^A agrees, as expected, with the MT in placing after 8:29 the passage concerning the altar on Mount Ebal. In slight contrast, however, the probably earlier Greek tradition is preserved by LXX^B. It also recounts the building of the first altar and reading of the Torah at Mount Ebal, but the combined narrative is placed after 9:2, not after 8:29 as in the MT and the hexaplaric LXX^A. The question remains, however, whether the reading of LXX^B, though it is probably earlier than that of LXX^A, preserves the original Greek translation or is itself already an early change in the Greek tradition.[19]

---

15 Noort argues that there are two pairs of mountains: one near Shechem and a second pair near Jericho (see below).

16 No one that I have encountered has provided a persuasive rationale for considering Mount Ebal the chosen site for Joshua's altar (see n. 55 below).

17 The direct object of כשמע ("when they heard") in 9:1 is not expressed, but it is clearly the destruction of Ai, not the building of the altar. In contrast, the object of כשמע in 5:1 explicitly refers to the drying up of the Jordan, displaying the divine power behind Israel.

18 See Noort, "4QJosh^a and the History of Tradition," 129. Tov (*Hebrew Bible, Greek Bible, and Qumran*, 217) agrees regarding the secondary placement here. Richard D. Nelson (*Joshua: A Commentary* [OTL; Louisville, Ky.: Westminster John Knox, 1997], 116) also comments: "This section is isolated from its context and clearly the product of deuteronomistic redaction. It begins abruptly with *ʾaz* and the imperfect, used to indicate a tenuous and appropriate chronological connection: 'about this time' (cf. 10:12; 22:1)." See Isaac Rabinowitz ("*ʾāz* Followed by Imperfect Verb-Form in Preterite Contexts: A Redactional Device in Biblical Hebrew," *VT* 34 [1984]: 53–62, esp. 54), who concludes: "*ʾāz* + imperfect in a preterite context is . . . a redactional usage, a device to which recourse is had for introducing into a text additional material from a source extraneous to, or other than, that from which the immediately foregoing bloc of material has been drawn or produced."

19 LXX^B, in my view, like Pap. Giessen, may not be the OG but an early revision of the OG, depending upon how early the "Mount Ebal" reading entered the MT. That the LXX here, as often elsewhere, was secondarily revised to agree with the MT (which, in this view, itself reflected a secondary or tertiary stage), is fully possible. The different placement after 9:2 in Vaticanus and half the minuscules, versus that of AFMNΘ and the other half with the MT at the end of chapter 8, shows either that LXX^B repositioned the passage generally in conformity with the MT edition but after 9:2 possibly for better sequence, or that LXX^A repositioned it for more exact conformity with the MT.

An analogy is offered by the insertion of the poetic Song of Hannah into the prose narrative of 1 Samuel 1–2 at slightly different points in 4QSam^a, MT, and LXX.[20] The placement of the Song at close but slightly different points in 4QSam^a, MT, and LXX betrays that it is a later insertion, but it is reflective of a single major editorial decision that was adopted in all three traditions. Analogously, the placement of the altar passage in Joshua at close but different points in the MT and the LXX^B causes us to suspect both that it is a later insertion into a formerly cohesive narrative, but also that its placement in the MT-LXX, even though at slightly different points, is to be viewed as reflective of a single major editorial decision which later was slightly adjusted in either the MT-LXX^A or LXX^B.

E. The Samaritan Pentateuch and the Old Latin

The Samaritans did not include the Book of Joshua in their Scriptures.[21] In the commandment at Deut 27:4, however, the SP stipulates that the placement of the altar should be on Mount Gerizim; thus it is likely that they envisioned that the first altar was in the north, in agreement with the MT-LXX of Joshua 8.

With regard to the individual *wording*, however, a very important clue emerges. The OL codex 100 reads *Garzin* at Deut 27:4.[22] An OL reading is normally a good translation of an LXX text; and indeed, though almost the entire LXX manuscript tradition reads a form of ἐν ὄρει Γαιβάλ, one single Greek witness attests "Mount Gerizim" for this verse: Papyrus Giessen[23] reads αργαρ[ι]ζιμ.[24] The writing of the pair of words without space

[20] See Frank Moore Cross, "51. 4QSam^a," DJD 17:30–38; Ulrich, *The Qumran Text of Samuel*, 120–21; and Tov, "Different Editions of the Song of Hannah and of Its Narrative Framework," in *The Greek and Hebrew Bible*, 433–55. The Song is discussed below in Ch. 6.

[21] Though a form of the Book of Joshua was later known to the Samaritan community, neither it nor any other Samaritan writings beyond the Pentateuch pre-date the fourth century C.E.; see Reinhard Pummer, "Samaritanism," in *The Eerdmans Dictionary of Early Judaism* (ed. John J. Collins and Daniel C. Harlow; Grand Rapids: Eerdmans, 2010), 1186–88.

[22] John W. Wevers, *Deuteronomium* (Septuaginta: Vetus Testamentum Graecum III.2; Göttingen: Vandenhoeck & Ruprecht, 1977), 287.

[23] Papyrus Giessen preserves fragments from Deuteronomy 24–29 dating from the fifth or sixth century; see Wevers, *Deuteronomium*, 16. Some Catenae manuscripts also attest that τὸ σαμ′ reads ἐν τῷ Γαριζείν. Tov provides a new edition and discussion of the papyrus, incorporating new readings and reconstructions: "Pap. Giessen 13, 19, 22, 26: A Revision of the Septuagint?" in *The Greek and Hebrew Bible*, 459–75. His analysis "suggests that the Giessen papyri do not reflect the Σαμαρειτικόν" but rather "a revision, possibly of Samaritan origin, of the OG" (459). Though he cautiously says, "possibly of Samaritan origin," he eventually does not prefer that possibility but argues rather for a (presumably Jewish or Christian) revision of the OG (cf. 473–74). See also Reinhard Pummer, "The Samareitikon Revisited," in *Essays in Honour of G. D. Sixdenier: New Samaritan Studies of the Société d'études samaritaines* (ed. Alan D. Crown and Lucy Davey; Sydney: Mandelbaum, 1995), 381–455; and S. Noja, "The Samareitikon," in *The Samaritans* (ed. Alan D. Crown; Tübingen: J. C. B. Mohr [Paul Siebeck], 1989), 408–12.

[24] Whereas Wevers (*Deuteronomium*, 287) presents the reading with a space between αρ and γαρ[ι]ζιμ, Tov ("Pap. Giessen," 472 n. 11) says that it "cannot be determined whether αργαρ[ι]ζιμ was written as one word, as in the Samaritan tradition." But he correctly suggests that Αρμαγεδων in Rev 16:16 "shows the wider use of this transliteration as do many additional transliterations of geographical terms in the LXX" (ibid.). His suggestion is confirmed by Reinhard Pummer ("ΑΡΓΑΡΙΖΙΝ: A Criterion for Samaritan Provenance?" *JSJ* 18 [1987]: 19–25), who perhaps understates, in light of his strong evidence, that "The results of these considerations are: In view of the recent age of Samaritan manuscripts, and the fact that

for word division is often considered the mark of a Samaritan author.[25] But since nothing we know leads us to think that the OL might be influenced by the SP, the question arises: Are this Greek papyrus reading and this OL reading witnesses to the SP specifically, or might they be witnesses to a Hebrew reading which circulated in the broader common Judean-Samarian milieu?

In favor of an ancient, non-sectarian witness, Reinhard Pummer notes that

> The Vetus Latina has twice the form *Argarzim*, i.e. in 2 Macc 5:23 and 6:2. It is well known that this translation has often preserved ancient variants, and it is most probable that this is the case also here.... Rather than assume that 2 Macc 5:23 and 6:2 go back to a Samaritan source or tradition, it can be argued that there existed Greek versions which transliterated and contracted הר גרזים as they did with other similar names.[26]

In editing 4QpaleoExod[m] and in further studies I have found a number of other putative "Samaritan" readings preserved in LXX manuscripts which strongly support Pummer's argument on a broader scale: that Greek readings that were initially considered "Samaritan" may well have derived from shared Judean-Samarian sources. For example, several LXX manuscripts attest the major expansions which are found in the SP but are not specifically Samaritan. That is, some expansions known primarily from the SP are also attested in LXX manuscripts, but those expansions are already found in 4QpaleoExod[m] and 4QNum[b], and thus are from commonly shared Judean-Samarian texts and are not specifically Samaritan.[27] Many other "Samaritan" readings are attested in the Syro-Hexapla[28] without LXX support,[29] while yet others are found in both LXX manuscripts and the Syro-Hexapla.[30] These ancient Greek readings, often attributed to "Samaritan" influence,[31] indicate that other Greek textual witnesses with expanded

there are instances where הר and the proper name following it were transliterated and contracted in Greek translations, LXX and others, without any conceivable sectarian basis for it, it is at least doubtful that the reading Αργαριζιν can at all times and in all writings where it is found be used as proof for Samaritan provenance or an underlying Samaritan tradition. It can only serve as one indicator among others. In itself it is insufficient to prove Samaritan provenance" (25).

[25] Pummer, "ΑΡΓΑΡΙΖΙΝ," 18.

[26] Pummer, "ΑΡΓΑΡΙΖΙΝ," 23–24; see also Ulrich, "47. 4QJosh[a]," DJD 14:146. Tov ("Pap. Giessen," 472) agrees: "While the importance of the agreement of P[ap.] G[iessen] with the most important sectarian reading of SP should not be underestimated, it could also be an ancient not yet sectarian reading. The fact that the Vetus Latina, never suspected as Samaritan, preserves the same variant, points in the same direction, since this source has preserved many important ancient variants." See also Tov, *Textual Criticism*, 87–88, n. 140.

[27] E.g., Exod 27:19[b] (see *BHS* note 19[e]); and 32:10[b] (*BHS* note 10[a]).

[28] The Syro-Hexapla (Syh) is an early seventh-century literal Syriac translation of Origen's fifth, (o′ = Septuaginta) column. Its close fidelity renders it equal to a Greek witness (Wevers, *Exodus* [Septuaginta II.1; Göttingen: Vandenhoeck & Ruprecht, 1991], 38) and "of great importance in recovering Origen's text of the LXX" (D. C. Parker, "Syro-Hexapla," *ABD* 6:285–86).

[29] E.g.: Exod 6:9[b]; 7:18[b]; 7:29[b] [LXX 8:4], etc.; Num 20:13[b] (*BHS* note 13[b]); 21:23[b]; etc.

[30] E.g.: Num 12:16[b] [LXX 13:1] (*BHS* note 12:16[b]); 21:12[a] [LXX 11[fin]]; 21:22[b]; 27:23[b]; 31:21[a] [LXX 20[fin]].

[31] Note, e.g., Wevers' annotation "ex Sam secundum Syh" after many of the Syh readings cited above. "Sam" is accurate insofar as the readings *appear* in the SP, but it is difficult to see how LXX manuscripts and the Syro-Hexapla would have *derived* them from ("ex") the SP specifically.

readings which used to be labeled "Samaritan" may rather be more accurately seen as general Judean-Samarian.

Ancient Hebrew manuscripts also confirm that view, demonstrating that numerous readings once considered Samaritan are not specifically Samaritan but commonly shared Judean-Samarian readings. 4QpaleoExod^{m} and 4QNum^{b}, both of which routinely display major "Samaritan" expansions, have taught us that the majority of such readings are not due specifically to the Samaritans but occur in general Judean-Samarian texts. These texts were simply "new and expanded editions" of scriptural books that were circulating within Judean and Samarian groups alongside the earlier editions that were transmitted in the Masoretic *textus receptus*. The Samaritans, in turn, simply happened[32] to adopt the later, expanded, equally valued edition,[33] rather than the earlier edition of those texts, as the basis for their (textually) only slightly altered version.

Returning to the OL at Deut 27:4, we can plausibly suggest that, even though only one surviving Greek witness attests "Mount Gerizim," the OL was translated from some form of an ancient LXX manuscript which read "Mount Gerizim." Based on what we know about the OL, it seems highly improbable that it was translated from a specifically Samaritan Hebrew or even from a Samaritan Greek manuscript.[34] Accordingly, even though only that single Greek witness survives,[35] it seems that the OL reading was based on an ancient Greek text which contained that reading. That in turn raises the question whether the Greek reading may have been based on an old Hebrew reading which circulated in broader Judaism, and so was not dependent on the SP specifically. Julio Trebolle in several studies has established that, when the OG has been lost, careful analysis of the OL can at times restore the OG, and this restored OG can at times reveal

[32] The Rabbis apparently did not choose or select the specific textual forms that they received and transmitted in the MT. That indicates that it is even less likely that the Samaritans, about two centuries earlier, consciously selected specific forms as opposed to others as the base text for their Torah. On the absence of deliberate selection of the text types for the MT see Talmon ("Aspects of the Textual Transmission of the Bible in the Light of Qumran Manuscripts," in *Qumran and the History*, 226–63, esp. 263), who says that "the combined evidence of Qumran and Rabbinic techniques proves the contention that variant readings in the Biblical textual traditions were viewed with relative equanimity by both groups and even were perpetuated by diverse manuscriptal and non-manuscriptal devices"; idem, ("The Old Testament Text," in *Qumran and the History*, 21): "[Kahle's] assumption that the *textus receptus* should be viewed as resulting from the concerted efforts of a rabbinic academy . . . is neither substantiated by any historical evidence nor plausible. The emergence of the *textus receptus* should be conceived of as a protracted process which culminated in its *post factum* acclamation in the first or at the latest in the second century A.D." See also Ulrich, "The Qumran Biblical Scrolls—The Scriptures of Late Second Temple Judaism," in *The Dead Sea Scrolls in Their Historical Context* (ed. Timothy H. Lim et al.; Edinburgh: T&T Clark, 2000), 67–87, esp. 86; and Tov, "The Coincidental Textual Nature of the Collections of Ancient Scriptures," *Congress Volume Ljubljana 2007* (VTSup 133; Leiden: Brill, 2010), 153–69; idem, *Textual Criticism*, 174–80.

[33] Note that the Jewish 4QPent (*olim* 4QRP) texts show agreements with this later edition (Ch. 12).

[34] See Tov's comment on the OL in n. 26 above and Ulrich, "The Old Latin Translation of the LXX and the Hebrew Scrolls from Qumran," in *Scrolls and Origins*, 233–74, esp. 270.

[35] A similar instance of only a single OG manuscript surviving is OG 88 (witnessed also by the Syro-Hexapla) for the entire Book of Daniel. For centuries all other surviving Greek manuscripts presented the revisionist Theodotionic text. Eventually Papyrus 967 of the Chester Beatty Papyri was found, which witnessed to a pre-hexaplaric text of the OG.

a form of an OH text that had otherwise been lost.[36] Thus, the ancient, otherwise inexplicable witnesses to a text reading "Mount Gerizim" in Papyrus Giessen and the OL codex 100 lead us to ask whether "Mount Gerizim" might have been a broader Judean-Samarian reading in certain Hebrew manuscripts that served as the basis for the SP.

F. A Recently Published Fragment

The reading בהרגרזים ("on Mount Gerizim") in Hebrew at Deut 27:4, long known from the SP, has recently surfaced in a small scroll fragment of uncertain origin, a solitary fragment measuring only 3.8 × 2.9 cm, containing text from Deut 27:4-6.[37] It is claimed that the fragment came from Cave 4, though some scholars may question whether it is genuine. Two questions arise.

First, is it genuine or a forgery? In particular, it is suspicious that בהרגרזים appears prominently and clearly in the center of this very small fragment with so few other words. That suspicion, however, is countered by the solitary fragment of 4QJudg^{a}, only slightly larger, which also clearly shows a highly significant variant (see Ch. 5). That small fragment has text from the Gideon story in Judges 6: vv. 3, 4, 5, 6 followed immediately by vv. 11, 12, 13. That is, it preserves an early, short text, without the theological insertion of vv. 7-10 added in the MT. Thus, that small Judges fragment provides an important witness to an earlier version of its narrative, just as the new Deuteronomy fragment would provide an important witness to an alternate and possibly earlier version of Deuteronomy 27. The authenticity of 4QJudg^{a}, if not definitively proving the authenticity of this newly surfaced fragment, does seriously counter the suspicion of inauthenticity due to its prominent important reading.

Moreover, although I have not seen the fragment itself but only a photograph, if it is a forgery, it appears to be a good forgery.[38] Materially, the fragment shows serious deterioration, and that deteriorated state would make forming the tiny tips of partial letters all around the edges very difficult for a forger, but all the letter-tips seem to have been well formed. Textually, whereas a forger would probably want to reproduce textual forms that generally agreed with MT-SP, there are both orthographic and morphological

---

36 See Julio Trebolle Barrera, "From the 'Old Latin' through the 'Old Greek' to the 'Old Hebrew' (2 Kings 10:23-35)," *Textus* 11 (1984): 17–36; idem, "Old Latin, Old Greek and Old Hebrew in the Books of Kings (1 Ki 18:27 and 2 Ki 20:11)," *Textus* 13 (1986): 85–95; and idem, "The Textcritical Value of the Old Latin in Postqumranic Textual Criticism: 1 Kgs 18:26-29, 36-37," in *From 4QMMT to Resurrection: Mélanges qumraniens en hommage à Émile Puech* (ed. Florentino García Martínez et al.; STDJ 61; Leiden: Brill, 2006) 313–31. I think his insight provides the essential key here as well.

37 On his website—http://www.ijco.org/?categoryId=46960—James H. Charlesworth presented photographs and an edition of the fragment. I thank Professor Charlesworth for collegially sharing this with me. He has now published it: "What Is a Variant? Announcing a Dead Sea Scrolls Fragment of Deuteronomy," *Maarav* 16/2 (2009): 201–12 and Pls. IX–X (pp. 273–74). In this article he sees "Mount Gerizim" as the original reading, with "Mount Ebal" a later variant. I agree that "Mount Gerizim" is the earlier of the two, but I suggest another, yet earlier reading without any place name.

38 Regarding authenticity, Charlesworth ("What Is a Variant?" 205) says, "The Arab who formerly owned the fragment belongs to the family through whom the Dead Sea Scrolls have come to scholars. He claims it is from Qumran Cave IV. The fragment appears to be genuine for the following reasons: The source is the same as that for almost all the Qumran fragments in the Shrine of the Book. The patina sparkles in the ink and in the leather. My attempts to prove that the fragment is a fake failed." Note also the agreement of Bruce and Kenneth Zuckerman (ibid., 205, n. 15).

variants from the MT and SP that would require sophisticated familiarity with Second Temple texts.

Second, if genuine, is the fragment from a specifically Samaritan or a more broadly general Judean-Samarian milieu? The available clues point toward a Judean-Samarian manuscript. Regarding provenance, it is highly unlikely that a specifically Samaritan manuscript would be found at Qumran:[39] one need only think of the Samaritan non-acceptance of the Nevi'im as authoritative Scripture, clashing with the intense Qumran emphasis on the Prophets. Regarding script, one would expect the Samaritans to use the Palaeo-Hebrew script (recall that 4QpaleoParaJoshua does use that script).[40] Regarding other Judean-Samarian texts, the MT-SP-LXX traditions all include a Mount Gerizim–Mount Ebal scribal stratum in Deut 11:29-30 and 27:11-13, in which Mount Gerizim is the mountain of blessings, but Mount Ebal is the mountain of curses. In addition, Abraham's first altar was at Shechem (Gen 12:7), and Mount Gerizim is always viewed positively in its few occurrences in the Hebrew Bible.[41] Moreover, as we have seen above, numerous putative "Samaritan" readings are not due specifically to the Samaritans but occur in general Judean-Samarian texts. Even the major "Samaritan" commandment added in Exodus 20 and Deuteronomy 5 is constructed with general Judean-Samarian passages, common to the MT-SP-LXX, from Deut 11:29a, 27:2-7, and 11:30.

Thus, this new fragment—if genuine, and if Jewish—would be an instance in which the OL witnesses to an ancient Greek reading entirely lost except for Pap. Giessen,[42] and ultimately to a (shared Judean-Samarian) OH text tradition also otherwise entirely lost.[43] Having discarded the Σαμαρειτικόν as the source of Pap. Giessen, it remains to determine whether the Greek reading is the original OG translation, or whether it is rather a very early revision of the OG. In either case it most probably reflects its Hebrew *Vorlage*

---

39 Although there were early statements by scroll editors about Samaritan manuscripts at Qumran, those views have evanesced in light of further research. For instance, Patrick Skehan entitled his first published announcement of 4QpaleoExod^m "Exodus in the Samaritan Recension from Qumran" (*JBL* 74 [1955]: 435–40), but he quickly revised that designation in "Qumran and the Present State of Old Testament Text Studies: The Masoretic Text," *JBL* 78 (1959): 21–25, esp. 22. See also Maurice Baillet, "Le texte samaritain de l'Exode dans les manuscrits de Qumrân," in *Hommages à André Dupont-Sommer* (ed. André Caquot and Marc Philonenko; Paris: Adrien-Maisonneuve, 1971), 363–81.

40 For the edition see Ulrich, "4Q123. 4QpaleoParaJoshua," in DJD 9:201–03; despite the title, this text may have been "simply a variant edition of the biblical book of Joshua" (p. 201).

41 Gary Knoppers ("Mt. Gerizim and Mt. Zion," 320) observes that "in the very texts that many Judeans cherished as in some sense foundational to the life of their own community, Mt. Gerizim occupied a favoured position."

42 See n. 36.

43 See now (without reference to the new fragment) the agreement of Magnar Kartveit (*The Origin of the Samaritans* [VTSup 128; Leiden: Brill, 2009], 300–05) that the OL and Pap. Giessen readings ultimately depend upon a Jewish Hebrew text, which had "the original reading 'Mount Gerizim'" (305) vis-à-vis "Mount Ebal." Again (see n. 37), rather than "the original reading," I would say "the earlier reading" that was inserted into the original form of Deuteronomy 27 which had no place name. Already in 1964, Gerhard von Rad (*Das fünfte Buch Mose: Deuteronomium* [ATD 8; Göttingen: Vandenhoeck & Ruprecht, 1964], 117; = *Deuteronomy* [OTL; Philadelphia: Westminster, 1966], 164) also appears to favor Mount Gerizim. Though the translation of Deut 27:4 that was used for the volume has "auf dem Berge Ebal," von Rad in his commentary continues, without explanation: "Das 27. Kapitel beginnt mit einer Aufforderung Mose, nach der Überschreitung des Jordan auf dem Berge Garzim 'alle Worte dieses Gesetzes' auf Steinen niederzuschreiben. . . ."

faithfully, since the variant originated at the Hebrew stage: either the OG was originally translated from a Hebrew *Vorlage* which already had the "Mount Gerizim" insertion, or the OG was translated from a Hebrew *Vorlage* with no place name but was secondarily revised to conform to a Hebrew manuscript which had that insertion. Again—if genuine, and if Jewish—the new fragment would at the same time provide additional support for the view that 4QJosh^a presents the earliest extant witness to the locality of the first altar built in the newly entered land. If, however the fragment is not genuine or not Jewish, such an old Hebrew reading is still quite likely in light of the OG and the OL.

G. Josephus, Pseudo-Philo, and Rabbinic Sources

Josephus and Pseudo-Philo are major witnesses, near the end of the first century C.E., to the scriptural text in the late Second Temple period. The Scriptures enjoyed a rich pluriformity in the textual and editorial forms of the various books in that period which endured certainly until the destruction of the Temple and arguably until the second century.[44] It has been demonstrated that for the Books of Samuel, Josephus used a form of the text that was closely aligned with 4QSam^a and the LXX in contrast to the MT.[45] Study of the *Jewish Antiquities* again yields rich results for the Book of Joshua. Josephus follows the account of the crossing of the Jordan (*Ant.* 5.16–19) with Joshua's building of an altar and sacrificing on it (βωμὸν . . . ἔθυεν ἐπ' αὐτοῦ, *Ant.* 5.20), exactly where it appears to be placed in 4QJosh^a. One could argue that Josephus is adding an "unscriptural" embellishment, overly describing the stones taken from the Jordan not only as a monument but also as an altar for sacrifice. But later in the narrative, between the conquest of Ai (*Ant.* 5.45–48; 8:1-29 in the MT) and the Gibeonites' ruse (*Ant.* 5.49–57; 9:3-27 in the MT), he makes no mention of a journey to Mount Ebal or an altar there (as in 8:30-35 in the MT). He does, however, eventually recount the building of the altar at Shechem, explicitly mentioning that it was commanded by Moses and that half the people were stationed on Mount Gerizim and half on Mount Ebal (*Ant.* 5.69); but this is not until *after* all the warfare and *after* the tabernacle was set up at Shiloh (= Josh 18:1).

Similarly, Pseudo-Philo states in the *Liber Antiquitatum Biblicarum* that "Joshua went down to Gilgal and built an altar with very large stones and did not lift an iron tool to them, as Moses had commanded."[46] It is true that Pseudo-Philo, just as Josephus, knows and mentions the altar at Shechem as well, but, just as Josephus, he places that report late in the Joshua narrative, not at the beginning or in the middle of the conquest. The point is that two separate early authors, with no hint of entering into "the altar locality debate," simply report as a matter of fact that Joshua's altar was built immediately at Gilgal.

---

[44] See Ulrich, "Pluriformity in the Biblical Text, Text Groups, and Questions of Canon," in *Proceedings of the International Congress on the Dead Sea Scrolls—Madrid, 18–21 March 1991* (ed. Julio Trebolle Barrera and Luis Vegas Montaner; STDJ 10; Madrid: Universidad Complutense; Leiden: Brill, 1992), 23–41; repr. in *Scrolls and Origins*, 79–98.

[45] See Frank Moore Cross, DJD 17:27; Ulrich, *The Qumran Text of Samuel and Josephus*, 165–91; and idem, "Josephus' Biblical Text for the Books of Samuel," in *Josephus, the Bible, and History* (ed. Louis H. Feldman and Gohei Hata; Detroit: Wayne State University Press, 1989), 81–96; repr. in *Scrolls and Origins*, 184–201.

[46] Pseudo-Philo, *L.A.B.* 21:7. I am grateful to Professor Christopher Begg for alerting me to this reference.

Moreover, as Alexander Rofé points out, "Both Mishna and Tosephta establish that the rites mentioned in Josh 8:30-35 were performed immediately after the crossing of the Jordan.... A text similar to 4QJosh^a could have been known to the Pharisaic masters."[47]

Thus three of our oldest texts (4QJosh^a, Josephus, and Pseudo-Philo), as well as rabbinic sources, have the first altar in the newly-entered land immediately at Gilgal, not later at Mount Ebal. A fourth text (LXX^B, which may not be the Old Greek translation but may be revised to agree with a text like the MT) reflects the same editorial tradition as the MT, but does not support the MT exactly.

II. The Plausibility of the Three Localities

What is described above as the first editorial stage is partly documented in 4QJosh^a, which, though no mention of a specific locality is preserved in the surviving fragments, clearly assumes Gilgal. The "Mount Gerizim" reading suggested as the second stage can be seen in the SP, the Greek Pap. Giessen, the OL codex 100, and (if genuine) the new scroll fragment. The proposed third-stage reading "Mount Ebal" occurs in the MT and also lies behind the main surviving LXX manuscript tradition and other versions such as the Targum, Peshitta, and Vulgate, which, however, are all dependent on the reading transmitted in the MT.

The oldest texts point to Gilgal as the site of the first altar. The oldest texts, however, are not necessarily the best texts, so one should ask which tradition represents the best, or superior, or original, or earlier form of the narrative? There are three key issues.

A. The Placement of the First Altar

Sanctuary ideology certainly has a strong role to play in these issues.[48] But prescinding for a moment from sanctuary ideologies and polemics by editors and redactors, the simplest and most natural narrative would be the sequence in 4QJosh^a. Even without the command in Deuteronomy 27, it would be appropriate to build an altar and offer sacrifices immediately after, and in thanksgiving for, the successful, long-delayed crossing into the promised land. Together with the circumcision ritual and the Passover observance following, these three rituals prepare for the conquest starting in Joshua 6. This is what we read clearly in Josephus and, to the extent that it is preserved, in 4QJosh^a. No name of the site is explicitly mentioned in the scroll because the beginning of the passage where one would expect it (the bottom of the previous column) is not preserved. With no place name stipulated, there is no cause for polemics; the polemics arise due to the specification of a particular sanctuary.

B. Mount Gerizim and Mount Ebal

Promotion of the sanctuary at Mount Gerizim could be envisioned in several time periods: the pre-monarchic, pre-Jerusalem-temple period; the period after the secession of the northern kingdom; the early post-exilic period when the Second Temple was being

---

[47] Alexander Rofé, "The Editing of the Book of Joshua in the Light of 4QJosh^a," in *New Qumran Texts and Studies* (n. 5), 73–80, esp. 79. The rabbinic sources are *m. Soṭah* 7:5 and *t. Soṭah* 8:7.

[48] Again, recall the altar polemics stirred by the building of the altar by the Transjordan tribes in Joshua 22 (see n. 4).

built in Jerusalem; the Hasmonaean period; plus other less-known situations.[49] But it seems impossible for either the Deuteronomy fragment from Qumran (if it is from Qumran), the Papyrus Giessen, or the OL to have been influenced by the SP itself; rather, the "Gerizim" (or "Ebal") reading appears to have been an intentional addition in some commonly shared Judean-Samarian manuscript tradition. In fact, the explicit mention in any text of a place name, whether "Mount Gerizim" or "Mount Ebal," would be suspicious as both a textual insertion and a rival claim. Note that Deut 27:4 reads perfectly smoothly without the place name, and that the MT inserts a number of other place names that are not present in the LXX: the MT inserts at Josh 6:26 the place name "Jericho" which is absent from the LXX, as well as from its quote in the Testimonia (4Q175) and the Apocryphon of Joshua (4Q379 22 ii 8). Similarly, the MT both adds "Gilgal" at Josh 10:15 and 10:43 where the LXX does not have it and adds the dubious place name "Bethel" at 8:17 where again the LXX does not have it.

The locale of Mount Ebal as a place where Joshua supposedly built the first altar has long troubled commentators, both militarily and religiously.[50] Militarily, Joshua has the entire population[51] march twenty miles north into hostile enemy territory unchallenged, build the altar, and then immediately abandon it, leaving it vulnerable to the autochthonous warriors and predators, and march with the entire population twenty miles back to Gilgal (Josh 9:6).

Religiously, Mount Ebal has no significance elsewhere in the Hebrew Bible except as the mountain of the curse. It is mentioned only five times in three closely interconnected passages: Deut 11:29; 27:4, 13; and Josh 8:30, 33, all in the context of this altar or (linked with "Mount Gerizim") the recitation of curses. Significantly, Mount Ebal is mentioned in the Joshua narrative only in this passage at 8:30, 33 and never again in the entire book, whereas the camp and the population are immediately back at Gilgal again (Josh 9:6). Adam Zertal claimed to have unearthed on Mount Ebal a structure that he described as "a cultic site," "founded in the second half of the 13th century B.C.E.," that was "presumably part of an earlier complex which undoubtedly bore a cultic character."[52] A number of archaeologists, however, dispute Zertal's claims.[53] Moreover, as Richard Nelson

---

49 See the various possibilities on the origins of the Samaritans in Kartveit, *The Origin of the Samaritans*, 17–43.

50 See the annotation at Josh 8:30-35 in *The New Oxford Annotated Bible: New Revised Standard Version* (New York: Oxford University Press, 1991), 280 OT: "Traveling to Ebal required the tribes to make a twenty-mile trip from Ai to Ebal and then to retrace their steps to encamp at Gilgal (9.6)." Noort ("4QJosh[a] and the History of Tradition," 129) calls the march "completely incomprehensible."

51 "All Israel, alien as well as citizen, with their elders" (Josh 8:33); "all the assembly of Israel, and the women, and the little ones, and the aliens" (8:35).

52 Adam Zertal, "Has Joshua's Altar Been Found on Mt. Ebal?" *BAR* 11/1 (Jan.-Feb. 1985): 26–43; idem, "Ebal, Mount," *ABD*, 2:255–58, esp. 256–57.

53 See Aharon Kempinski, "Joshua's Altar—An Iron Age I Watchtower," *BAR* 12/1 (Jan.-Feb. 1986): 42; idem, "Zertal's Altar—19th Century Biblical Archaeology," *BAR* 12/4 (July-Aug. 1986): 64; Amihai Mazar, *Archaeology of the Land of the Bible* (New York: 1990), 348–50. See also n. 55 below. I thank Professor Ephraim Stern for an enlightening discussion on this topic. Regarding Mount Gerizim, however, Knoppers ("Mt. Gerizim and Mt. Zion," 312) relates that the "archaeological excavations of Yizhaq Magen attest to the construction of an impressive city and sacred precinct on Mt. Gerizim in Hellenistic times.... Beneath the Hellenistic sacred precinct on Mt. Gerizim, Magen . . . discovered an older layer, which he dates to the 5th century and identifies as the Samari(t)an Temple mentioned (but misdated) by Josephus

observes, it "must be stressed that this particular text relates exclusively to Deuteronomy [literarily and thematically] and not directly to any tradition about any actual sanctuary" historically or archaeologically.[54]

In short, "Mount Ebal" has nothing to recommend it, other than its presence in the MT, and no one has presented a plausible rationale for its selection.[55] If "Mount Gerizim" can be characterized as "the most important sectarian reading of SP,"[56] then "Mount Ebal" should be equally considered as a possibly sectarian reading.[57]

A major problem in scholars' deliberations is the geographical confusion about Mount Gerizim and Mount Ebal in Deut 11:30: "These are beyond the Jordan, on the other side of the western road in the land of the Canaanites who live in the Arabah, opposite Gilgal beside the oak of Moreh" (*NABRE*). This verse leads some to think that there were two pairs of mountains. Noort even says, "All our problems ... have to do with the general presupposition that we know where the 'real' Gerizim and 'real' Ebal are located," and "this is a mystery for exegetes."[58] Gerhard von Rad tersely states: "The rest of the statement about localities in v. 30 are obscure, indeed difficult...."[59] Samuel Driver devotes two pages, one in fine print, seriously trying to understand scholars' futile attempts to make sense of the geography of the verse as transmitted in the MT. He correctly explains "behind" the western road: "i.e., on the other side of the great westerly

(i.e., to the time of Alexander the Great: *Ant.* 11.302–347, 13.254–56; *J.W.* 1.62–65)." For Magen's publication references, see Knoppers, "Mt. Gerizim and Mt. Zion," 335. Magen's conclusions may still be developing; see Kartveit, *The Origin of the Samaritans*, 206–8.

[54] Nelson, *Joshua*, 118 n. 5; see also the following note.

[55] Ralph K. Hawkins, in *The Iron Age I Structure on Mt. Ebal: Excavation and Interpretation* (Winona Lake, Ind.: Eisenbrauns, 2012), "provides the most thorough analysis to date of this important Iron I site...," according to Robert D. Miller II in his *RBL* review (http://www.bookreviews.org 8/14/2014). But Hawkins has textual and genre weaknesses. He uses only "Mount Ebal" as in the MT, with no reference to "Mount Gerizim" in the SP, Pap. Geissen, and the OL. Moreover, he presumes that the Deuteronomy 27 and Josh 8:30-35 texts function as historical reports. But see Martin Noth (*Überlieferungsgeschichtliche Studien* [3d ed.; Tübingen: Max Niemeyer, 1967], 43): "Hinter der Ai-Geschichte hat Dtr einen ganzen Abschnitt von eigener Hand eingeschoben (Jos. 8, 30-35); dieser Abschnitt is vollkommen deuteronomistisch formuliert und restlos aus den besonderen Voraussetzungen von Dtr heraus zu verstehen, so daß gar kein Grund vorliegt, hier eine ältere Quellengrundlage anzunehmen. ... es nicht um die Vorgeschichte und Geschichte der altern Überlieferungen, sondern um die Arbeit von Dtr geht. ..." At any rate, Miller closes his detailed review by concluding that the structure "is not Joshua's altar" and "gives no indication of belonging to all Israel."

[56] The quote is from Tov ("Pap. Giessen," 472), but he does conclude that, though it is also an "important sectarian reading of SP," in this case it is "an ancient not yet sectarian reading" in origin.

[57] Though in his earlier edition Tov (*Textual Criticism*, 2d ed., 266, n. 37) wrote that "the probability that *Ebal* in MT in Deut 27:4 is an anti-Samaritan reading ... is very slight," in the third edition (254, n. 96) he rephrases, saying that it "is probably not anti-Samaritan, but reflects an ancient reading." In neither edition is an explanation given for that view; rather, he states that Gerizim "should probably be considered non-sectarian and possibly original" (88, n. 140). If that is the case, then it would seem that Ebal is secondary, and no one has, to my knowledge, offered a rationale for that curious variant other than as a tendentious substitution for Gerizim. Kartveit (*The Origin of the Samaritans*, 300–305) also concludes in favor of Gerizim: "The change to 'Ebal' must have been made at the hands of the Jews and could be a polemical alteration..." (303).

[58] "4QJosh^{a} and the History of Tradition," 135 and 141.

[59] Von Rad, *Deuteronomy*, 86.

road, leading through Palestine from N[orth] to S[outh], which must have passed formerly, as it passes still, through the plain E[ast] of Shechem. . . ."[60] He also identifies "beside the oak of Moreh" with Shechem (cf. Gen 12:6; 35:4; Josh 24:26).

I propose that the problem is caused by a tertiary insertion into an already secondary "topographical gloss."[61] The clear identification in the secondarily inserted topographical gloss was Shechem:[62] "Are these not beyond the Jordan, on the other side of the western road, beside the oak of Moreh?" A later scribe is responsible for the tertiary insertion: "in the land of the Canaanites who live in the Arabah, opposite Gilgal," clearly pointing to a different setting near Jericho and thus creating the geographic doublet. The latter may perhaps be reminiscent of the older tradition as witnessed in 4QJosh[a], Josephus, and Pseudo-Philo. The final, confused, double form of the verse was taken up as the "biblical word" by early exegetes such as Eusebius in his "Onomasticon,"[63] and it eventually appeared in the Madaba map, with the result that in the map Mount Gerizim and Mount Ebal are depicted twice—once near Shechem and again near Jericho.[64] Curiously, the two sets of names are stylistically different in the map. The two near Shechem are listed as ΤΟΥΡΓΑΡΙΖΙΝ and ΤΟΥΡΓΩΒΗΛ, whereas the two near Jericho are listed as ΓΑΡΙΖΕΙΝ and ΓΕΒΑΛ. Here one can only speculate, but since ΤΟΥΡ is clearly the Aramaic טור (= "mountain," Hebrew צור),[65] it presumably goes back to a Semitic source, whereas the latter pair may be based on a Greek (= Christian) tradition that simply rested on the conflated "biblical text" which included Gilgal.

C. Deuteronomy 27:4

Joshua's building of the first altar is the fulfillment of the command given by Moses in Deut 27:1-8. There is no mention of a specific place in v. 2 where one might expect it, and the clear assumption (prior to v. 4) is that Joshua should build an altar not far from the site—wherever it be—of the crossing of the Jordan, on the day that Israel crossed (though, to be sure, ביום need not be taken literally).[66] No specific place is mentioned

---

60 Samuel R. Driver, *Deuteronomy* (ICC; Edinburgh: T&T Clark, 1895), 132–34, esp. 133; see also the discussion by Gary N. Knoppers, *Jews and Samaritans: The Origins and History of Their Early Relations* (Oxford: Oxford University Press, 2013), 200–4.

61 Moshe Weinfeld, *Deuteronomy 1–11* (AB 5; New York: Doubleday, 1991), 452. Weinfeld also notes the similar "gloss that also opens with the word *halô* in Deut 3:11."

62 This secondary gloss in Deut 11:30, without the tertiary insertion, was possibly linked with the stratum commanding blessings and curses on Mount Gerizim and Mount Ebal in Deut 11:29 + 27:12-13.

63 Though Eusebius mentions both pairs, he endorses the pair near Jericho and proclaims the pair near Shechem to be in error; see Noort, "4QJosh[a] and the History of Tradition," 130 n. 9; and Glen W. Bowersock, *Mosaics as History: The Near East from Late Antiquity to Islam* (Cambridge, Mass.: Belknap Press of Harvard University Press, 2006), 13–28, esp. 26.

64 Bowersock, *Mosaics as History*, 25.

65 See *HALOT*, 1883; and Bowersock, *Mosaics as History*, 26.

66 In contrast to my starting text critically with a less specified, unnamed place as in Deut 27:2 and a possibly later v. 4 with or without the insertion of "Mount Gerizim" or "Mount Ebal," Noort ("4QJosh[a] and the History of Tradition," 127) takes the MT text as it stands and starts with 27:4, 8, 5-7, which emphasizes the *location* near the two mountains, and he considers 27:2-3 as a later stage, emphasizing the *time* ("on the day you cross"). But "the time" (ביום) is vague, not a new emphasis, and methodologically, the more vague element should be seen as earlier, and the more specific (introducing Mount Gerizim/Ebal)

until v. 4, and indeed, if בהר עיבל ("on Mount Ebal") were absent from the verse, the passage would read perfectly smoothly, again implying that the altar should be built immediately at Gilgal. The suspicion is strong that the mention of a specific place is a secondary insertion,[67] and that whichever mountain was first inserted, Gerizim or Ebal, the other is a tertiary, polemical substitution. One tends to see בהר גרזים as the earlier form of the insertion, since הר עיבל has no other significant function in the Hebrew Bible, and the only readily apparent rationale for it here is as a polemical replacement for הר גרזים.

CONCLUSION

In sum, there are three sets of texts witnessing to the placement of the initial altar after crossing the Jordan into the land, and the question focuses on the order in which the traditions were developed. 4QJosh[a] is arguably the oldest extant witness with the altar naturally and neutrally at Gilgal, joined by Josephus, Pseudo-Philo, *m. Soṭah*, and *t. Soṭah*. A second set of texts joins the SP: an ancient Greek papyrus and an OL reading (with or without a possible Qumran Hebrew fragment) displaying the reading "Mount Gerizim," presumably prior to and apart from influence by the SP specifically. A third set includes the MT plus the versions routinely dependent on it. The MT, which often exhibits a more expanded text of the book and includes the insertion of several other place names, reads "Mount Ebal." That site is odd and has nothing to recommend it, whereas the passage 8:30-35 is acknowledged to be out of place in the MT.

Thus, the three-stage solution as sketched above seems to be at least fully plausible if not compelling. 4QJosh[a], presumably specifying no locality and supported by the independent first-century witnesses Josephus and Pseudo-Philo, plus (non-Qumran) rabbinic sources, presents the earliest preserved and most logical stage of the narrative. The simple and natural narrative with an unnamed, and thus unobjectionable, site ("when you cross over") would seem to be the earliest form. The occurrence of a specific place name was probably an intentional secondary insertion, designed to promote some site other than the original, thus introducing a theological claim. Such a secondary insertion, whether "Gerizim" or "Ebal," would require a third stage with the opposite name to replace it. Which order of the two names, Gerizim and Ebal, would be more likely? The replacement of "Ebal" with "Gerizim" would be expected only by the Samarians or

should be seen as the later element. Noort says (130), on "the basis of the presupposition that 'Ebal' in Joshua 8:30ff. belonged to the original text, . . . it may be presumed that the author of Joshua 8:30-35 understood 'his' Ebal to be in the neighbourhood of Jericho." Regarding the later stage, "The erection of stones and altar directly after the crossing of the Jordan (Deut 27:2-3) is the stage where the mountains Ebal and Gerizim are moved to a position in the neighbourhood of Jericho/Gilgal (Deut 11:30; 4QJosh[a])." Verse 4, however, with "you shall set up *these* stones," requires that the stones have already been mentioned (as they are in v. 2, which must be earlier) and would also require that the stones from the Jordan be carried all the way to Mount Ebal. It is difficult to imagine that the original "author" of this passage thought that the mountains were near Gilgal. Rofé ("The Editing of the Book of Joshua in the Light of 4QJosh[a]," 79) recognizes the implausibility; he helpfully notes that "the Tanna Rabbi Eliezer (ben Hyrcanus, 2nd half of the 1st century C.E.) reacted against the prevailing view with an original *ruse*: he 'transferred' Gerizim and Ebal to two artificial mounds which had allegedly been heaped up by the Israelites near Gilgal" (*y. Soṭah* 7:3; emphasis mine).

[67] Recall the other place names mentioned above that are added in the MT but lacking in the LXX at Josh 6:26; 8:17; 10:15, and 10:43.

Samaritans (but then how explain the broader Jewish reading attested by Pap. Giessen and the OL?), whereas the replacement of "Gerizim" with "Ebal" can probably be explained only as a polemical counterclaim by southerners against the northern shrine. To date there appears to be no other cogent explanation of the anomalous "Mount Ebal." Thus, the sequence appears to be: Gilgal (4QJosh[a], Josephus, Pseudo-Philo, *m. Soṭah*, and *t. Soṭah*), then Mount Gerizim (either non-extant Jewish manuscripts or the newly surfaced fragment, SP, Pap. Giessen, and the OL), replaced in most texts by Mount Ebal (MT and revised LXX).

CHAPTER 5

A SHORTER TEXT OF JUDGES AND A LONGER TEXT OF KINGS

I. 4QJUDG^A

THE OLDEST PRESERVED MANUSCRIPT of the book of Judges is 4QJudg^a. The manuscript dates from ca. 50–25 B.C.E. and survives in only a single fragment 7.6 x 4.8 cm.[1] But this small fragment offers an important piece of evidence. It contains text from eight verses in chapter 6 of Judges: vv. 2, 3, 4, 5, 6 followed directly, without interval, on this same fragment by vv. 11, 12, 13. Verses 7-10 are not present. Julio Trebolle, the editor of this manuscript, notes that since the time of Wellhausen vv. 7-10 have been "generally recognized by modern critics as a literary insertion" and that they are now seen as "a piece of late Dtr. redaction." On the basis of the 4QJudg^a evidence he correctly concludes that "4QJudg^a can confidently be seen as an earlier literary form of the book than our traditional texts."[2] Into the earlier form of the text, witnessed by 4QJudg^a, the text form witnessed by the MT inserts a theological passage featuring a nameless prophet (see Table 1).

This part of the original scroll narrated the story of the Midianite oppression of the Israelites and the call of Gideon to deliver them. The Midianites were repeatedly raiding and destroying Israel's crops, leaving them no sustenance. In the early form of the story, the Israelites cry out to the Lord, and the angel of the Lord comes to commission Gideon, who at first challenges the angel.[3] The secondary text as preserved in the MT inserts a stereotypical passage which indicts the Israelites[4] and thus makes Gideon's impertinent challenge out of place. Thus, when the Israelites cried out to the Lord for help (v. 6), the original answer to that cry came in the form of the angel of the Lord in (the immediately following) v. 11. In the MT version the inserted passage thus forms a conflicted duplicate: in answer to the Israelites' cry, the Lord first sends a (nameless) prophet (v. 7, to which episode there is no conclusion), and then sends the angel of the Lord (v. 11), and the story continues.

---

[1] See Julio Trebolle Barrera, "49. 4QJudg^a," in DJD 14:161–64 (*The Biblical Qumran Scrolls*, 255); and idem, "Textual Variants in 4QJudg^a and the Textual and Editorial History of the Book of Judges," *RevQ* 14/2 (1989): 229–45. Trebolle argues for a variant edition of Judges in the OG and OL.

[2] Trebolle, "49. 4QJudg^a," 162. Note that the passage is set off by פ both before and after it in the MT.

[3] "But sir, if the LORD is with us, why then has all this happened to us? And where are all his wonderful deeds. . . ?" (Judg 6:13).

[4] "I led you up from Egypt, . . . but you have not given heed to my voice" (6:8, 10).

TABLE 1: *Judges 6:6-11*

4QJudg[a]

] [6] וידל ישראל מאד מפני מדין]וׄיזעקו בני יש[ראל אל] יהוה

] [11]ויבא מלאך יהוה וישב תחת האלה אשר בעפרה]אשר ליואש האביעזרי

MT Judg 6:6-11

[6]וידל ישראל מאד מפני מדין ויזעקו בני ישראל אל יהוה: פ

[7]ויהי כי זעקו בני ישראל אל יהוה על אדות מדין:
[8]וישלח יהוה איש נביא אל בני ישראל ויאמר להם כה אמר יהוה אלהי ישראל
אנכי העליתי אתכם ממצרים ואציא אתכם מבית עבדים:
[9]ואצל אתכם מיד מצרים ומיד כל לחציכם ואגרש אותם מפניכם ואתנה לכם את ארצם:
[10]ואמרה לכם אני יהוה אלהיכם לא תיראו את אלהי האמרי
אשר אתם יושבים בארצם ולא שמעתם בקולי: פ

[11]ויבא מלאך יהוה וישב תחת האלה אשר בעפרה אשר ליואש אבי העזרי

4QJudg[a]

[... [6]Thus Israel was greatly impoverished because of Midian];
and the Is[rael]ites cried out [to] the LORD.

[[11]Then the angel of the LORD came and sat under the oak...]
which belonged to Joash the Abiezrite

MT Judg 6:6-11

... [6]Thus Israel was greatly impoverished because of Midian;
and the Israelites cried out to the LORD.

> [7]*When the Israelites cried out to the LORD on account of the Midianites,*
> [8]*the LORD sent a prophet to the Israelites; and he said to them,*
> *"Thus says the LORD, the God of Israel: I led you*
> *up from Egypt, and brought you forth from the house of slavery;* [9]...
> [10]*... But you have not given heed to my voice."*

[11]Then the angel of the LORD came and sat under the oak ...
which belonged to Joash the Abiezrite

The deuteronomistic character that imbues the insertion of vv. 7-10 is unmistakable both in the general message and in the individual phrases employed. It is difficult not to think of the other Dtr-narrated nameless prophet in 1 Kings 13. Moreover, the claim of later insertion is supported by the fact that נביא ("prophet") occurs nowhere else in the book of Judges. In addition, the overall passage reiterates the Deuteronomist's general cyclical view of the era of the Judges (Judges 2–3)—of apostasy, punishment, cry to Yhwh, deliverance. Finally, the individual phrases are echoes of other Deuteronomistic passages:

"the Israelites cried out to the LORD" (cf. Judg 3:15)
"the LORD sent a prophet" (cf. 2 Sam 12:1; the Dtr layer in Amos 2:11; and the nameless prophet in 1 Kings 13)
"brought you up out of Egypt" (cf. Judg 2:1, 12)
"you have not obeyed my voice" (cf. Judg 2:2, 20)

Natalio Fernández Marcos, while accepting "the importance of the Qumran documents, and particularly of 4QJudg^{a}, for the textual criticism of the book," has cautioned that we "cannot rely on such tiny fragments as those contained in 4QJudg^{a} to support such diverse issues as... the existence of 'independent texts' at Qumran [and] the theory of a different, shorter edition of the book...."[5] Trebolle and Fernández Marcos are both correct. It is important to distinguish between this passage and the entire book. For example, a scroll of Jeremiah, 4QJer^{b}, witnesses to a variant edition of its entire book, as seen in the OG, though it too survives in only a single small fragment. In addition to textual criticism one must consider literary, source, and redaction criticism. The convergence here of experienced literary-critical methodology applied to the composition and redaction of Judges, plus the new manuscript evidence documenting other variant editions of biblical books, makes it possible that 4QJudg^{a} could be part of an earlier edition. We cannot know, however, about the full scroll; but 4QJudg^{a} witnesses, if not to an earlier edition of the entire book of Judges, at least to an "earlier literary form" of this passage.

With regard to date, it is difficult to know when the insertion was made; but it seems inconceivable that 4QJudg^{a} would still preserve in the first century B.C.E., against all other witnesses, a seventh-century B.C.E. pre-DtrH text. It is, rather, far more likely that the short text represented by 4QJudg^{a} was the dominant text during the early Second Temple period, and that this deuteronomistically inspired insertion in MT is part of the late, widespread, developmental growth at the hands of numerous scribes seen in many biblical books. And though the designation "deuteronomistic" is used, it is less likely to be the result of the specific "Deuteronomistic school" that flourished in the seventh and sixth centuries, and more likely to be the general Second Temple Judean theology that, as has been increasingly recognized, had widely endorsed the traditional Deuteronomistic mode of theology. For example, Carol Newsom has observed that in "Second Temple Judaism... one can note the spread of several discourses.... The language of the Deuteronomic movement becomes broadly influential...."[6]

---

[5] Natalio Fernández Marcos, "The Hebrew and Greek Texts of Judges," in *The Earliest Text of the Hebrew Bible: The Relationship between the Masoretic Text and the Hebrew Base of the Septuagint Reconsidered* (ed. Adrian Schenker; Atlanta: Society of Biblical Literature, 2003), 1–16, esp. 15; see also idem (ed.), *BHQ* 7: *Judges* (Stuttgart: Deutsche Bibelgesellschaft, 2011), 65*–66*. The arguments for caution expressed by Richard S. Hess ("The Dead Sea Scrolls and Higher Criticism of the Hebrew Bible: The Case of 4QJudg^{a}," in *The Scrolls and the Scriptures: Qumran Fifty Years After* [JSPSS 26; ed. Stanley E. Porter and Craig A. Evans; Sheffield: Sheffield Academic Press, 1997], 122–28) should indeed be considered but are not persuasive.

[6] Carol Newsom, *The Self as Symbolic Space: Constructing Identity and Community at Qumran* (STDJ 52; Leiden: Brill, 2004), 9. See also Linda S. Schearing and Steven L. McKenzie, eds., *Those Elusive Deuteronomists: The Phenomenon of Pan-Deuteronomism*; JSOTSup 268; Sheffield: Sheffield Academic Press, 1999); H. J. M. Van-Deventer, "The End of the End, or, What is the Deuteronomist (Still) Doing

The prophetic nature of the insertion may offer a clue regarding the recognition of the book as Scripture. At some point the book of Deuteronomy was separated from the rest of the Deuteronomistic History Work to become one with Genesis–Numbers as the Mosaic Torah. The remaining books of the History—which was probably seen in early centuries not as Scripture but as historical *literature*—apparently continued to be considered national literature after (and even though) Deuteronomy had become part of the "Torah."[7] One factor in the eventual reclassification of Joshua–Kings from being seen simply as national historical literature to being recognized as "Scripture" may have been the increasing focus on prophets, helped by insertions such as the one in the MT highlighted by 4QJudg[a]. By genre, the corpus is a history, or better, a theological interpretation of history (thus the Christian classification as "Historical Books"). But eventually, the shift of focus may have moved from "literature" to "Scripture" in light of appreciation that the religious high-points centered on the narratives of the great prophets Samuel, Nathan, the (nameless) "man of God" in 1 Kings 13, Elijah, Micaiah, and Elisha (thus the Jewish classification as the "Former Prophets").[8]

In summary, 4QJudg[a] witnesses to the short, "original" text of this passage in Judges during the late Second Temple period, whereas some scribe added a late, deuteronomistically inspired insertion into a variant form of the text which now appears in the MT, the LXX, and all other texts dependent on them.[9]

II. 4QKINGS

The text of Kings does not enjoy either the generous preservation at Qumran (such as 4QSam[a]) or the enlightening readings (such as 4QJosh[a]) that some of the other more fortunately preserved books enjoy.[10] 4QKgs, however, which dates from about the middle of the first century B.C.E., does provide eight fragments that offer two modest

in Daniel?" in *Past, Present, Future: The Deuteronomistic History and the Prophets* (ed. J. C. de Moor and H. F. van Rooy; Leiden: Brill, 2000), 62–75; and Hanne von Weissenberg "4QMMT — Towards an Understanding of the Epilogue," *RevQ* 21 (2003): 29–45, esp. 29; eadem, *4QMMT: Reevaluating the Text, the Function, and the Meaning of the Epilogue* (STDJ 82; Leiden: Brill, 2009). Von Weissenberg shows that the structure of MMT is based on the covenant pattern in Deuteronomy.

[7] Note both the very few Qumran copies of Joshua–Kings in comparison with the many copies of the Torah (especially Deuteronomy!) and Prophets, as well as the lack of quotations from those books (except for the single passage 2 Sam 7:10-14 — a prophetic passage that is used and interpreted prophetically in 4QFlorilegium); see Ulrich, "Qumran and the Canon of the Old Testament," in *The Biblical Canons*, 57–80, esp. 80; and VanderKam and Flint, *The Meaning of the Scrolls*, 178–80.

[8] Note also the explicit mention of "prophecy" in relation to the Psalter's reclassification from "hymnbook of the Temple" to "book of Scripture" in 11QPs[a] 27:11 (see Chapter 12).

[9] For another deuteronomistically inspired insertion into a prophetic text, note the lengthy marginal insertion of Jer 7:30–8:3 by a later hand into 4QJer[a] between Jeremiah 7 and 8; see DJD 15:152–56, Pl. XXIV; *The Biblical Qumran Scrolls*, 559–60; and Ch. 9 below.

[10] See Julio Trebolle Barrera, "Kings, First and Second Books of," *Encyclopedia of the Dead Sea Scrolls*, 1:467–68.

TABLE 2: *1 Kings 8:16*

4QKgs ≈ 2 Chr 6:5-6

[[16]מן היום אשר הוצאתי את עמי את ישראל ממצרים לא בחרתי בעיר מכל שבטי]
[ישראל לבנות בית להיות שמי שם ולא בחרתי באיש ל]היות נגיד על עמ[י ישראל]
[ואבחר בירושלם להיות שמי שם ואבחר בדוד] להיות על עמי על [ישראל [17]ויהי]

MT 1 Kgs 8:16

[16]מן היום אשר הוצאתי את עמי את ישראל ממצרים לא בחרתי בעיר מכל שבטי
ישראל לבנות בית להיות שמי שם
ואבחר בדוד להיות על עמי ישראל [17]ויהי

4QKgs ≈ 2 Chr 6:5-6

[[16]. . . I have not chosen a city from any of the tribes of Israel
in which to build a house, that my name might be there;
and I chose no one] *to be ruler over* [*my*] *people* [*Israel;*
but I have chosen Jerusalem that my name might be there,
and I chose David] to be over my people, over [Israel.]

MT 1 Kgs 8:16

[16]. . . I have not chosen a city from any of the tribes of Israel
in which to build a house, that my name might be there;

but I chose David to be over my people Israel.

pieces of information.[11] First, the fragments often agree with "the Masoretic Text of Kings (and Chronicles) against the Septuagint in all the minuses and transpositions that give the Old Greek its peculiar textual character."[12] Second, while in general supporting the Hebrew text of Kings that the MT inherited, frg. 7 shows that the MT has lost a full line from 1 Kgs 8:16 (see Table 2). As Trebolle points out, "The most important reading of 4QKgs is the preservation of a substantial original reading of Kings, lost by homoioteleuton in 1 Kgs 8:16, but preserved in the parallel text of 2 Chr 6:5b-6a and partially preserved in the Old Greek text of 1 Kgs 8:16."[13]

A scribe, in the transmission process after 4QKgs was copied and prior to the medieval MT, apparently skipped from the first occurrence of להיות שמי שם to the second occurrence, losing the text in italics above. This Qumran witness to a full line that has been lost in the MT is most likely paralleled by two similar examples in 1 Samuel, one certain and one probable. First, the MT has clearly lost a large amount of text in 1 Sam 14:41. Second, column X fragment b of 4QSam^{a} includes the beginning words of three

[11] See Trebolle, "54. 4QKgs," in DJD 14:171–83.

[12] Trebolle, "Kings, First and Second Books of," 1:467.

[13] Trebolle, "54. 4QKgs," 183, and text on 180; see also *The Biblical Qumran Scrolls*, 325–26.

lines that attest to a text of 1 Sam 11:9 with one full line more than the MT and the versions have (see Chapter 6.III.B).[14] No other witnesses, however, offer any clues helpful for discovering the longer text there, and thus it is impossible to know whether it is an addition in 4QSam[a] or a loss in the MT. We can, however, be grateful to 4QJudg[a] and 4QKgs for providing both shorter and longer texts, respectively, that are earlier than the forms that have been transmitted in the MT.

[14] Frank Moore Cross, "51. 4QSam[a]," in DJD 17:67–68; Ulrich, *The Qumran Text of Samuel*, 133; *The Biblical Qumran Scrolls*, 272.

CHAPTER 6

THE SAMUEL SCROLLS

TWENTY-SEVEN leather fragments in Hebrew, later to be identified as fragments from a manuscript of the Book of Samuel, were retrieved, along with thousands of fragments of perhaps a hundred manuscripts, from the deepest level of excavation in Cave 4 at Qumran. The Samuel manuscript would prove to be one of the most important and most instructive of the biblical manuscripts. It was discovered between 22 and 29 September 1952, and in early summer of 1953 the fragments were assigned for identification to Frank Moore Cross, the first member of the new Cave 4 team of editors to arrive in Jerusalem. They were "wholly illegible" as well as "darkened and mostly covered with yellow crystals—evidently animal urine."[1] But once they were cleaned, Cross pieced them together to form generous parts of chapters 1–2 of 1 Samuel and published his results already in 1953.[2]

The excavations by the scholars, however, were occasioned by the prior successes of the enterprising Bedouin in early September 1952. The Bedouin had recovered the vast majority of the fragments of 4QSam^a and, from 1952 until 1958, gradually brought them and the fragments of two other scrolls of Samuel, 4QSam^b and 4QSam^c, for purchase.[3] The fact that the fragments excavated from Cave 4 by the scholars proved to be part of the same manuscript offered by the Bedouin confirmed the provenance of the fragments purchased from the latter. Cave 1 contained another manuscript of Samuel, but only a few small fragments were preserved.

Due to its size, 4QSam^a teaches us much about the history of the text. Although "only just under fifteen percent of the text of Samuel is extant on the leather fragments," 4QSam^a is still "the most extensively preserved of the biblical manuscripts from Cave 4" (DJD 17:3) and the fourth most extensively preserved of the entire corpus of scriptural scrolls.[4] Since it is so well preserved, it is a potentially rich candidate for examining the four distinct types of manuscript variation: orthography, individual variants, isolated insertions, and variant or successive editions.

[1] Frank Moore Cross, Donald W. Parry, Richard Saley, and Eugene Ulrich, DJD 17:2, n. 3.

[2] Frank Moore Cross, "A New Qumran Biblical Fragment Related to the Original Hebrew Underlying the Septuagint," *BASOR* 132 (1953) [C. C. Torrey Volume]: 15–26.

[3] A preliminary edition of 4QSam^b was also quickly published by F. M. Cross, "The Oldest Manuscripts from Qumran," *JBL* 74 (1955): 147–72. Eugene Ulrich received the third manuscript in summer 1977, edited it in a year and published it in 1979: "4QSam^c: A Fragmentary Manuscript of 2 Samuel 14–15 from the Scribe of the *Serek Hay-yaḥad* (1QS)," *BASOR* 235 (1979): 1–25.

[4] Martin Abegg (DJD 32, Part 2:25) reports that there are more than 94,000 extant words in the corpus of the preserved biblical scrolls. 1QIsa^a is virtually completely intact, containing 22,696 words (24% of the entire biblical corpus); MurXII is the second largest manuscript with 4,834 words (ca. 5.1%); 1QIsa^b is the third largest with 4,603 words (almost 5%); and 4QSam^a is fourth with 3,656 words (almost 4%).

The four parts of this chapter will analyze the different levels of variation in the texts of Samuel. Part I will present some characteristics and differences in orthography. Part II will review a selection of the smaller individual variants for each of the scrolls. Part III will then present the larger intentional isolated insertions, and Part IV will analyze possible variant editions.

I. Orthography of the Samuel Scrolls

Cross dates 4QSam^{a} palaeographically to approximately "50–25 B.C.E., that is, in the transition from Late Hasmonaean to Early Herodian scripts" (DJD 17:5). He dates 4QSam^{b} to approximately 250 B.C.E. (17:220) and the "semiformal" script of 4QSam^{c} (the same hand as in 1QS, 4QTest, etc.) to approximately 100–75 B.C.E. (17:249).

Table 1 presents in the upper section a brief, impressionistic comparison of orthographic forms exhibited by the various texts for common words. The lower section of the table lists forms that are somewhat contrary to the regular practices of one or another manuscript. The orthography of 4QSam^{a} exhibits a somewhat fuller use of internal *matres lectionis* than the MT: 4QSam^{a} has 210 fuller readings than the MT, compared with 19 readings in the MT that are fuller than 4QSam^{a} (DJD 17:5); note, however, that the MT has לוא at 1 Sam 2:24. In contrast, 4QSam^{b}, probably due to the fact that it is two centuries older than 4QSam^{a}, is copied "in a surprisingly archaic orthography" (17:220), with only a single instance of a reading fuller than MT: רוץ at 1 Sam 20:38. The orthography of 4QSam^{c} is consistently the fullest, often termed "baroque," using forms such as מאודה (2 Sam 14:25 מאד MT) and היאה (14:27 היא MT); note, however, in 4QSam^{c}

Table 1: *Orthographic Characteristics*

4QSam^{a}	4QSam^{b}	4QSam^{c}	MT Sam	MT Chr
כול	כל	כול	כל	כל
כיא/כי	כי	כיא	כי	כי
לוא/לא	לא	לוא	לא	לא
אלוהי	אלהי	אלוהי	אלהי	אלהי
ויאמר	ויאמר	ויאומר	ויאמר	ויאמר
לאמור	לאמר	לאמור	לאמר	לאמר
דויד	דוד		דוד	דויד
אפוד	אפד		אפוד	אפוד
הכוהן			הכהן	הכהן
		עוון	עון	עוון
גויים			גוים	גוים
פלשתיים			פלשתים	פלשתים
לוא/לא	לא	לוא	לוא	לא
בא	ויבא, בבאם		ויבוא, בבואם	ויבא, בבאם
לעזר			לעזיר	לעזר
	רוץ		רץ	
אליו		אלו	אליו	אליו

at 2 Sam 14:30 the shorter form אלו (אליו MT, but ועלו MT^ketiv at 2 Sam 20:8).[5] Beyond what has been said, it is difficult to formulate any meaningful specific conclusion regarding the general trends and inconsistencies in orthography of the various manuscripts that would not be countered by further examples.

II. Individual Textual Variants

From the very first publication of the 4QSam^a fragments, the claim was made that they were "related to the original Hebrew underlying the Septuagint."[6] This section will review a sampling of the smaller individual variants for the Samuel scrolls. For each it will survey "original" (i.e., earlier in the manuscript transmission) readings as well as secondary or erroneous readings, watching the affiliation of the Old Greek, that is, whether the Greek is translating a text in the MT tradition, or a text in the tradition of one of the scrolls, or neither.

A. Variants in 1QSam

The Cave 1 manuscript of Samuel survived in only a few fragments, containing 1 Sam 18:17-18; 2 Sam 20:6-10; 21:16-18; and 23:9-12.[7] The variants they exhibit appear minor and insignificant, but they offer two learnings. First, tiny frg. 1, though containing only six letters of 1 Sam 18:17-18 on one line and four on the following line, demonstrates that the manuscript contained the longer edition of the narrative of David's entrance into Saul's service, in agreement with the MT against the short OG (see IV.D below). Second, fragments 2–3 attest that the scribe erroneously lost a full line from 2 Sam 20:8:

2 Sam 20:8 *(DJD 1:65; The Biblical Qumran Scrolls [BQS] 316)*[8]

1QSam

1 [ ] בצ]רות והציל עיננו [7]ויצאו אחריו א]נשי יוא]ב והכרתי והפלתי]
2 [וכל הגברים וי]צאו מירו̇]שלם לרדף אחרי שבע בן בכרי [8]]ה̇מה עם ה]אבן הגדולה אשר]
3 [בג]ב̇עון ותפל [9]ויאמר יואב̇] לעמשא השלום אתה א]חי ותאחז יד ימין] יואב בזקן עמשא]
4 [ ]ל[נש]ק ל[ו [10]ועמש]א ל]א נשמר בחרב אשר ביד יואב וי]כהו בה אל ה̇]חמש [

MT OG

1 פן מצא לו ערים בצרות והציל עיננו [7]ויצאו אחריו אנשי יואב והכרתי והפלתי
2 וכל הגברים ויצאו מירושלם לרדף אחרי שבע בן בכרי [8]הם עם האבן הגדולה אשר
3a בגבעון ועמשא בא לפניהם ויואב חגור מדו לבשו ועלו חגור חרב מצמדת על מתניו בתערה
3b והוא יצא ותפל [9]ויאמר יואב לעמשא השלום אתה אחי ותחז יד ימין יואב בזקן עמשא
4 לנשק לו [10]ועמשא לא נשמר בחרב אשר ביד יואב ויכהו בה אל החמש

---

5 For fuller descriptions of the orthography of 4QSam^a and 4QSam^b see Cross, DJD 17:5–15 and 17:220–21; for 4QSam^c see Ulrich, DJD 17:250–51.

6 Cross, "A New Qumran Biblical Fragment Related to the Original Hebrew Underlying the Septuagint."

7 See DJD 1:64–65, revised in Ulrich, *The Biblical Qumran Scrolls* [*BQS*].

8 The readings throughout (except for 1QSam in DJD 1) are taken from DJD 17 and *BHS*. For fuller discussion of the variants see Cross's final edition in DJD 17; Ulrich's preliminary study in *The Qumran Text of Samuel and Josephus* [*QTSJ*] (which owes a significant debt to Cross's unpublished notes); and the magisterial commentary by P. Kyle McCarter, *I Samuel* and *II Samuel*.

The loss of text in 1QSam is clear, since it contains no subject for ותפל. An analogous loss of a full line of text occurs in 4QSam^c at 2 Sam 15:1, although there the scribe caught his error immediately and filled in the missing line.[9] In neither case is the parablepsis caused by homoiarchton or homoioteleuton, that is, by the scribe's skipping from one word to another, but rather by his skipping from one line (in the text from which he is copying) to the next. In addition, another instance of the possible loss in the MT of an entire line (but possible addition in 4QSam^a) will be presented below in III.B. at 1 Sam 11:9.

B. Variants in 4QSam^a

1 Sam 1:23 *(DJD 17:31; BQS 260; Qumran Text of Samuel and Josephus [QTSJ] 71)*

4QSam^a	[ויקם יהו]הׄ היוצאׄ מפׄיך
MT	יקם יהוה את דברו
OG	στήσαι κύριος τὸ ἐξελθὸν ἐκ τοῦ στόματός σου

The scroll and the OG retain the earlier text: Hannah has made a vow to dedicate Samuel to the Lord, and Elkanah says "may the LORD bring about what you have said" (i.e., your request and your vow). The tradition behind the MT has been revised according to routine Deuteronomistic theology (which perdured down through the late Second Temple period), emphasizing the prophecy-fulfillment theme—even though the Lord has not pronounced any prophetic word.[10] Note that the OG agrees with 4QSam^a against the MT in this "original" reading.

1 Sam 17:4 *(DJD 17:78; BQS 277; QTSJ 79)*

4QSam^a	[גבהו]אׄרבע[א]מות וזרת
MT	גבהו שש אמות וזרת
OG	ὕψος αὐτοῦ τεσσάρων πήχεων καὶ σπιθαμῆς

On the principle that traditions tend to become more exaggerated, the scroll and the OG presumably retain the earlier text, with Goliath's height at four cubits and a span, and Josephus (*Ant.* 6.171), who was using a Greek text in the 4QSam^a tradition,[11] also has the number four. Some Greek manuscripts (LXX^{N++}) report five cubits, while the MT followed by the Hexaplaric tradition (LXX^{Acx}, σ′) raises the number to six.

1 Sam 1:24 *(DJD 17:31; BQS 260, QTSJ 48–49)*

4QSam^a	[בפר בן]בקר משלש
MT	בפרים שלשה
OG	ἐν μόσχῳ τριετίζοντι = בפר משלש*

---

9 See DJD 17:260, and *The Biblical Qumran Scrolls*, 308.

10 I first heard this point argued by Robert Kugler in "The Deuteronomist's Text of 1 Samuel 1," presented at the meeting of the Society of Biblical Literature in San Francisco, November 1992. It is persuasively in line with Gerhard von Rad, "The Deuteronomic Theology of History in I and II Kings," in *The Problem of the Hexateuch and Other Essays* (trans. E. W. T. Dicken; London: SCM Press, 1966), 205–21.

11 Ulrich, *The Qumran Text of Samuel*, 165–91.

In this instance the OG alone retains the "original" reading, presumably reflecting its short Hebrew *Vorlage* בפר משלש*. A form of that early tradition which was inherited by the Masoretic *textus receptus* erred by misdividing: בפרם שלש* and was later revised to בפרים שלשה.[12] 4QSam^a^ also contains the "original" reading but secondarily expands it with בן בקר (cf. בפר בן בקר Lev 16:3 and 2 Chr 13:9). Here we can see that the OG has faithfully translated an early, undisturbed form of the Hebrew tradition, which 4QSam^a^ has transmitted though it also inserted an expansion, and which the MT has mistaken.

Just as the MT presented that erroneous reading, 4QSam^a^ also includes erroneous readings, and it is instructive to study the OG in these cases. The first has a triple occurrence:

2 Sam 4:1 *(DJD 17:113, 118; BQS 294, 295; QTSJ 42–44)*

4QSam^a^	[וי]שמע מפיב[ש]ת בׄ[ן שאול	
MT	וישמע בן שאול	
OG	Καὶ ἤκουσεν Μεμφιβοσθε υἱὸς Σαουλ	(LXX^MN++^ Ιεβοσθε)

2 Sam 4:2

4QSam^a^	למפיבשת	
MT	היו	
OG	τῷ Μεμφιβοσθε	(LXX^MN++^ Ιεβοσθε)

2 Sam 4:12

4QSam^a^	מפיבשת	
MT	אישבשת	
OG	Μεμφιβοσθε	(LXX^MN++^ Ιεβοσθε)

The passage involves Saul's son, an individual named אישבעל, though it includes a parenthesis (2 Sam 4:4) about Jonathan's lame son מפיבעל/מריבעל, which causes the confusion here. The Hebrew tradition often replaces the בעל ("Baal") element of names with the denigrating בשת ("shame"). In all three readings 4QSam^a^ errs, substituting מפיבשת for אישבשת (some Greek manuscripts have Ιεβοσθε, and the Peshitta has אשבשול*), presumably due to the occurrence of מפיבשת in v. 4. It is difficult to know whether the MT preserves the original short reading in 4:1 or deletes the name since it is incorrect, although the latter is quite plausible, since some Greek manuscripts and the Peshitta (almost) somehow inherited the correct name. The MT, however, errs in the second reading with disturbed syntax, though its third reading is correct. A point to notice is that the OG follows 4QSam^a^ in all three errors, a strong sign of textual affiliation: "Agreement in error is the best indication of textual affinity" (DJD 17:130–31).

2 Sam 7:23 *(DJD 17:130; BQS 298; QTSJ 71, 161)*

4QSam^a^	[גוים] ואהלים
MT	גוים ואלהיו
OG, OL	ἔθνη καὶ σκηνώματα

---

[12] For a similar error in word division (plus palaeographic confusion) see ἐν Νασιβ (= בנציב*) for בן־צוף in 1 Sam 1:1, as well as [א]יׄשטוב at 2 Sam 10:6 below.

The metathesis of *lamed-he* earlier in the Hebrew tradition behind 4QSam^a influenced the OG, again showing that the OG faithfully translates a Hebrew text independent from the MT, at times even when that Hebrew text contains an error. MasPs^a with אלהי displays a similar metathesis for MT-LXX אהלי at Ps 83:7.

2 Sam 10:6 *(DJD 17:136; BQS 300; QTSJ 152–56)*

4QSam^a	[א]י̊שטוב
MT	ואיש טוב
OG, Pesh., Vulg.	καὶ Ιστωβ

The MT correctly lists "the men of Tob" among the military allies of the Ammonites. At the end of its line 4QSam^a cramps the two words together without obvious space division, and the OG, followed by Josephus ("Ιστοβον, *Ant.* 7.121), as well as the Peshitta and the Vulgate interpret the reading as the proper name of an individual.

C. *Variants in 4QSam^b*

1 Sam 21:3 *(DJD 17:231; BQS 279)*

4QSam^b	לכהן
MT, LXX^A	לאחימלך הכהן
OG^B	τῷ ἱερεῖ

The OG reflects the earlier Hebrew text exemplified by 4QSam^b, in contrast to the explicating plus in the MT, reflected in the revision toward the MT in LXX^A.

1 Sam 20:27 *(DJD 17:230; BQS 278)*

4QSam^b	על השלחן
MT	אל הלחם
OG	ἐπὶ τὴν τράπεζαν

The two synonymous variants occur several times in the passage; see על הלחם 20:24, אל שלחן 20:29. Here the OG clearly reflects a Hebrew text of the 4QSam^b tradition against the MT.

1 Sam 20:30 *(DJD 17:230; BQS 278)*

4QSam^b	בן נערות המרדת
MT	בן נעות המרדות
OG	Υἱὲ κορασίων αὐτομολούντων

Although it is difficult to decide with certainty, it seems that *בן נערת המרדת ("son of a rebellious slave woman") was probably the original reading, with 4QSam^b adding a *mater lectionis*, leading the OG to read the plural, and with the MT ("son of a perverse, rebellious woman"; √עוה Niphal) making the predictable mistake of confusing thin ר/ד and ו/ז/י (see, e.g., the final *resh* of למישור in 1QIsa^a XXXIII 3 [Isa 40:4]). Here the OG again reflects a Hebrew text of the 4QSam^b tradition against the MT reading, and Josephus (*Ant.* 6.237) mirrors the OG with ἐξ αὐτομόλων.

1 Sam 16:4 *(DJD 17:226; BQS 276)*

4QSam^b	]השלם בואך[הראה
MT	שלם בואך
OG	Εἰρήνη ἡ εἴσοδός σου, ὁ βλέπων;

The 4QSam^b tradition apparently adds the vocative to the short MT tradition, and the OG clearly agrees in the secondary reading.

1 Sam 20:32 *(DJD 17:230; BQS 279)*

4QSam^b	] [אביו ויאמר למה
MT	שאול אביו ויאמר אליו למה
OG^B	τῷ Σαουλ Ἵνα τί
LXX^L	τῷ Σαουλ πατρὶ αὐτοῦ καὶ εἶπεν Ἵνα τί
LXX^O	τῷ Σαουλ πατρὶ αὐτοῦ καὶ εἶπεν πρὸς αὐτὸν Ἵνα τί

This example captures some of the complexity of the history of the text as well as some of the clarity that can be gained. The OG translation transmitted in codex B alone retains the earliest, short, reading, though its Hebrew basis no longer survives in preserved manuscripts. The 4QSam^b tradition adds the pleonastic אביו ויאמר and the Lucianic tradition reflects that text. The MT tradition further adds אליו to those two words and the Hexaplaric tradition revises toward the expanded MT. This example offers additional confirmation for trusting the OG as an ancient, accurate witness.

D. Variants in 4QSam^c

2 Sam 14:7 *(DJD 17:256–58; BQS 306)*

4QSam^c	]הנחלת אשר[ה̊]ש[א̊רתי
MT	נחלתי אשר נשארה
LXX^B	τὸν ἄνθρακά μου τὸν καταλειφθέντα
LXX^L, OL^V, Pesh.	ὁ σπινθήρ ὁ ὑπολελειμμένος μοι

Codex Vaticanus (LXX^B, which in this last section of 2 Samuel presents the *kaige* revision toward the MT in place of the mostly lost OG) agrees with the MT, as expected. The 4QSam^c reading, as *lectio difficilior*, represents either the earlier text or a synonymous variant, and the early Lucianic text, plus probably a form of the Old Latin and the Peshitta, agrees with the 4QSam^c reading.

2 Sam 14:23 *(DJD 17:260; BQS 308)*

4QSam^c	ויאב
MT	ויקם יואב
OG	καὶ ἀνέστη Ιωαβ

4QSam^c here makes a simple error of parablepsis, skipping from one part of one word to a similar part of the next: וי<קם יו>אב. The Greek is unaffected by the error.

*2 Sam 14:30^fin^* *(DJD 17:260; BQS 308)*

4QSam[c]	[בא]ש [ויבואו י]לדי יואב אלו קרועי ב[נ]גדיהם ויאומרו הציתו עב[ד֯י אבשלום א֯ת֯ ה]ח֯לקה באש
MT, Targ., Pesh.	באש
OG	(καὶ ἐνέπρησαν ...) καὶ παραγίνονται οἱ δοῦλοι Ιωαβ πρὸς αὐτὸν διερρηχότες τὰ ἱμάτια αὐτῶν καὶ εἶπαν 'Ενεπύρισαν οἱ δοῦλοι Αβεσσαλωμ τὴν μερίδα ἐν πυρί.

In contrast to the previous example, in this one it is the MT which probably betrays parablepsis, skipping from the second occurrence of באש in this verse to the third באש, thus omitting the seemingly required sentence narrating how Joab learned of Absalom's violent plea for attention. Again, the Greek maintains the sound text, unaffected by this error on the part of the MT.

2 Sam 15:2 *(DJD 17:260, 154; BQS 308, 309)*

4QSam[c]	וענה [האיש ואמר]
4QSam[a]	[וענה האיש] ואמר
MT	ויאמר
LXX[B]	καὶ εἶπεν
LXX[L], Vulg.	καὶ ἀπεκρίθη ὁ ἀνήρ καὶ εἶπεν

The MT presents the early, short text and Vaticanus agrees with the MT. Both 4QSam[c] and 4QSam[a], in a rare case of overlap, show a predictable expansion, reflected in the old Lucianic text.

The examples above were selected to show both "original" or earlier correct readings as well as secondary or erroneous readings in order to examine the affiliation of the Greek. The OG repeatedly demonstrates that it faithfully translates a Hebrew text that is simply at variance with the MT. Thus, sound Greek readings which differ from the MT but lack extant Hebrew manuscript support should be seriously considered as based on an alternate Hebrew manuscript and thus as a serious candidate for the "original" text.

The preserved fragments of each of the three Cave 4 manuscripts display a form of the text that is generally superior to the MT. The textual character of 4QSam[a] is too complex for brief description, but, as the examples in this study demonstrate, it contains original readings, intentional additions, and errors, but, more often than not, it is superior to the faulty MT, which has suffered numerous confusions in its transmission. The scroll exhibits frequent agreements with the Hebrew text behind the OG, and is noticeably closer than is the MT to the Samuel text tradition used as a base by the Chronicler and the tradition used by Josephus for his *Antiquities*.[13]

4QSam[b] is also superior in general to the MT. It "exhibits 142 superior readings, of which ninety are in agreement with the Old Greek..., [and] is in agreement with the

[13] For detailed analysis see examples throughout Cross, DJD 17; Ulrich, *The Qumran Text of Samuel*; and McCarter, *I Samuel* and *II Samuel*. There are also recent articles treating both the quantitative and qualitative aspects of the scroll: see Frank Moore Cross and Richard J. Saley, "A Statistical Analysis of the Textual Character of 4QSamuel[a] (4Q51)," *DSD* 13/1 (2006): 46–54; and Eugene Ulrich, "A Qualitative Assessment of the Textual Profile of 4QSam[a]," in *Flores Florentino: Dead Sea Scrolls and Other Early Jewish Studies in Honour of Florentino García Martínez* (ed. A. Hilhorst et al.; JSJSup 122; Leiden: Brill, 2007), 147–61.

MT seventy-eight times, of which sixty-three readings are superior.... [I]n an overwhelmingly large number of cases, the readings of 4QSam^b agree with the Old Greek when it is superior, but agree with the Masoretic tradition when it is superior" (DJD 17:223). Finally, 4QSam^c, despite being copied by "a scribe with quite surpassable skill" who made "twenty-one lapses in sixty-seven partially surviving lines," nonetheless presents "a text noticeably superior to our Masoretic *textus receptus*, with seventeen superior readings preserved..., in contrast to twelve readings in which the MT is superior" (17:253).

III. Isolated Insertions in 4QSamA

In addition to the mostly meaningless differences in orthography and the hundreds of individual textual variants of varying importance that penetrate the Samuel transmission, there are a number of longer, intentional insertions into the text of 4QSam^a which add information or more details.

A. Intentional Insertions in 4QSam^a

1 Sam 1:22 *(DJD 17:31; BQS 260; QTSJ 165–66)*

4QSam^a ≈ Josephus [ונת]תֿיהו נזיר עד עולם כול ימי [חייו]
MT >

This reading, since it preserves the word נזיר, is placed here before the following reading of 1 Sam 1:11 in which the word is reconstructed. The reading is probably a secondary addition, though it is attested by Josephus (*Ant.* 5.347). He uses the more common προφήτην instead of "nazir" in view of his Greco-Roman audience, just as he does regarding the nazir Samson (*Ant.* 5.285), since his audience would not be familiar with the concept of nazir.

1 Sam 1:11 *(DJD 17:29; BQS 259; QTSJ 39–40)*

4QSam^a ≈ LXX ונתתיהו ל̊[פניך נזיר עד יום מותו ויין ושכר לוא ישתה ו]מורה לא יעבור ע̊[ל ראשו]
MT ונתתיו ליהוה כל ימי חייו > ומורה לא יעלה על ראשו

This reading should be analyzed in tandem with the preceding reading and also appears to be a secondary addition. The reconstruction of "nazir" is based on the Greek word δοτὸν here and the occurrence of "nazir" in v. 22 (cf. also Josephus, *Ant.* 5.344 and the variant עד יום מותו in the nazir passage at Judg 13:7).[14] The reconstruction of the longer reading is based on the requirements of space in the manuscript and the longer Greek text. In light of these first two readings, one could suspect an intentional pattern of variants; but the emphasis on Samuel as a nazir is seen nowhere else in the scroll.

[14] The Greek form δοτός occurs only here in the LXX, but note the related δῶρον = נדר in Deut 12:11. Note also the interplay of נזר/נדר in the passage about nazirite vows in Num 6:2: לנדר נדר נזיר להזיר. Phonologically, see נדר and נזר in *HALOT* 674, 684; and palaeographically, a thin or marred ד could cause נזר/נדר confusion (see discussion of 1 Sam 20:30 in II.C. above).

1 Sam 2:9 *(DJD 17:32; BQS 260; QTSJ 119)*

4QSam^a = LXX	[9] נתן נ̇ד̇[ר]ל̊[נוד]ר̊ ויברך ש[נות צדיק]
MT	>

The tradition behind 4QSam^a and the OG adds a stich in Hannah's song, possibly prompted by the vow theme in the previous story (see Ch. IV.B.1.f below). There are two further additions in verses 8 and 9 that are required in 4QSam^a by the spatial requirements, one witnessed by the MT, the other by the LXX, but neither is preserved on the manuscript due to its fragmentary condition.

1 Sam 2:22^{init} *(DJD 17:39; BQS 262; QTSJ 133)*

4QSam^a	[22] ועלי זקן מאד בן תשעים שנ̇ה̇ [ושמונה שנים] וישמ̇ע̇
MT = LXX	[22] ועלי זקן מאד > ושמע

The MT and the LXX probably retain the short "original text," whereas the explicit mention of Eli's age is quite probably a secondary addition, drawn from the information present in all witnesses at 4:15 (note also a second variant at 1 Sam 2:22^{fin} under III.C. below).

2 Sam 6:2 *(DJD 17:123; BQS 297; QTSJ 194)*

4QSam^a ≈ Chr	בעלה היא קר̊י[ת יערים אשר] ליהו⌈ד⌉ה
MT	מבעלי > יהודה

The scroll adds a "footnote," a secondary identification of the place (cf. Josh 15:9), found also in 1 Chr 13:6. The LXX lacks the insertion but is problematic; see note 27.

2 Sam 8:7 *(DJD 17:132; BQS 299; QTSJ 45–48)*

4Q^a ≈ LXX	[ירוש]ל[י]ם̊ נמ[ ]אותם ל[קח אחר שושק מלך מצרים ב[ע̊ל̊ותו אל יר̊[ושלים] בימי רחבעם בן שלו[מה]
MT	ירושלם: >

This reading is an intentional addition, incorporating a later, related historical detail (cf. 1 Kgs 14:25-26) which influenced 1 Chr 18:8 as well; see the discussion in IV.E.2.(c).

2 Sam 10:6 *(DJD 17:136; BQS 300; QTSJ 152–56)*

4Q^a ≈ Jos	[עמון]אלף ככר כסף [... צוב]ה̊ רכב ופרשים [... שנים ושלושי]ם אלף רכב̊ [ואת מלך ...] עמון נאספו
MT = LXX	עמון > ... צובא > ... > ואת מלך ... >

The scroll, supported by 1 Chr 19:6-7, has a longer list of differing details about the Ammonites' military allies, partly reflected by Josephus (*Ant.* 7.121). The revisional Greek agrees with the shorter readings in the MT.

B. Possible Insertions in 4QSam^a^ or Possible Losses in the MT

1 Sam 11:9 *(DJD 17:67; BQS 272; QTSJ 133)*

4QSam^a^	[מיהוה התשׁ]ועה ...	MT = LXX	תהיה לכם תשועה ...
	[לכם פתחו השׁ]ער ...		
	[[10]ויאמר̊]ו אנש]י יביש ...		[10]ויאמרו אנשי יביש ...

Quantitatively, the scroll has a noticeably longer reading: three lines of text in contrast to two lines in the MT; thus, as seen again in 1 Sam 1:24 below, it has an entire line not in the MT. Neither the LXX nor Josephus (*Ant.* 6.76) supplies any clues as to the possible text of the plus. Because so little text is preserved it is impossible to determine whether the extra text is an addition in the scroll or a loss by the MT, but either way it is a major difference in length.

2 Sam 6:7 *(DJD 17:124; BQS 297; QTSJ 195)*

4QSam^a^	האלוהי]ם על] אשׁ]ר שלח ידו] ע̊ל [ה]ארון
MT	האלהים על השל
LXX	>

The LXX, which does not specify the reason for Uzzah's death, probably has the original reading. Both 4QSam^a^ and MT add a reason, perhaps a simple corruption in the MT, or perhaps a more explicit reason in the scroll.

2 Sam 13:21 *(DJD 17:147; BQS 304; QTSJ 84)*

4QSam^a^ = LXX	[ויחר לו מאד ולוא עצב את רוח אמנון בנו כי אה]בו כי בכור]ו הוא [22]ולוא]
MT	ויחר לו מאד [22]ולא

Although the MT might have lost the longer reading due to parablepsis ולא[22]∩ולא, it seems more likely that the scroll inserted a secondary addition, attested by the LXX and Josephus (*Ant.* 7.173), about David's emotions.

2 Sam 13:27 *(DJD 17:147; BQS 304–5; QTSJ, 85)*

4QSam^a^ = LXX	[כו]ל בני המלך [ויעש אבשלום משתה כמשתה ה]מ̊[ל]ך̇
MT	כל בני המלך:

Again, though the MT might have lost the longer reading due to parablepsis המלך∩המלך, it seems more likely that the scroll inserted a secondary addition, attested by the LXX and Josephus (*Ant.* 7.174), embellishing Absalom's feast (for the wording, cf. ironically, another feast in ominous circumstances: משתה בביתו כמשתה המלך in 1 Sam 25:36).

C. Intentional Insertions in the MT

In contrast to 4QSamª, which intentionally added at least seven and possibly eleven longer insertions, the MT seems to have added only two.

*1 Sam 2:22^fin^* *(DJD 17:39–47; BQS 262; QTSJ, 57–58)*

4QSamª = OG	לבני ישׂראׂלׂ ... [23]וׂ]יאמר
MT = LXX^O^	לכל ישראל ואת אשר ישכבון את הנשים הצבאות פתח אהל מועד [23]ויאמר

Whereas 4QSamª inserted one addition, Eli's age, at the beginning of this verse (see 1 Sam 2:22^init^ in III.A above), the MT inserts a different addition, the sin of Eli's sons, at the end of the verse.

2 Sam 5:4-5 *(DJD 17:118–23; BQS 295; QTSJ, 60–62)*

4QSamª	>
MT = LXX	[4]בן שלשים שנה דוד במלכו ארבעים שנה מלך: [5]בחברון מלך על יהודה שבע שנים וששה חדשים ובירושלם מלך שלשים ושלש שנה על כל ישראל ויהודה:

This passage is lacking in 4QSamª, the Old Latin (and thus probably the OG), Josephus (see *Ant.* 7.54, 61, 65), and the parallel in 1 Chr 11:3-4. Thus, it is safe to assert that the MT, reflected in the transmitted LXX, inserts a lengthy notation of the chronological details about David's age and reign, possibly drawn from 1 Kgs 2:11.

D. Problems, Not Insertions

There are other longer differences in text which are not intentional insertions but rather are simple errors: either accidental loss of text or conflation of double renditions.

1 Sam 1:24 *(DJD 17:30–37; BQS 260; QTSJ, 40–41)*

4Qª≈LXX	והנער]עמם ויביאוהו לפני יהוה וישחט אביהו את]הׄזבחׂ [כ]אשר]יעשה מימים ימימה ליהוה [25]וי]שחט
MT	והנער ... נער [25]וישחטו

This appears to be a simple inadvertent loss of text by the MT, though not by normal homoioteleuton; see the possible example in III.B above of another loss of text at 1 Sam 11:9, as well as the clear case of loss by homoioteleuton in the MT at 1 Sam 14:41.

1 Sam 2:24 *(DJD 17:39–47; BQS 262; QTSJ 41–42)*

4QSamª = LXX	כי לוא טובה הש]מׄועה אשר אנׄכי שׁוׂמׂ]ע אל תעשון כן כי לו]אׄ טובנ]ות השמועות]אשר אנׄי שומע
MT	כי לוא טובה השמעה אשר אנכי ... שמע

This longer reading appears to be simply a double rendering in the scroll, not loss by parablepsis שמע∩שמע, and the LXX contains the longer, secondary reading.

1 Sam 2:31-32 *(DJD 17:40; BQS 262–63; QTSJ 58–59)*

4QSam[a] = LXX 31[הנה י]מׄ[י]ם באים ונדעת[י את זרעך וזרע בית אביך
32ולוא] יׄהיה לך זקן בׄביתי כול [הימים]

MT 31הנה ימים באים וגדעתי את זרעך ואת זרע בית אביך
מהיות זקן בביתך
32והבטת צר מעון בכל אשר ייטיב את ישראל
ולא יהיה זקן בביתך כל הימים

This is not so much an intentional insertion but scribal confusion in the MT. See Cross's discussion in DJD 17:44 about this large-scale expansion in the MT. In addition to the double rendering מהיות זקן בביתך and ולא יהיה זקן בביתך, MT 2:29-32 is replete with expansion and corruption: for example, note תבעטו . . . צויתי מעון . . . ישראל in v. 29a compared with MT v. 32a.

IV. Variant Editions in 4QSam^a?

Although few, to my knowledge, have claimed that there are variant editions of the entire book of Samuel,[15] some scholars have proposed that certain passages survive in variant editions. At least five passages have been proposed as variant editions: the story of Hannah's vow and the birth of Samuel in 1 Samuel 1; the Psalm of Hannah in 1 Samuel 2; the Nahash passage introducing 1 Samuel 11; the accounts of David's entering Saul's camp in 1 Samuel 17–18; and David's bringing the plague on Israel in 2 Samuel 24.

A. Hannah and Anna: 1 Samuel 1

(DJD 17:29–36; BQS 259–61; QTSJ 39–41, 48–49, 133–34, 165–66)

Stanley D. Walters[16] proposes that in 1 Samuel 1 the MT and the LXX present two separate narratives of the role of Hannah (MT)/Anna (LXX) in dedicating her son to God's service. He sees two "separate stories, each informed and shaped by its own distinctive interests" (387), "each with its own *Tendenz*" (409). "B's [= LXX^B's] story is a tale with its own shape and emphasis" (403–4), which "minimizes the woman's role and portrays her less sensitively than does M [= MT]" (407). In contrast, "M portrays Hannah much more sympathetically and respectfully than does B" (396–97).

Moreover, he argues that the two stories are so consistently diverse that they have "been largely obscured," because in the wake of Thenius, Wellhausen, and others "text-critical interests have operated more and more freely to create a text that is neither M nor B but a blend of both" (409). He expresses "doubt that there ever was an original text

[15] Alexander Rofé has suggested that 4QSam[a] is sufficiently reworked that it should be entitled, not "4QSamuel," but "4QMidrash Samuel"; see "4QMidrash Samuel?—Observations Concerning the Character of 4QSam[a]," *Textus* 19 (1998): 63–74. I will analyze below, with different conclusions, two of the three passages he treats for support for this title. By his criterion, should not a number of biblical books have to be relabeled "Midrash X"? Should, e.g., MT Judges and MT Jeremiah, in light of 4QJudg[a] and 4QJer[b,d]-OG, be entitled "Midrash Judges" and "Midrash Jeremiah"?

[16] Stanley D. Walters, "Hannah and Anna: The Greek and Hebrew Texts of 1 Samuel 1," *JBL* 107 (1988): 385–412.

which has given rise—by known processes of transmission—to the two stories M and B" (410). He concludes, "Let us allow both women to live" (412).

Walters writes interestingly and clearly, and the article is replete with good literary sensitivity and accurate syntactic points, built on wide-ranging reading and impressive learning. One can learn much from reading it, and he gives a delightfully imaginative interpretation of each of the two forms of the story.

Principal points in his argumentation, to be discussed in order, are:

1. the "most puzzling sentence," יקם יהוה את דברו (1 Sam 1:23) which cannot be explained as a variant of στῆσαι κύριος τὸ ἐξελθὸν ἐκ τοῦ στόματός σου through text-critical procedures
2. the emphasis on Hannah's childlessness in the LXX
3. the emphasis on Peninnah's abuse and harassment in the MT vs. Anna's silent depression and deference in the LXX
4. the doubt in the LXX whether Hannah would carry out what she has promised
5. the difference in who performs the sacrifice
6. the claim that textual criticism cannot trace the two stories back to a common original

1. No Simple Variant

I agree with Walters (against Thenius and Wellhausen) in the one point that יקם יהוה את דברו and the Greek reading στῆσαι κύριος τὸ ἐξελθὸν ἐκ τοῦ στόματός σου in 1:23 cannot be explained in the narrow text-critical sense as a simple scribal variant in one text mistakenly derived from the other, but should instead be viewed as an intentional variant "belonging to a different universe of discourse. The MT's expression belongs to the world of the divine promise, while the Greek's belongs to the world of the human vow" (387). He correctly compares the MT reading to similar expressions "in 'deuteronomic' contexts" and in promises concerning the "Davidic dynasty" (410–11).

My own conclusions are similar to those of Walters; see 1:23 in II.B above, where I specify further. I judged that the "tradition behind the MT has been revised according to routine Deuteronomistic theology (which perdured down through the late Second Temple period), emphasizing the prophecy-fulfillment theme—even though the LORD has not pronounced any prophetic word." Some theologically motivated scribe in the tradition inherited by the MT intentionally replaced the earlier "what went out of your mouth" (the human vow) with "his word" (the divine promise theme). But it is important to point out both that the OG here faithfully translates a Hebrew text like 4QSam[a] (יקם יהו[ה היוצא מפיך]), and that Walters does not advert to the Hebrew basis of the Septuagint but attributes the reading to the translator.

It is from this variant that Walters raises "the possibility that these are separate stories, each informed and shaped by its own distinctive interests" (387). And it is here where I disagree. Does this single variant in fact share a similar pattern together with a number of other variants to warrant judging the MT and the LXX as two irreducibly different stories, as Walters suggests? Or has he taken this one intentional variant and then stretched it too far, to imbue the remainder of the variants with meaning that the Hebrew author and the OG translator did not intend? It is important to distinguish between exegesis, attempting to discern what the author presumably intended, and eisegesis, reading into the final texts as transmitted various interpretations that one might divine.

2. Hannah's Childlessness

Walters is again correct that the LXX emphasizes Hannah's childlessness, saying six times that "she had no child" or that "the Lord had closed her womb"; thus, "B has chosen greatly to heighten the barrenness motif" (394). But the MT also emphasizes that theme, mentioning it three times in five verses (1:2-6). So it is merely a small difference of degree, and the purpose in both versions is similarly to heighten the sense of marvel at the eventual birth. Text-critically the narratives are routine storytelling embellishments[17] of a Hebrew text similar to the MT, typical of those seen in other narratives.[18]

3. Peninnah's Abuse

Walters overinterprets the theme of Peninnah's provocation, stating that "In M it is the harassment that goes on and on; in B it is Anna's passive resistance that goes on and on." In addition, "In M there is provocation but no response; in B there is depression but no provocation" (392).

One can suspect that interpretations may be stretched when coming across phrases such as "the bitchy other woman" for Peninnah, and "the hunger strike and the cerulean funk" (392) when Hannah "would become depressed, would weep, and could not eat" (v. 7).

Regarding the provocation in the MT, Walters' interpretation of בעבור הרעמה in v. 6 is that Peninnah "intended to make Hannah thunder" (392), but Hannah does not respond. Walters avers, "The thunder finally comes, but not against Peninnah. 'Reversèd thunder' (to borrow George Herbert's conceit) sounded in YHWH's ears and moved the divine to action" (392). "Thunder" from Hannah in God's ears, however, is clearly hyperbole. But more pointedly, the OG translator probably did not recognize the concrete meaning of צרה^{II} "co-wife, rival wife," as Walters agrees (396), or simply assumed the abstract meaning of צרה^{I} "distress."[19] Peninnah is absent from the LXX story after v. 5, so "Anna's passive resistance" does not go "on and on"; and there is, of course, no need of response, since צרה is interpreted as "distress," not "rival wife."

Regarding Hannah's alleged deference in the LXX, Walters says that her response, ἰδοὺ ἐγώ κύριε, to Elkanah's inquiry (v. 8) is a response "of extreme deference" (392), used "primarily when subordinates reply to someone over them, and in dialogue entirely in the mouths of inferiors to superiors" (391–92). This latter is accurate (see 1 Sam 22:12), but in the Israelite system wives are "naturally" subordinate to their husbands. Nonetheless, "extreme deference" is hyperbole: the response of Bathsheba, as proud and

---

[17] One addition in the LXX, e.g., is a typical scribal explanation: "to Anna he gave one portion, *because she had no child*" (v. 5). That last clause is an innocent explanation of why Hannah received only one portion; it is hardly noteworthy "emphasis" in the LXX, especially since the MT (just as the LXX) ends that same verse with "the LORD had closed her womb."

[18] See, e.g., Ch. 15 and Ulrich, "The Parallel Editions of the Old Greek and Masoretic Text of Daniel 5," in *A Teacher for All Generations: Essays in Honor of James C. VanderKam* (ed. E. F. Mason et al.; 2 vols.; JSJS 153; Leiden: Brill, 2012), 1:201–17, esp. 206.

[19] Similarly, the OG may not have recognized אפים in v. 5 (if that were in fact the form present) or הרעמה in v. 6.

confident queen, is similarly "κύριε" (1 Kg 1:17, 18) when she boldly confronts King David. Upon learning of Adonijah's attempt at coronation, she asserts that—whereas "Adonijah has become king, though you, my lord (κύριε) the king, do not know it"(!)—he had promised her that her own son Solomon would succeed him as king. As a result of her claim, the king acquiesces to her demand. A thought perhaps more apropos for consideration is that Hannah's response anticipates her son Samuel's reply (ἰδοὺ ἐγῶ in 3:4, 5, 6, 8) when God calls him for his initial prophetic message.

Finally, if yet another clue is desired to counter Walters' interpretation that "M portrays Hannah much more sympathetically and respectfully than does B" (396–97), note that in v. 5, against the silence of the MT, it is the Greek which adds: "however, Elkanah loved Hannah more than [Peninnah]."

4. Doubt about Hannah's Vow

Walters claims that there is "doubt in the LXX whether Anna would carry out what she has promised" (408) and that "in B's story it has never been perfectly clear that Anna was actually going to part with Samuel"; instead, Anna was "fulfilling her vow with a reticent heart and a calculating eye" (407). But these claims seem overstretched and tendentious:

- Hannah is *obliged* to nurse the boy until he is weaned; for that reason she did not go to Shiloh for the first feast after the baby's birth (v. 22).
- Elkanah says, "May the LORD establish what has gone out of your mouth" (v. 23). He could have nullified her vow (cf. Num 30:6-15) but leaves it up to her to perform, and she carries it out admirably.
- After weaning the child, "she went to Shiloh with him," and all the remaining actions happen in rapid succession, with no hesitations on her part.[20]
- The words χράω/κίχρημι are often translated "lend," and thus Walters says that it "is less generous" than the MT, "replacing a clearly promised gift [in the MT] with an equally clearly expressed loan" (406) in the OG. But there is a play on the root שאל in the Hebrew text (which also means "to lend, borrow"),[21] used four times in vv. 27-28. For the first two in v. 27, the OG uses forms of αἰτέω and for the second two in v. 28 forms of χράω/κίχρημι. That is because the first two mean "request": God gave Hannah the request that she requested. But for v. 28, Hannah gives the boy to God. The MT has available the Hiphil of שאל, but the Greek does not, and so, following Pentateuchal precedent, it uses the root χράω/κίχρημι which is used for the only other instance of the Hiphil of שאל (in Exod 12:36). In that passage leading to the Exodus, the meaning is not at all negative or "calculating," but positive: God had given the Israelites "favor in the eyes of the Egyptians, so that *they let them have* what they asked." The "Radic[al]

[20] Walters thinks that "she went up with him" (v. 24) refers to Elkanah ("Hannah and Anna," 402). But the previous sentence is "The woman remained and nursed her son until she weaned him. [24]And she went up with him to Shiloh. . . ." Thus, the presumed referent is Samuel, not Elkanah. It could, however, be seen as ambiguous, because the Hebrew text behind the LXX is ambiguous: ותעל אתו (Qal "she went up with him," or Hiphil "she took him up"). The OG translated one possible meaning (Qal) faithfully: καὶ ἀνέβη μετ' αὐτοῦ. 4QSam^a orthographically made the alternate reading (Hiphil) explicit and unambiguous: ותעל אותו, whereas the MT made it even more explicit with the conflation: ותעלהו עמה.

[21] See *HALOT*, "שאל."

> sense" of χράω/κίχρημι is "to give what is needful"; it is used of "the gods [giving] needful answer" (LSJ). Because of her vow Hannah "needs" to give the promised child to the Lord, and she does so, but there is no hint of "a reticent heart and a calculating eye."

As one reads the story in the LXX, there is no indication, unless one is tendentiously looking for it, that there is any reluctance on Hannah's part.

5. Performing the Sacrifice

In the MT both Elkanah and Hannah perform the sacrifice, whereas in the LXX "his [Samuel's] father" alone does (401–2); thus, Walters states that "B intends to exclude Anna from participation in the cult" (404).

At the surface that seems like a clear argument. But the MT does not explicitly say "Elkanah and Hannah sacrificed," but simply has the verb וישחטו. The subjects are presumably Elkanah and Hannah, but they are implied; there is no emphasis on the actors. In fact, where the MT has the plural וישחטו, 4QSam[a] has the singular [וי]שחט, for which the Greek καὶ ἔσφαξεν is a perfect translation.[22] Moreover, that word is the first word after a major confused loss of text in the MT (והנער⌒נער).[23] The inclusion in the LXX of ὁ πατὴρ αὐτοῦ = אביו could simply be a scribal explication (whether correct or not), or it could be deliberate. For a scribal explication, see 1 Sam 20:32 in II.C above, where אביו is an unnecessary secondary addition in all texts except Codex Vaticanus, which retains the short original without it. If it is simply a secondary scribal explication, then it is meaningless for the basic story. If the insertion is deliberate, then καὶ ἔσφαξεν . . . τὴν θυσίαν ἣν ἐποίει ἐξ ἡμερῶν εἰς ἡμέρας τῷ κυρίῳ as the conclusion of the story could simply be the reiteration of the ἐξ ἡμερῶν εἰς ἡμέρας . . . καὶ θύειν τῷ κυρίῳ which began the story (1 Sam 1:3).

From a broader perspective, two main currents are interwoven in this chapter: the introduction which sets the frame describes Elkanah's yearly pilgrimage and sacrifice at Shiloh, and within that frame is interwoven the story of childless Hannah, who prays for a child, vows to devote him to the Lord, gives birth to the child, and takes him to Shiloh to give him to the Lord. The two currents are woven together as integral, interrelated parts of a single story, and Elkanah and Hannah do most things together (except that Hannah remains at home until the weaning). Walters, however, claims that when Hannah takes the boy to Shiloh with the sacrificial elements, "[t]he text does not mention Elkanah, and he does not seem to be along" (401). But that is tendentious: no one envisions that Hannah and the boy would travel alone to Shiloh without Elkanah, and regardless, both texts clearly assume Elkanah's presence, reporting that he goes home after Hannah's prayer (2:11).[24]

---

[22] Singular vs. plural variants are commonplace in Hebrew narrative, and masculine vs. feminine forms are not infrequent: note, for example, even in the Book of Ruth, where the feminine ought to be expected, לכם in the MT for לכן at 1:11, and קולם in 4QRuth[a] for קולן MT at 1:9.

[23] Walters (403) defends the implausible MT reading 1 Sam 1:24 (see under III.D.) with the non-parallel and equally non-convincing example of ידדון ידדון in Ps 68:13.

[24] See analogous textual complexity in nn. 20 and 22.

6. Textual Criticism

Walters concludes that there was no common Hebrew text from which the MT and the LXX could develop. Despite the frequently erroneous and confused condition of the MT of Samuel, and despite the multifaceted illumination shed by the Qumran Samuel scrolls on the textual situation, he does not even mention Qumran in his first eighteen pages. On that page of first mention (403), he decides that the 4QSam[a] reading at 1 Sam 1:24 is incorrect and endorses the MT (see III.D above). To help decide the broader issue, let us analyze one of the most difficult textual problems with respect to whether there was a common Hebrew text shared by both the MT and the OG *Vorlage*, v. 6:

MT וכעסתה צרתה גם כעס בעבור

LXX κατὰ τὴν θλῖψιν αὐτῆς
καὶ κατὰ τὴν ἀθυμίαν τῆς θλίψεως αὐτῆς, καὶ ἠθύμει διὰ τοῦτο

Walters' solution to the problem is that "B rests on a Hebrew text which was clearly different from M" (396) and proposes "a euphonious proverb" behind the Greek (395)—"a proverb about rival wives and distress" (397). He suggests "a *Vorlage* reading כצרה וכמצוק הצרה, 'Her distress was like the stress caused by a co-wife' " (396), though the LXX translation of it "still does not make sense" (395). Although he says that "the translator . . . did not recognize the homophone 'co-wife'" צרה (396), he nonetheless translates the LXX as "Her distress was equal to the depression caused by {her} a co-wife" (389).

As opposed to two "clearly different" Hebrew texts, I propose a common Hebrew behind the MT and the OG, presuming some minor scribal difficulties, but also noting that in numerous instances the OG faithfully and correctly translates (1) earlier forms where the MT has secondary insertions, (2) extant Hebrew texts (e.g., Qumran scrolls or the SP) that vary from the MT, (3) ambiguous or alternate Hebrew forms, and (4) plausible but non-extant or misread Hebrew forms.[25]

Two observations counter Walters' interpretation. First, the OG translator probably did not recognize the concrete meaning of צרה "co-wife," as Walters agrees, or simply presumed the abstract meaning "distress." Similarly, he may not have recognized **אפים** in v. 5 (if that were in fact the form present) or הרעמה in v. 6.[26]

Second, κατὰ τὴν θλῖψιν αὐτῆς and καὶ κατὰ τὴν ἀθυμίαν τῆς θλίψεως αὐτῆς are quite likely two elements of a doublet: two different translations conflated here (just as 4QSam[a] at 1 Sam 2:24 and the MT at 2:31-32 in D.III. above). The former element is a free translation of (כ)כעסת צרתה, and the latter is a closer translation of the same. See a similar double translation at 2 Sam 20:8, where for MT והוא יצא ותפל, LXX[B] has καὶ ἡ μάχαιρα ἐξῆλθεν καὶ αὐτὴ ἐξῆλθεν καὶ ἔπεσεν. The former element translates more freely and the latter more closely (if erroneously).[27] If κατὰ τὴν θλῖψιν αὐτῆς is removed as a doublet, then (1) forms of ἀθυμία correspond to כעס in all three occurrences in vv. 6-7,

[25] See lists of examples in DJD 32, 2:93–94.

[26] Henry Preserved Smith (*The Books of Samuel* [ICC; Edinburgh: T&T Clark, 1904], 7–8) states that the form **אפים** "is impossible. . . . There is reason to suppose, therefore, that the corruption is incurable." McCarter (*I Samuel*, 52) concludes that it is "an obscure term or an early corruption." Smith also calls הרעמה in v. 6 "an abnormal form" (*The Books of Samuel*, 8); see GKC 20*h*, 22*s*.

[27] See yet another doublet at 2 Sam 6:2: for מבעלי יהודה להעלות in the MT, the LXX has ἀπὸ τῶν ἀρχόντων Ιουδα ἐν ἀναβάσει τοῦ ἀναγαγεῖν.

(2) θλῖψις equals צרה as expected, (3) καὶ κατὰ τὴν ἀθυμίαν τῆς θλίψεως αὐτῆς faithfully translates ו(כ)כעסת(ה) צרתה, and (4) the OG is a fitting translation of a Hebrew text very close to that behind the MT. Walters did not recognize the doublet in the LXX and thus proposed כצרה וכמצוק הצרה for the longer reading. But that is more hypothetical than ו(כ)כעסת(ה) צרתה proposed here. Note that ו(כ)כעסת(ה) צרתה diverges by only one or two letters from the MT, whereas neither the overall structure nor the second word of Walters' כצרה וכמצוק הצרה resembles the MT, and only the last word comes within two letters of agreeing with the MT.[28]

I agree that there are a large number of variants in 1 Samuel 1, but I do not see them as intentionally introduced or as all moving in a single direction; thus, I would argue that there is no intentionally unified variant edition such as Walters suggests.[29] It is true that communities hearing the two stories separately might get slightly different impressions of Hannah; the question is whether the difference is significant or not. That is, is the difference due to an editor's intention to paint a different portrait or due to disparate changes that each form has innocently picked up over the course of its transmission?

The OG agrees with 4QSam^a specifically in the pivotal verse 1:23 and generally in many other readings, demonstrating that it is a faithful translation of a Hebrew text which is simply different from the MT. Thus, if the Greek is telling a different story, it is based on a Hebrew *Vorlage*, and the differences arise within the Hebrew tradition. Walters sees all the Greek variants, each of which can be explained in more than one way, as intentionally aimed in a single direction; but he repeatedly stretches the interpretation of the variants and regularly chooses the denigration of Hannah motif. Each of the variants, however, can be explained in different ways, and as each is judged most naturally and plausibly, it seems clear that they are due to diverse textual causes and simply go in different, unrelated directions.

Viewing the arguments above, and keeping in mind the typical scribal changes that mark virtually all textual traditions, one can affirm that the two Hebrew texts—the one behind the OG (≈ 4QSam^a) and the MT—share a close common ancestor. The two Hebrew texts are genetically related, reflecting a common original, with predictable,[30] mostly insignificant, scribal variants.

B. The Prayer/Song[31] of Hannah: 1 Samuel 2

(DJD 17:31–34; BQS 260–61; QTSJ 120–22)

Viewing a bit more broadly the story of Hannah and the birth of Samuel, Emanuel Tov sees "different recensions" in the Song of Hannah (1 Sam 2:1-10) connected to themes in

---

28 Whereas Walters criticizes textual critics' "amazing predilection for the hypothetical over the real" (387), saying that you "cannot simply replace the actual texts with a theoretical one. . . ; you must account for the given texts" (386), he himself "has replaced two actual texts with a hypothetical one," "in fact a third text that is neither the Greek nor the Hebrew" (385).

29 Emanuel Tov finds similar difficulties with Walters' argument: "Different Editions of the Song of Hannah and of Its Narrative Framework," in *The Greek and Hebrew Bible*, 433–55, esp. 439, n.18.

30 The variants are generally predictable, except for את דברו (MT) replacing היוצא מפיך (4QSam^a OG) in 1 Sam 1:23, which is intentional but unrelated to other variants.

31 Regarding the term "Prayer" or "Song" see below.

the story in chapter 1 leading up to the Song.[32] He suggests that the "three different texts of the Song of Hannah do not merely reflect scribal differences such as are created in the course of the transmission of any text, but reflect three different editions (recensions) of the Song and its narrative framework" (434).

More recently, Anneli Aejmelaeus has also posited an intentional new edition presented by 4QSam[a].[33] She examines the major differences between the scroll, the LXX, and the MT and notes that when the LXX and the MT have different pluses, the scroll often contains both forms. Thus, she plausibly envisions a new edition formed not by theological or ideological motives but by "the technique of complementing the text," and concludes that the "connecting motive behind variants may have been the ambition of the scribe to produce a perfect manuscript with the most complete collection of material, not lacking anything. . . ."[34]

Both studies are rich with textual, philological, and literary insights. Our focus here will be solely on the definition of and criteria for "a new edition" and whether the scroll, the LXX, or the MT represents "a new edition." Tov wisely says, "The difference between scribal and editorial activity is difficult to define and even scholars who agree in principle that there is a category of editorial differences often do not agree with regard to individual instances" (434). His observation will prove to be helpful in our exploration of his and Aejmelaeus' views.

It will be important to define our terms first. There may be a large number of insertions in a manuscript, but they may or may not constitute an "edition" or "recension." If the insertions are random or sporadic, showing no unity, they remain "isolated insertions." The criterion for an edition is that a substantial number of insertions by a single editor form an intentional pattern with discernible principles of development, as visible in 4QpaleoExod[m] or the SP. The use of the designation "recensions" by William Foxwell Albright for the MT versus the LXX versus the scrolls was correctly replaced with "text traditions" by Frank Moore Cross, endorsed also by Tov, because the developments were not so much according to set principles by an individual but were more incremental and unsystematic.[35] Thus, the question to ask as we analyze the Song will be: do the secondary readings exhibit a unified intentional pattern according to discernible principles or simply a series of incremental and unsystematic variants?

---

[32] Tov, "Different Editions of the Song of Hannah," 433–55.

[33] Anneli Aejmelaeus, "Hannah's Psalm in 4QSam[a]," in *Archaeology of the Books of Samuel: The Entangling of the Textual and Literary History* (ed. Philippe Hugo and Adrian Schenker; VTSup 132; Leiden: Brill, 2010), 23–37.

[34] Aejmelaeus, "Hannah's Psalm," 37.

[35] See William F. Albright, "New Light on Early Recensions of the Hebrew Bible," *BASOR* 140 (1955): 27–33; Frank Moore Cross, "The Contribution of the Qumrân Discoveries to the Study of the Biblical Text," *IEJ* 16 (1966): 81–95, esp. 86 [repr. in *Qumran and the History*, 278–92, esp. 283]; Emanuel Tov, *Textual Criticism*, 173–74; and Ulrich, "Biblical Scrolls Scholarship in North America," in *The Dead Sea Scrolls in Scholarly Perspective: A History of Research* (ed. Devorah Dimant; STDJ 99; Leiden: Brill, 2012), 49–74, esp. 63–64.

1. Tov's View

Let us begin with Tov's analysis. He lists the principal differences between the MT, 4QSam[a], and the LXX in his points "a"–"g"(453–54):

a. "The Song of Hannah is located in two slightly different positions in MT vs. the LXX and 4QSam[a]."
b. "The three texts present different concepts of the events occurring before and after the Song (1:28; 2:11).... MT reflects a revision which shifts to Elkanah a role which was originally ascribed to Hannah."

Points "a" and "b" can be discussed together, since most scholars, including Tov, view the Prayer as a later insertion. Without the inserted Prayer (which precedes 2:11) the texts of the three traditions are:

4QSam[a]	[ותעזב]הו שם ותשתח]ו ליהוה ‸ 2:11 ? [
MT	וישתחו שם ליהוה ‸ 2:11 וילך אלקנה הרמתה על ביתו
LXX[B]	‸ 2:11* ותעזבהו שם לפני יהוה ותלך הרמתה

Thus, in 4QSam[a]:	Hannah leaves the boy and prostrates, [...prayer,...?];
in the MT:	"he/they" prostrate(s),[36] [prayer], then Elkanah goes home;
in the LXX[B]:	[prayer], she leaves the boy, and she goes home.

When secondary passages are inserted into a narrative, different manuscript traditions occasionally preserve them at slightly different points.[37] Here it appears likely that the prayer was inserted at one point early in the common transmission process, and that one or another scribe in the diverging processes of transmission changed the insertion point slightly, whether inadvertently or intentionally; but it is difficult to see any significance in the slightly different positions.

Without the Prayer the texts are quite similar, each with only minor variants. The text behind 4QSam[a] and LXX added ותעזבהו, while 4QSam[a] and MT added וישתחו/ותשתחו. But no matter which actions are mentioned explicitly and in which order in each tradition, each story assumes in common that both Hannah and Elkanah are at Shiloh, they leave Samuel with Eli, both Hannah and Elkanah worship, Hannah prays, and both go home.

In my view it is important to recall the two main currents of the narrative proposed above: the Elkanah-yearly-worship current that frames the chapter, as opposed to the

---

[36] Note that for וישתחו (1:28) in Leningradensis and *BHS*, some Masoretic manuscripts as well as the Lucianic Greek and the proto-MT witnesses Peshitta and Vulgate have the plural; moreover, the form וישתחו can be plural as well as singular (*HALOT*, חוה, 296), as noted by Tov ("Different Editions of the Song of Hannah," 437, n. 14) for Gen 43:28 (*ketib*). The form וישתחו (or והשתחו) is also clearly used twice in 1QIsa[a] as a plural where the MT has וישתחוו or והשתחוו (Isa 27:13 and 46:6; see also 45:14 and *BHS* note 14[d]).

[37] The MT passage Josh 8:30-35 appears in 4QJosh[a] at the end of chapter 4 and in LXX[B] after 9:2. Tov ("Different Editions of the Song of Hannah," 435), following Wellhausen (*Der Text der Bücher Samuelis* [Göttingen: Vandenhoeck & Ruprecht, 1871], 42), adds other examples: "the Song of the Ark (MT: Num 10:34-36),... Solomon's benediction for the dedication of the temple (MT: 1 Kgs 8:12-13), the story of Naboth (MT: 1 Kgs 20/21), and the oracles against the foreign nations in Jeremiah (MT: chapters 46–51)."

Hannah-vow-son current that is the main point of the chapter. The MT is simply ending the story the way it began, with Elkanah coming to worship (1:3), then worshiping and returning home, according to the Elkanah-framing current. The LXX is simply ending with more focus on the Hannah-vow-son current. The two currents are interwoven through the narratives, however, and thus elements from one current sporadically influence elements in the other current because the two are interwoven. But the lack of intentionality in "assigning roles" can be appreciated in LXX 1:24-25:

> *Hannah* went up with the boy and the sacrificial elements, "and the boy was with *them*," [25]*they* brought him before the Lord, and his *father* slaughtered the sacrifice *as he used to do yearly*, and *he* brought the boy near and slaughtered.... And *Hannah* brought him to Eli.

If (presuming the singular vs. the plural for וישתחו) the "MT reflects a revision which shifts to Elkanah a role which was originally ascribed to Hannah" (i.e., ותשתחו̇[ו > וישתחו) in 1:28, the LXX (which should do the opposite if there is intentional design at work) also shifts to Elkanah a role which was originally ascribed to both Hannah and him (וישחטו > καὶ ἔσφαξεν ὁ πατὴρ αὐτοῦ) in 1:24-25. Notice that the introduction of "his father" here may be due not so much to intentional role-assignment as to the literary current: "his father ... *as he used to do yearly*." Again, it appears difficult to detect significant and consistent editorial intention here.

c. "The edition of MT adapted the Song to the context by an addition which makes the Song into a prayer" by adding ותתפלל at the beginning of 2:1.

In 4QSam^a the line with the beginning of chapter 2 is mostly lost, and the edition correctly reconstructs the preferable, short reading ותאמר on the basis of LXX^B. But there would be space in the lacuna for the possible addition of ותתפלל חנה, and it is simply unknown whether the scroll had it or not.[38] Moreover, it should be noted that the designation "Song" is a modern commentator's word.[39] The texts never call 2:1-10 a "Song," whereas the story in chapter 1 has already used the פלל root often for Hannah praying, in vv. 10, 12, (15 implicitly), and 27; and so, "Prayer" or even "Psalm"[40] seems more appropriate than "Song." Thus, MT's addition of ותתפלל seems to add little new meaning. It seems rather to be a simple scribal explication of the evident, which does not change the meaning.

d. "2:2 has been preserved in three different editorial forms."
e. "2:8c ... was added in MT and 4QSam^a, in order to stress the universal power of God.... This universal power is also referred to in v. 10...."

There are indeed three different forms of 2:2, with the MT and the LXX having two virtually identical lines as well as each having a distinct third line, but in a different

---

[38] See DJD 17, Plate II and p. 31, line 16. The bracket after ותאמר in line 16 should more accurately be placed farther to the left, under the bracket in ותעזב[הו in line 15. Thus, ותתפלל חנה may or may not have been included in the scroll.

[39] See DJD 17:32, 37; McCarter, *I Samuel*, 67; and Tov, "Different Editions of the Song of Hannah."

[40] Aejmelaeus, "Hannah's Psalm in 4QSam^a."

order.[41] The fragmentary 4QSam[a] probably has all four lines, conflating the MT and LXX. The thoughts expressed are: "there is none as holy as the Lord; none besides you; no rock like our God; none holy besides you." It is difficult to see any notable differences among the four thoughts or that the differences pertain "to major details" or "reflect different versions (editions) of the biblical verse" (442). Many psalmic phrases are similar, commonplace, and interchangeable. In addition to the well-known variants between the parallel psalms, 2 Samuel 22 and Psalm 18, another illuminating parallel is the Yahwistic Psalm 14 with its Elohistic counterpart Psalm 53. Verses 1-4 of Psalm 14 are mostly identical to vv. 2-5 [Eng. 1-4] of Psalm 53, but there are minor variants in every verse. Interestingly, the variants found in Codex Leningradensis for one Psalm are found in other MT manuscripts for the corresponding Psalm. For example,

MT^L	יהוה לא קראו[14:4]	MT^L	אלהים לא קראו[53:5]
MT^{mss}	אלהים לא קראו[14:4]	MT^{mss}	יהוה לא קראו[53:5]

In my view, the forms in Leningradensis for this example are preferable, and the variants in the other manuscripts are due to inadvertent cross-influence from similar texts.[42] They represent "scribal differences such as are created in the course of the transmission of any text," not intentionally "different editions" (434) or recensions. More importantly, before the texts resume their similarity in 14:7 and 53:7, the long verses 14:5-6 and 53:6 (after sharing the first three words) differ entirely from each other: 14:5-6 stresses that God will protect the poor against those who would confound them, whereas 53:6 assures that God will scatter the bones of the enemies. It is uncertain whether there is significant intentionality behind the variants, since both themes are commonplace.[43]

These arguments apply to 2:8c as well. Someone did add 8c, but it is difficult to perceive an editorially intentional relationship to the story of Hannah.[44] Rather, it may have been prompted by the "universal power . . . also referred to in v. 10" in all texts of the Prayer, which again has no particular relationship to the story.

---

[41] These differences in the order of cola seem insignificant in this context in light of the differences in the order of some commandments of the Decalogue in certain manuscripts; cf. Deut 5:17-21 in 4QDeut[n]-MT-SP vs. LXX[B]-Nash Pap. vs. LXX[B] of Exodus 20:13-15; DJD 14:125–26; *BQS* 185–88.

[42] For similar cross-influence see ודרך vs. רגלי in 1 Sam 2:8-9 in section "f." just below, and ודרך חסידו ישמר in Prov 2:8.

[43] Hans-Joachim Kraus (*Psalms 1–59: A Commentary* [trans. Hilton C. Oswald; Minneapolis: Augsburg, 1988], 218–24) does not seem to note any intentional or "editorial" significance in those two major variants. In fact, his suggestion of עצמות in Ps 53:5 as an error for עצות (cf. עצת in 14:6), if combined with seeing לא היה פחד in Ps 53:5 as a gloss and פזר/*בדר as a palaeographic error, may transform "the two totally different major variants in meaning" into the same pair of lines which simply suffered several scribal errors. This possibility receives support from the example of 1 Sam 1:6 in section IV.A.6 above. For a similar, recent comparison of Psalms 14 and 53, see Tov's 3rd edition of *Textual Criticism*, 14–15.

[44] Aejmelaeus ("Hannah's Psalm in 4QSam[a]," 31) agrees: "Reference to the creation seems, however, to be misplaced in this context."

f. "... 2:8-9 consisted of 8ab and 9b only ... [and] was interpreted in two different ways in MT and the *Vorlage* of the LXX." "The counterpart to 2:9a in the LXX, v. 9a', reflects an attempt to accommodate the Song more closely to Hannah's position by adding a reference to God's granting the vow to the person who vows" (454):

4QSam^a	ודרך ח]סידיו ישמור ורשעים בחשך ידמו] נתן נד̇]ר]ל̊]נוד]ר̊ ויברך ש]נות צדיק]
MT	רגלי חסידו ישמר ורשעים בחשך ידמו
LXX^*Vorl.*	*נתן נדר לנודר ויברך שנות צדיק

This would be the strongest example for making the claim that the editing of the Prayer was intentional. It seems plausible that some Hebrew scribe would have added this line which is suggested by the theme of the story, Hannah's vow. It is important to note, however, that the masculine is used in all texts, not the feminine for Hannah, thus arguing against intentional shaping due specifically to Hannah's vow. Moreover, Aejmelaeus argues that the line was original on linguistic grounds.[45] At any rate, if this is judged a scribal addition, it has no apparent connection to any of the other variants in the story or the Prayer.

g. "2:10 in MT differs completely from the LXX and 4QSam^a. The latter two texts add a long plus..." (454).

4QSam^a and the LXX do indeed introduce a lengthy addition with the theme, "Let not the clever boast..." (similar to Jer 9:22-23). These lines, however, are suggested—not by the story, as in the preceding example—but by previous verses in the Prayer itself: "Talk no more so very proudly" (2:3) and "not by might does one prevail" (2:9), both of which are common to the MT as well as to 4QSam^a-LXX. Thus, the addition does not contribute to the hypothesis of a variant edition of the Prayer in light of the story. Moreover, it is important to note that this addition in the Prayer in the LXX does not align with the details of the story. That is, although 1:6 in the MT could be interpreted as "boasting" by Peninnah, as noted with Walters above, Peninnah does no "boasting" in the LXX. Thus, the "boasting" addition in 2:10 of 4QSam^a-LXX does not relate to "boasting" in their text of the story.

In reviewing the variants above I wish to stress first the value generally of the enlightening full analyses of these passages by Tov. On the single issue, however, of whether they "reflect three different editions (recensions) of the Song and its narrative framework," I must admit that I cannot detect significant intentional revision in any example that coheres with the revision in other variants. The addition נתן נדר לנודר (2:8b/9) in 4QSam^a-LXX appears to be the only variant related to the story in a meaningful way, so it could have been added secondarily. But Aejmelaeus may well be correct

[45] Aejmelaeus ("Hannah's Psalm in 4QSam^a," 32) makes the case that "the couplet found in the Septuagint is a good match for the first part of v. 8," since "the Septuagint presupposes a participle in the *Vorlage*, being thus linked with the participial style of the beginning of v. 8 and forming a stanza with the first two couplets of the verse."

regarding its originality.[46] Either way, the remaining variants appear to be unrelated scribal developments in the transmission of the common story and the common Psalm.[47]

2. Aejmelaeus' View

We turn now to Aejmelaeus' detailed analysis of the Psalm. She first examines several variants in the Psalm for which 4QSam^{a} and the LXX agree in original readings against the MT (1 Sam 2:3, 4, 10), confirming that 4QSam^{a} does have numerous agreements with the LXX. But, noting correctly that "affiliation between textual witnesses is determined by secondary—not by original—readings" (26), she examines the major variants which seem to be secondary insertions: 1 Sam 2:2, 8b-9a, and 10. In each of these cases she concludes that 4QSam^{a} is longer than both the LXX and the MT, conflating readings from both.

Writing for a symposium in 2008, she cites my distinction made in 2007 "between orthographic differences, textual variants, and variant literary editions as three independent levels of variation due to different factors."[48] She quite logically concludes from that threefold distinction that 4QSam^{a} is a variant literary edition with sustained major differences from the LXX and from the MT. She advances the conversation by adding to my descriptions of "theological or ideological motives behind such variants" (36) a third possibility which emerges from her analysis: "the technique of complementing the text. The connecting motive behind variants may have been the ambition of the scribe to produce a perfect manuscript with the most complete collection of material, not lacking anything, which is exactly how I see the textual profile of 4QSam^{a}" (37). Her position can be supported by comparison with other examples of variant editions, such as 4QpaleoExod^{m}-SP, 4QNum^{b}-SP, and MT Jeremiah, each of which show repeated intentional literary expansion beyond earlier editions of their respective books.

In light of my more recently observing a number of large additions in the MT of Isaiah,[49] however, I identified yet another category of variation between manuscript traditions, "isolated insertions"(see Ch. 3.V.2), with the following distinction:

> [If such] insertions are isolated and not linked with other insertions as a part of a patterned series, they are classified in this category of isolated . . . insertions. If there are a number of coordinated insertions with the same pattern, showing substantial harmonizations, revisions, or tendencies by a single scribe (as seen, e.g., in 4QpaleoExod^{m}, 4QNum^{b}, the Samaritan Pentateuch, etc.), these would form a new edition of a book.[50]

Comparison of 1QIsa^{a} with the MT highlighted seven isolated insertions in the MT of Isaiah that had not yet entered the text tradition when 1QIsa^{a} and its source text were formed (see Ch. 7.III). The short OG exposed two further insertions in the MT.[51]

[46] See the previous note.

[47] See the similar long pluses in 4QSam^{a}-LXX against the short MT in 1 Sam 1:22; 2 Sam 8:7; 10:6; 13:21; 13:27 in III.A.–B. above, none of which appear to show similar tendencies, with the possible exception of the last two, both within the Absalom story.

[48] Aejmelaeus, "Hannah's Psalm in 4QSam^{a}," 36, citing my "A Qualitative Assessment," [n. 12 above], 152–53.

[49] See Ch. 7.

[50] DJD 32, 2:90.

[51] Isa 2:22 and 36:7b.

These insertions betray no features in common to suggest unity in origin or motivation; they rather appear to have been produced by different scribes at different times for different reasons.

In response to Aejmelaeus' helpful advancement of our analysis by adding the idea of "complementing" the text to the possibilities for assigning a text to the category of variant literary editions, I propose considering the category of isolated insertions for understanding the additions in 4QSam^a. After acknowledging virtually full agreement with her individual analyses, my concluding question is: one scribe or many scribes? That is, are the many additions and conflations in 4QSam^a the work of a single scribe at the time of production of the scroll (and thus a new edition), or the accumulated results of a series of scribes who inserted them at different times for different reasons (and thus a series of isolated insertions)?

Prior to knowing of this distinction, Aejmelaeus appears to have envisioned a single scribe responsible for the conflated text of the scroll: "The ambitious scribe who produced this manuscript. . ."; "he had some other manuscripts and sources out of which he complemented his text. . ." (37). Her scenario is entirely plausible,[52] and if all the additions can be assigned to a single scribe, then her conclusion of "an independent edition of the text in the case of 4QSam^a" (37) is fully warranted.

If, however, one could distinguish multiple scribes or different scribal activity in different circumstances, then one would assign the series of additions in 4QSam^a to the category of isolated insertions, insofar as they would be unrelated to each other.

First, one can observe that, though Aejmelaeus agrees with certain individual points of Tov's article, she does not engage with (does not endorse?) his larger view that the "three different texts of the Song of Hannah . . . reflect three different editions (recensions) of the Song."[53] That is, she does not appear to see in her "complementing" editor the same editors as seen by Tov.

Moreover, the additions in 4QSam^a differ literarily from those in editions such as 4QpaleoExod^m, 4QNum^b, and the SP, in that the additions in these latter texts show a distinct unity. Repeatedly 4QpaleoExod^m expands by adding a report of the execution of the Lord's command explicitly when the MT edition only tacitly presumes it, and 4QpaleoExod^m and 4QNum^b repeatedly insert into their texts appropriate verses from Deuteronomy that are lacking in the Masoretic editions of Exodus or Numbers. The SP consistently emphasizes Mount Gerizim as opposed to Jerusalem. That is, the additions or variants in each display identifiable patterns.

In the attempt to distinguish the additions in 4QSam^a from each other and attribute them to different scribes, one could raise the problem of additions contained in the MT that are not in 4QSam^a (1 Sam 2:22^{fin}; 2 Sam 5:4-5; see III.C), arguing that the scribe did not succeed in his goal of collecting all available Samuel material. The counter-argument, however, could be made that those MT additions were simply later or in manuscripts not available to the 4QSam^a editor. Chronologically, since the OG was translated a century or so before 4QSam^a was copied, one could point to certain additions

52 One could envision a Second-Temple parallel to Origen's collecting a number of manuscripts for producing the Hexapla.

53 Tov, "Different Editions of the Song of Hannah," 434.

in 4QSam^a that are shared with the LXX[54] in contrast to others that are lacking in the LXX (1 Sam 2:22^{init}; 11:9), arguing that the additions shared with the LXX entered the 4QSam^a tradition early and the others entered only later. The similar counterargument would be that the former were, but the latter were not, available to the editor. The lack of unity in content and style among the insertions, however, does distance 4QSam^a from manuscripts such as 4QpaleoExod^m and 4QNum^b.

Again, Aejmelaeus introduces another promising factor for exploring: "the liturgical use of the text" (35). This raises the related factor of oral influence. Since some additions appear to have the flavor of exegetical piety, it is quite possible that they originated orally in liturgical or "Bible study" situations. The oral origin of such interpretive additions can easily be imagined as occurring in the scenes behind the writing of *The Community Rule*, the Gospels, and the *pesharim*. Community study or worship may have produced a certain interpretive or pious reflection that became commonly associated with the text, became repeatedly expressed at that point in the recitation of the text, and then eventually became inserted into a manuscript. The *Community Rule* directs the members to study the Law continually; they are "to read out the [scriptural] text, to study the ruling [or, interpret the correct application], and to pray together" (1QS 6:6-7). The interpretations, perhaps often repeated in subsequent readings of the text, might easily be copied into the margins of manuscripts, and eventually into the text itself. A clear and instructive example can be seen in Greek manuscripts of Matthew 6. After the "Our Father" (Matt 6:9-13), which Christians presumably prayed in common worship, a doxology ("For thine is the kingdom . . .")—undoubtedly oral—gradually became a fixed conclusion, and the doxology eventually came to be inserted into many manuscripts. In this light, it is worth considering, for example, whether the similarities and variants between the three or four cola in 1 Sam 2:2 (see the discussion of Tov's "d" and "e" above) could be due to varying oral recitations of the Psalm as easily as to "comparison between two manuscripts," as Aejmelaeus suggests (31).

In sum, her proposal of the idea of literary "complementing" advances our discussion of the types of scribal development of the scriptural texts in the Second Temple period. In light of her advance, the question now becomes whether the insertions are the product of a single complementing scribe who copied 4QSam^a (or its source manuscript), or rather of a sporadic series of scribal insertions that accumulated at different times during the transmission process. The former could be classified as a new edition of the book of Samuel; the latter would be classified as an exemplar of the single edition of Samuel common to the MT and the LXX but developed with isolated insertions by various scribes. I repeat that Aejmelaeus' option for the former is logical and plausible. But, as I weigh the combination of factors—

- the phenomenon of the category of isolated insertions in contrast to the category of patterned new editions;
- the analogous example of the nine MT insertions into the developing text of Isaiah, which show no unity in origin or motivation;
- the lack of unity in content or style of the 4QSam^a additions (cf. my similar arguments against the editorial unity suggested by Tov);

---

[54] See especially secondary readings: 1 Sam 1:11?; 2:8-9, 24; 2 Sam 8:7; 13:21, 27.

- the likelihood of a single "complementing" scribe's possible access to some but not all of the insertions seen in the MT;
- his insertions shared with the LXX in contrast to others that are not shared;
- the possibility that some insertions arose in oral, rather than written, situations—

I am inclined rather to think that the additions were not the work of a single scribe at one time but reflect a sporadic series of additions at various times, and thus they do not constitute a new literary edition.

C. Nahash the Ammonite: 1 Samuel 11[init]

(DJD 17:65–67; QTSJ, 69–70, 166–170)

4QSam[a] = Josephus [ ] *vacat* [זה וי]ב֯זוהו ו֯לוא הביאו לו מנח֯ה

[ונ]ח֯ש מלך בני ע֯מון הוא לחץ את בני גד ואת בני ראובן בחזקה ונקר להם כ֯[ול]

[ע]י֯ן ימין ונתן אי֯[ן מושי]ע֯ ל[י]שראל ולוא נשאר איש בבני ישראל אשר בע֯[בר הירדן]

[אש]ר֯ ל[וא נ]ק֯ר֯ לו נח֯[ש מלך] בני[ע]מ֯ון כול עין ימין ו[ה]ן שבעת אלפים איש

ויהי כמו חדש [11:1]ויעל נחש העמוני ויחן על יביש[גלעד]

[נצלו מיד] ב֯נ֯י עמון ויבאו אל [י]בש ג֯לעד ויאמרו כול אנשי יביש אל נחש מ֯[לך]

MT = LXX זה ויבזהו ולא הביאו לו מנחה ויהי כמחריש: [11:1]ויעל נחש העמוני ויחן על יבש גלעד

The only occurrence of this paragraph in biblical manuscripts is in 4QSam[a], though it is also attested detail by detail in Josephus (*Ant.* 6.67–69).[55] It presents the context for the otherwise abrupt account of Nahash's violence against Jabesh Gilead. The passage appears to be an original reading accidentally lost from the MT by skipping a paragraph (cf. also 2 Sam 24:16, 20 below). The sudden appearance of Nahash in the MT, without the royal title and without motivation for his violent action, is in contrast with similar narratives: the normal style in introducing a king into a narrative is to list the personal name followed by the title, "king of" his country (see 1 Chr 19:1).[56] Other scholars, however, judge the passage to be a secondary intentional addition. Note that the *New Revised Standard Version* of the Bible includes the passage in its text, whereas the *New American Bible: Revised Edition* does not. Whichever view is correct—whether dramatic loss of text or smoothing addition—it is a one-time occurrence, and no other similarly motivated additions are found. The Nahash passage appears to be simply a single, inadvertent loss of this paragraph in the MT—thus no intentional new edition. If the paragraph were in fact shown to be a deliberate addition in 4QSam[a], that would still not constitute a variant edition of the book Samuel, because it is an isolated, unrepeated phenomenon. Either way it simply points to two noticeably different text traditions, only distantly related.

---

[55] Josephus moves the introductory time specification ("about a month later") from the end to the beginning of the paragraph. Cross (DJD 17:66) notes this as a possible problem, but Josephus is focusing on his larger story (Saul's rise to kingship), and puts the "month" in his topic sentence: after some "knaves" held Saul in contempt, "a month later, he began to win the esteem of all by the war with Naas, King of the Ammonites" (*Ant.* 6.68; see Ulrich, *The Qumran Text of Samuel*, 168).

[56] Cf. also Agag king of Amalek (1 Sam 15:8); Achish king of Ziklag (1 Sam 21:11; 27:2); Hadadezer son of Rehob king of Zoba (2 Sam 8:3); Shishak king of Egypt (2 Sam 8:7; cf. also 1 Kgs 4:19; 5:15). See Cross, DJD 17:65–67, and Ulrich, *The Qumran Text of Samuel*, 69–70, 166–170.

D. David and Goliath: 1 Samuel 17–18

(DJD 17:80; BQS 277–78)

In contrast to the negative conclusions regarding variant editions in the preceding passages, the David and Goliath episode in 1 Samuel 17–18 is now probably accepted by virtually all as displaying variant literary editions of that passage in the OG and the MT.[57] Thus, it needs little discussion here. The OG version has the short original text, whereas the MT displays an intentional double version. The MT tradition has inserted a "romantic tale" into the earlier "heroic tale" seen in the OG;[58] the details of the romantic tale have been interspersed into the heroic tale the same way the Priestly flood story was interspersed into the Yahwistic flood story in Genesis 6–8.[59] But no parallel phenomena with similar motivations are visible anywhere else in the Book of Samuel.

Two tiny fragments of 4QSam[a], frg. 16 (with parts of eight letters from 1 Sam 17:40-41) and frg. 17 (with parts of nine letters from 1 Sam 18:4-5) survive from 4QSam[a]; similarly one of the few fragments of 1QSam has ten letters from 18:17-18. These fragments demonstrate that both scrolls contained the longer edition of this passage, since none of those verses appear in the OG.[60]

Thus chapters 17–18 are an example of a variant literary edition of a single passage, but 4QSam[a] and the OG are not examples in contrast to the MT of variant literary editions of the full book.

E. David, the Plague, and the Angel: 2 Samuel 24 and 1 Chronicles 21

(DJD 17:192–95; BQS 322)

The final passage involving a possible variant edition is the curious story in 2 Samuel 24, paralleled in 1 Chronicles 21, of God's anger inciting David to order a census of the people and thus to bring punishment upon the people. The discovery of 4QSam[a], which presents a number of agreements with Chronicles against MT-Samuel, has brought to light two questions: (1) Do the disagreements between 4QSam[a] and the MT constitute a variant edition in 4QSam[a] for 2 Samuel 24? and (2) Is 4QSam[a] dependent upon Chronicles, or vice-versa, for the passages in which those two agree against MT-Sam?[61] The case

---

57 For detailed discussions of the two editions, see Dominique Barthélemy, David W. Gooding, Johan Lust, and Emanuel Tov, *The Story of David and Goliath: Textual and Literary Criticism: Papers of a Joint Research Venture* (OBO 73; Fribourg, Suisse: Éditions Universitaires; Göttingen: Vandenhoeck & Ruprecht, 1986). I agree with the position of Tov and Lust that the OG is the earlier edition and the MT is a composite of two variant accounts, and disagree with the position of Barthélemy and Gooding, who see the LXX as abbreviated from the MT. For a more recent and clearly presented exposition see Tov, "The Composition of 1 Samuel 16–18 in Light of the Septuagint," in *The Greek and Hebrew Bible*, 333–62.

58 The terms "heroic tale" and "romantic tale" were proposed by Lust (*The Story of David and Goliath*, 14).

59 On the literary sophistication of the editor see Julio Trebolle Barrera, "The Story of David and Goliath (1 Sam 17–18): Textual Variants and Literary Composition," *BIOSCS* 23 (1990): 16–30.

60 Josephus (*Ant.* 6.175–78), again working from a text in the tradition of 4QSam[a], knows the longer edition.

61 For discussion prior to the discovery of 4QSam[a] see, e.g., Julius Wellhausen, *Der Text der Bücher Samuelis*; and Samuel R. Driver, *Notes on the Hebrew Text and the Topography of the Books of Samuel* (2d ed.; Oxford: Clarendon, 1913). For the edition and analysis of 4QSam[a] see Cross, DJD 17. For early

here centers primarily on the two large pluses in 2 Samuel 24 || 1 Chronicles 21 at verses 16 and 20, present in 4QSam[a] and MT-Chr but lacking in MT-Sam.

1. A Variant Edition in Chronicles

We may begin by focusing on several pluses in Chronicles (for 4QSam[a] the letters partially or fully preserved on the fragment are in black, with reconstructed letters in half-tone):

2 Samuel 24	**4QSam[a]**	**1 Chronicles 21**
24:1 אף יהוה לחרות ... ויסת את דוד		21:1 ויעמד שטן ... ויסת את דויד
13 ... דבר בארצך ...		12 ... חרב יהוה ודבר בארץ ומלאך יהוה משחית ...
16 וישלח ידו המלאך	16	15 וישלח האלהים מלאך
	וישא דו**יד** את עיניו וירא את מלאך יהוה עומד בי**ן הארץ ובין ה**ש**מ**י**ם וחרבו** **שלופה בידו** וי**דו נטוא**ה על ירושלים ויפל דויד והזקנים ע**ל** פ**ניהם מתכ**סים ב**שקים**	16 וישא דויד את עיניו וירא את מלאך יהוה עמד בין הארץ ובין השמים וחרבו שלופה בידו נטויה על ירושלם ויפל דויד והזקנים מכסים בשקים על פניהם:
17	17	17 הלא אני אמרתי למנות בעם
18 ויבא גד אל דוד ביום ההוא ויאמר לו עלה	18 ויבא גד אל דוד בי**ום ההוא** **ויאמר עלה**	18 ומלאך יהוה אמר אל גד לאמר לדויד כי יעלה דויד
20 וישקף ארונה וירא את המלך	20 **וישקף** ארנה וירא את המלאך	20 וישב ארנן וירא את המלאך
25		26 ויקרא אל יהוה ויענהו באש מן השמים על מזבח העלה: פ
ותעצר המגפה מעל ישראל		27 ויאמר יהוה למלאך וישב חרבו אל נדנה:
		21:28, 29, 30
— — —		22:1 ויאמר דויד זה הוא בית יהוה האלהים וזה מזבח לעלה לישראל

analysis see Ulrich, *The Qumran Text of Samuel*; and Stephen Pisano, *Additions or Omissions in the Books of Samuel: The Significant Pluses and Minuses in the Massoretic, LXX and Qumran Texts* (OBO 57; Fribourg: Universitätsverlag, 1984). For incorporation into an excellent commentary see McCarter, *II Samuel*. For focus on the Septuagint see Anneli Aejmelaeus, "Lost in Reconstruction? On Hebrew and Greek Reconstructions in 2 Sam 24," *BIOSCS* 40 (2007): 89–106. See also Paul E. Dion, "The Angel with the Drawn Sword (1 Chr 21,16): An Exercise in Restoring the Balance of Text Criticism and Attention to Context," *ZAW* 97 (1985): 114–17; Alexander Rofé, "Midrashic Traits in 4Q51 (so-called 4QSam[a])," in *Archaeology of the Books of Samuel* [see n. 33], 75–88, esp. 76–79; idem, "4QMidrash Samuel?"; and Graeme Auld, "Imag[in]ing Editions of Samuel: The Chronicler's Contribution, in *Archaeology of the Books of Samuel*, 119–31. See also Eva Mroczek, "What Did Arna the Jebusite See? Reconstructing 4QSam[a] for 2 Samuel 24:20 on the Basis of 1 Chronicles 21:20" (paper presented to the Canadian Society of Biblical Studies, Saskatoon, June 2, 2008).

It seems clear that the framing of chapter 21 in Chronicles shows that it is generally a revised edition based on the narrative from Samuel.[62] Passing over for the moment a number of individual variants and isolated insertions—common embellishments which enhance but do not change the story—we note that the pluses in Chronicles exhibit a common pattern and seem intentionally motivated to give a different perspective to the story. It is clear that some form of the Samuel narrative, not necessarily as witnessed exactly by either MT-Sam or 4QSam^{a}, provides the earlier version of the story. The Chronicler's narrative is a later retelling of the Samuel story, as happens frequently throughout Chronicles. At the beginning, in 2 Samuel 24:1, it is God's anger that instigates the census, whereas 1 Chr 21:1 has the intermediary Satan incite David, thus relieving God of the initiative in causing a plague among his people.[63] At the end, 2 Samuel concludes with the plague simply averted, whereas 1 Chr 21:26–22:1 greatly expands, establishing the threshing-floor altar as the place of the future Temple and even referring to Moses' Tabernacle in the wilderness.

Several features already in Samuel are further emphasized in Chronicles, while yet others are introduced. There are twelve readings, all lacking in Samuel, that highlight the revised edition in Chronicles:

a. Emphasis on the angel and his sword: 1 Chr 21:12, 27, 30
b. Intermediaries between God and humans: 21:1, 12, 18
c. The census as David's sin and as the cause of the plague: 21:3bβ, 6b, 17
d. Relationship to the Pentateuch: 21:26 (cf. Lev 9:24), 29
e. David's establishment of the Jerusalem altar:[64] 22:1 and all of chapter 22[65]

None of those twelve readings occurs in MT-Sam, and all but one are additions in the MT-Chr text. This collection of different types of variants, when seen together—the distinctive framing of the chapter, beginning with the Satan and ending with the threshing-floor as the place for the future Temple; the twelve principal additions illustrating five characteristic themes, with the repeated emphasis on the angel—provides a sufficiently unified approach to a fresh version of the story to consider it a revised edition of 2 Samuel 24. Note, however, that it is Chronicles that displays a revised edition based on its source text in Samuel; this is not a variant edition within the Samuel tradition.

2. Major Variants within the Chapter

Within the chapter itself the decision whether Samuel or Chronicles was the source for the readings in 4QSam^{a} should be informed by three sets of evidence: (a) distinctive variants between 4QSam^{a}, MT-Sam, and Chr in the chapters under discussion; (b) the two large passages, 1 Chr 21:16 and 20aβ-21aα; and (c) other large passages in the books of Samuel or Chronicles shared by 4QSam^{a} and MT-Chr.

---

[62] Here Chronicles is treated as though it were an additional manuscript of its source text, Samuel.

[63] Note the parallel with Job 1–2.

[64] The recensional version LXX^{R} (= LXX^{BAMN}) at 2 Sam 24:25, which possibly reflects a developed Hebrew text of Samuel, had already introduced a link with Solomon's altar. If the link was in its Hebrew parent text, it is difficult to assign a date to it.

[65] 1 Chronicles 22:1 quotes David: ויאמר דויד זה הוא בית יהוה האלהים וזה מזבח לעלה לישראל.

(a) There are five distinctive variants:

	2 Samuel 24	4QSam[a]	1 Chronicles 21
(1)	17 בראתו את המלאך המכה בעם	17 בראתו את המלאך המכה בעם	17 >
(2)	>	>	הלא אני אמרתי למנות בעם
(3)	ואנכי	ואנכי	>
(4)	18 ויבא גד אל דוד ביום ההוא ויאמר לו עלה	18 ויבא גד אל דויד ביום ההוא ויאמר עלה	18 ומלאך יהוה אמר אל גד לאמר לדויד כי יעלה דויד
(5)	19 כאשר צוה יהוה:	19 כאשר צוה יהוה	19 אשר דבר בשם יהוה:

In all five distinctive variants, with none to the contrary, 4QSam[a] agrees with the MT-Sam against MT-Chr.[66] Thus, from this first set of evidence 4QSam[a] appears to be linked with the Samuel tradition and distinct from Chronicles.[67]

(b) The two large passages (vv. 16 and 20):

	2 Samuel 24	4QSam[a]	1 Chronicles 21
(1)	16 וישלח ידו המלאך . . . ומלאך יהוה היה עם גרן האורנה היבסי: ס	16 . . . ומלאך יהוה עומד עם גרן ארנא היבוסי	15 וישלח האלהים מלאך . . . ומלאך יהוה עמד עם גרן ארנן היבוסי: ס
	[וישא דוד⁀ויאמר דוד ?]	וישא דויד את עיניו וירא את מלאך יהוה עומד בין הארץ ובין השמים וחרבו שלופה בידו וידו נטואה על ירושלים ויפל דויד והזקנים על פניהם מתכסים בשקים	16 וישא דויד את עיניו וירא את מלאך יהוה עמד בין הארץ ובין השמים וחרבו שלופה בידו נטויה על ירושלם ויפל דויד והזקנים מכסים בשקים על פניהם:
	17 ויאמר דוד אל יהוה	17 ויאמר דויד אל יהוה	17 ויאמר דויד אל האלהים
(2)	20 וישקף ארונה [וירא את המלאך⁀וירא את המלך ?]	20 וישקף ארנא וירא את המלאך וארבעת בניו עמו מתחבאים מתכסים בשקים וארנא דש חטים	20 וישב ארנן וירא את המלאך וארבעת בניו עמו מתחבאים וארנן דש חטים:
		(21) ויבא דויד ויבט ארנא	21 ויבא דויד עד ארנן ויבט ארנן
	וירא את המלך ואת עבדיו עברים עליו ויצא ארונה וישתחו למלך אפיו ארצה:	וירא את המלך דויד ועבדיו מתכסים בשקים באים אליו ויצא ארנא וישתחו לדויד אפים ארצה	וירא את דויד ויצא מן הגרן וישתחו לדויד אפים ארצה:

66 The second occurrence of ואנכי is admittedly weak evidence, but it is corroborative evidence.

67 Alexander Rofé ("Midrashic Traits in 4Q51," 79), though suspicious of 4QSam[a] as tending toward the "midrashic," nonetheless agrees that "most of the modifications to 2 Samuel 24 that show in 1 Chronicles 21 were introduced in a text sometime between the composition of the Book of Samuel and that of Chronicles." I understand him to mean: introduced in a *Samuel* text sometime after the composition of the Book of Samuel and *before* the composition of Chronicles.

Does the absence of the two large passages in MT-Sam indicate that 4QSam[a] derived the passages from MT-Chr? As was seen in sections II and III above, 4QSam[a] generally both preserves text that MT-Sam has lost and adds material beyond MT-Sam. This is true for large passages as well as for individual words or phrases. The long pluses in vv. 16 and 20 can be viewed either as losses through parablepsis by MT-Sam or as additions in 4QSam[a]. That is, parablepsis is quite possible in MT-Sam:

וישא דוד∩ויאמר דוד (16-17)
וירא את המלאך∩וירא את המלך (20-21);

or 4QSam[a] could have added the sight of the angel (v. 16) and the description of the various personages: angel, sons, Araunah, and David (v. 20). Both possibilities have reasonable arguments in support: parablepsis is quite plausible, since the MT in Samuel is guilty of other such losses. On the other hand, additions are frequent, and both vv. 16 and 20 mention the angel, which is a main concern of Chronicles.[68]

The same explanation does not need to apply to both passages, but the similarities suggest that they are both due to the same cause. Literarily, v. 16 would seem to be a good candidate for an intentional insertion, since it features a dramatic appearance of the destroying angel who is emphasized repeatedly by Chronicles. In contrast, v. 20 seems more pedestrian and less likely to be an intentional insertion. Although there is a brief mention that Araunah sees the angel, briefly mentioned also are the sons, the threshing, and David's approach; but nothing more is said of them. They are unimportant elements in the narrative, and the sight of the angel does not even interrupt Araunah from his threshing. What would be the point adding this material? Thus, while v. 16 might be considered a dramatic addition, there is no apparent reason why v. 20 would have been added, whereas וירא את המלאך∩וירא את המלך could well be due to parablepsis.

There seem to be three possibilities for each: (1) The longer text is original in the Samuel tradition (preserved in 4QSam[a]), MT-Sam lost it, and Chronicles copied the original sound text of Samuel; (2) the MT of Samuel preserves the original short text, other Samuel texts (represented by 4QSam[a]) introduced the addition, and Chronicles copied the Samuel addition;[69] or (3) the MT of Samuel preserves the original short text, the Chronicler introduced the addition, and the late 4QSam[a] copied it from the parallel Chronicles text.

If the two passages appear as pluses in 4QSam[a] and MT-Chr simply because they were lost in MT-Sam, then the argument for 4QSam[a] dependence on Chronicles has no validity, since both passages were originally in Samuel. If the two represent secondary additions, they could have originated either in Samuel or in Chronicles, since the angel has already appeared as an actor in MT-Sam. The likelihood seems slightly stronger for addition in v. 16, but for parablepsis in v. 20, though the same explanation probably holds for both. Finally, it is important to note that, if the two large passages were lost due

---

[68] Recall that in Josh 5:13-15 a probably secondary, but early, insertion similarly narrates that Joshua sees "a man" who turns out to be the שר צבא יהוה ("the commander of the army of the LORD") with a sword outstretched, just before the battle of Jericho.

[69] Note that Chronicles is non-Masoretic in its source text, i.e., it characteristically agrees with 4QSam[a] against MT-Sam; see Ulrich, *The Qumran Text of Samuel*, 151–64.

to parablepsis, then 4QSam^a agrees, apart from a few minor individual variants, virtually completely with MT-Sam against Chonicles.

Thus, also from this second set of evidence 4QSam^a appears to be linked with the Samuel tradition and distinct from Chronicles in two out of the three possible scenarios.

(c) Other large passages

4QSam^a appears to be a more developed text than MT-Sam (see section III above). Though it occasionally preserves text that MT-Sam has lost (e.g., 1 Sam 1:24;[70] and possibly 1 Sam 11:9 and 2 Sam 13:27), more frequently it inserts additional details beyond MT-Sam (1 Sam 1:11, 22; 2:22^{init}; 2 Sam 6:2; 8:7; 10:6; and possibly 1 Sam 11:9 and 2 Sam 13:27). In contrast, MT-Sam inserts only two additions beyond 4QSam^a (1 Sam 2:22^{fin}; 2 Sam 5:4-5). In three (2 Sam 6:2; 8:7; 10:6) of the six (or eight, depending on 1 Sam 11:9 and 2 Sam 13:27) secondary insertions by 4QSam^a, MT-Chr joins 4QSam^a in the added material. All of those passages seem at home in the developing Samuel tradition. None of the three joint readings betrays characteristics commonly ascribed to the Chronicler's specific interests (e.g., Levites, cultic matters, genealogies) or displays new patterns of variation from MT-Sam due to the fact that MT-Chr provides a parallel.

Since Chronicles is generally based on a text of Samuel, since none of the insertions betray specific influence by the Chronicler, and since the 4QSam^a insertions shared with MT-Chr show no difference from those in 4QSam^a alone with no Chronicles parallel, a developed Samuel text like 4QSam^a appears to be the source for the MT-Chr longer texts.

One further indication strengthening the claim that 4QSam^a is not dependent upon Chronicles comes surprisingly from a reading in which 4QSam^a and MT-Chr agree against MT-Sam. At 2 Sam 5:4-5, MT-Sam adds a lengthy chronological summary about David's age and the length of his reign over Judah and then over united Israel. The two verses are not in 4QSam^a, the OL, MT-Chr, or Josephus (*Ant.* 7.53–61), which preserve the earlier text; they are clearly a secondary informational insertion into MT-Sam, using data from 2 Sam 2:11 and 1 Kgs 2:11.[71] The OL of Samuel virtually demands that the OG also lacked these verses,[72] even though the received LXX[73] contains them in agreement with MT-Sam.

---

70 Note also the clear parablepsis in MT at 1 Sam 14:41.

71 See conversely the chronological addition of Eli's age at 1 Sam 2:22 (based on 4:15) in 4QSam^a, which is lacking in MT.

72 See Julio Trebolle Barrera, "From the 'Old Latin' through the 'Old Greek' to the 'Old Hebrew' (2 Kings 10:23-35)," *Textus* 11 (1984): 17–36; idem, "Old Latin, Old Greek and Old Hebrew in the Books of Kings (1 Ki 18:27 and 2 Ki 20:11)," *Textus* 13 (1986): 85–95; idem, "The Textcritical Value of the Old Latin in Postqumranic Textual Criticism: 1 Kgs 18:26-29, 36-37," in *From 4QMMT to Resurrection: Mélanges qumraniens en hommage à Émile Puech* (ed. Florentino García Martínez et al.; STDJ 61; Leiden: Brill, 2006) 313–31. Pierre-Maurice Bogaert, "*La vetus latina* de Jérémie: texte très court, témoin de la plus ancienne Septante et d'une forme plus ancienne de l'hébreu (Jer 39 et 52)," in *The Earliest Text of the Hebrew Bible: The Relationship between the Masoretic Text and the Hebrew Base of the Septuagint Reconsidered* (ed. Adrian Schenker; SBLSCS, 52; Atlanta: SBL, 2003), 51–82; and Eugene Ulrich, "The Old Latin Translation of the LXX and the Hebrew Scrolls from Qumran," in *Scrolls and Origins*, 233–74.

73 See discussion of the OG vs. the recensional LXX in DJD 17:25–26; Ulrich, *The Qumran Text of Samuel*, 1–37; and Aejmelaeus, "Lost in Reconstruction," 90–100.

The two alternative arguments for dependency are: (a) 4QSam^a retains the earlier, short Samuel reading followed by (OG), OL, and Josephus; MT-Chr bases its narrative on this short Samuel reading; in the MT-Sam transmission a scribe adds a chronological note. (b) Alternatively, though the scroll is clearly and unambiguously a text of Samuel, not Chronicles, and frequently adds new Samuel material not in MT-Chr, here 4QSam^a omits a pair of correct informational verses in MT-Sam simply because MT-Chr lacks them. The former is persuasive; the latter is not.

In contrast, MT-Chr inserts two long pluses in 1 Chr 15:27-28 that are lacking in 4QSam^a and MT-Sam at 2 Sam 6:14-15. The first is a ten-word specification about the Levites and singers, and the second adds a list of musical instruments for the liturgical procession—both characteristic of the Chronicler. Though 4QSam^a agrees with MT-Chr against MT-Sam concerning the number of sacrificial animals in the preceding verse (2 Sam 6:13 || 1 Chr 15:26), that is not a specific characteristic of the Chronicler;[74] it is clear that 4QSam^a is a Samuel text for the whole passage and that MT-Chr has used a text in that same tradition, inserting two long characteristic pluses.

In a mixed case, 4QSam^a has two long additions beyond MT-Sam at 2 Sam 8:7-8; 1 Chr 18:7-8 contains the second but not the first (see III.A above). The first is added to the MT-Sam report that David took gold shields from Hadadezer; the second is added to the report that David took much bronze from Hadadezer's towns. The first insertion in 4QSam^a adds that Shishak in turn took away the gold shields when he subsequently attacked Rehoboam. The second adds that Solomon used the bronze from Hadadezer's towns to make the bronze sea, the pillars, and bronze vessels in the Temple. It is likely that MT-Sam has the original short text, that the developing Samuel transmission process inserted into the David narrative this twofold update regarding Solomon's time, and that 4QSam^a attests the updated tradition. Chronicles then made use of that updated Samuel text, choosing not to include the first addition because it was negative concerning the Davidic-Solomonic regime, but it did include the second because it was positively related to the Temple. Chronicles could be dependent on 4QSam^a, but 4QSam^a could not have depended on Chronicles here.

Finally, the OG of Samuel (or a slightly developed form of it) as well as Josephus' retelling of the Samuel story repeatedly agree with 4QSam^a against MT-Sam in the joint 4QSam^a-Chr passages as well as in the passages without parallel in MT-Chr. These witnesses further support the joint 4QSam^a-Chr readings as deriving from the Samuel tradition.

Thus, as in the first and second sets of evidence, also in the third set it appears that Chronicles depends on a Samuel source distant from the MT of Samuel but close to the expanded 4QSam^a and the *Vorlage* of the OG of Samuel.[75]

Conclusion

Once we view these larger instances of pluses and minuses in 4QSam^a and the MT and also think of the hundreds of other textual variants between these two texts, the question

74 Note that 4QSam^a also disagrees with MT about the number and age of the sacrificial animal(s) in 1 Sam 1:24, where Chronicles is not extant.

75 In support of Chronicles' dependence on a Samuel tradition and not vice-versa, see T. Michael Law, "How Not to Use 3 Reigns: A Plea to Scholars of the Books of Kings," *VT* 61 (2011): 280–97, esp. 291.

rises: do these two Hebrew text traditions display simply a large number of individual textual variants or rather two variant editions of the book of Samuel?

I think that a survey of these examples—and the same would hold true for the bulk of the remaining variants—indicates not an intentional new edition in either the scroll or the MT, but rather two exemplars of the same general edition, simply distantly related due to separate transmission, where each has gained numerous innocent and predictable, but not patterned or coordinated, additions, and each has suffered either losses or double renderings or corruption. But they do not represent intentionally produced variant literary editions. No significant intentional pattern of similarly motivated variants emerges to indicate a new edition.

The most promising passages that might suggest two variant literary editions would be the Nahash passage as an introduction to 1 Samuel 11, the Hannah-Elkanah narrative of the birth of Samuel in 1 Samuel 1–2, and the David-Saul episode in 1 Samuel 17–18.

But the Nahash passage appears to be simply a single, inadvertent loss of this paragraph by the MT—thus no intentional new edition. If the paragraph were in fact shown to be a deliberate addition in 4QSam[a], that would still not constitute a variant edition of the book Samuel, because it is an isolated, unrepeated phenomenon. Either way it simply points to two noticeably different text traditions, only distantly related.

Regarding the Hannah episode, I agree with Stanley Walters, Emanuel Tov, and Anneli Aejmelaeus that there is a significant cluster of variants between the various texts. But since the variants do not form an intentional pattern, I do not find that they constitute an intentional new edition of the passage by a single editor, whether for misogynist or any other purpose. Nor do all the complementary additions in 4QSam[a] appear to be inserted by a single scribe at a single time. Rather, some appear early and others late, and all are due to a scattered variety of influences.

Finally, the David–Goliath episode in 1 Samuel 17–18 presents variant literary editions of the passage. The Old Greek version has the short original text, whereas the MT displays an intentional double version. The MT tradition has interspersed a "romantic tale" into the earlier "heroic tale" attested in the Old Greek the same way the Priestly flood story was interspersed into the Yahwistic flood story in Genesis 6–8. But no parallel phenomena with similar motivations are visible anywhere else in the book of Samuel. Thus chapters 17–18 are an example of variant literary editions of a single short passage, but 4QSam[a] and MT-Samuel are not examples of variant literary editions of the full book.

4QSam[a] and the Old Greek are close members of one text tradition of Samuel, a tradition that was used by the Chronicler and by Josephus; and they are quite removed from the text tradition used by the MT and by the *kaige* and Hexaplaric Greek texts. Thus 4QSam[a] and the MT are distant representatives of the same general edition of the book of Samuel.[76]

---

[76] The conclusions of this qualitative analysis coincide well with the conclusions reached by Cross and Saley in their statistical analysis, "A Statistical Analysis," 46–47, 53–54 (see n. 13).

CHAPTER 7

THE GREAT ISAIAH SCROLL: LIGHT ON ADDITIONS IN THE MT

THE BOOK OF ISAIAH appears to have been one of the most important, revered, and influential works for the community gathered at Qumran. This is not at all surprising, since the same can be affirmed for the early Christians, who used Isaiah heavily in understanding and depicting Jesus.

One complete copy of the book (1QIsa[a]) was found in Cave 1 at Qumran, the only scriptural manuscript that survived intact over the intervening two millennia. It was found inside a pottery jar, presumably placed there, quite effectively, for safe preservation. Though there are a few small damaged places, its text is virtually completely preserved. Generous fragments from a second copy of the book (1QIsa[b]) were also found in that cave.[1] The fragmentary remains of eighteen more manuscripts were recovered from Cave 4, as well as a couple fragments from an additional copy in nearby Cave 5, for a total of twenty-one at Qumran. One more was found at Murabbaʿat a few miles south, and yet another with two fragments of unknown provenance is reported.[2]

The total of twenty-one manuscripts at Qumran places Isaiah as one of the most popular books there, surpassed only by Psalms (36 manuscripts), Deuteronomy (36), Genesis (24), and Exodus (22). The popularity of these books was presumably shared among a wider group within general Judaism as well, since (1) the scrolls at Qumran appear to be representative of the Scriptures of general Judaism of the period (see Ch. 11), (2) the biblical scrolls, though found at Qumran, were probably in large part copied in Jerusalem and elsewhere and brought to Qumran by those entering the community; and (3) quotations from these books rank statistically as the highest in the New Testament as well. Authors in the Qumran community, believing that Isaiah had foretold God's plan for the period in which the community lived, explicitly quoted the book as authoritative Scripture, wrote commentaries on it, and even quoted Isa 40:3 to give expression to their self-identity: "when these have become a community in Israel . . . , they are to be segregated . . . to walk to the desert to open there his path, as it is written: 'In the desert, prepare the way of ••••'" (1QS VIII 12–14).[3]

It is probably accurate to say that the majority of scholars view the text encountered in 1QIsa[a] as secondary to that in the MT. This is no doubt due in part to the scroll's very full orthography and other linguistic features and to E. Y. Kutscher's early and exhaustive study of that scroll which concluded:

---

[1] See Ch. 6 n. 4.

[2] These last-mentioned fragments are not yet published; see Emanuel Tov, *Revised Lists of the Texts from the Judaean Desert* (Leiden: Brill, 2010), 110.

[3] The four dots are this scribe's replacement for the Tetragrammaton.

> A comprehensive and thorough examination of all these details will, I am convinced, prove that [1Q]Isa^{a} reflects a later textual type than the Masoretic Text. Further, it will be seen that the linguistic anomalies of [1Q]Isa^{a} reflect the Hebrew and Aramaic currently spoken in Palestine towards the end of the Second Commonwealth. Hence, it is possible to postulate that [1Q]Isa^{a} (or its predecessors) is descended from a text identical (or at least very similar) to that of the Masoretic Text, but by no means can we assume the converse—i.e., that the Masoretic Text is descended from a text of the type of [1Q]Isa^{a}.[4]

The clarity and force of his conclusion, however, may not be matched by scholars' attention to his context. His preceding sentence, enumerating "these details" that issued in his conclusion, is: "The orthography, pronunciation, morphology, vocabulary, syntax, and even the proper nouns must all be carefully studied."[5] That is, his conclusion refers to the philological stratum of the scroll, not the textual character. In fact, when in an Appendix he lists data relevant to the textual character and comments on the many instances in which 1QIsa^{a} is fuller than the MT, he is careful to state that "It shall be up to the students of Bible to determine the nature of this added portion."[6] Thus, the linguistic level of the scroll, dated in the late Second Temple period, reflects a later stage than does the predecessor of the MT, but as will be seen below, the *textual* character of the scroll is earlier than that of the MT for many long readings.

I would also add that the assumption that 1QIsa^{a} was copied at Qumran or reflects issues of that covenant community is only an assumption. It seems to be a widespread assumption, but it remains unproved and, to my mind, unwarranted. The scroll was certainly used at Qumran, as several aspects indicate: marginal signs by readers; frequent insertions by later scribes, at least one of whom was presumably at Qumran;[7] and the darkening of much of the scroll midway between the top and bottom where the readers' hands would have held it. But though used at Qumran, if it were copied there, its age, ca. 125–100 B.C.E., means that it would have to have been produced by the first generation at Qumran. But even on that hypothesis, it was nonetheless copied from an earlier text—prior to the Qumran settlement—very much like it. In either case, this text form is not dependent on Qumran factors; it is a general Jewish manuscript.

Again, we can briefly examine the orthographic, or philological, stratum of 1QIsa^{a}, review a few select textual variants, explore the phenomenon of isolated insertions, and consider whether more than one edition of Isaiah has been preserved.

I. ORTHOGRAPHY

There is no clear system of orthography in 1QIsa^{a}, just as there is none in the MT or in other Qumran manuscripts, though there are clear tendencies toward shorter or fuller spelling in each. 1QIsa^{a} usually exhibits longer forms than those of the MT (see Table 1); there are many forms, however, for which the MT is longer (see Table 2).

---

[4] Edward Yechezkel Kutscher, *The Language and Linguistic Background of the Isaiah Scroll (1 Q Isa^{a})* (STDJ 6, 6a; Leiden: Brill, 1974, 1979), 2–3.

[5] Kutscher, *The Language*, 2.

[6] Kutscher, *The Language*, 545.

[7] The secondary insertion in Isa 40:7 was made by the scribe of 1QS, arguably the Maskil. Since the scroll was probably kept at Qumran, it is likely that other scribal insertions were also made there.

TABLE 1: *Characteristic Orthography and Morphology*

Col., line	Isaiah	1QIsa[a]	MT[L]
1 6	1:5	כול	כל
1 4	1:3	לוא	לא
1 3	1:2	כיא	כי
29 5	36:5	ביא	בי
32 9	38:17	ליא	לי
41 20	49:21	מיא	מי
1 13	1:11	יואמר	יאמר
3 10	3:7	לאמור	לאמר
1 14	1:12	זואת	זאת
1 12	1:10	אלוהים	אלהים
4 8	4:4	אדוני	אדני
3 20	3:15	נואם	נְאם
2 10	2:3	יעקוב	יעקב
6 13	7:2	דויד	דוד
1 16	1:13	חודש	חדש
1 27	1:24	נאום	נאם
1 6	1:5	ראוש	ראש
33 20	40:21	רוש	ראש
1 29	1:26	ראישון	ראשן
1 5	1:4	עוון	עון
2 9	2:2	גואים	גוים
4 24	5:9	גדול	גדל
4 29	5:14	חוק	חק
5 6	5:20	חושך	חשך
5 26	6:5	אנוכי	אנכי
6 4	6:10	אוזן	אזן
6 9	6:13	קודש	קדש
7 20	8:2	כוהן	כהן
8 29	9:10	אויב	איב
9 27	10:13	כוח	כח
10 3	10:16	כבוד	כבד
1 9	1:7	אות-	את-
6 9	6:13	מה-	ם-
6 2	6:9	תה-	תָּ-
4 17	5:5	כמה-	כם-
1 3	1:2	המה-	הם-
2 17	2:7	(למרכבותיו) fem. pl.	(למרכבתיו)
4 2	3:25	(יפולו) Q impf.	יפלו
1 9	1:7	(אוכל-) Q ptcp.	(אכל-)
7 18	8:1	(כתוב) Q psv. ptcp.	(כתב)
2 26	2:19	(לערוץ) Q inf.	(לערץ)
3 14	3:10	(אמורו) Q imptv.	(אמְרו)

TABLE 2: *Orthography and Forms Where MT Is Longer than 1QIsa*[a]

Col., line	Isaiah	1QIsa[a]	MT[L]	Col., line	Isaiah	1QIsa[a]	MT[L]
2 3	1:29	מאלים	מאילים	32 6	38:14	עוגר	עָגור
2 16	2:7	קץ	קצה	33 11	40:11	טלים	טלאים
3 5	3:3	ונשא	ונשוא	33 15	40:15	מזנים	מאזנים
3 6	3:3	ויעץ	ויועץ	34 1	40:28	יעף	יִיעף
3 16	3:11	ידו	ידָיו	34 1	40:28	יגע	יִיגע
3 16	3:12	נגשו	נגשָיו	35 5	41:26	צדק	צדִיק
5 4	5:18	השי	השוא	36 7	42:25	ועוזז	ועֱזוז
5 6	5:19	ונדע	ונדעה	37 5	43:25	פשעכה	פשעיךָ
6 14	7:2	כנע	כנוע	37 7	43:28	לגודפים	לגִדופים
7 1	7:15	ובחר	ובחור	38 4	44:26	תשב	תושב
7 21	8:3	הנביא	הנביאה	38 8	45:2	והררים	והדורים
9 16	10:3	ולשאה	ולשואה	38 17	45:11	האותות	האתיות
9 28	10:13	נבלות	גבולת	39 11	46:6	ישתחו	ישתחוו
9 29	10:14	בצים	ביצים	40 1	47:11	שאה	שואה
10 3	10:16	יקוד כיקד	יקד כיקוד	40 3	47:13	מודעים	מודיעִם
10 17	10:32	בת	בית	41 27	49:26	ישכרו	ישכרון
10 21	11:3	עניו	עיניו	42 3	50:2	תיבש	תִבאַש
11 14	13:4	נספים	נאספים	42 13	50:11	תשכבו	תשכבון
11 20	13:12	אוקר	אוקיר	42 25	51:9	מחללת	מחוללת
11 29	13:22	א'ם	איים	42 26	51:11	ישובו	ישובון
12 10	14:9	לקרת	לקראת	42 27	51:11	ישיגו	ישיגון
12 20	14:19	לבש	לבוש	43 9	51:20	כתו	כתוא
12 23	14:21	ומלו	ומלאו	43 16	52:2	צורך	צוארך
13 4	14:32	מלכי	מלאכי	44 16	53:9	בומתו	במתיו
13 8	15:2	יליל	ייליל	44 22	53:12	יפגע	יפגִיע
15 10	19:6	והזניחו	והאזניחו	45 1	54:5	בעלכי	בעליך
15 11	19:7	יבש	ייבש	45 14	54:15	מאתי	מאותי
15 11	19:8	הדגים	הדַיגים	45 24	55:5	ידעכה	ידעוךָ
16 9	20:4	גולת	גָלות	46 7	55:12	תלכו	תובלון
17 4	22:1	גי	גיא	46 26	56:12	ונסבה	ונסבאה
17 9	22:5	בגי	בגיא	47 13	57:13	וירש	ויירש
18 8	23:4	צידן	צידון	47 19	57:19	ורפתיהו	ורפאתיו
18 12	23:8	המעטרה	המעטירה	47 24	58:2	יחפצו	יחפצון
20 18	26:7	צדק	צדיק	48 6	58:11	בצצחות	בצחצחות
21 27	27:13	והשתחו	השתחוו	48 11	58:14	בומתי	במֳותי
22 8	28:7	ונבי	ונביא	48 15	59:4	שו	שָוְא
23 24	29:14	להפלה	להפליא	49 24	60:21	ירשו	יירשו
27 25	33:21	שט	שיט	50 27	63:1	הדר	הדור
28 13	34:13	חצר	חציר	52 10	65:9	ירש	יורש
28 26	35:10	ישובו	ישִבון	53 5	65:23	יגעו	ייגעו
30 14	37:10	תומרו	תאמרון	53 7	65:25	זב	זאב
31 8	37:29	בתה	בָאתָ	54 8	66:19	האים	האיים

Characteristic, but not consistent, are full forms for כול, לוא, יאומר, קוטל (for Qal participles), and the morphological affixes -תה, -כה (for the anomalous -תָ, -ךָ in MT[L]) and -המה, -כמה. The form לוא is used for both MT לא frequently and for לו occasionally. Similarly, בוא is used for both בא and בו.

The demonstrative זואת is very common in both sections[8] of 1QIsa[a], but זאות occurs in four instances (3:6; 5:25; 9:6; and 37:33 in the second section). The alternate forms ירושלם and ירושלים also occur in both parts of the scroll (e.g., ירושלם in 1:1; 3:1 and in 52:1; ירושלים in 2:1; 8:14 and in 36:2; 44:28). These and other characteristic forms such as אנוכי (אנכי MT), מאדה (מאד MT), and יחדיו (יחדו MT) are not listed in Table 1. Many of the forms in Table 1 occur in both the first and the second sections of the manuscript.[9]

The fuller spelling should not be labeled "Qumran orthography" but is probably reflective of the increasingly fuller spelling of the late Second Temple period, visible also in the nonbiblical scrolls, Targumic Aramaic, and elsewhere. It is unlikely that the orthographic style characteristic of the scrolls was limited to Qumran, since many "Qumranic" features can be found replicated in the MT in different loci, in general Jewish literature, and in a variety other sources. The fact that the scrolls were found at Qumran does not mean that all, or even most, were copied there. Kutscher's conclusion was quoted above, that "the linguistic anomalies of 1[Q]Isa[a] reflect the Hebrew and Aramaic currently spoken in Palestine." Eleazar Sukenik concurred: "as early as the period of the Second Temple, it had become customary to facilitate reading through the extensive use of the *plene* spelling, not only in books composed at the time but also in the ancient books of the Bible."[10]

II. Individual Textual Variants

The full list of individual textual variants for 1QIsa[a] extends to seventy-five exhausting pages in DJD 32. Since the number of textual variants is well over 2,600, detailed analysis is impossible here, but the full list now provides the possibility of, and indeed invites, systematic study. The full panoply of routine variants can be seen in 1QIsa[a] as well as in each of the other witnesses. Sometimes 1QIsa[a] contains the superior reading, and sometimes MT[L], MT[q], MT[mss], the LXX, or another scroll contains the superior reading. Thus, all witnesses, including the MT, must be evaluated word-by-word on an egalitarian basis, with none privileged over others (see Ch. 2).

Occasionally, all witnesses display erroneous or implausible readings, showing that the problem entered the text prior to any of the preserved witnesses. The *JPS Hebrew-*

[8] Some think that two different scribes copied 1QIsa[a], a Scribe A who copied Isaiah 1–33 (cols. I–XXVII) and a Scribe B who copied 34–66 (cols. XXVIII–LIV). The reasons, with bibliography, are conveniently listed in Tov, *Scribal Practices*, 21; see also Tov, *Textual Criticism*, 103–5. However, the palaeographic style, i.e., the way the scribe shaped the letters, not orthography or textual character, is the primary criterion for distinguishing scribes, and the palaeographic style of both sections is identical, indicating a single scribe for both sections; see DJD 32, 2:61–65.

[9] For more details see Martin G. Abegg, Jr., "The Linguistic Profile of the Isaiah Scrolls," in the main Introduction to DJD 32, 1:25–41, and "Orthography," in DJD 32, 1:65–82.

[10] Eleazar L. Sukenik, *The Dead Sea Scrolls of the Hebrew University* (ed. N. Avigad and Y. Yadin; Jerusalem: Hebrew University and Magnes Press, 1955), 31.

English Tanakh[11] in its translation of Isaiah lists “Meaning of Heb. uncertain” or “Meaning of verse uncertain” over one hundred times, and suggests “Emendation yields…” approximately as often. If a committee of eminent specialists with a neatly printed Hebrew text and with all the scholarly tools available today finds the text “uncertain” at multiple places, we should not be surprised that ancient scribes as well as the Greek translator also felt challenged by the handwritten text they were using. They often had to choose either to copy a form which they may not have recognized or may have thought erroneous or to replace it with their *lectio facilior* to achieve a sentence that made sense.

A brief sampling of some variants can be presented here:

6:2 שש כנפים 1QIsa^{a}] שש כנפים שש כנפים 𝔐

6:3 קדוש קדוש 1QIsa^{a}] ואמר קדוש קדוש קדוש 𝔐 𝔊

8:9 התאזרו וחותו 1QIsa^{a} 4QIsa^{e}(vid) 4QIsa^{f}(vid)] התאזרו וחתו התאזרו וחתו 𝔐 𝔊 γ′

3:17 ·אֲדֹנָי· יהוה 1QIsa^{a}] אֲדֹנָי 4QIsa^{b} 𝔐; יוי 𝔗; ὁ θεὸς 𝔊; κύριος 𝔊^{C}

3:18; 8:7 ·יְהוָה· אדוני 1QIsa^{a}] אדני 𝔐; κύριος 𝔊

28:16 יהוה^{אדוני} 1QIsa^{a}] אדני יהוה 𝔐; κύριος 𝔊

28:22 יהוה 1QIsa^{a} 𝔐^{mss} 𝔊 𝔖] אדני יהוה 𝔐^{L}

9:16[17] יחמ֯ל 1QIsa^{a}] ישמח 𝔐𝔊 (cf v 18)

13:16 תשׁכבנה 1QIsa^{a} 𝔐^{q} 𝔗(vid)] תשג[ל]נה 4QIsa^{a} 𝔐 𝔖 𝔙; ἕξουσιν 𝔊; συγκοιτασθησονται α′; παραχρησ-θησονται σ′; σχεθησονται θ′ (cf 4QDeut^{c} 𝔐 at Deut 28:30 and see *b. Meg.* 25b)

21:16 שלוש שנים 1QIsa^{a}] שנה 𝔐 𝔊

26:5 ישפילנה 1QIsa^{a} 𝔊 𝔖] ישפילה ישפילנה 𝔐

53:11 יראה אור 1QIsa^{a} 1QIsa^{b} 4QIsa^{d}(יראה או̊[ר]) 𝔊] יראה 𝔐 (err for ירוה // ישבע; note יראה in v. 10)

The 53:11 variant will be discussed in relation to 1QIsa^{b} in the next chapter. There are also numerous instances in which 1QIsa^{a} agrees with one or other of MT^{L}, MT^{q}, MT^{mss}, or MT^{Cairo}, where the Masoretic witnesses disagree among themselves: 22:5, 15; 25:10; 26:15, 20; 28:16; 29:3, 8 are a few examples.[12]

Two large quantitative variants are not to be confused with intentional isolated insertions:

4:5-6 יומם 1QIsa^{a} (יומם⁀יומם)] [יומם ועשן] ונגה אש להבה ל◦[ ]◦(לילה σ′ 𝔊 𝔐) כי על כל כבוד חפה ^{6}וסוכה(וסכה 𝔐) [תהיה] לצל יוֹמ̇ם] 4QIsa^{a} 𝔐 𝔊

16:8-9 גפן שבמה 1QIsa^{a} (שבמה⁀שבמה)] גפן שבמה בעלי גוים חלמו שרוקיה עד יעזר נגעו תעו מדבר שלחותיה נטשו עברו ים ^{9}על כן אבכה בבכי יעזר גפן שבמה 1QIsa^{b} 𝔐 𝔊

These two readings, though large, should be classified merely as individual textual variants, since 1QIsa^{a} has simply lost through parablepsis text correctly preserved in the MT and LXX traditions.

---

11 *JPS Hebrew-English Tanakh* (Philadelphia: Jewish Publication Society, 1999).

12 See these and other examples in DJD 32, 2:119–93.

III. Isolated Insertions

Isolated insertions are larger amounts of text intentionally inserted into one manuscript or tradition in contrast to an earlier short text; they are complete thoughts or verses that learned scribes inserted into the text when they considered it appropriate. Such passages range from a single sentence or clause to full paragraphs, from part of a verse to seven or eight verses.[13] They may have been created in various ways: as scribal notes, through oral commentary that had become customary in a certain community, from passages with similar or contrasting ideas, or as expressions of a liturgical, pious, or apocalyptic nature.[14] If such insertions are isolated—that is, inserted by different scribes at different times and not linked with other insertions as a part of a patterned series — they are classified in this category of isolated insertions. If there is a substantial number of coordinated insertions consistently showing the same pattern, these would form a new edition of a book. The Hebrew and Greek manuscripts of Isaiah do not show this latter pattern; rather they all witness to single edition.

Within this single edition, however, 1QIsa^{a} and MT contain two isolated insertions highlighted by the shorter Greek text (see 2:22 and 36:7b below). 1QIsa^{a} in turn highlights seven more isolated insertions in the MT that apparently had not yet entered the text when 1QIsa^{a} and its source text were formed. The double attestation should be noted that the OG agrees with 1QIsa^{a} in not yet having the insertion that occurs in the MT at 40:7.

The focus in the following examples will be on the presence or absence of the large pluses or minuses; minor variants within them will mostly be ignored so that they do not distort or distract from our primary focus.

Isa 2:9b-10 *(DJD 32, 1:4–5; BQS 334)*

The major quantitative difference in Isa 2:9b-10 between 1QIsa^{a}, the MT, and the LXX highlights a plus, present in the MT and the LXX but absent from 1QIsa^{a}. There appears to be no obvious trigger for parablepsis by homoiarchton or homoioteleuton, whereas the material seems jarring in the context, both in content and in syntax. Verses 9a and 11 are both concerned with the humbling of human pride and use similar diction, expressed in the third person. In contrast, vv. 9b and 10 are second-person negative and positive commands which sit uneasily in the context. Moreover, the commands do not even fit well with each other: v. 9b seems most appropriately addressed to God, an exclamatory coda on the excesses (perhaps especially the idolatry) just mentioned, whereas v. 10 is an apocalyptic directive addressed to humans, that they should hide from the terror of the Lord. Thus, vv. 9b and 10 seem to be two separate late insertions into the Isaiah text, possibly in two moves. In fact, Joseph Blenkinsopp sees yet more secondary accretions in this chapter, including 2:8b, 9a, 20, and 22 (below),[15] and notes

[13] See Ch. 3.V.2; see also the large insertion of eight verses (7:30–8:3) in 4QJer^{a} (DJD 15:155 and Pl. XXIV) discussed in Ch. 9.

[14] For an insertion of liturgical origin see the discussion in Ch. 6.IV.B.2 of Greek manuscripts of the Lord's Prayer in Matthew 6.

[15] Joseph Blenkinsopp, *Isaiah 1–39: A New Translation with Introduction and Commentary* (AB 19; New York: Doubleday, 2000), 194: "Picking our way through the editorial debris that has gradually accumulated in this passage. . . ."

TABLE 3

Isa 2:9b-10

MT LXX [4QIsa^a 4QIsa^b]

9 וישח אדם וישפל איש
ואל תשא להם
10 בוא בצור והטמן בעפר
מפני פחד יהוה ומהדר גאנו (+ בקומו לערץ הארץ LXX)
11 עיני גבהות אדם שפל ושח רום אנשים
ונשגב יהוה לבדו ביום ההוא

1QIsa^a (col. II 18)

9 וישח אדם וישפל איש

11 ועיני גבהות אדם תשפלנה וישח רום אנשים
ונשגב יהוה לבדו ביום ההוא

9 So humankind is humbled,
and everyone brought low—
Do not forgive them!
10 *Enter into the rock and hide in the dust*
from the terror of the LORD and from the glory of his majesty
(+ when he rises to terrify the earth LXX*).*
11 The haughty eyes of humankind will be brought low
and human pride will be humbled;
the LORD alone will be exalted on that day.

that "harsh sentiments excluding the possibility of intercession or pardon on judgment day" such as 9b are "characteristic of a certain strand of apocalyptic thinking (cf. 2 Esd 7:102-115)."[16]

An indicator of the secondary nature of v. 9b is the variants: ואל תשא MT; ולא]שא[4QIsa^a, and [ ]ולא 4QIsa^b. Since the LXX also varies with the first person καὶ οὐ μὴ ἀνήσω ("and I will not forgive"), the original form cannot be reconstructed with certainty.

The OG was translated from (or, the transmitted Greek text secondarily reflects) the already expanded text, but it expands yet further, adding ὅταν ἀναστῇ θραῦσαι τὴν γῆν which occurs also in 2:19 and 21, in each verse following the identical clause in v. 10b ". . . from the glory of his majesty." This third added element is as likely to have occurred in the Hebrew *Vorlage* as in the Greek transmission.

In sum, the indications are that 2:9b and 10 are secondary insertions into the developing text of Isaiah, with 1QIsa^a exhibiting the earlier form and the MT, 4QIsa^a, 4QIsa^b, and the LXX all displaying slightly varying forms of the expansions.

---

16 Blenkinsopp, *Isaiah 1–39*, 194. Note that the *New American Bible* translation puts 2:9b in brackets.

TABLE 4

	Isa 2:22
MT	22חדלו לכם מן האדם אשר נשמה באפו כי במה נחשב הוא
1QIsa^{a} (III 1-2)	22חדלו לכמה מן האדם אשר נשמה באפו כיא במה נחשב הוא
LXX	>

22 *Avoid mortals, who have only breath in their nostrils, for of what account are they?*

Isa 2:22 *(DJD 32, 1:6–7; BQS 335)*

The second major quantitative variant occurs at the end of the same chapter, Isa 2:22. The Greek concludes its chapter with 2:21 and the repeated formula "... when he rises to terrify the earth" (as after 2:10b above), but the MT and 1QIsa^{a} continue with the imperative of v. 22.

Again, there is no trigger for parablepsis, whereas the change to second person in the imperative contrasts with the previous two verses and suggests that it too is a later expansion. Blenkinsopp also considers this verse among the "probable editorial additions" to the chapter.[17]

It is interesting, however, to note that both Brevard Childs and Marvin Sweeney judge v. 22 to be somehow integral to the Isaianic text. Childs sees 2:6-22 as a unit, "in spite of the unresolved problems of its literary composition," and criticizes

> all the various literary reconstructions [by scholars] ... as pale and insipid in contrast to the rough, awesome terror produced by the received text. This effect is only enhanced by the imperative interpolations: "do not forgive them" (v. 9); "go into the rocks" (v. 10), "stop glorifying man, who has a only a breath in his nostrils" (v. 22). With this utterly theocentric focus, the reader finds the central pulse beat of Isaianic theology....[18]

If all these imperatives, however, are quite late additions, is "the central pulse beat of Isaianic theology" to be found in the approximately third- or second-century additions, while the early text of the prophet Isaiah is "pale and insipid"?

Sweeney adverts both to the "composite nature of this text" (Isa 2:22–4:6) and to the "absence [of 2:22] in the LXX," but nonetheless judges that v. 22 "plays a determinative role in the structure of chs. 2–4." Moreover,

> Its wisdom character makes it a potential candidate for Isaianic authorship, since the prophet frequently employs wisdom forms. Unfortunately, there is no other clear evidence to date this text. Its date of composition could be any time from the late 8th century to the late 6th or early 5th century when the basic structure of chs. 2–4 was established.[19]

---

[17] Blenkinsopp, *Isaiah 1–39*, 193.

[18] Brevard S. Childs, *Isaiah* (OTL; Louisville: Westminster John Knox, 2001), 33.

[19] Marvin A. Sweeney, *Isaiah 1–39 with an Introduction to Prophetic Literature* (FOTL 16; Grand Rapids, Mich.: Eerdmans, 1996), 109.

TABLE 5

Isa 34:17–35:2

MT LXX

17 והוא הפיל להן גורל
וידו חלקתה להם בקו עד עולם יירשוה
לדור ודור ישכנו בה
35:1 ישׂשום מדבר וציה ותגל ערבה ותפרח
כחבצלת 2 פרח תפרח ותגל אף גילת ורנן
כבוד הלבנון נתן לה הדר הכרמל והשרון
המה יראו כבוד יהוה הדר אלהינו
3 חזקו ידים רפות וברכים כשלות אמצו

1QIsaª (XXVIII 18–20)

17 והואה הפיל להנה גורל
וידיו חלקת לה{מ}[נ]ה בקו עד עולם[ירשוה]
לדור ודור ישכנו בה 35:1 ישׂשום מדבר וציה ותגל ערבה ותפרח
כחבצלת 2 פרח תפרח ותגל אף גילת ורנן כבוד לבנון
נתן לה הדר הכרמל והשרון המה יראו כבוד יהוה הדר אלהינו
3 חזקו ידים רפות וברכים כושלות אמצו

17 He has cast the lot for them,
his hand has portioned it out to them with the line forever.
(Forever) they shall possess it,
from generation to generation they shall live in it.
35:1 *The wilderness and the dry land shall be glad,*
the desert shall rejoice and blossom;
like the crocus 2 *it shall blossom abundantly,*
and rejoice with joy and singing.
The glory of Lebanon shall be given to it,
the majesty of Carmel and Sharon.
They shall see the glory of the LORD, the majesty of our God.
3 Strengthen the weak hands, and make firm the feeble knees.

One clue, however, that this analysis may not be quite on target is that the structure of the unit he defines (Isa 2:22–4:6) has two parts: part "I" contains only this isolated verse (2:22) which is a "wisdom saying," whereas part "II" contains all of chapters 3–4 but apparently contains no wisdom sayings.

Curiously, this verse occurs in yet another secondary situation. The Rule of the Community (1QS V 17) quotes it, using it as a basis for avoiding those who are "not included in his covenant." This quote from Scripture, however, is not in the Rule manuscripts 4QS[b,d]. According to Sarianna Metso's hypothesis that the shorter texts of

4QS^{b,d} represent an earlier edition of the *Rule*, the inclusion of Isa 2:22 is secondary in the Cave 1 copy, just as it is in the text of Isaiah itself.[20]

Isa 34:17–35:2 *(DJD 32, 1:56–57; BQS 397)*

The scribe of 1QIsa^a concluded Isa 34:17 at עד עולם, skipped one full line, entered a paragraphos sign in the right margin, and resumed the next section with 35:3. Subsequently, another scribe wrote יירשוה above the line after עד עולם in the left margin. Yet a third scribe wrote the remaining words as in the MT, squeezing two lines of very small Herodian script within the space of that single blank line (DJD 32, 2:108).

Did the 1QIsa^a scribe *omit* the text which was then correctly restored, or did the subsequent scribes *add* the text, secondarily expanding? Once again there is no apparent trigger for parablepsis, while the text as in 1QIsa^a reads smoothly, complete in itself; and once again there appear to be two different textual units that may have been inserted independently.

First, the final words עד עולם, which may originally have looked backward to describe the apportioned lot of the wild animals who have taken over the desolated Edom, seem to have been secondarily severed and used to look forward as the beginning of the expanded parallel

עד עולם יירשוה
לדור ודור ישכנו בה

perhaps influenced by similar passages in Isa 13:20 and Jer 50:39.

Second, 35:1-2 can be seen as an independent poetic unit. Even though chs. 34 and 35 function as a "diptych in which the final annihilation of Edom is contrasted with the ultimate well-being of Zion,"[21] the movement of chapter 35, beginning with v. 3, can be understood to flow logically from the "weak hands" and "feeble knees" in a crescendo to the full orchestration of jubilant entrance into Zion "crowned with everlasting joy." According to this hypothesis, 35:1-2 would be seen as secondarily placed there in anticipation of vv. 8-10, perhaps influenced by the similar passage in 40:3-4 crowned by 40:9-11. At any rate, a case can be made for seeing once again a two-stage insertion into the developing text of Isaiah.

In fact, 34:16a ("Seek and read from the book of the LORD..."!) also seems to be a late and unusual insertion in 1QIsa^a-MT, absent from the OG.

Isa 36:7 *(DJD 32, 1:58–59; BQS 399)*

Between the protasis in 36:7a and the apodosis of the Greek text in 36:8, a complex question is found in 1QIsa^a and the MT but not in the LXX. Mechanically one could point to the possible loss through homoioteleuton from בטחנו to תשתחוו in the Hebrew *Vorlage* behind the Greek. But the lengthy and pointed question that the Rabshakeh asks

[20] See Sarianna Metso, *The Textual Development of the Qumran Community Rule* (STDJ 21; Leiden: Brill, 1997), 151–55. Note moreover that the scribe of 1QS also knows an expanded text at 40:7 (see below) and inserted it into 1QIsa^a.

[21] Blenkinsopp, *Isaiah 1–39*, 450.

TABLE 6

Isa 36:7

MT

7 וכי תאמר אלי אל יהוה אלהינו בטחנו
הלוא הוא אשר הסיר חזקיהו את במתיו ואת מזבחתיו
ויאמר ליהודה ולירושלם לפני המזבח הזה תשתחוו
8 ועתה התערב נא את אדני המלך אשור

1QIsa[a] (XXIX 8-12)

7 וכיא תואמרו אלי על יהוה אלוהינו בטחנו
הלוא הואה אשר הסיר חזקיה את במותיו ואת מזבחותיו
ויואמר ליהודה ולירושלים לפני המזבח הזה תשתחוו {בירושלים}
8 ועתה התערבו נא את אדוני המלך אשור

LXX

7 εἰ δὲ λέγετε Ἐπὶ κύριον τὸν θεὸν ἡμῶν πεποίθαμεν,

8 νῦν μείχθητε τῷ κυρίῳ μου τῷ βασιλεῖ Ἀσσυρίων,

7 But if you say to me, "We rely on the LORD our God,"
—*is it not he whose high places and altars Hezekiah has removed,*
saying to Judah and to Jerusalem, "you shall worship before this altar"?—
8 come now, make a wager with my master the king of Assyria. . . .

seems unlikely on Assyrian lips; it presumes a knowledge of internal Judahite religious politics. That argument is not altogether persuasive, however, since the words are those of the author of the story, and not a historical quote of the Rabshakeh himself. At any rate, the argument can be made that a rhetorically forceful question has been inserted into one Hebrew text family of Isaiah that was not included in the text tradition translated by the LXX. Both the MT and the LXX have the fuller reading in 2 Kgs 18:22.

Inasmuch as a number of these secondary expansions have displayed a two-stage addition, note here that בירושלים (as in 2 Kgs 18:22) had been either added in the text used by the scribe of 1QIsa[a] or possibly added by him, but he (or a later corrector) marked it as not to be included.

Isa 37:4-7 (*DJD 32, 1:60–61; BQS 401*)

The scribe of 1QIsa[a] concluded v. 4 with השארית הנמצאים (or at least some form of the latter word), leaving blank the remainder (more than half) of line 10 plus the entire next line. He resumed his text on line 12 with v. 8. Both the MT and the LXX have the longer text as in Isa 37:5-7. Sometime after line 12 was written, a scribe with a hand very similar to the main scribe's (and possibly the main scribe himself) added בעיר הזואת to the end of v. 4 and continued writing vv. 5-7, squeezing two lines of text into the space of line 11, with the last three words trailing across the stitching of the manuscript and down the margin of the next skin.

TABLE 7

Isa 37:4-7

MT LXX

4 אולי ישמע יהוה אלהיך את דברי רב שקה
אשר שלחו מלך אשור אדניו לחרף אלהים חי
והוכיח בדברים אשר שמע יהוה אלהיך ונשאת תפלה בעד
השארית הנמצאה 5 ויבאו עבדי המלך חזקיהו אל ישעיהו
6 ויאמר אליהם ישעיהו כה תאמרון אל אדניכם כה אמר יהוה
אל תירא מפני הדברים אשר שמעת אשר גדפו נערי מלך אשור אותי
7 הנני נותן בו רוח ושמע שמועה ושב אל ארצו והפלתיו בחרב בארצו
8 וישב רב שקה

1QIsa[a] (XXX 10–11b)

4 אולי ישמע יהוה אלוהיכה את דברי רב שקה
אשר שלחו מלך אשור אדוניו לחרף אלוהים חי
והוכיח בדברים אשר שמע יהוה אלוהיכה ונשאתה תפלה בעד
השארית הנמצאים בעיר הזואת 5 ויבואו עבדי המלך יחוזקיה אל ישעיה
6 ויואמר להמה ישעיה כוה תואמרו אל אדוניכמה כוה אמר יהוה
אל תירא מפני הדברים אשר שמעתה אשר גדפו נערי מלך אשור אותי
7 הנני נותן רוח בוא ושמע שמועה ושב לארצו והפלתיו בחרב בארצו
8 וישוב רב שקה

“. . . 4 It may be that the LORD your God hears the words of the Rabshakeh, whom his master the king of Assyria has sent to mock the living God, and will rebuke the words that the LORD your God has heard; therefore lift up your prayer for the remnant that is left *(in this city)*.”

5 *When the servants of King Hezekiah came to Isaiah,* 6 *Isaiah said to them, “Say to your master, ‘Thus says the Lord: Do not be afraid because of the words that you have heard, with which the servants of the king of Assyria have reviled me.* 7 *I myself will put a spirit in him, so that he shall hear a rumor and return to his own land; I will cause him to fall by the sword in his own land.’”*

8 The Rabshakeh went back. . . .

There is nothing to elicit suspicion of parablepsis except the initial *waw-yod* in ויבאו and וישב. On the other hand, the content of Isa 37:5-7 can be suspected as a prophetic word secondarily inserted here to correspond with the conclusion of this narrative in 37:36-38, recording that Sennacherib died “by the sword in his own land.”

On the hypothesis that 37:5-7 is a secondary element in the Isaian narrative, one can note that again two separate insertions are found here: the prophecy of vv. 5-7 and the explicative expansion בעיר הזואת at the end of v. 4. While 2 Kings 19 does not have בעיר הזואת, it does include the prophecy.

TABLE 8

Isa 38:20b-22

MT LXX	19 חי חי הוא יודך כמוני היום אב לבנים יודיע אל אמתך 20 יהוה להושיעני ונגנותי ננגן כל ימי חיינו על בית יהוה 21 ויאמר ישעיהו ישאו דבלת תאנים וימרחו על השחין ויחי 22 ויאמר חזקיהו מה אות כי אעלה בית יהוה
1QIsa[a] (XXXII 11–14)	19 חי חי הוא יודכה כמוני היום אב לבנים יודיע אל אמתכה 20 יהוה להושיעני 19 חי חי יודך כמוני היום אב לבנים יהודיע אלוה אמתך 20 יהוה להושיעני ונגנותי ננגן כול ימי חיינו על בית יהוה 21 *ויאומר ישעיהו דבלת תאנים וימרחו על השחין ויחי* 22 *ויאמר חזק'ה מה אות כי אעלה בית יהוה*

19 The living, it is the living who thank you, as I do today.
A father instructs children to your truth
20 The LORD will save me, *and we will sing to stringed instruments*
all the days of our lives at the house of the LORD.
21 *Now Isaiah had said, "Let them take a lump of figs, and apply it to the boil, so that he may recover."*
22 *Hezekiah also had said, "What is the sign that I shall go up to the house of the LORD?"*

Isa 38:20b-22 (*DJD 32*, *1:64–65; BQS 405*)

Verse 20 is the traditional conclusion of Hezekiah's prayer. Verses 21-22 seem "cut and pasted" here, and a glance at the logical order of 2 Kgs 20:1-10 as compared with Isaiah 38 will make clear that vv. 21-22 are out of place here in the Isaiah text.[22]

The scribe of 1QIsa[a] wrote the first two words of 38:20 on one line (XXXII 12) and apparently left two and a half lines blank, then resumed with 39:1 on line 15. Though it is possible that the original scribe continued with the repetition of v. 19, it looks rather that another scribe with a quite similar but larger script continued with a repetition (with variants) of v. 19 and all of traditional v. 20. Clearly, a yet later, Herodian hand continued on line 14 with traditional vv. 21-22, eventually running it down the left margin, since there was insufficient space.

It is probably true that a variety of scholars would give a variety of guesses concerning precisely where Hezekiah's prayer "originally" ended, and it is unlikely that any one would convince another. The prayer includes numerous topoi, but v. 19a is the last line that clearly fits into the preceding, though even that is not a firm argument. Verse 19b could be seen as an addition, as could 20a. Verse 20b was not originally included by the scribe of 1QIsa[a], and thus the subsequent addition, which apparently started a line or so too soon, caused the dittography. We need not speculate here whether

22 Childs (*Isaiah*, 283) agrees: "Quite correctly, most critical commentators speak of a dislocation caused by a later redactor's attempt to supplement Isaiah's shorter version from 2 Kings (cf. Delitzsch)."

vv. 21-22 were in the original story. They could have been an addition, since Isa 38:1-8 reads smoothly without them and the verses could be seen as later narrative embellishment. On the other hand, homoiarchton (ויאמר ישעיהו beginning both v. 7 and v. 9 of 2 Kings 20) could explain a loss of original text. At any rate, to the text penned by the scribe of 1QIsa^{a} there are two subsequent additions which supplement the text and attempt to bring it into conformity with the secondarily expanded tradition inherited in the MT.

Isa 40:7-8 *(DJD 32, 1:66–67; BQS 407)*

Isaiah 40 has been dear to many, from Second Isaiah, to the Qumran covenanters and the four evangelists, to Händel's *Messiah*, and to the present day; thus one might expect resistance to the suggestion of a variant text. Nonetheless, it can be claimed that the original scribe of 1QIsa^{a} copied a short text which reads perfectly both in itself and as a balanced poem worthy of Second Isaiah, that the OG has faithfully translated a Hebrew text virtually identical with that of 1QIsa^{a}, and that the MT includes an expansion.

Sometime after 1QIsa^{a} was copied, the easily identifiable scribe who copied 4QSam^{c}, 1QS, and 4QTest (4Q175) inserted what he probably thought was erroneously missing text. He presumably thought that v. 7 was "original" and had been lost through parablepsis, the 1QIsa^{a} scribe having skipped from the first occurrence of יבש חציר נבל ציץ to the second, thus losing a line. He placed the insertion after what he considered v. 7a, because (with 8a identical to 7a) it is only with traditional 7b that the variant became noticeable. As one would expect from that scribe, he makes several errors, misspelling חציר (חציל) and אכן (הכן), and continuing his insertion beyond where he should have ended it.

The possibility of parablepsis, however, leaves the alternative of a loss of text as a viable explanation; either conclusion is reasonable. In fact, both Childs and (with qualification) Baltzer treat v. 7 as integral in their translation and commentary. Childs agrees with Christopher Seitz that "[First] Isaiah's preaching of judgment has been summarized in 40:6b-7 by means of an intertextual reference to 28:1-4."[23] Klaus Baltzer labels v. 7 a "communal lament" and says that "the vocabulary is DtIsa's own." But, whereas Childs does not mention the 1QIsa^{a}-LXX reading, Baltzer does add that "Textually, the sentence could be a gloss, and has been presumed to be such ever since the eighteenth century, with Koppe. The sentence is missing in the LXX. That it is a later gloss would seem to be confirmed by 1QIsa^{a}, where it has been interpolated between the lines and in the margin." Nonetheless, Baltzer then moves on, presenting v. 8 as "the reversal of 7a both in its form and its content."[24]

---

[23] Childs, *Isaiah*, 300.

[24] Klaus Baltzer, *Deutero-Isaiah: A Commentary on Isaiah 40–55* (trans. Margaret Kohl; Hermeneia; Minneapolis: Fortress, 2001), 58.

TABLE 9

Isa 40:7-8

MT

6 קול אמר קרא ואמר מה אקרא
כל הבשר חציר וכל חסדו כציץ השדה
7 יבש חציר נבל ציץ כי רוח יהוה נשבה בו אכן חציר העם
8 יבש חציר נבל ציץ ודבר אלהינו יקום לעולם

1QIsa[a] (XXXIII 6–7) LXX

6 קול אומר קרא ואומרה מה אקרא
כול הבשר חציר וכול חסדיו כציץ השדה
כי רוח •••• נשבה בוא הכן חציר העם יבש חציל נבל ציץ ודבר אלוהינו
8 יבש חציר נבל ציץ ודבר אלוהינו יקום לעולם

LXX 6 φωνὴ λέγοντος Βόησον· καὶ εἶπα Τί βοήσω;
Πᾶσα σὰρξ χόρτος, καὶ πᾶσα δόξα ἀνθρώπου ὡς ἄνθος χόρτου·

8 ἐξηράνθη ὁ χόρτος, καὶ τὸ ἄνθος ἐξέπεσε,
τὸ δὲ ῥῆμα τοῦ θεοῦ ἡμῶν μένει εἰς τὸν αἰῶνα.

6 A voice says, "Cry out!" And I said, "What shall I cry?"
All flesh is grass, their constancy is like the flower of the field.
7 The grass withers, the flower fades,
when the breath of the LORD blows upon it;
surely the people is "the grass."
8 *The grass withers, the flower fades, but the word of our God*
but the word of our God will stand forever.

At least it is clear that one Hebrew tradition, witnessed by 1QIsa[a] and the LXX, contained the shorter text, while another tradition contained the fuller text. The 1QS scribe knew the longer tradition and revised 1QIsa[a] according to it. But again, was the shorter text "the original" and the longer text a subsequent expansion? Or was the longer text "original" and then apocopated?

In favor of the longer text as original are: (1) the clear possibility of parablepsis, and (2) the traditional view that the text as preserved in the MT is correct.

In favor of the short original are: (1) that the short text is smoother than, or at least as smooth as, the longer text; (2) that the LXX also attests the same short reading, providing double attestation; (3) that there is a clear tendency to supplementation in the developing text of Isaiah; and (4) that at least part of v. 7 ("surely the people is 'the grass'") is widely considered a supplementary gloss. The arguments favor the short original that has been glossed.

TABLE 10

Isa 40:14b-16

MT LXX

14 את מי נועץ ויבינהו וילמדהו בארח משפט
וילמדהו דעת ודרך תבונות יודיענו
15 הן גוים כמר מדלי וכשחק מאזנים נחשבו
הן איים כדק יטול
16 ולבנון אין די בער וחיתו אין די עולה
17 כל הגוים כאין נגדו

1QIsa[a] (XXXIII 14–16)

14 את מי נועץ ויבינהו וילמדהו באורח משפט
וילמדהו דעת ודרך תבונות יודיענו
15 הן גואים כמר מדלי וכשחק מזנים נחשבו
הן איים כדק ייטול
16 ולבנון אין די בער וחיתו אין די עולה
17 כול הגואים כאין נגדו

14 Whom did he consult to enlighten him? Who instructed him in the path of justice?
Who taught him knowledge (MT; > LXX) *or showed him the way of insight?*
15 *Look, the nations are like a drop from a bucket and considered as dust in the scales;*
he weighs the islands like fine powder.
16 *Lebanon is not enough for firewood, or its animals enough for burnt offering.*
17 All the nations are as nothing before him. . . .

Isa 40:14b-16 *(DJD 32, 1:66–67; BQS 408)*

The original scribe stopped with משפט at the end of 40:14a, left two and a half lines blank, and resumed with v. 17. The MT and the LXX include the longer text, though וילמדהו דעת is not reflected in the LXX and may be a doublet. There is no obvious cause for parablepsis, whereas the extra text as in MT-LXX can be seen as expansions on the two themes of 14a and 17. Someone with a noticeably later hand inserted the longer text into 1QIsa[a].

The amount of space the scribe left blank, however, is puzzling (see also col. XXXII above). The only larger interval, three full lines at the bottom of col. XXVII, occurs at the end of Isaiah 33, which probably signaled the conclusion of the book of (First) Isaiah. That interval probably served as the division between two "books," as paralleled by the almost four-line lacuna in 4QpaleoGen-Exod[l] between Genesis and Exodus.[25]

The only other interval of more than one line in 1QIsa[a] occurs in the very next column (34:15-16) between 41:11 and 12; it extends to more than one and three-fourths

[25] See DJD 9:25 + Pl. I, frg. 1.

TABLE 11

Isa 63:3

MT LXX	3 פורה דרכתי לבדי ומעמים אין איש אתי ואדרכם באפי וארמסם בחמתי ויז נצחם על בגדי וכל מלבושי אגאלתי
1QIsa^a (L 29)	3 פורה דרכתי לבדי ומעמי אין איש אתי וכול מלבושי גאלתי

3 The winepress I have trod alone, and from the peoples (my people) there was none with me.
I trod on them in my anger and crushed them in my fury;
their juice splattered over my garments,
and all my robes I have stained.

lines and includes a **X** (Palaeo-Hebrew *tav*) in the left margin. The text looks a bit troubled there, if one judges with the MT as the criterion: 1QIsa^a "omits" יהיו כאין and תבקשם ולא תמצאם (41:11-12). But the scroll there may also be interpreted as reading smoothly, with the MT having added those phrases.

One possible consideration at 40:14b-16 is that the scribe knew that another tradition inserted a Hebrew expansion here and left room for it, just in case it should be added. In this case, the scribe may have been aware that expansions of a verse or two were a phenomenon that was to be expected in the developing text of Isaiah.

Isa 63:3 *(DJD 32, 1:100–101; BQS 455)*

1QIsa^a presents a shorter Hebrew text in which the pattern is a triple noun + verb (or verbal equivalent). The MT presents a longer text (63:3aβ-bα) in which the pattern for the additional text is a triple verb + noun. The Greek knows and reflects a form of the longer text but does not translate this specific text. To argue for loss of text by 1QIsa^a from a longer original, one could point to the final *yod* in אתי and בגדי. But perhaps more persuasive is the set of facts (1) that both the shorter text and the additional text can each stand on its own as a complete verse; (2) that they each have a consistent pattern distinct from the other; (3) that the additional text is a close variant of v. 6 only a few verses later (ואבוס עמים באפי ואשכרם בחמתי ואוריד לארץ נצחם); and (4) that the Greek translation of the final clause is closer to the Hebrew text in v. 6 than in v. 3. These factors weigh in favor of a secondary insertion into the MT tradition, early enough to be reflected in the received LXX.

Table 12

Isa 51:6

MT LXX	6 שאו לשמים עיניכם והביטו אל הארץ מתחת כי שמים כעשן נמלחו והארץ כבגד תבלה וישביה כמו כן ימותון וישועתי לעולם תהיה וצדקתי לא תחת
1QIsa^{a} (XLII 19–21)	6 שאו שמים עיניכמה והביטו אל הארץ מתחתה וראו מי ברא את אלה *vacat* ויושביה כמו כן ימותון וישועתי לעולם תהיה וצדקתי לוא תחת

6 Lift your eyes to the heavens and look at the earth beneath,
(MT LXX:) *for the heavens will disappear like smoke,*
and the earth will wear out like a garment.
(1QIsa^{a}:) *and see who created these.*
Its inhabitants will die like gnats, but my saving power will be forever,
and my vindication will never fail.

Isa 51:6 (*DJD 32*, 1:84–85; *BQS* 421)

One final example may be presented, although it does not qualify as an insertion into the MT. Verse 6b of Isaiah 51 presents what could be viewed as one insertion into the MT and a different insertion into 1QIsa^{a}.

Of the three segments of Isa 51:6, the major witnesses agree on the first and third, but for the second, 1QIsa^{a} and MT-LXX present two very different ideas, both of which could be seen as logical supplements. 1QIsa^{a} looks back, focusing on the creator of the heavens and earth, whereas the MT-LXX looks forward, focusing on the transitory nature of the created order. That the variant in 1QIsa^{a} might be expansionist is signaled by the feminine singular suffix on וישביה, whose antecedent is the earth, not the creator. Though one could suspect the same regarding the MT-LXX, no clue remains, since "the earth" is repeated in the MT-LXX parallel clause. Several clues, however, indicate that the MT should be judged original. MT, with "the earth," could well be original, and its text fits the immediate context better. Verses 6b-6c with וישועתי לעולם תהיה וצדקתי לא תחת in the MT form a prophetic salvation promise parallel to Isa 40:6+8 (omitting v. 7 with 1QIsa^{a}-LXX):

40:6 . . . כול הבשר חציר וכול חסדיו כציץ השדה
8 יבש חציר נבל ציץ ודבר אלוהינו יקום לעולם

Finally, the possibility that 1QIsa^{a} has been influenced by 40:26

40:26 שאו מרום עיניכם
וראו מי ברא אלה

further confirms the soundness of the MT verse as original and the 1QIsa^{a} as a variant.

Conclusion

The very first scriptural manuscript discovered at Qumran and published already by 1950 is, in a condensed form, a compendium of most of the learnings to be gained about the Scriptures in the Second Temple period.

1QIsa[a] is so different from the familiar Masoretic *textus receptus* of Isaiah that scholars were simply unprepared to see that it was not a "vulgar" text impaired by the Qumran community. It is a beautiful manuscript of the commonly shared edition of the book of Isaiah. Though found and used at Qumran, it may well not have been copied there but in Jerusalem or elsewhere in Judah and brought to Qumran. Its age indicates that, if it had been copied at Qumran, it must have been copied by the first generation there, and it must have been copied from a pre-Qumran source text.

There is no clear system of orthography in 1QIsa[a], just as there is none in the MT or in most other Qumran manuscripts. In general 1QIsa[a] employs longer forms than those of the MT, but the MT also displays the longer form occasionally. We agree with Kutscher and Sukenik that the orthography and other "Qumranic features" were not peculiar to Qumran but reflect the language and spelling common in Palestine at the time.

The more than 2,600 textual variants compared with other Qumran manuscripts, the MT, and the LXX span the full panoply of known types of variants within each tradition. Sometimes the scroll is superior, sometimes the MT, the LXX, or another scroll is superior. This teaches us that all manuscripts, including the MT, must be seriously weighed on an egalitarian basis, word-by-word.

Nine large insertions of text—of a sentence or a verse, or even several sentences or verses—were discovered in the MT, seven of which were not yet present in the text of 1QIsa[a], and three not yet in the LXX (for one insertion at 40:7 both 1QIsa[a] and the LXX preserve the unexpanded form). This requires that we clarify Kutscher's judgment that "1[Q]Isa[a] reflects a later textual type than the Masoretic Text."[26] His judgment centered on linguistic clues: "orthography, morphology, syntax," and we can fully agree with him that with regard to the majority of individual linguistic features, 1QIsa[a] does exhibit a later profile. With regard to the development of the *text*, however, the case is the reverse. 1QIsa[a] appears in many, if not all, of those seven major secondary additions in the MT to be the earlier textual form from which the MT descended. The MT routinely represents the later, secondary textual form, even if the linguistic features of the MT did not undergo as much updating as those of 1QIsa[a].

The reading in 51:6 in which the first and third clauses in each tradition agree while the second is quite different may also be enlightening. If the second clause in each was secondarily added to an earlier version which contained only the first and third, that would provide a helpful example of the developmental composition of the book. It would indicate that, at any given moment in the development of the text of what the current community held as the book of Isaiah, short insights derived from reflections on the prophetic word were occasionally added. These would have been expansions based on

---

[26] See note 4.

thoughts similar to the thoughts of the "prophet"—whether Isaiah of Jerusalem, Second Isaiah, Third Isaiah, or any of the accumulated supplements.

The realization that the book of Isaiah was composite, which became common knowledge with Bernhard Duhm's separation of First, Second, and Third Isaiah,[27] continues to expand. William L. Holladay's subtitle, *Isaiah: Scroll of a Prophetic Heritage*,[28] is insightful and instructive: the book continually experienced growth and development. The recognition has also long been operative that the composite nature of the book extends even to short exclamations such as "There is no peace for the wicked, says the LORD" (Isa 48:22). But even when the additions are not so unrelated to the preceding material, we should expect that numerous hands have contributed in a wide variety of styles to the developing text that eventuated in the book of Isaiah. We should not be surprised that there are numerous late insertions into the text of Isaiah. Nor should we be surprised that, when we are able to detect an expansion in an extant manuscript, we may find two or even three expansions added together.

Sometimes there are clear categories of inserted reflections or comments, such as "a prose comment on a verse oracle beginning 'on that day' (*bayyôm hahû'*)" which is a "frequent occurrence throughout the book."[29] But often the insertions are simply ad hoc.

The fact that manuscripts that are still extant witness at times to both the earlier unexpanded text and the later expanded text suggests that those expansions are relatively late, perhaps from the third or second or even first centuries B.C.E. Moreover, the fact that sometimes 1QIsa^{a} preserves the earlier unexpanded text in contrast to the LXX, while sometimes the LXX does so in contrast to 1QIsa^{a}, suggests that the nine expansions presented do not all stem from the same source and were not all added at the same time. It should also be stated explicitly that there is no reason to doubt that the LXX of Isaiah simply translated as faithfully as possible its Hebrew *Vorlage*, and that it either lacked or included the expansions depending upon whether its *Vorlage* lacked or included them. We should also not discount the possibility that the Greek text has at certain points been secondarily revised to agree with the MT.

Finally, we can note that neither the nine large expansions in the MT nor any other set of variants show an intentional pattern such as that observable in 4QpaleoExod^{m}, 4QNum^{b}, or the SP. Thus, we have only a single edition of the book—recall Kutscher's comment that "the Masoretic Text is descended from a text of the type of [1Q]Isa^{a}." The time and circumstances of the nine isolated insertions were varied, showing no signs of coordination. All Isaiah manuscripts are genetically related; but the various exemplars, despite the numerous and significant variants, are not differentiated by a pattern of variants defined enough to indicate a variant edition.

---

[27] Bernhard Duhm, *Das Buch Jesaja* (Göttingen: Vanderhoeck & Ruprecht, 1892).

[28] William L. Holladay, *Isaiah: Scroll of a Prophetic Heritage* (Grand Rapids: Eerdmans, 1978).

[29] Blenkinsopp, *Isaiah 1–39*, 194.

Chapter 8

1QIsaiah^{B} and the Masoretic Family

1QIsa^{B} was the first biblical scroll from Qumran recognized as genuinely ancient, although 1QIsa^{a} had been discovered several months before it.[1] The original scroll contained twenty-eight columns of about fifty-one lines, copied in a late Hasmonaean or early Herodian hand from about the third quarter of the first century B.C.E. Nothing remains of the first two columns. One or more fragments survive for each of columns III–XV, and generous portions survive for columns XVI–XXVIII.

From the time of the initial discovery of 1QIsa^{b} and the publication by Eleazar Sukenik in 1954 and 1955,[2] the scroll has been generally described as very close to the Masoretic text of Isaiah. Now that a critical edition has been published in DJD 32, a more precise assessment of its relation to the MT is possible.

In addition to examining the usual four categories of orthographic features, individual textual variants, isolated insertions, and literary editions, for 1QIsa^{b} a more focused look may be added into text-family groupings. Whereas the four categories usually operate independently and do not influence each other, text-family groupings are determined precisely according to those four classes of variation.

I. Orthography

Although the orthographic practice of 1QIsa^{b} displays widespread agreement with that transmitted in MT^{L}, MT^{q}, MT^{mss}, and MT^{Cairo}, there yet remain approximately 161 words that are spelled differently in the preserved parts of the text (see Table 1); because of the closeness to the MT of Isaiah it seems helpful to list all forms. The fuller spelling is found sometimes in 1QIsa^{b}, sometimes in the MT, in roughly equal measure. In general 1QIsa^{b} tends to spell the Qal participle with *vav*, whereas the MT does not (note, however, פשעים in 1QIsa^{b} vs. פושעים in the MT at XX 6 [46:8]). In contrast, the MT tends to mark the feminine plural noun with *vav* noticeably more often than does 1QIsa^{b}. Otherwise, there are few patterns of differentiation. Instructive is the vacillation, for example, between לאמים followed by לאומ̊[ים] in 1QIsa^{b} vs. לאומים followed by לאמים in the MT at XXIV 3 (55:4), and between הם followed by המה in 1QIsa^{b} vs. המה followed by הם in the MT at XXVIII 7 (65:23-24).

---

[1] Weston W. Fields, *The Dead Sea Scrolls: A Short History* (Leiden: Brill, 2006), 109–11.

[2] Eleazar L. Sukenik, אוצר המגילות הגנוזות שבידי האוניברסיטה העברית (Jerusalem: Bialik Foundation and the Hebrew University, 1954); idem, *The Dead Sea Scrolls of the Hebrew University* (ed. Nahman Avigad and Yigael Yadin; Jerusalem: Hebrew University and Magnes Press, 1955). Seven more fragments of the same scroll were excavated from Cave 1, proving the provenance of the main scroll, and were published by Dominique Barthélemy, "8. Isaïe," in DJD 1:66–68 and Pl. XII.

TABLE 1: *Orthography*

Col. frg. line	Isaiah	1QIsa[b]	𝔐[L]	𝔐[q mss]
4 2	8:8 or 8:10?	עמנוא]ל	עמנו אל	
5 b 6	13:3	גברי	גבורי	
6 c-d 4	15:5	הלחׄית	הלוחית	
6 c-d 6	15:7	ישאום	ישאום	ישאֱם
7 c 1	19:7	יאר֯	יאור	
7 c 2	19:8	ביאר	ביאור	
8 c-e 7	22:15	בו֯א	בא	
8 c-e 9	22:17	גׄבור	גָּבֶר	
9 b-f 2	24:19	רוׄע	רעה	רוע
9 b-f 2	24:19	התרו[ע]עׄה	התרעעה	
9 b-f 3	24:20	והתנודׄא	והתנודדה	
11 a-c 1	28:15	יבאנו	יבואנו	
11 a-c 2	28:16	יוסד	יִסַּד	
11 d-e 7	29:5	עובר	עבר	
15 a-f 7	37:12	אב֯ת֯י	אבותי	
16 7	38:19	יודע	יודיע	
16 7	38:20	להשיעני	להושיעני	
16 15	39:3	ויבוא	ויבא	
16 18	39:4	[הר]א֯י֯ת֯םׄ	הראיתים	
16 18	39:4	ב֯אׄצׄרׄ◦◦◦	באוצרתי	
17 4	41:7	א֯[ומ]רׄ	אמר	
17 4	41:7	ט'ב	טוב	
17 18	41:19	ותשור	ותאשור	
17 18	41:19	יחדׄיׄוׄ	יחדו	
18 1	43:1	בוראך	בראך	
18 3	43:2	[ב]מואש	במו אש	
18 6	43:6	אומר	אמר	
18 7	43:6	ובנתיך	ובנותי	
18 8	43:7	ולכבד֯י	ולכבודי	
18 9	43:9	יחדיו	יחדו	
19 5	44:24	גואלך	גאלך	
19 5	44:24	ויוצרו]ך	ויצרך	
19 6	44:24	רוקע	רקע	
19 6	44:25	אתת	אתות	
19 6	44:25	וקוסמ]ים	וקסמים	
19 7	44:25	יסכל	ישׂכל	
19 8	44:26	האו֯מ֯ר	האמר	
19 8	44:26	תשב	תושב	
19 8	44:26	וחרבתיה	וחרבותיה	
19 9	44:27	הא[ו]מר	האמר	
19 9	44:28	האומׄ]ר	האמר	
19 10	44:28	ישלים	ישלם	
19 14	45:3	אוצרת	אוצרות	

Table 1: *Orthography (cont.)*

Col. frg. line	Isaiah	1QIsa^{b}	𝔐^{L}	𝔐$^{q\ mss}$
19 23	45:9	ליוצרוׄ	ליצרו	
19 24	45:10	ה]א֯ומר	אמר	
19 25	45:11	ויוצרו	ויצרו	
19 28	45:13	וגלתי֯	וגלותי	
20 1	46:4	אסבול	אסבל	
20 5	46:7	וינחה]ו	ויניחהו	
20 6	46:8	פשעים	פושעים	
20 11	46:12	הרחקים	הרחוקים	
20 27	47:11	שאה	שואה	
21 2	48:17	מדרכיך	מדריכך	
21 3	48:18	וׄלׄאׄ	לוא	
21 3	48:18	שלמך	שלומך	
21 7	48:21	צר	צור	
21 12	49:4	כלתי	כליתי	
21 12	49:5	יוצרי	יצרי	
21 17	49:7	גואל	גאל	
21 19	49:7	קדוש	קדש	
21 21	49:8	[ש]ממׄת	שממות	
21 23	49:10	מבע֯]י	מבועי	
22 13	51:4	ולאׄמׄי	ולאומי	ולאומים
22 17	51:6	כׄמוכן	כמו־כן	
22 18	51:7	יודעי	ידעי	
22 23	51:11	ופדויׄ	ופדויי	
23 1	52:8	י֯ח֯ד֯י֯ו֯	יחדו	
23 1	52:8	בׄשׄב	בשוב	
23 2	52:9	יחדיו	יחדו	
23 5	52:12	ובמנסה	ובמנוסה	
23 6	52:12	הולך	הלך	
23 7	52:14	משחת	משחת	מושחת
23 8	52:14	ותרו	ותארו	
23 12	53:3	וידע	וידוע	
23 15	53:5	מפשעי֯נ֯ו	מפשענו	
23 15	53:5	שלמנו	שלומנו	
23 17	53:7	לטבוח	לטבח	
23 23	53:11	יסבול	יסבל	
23 28	54:2	מתרי֯[ך]	מיתריך	
23 30	54:4	תבשי	תבושי	
23 30	54:4	תחפר[י]	תחפירי	
23 31	54:4	אלמנתך	אלמנותיך	
23 32	54:5	וגואלך	ונאלך	
24 2	55:3	דויד	דוד	
24 3	55:4	לאמים	לאומים	
24 3	55:4	לאומ֯[י]ם	לאמים	

TABLE 1: *Orthography (cont.)*

Col. frg. line	Isaiah	1QIsa^b	$\mathfrak{M}^{L}$	$\mathfrak{M}^{q\ mss}$
24 7	55:8	מחשבתי	מחשבותי	
24 17	56:2	שומר	שמר	
24 20	56:4	שבתתי	שבתותי	
24 21	56:5	ו֯ב֯חמתי	ובחומתי	
24 24	56:7	והביאתים	והביאותים	
24 24	56:7	עלתיהם	עולתיהם	
24 26	56:8	לנקבצו	לנקבציו	
24 28	56:10	יכלו	יוכלו	
24 29	56:11	והם	והמה	
24 30	56:12	אקח	אקחה	
24 33	57:2	מׄשכבתם	משכבותם	
24 33	57:2	הולך	הלך	
25 2	57:18	ואשלמה	ואשלם	
25 6	58:2	אתי	ואותי	
25 8	58:3	ראיתה	ראית	
25 9	58:3	עצבכם	עצביכם	
25 13	58:6	חרצבת	חרצבות	
25 13	58:6	אגדת	אגדות	
25 13	58:6	מטה	מוטה	
25 14	58:6	רצצים	רצוצים	
25 14	58:6	מטה	מוטה	
25 14	58:7	פרוס	פרס	
25 15	58:7	מרדים	מרודים	
25 15	58:7	ערום	ערם	
25 16	58:8	ארוכתך	וארכתך	
25 18	58:9	מטה	מוטה	
25 20	58:11	בצׄחצחת	בצחצחות	
25 20	58:11	ועצמתיך	ועצמתיך	ועצמתך
25 20	58:11	יחלצו	יחליץ	
25 22	58:12	גודר	גדר	
25 23	58:13	חפצך	חפציך	
25 24	58:13	דרכך	דרכיך	
25 25	58:14	במתי	במותי	במתי
25 27	59:2	מבדילים	מבדלים	
25 28	59:2	וחטאתיכם	וחטאותיכם	
25 29	59:3	ואצבעתיכם	ואצבעותיכם	
25 30	59:4	קורא	קרא	
25 31	59:5	בצי	ביצי	
25 32	59:5	האוכל	האכל	
25 32	59:5	מבציה֯ם	מביציהם	
25 34	59:7	מחשבתי[הם]	מחשבותיהם	
26 5	60:2	וכבדו	וכבודו	
26 8	60:5	תראי	תראי	תיראי

TABLE 1: *Orthography (concl.)*

Col. frg. line	Isaiah	1QIsa^b	$\mathfrak{M}^{L}$	$\mathfrak{M}^{q\ mss}$
26 9	60:5	יבוא	יבאו	
26 10	60:6	ולבנה	ולבונה	
26 12	60:8	תעפינה	תעופינה	
26 15	60:10	וברצני	וברצוני	
26 18	60:12	חרוב	חרב	
26 19	60:13	בראש	ברוש	
26 19	60:13	יחדיו	יחדו	
26 24	60:16	וגואלך	וגאלך	
26 27	60:18	בגבולך	בגבוליך	
26 28	60:18	חמ[ת]יׄך	חומתיך	
26 30	60:21	מטעיו	מטעו	מטעי
26 34	61:1	]פׄקחקח	פקח קוח	פקחקוח
27 2	62:3	מלכה	מלוכה	
27 4	62:6	חמׄתׄיׄך	חומתיך	
27 5	62:6	המזׄכׄיׄרׄ]ים	המזכרים	
27 7	62:9	בחצרת	בחצרות	
27 12	63:2	כדורך	כדרך	
27 14	63:5	ואשתוממה	ואשתומם	
27 15	63:6	ואשכירם	ואשכרם	
27 15	63:6	וארידה	ואוריד	
27 16	63:7	תהלות	תהלת	
28 6	65:23	יגעו	ייגעו	
28 6	65:23	ברכי	ברוכי	
28 7	65:23	הם	המה	
28 7	65:24	המה	הם	
28 10	66:1	איזה	אי־זה	
28 10	66:1	ואיזה	ואי־זה	
28 10	66:1	מנחתי	מנוחתי	
28 11	66:2	ונכאה	ונכה	ונכא
28 11	66:3	עורף	ערף	
28 13	66:4	ו]במגרתם	ומגורתם	
28 21	66:12	נוטׄ]ה	נטה	

II. INDIVIDUAL TEXTUAL VARIANTS

In addition to those 161 orthographic differences, there is a total of 622 textual variants in 1QIsa^b against other Hebrew manuscripts or the LXX. Some variants consist of several words, thus increasing the number of variant words. The full list is provided in the 1QIsa^b edition, and a brief analysis is offered here.

Many of the variants between 1QIsa^b and MT^{L, q, mss, Cairo} are very minor, involving little change of meaning; but it may prove helpful to select those that show the upper range of variation. Generally not listed below are: the presence vs. the lack of the definite article, copulative, or common words such as כי or כה; routine palaeographic confusion of letters such as כ/ב, ר/ד, י/ו; phonological confusion of א/ע, ה/ח, ע/ח; minor differences in verbal form; or differences in vocalization.

There are only two quantitatively large variants between 1QIsa^{b} and the MT. Although it is possible that both are long additions in the text inherited by 1QIsa^{a}, MT, and LXX, they are quite probably instances of simple parablepsis in 1QIsa^{b} (see similar parablepses in MT^{L}, e.g., at Josh 21:36-37 and 1 Sam 14:41):

38:12-13 om v 13 1QIsa^{b}] hab 1QIsa^{a} 𝔐 𝔊 (תשלימני[12]⋂תשלימני[13]? or add?)
60:19-20 לאור עולם ושלמו 1QIsa^{b}] לאור עולם ואלוהיך לתפארתך [20]לוא יבוא שמשך וירחך לוא יאסף כיא יהוה יהיה לך לאור עולם ושלמו 1QIsa^{a} 𝔐(... כי ... לא ... [20]לא יבוא עוד ... ואלהיך)
(לאור עולם⋂לאור עולם? or add?)

Different names for God are used:

22:15 אדני 1QIsa^{b} 1QIsa^{a}(אדוני) 𝔐^{L}] > 𝔐^{mss} 𝔊 θ′ 𝔖
38:14 י]הֿוה חשקה 1QIsa^{b} 𝔊(πρὸς τὸν κύριον ὅς ἐξείλατό με)] אדוני עושקה 1QIsa^{a}; אדני עָשְׁקָה 𝔐^{L} (cf v 17)
38:19 אלה 1QIsa^{b}] אל 1QIsa^{a*}; אלוה 1QIsa$^{a\ dittog\ 2m}$; אֶל 𝔐^{L}
49:7 אדני 1QIsa^{b} 1QIsa^{a}(אדוני)] > 𝔐
57:21 אלה]י 1QIsa^{b} 1QIsa^{a}(אלוהי) 𝔐^{L}] יהוה 𝔐^{mss}; κύριος ὁ θεός 𝔊; ὁ θεός 𝔊^{mss}
61:1 יה]וה אלהים 1QIsa^{b}] יהוה 1QIsa^{a} 𝔊(vid) 𝔙(vid); אֿד]ני יהוה 4QIsa^{m} 𝔐 𝔊^{Qmg}

Differences in meaning:

44:25 יסכל 1QIsa^{b} 1QIsa^{a} 4QIsa^{b} 𝔊(μωρεύων)] ישׂכל 𝔐 (err)
48:17 מדרכיך 1QIsa^{b}] הדריכה 1QIsa^{a}; מדריכך 4QIsa^{d} 𝔐 𝔗 𝔖 𝔙
51:4 עמי 1QIsa^{b} 1QIsa^{a} 𝔐^{L} 𝔊] עמים 𝔐^{mss} 𝔖
51:4 ולאֿמֿי 1QIsa^{b} 1QIsa^{a}(ולא˚מי) 𝔐^{L}(ולאומי)] ולאומים 𝔐^{mss} 𝔖; καὶ οἱ βασιλεῖς 𝔊
58:14 והרכֿיבך 1QIsa^{b} 1QIsa^{a}(-כה) 4QIsa^{n}(ו]הֿרכבךֿ) 𝔗(וישרינך) 𝔊(καὶ ἀναβιβάσει σε)] והרכבתיך 𝔐 θ′
59:4 בטחו ... ודברו ... הרו ... והולידו 1QIsa^{b} 𝔊 (3 pl)] בטחו ... ודבר ... הרוה ... והולידו 1QIsa^{a};
בטוח ... ודבר ... הרו ... והוליד 𝔐 (inf abs)
60:5 תראי 1QIsa^{b} 1QIsa^{a} 𝔐^{L} 𝔊(ὄψῃ)] תיראי 𝔐^{mss} (orth or √ ירא?; see ופחד two words later)

Parallel words are substituted:

49:6 להש]יֿב 1QIsa^{b} (cf v 6aβ)] להֿקים 1QIsa^{a}; להֿקים 4QIsa^{d} 𝔐 (see NOTE)
52:9 ירושלם 2° 1QIsa^{b} 𝔐^{L} 𝔊] ישראל 𝔐^{mss}
58:10 נפשך 1QIsa^{b} 1QIsa^{a}(נפשכה) 𝔐^{L}] לחמך 𝔐^{mss} 𝔖; τὸν ἄρτον ἐκ ψυχῆς σου 𝔊
60:4 תנשינה 1QIsa^{b} 𝔊(ἀρθήσονται)] תאמנה 1QIsa^{a} 𝔐
62:8 עזו 1QIsa^{b} 1QIsa^{a}(עוזו) 𝔐 𝔊] קדשו 𝔗
63:5 איש 1QIsa^{b}] עוזר 1QIsa^{a} 𝔐(עזר) 𝔊(βοηθός)

Words are added or lost:

49:3 ישראל 1QIsa^{b} 1QIsa^{a} 4QIsa^{d} 𝔐 𝔊] > 𝔐^{ms}
52:11 תגעו 1QIsa^{b}] + צאו מתוכה 1QIsa^{a} 𝔐 𝔊
53:4 ומכא בינו 1QIsa^{b} 1QIsa^{a}(ומכאובינו) 𝔐^{L}] + הוא 𝔐^{mss} 𝔖 𝔙
53:11 אור 1QIsa^{b} 1QIsa^{a} 4QIsa^{d}(אֿו]ר) 𝔊 (add?)] > 𝔐 (יראה = err for ירוה || ישבע?)
55:5 אשר [ל]אֿ 1QIsa^{b}] לוא 1QIsa^{a} 4QIsa^{c}(לֿ]ו]אֿ) 𝔐(לא)
56:8 לנקבצו 1QIsa^{b}] עליו לנקבציו 1QIsa^{a} 𝔐; ἐπ’ αὐτὸν συναγωγήν 𝔊
59:2 כי 1QIsa^{b}] כיא אם 1QIsa^{a} 𝔐(כי אם)
60:7 רֿצון 1QIsa^{b}] לרצון על 1QIsa^{a} 𝔐^{mss} 𝔊 𝔖 𝔗; על רצון 𝔐^{L}
60:14 כל 1° 1QIsa^{b} 1QIsa^{a}(כול)] > 𝔐 𝔊

60:21 ארץ 1QIsa^{b} 𝔐^{ms}] + נצר 1QIsa^{a} 4QIsa^{m}(נצ]ר̊) 𝔐^{L}(נֵצֶר); + φυλάσσων (= נֹצֵר) 𝔊
62:6 הל]י̊לה 1QIsa^{b} 1QIsa^{a}] + תמיד 𝔐 𝔊
62:7 ע̇]ד ישי]ם 1QIsa^{b}] עד יכין ועד יכונן ועד ישים 1QIsa^{a}; עד יכונן ועד ישים 𝔐 𝔊
62:8 ב̇]ימ̊ין 1QIsa^{b}] בימינו ובזרוע 1QIsa^{a} 𝔐 𝔊
66:19 מ]שכי [ק̊שת 1QIsa^{b} 𝔐^{L}] משוך] [קשת 1QIsa^{a}; > קשת 𝔐^{ms}; καὶ Μοσοχ 𝔊

Transpositions:

38:19 ה]י]ו̇ם כמוני 1QIsa^{b}] כמוני היום 1QIsa^{a*} 1QIsa$^{a\ dittog\ 2m}$ 𝔐 𝔊(vid)
52:13 וגבה/ונשא 1QIsa^{b}] tr 1QIsa^{a} 𝔐; καὶ δοξασθήσεται 𝔊
55:8 מ̊]חשבת]יכ̊ם מחשבתי 1QIsa^{b}] מחשבותי מחשבותיכם 1QIsa^{a} 𝔐 𝔊(αἱ βουλαί μου ὥσπερ αἱ βουλαὶ ὑμῶν)
57:20 נר̊ג̊]ש ?] 1QIsa^{b}] נגרשו 1QIsa^{a}; נגרש 𝔐
62:8 עוד א̊ת̊ ד̊גנך 1QIsa^{b}] עוד דגנך 1QIsa^{a}; את דגנך עוד 𝔐; ἔτι ... τὸν σῖτόν σου 𝔊

Differences in pronoun:

13:19 ממלכתו 1QIsa^{b}] ממלכת 1QIsa^{a}; ממלכות 𝔐; ὑπὸ βασιλέως 𝔊
43:6 הביא]ו ב]ניך ... ובנתיך 1QIsa^{b}] הביאו בני ... ובנותי 1QIsa^{a}; הביאי בני ... ובנותי 𝔐 𝔊
43:10 ו]א̊חריו לא יהיה 1QIsa^{b}] ואחרי לוא היה 1QIsa^{a}; ואחרי לא יהיה 𝔐 𝔊
46:11 עצתי 1QIsa^{b} 𝔐^{q}; βεβούλευμαι 𝔊] עצתו 1QIsa^{a} 4QIsa^{d}(עצת̇ו) 𝔐^{L}
53:12 ולפשעיהם 1QIsa^{b} 1QIsa^{a}(-יהמה) 4QIsa^{d}(-יה]ם) 𝔊] -עים 𝔐 σʹ
58:5 ראשך 1QIsa^{b}] רואשו 1QIsa^{a} 𝔐(ראשו); τὸν τράχηλόν σου 𝔊
60:21 מטעיו 1QIsa^{b}] מטעי יהוה 1QIsa^{a}; מטעי 𝔐^{q}(cf ℭ 𝔖 𝔙); מטעו 𝔐^{L}; τὸ φύτευμα 𝔊
62:7 לכם 1QIsa^{b}] לו 1QIsa^{a} 𝔐

Differences in preposition:

55:5 וקדוש 1QIsa^{b} 1QIsa^{a*}] ו^{ל}קדוש 1QIsa$^{a\ corr\ 1m}$ 𝔐(ולק׳)
58:4 ולמצה 1QIsa^{b} 1QIsa^{a}(-צא)] ומצה 𝔐
59:2 ובין 1QIsa^{b}] לבין 1QIsa^{a} 𝔐
62:10 אבן 1QIsa^{b}] מאבן הנגף 1QIsa^{a}; מאבן 𝔐
65:20 שם 1QIsa^{b}] משמה 1QIsa^{a}; משם 𝔐
66:4 ו]במגרתם 1QIsa^{b} 1QIsa^{a}(ובמגורותיהםה)] ומגורתם 𝔐; καὶ τὰς ἁμαρτίας 𝔊

Singular vs. plural:

26:2 ויבאו 1QIsa^{b}] ויב(ו)א 1QIsa^{a} 𝔐
43:9 יגידו 1QIsa^{b}] ויגידו 1QIsa^{a}; יגיד 𝔐 𝔊(ἀναγγελεῖ)
53:8 לקחו 1QIsa^{b}] לוקח 1QIsa^{a} 𝔐(לקח) 𝔊
53:12 חטא]י 1QIsa^{b} 1QIsa^{a} 4QIsa^{d} 𝔊] חֵטְא 𝔐; חובין ℭ
54:3 יירשו 1QIsa^{b} 1QIsa^{a}] יירש 𝔐
57:2 יבו]א̊ו 1QIsa^{b}] ויבוא 1QIsa^{a}; יבוא 𝔐; ἔσται 𝔊
58:3 נפשתינו 1QIsa^{b} 1QIsa^{a}(נפשותינו) 𝔊] נפשנו 𝔐
58:11 יחלצו 1QIsa^{b} 1QIsa^{a}(יחליצו)] יחליץ 𝔐
59:21 י̊מ̊]ו[ש 1QIsa^{b}] ימושו 1QIsa^{a} 𝔐; ἐκλίπῃ 𝔊
60:5 יבוא 1QIsa^{b} 𝔙] יבואו 1QIsa^{a} 𝔐(יבאו); καὶ ἥξουσί 𝔊

Masculine vs. feminine:

26:1 השירה הזאת 1QIsa^{b}] השיר הזואת 1QIsa^{a}; השיר ה̊ז[4QIsa^{c}; השיר הזה 𝔐
29:3 מ]צ̊בה̇ 1QIsa^{b}] מצב 1QIsa^{a} 𝔐
53:3 מכאבים 1QIsa^{b}] מכאובות 1QIsa^{a} 𝔐(מכאבות)
66:17 אחר אח]ת 1QIsa^{b} 1QIsa^{a} 𝔐$^{q\ mss}$] אחר אחד 𝔐^{L}; > 𝔊

One example of the complexity of manuscript transmission and the growth and multiplication of errors can be seen in the variant at 53:11 listed under "Words are added or lost" above:

53:11 אור 1QIsa^b 1QIsa^a 4QIsa^d(א̊ו[ר]) 𝔊 (add?) **]** > 𝔐 (יראה = err for ירוה || ישבע?)

The MT reads מעמל נפשו יראה ישבע בדעתו ("out of his anguish he shall *see*; he shall find satisfaction with his knowledge"), whereas, surprisingly, 1QIsa^b agrees with 1QIsa^a, 4QIsa^d, and the LXX in reading מעמל נפשו יראה אור יש[בע בדעתו] (". . . he shall see *light*").[3] In light of the 1QIsa^b reading, one's immediate judgment might be that the MT has simply lost the word אור, and this could be supported by the fact that ראה ("see") virtually never occurs without a direct object. On the other hand, one might be suspicious of יראה אור as a *lectio facilior*.

Bible translations and commentators offer their interpretations, most, quite understandably, apparently attempting to stay with the preserved textual evidence:

JPS	Out of his anguish he shall see it [i.e., "the arm of the LORD"]; he shall enjoy it to the full. . . .
NRSV	Out of his anguish he shall see light; he shall find satisfaction. . . .
NAB/RE	Because of his anguish he shall see the light; . . . he shall be content.
Baltzer	After the trouble of his life he shall see light and be satisfied.[4]
Barthélemy	Emergeant de ce qu'il a souffert, il verra la lumière, il s'en rassasiera.[5]
Blenkinsopp	After his painful life he will see light and be satisfied.
Paul	Because of his anguish he shall be sated and saturated with light.[6]

The Jewish Publication Society translates the MT (without אור), whereas most others choose to include "light." Examination of the context reveals that the form יראה also occurs in the previous verse, that in this poem the parallel to יראה is ישבע, and that the LXX, though reading φῶς, divides the verses differently and interprets יראה as a Hiphil. These various problems, especially the poetic parallelism, have led some scholars (see Paul's translation and *BHS* n. 11^a) to suggest רוה in place of ראה. The word רוה ("be filled, refreshed") is used several other times in Isaiah (34:5, 7; 43:24; 55;10), and, as Jer 31:14; 46:10 and Lam 3:15 indicate, it would be the expected parallel to שבע ("be sated, satisfied"). A final clue is that 1QIsa^a makes the identical error in 34:5, writing תראה for רותה.[7] Thus, it appears that the original text was מעמל נפשו ירוה ישבע בדעתו; that no manuscript survives to attest it; that an early form of the MT erred with the *lectio facilior* יראה

[3] Note that the OG should read πλῆσαι ("fill"), not πλάσαι ("form, mold") as in Ziegler's edition. No Greek manuscript preserves πλῆσαι, since it seems that πλάσαι infested the entire LXX transmission at an early stage; but Aquila and Theodotion attest ἐμπλησθήσεται.

[4] Klaus Baltzer, *Deutero-Isaiah: A Commentary on Isaiah 40–55* (Hermeneia; trans. Margaret Kohl; ed. Peter Machinist; Minneapolis: Fortress, 2001), 393; his full translation is: "After [or 'because of'?] the trouble/anguish of his life/soul he shall see <light> < and> be satisfied."

[5] Dominique Barthélemy chooses this conclusion even though he notes that a scholar as early as Cappel suggested a "glissment" from רוה to ראה: *Critique textuelle de l'Ancien Testament: 2. Isaïe, Jérémie, Lamentations* (Fribourg: Éditions Universitaires; Göttingen: Vandenhoeck & Ruprecht, 1986), 405.

[6] Shalom M. Paul, *Isaiah 40–66: Translation and Commentary* (Grand Rapids: Eerdmans, 2012), 412.

[7] Paul (*Isaiah 40–66*, 412) adduces two other instances in which ראה appears in place of רוה: Ps 91:16 and Job 10:15.

(possibly influenced by יראה in v. 10); and that most manuscript traditions filled in a suitable object, אור (cf. 9:1; 44:16; and יהוה אורי Ps 27:1).

Viewing the 1QIsa^{b} variants in general, it seems that the two extensive variants between 1QIsa^{b} and the MT (38:12-13 and 60:19-20) are due to accidental parablepsis and thus are textually meaningless. On that assumption, the remaining variants indicate that 1QIsa^{b} is a close member of the Masoretic text family. Most of the variants between 1QIsa^{b} and MT^{L} mirror the frequent minor disagreements between MT^{L}, MT^{q}, and MT^{mss} in degree and in kind. This conclusion is corroborated by the following section.

III. Isolated Insertions

1QIsa^{b} does not preserve any major isolated insertions compared with other members of the MT tradition, although the composite Masoretic tradition does contain at least nine such insertions as compared with 1QIsa^{a} and the OG (see Ch. 7). The fragments of 1QIsa^{b} are extant for only three of those passages and they contain all three insertions; thus the original manuscript presumably contained the others as well. With respect to literary editions, all ancient Hebrew manuscripts as well as the OG translation witness to a single edition of the book of Isaiah. That is, even though the book of Isaiah developed through a series of major new editions (the traditions of Isaiah of Jerusalem, plus the parallel from 2 Kings, plus Second-Third Isaiah) and attracted countless smaller interpretive expansions as it was transmitted, all the manuscript witnesses exhibit the final edition of the book, despite the great amount of individual textual variants.

Conclusion

Among the witnesses to that final edition there are quite divergent family groupings. 1QIsa^{a} and the LXX display enough textual variation between themselves and against 1QIsa^{b} that each should be classified as belonging to different text families within the single literary edition. A general assessment of the textual character of 1QIsa^{b} relative to 1QIsa^{a} can be seen in DJD 32, 2:88-92, which compares 1QIsa^{a} to 1QIsa^{b} and the MT.

On the whole, 1QIsa^{b} shows close agreement with MT^{L}, MT^{q}, MT^{mss}, and MT^{Cairo} in orthographic profile, in minor textual variants, and in isolated insertions. This classifies it as belonging to the textual group that eventually emerges as the Masoretic family. That is, from among the Isaiah texts circulating in the late Second Temple period, 1QIsa^{b} is one ancient witness, fortuitously preserved, to that form of text which continued to be copied carefully by the Rabbis and future scribes from antiquity through the Middle Ages and which eventually appeared with minimal variation in the surviving Masoretic witnesses. Nonetheless, 1QIsa^{b} does exhibit 183 textual variants (in addition to the 161 differences in orthography) from other preserved witnesses to the Masoretic family. Thus, previous descriptions of the closeness of 1QIsa^{b} to the MT are both correct and now able to be articulated with more precision.

CHAPTER 9

ADDITIONS AND EDITIONS IN JEREMIAH

1QISA^A AND THE OG of Isaiah, as we have seen, have highlighted nine large intentional insertions into the MT of Isaiah, and manuscripts of Exodus, Numbers, and Joshua have exhibited variant editions of their respective books. Since the MT form of Jeremiah is about sixteen percent longer than the text transmitted in the LXX, suspicions may be raised that the MT of Jeremiah may also show intentional insertions or variant editions.[1]

In fact, the book of Jeremiah itself tells us that it grew by stages (36:4-26, 32; 45:1). Analysis by modern scholars reaches similar results: for example, the well-known A source (the poetic sayings of the prophet), B source (the historical and biographical materials), and C source (the deuteronomistic layer of the book). The Qumran scrolls also now provide documentation for two examples of the developmental growth of the book.

I. INSERTION IN 4QJER^A

4QJer^a is one of the oldest manuscripts among the scrolls, palaeographically dated to approximately 200 B.C.E.[2] It generally presents a text form very close to the MT.[3] One of the more intriguing features of this manuscript is a lengthy insertion of Jer 7:30–8:3 by a later hand (4QJer^a 2m) between chapters 7 and 8 as penned by the original scribe (see TABLES 1–2).[4] The insertion is in a Hasmonaean script (ca. 100–50 B.C.E.), so roughly a century or more later than the original manuscript. Emanuel Tov, the editor of 4QJer^a, describes it thus:

> The first scribe wrote an incomplete line (III 3) in this column [line 6 in the reconstruction of column III], indicating an open paragraph, and this space enabled the corrector to add the long text, in three lines of small writing, similar to col. XXVIII of 1QIsa^a. Since this space did not suffice for the omitted text, the scribe continued to write vertically in the margin between this and

[1] Section II. below will argue that the OG presents an early edition and the MT a secondary, expanded edition; see William McKane, *A Critical and Exegetical Commentary on Jeremiah* (2 vols.; ICC; Edinburgh: T&T Clark, 1986), 1:xv–xxvii; William L. Holladay, *Jeremiah 2* (Hermeneia; Philadelphia: Fortress, 1989), 2–4. Defending the opposite position is Jack R. Lundblom, *Jeremiah 1–20* (AB 21A; New York: Doubleday, 1999); *Jeremiah 26–36* (AB 21B; New York: Doubleday, 2004); *Jeremiah 37–52* (AB 21C; New York: Doubleday, 2004). There are, of course, many small-scale exceptions to the general overview, and both editions have acquired subsequent developments.

[2] See Frank Moore Cross, "Palaeography and the Dead Sea Scrolls," in *The Dead Sea Scrolls after Fifty Years*, 1:379–402 and Pl. 8–14, esp. Pl. 9, Line 5; and similarly Ada Yardeni, "The Palaeography of 4QJer^a: A Comparative Study," *Textus* 15 (1991): 233–68, esp. 268.

[3] For the edition of 4QJer^a see Emanuel Tov, "70. 4QJer^a," DJD 15:145–70.

[4] Tov, DJD 15:155 and Plate XXIV. I thank Dr. Catherine Murphy for her computer production of p. 155 in DJD 15, reproduced here.

TABLE 1: *Jer 7:28–9:2* *4QJer^a, col. III*

1 [היום הזה ואשלח אליכם את כל עבדי הנביאים יום השכם ושלח 26ולוא שמעו אלי]

2 [ולא הטו את אזנם ויקשו את ערפם הרעו מאבותם 27ודברת אליהם את כל הדברים]

3 [האלה ולא ישמעו אליך וקראת אליהם ולא יענוכה 28ואמרת אליהם זה]הג̇[וי אשר] f.3

4 [לוא שמעו בקול יהוה אלהיו ולא לקחו מוסר אבדה האמונה ו]נ̇כרתה מפ̇[יהם]

5 [*vacat* 29גזי נזרך והשליכי ושאי על שפים קינ]ה̇ כי מאס f.4

6a [30כי עשו בני יהודה הרע בעיני נא]ם̇ יהוה שמו שקוציהם ב̇[בית אש]ר̇

6 [יהוה ויטש את דור עברתו *vacat* נקרא שמי עליו לטמאו *vac?* 31ובנ]ו̇ במות התפת אשר בגיא

6b [בן הנם לשרף את בניהם ואת בנת]יהם באש אשר לא צויתי

7 **8** [4ואמרת אליהם כה אמר יהוה היפלו ולא יקומו אם ישוב 5מדוע שוב]בה העם הזה

8 [ירושלם משבה נצחת החזיקו בתרמית מאנו לשוב *vacat* 6]הקשבתי ואשמע

9 [לוא כן ידברו אין איש נחם על רעתו לאמר מה עשיתי כלה שב]ב̇מ̇רצתם כסוס

10 [שוטף במלחמה 7גם חסידה בשמים ידעה מועדיה ותר וסוס ו]ע̇גור ישמרו את

11 [עת באנה ועמי לא ידעו את משפט יהוה *vac[at*

12 [8איכה תאמרו חכמים אנחנו ותורת יהוה אתנו אכן הנ]ה לשק̇ר עשה עט שקר ספרים

13 [9הבשו חכמים חתו וילכדו הנה בדבר יהוה מאסו]וחכמת מ[ה ל]ה̇ם̇ *vacat*

14 [10לכן אתן את נשיהם לאחרים שדותיהם ליורשים כי]מ̇קטן וע̇ד̇ ג̇דול כלה בצע ב̇צ̇ע̇

15 [מנביא ועד כהן כלה עשה שקר 11וירפו א]ת̇[שבר בת]עמי על̇[נקלה לאמר שלום] f.5

16 [שלום ואין שלום 12הבשו כי תועב]ה גם בוש[עשו] לא יבשו והכלם ולא ידעו לכן יפלו]

17 [בנפלים בעת פקדתם יכשלו אמר יהוה *vacat*]

18 [13אסף אסיפם נאם יהוה אין ענבים בגפן ואין תאנים בתאנה והעלה נבל ואתן]

19 [להם יעברום 14על מה אנחנו ישבים האספו ונבוא אל ערי המבצר ונדמה שם כי]

20 [יהוה אלהינו הדמנו וישקנו מי ראש כי חטאנו ליהוה 15קוה לשלום ואין טוב]

21 [לעת מרפה והנה בעתה 16מדן נשמע נחרת סוסיו מקול מצהלות אביריו רעשה כל]

22 [הארץ ויבואו ויאכלו ארץ ומלואה עיר וישבי בה 17כי הנני משלח בכם נחשים]

23 [צפענים אשר אין להם לחש ונשכו אתכם נאם יהוה *vacat*]

24 [18מבליגיתי על]י̇[יגון עלי לבי דוי *vacat?* 19הנה קול שועת בת עמי מארץ] f.6

25 [מרחקים הי]הוה אין ב̇[ציון אם מלכה אין בה מדוע הכעסוני בפסליהם בהבלי נכר]

26 [20עבר קציר כלה קיץ ואנחנו לא נושענו 21על שבר בת עמי השברתי קדרתי שמה]

27 [החזקתני 22הצרי אין בגלעד אם רפא אין שם כי מדוע לא עלתה ארכת בת עמי]

28 **9** [23מי י]ת̇ן̇ ר̇א̇[שי מים ועיני מקור דמעה ואבכה יומם ולילה את חללי בת עמי 1מי] f.7

29 [י]ת̇נני במדבר̇[מלון ארחים ואעזבה את עמי ואלכה מאתם כי כלם מנאפים עצרת]

30 [ב]ג̇דים 2וידרכו א̇[ת לשונם קשתם שקר ולא לאמונה גברו בארץ כי מרעה אל]

31 רעה יצאו ואת̇י̇[לא ידעו נאם יהוה 3איש מרעהו השמרו ועל כל אח אל תבטחו]

bottom margin

6c [ול]א̇ עלתה על לבי [32 לכן הנ]ה ימים באים נאם יהוה ולא יאמר ע̇[וד התפת וגיא בן הנם כי אם גיא ההרגה וקברו בתפת מאין מקום 33 והיתה נבלת העם הזה למאכל לעוף השמים]

6d ולבהמת הא[ר]ץ וא̇[ין מח]ריד 34 והשבתי מערי יהודה ומ̇[חצות ירושלם קול ששון וקול שמחה קול חתן וקול כלה כי לחרבה תהיה הארץ 8:1 בעת ההיא נאם יהוה]

6e יוציאו את עצמות מלכי יהודה ואת עצמות שריו ואת [עצמות הכהנים ואת עצמות הנביאים ואת עצמות יושבי ירושלם מקבריהם 2 ושטחום לשמש ולירח ולכל צבא]

6f השמים אשר אהבום ואשר עבדום ואשר [הלכו אחריהם ואשר דרשום ואשר השתחוו להם ולא יאספו ולא יקברו לדמן על פני האדמה יהיו 3 ונבחר מות מחיים לכל השארית הנשארים]

6g [מן המשפחה הרעה הזאת בכל המקמות הנשארים אשר הדחתים שם נאם י]הוה צבאות

TABLE 2: *Jer 7:27–8:5 4QJer[a], col. III*

7 . . . [27]So you shall speak all these words to them, but they will not listen to you. You shall call to them, but they will not answer you. [28]You shall say to them: This is the nation that did not obey the voice of the LORD their God, and did not accept discipline; truth has perished; it is cut off from their lips.

[29]Cut off your hair and throw it away;
raise a lamentation on the bare heights,
for the LORD has rejected and forsaken
the generation that provoked his wrath.

[30]For the people of Judah have done evil in my sight, says the LORD; they have set their abominations in the house that is called by my name, defiling it. [31]And they go on building the high place of Topheth, which is in the valley of the son of Hinnom, to burn their sons and their daughters in the fire—which I did not command, nor did it come into my mind. [32]Therefore, the days are surely coming, says the LORD, when it will no more be called Topheth, or the valley of the son of Hinnom, but the valley of Slaughter: for they will bury in Topheth until there is no more room. [33]The corpses of this people will be food for the birds of the air, and for the animals of the earth; and no one will frighten them away. [34]And I will bring to an end the sound of mirth and gladness, the voice of the bride and bridegroom in the cities of Judah and in the streets of Jerusalem; for the land shall become a waste.
8 *[1]At that time, says the LORD, the bones of the kings of Judah, the bones of its officials, the bones of the priests, the bones of the prophets, and the bones of the inhabitants of Jerusalem shall be brought out of their tombs; [2]and they shall be spread before the sun and the moon and all the host of heaven, which they have loved and served, which they have followed, and which they have inquired of and worshiped; and they shall not be gathered or buried; they shall be like dung on the surface of the ground. [3]Death shall be preferred to life by all the remnant that remains of this evil family in all the places where I have driven them, says the LORD of hosts.*

[4]You shall say to them, Thus says the LORD:
When people fall, do they not get up again?
If they go astray, do they not turn back?
[5]Why then has this people turned away
in perpetual backsliding?

> the next column and, finally, the remaining text was written in the bottom margin, in inverted writing. . . .[5]

The question is whether the later insertion (printed in indented italics in TABLE 2) was an original part of the text that was accidentally skipped through parablepsis by the principal scribe and then restored a century or more later by a "corrector," or whether it was only a secondary passage simply added by a later scribe in the course of the growth of the tradition. Tov judiciously weighs both options for this omission-or-addition: "The possibility that a shorter text served as the *Vorlage* of 4QJer[a] should be considered, especially the possibility that 7:30–8:3 was lacking in the earlier text . . . [and] from a contextual point of view it is attractive to assume that this section was lacking in the *Vorlage* of the Jeremiah scroll. On the other hand, it "appears that the sole reason for this

[5] Tov, DJD 15:154.

omission was technical, a mere scribal error," and he eventually decides that "a technical solution such as parablepsis . . . seems more likely."[6]

Further examination of the context and the content, however, may turn the decision in the other direction. Both William McKane and William Holladay see multiple disjunctions throughout chapters 7 and 8,[7] and the presence of two prose paragraphs (7:30-34; 8:1-3) between poetic verses (7:29, which raises a lament because the Lord has rejected the people, and 8:4-5, which accuses the people of backsliding) raises suspicion. Moreover, a number of the words in the passages are strongly reminiscent of the deuteronomistic style that pervaded much of Second Temple Judaism, including and especially the book of Jeremiah.

When one considers how well, or not, the inserted section fits the context, many problems surface. Whereas divisions in the MT are marked with ס before 7:29 (not before 7:30), before 7:32, and after 8:3, literarily the elements of chapters 7–8 can be characterized thus:

7:1-28	a prose address of God to Jeremiah, pronouncing judgment against Judah
7:29	a poetic introductory command (fem. sing.) to raise a lamentation, for the Lord has rejected Judah
7:30-34	a prose passage: Judah has done evil, therefore their corpses will be devoured
8:1-3	a different but related prose passage threatening that the bones of all will be defiled
8:4–9:11	a poetic passage about the people failing to repent

McKane sees disjunctions between all of those sections: he does not think that v. 29 "integrates with the verses which precede it" or with the following verses, and he even questions whether 29b was originally linked with 29a. He sees 29a as a "snatch of poetry [that] has invited secondary exegetical elaboration: in v. 29b it has attracted an observation that Yahweh has rejected his people and in vv. 30-34 a speech by Yahweh to a third party in which he describes the abominable cultic practices. . . ." He sees 8:1-3 as "introduced by a formula . . . which elsewhere introduces prose units in the book of Jeremiah" and favors the "disengaging of 8.1-3 from 7.1-34," since it "introduces a new train of thought and is not intrinsically related to 7.30-34. . . ."[8]

Holladay similarly sees "a small tangle of interrelated textual, form-critical, and literary problems between vv 27 and 30" as well as "the necessity of separating vv 29-34 from 8:1-3," which in turn is separated from 8:4-13.[9]

When analyzing for deuteronomistic phraseology, we can begin by noting that Tov had already described the passage as "deuteronomistic,"[10] and by remembering the consensus view that deuteronomistic theology spread as one of the principal approaches to theology throughout the Second Temple period (as seen, e.g., in the prayer in Dan 9:4-19). Numerous key words in Jer 7:30–8:3, while not necessarily unique to DtrH, have strong echoes of deuteronomistic phraseology:

---

[6] Tov, DJD 15:152, 154.

[7] McKane, *Critical and Exegetical Commentary*, 1:176–77, 181–82; Holladay, *Jeremiah 1* (Hermeneia; Philadelphia: Fortress, 1986), 259, 265.

[8] McKane, *Critical and Exegetical Commentary*, 1:176–77, 181–82.

[9] Holladay, *Jeremiah 1*, 259, 265.

[10] Tov, DJD 15:152.

תפת (Jer 7:31, 32bis) occurs elsewhere only in the Dtr passage in 2 Kgs 23:10 (which similarly refers to offering sons and daughters by fire) and in the parallel in Jeremiah 19.[11]

שקוץ (Jer 7:30) occurs in Deut 29:17, three times each in 1 Kings and 2 Kings, and in four other loci in Jeremiah, though it also occurs once in 2 Chr 15:8 and in several prophetic texts.

נבלה (Jer 7:33) occurs frequently in Leviticus legislation, once in Ps 79:2, and twice each in Deuteronomy, Isaiah, and Ezekiel in varying contexts; but the entire verse 7:33 is virtually identical with the curse in Deut 28:26; see in addition the parallel Jer 19:7 as well as 16:4 and 34:20.

עצמות (Jer 8:1) occurs frequently, of course, but there is a similar concentration on the proper burial or defilement of "bones" in 2 Samuel 21, 1 Kings 13, and 2 Kings 23.

דמן (Jer 8:2) occurs only once in 2 Kings, three other times in Jeremiah, and once in Ps 83:10.

Thus, the passage is well characterized as deuteronomistic, but it does not seem possible to determine whether it is due to the principal deuteronomistic stratum of the book of Jeremiah or to a later Second Temple person imbued with the broadly influential theology inspired by the Deuteronomists' tradition.[12] Nothing specifically signals this passage as early or late, though the human sacrifice at Topheth and the reference to the bones of the kings may argue for an earlier date. But the question is less about the *date of composition* of this passage and more about the *date of its insertion* into the developing text of Jeremiah.

There do not appear to be any compelling reasons to consider 7:30–8:3 an integral part of the Jeremiah text here. In contrast, there are three opposing factors to consider: (1) The size of the parablepsis required for the skipping of the scribe's eye would have involved the unprecedented amount of approximately twelve lines of text;[13] (2) the poem in 8:4 flows logically after 7:29; and (3) despite the fact that the original scroll had been corrected early toward the proto-MT in many loci, it existed for over a century in a plausibly sound form without this passage. The more likely explanation in my view is that 7:30–8:3 is a later intentional insertion into what McKane terms the "rolling corpus" of prophetic oracles ascribed to Jeremiah.[14]

On the other hand the LXX presents a problem.[15] The entire preserved Greek manuscript tradition contains the passage, which indicates that it was part of the OG translation and thus derives from the Hebrew edition from which the OG was translated. If it was part of the original OG, the view that the short Hebrew edition behind the OG contained the passage while the longer edition seen in 4QJer^{a} and proto-MT did not requires explanation.

One solution lies in the combination of McKane's contextual view of a "rolling corpus" together with the distinction between different categories of textual variation,

---

[11] In accord with the dictionaries, the occurrences of תפת in Job 17:6 and Isa 30:13 are judged to be questionable.

[12] McKane (*Critical and Exegetical Commentary*, xliv) cautions that there is "a danger of making too much of comparisons of vocabulary in the prose of the book of Jeremiah, on the one hand, and the book of Deuteronomy and the Deuteronomistic historical literature on the other."

[13] To my knowledge, twelve lines of text is more than double the size of any other loss of text through parablepsis.

[14] McKane, *Critical and Exegetical Commentary*, l–li.

[15] I thank Joseph Riordan, S.J., for bringing this aspect to my attention. See his "Sin of Omission or Commission: An Insertion in 4QJer^{a}?" in *Gottes Wort im Menschenwort: Festschrift für Georg Fischer zum 60. Geburtstag* (ed. Dominik Markl, Simone Paganini, and Claudia Paganini; Frankfurt am Main: Peter Lang, 2014), 99–112.

namely large-scale edition versus isolated insertion. McKane concludes that "the book of Jeremiah has arrived at its extant form as a consequence of long and complicated processes of growth" and cautions that "there is a tendency to underestimate the untidy and desultory nature of the aggregation of material which comprises the book of Jeremiah."[16]

The evidence thus suggests that there were various oral "Jeremiah" sayings and traditions in circulation during the Second Temple period, many of which were in written texts but not necessarily all in every text tradition. Here specifically, the two passages 7:30-34 and 8:1-3 were in one tradition (the OG *Vorlage*), but not in all traditions (4QJer^{a}–proto-MT).

By around 200 B.C.E. there were two Hebrew editions: the OG *Vorlage* and the forerunner of the MT. Keeping in mind the distinction between a large-scale edition and an isolated insertion, the OG *Vorlage* had the earlier, short edition (edition $n + 1$) that the OG translated, but it also contained this pair of isolated insertions. The proto-MT tradition had the later, expanded edition (edition $n + 2$) that 4QJer^{a} copied, but (unless there was unusual parablepsis) it lacked (and therefore 4QJer^{a} lacked) the isolated insertion.

The OG *Vorlage* and the OG translation maintain their edition $n+1$ permanently. Quite early a correcting scribe (4QJer$^{a\ corr}$) makes a number of proto-MT corrections in 4QJer^{a} but importantly does not "correct" by adding this passage, indicating that it was not yet in the proto-MT. During the next century the proto-MT tradition subsequently picks up the extra passage and adds it as an isolated insertion while maintaining edition $n + 2$ in general. In the early or mid first century B.C.E. a much later scribe (4QJer$^{a\ 2m}$) inserts the passage into 4QJer^{a} based on proto-MT. Just as OG maintains edition $n + 1$ with the insertion, so too the final 4QJer^{a} and its basis, proto-MT, maintain edition $n + 2$ now somewhat further expanded with this isolated insertion.

This explanation is somewhat complex but, in light of the lengthy and complex process of the formation of the prophetic books in general, of McKane's cautions specifically regarding Jeremiah, and the fact that we have only a few of the many developing manuscripts from the Second Temple period, it is entirely plausible.

Another much simpler and also fully plausible explanation would be that, though the entire LXX tradition now includes the passage, it was not part of the OG but—like the passage in 4QJer$^{a\ 2m}$ itself and perhaps around the same time—was secondarily inserted to agree with a fuller proto-MT text; this is what occurred in the LXX at Ezek 36:23c-38 as shown by the short Greek Papyrus 967 and an OL manuscript (see Chs. 15 and 8 n. 3).

II. 4QJER^{B} AND AN EXPANDED EDITION IN THE MT

It is widely affirmed that the short OG of Jeremiah in contrast to the longer MT reveals a pair of variant editions. Emanuel Tov and Pierre-Maurice Bogaert have cogently described the editorial and exegetical aspects of the complete MT second edition.[17]

The single surviving fragment of 4QJer^{b} preserves only the ends of thirteen lines of text (see TABLES 3 and 4 for lines 4–8 with Jer 10:1-11), but reconstruction according to the demands of space indicates that for Jer 10:1-11 the scroll almost certainly agreed

---

[16] McKane, *Critical and Exegetical Commentary*, xlviii–xlix.

[17] Emanuel Tov, *The Greek and Hebrew Bible*, 363–84; Pierre-Maurice Bogaert, "Le livre de Jérémie en perspective: Les deux rédactions antiques selon les travaux en course," *RB* 101 (1994): 363–406.

TABLE 3: *Jer* 9:22–10:5a, 9, 5b, 11 *4QJer*^{b}

top margin?

Line	Ch.	Verses		Text
1			]	בח]כ֯מתו ואל֯ יתהל֯[ל]
2		(23)	]	משפ]ט֯ וצדקה בארץ כי
3		(24,25)	]	]ק֯צ֯ו֯צ֯י֯ פ֯א֯ה הישׁב[י]ם
4	10	(1,2)	]	] אל דרך הגוים
5		(3,4)	]	ובז]ה֯ב ייפהו במקבות
6		(5a,9)	]	]ת֯כלת וארגמן
7		(5b,11)	]	]י֯אבדו מן ארעא
8		(12,13)	]	מק]צה א֯ר֯ץ ברקים

Jer 9:22–10:5a, 9, 5b, 11-13 4QJer^{b} [reconstructed]

1 [[21]דבר כה נאם יהוה ונפלה נבלת האדם כדמן על פני השדה
וכעמיר מאחרי הקצר ואין מאסף [22]כה אמר יהוה אל יתהלל חכם בח]כ֯מתו ואל֯ יתהל֯[ל]

2 [הגבור בגבורתו אל יתהלל עשיר בעשרו [23]כי אם בזאת יתהלל
המתהלל השכל וידע אותי כי אני יהוה עשה חסד משפ]ט֯ וצדקה בארץ כי

3 [באלה חפצתי נאם יהוה [24]הנה ימים באים נאם יהוה ופקדתי על כל מול בערלה
[25]על מצרים ועל יהודה ועל אדום ועל בני עמון ועל מואב ועל כל]ק֯צ֯ו֯צ֯י֯ פ֯א֯ה הישׁב[י]ם

4 [במדבר כי כל הגוים ערלים וכל בית ישראל ערלי לב
10 [1]שמעו את הדבר אשר דבר יהוה עליכם בית ישראל [2]כה אמר יהוה] אל דרך הגוים

5 [אל תלמדו ומאתות השמים אל תחתו כי יחתו הגוים מהמה [3]כי חקות העמים
הבל הוא כי עץ מיער כרתו מעשה ידי חרש במעצד [4]בכסף ובז]ה֯ב ייפהו במקבות

6 [ובמסמרות יחזקום ולא יפיק [5a]כתמר מקשה המה לא ידברו
[9]כסף מרקע מתרשיש יובא וזהב מאופז וידי צורף מעשה חכמים כלם ?]ת֯כלת וארגמן

7 [לבושם [5b]נשוא ינשוא כי לא יצעדו אל תיראו מהם כי לא ירעו וגם היטיב אין אותם
[11]כדנה תאמרון להום אלהיא די שמיא וארקא לא עבדו]י֯אבדו מן ארעא

8 [ומן תחות שמיא אלה [12]עשה ארץ בכחו מכין תבל בחכמתו ובתבונתו נטה שמים
[13]לקול תתו המון מים בשמים ויעלה נשאים מק]צה א֯ר֯ץ ברקים

with the short OG against the MT. The OG text lacked vv. 6-8 and 10 as in the MT and also showed a different order of verses: vv. 5aα, 9, 5aβ-b.

Comparison of the short 4QJer^{b}-OG text in contrast to the long MT text shows a unified poem in 4QJer^{b}-OG ridiculing idols, in contrast to a composite poem with both ridicule of idols and praise of the Lord in the MT. The elements in the MT that are lacking in the 4QJer^{b}-OG form a coherent poem in praise of the Lord (in indented italics in TABLE 4) and are easily separable from the 4QJer^{b}-OG text. A strong argument against the originality of the longer text with praise of the Lord is the introduction to the passage: the poem of praise clearly does not fit as part of "the word that the LORD speaks against you, O house of Israel" (10:1). Note also the close parallel consisting of ridicule of

TABLE 4: *Jer* 10:1-5a, 9, 5b, 11 *4QJer*[b]

1Hear the word that the LORD speaks against you, O house of Israel.
2Thus says the LORD:
Do not learn the way of the nations,
or be dismayed at the signs of the heavens;
for the nations are dismayed at them.
3For the customs of the peoples are false:
a tree from the forest is cut down,
and worked with an ax by the hands of an artisan;
4they deck it with silver and gold;
they fasten it with hammer and nails
so that it cannot move.
5aα Their idols are like scarecrows in a cucumber field,
and they cannot speak;
9Beaten silver is brought from Tarshish,
and gold from Uphaz.
They are the work of the artisan and of the hands of the goldsmith;
their clothing is blue and purple;
they are all the product of skilled workers.
5aβthey have to be carried,
for they cannot walk.
Do not be afraid of them,
for they cannot do evil,
nor is it in them to do good.

> *6There is none like you, O LORD;*
> *you are great, and your name is great in might.*
> *7Who would not fear you, O King of the nations?*
> *For that is your due;*
> *among all the wise ones of the nations*
> *and in all their kingdoms*
> *there is no one like you.*
> *8They are both stupid and foolish;*
> *the instruction given by idols*
> *is no better than wood!*
> *10But the LORD is the true God;*
> *he is the living God and the everlasting King.*
> *At his wrath the earth quakes,*
> *and the nations cannot endure his indignation.*

11Thus shall you say to them:
The gods who did not make the heavens and the earth
shall perish from the earth and from under the heavens.

idols in Isa 44:9-20 which also is not broken by contrasting praise of the Lord.[18] It seems certain that the contrasting poem in praise of the Lord has been secondarily inserted into the original short poem ridiculing idols.

18 Note, however, the positive poem of praise in Isa 40:18-20 similar to Jer 10:6-8, 10 which includes, parallel to Jer 10:8, a brief comparison of God with idols.

4QJer^b thus demonstrates, by providing a Hebrew text which displays the short edition, that the OG is not responsible for a "shortening of the original text" but is a faithful translation of an alternate Hebrew text that was simply different from the MT.

III. Expanded Edition in the MT for Jer 27[34𝔊]:1-10

As an additional example of the larger variant edition by which the MT expands the short Hebrew edition on which the OG is based, we can present a comparative passage from Jer 27[34𝔊]:1-10 (see Table 5).

The edition in the MT is characterized by frequent additions sparked by a variety of categories, such as additional information, expanded titles of God and rulers, clarifications, aggrandizement, and so forth.

Table 5: *Variant Editions of Jeremiah for Jer 27[34𝔊]:1-10*

Later Edition in the MT	*Earlier Edition Reconstructed from the OG*
27:1 בראשית ממלכת יהויקם בן יאושיהו	27[34𝔊]:1
מלך יהודה היה הדבר הזה אל ירמיה	
מאת יהוה לאמר: [2]כה אמר יהוה	[2]כה אמר יהוה
אלי עשה לך מוסרות ומטות ונתתם על צוארך:	עשה לך מוסרות ומטות ונתתם על צוארך:
[3]ושלחתם אל מלך אדום ואל מלך מואב	[3]ושלחתם אל מלך אדום ואל מלך מואב
ואל מלך בני עמון ואל מלך צר ואל מלך צידון	ואל מלך בני עמו ואל מלך צר ואל מלך צידו
ביד מַלְאָכִים הבאים ירושלם אל צדקיהו מלך יהודה:	ביד מַלְאֲכֵיהֶם הבאים ירושלם אל צדקיהו מלך יהודה:
[4]וצוית אתם אל אדניהם לאמר כה אמר	[4]וצוית אתם אל אדניהם לאמר כה אמר
יהוה צבאות אלהי ישראל כה תאמרו אל אדניכם:	יהוה אלהי ישראל כה תאמרו אל אדניכם:
[5]אנכי עשיתי את הארץ את האדם ואת הבהמה	[5]אנכי עשיתי את הארץ
אשר על פני הארץ בכחי הגדול ובזרועי הנטויה	בכחי הגדול ובזרועי הנטויה
ונתתיה לאשר ישר בעיני:	ונתתיה לאשר ישר בעיני:
[6]ועתה אנכי נתתי את כל הארצות האלה	6 נתתי את הארץ
ביד נבוכדנאצר מלך בבל	ביד נבוכדנאצר מלך בבל
עבדי וגם את חית השדה נתתי לו לעבדו:	וגם את חית השדה לעבדו:
[7]ועבדו אתו כל הגוים ואת בנו ואת בן בנו	7
עד בא עת ארצו גם הוא ועבדו בו גוים רבים	
ומלכים גדלים: [8]והיה הגוי והממלכה	8 והגוי והממלכה
אשר לא יעבדו אתו את נבוכדנאצר מלך בבל	
ואת אשר לא יתן את צוארו בעל מלך בבל	אשר לא יתן את צוארו בעל מלך בבל
בחרב וברעב ובדבר אפקד	בחרב וברעב אפקד
על הגוי ההוא נאם יהוה עד תמי אתם בידו:	עליהם נאם יהוה עד תמי אתם בידו:
[9]ואתם אל תשמעו אל נביאיכם ואל קסמיכם	[9]ואתם אל תשמעו אל נביאיכם ואל קסמיכם
ואל חֲלֹמֹתֵיכֶם ואל ענניכם ואל כשפיכם אשר	ואל חֹלְמֵיכֶם ואל ענניכם ואל כשפיכם אשר
הם אמרים אליכם לאמר לא תעבדו את מלך בבל:	הם אמרים לא תעבדו את מלך בבל:
[10]כי שקר הם נבאים לכם למען הרחיק אתכם	[10]כי שקר הם נבאים לכם למען הרחיק אתכם
מעל אדמתכם והדחתי אתכם ואבדתם:	מעל אדמתכם:

A blatant example of an insertion that is incorrect is the introduction found in the MT in 27:1: "In the beginning of the reign of Jehoiakim. . . ." The later editor has also added other introductions at 7:1 and 16:1. Here, in contrast to the OG which has no historical introduction, he imports an introduction virtually identical to that found in Jeremiah 26. In that chapter the correct historical setting is the reign of Jehoiakim. In chapter 27, however, the setting is the reign of Zedekiah, as vv. 3 and 12 make clear.

An example of an incorrect individual variant is מַלְאָכִים MT for *מַלְאֲכֵיהֶם LXX in v. 3 (see *BHS* n. 3^{b}), as indicated by the unusual syntax and by the context, which mentions the kings of whom these are "their messengers who have come to Jerusalem."

In addition to making frequent predictable or routine expansions, the later editor also considered Nebuchadnezzar to be God's עבד, adding this word in v. 6 as he did also in 25:9 and 43:10, all of which are lacking from the OG edition.

Thus the OG of Jeremiah proves to be a faithful translation of a current alternate Hebrew edition of Jeremiah which was secondarily amplified and rearranged to form the edition transmitted in the traditional MT. Whatever "shortening" or "lengthening" that took place did so at the Hebrew level, not the Greek. It is important to remember the faithful character of the Greek translation, especially for those parts where no Hebrew testimony is available.

With this vindication of the Old Greek of Jeremiah, we can now turn to the Septuagint manuscripts found at Qumran.

CHAPTER 10

THE SEPTUAGINT SCROLLS

THE LESSONS GAINED from 4QJer^{b} in the previous chapter and the vindication of the OG as a faithful translation of its Hebrew source for that book suggest that an inquiry into any further lessons the Greek scrolls may provide might offer useful results. This chapter seeks to demonstrate that the scrolls have greatly enhanced our understanding of the Septuagint, and that the Septuagint has significantly enhanced our understanding of the scrolls.

The Septuagint (Greek numeral o′ = 70; Latin *Septuaginta* or LXX; 𝔊 in *BHS*/*BHQ*) is the collection of ancient Greek texts transmitted through the centuries, based on original translations of the sacred Hebrew books plus several additional compositions originally in Greek. The translations were made by a number of different Jewish translators over the course of the third, second, and perhaps early first centuries B.C.E. Some later, systematically revised versions for certain books or sections have been substituted for the originals, making the collection even more diverse.

The origin of the term can be traced to the legendary *Letter of Aristeas*, which narrates that seventy-two (or according to some traditions, seventy) scholars translated into Greek the five scrolls of the books of Moses brought from Jerusalem at the request of Ptolemy Philadelphus (285–247 B.C.E.). Rather quickly the tradition grew to embrace the translations of all the books of the Hebrew Bible, as well as translations of some Hebrew books excluded from the rabbinic Bible, and even certain sacred Jewish books originally composed in Greek. Thus, an excessively strict use of the term (since it has not been so used in the last 1800 years) denotes only the Pentateuch, whereas the broad and common use denotes the entire Greek version of the Jewish Scriptures, without regard to textual character, including the deuterocanonical or apocryphal books.

Thus, regarding terminology, the "Septuagint" generally refers to the Jewish Scriptures in Greek without specifying the precise form. More precisely, "the Old Greek" (OG) is used specifically to denote the original Greek translation, as opposed to later developments, revisions, or recensions. This can be either ideal or practical: ideally, it is the original Greek "text as it left the hand of the translator";[1] but practically, since the original is usually not preserved purely, it is the earliest Greek form recoverable through the surviving evidence. The Hebrew *Vorlage* used for the translation is sometimes close to the tradition inherited in the MT, sometimes quite different. 𝔊 or 𝔊^{ed} usually refers to the text presented in a critical edition, whereas 𝔊*, or "more original Greek," is sometimes used to distinguish a reading which a scholar thinks is more likely to have been

[1] Sidney Jellicoe, *The Septuagint and Modern Study* (Oxford: Clarendon, 1968), 1, 359; see also John W. Wevers, "Die Methode," in *Das Göttinger Septuaginta-Unternehmen* (ed. Robert Hanhart and John W. Wevers; Göttingen: Septuaginta-Unternehmen, 1977), 12–19, esp. 19.

original than the reading presented as $\mathfrak{G}^{ed}$. The terms for the various recensions will be discussed below.

The illumination between the scrolls and the LXX is reciprocal and multifaceted. On the one hand, several Greek scrolls were discovered in various caves, providing some of the earliest extant LXX manuscripts (alongside the second-century B.C.E. John Rylands papyrus of Deuteronomy), approximately four centuries earlier than our oldest surviving LXX codices, such as Vaticanus (fourth century C.E.), Alexandrinus and Sinaiticus (fifth century). Among other things, these scrolls thus confirm that the OG is pre-Christian, dating from at least the second century B.C.E.

On the other hand, certain Hebrew scrolls, at variance with the MT, proved to exhibit text forms similar to the Hebrew *Vorlage* from which the LXX had been translated. Moreover, it frequently happens that, though a particular scroll may not have been the exact form of Hebrew text from which the LXX was in the main translated, it may display individual readings that have influenced readings in the LXX text. In turn, the LXX, now generally exonerated and shown to be basically a faithful translation of one ancient Hebrew text form of each book, sometimes earlier than or superior to the MT, may be used to reconstruct the text of lacunae in the fragmentary scrolls.[2]

I. Analysis of the Septuagint Scrolls

Eight highly fragmentary manuscripts of the LXX, plus two LXX-like manuscripts, were among the texts found in Qumran Caves 4 and 7 and at Naḥal Ḥever.

4QLXXLev^a^ (4Q119; Rahlfs 801)[3]

Scraps from a Leviticus manuscript on leather dating from "the late second or the first century B.C.E." were found in Cave 4.[4] The handful of fragments can be pieced together to form a mostly vertical strip preserving the full height of a column containing Lev 26:2-16; about a third of the width of the column is preserved. The text is generally close to the manuscript tradition of LXX Leviticus, but it presents fifteen variants from the text presented in the Göttingen Greek critical edition. In general, this scroll appears to be a reasonably literal and quite faithful translation of a Hebrew *Vorlage* from which the text preserved in the MT varied only slightly, whereas the later LXX manuscript tradition shows occasional revision toward the MT tradition.

---

2 For judicious expositions of the possibilities and limitations of retroversion see Tov, *The Text-Critical Use of the Septuagint in Biblical Research* (2d ed.; Jerusalem: Simor, 1997); and Anneli Aejmelaeus, *On the Trail of the Septuagint Translators* (2d ed.; Leuven: Peeters, 2007).

3 The classic catalogue of Septuagintal manuscripts is Alfred Rahlfs and Detlef Fraenkel, *Verzeichnis der griechischen Handschriften des Alten Testaments* (Göttingen: Vandenhoeck & Ruprecht, 2004). For an updated version on the IOSCS website, see http://septuaginta-unternehmen.adw-goe.de/ .

4 Patrick W. Skehan quickly provided a preliminary publication of this manuscript in "The Qumran Manuscripts and Textual Criticism," in *Volume du congrès, Strasbourg 1956* (VTSup 4; Leiden: Brill, 1957), 148–60, esp. 157–60. The full publication of this and the other Cave 4 Greek manuscripts is in DJD 9:161–97, 219–42. The dates for the individual scrolls given in quotation marks are either from Peter J. Parsons' palaeographic descriptions in the General Introduction (DJD 9:7–13) or from the Introductions to the individual scrolls.

Comparison of 4QLXXLev^a with the critical text in the Göttingen edition of Leviticus raised some questions.[5] The first was its relation to the OG. Though in twenty-eight half-preserved lines it has fifteen readings different from those selected for $\mathfrak{G}^{ed}$, it nonetheless clearly exhibits the OG translation generally, with the two texts showing only routine, predictable variants. But were its readings closer than $\mathfrak{G}^{ed}$ to the original or secondary? Of the fifteen variants from $\mathfrak{G}^{ed}$ some have good support in the manuscript tradition, three are attested by only one or two other manuscripts, and seven are unique readings. Not one is an error, while some appear clearly preferable as the OG. None of these readings, however, was selected for the critical text in the Göttingen edition of Leviticus, even though the scroll is four centuries older and closer to the original than other LXX witnesses.

Though older is not necessarily better, and though for some of the variants priority cannot be determined, one especially could be judged OG. For לעם ("people") in Lev 26:12, the scroll has ἔθν[ος] ("people, nation"), against λαός ("people") in $\mathfrak{G}^{ed}$. With very few exceptions, both the LXX and the later recensions use λαός for עם when referring to the people Israel and ἔθνος for גוי ("nation") and for עם when referring to peoples other than Israel. One other time in Leviticus (Lev 19:16) the entire LXX tradition uses ἔθνος for Israel and that word is thus chosen for $\mathfrak{G}^{ed}$ (see also Gen 18:18; 46:3). Substitution of λαός in place of ἔθνος would be routine and expected, whereas substitution of ἔθνος in place of λαός is highly unlikely. Thus, the scroll's ἔθνος is probably the OG, and the Göttingen editor has now accepted it as well as some other readings of 4QLXXLev^a as superior candidates for the OG.[6]

4QpapLXXLev^b (4Q120; Rahlfs 802)

Nearly a hundred small fragments from a papyrus manuscript of Leviticus (DJD 9:167–86) were also found in Cave 4. The thirty-one fragments with identifiable text come from the first thirteen columns of the scroll and contain parts of Lev 1:11–6:5[5:24 LXX]. The scroll, which "could reasonably be assigned to the first century B.C.E.," exhibits only two important variants: First, ΙΑΩ occurs at Lev 4:27 (and probably again at 3:12) where the MT and SP have the Tetragrammaton and the later LXX tradition has κύριος. Second, for העלה ("burnt offering") at Lev 4:7, 10, 18 it attests κάρπωσις ("burnt offering") as opposed to the more frequent ὁλοκαύτωμα ("whole burnt offering") in $\mathfrak{G}^{BA}$ which was thus chosen for $\mathfrak{G}^{ed}$. Otherwise, it has only minor, routine variants.

Which form is closer to the OG and which is secondary? Neither ΙΑΩ nor κύριος occurs in 4QLXXLev^a or 4QLXXNum to help add light. Although the oldest papyrus apart from the scrolls, Rylands Greek Papyrus 458 (Rahlfs 957, second century B.C.E.),[7] does not contain the divine name, Papyrus Fouad 266 (Rahlfs 848, first century B.C.E.)

---

[5] Eugene Ulrich, "The Septuagint Manuscripts from Qumran: A Reappraisal of Their Value," *Septuagint, Scrolls and Cognate Writings* (ed. George J. Brooke and Barnabas Lindars; SBLSCS 33; Atlanta: Scholars Press, 1992), 49–80.

[6] John W. Wevers, *Notes on the Greek Text of Leviticus* (SBLSCS 44; Atlanta: Scholars Press, 1997), 439, 443; see also Leonard J. Greenspoon, "The Dead Sea Scrolls and the Greek Bible," in *The Dead Sea Scrolls after Fifty Years* (ed. P. W. Flint and J. C. VanderKam; Leiden: Brill, 1998), 101–27, esp. 109–110.

[7] C. H. Roberts, *Two Biblical Papyri in the John Rylands Library, Manchester* (Manchester: 1936), 47–62.

regularly writes the divine name with Hebrew letters in the Aramaic (square) script (יהוה).[8] Moreover, the Greek Minor Prophets scroll (8ḤevXII gr, mid-first century B.C.E. to mid-first century C.E.; see below) has the divine name in Palaeo-Hebrew characters (𐤉𐤄𐤅𐤄). In a masterful article Patrick Skehan, surveying the occurrences of the divine name in ancient Hebrew and Greek texts, traces the development of the writing of the divine name in the LXX: (1) IAΩ, (2) יהוה, (3) 𐤉𐤄𐤅𐤄, (4) κύριος.[9]

Albert Pietersma offers a learned and detailed, but not altogether convincing counter-argument, that κύριος was the OG usage. He acknowledges that "we have early, even pre-Christian, MS evidence for the tetragram [IAΩ] and no such MS evidence to the contrary"[10] (i.e., for κύριος). In addition to his argument's going against the evidence,[11] it is difficult to imagine a scribe introducing the not-to-be-pronounced divine name where the more reverent κύριος was already in the text. The scrolls even more than the MT and the SP show that there was widespread and frequent scribal replacing of יהוה with אדני, אלהים, אל, 𐤉𐤄𐤅𐤄, and even four dots, occurring in different manuscripts of the same era.[12] Thus, it is plausible that Skehan's four stages overlapped to a large degree; but IAΩ was undoubtedly very early, gradually dropping out, while κύριος began as a translation of the Hebrew substitute אדני and was gradually standardized throughout the LXX.[13]

Similarly, the scroll's use of κάρπωσις for העלה is probably OG, since ὁλοκαύτωμα became the routine word in the LXX and became the recensional standard for Theodotion and Aquila. Thus, at least for these two readings 4QpapLXXLev[b], just as 4QLXXLev[a], appears to be an earlier witness to the OG.[14]

4QLXXNum (4Q121; Rahlfs 803)

Fragments from a Numbers manuscript (DJD 9:187–94) dating from "the late first century B.C.E. or the early first century C.E.," contain text from Num 3:40–4:16 from

---

[8] William G. Waddell, "The Tetragrammaton in the LXX," *JTS* 45 (1944): 158–61.

[9] Patrick W. Skehan, "The Divine Name at Qumran, in the Masada Scroll, and in the Septuagint," *BIOSCS* 13 (1980): 14–44, esp. 28–29 and 34.

[10] Albert Pietersma, "Kyrios or Tetragram: A Renewed Quest for the Original Septuagint," in *De Septuaginta: Studies in Honour of John William Wevers on His Sixty-Fifth Birthday* (ed. A. Pietersma and C. Cox; Mississauga, Ontario: Benben Press, 1984), 85–101, esp. 88.

[11] Additional strong evidence for IAΩ as an early, and possibly the earliest, Greek rendering of the Tetragrammaton comes from the Aramaic Papyri from Elephantine. One letter in two drafts is published as TAD A4.7–8 in Bezalel Porten and Ada Yardeni, *Textbook of Aramaic Documents from Ancient Egypt* (Jerusalem: Hebrew University, Dept. of the History of the Jewish People, 1986); as AP 30–31 in Arthur E. Cowley, *Aramaic Papyri of the Fifth Century B.C.* (Oxford: Clarendon Press, 1923); and as B19–20 in Bezalel Porten et al., *The Elephantine Papyri in English: Three Millennia of Cross-Cultural Continuity and Change* (Documenta et monumenta Orientis antiqui 22; Leiden: Brill, 1996). The letter mentions "the Temple of YHW" (יהו = Greek IAY or IAΩ), and it is dated 407 B.C.E.

[12] For an educative example warranting great caution, see 1QIsa[a] col. III lines 20–25, where within six lines יהוה is marked with cancellation dots and replaced by אדוני once and replaced without dots by אדוני once again, whereas אדוני is marked with dots and replaced by יהוה once. For a scribe using four dots for the Tetragrammaton, see 4QSam[c], 1QS, and 4QTest, as well as that scribe's insertion into 1QIsa[a] at Isa 40:7-8.

[13] See similarly Emanuel Tov, *Textual Criticism*, 132, n. 218.

[14] See in agreement Tov, *Textual Criticism*, 132, nn. 217, 219.

three contiguous columns of a leather scroll.[15] There are seventeen variants in 4QLXXNum, thirteen of which are unique, only four finding support in other Greek manuscripts. Most are minor or ambiguous. Like 4QLXXLev^{a}, it does not preserve the divine name. Again, only one variant—where $\mathfrak{G}^{B}$ has an obvious error and 4QLXXNum has strong support from the manuscript tradition—is accepted in the Göttingen critical edition as the OG.

John Wevers, as editor of the Göttingen edition of the Pentateuch, and Patrick Skehan, as early editor of the Greek Cave 4 manuscripts, shared their work with each other. Whereas Wevers and the later Skehan viewed 4QLXXNum as representing a revision of the OG, Ulrich and the earlier Skehan viewed the scroll as an earlier form which the subsequent LXX tradition revised in some readings.

Most of the seventeen variants in 4QLXXNum offer no help in deciding the OG, but one does seem solid. At Num 3:40 Moses is commanded to take a census of the Israelites. 4QLXXNum has ἀρίθμησον ("to number, count") for פקד ("inspect, review") where $\mathfrak{G}^{ed}$ has ἐπισκέψαι ("inspect"). The title 'Αριθμοί ("Numbers") is apparently the original Greek title of the book, and the title surely derives from occurrences of the word in the text.[16]

Examination of the patterns in Hatch-Redpath[17] reveals that ἐπισκέπτειν became the standard equivalent for פקד for the recensionists Theodotion, Aquila, and Symmachus, while they used ἀριθμεῖν for מנה ("to count"). Thus, ἀρίθμησον, which more dynamically translates the meaning, is likely the OG, whereas ἐπισκέψαι is more likely the routine revision toward agreement with the MT.

The clues in these three Greek scrolls, four centuries earlier than most other witnesses, all point in the same direction: the scrolls are often closer witnesses to the OG than the text presented in the Göttingen editions.

4QLXXDeut (4Q122; Rahlfs 819)

Only five small fragments of this early- or mid-second century B.C.E. manuscript survive (DJD 9:195–97). The only clue to its identification as LXX Deuteronomy (Deut 11:4) is the lone word ἐρυθρᾶς for "Red" (Sea).[18]

The main value of this manuscript is its witness to the existence of the Greek Deuteronomy at Qumran and its ancient date in the early- or mid-second century B.C.E. Since LXX manuscripts of Exodus, Leviticus, Numbers, and Deuteronomy were at Qumran, it is safe to presume that LXX Genesis was represented as well. And the early date of 4QLXXDeut makes it vie with the Rylands Papyrus 458 of Deuteronomy for the oldest LXX manuscript extant.

---

[15] Skehan also included a partial publication of 4QLXXNum in "The Qumran Manuscripts," 155–57.

[16] H. B. Swete (*An Introduction to the Old Testament in Greek* [rev. ed. by R. R. Ottley; New York: Ktav, 1968], 214–15) considers the Greek titles "probably of Alexandrian origin and pre-Christian in use" and notes that some of them are used in Philo and the NT.

[17] Edwin Hatch and Henry A. Redpath, *A Concordance to the Septuagint and the Other Greek Versions of the Old Testament* with a "Hebrew/Aramaic Index to the Septuagint" by Takamitsu Muraoka (2d ed.; Grand Rapids: Baker, 1998).

[18] Ulrich, "The Greek Manuscripts of the Pentateuch from Qumran, Including Newly-Identified Fragments of Deuteronomy (4QLXXDeut)," in *De Septuaginta* (n. 10), 71–82.

7QpapLXXExod (7Q1; Rahlfs 805)

This pair of small papyrus fragments (DJD 3:142–43) containing text from Exodus 28:4-7 dates from around 100 B.C.E. Only nineteen words survive, of which fourteen are only partly preserved, while the five complete words are: καί/"and" (twice), τό/"the" (twice), and χρυσίον/"gold" (once). This last, together with κόκκι[νον]/"scarlet" and the remaining letters, is sufficient to identify the text. The small amount of text is basically the OG with a few minor, insignificant variants.

The editor of this papyrus of Exodus, Maurice Baillet, characterizes it as "in general closer to the MT than to the LXX," agreeing several times with the Greek manuscripts c and m.[19] The conclusion, however, that 7QpapLXXExod is "closer to the MT than to the LXX" is tenuous at best, and virtually meaningless, with only two distinctive words (neither of which are variants) and a small number of partial words preserved. In fact, only one variant is clearly preserved, while a second is barely visible and thus speculative. For the clear variant, 7QpapLXXExod and Vaticanus present two slightly different forms of the infinitive (ἱερα[τεύειν] "to serve" 7Q, vs. εἰς τὸ ἱερατεύειν 𝔊^{B}), both of which accurately translate the text as in the MT (לכהנו "to serve as priest"); but the former is typical OG whereas the use of the preposition to represent the preposition in the MT is characteristic of α´θ´ (cf. ἁγιάσαι OG vs. εἰς το ἁγιάσαι α´θ´ for לקדש ["sanctify"] in nearby Exod 29:1).[20] For the barely visible possible variant, after "Aaron" in Vaticanus the MT and perhaps 7QpapLXXExod add "your brother"; the cause for this common reading could indeed be MT influence, but it could just as easily be an independent scribal commonplace.

7QpapEpJer (7Q2; Rahlfs 804)

Only two complete and seven partially preserved words remain of this papyrus from around 100 B.C.E. (DJD 3:143), with text from verses 43-44 of the Letter of Jeremiah. This apocryphal or deuterocanonical letter of seventy-three verses was later placed in different sequences in different codices of the LXX. Since no Hebrew or Aramaic original (if there ever was one) survives, comparison with a possible *Vorlage* is not possible. The Greek text of the small fragment appears to have affiliation with Lucianic manuscripts and the Syriac.

7QpapEnoch (7Q4)

Émile Puech in 1996 confirmed G.-Wilhelm Nebe's identification of a pair of Greek papyrus fragments—which had formerly been alleged to be from the NT (1 Tim 3:16–4:3)—as from a Greek translation of 1 Enoch 103 and 105.[21] The text would then be considered part of the LXX, since this book was somewhat widely considered Scripture, as indicated by the large number of Enoch manuscripts at Qumran, by quotations or

[19] "Le texte est en général plus proche du TM que de la LXX . . ." DJD 3:142.

[20] Note also ἱερατεύειν OG (without preposition) immediately following in Exod 29:1, though no attestation for α´ θ´ is preserved.

[21] G.-Wilhelm Nebe, "7Q4. Möglichkeit und Grenze einer Identifikation," *RevQ* 13 (1988): 629–33; Émile Puech, "Notes sur les fragments grecs du manuscrit 7Q4 = 1 Hénoch 103 et 105," *RB* 103/4 (1996): 592–600.

allusions in the Qumran writings and in the NT Epistle of Jude, and by its continuing inclusion in the Ethiopian canon.

4QUnid gr (4Q126)

Cave 4 also yielded two other unidentified Greek texts, one on leather and one on papyrus. The former (DJD 9:219–21), with only eight small fragments dating from the same period as 4QpapLXXLev^{b} and 4QLXXNum, contains κυριο[ ], [ ]σποδ[ ], and [ ]κορπιδ[ ] (possibly [ ]σκορπιδ[ ]), as the most distinctive words. It would not be surprising if this were an LXX-related text or a Greek version of an otherwise known or unknown religious text.

4QpapParaExodus gr (4Q127)

This papyrus text (DJD 9:223–42) looks similar to and dates from about the same period as 4QpapLXXLev^{b}. Its largest fragment mentions Egypt, Pharaoh, Moses, Red [Sea], probably Aaron, and possibly Miriam, and so it would seem to be from Exodus. But other fragments mention angels, sins, and possibly lawlessness and the hidd[en things]. None of the remaining fragments have connected text that could aid in identification. Thus Devorah Dimant may well be correct in suggesting that it is a lost apocalyptic work recalling God's salvific deeds at the Exodus and urging the faithful toward righteous action in the future.[22]

8ḤevXII gr (Rahlfs 943)

Dominique Barthélemy quickly published preliminary parts of this manuscript and a highly insightful analysis of it, and Emanuel Tov completed a thorough edition and study of it in DJD 8.[23] Its generous fragments contain many parts of the Twelve Minor Prophets, interestingly in the order of the Murabbaʿat Hebrew scroll and the MT, not in the LXX order. Barthélemy dated the manuscript to the middle of the first century C.E., whereas C. H. Roberts dated it to 50 B.C.E.–50 C.E., and Peter Parsons cautiously dated it to the later first century B.C.E. ("such a dating is possible, though not of course necessary"; DJD 8:26). The Tetragrammaton is inscribed in Palaeo-Hebrew characters throughout.

This Greek text of the Minor Prophets from Naḥal Ḥever, Barthélemy and Tov convincingly demonstrate, is a revision of the OG translation whose intention was to bring the OG into more precise quantitative, lexical, and syntactical conformity with a Hebrew text which was close to, though not identical with, the text eventually appearing in the MT (the "proto-MT"). One may presume that it adjusted also the order of the twelve books to conform with the order in that Hebrew manuscript, rather than leave the

---

22 Devorah Dimant, "4Q127: An Unknown Jewish Apocryphal Work?" in *Pomegranates and Golden Bells: Studies in Biblical, Jewish, and Near Eastern Ritual, Law, and Literature in Honor of Jacob Milgrom* (ed. David P. Wright et al.; Winona Lake, Ind.: Eisenbrauns, 1995), 805–13.

23 Dominique Barthélemy, "Redécouverte d'un chaînon manquant de l'histoire de la Septante," *RB* 60 (1953): 18–29; idem, *Les devanciers d'Aquila* (VTSup 10; Leiden, Brill, 1963); Emanuel Tov with the collaboration of Robert A. Kraft, *The Greek Minor Prophets Scroll from Naḥal Ḥever (8ḤevXIIgr)* (DJD 8; Oxford: Clarendon, 1980).

books in the LXX order. The recension, labeled the *kaige* recension, due to its routine rendering of גם(ו) by the Greek καί γε, was close to the one associated with the name Theodotion.

Barthélemy recognized in this scroll a "missing link" between the OG and the later, slavishly literal recension of Aquila based on this intermediate text form.[24] Thus, this manuscript is perhaps the most richly instructive of the Greek scrolls with respect to the history of the Greek textual development (see III below).

Regarding the scroll's agreement with the MT, two alternate possibilities suggest themselves, though evidence is unfortunately lacking to determine which of the two to endorse. On the one hand, it is quite possible that the rabbinic text (or "proto-MT") specifically, as opposed to another text form, was intentionally selected to serve as the basis of the Greek revision. On the other, it is also quite plausible that the situation was simply coincidental.[25] The reviser may simply have happened to have available the form of Hebrew edition of the book that was also found at Murabbaʿat and judged that it was important that the Greek agree with that inspired "original." Whether intentional or coincidental, the scroll witnesses to the earliest systematic recension which attempted to revise the OG to conform with a Hebrew text and which served as the basis for Aquila's even more rigorous recension. Thus, whereas the other LXX scrolls shed light on the OG and its early transmission, this scroll serves as the key to understanding the Greek recensional history. Moreover, the fact that a major effort was expended to revise the Greek form of the book (and the same was done yet again by Aquila) underscores the use and importance of the LXX within Judaism at this time.

II. Hebrew Scrolls and the Septuagint *Vorlage*

While the Greek manuscripts provide ancient samples of the pre-Christian LXX, numerous Hebrew scrolls shed light on the textual character and reputation of the LXX.

4QJer^b

Shortly after the discoveries in Cave 4 Frank Moore Cross reported that a Hebrew fragment of Jeremiah displayed the same shorter and rearranged text known from the LXX translation of Jeremiah.[26] As was seen in the previous chapter, the fragment preserves text from Jer 9:22–10:21, though it is not the Hebrew text as in the MT but the type of Hebrew text from which the LXX had been translated. This fragment demonstrates clearly that part of the LXX text, and presumably the full LXX text of Jeremiah is faithfully translated from an ancient Hebrew text from which the MT differs substantially (see Ch. 9). Further analysis leads to the conclusion that the (4QJer^b-)LXX text is a more original, short edition of the book with an intelligible order, and that the MT

[24] Barthélemy, "Redécouverte d'un chaînon manquant de l'histoire de la Septante."

[25] On the coincidental or chance nature of the selection of the text forms found in the MT collection, see Ch. 2 "Coincidental Nature." Against the notion that the "proto-MT" was intentionally selected is the fact that the θ′ recension of Daniel includes the longer text with the Additions, as opposed to the short MT.

[26] Frank Moore Cross, *The Ancient Library of Qumran* (1958; 3d rev. and enl. ed.; Minneapolis: Fortress, 1995), 137 n. 4.

contains a later, longer edition of the book based on that earlier edition but amplified and rearranged so that the Oracles against the Nations occur in connection with chapter 25 in the LXX but near the end of the book in the MT.[27]

Once the 4QJer^b-LXX text and the MT are seen as two successive editions of the book, the phenomenon can be recognized as parallel to the Book of Daniel, though the situation is reversed. The MT of Daniel presents one early edition in the growth of the Daniel collection, and the LXX and Theodotionic texts present a later, longer edition. The LXX of both Jeremiah and Daniel should be seen as faithful translations of current Semitic texts that were simply variant editions different from those preserved in the traditional *textus receptus*.

4QSam^a and 4QSam^b

Cross also published early articles announcing scrolls of Samuel (see Ch. 6) which showed close relationships with the LXX.[28] Neither Hebrew scroll presents the exact text from which the LXX was translated, but both repeatedly display distinctive readings showing that the LXX translation of Samuel was based on, and faithfully translated from, a Hebrew text which not only was frequently different from, but was often superior to, the MT. Moreover, the Chronicler also used a form of Samuel closer to the Qumran texts than to MT-Sam, as did Josephus for his *Jewish Antiquities* (see Ch. 6).

4QDeut^q

4QDeut^q (DJD 14:137–42, see Table 1) survives in only a few fragments with text from Deut 32:37-43 and 32:9-10(?) and dates from approximately the latter part of the

TABLE 1

LXX	MT	4QDeut^q	
=	ולמשנאי אשלם	[ולמשנ]אי אשלם	1
=	42 אשכיר חצי מדם	[42 אשכיר]ה חצי מדם	2
=	וחרבי תאכל בשר	[וחרבי תא]כל בשר	3
=	מדם חלל ושביה	[מדם חלל ו]שביה	4
=	מראש פרעות אויב	ומׄראׄשׄ פׄ[ר]עׄות איׄוב	5
= 4Q + MT	43 הרנינו גוים עמו	43 הרנינו שמים עמו	6
= 4Q		והשתחוו לו כל אלהים	7
=	כי דם עבדיו יקום	כי דם בניו יקום	8
=	ונקם ישיב לצריו	ונקם ישיב לצריו	9
= 4Q		ולמשנאיו ישלם	10
=	וכפר אדמתו עמו	ויכפר אדמת עמו	11

[27] For discussion, including counter-suggestions, see Tov, *Textual Criticism*, 286–94.

[28] Frank Moore Cross, "A New Qumran Biblical Fragment Related to the Original Hebrew Underlying the Septuagint," *BASOR* 132 (1953): 15–26; idem, "The Oldest Manuscripts from Qumran," *JBL* 74 (1955): 147–72. Full publications are in DJD 17.

first century B.C.E. It is safe to conclude that this small scroll contained only the poetic Song of Moses (Deut 32:1-43) and not the complete large book of Deuteronomy. Its height is only 11.4 cm., and it contains only eleven lines per column; moreover, the left margin of the final column is broad and blank with no stitching along the left side for additional columns. Thus, the text ends with 32:43, the last verse of the poem, and the final prose verses of chapter 32 as well as chapters 33 34 are not included. The scroll's affiliation with the Hebrew *Vorlage* of the OG, rather than with the MT, is quite clear.

For this passage, all three texts agree for lines 1–5, 9, and 11, with only insignificant deviations. The salient readings are in lines 6–8 and 10, for which LXX = 4QDeut[q] ≠ MT in two individual variants (שמים and בניו) and two pluses, indicating the main textual affiliation. For lines 6–7 the Greek tradition has a double rendering:

> εὐφράνθητε, οὐρανοί, ἅμα αὐτῷ,
> καὶ προσκυνησάτωσαν αὐτῷ πάντες (> πάντες B) υἱοὶ θεοῦ·
> εὐφράνθητε, ἔθνη, μετὰ τοῦ λαοῦ αὐτοῦ,
> καὶ ἐνισχυσάτωσαν αὐτῷ πάντες ἄγγελοι θεοῦ·

The more mythic and polytheistic words שמים/οὐρανοί ("heavens" as personified) and כל אלהים/υἱοὶ θεοῦ ("gods") are clues that the scroll contains the original Hebrew and that the rendering in the first pair of lines is probably the OG translation (see Hebrews 1:6). The MT represents a more monotheistic revision, and the latter two Greek lines conform to that later revision, subsequently inserted into the LXX (see Rom 15:10). But note that the later Greek rendering, just as the earlier one, also presumed a Hebrew text containing a plus similar to line 7 of 4QDeut[q].[29] Once again, the scroll demonstrates that the OG is a faithful translation of an ancient Hebrew text that was simply at variance with that preserved in the MT.

III. INDIVIDUAL AGREEMENTS OF SCROLLS AND THE SEPTUAGINT

Whereas some manuscripts, such as 4QJer[b], provided copies of the Hebrew parent text from which the LXX had been translated, and others, such as 4QSam[a] and 4QSam[b], displayed a preponderance of readings in agreement with the LXX as opposed to the MT, such qualitatively dramatic evidence is supplemented by the great quantity of sporadic readings exhibiting a pattern of Q = LXX ≠ MT in a wide variety of manuscripts.

Many of the editors of the Hebrew biblical scrolls have pointed out the interrelationships between the Hebrew and Greek texts of the books they edited. For example, James Davila urged that scholars should "take the LXX of Genesis very seriously as a source for a Hebrew tradition alternate to the MT."[30]

---

[29] The word ἐνισχυσάτωσαν ("be strong") presents an anomaly in the context. Noting that it is in poetic parallelism with εὐφράνθητε ("rejoice") or προσκυνησάτωσαν ("bow down"), one looks for Hebrew parallels for רנן ("rejoice") or [השת]חוה ("bow down"). The root עלז ("exult") parallels with רנן in Pss 96:12 and 149:5. Alexander Rofé ("The End of the Song of Moses [Deuteronomy 32.43]," in *Deuteronomy: Issues and Interpretation* [ed. Alexander Rofé; London: T&T Clark, 2002], 47–54) suggests a Hebrew ויעלזו corrupted by metathesis to ויעזו לו, for which καὶ ἐνισχυσάτωσαν αὐτῷ is a perfect translation of that error. Moreover, עלז is textually suspect in several other loci, e.g., Ps 60:8 (see *BHS* n. 8[a] and Num 13:17); 108:8 (see *BHS* n. 8[a]); and Jer 11:15 (see *BHS* n. 15[f]); note also עלץ for עלז in the parallel 1 Chr 16:32.

[30] James R. Davila, "New Qumran Readings for Genesis One," in *Of Scribes and Scrolls: Studies on the Hebrew Bible, Intertestamental Judaism, and Christian Origins presented to John Strugnell on the Occasion*

For Exodus, Anneli Aejmelaeus had already demonstrated that "All in all, the scholar who wishes to attribute deliberate changes, harmonizations, completion of details and new accents to the translator is under the obligation to prove [that] thesis with weighty arguments and also to show why the divergences cannot have originated with the *Vorlage*."[31] The DJD editors of Exodus, Frank Cross, Patrick Skehan, Judith Sanderson, and Eugene Ulrich, confirmed this, showing that many of the Greek variants were quite likely accurate translations of alternate Hebrew texts.

For Deuteronomy, Skehan and Ulrich concluded that, though "not identical to 𝔊, 4QDeut[q] shares several unique readings with the Septuagint version of Deuteronomy and bears witness to the existence of the variant Hebrew *Vorlage* used by the Septuagint translator" (DJD 14:138). The DJD co-editors, Sidnie White Crawford and Julie Duncan, also showed numerous agreements between the scrolls and the LXX in Deuteronomy manuscripts. For Joshua, Ulrich and Tov showed similar agreements, with Tov especially pointing out that a correction made in 4QJosh[b] took that manuscript further away from the MT and brought it into closer agreement with the Hebrew behind the LXX (DJD 14:155–57).[32]

Due to the fragmentary, non-sustained nature of most of the evidence, it may rather prove helpful to give a few classified examples of the types of LXX readings provided by the scrolls.

1. Correct readings in Hebrew scrolls preserved by the LXX, where the MT errs:

Deut 33:8 *(DJD 14:68–69; BQS 244)*

4QDeut[h]	הבו ללוי[י]	Give to Levi
MT	>	(see *BHS* n. 8[a])
LXX, OL	Δότε Λευι	Give to Levi

1 Sam 10:27–11:1 *(DJD 17:66–67; BQS 271)*

4QSam[a]	כמו חדש	[11:1]In about a month ...
MT	כמחריש	... (he was) like one silent. [11:1]
LXX, OL	ὡς μετὰ μῆνα	[11:1]After about a month ...

2. Intentional variants between the Hebrew text translated by the LXX and the MT:

Exod 1:5 *(DJD 12:18, 84; BQS 27, 28)*

4QExod[b]	חמש ושבעים נפש	five and seventy persons
4QGen-Exod[a]	[שבעים] וחמש נפש	[seventy] and five persons
MT	שבעים נפש	seventy persons
LXX	ψυχαὶ...πέντε καὶ ἑβδομήκοντα	five and seventy persons

of His Sixtieth Birthday (ed. Harold W. Attridge, et al.; Lanham, Md.: University Press of America, 1990), 3–11, esp. 11.

31 Anneli Aejmelaeus, "What Can We Know about the Hebrew *Vorlage* of the Septuagint?" in *On the Trail of Septuagint Translators: Collected Essays* (rev. ed.; Leuven: Peeters, 2007), 71–106, esp. 86.

32 For many examples from 1QIsa[a] and 1QIsa[b] see DJD 32, 2:92–95 and 209–11.

The total in the scrolls, followed by the LXX, is different from that in the MT due to the five additional descendants of Joseph born in Egypt (see LXX-Gen 46:20, 27; Acts 7:14).[33]

Deut 32:8 *(DJD 14:90; BQS 240)*

4QDeut[j]	בני אלוהים	the sons of God
MT	בני ישראל	the sons of Israel
OG	υἱῶν θεοῦ	the sons of God

The MT intentionally replaces the polytheistic term, just as it did the more mythic and polytheistic readings in 4QDeut[q] at Deut 32:43 noted in the previous section.

Isa 40:7-8 *(DJD 32, 2:91; BQS 407)*

1QIsa[a*]	>	
1QIsa[a 2m], MT	יבש חציר ... רוח יהוה ...	the grass withers ... when the breath of the LORD ...
OG	>	

A later scribe has inserted this statement into 1QIsa[a] at Isa 40:7-8, and the MT also contains it, whereas the original scroll in agreement with the LXX did not have it.

3. Correct readings in the MT vs. errors in Hebrew scrolls reflected in LXX:

2 Sam 4:12 *(DJD 17:118; BQS 295)*

4QSam[a]	מפיבשת	Mephibosheth
MT	איש בשת	Ishbosheth
LXX	Μεμφιβοσθε	Mephibosheth

The MT has the correct reading here, whereas the scroll continues the confusion concerning the son and the grandson of Saul (cf. 2 Sam 4:1, 2, 4) and the LXX faithfully translates the Hebrew error (see Ch. 6.II.B).

2 Sam 7:23 *(DJD 17:130; BQS 298)*

4QSam[a]	[גוים] ואהלים	nations and tents
MT	גוים ואלהיו	nations and its gods
OG, OL	ἔθνη καὶ σκηνώματα	nations and tents

The scroll betrays a metathesis of *lamed-he* in one Hebrew tradition of Samuel, and the LXX translates from a *Vorlage* like the scroll. Cf. אהלי/אלהי in MasPs[a] II 19 at Ps 83:7.

[33] See Cross, *The Ancient Library of Qumran* (3d ed.), 135–36, n. 1.

4. Corrections inserted into Hebrew scrolls, by either the original or a subsequent scribe, which go against the MT and toward an alternate Hebrew text from which the LXX was translated:

Deut 7:15 *(DJD 3:170; BQS 193)*

5QDeut	אשר ראיתה ואשר ידעת	that$^{\text{you saw and that}}$ you knew
MT	אשר ידעת	that you knew
LXX	ἃς ἑώρακας καὶ ὅσα ἔγνως	that you saw and that you knew

5QDeut corrected away from the reading retained in the MT toward a Hebrew that was the basis of the LXX. The few fragments of 5QDeut show two additional insertions, plus a tenuous fourth, correcting toward the *Vorlage* of LXX, away from the MT.

Josh 3:15 *(DJD 14:155; BQS 248)*

4QJosh[b]	קציר חטים	the^{wheat} harvest
MT	קציר	the harvest
LXX	θερισμοῦ πυρῶν	the wheat harvest

The scroll inserted a specification also contained in the LXX *Vorlage*, moving away from the MT.

Isa 5:25 *(DJD 15:25; BQS 470)*

4QIsa[b]	יהוה צ]באות[	the LORD$^{\text{of h[osts]}}$
MT	יהוה	the LORD
LXX	κύριος σαβαωθ	the LORD of hosts

The scroll inserted צבאות in agreement with the LXX *Vorlage*, again moving away from the MT.

The first category is important and helpful for attaining a better form of the biblical text. The second and third categories are significant for determining textual affiliation and the reliability of the LXX as a translation, for providing at times superior readings, and for witnessing to the accepted pluriformity of the text. The significance of the fourth category is complex and must be decided case-by-case; at a minimum, it neutralizes contentions that corrections in the scrolls were made "on the basis of the MT." The texts of the books of Scripture were pluriform; scribes were, of course, concerned that texts be accurate, and so they or subsequent readers checked their texts and corrected them when seen as inaccurate. The corrections were based on memory or other texts available. Sometimes these involved readings that were embedded in the texts preserved by the Rabbis and Masoretes, while sometimes they involved readings embedded in the texts translated as the LXX; at other times they involved genuine readings current then but no longer preserved in any extant witnesses.

IV. HISTORICAL DEVELOPMENT OF THE SEPTUAGINT

The Greek Minor Prophets scroll from Naḥal Ḥever (8ḤevXII gr) provided highly significant information enabling scholars to paint a more accurate picture of the historical development of the ancient Greek text.[34] That history is now well known and can be briefly sketched here.

The Old Greek, the original single (or singly-influential) translation of each book began with the Pentateuch in the first half of the third century B.C.E., a generation or two after the introduction of Hellenism, and the other books followed over the next century or so. The date is based on the combination of manuscripts found in Palestine and Egypt in the second and first centuries B.C.E., and on quotations in Jewish Hellenistic literature. In the second century B.C.E., 4QLXXDeut and possibly 4QLXXLev[a] circulated in Palestine and the Rylands Greek Papyrus 458 in Egypt. In the first century B.C.E., 4QpapLXXLev[b] was available in Palestine and Papyrus Fouad 266 in Egypt. In addition, Demetrius the Chronographer quoted the Greek Genesis and Exodus in the last quarter of the third century B.C.E.[35] The wide range of these early manuscripts and quotations require that the OG Pentateuch must have been translated significantly earlier.

The early Greek texts ($\mathfrak{G}_2$): The original translation quickly began to show variants and continued to do so through the next couple centuries. Undoubtedly, from the first copying of the Greek translation the text began to incorporate scribal errors as well as attempts to correct the text and improve it with clarifications. It is unlikely that the original Greek text is fully preserved for any book; rather, ideally the Göttingen critical editions ($\mathfrak{G}^{ed}$) seek to attain the OG, but practically they usually can present only the best and earliest preserved of the gradually evolving forms ($\mathfrak{G}_2$) which developed from that original translation.[36]

The early recensions: What Barthélemy discovered in the Greek Minor Prophets scroll was, first, that its many agreements with the OG showed that it was based on a form of the OG text (probably $\mathfrak{G}_2$) and, second, that it was a systematic attempt to bring the OG into more precise quantitative, lexical, and syntactical conformity with a type of Hebrew text edition that the MT eventually inherited. That is, whereas the Greek texts known as Theodotion, Aquila, and Symmachus (θ′, α′, σ′) had been considered fresh translations, this scroll provided the "missing link," demonstrating that they were rather recensions ($\mathfrak{G}^{R}$) or intentional revisions of the OG. Aquila's recension was based on this type of text but carried the systematic revision to even further levels of mechanical conformity toward the rabbinic text of the second century C.E.[37]

---

[34] For further detail on the early history of the Septuagint, see Jellicoe, *The Septuagint and Modern Study*, 59–171; Leonard Greenspoon, "Septuagint," in *The New Interpreter's Dictionary of the Bible* (5 vols.; Nashville: Abingdon, 2006–2009), 5:170–77; Tov, *Textual Criticism*, 127–47; and Ulrich, *Scrolls and Origins*, 202–32.

[35] See Carl R. Holladay, "Demetrius the Chronographer," in *ABD* 2:137–38; and J. Hanson, "Demetrius the Chronographer," in *The Old Testament Pseudepigrapha* (2 vols.; ed. James H. Charlesworth; New York: Doubleday, 1985), 2:843–54.

[36] See Wevers, *Das Göttinger Septuaginta-Unternehmen*, 19; and Jellicoe's first and last pages (*The Septuagint and Modern Study*, 1, 359).

[37] On the Greek recensions see Dominique Barthélemy, *Les devanciers d'Aquila* (VTSup 10; Leiden: Brill, 1963); and Kevin G. O'Connell, "Greek Versions (Minor)," *IDBSup* (Nashville: Abingdon, 1976), 377–81. Aquila's recension is so systematic that Joseph Reider and Nigel Turner were able to compile *An Index to Aquila* (VTSup 12; Leiden: Brill, 1966), which gives the Greek equivalents used by Aquila for the Hebrew roots in the biblical text.

The Hexaplaric recension ($\mathfrak{G}^{O}$, *O′*) was the fifth column in the monumental six-column tome which Origen (185–254), due to the proliferation and confusion of multiple Greek text forms, produced in the attempt to restore the original text of the "Seventy." He (and everyone else by his time), however, thought that the rabbinic Bible was the "original" Hebrew text; but, whereas some books of the OG had been translated from such a text, other books had been translated from a different *Vorlage*. For these latter, he frequently departed further from the "original" by correcting the true OG toward the rabbinic Hebrew.

"The Lucianic recension" ($\mathfrak{G}^{L}$, *L′*) is named for the fourth-century Antiochene martyr and recension.[38] For some books it is based on the OG (or $\mathfrak{G}_2$), but it is also heavily influenced by the Hexaplaric recension. Since some of its readings occur in pre-Hexaplaric texts and even agree with readings from the late Second Temple period (e.g., 4QSam[a]), scholars recognize a "proto-Lucian" substratum to this recension.[39]

It is important to keep in mind that the preserved LXX manuscripts may individually display their own mixture of multiple influences. One may find in the same sentence, (1) some original OG readings based on an alternate Hebrew, (2) other OG readings in agreement with the MT and the general LXX text tradition, (3) later minor errors or clarifications (with $\mathfrak{G}_2$), and (4) revisions influenced by the recensions (θ′, α′, σ′, $\mathfrak{G}^{O}$).

Conclusions

A few final observations can be made concerning the LXX manuscripts found at Qumran and related sites. The finds are random, fragmentary, and mutely ambiguous, and so, while some conclusions are certain, it must be recognized that many are more or less educated attempts at reconstructing what may have been the situation.

First, if fragments of Exodus, Leviticus, Numbers, and Deuteronomy were found, it is a safe bet to wager that Genesis had also been at Qumran. As Martin Hengel[40] and many before him have shown, the Greek language as well as Hellenistic culture had deeply penetrated Palestinian Judaism in the late Second Temple period. And as Nicholas de Lange[41] has observed, there was always more Greek in Jewish life and literature than Jewish tradition cares to admit. At a minimum we can say that more than one person—it is unlikely that the same individual brought both 4QLXXLev[a] and 4QpapLXXLev[b]—thought that the Greek Scriptures were important and brought copies to Qumran. How much use they received is open to speculation. On the one hand, the conservative nature of the Qumran community members may have caused them to be

[38] See Melvin K. H. Peters, "Septuagint," in *ABD* 5:1093–1104, esp. 1099–1100; Frank Moore Cross, "The Evolution of a Theory of Local Texts," in *Qumran and the History*, 306–315, esp. 311–15; Emanuel Tov, "Lucian and Proto-Lucian: Toward a New Solution of the Problem, *RB* 79 (1972): 101–13; Ulrich, *The Qumran Text of Samuel*, 15–28.

[39] See recently Richard Saley, "Greek Lucianic Doublets and 4QSam[a]," *BIOSCS* 40 (2007): 63–73; and idem, "Proto-Lucian and 4QSam[a]," *BIOSCS* 41 (2008): 34–45.

[40] Martin Hengel, *Judaica et Hellenistica* (Tübingen: J. C. B. Mohr, 1996); idem, *The Septuagint as Christian Scripture* (Edinburgh: T&T Clark, 2002).

[41] Nicholas de Lange, *Jewish Reception of Greek Bible Versions: Studies in Their Use in Late Antiquity and the Middle Ages* (Tübingen: Mohr Siebeck, 2009).

suspicious and to see Greek forms of the Scriptures as part of unacceptable Hellenistic tendencies. On the other, the educated priests in Jerusalem probably knew Greek, and the Zadokite leaders who moved out to Qumran may have studied the Scriptures also in Greek or at least may have been open to those members who would have profited from reading them in Greek; moreover, the Books of the Torah in Greek may have been seen as part of the hedge against Hellenizing antinomian tendencies.[42]

In addition to the Torah, the Prophets in Greek were also represented among the scrolls, as well as other religious literature in Greek (in Cave 7) which may, or may not, or may not yet, have been considered Scripture. The Book of the Minor Prophets was certainly considered among the Prophets, as the *pesharim* demonstrate. It is uncertain but likely that 1 Enoch (just as Daniel) was also considered among the Prophets;[43] note that (parallel to Matt 24:15 calling Daniel a prophet) the Epistle of Jude explicitly says Enoch "prophesied" (Jude 14) and quotes (14-16) the prophecy from 1 Enoch 1:9. It is difficult to know whether the Letter of Jeremiah was considered among the Prophets, but its presence in Greek strongly suggests that the book of Jeremiah was available in Greek, and it would have been considered Scripture. Thus, it does not seem unduly speculative to assume further that there were Greek translations of other major prophetic books such as Isaiah that simply have not survived. As yet it cannot be determined whether 4QUnid gr (4Q126) was part of the LXX, though 4QpapParaExodus gr (4Q127) most likely was not considered such.

The Greek scrolls also generally confirm the approach of Paul de Lagarde, as opposed to that of Paul Kahle.[44] De Lagarde thought that there was a single OG translation which gradually diversified as errors and intentional additions crept in during the transmission process. The task was to trace the widespread variation in our extant manuscripts back to three major recensions of the Greek text and then compare those three to arrive at the original translation. Kahle, in contrast, thought that the origins of the LXX mirrored those of the Targumim, from a plethora of individual partial translations which were eventually supplanted by a single translation. He proposed that the Letter of Aristeas, with a third century B.C.E. setting, was written as propaganda for one official translation which was to replace competing Greek texts in the late second century B.C.E.[45]

De Lagarde's view appears confirmed both by the Greek scrolls from Qumran and by the Greek Minor Prophets scroll from Naḥal Ḥever. The Qumran LXX scrolls all present basically an OG text close to that in the Göttingen editions, with only minor, routine variants, some of which are closer to the OG than the readings chosen for the critical editions. Moreover, the Minor Prophets scroll, though significantly different from the OG, confounds Kahle's view of different translations by showing that it is not an alternate translation but an intentional revision of precisely the single OG translation.

---

[42] Recall the attestation of the continuing use of Greek by θ′, α′, σ′. An additional reason to think that these manuscripts were used by community members is the appearance of important legal and marriage documents in Greek in the caves at Naḥal Ḥever.

[43] See "7QpapEnoch" above.

[44] See Jellicoe, *The Septuagint and Modern Study*, 5–9; Ulrich, *Scrolls and Origins*, 209–10.

[45] Paul Kahle, "Untersuchungen zur Geschichte des Pentateuchtextes," in *Theologische Studien und Kritiken* 88 (Gotha: F. A. Perthes Aktiengesellschaft, 1915), 399–439, esp. 410–26; and *The Cairo Geniza* (2d ed.; Oxford: Blackwell, 1959), 211–12. But see Jellicoe, *The Septuagint and Modern Study*, 61–63.

Thus, for each biblical book there seems to have been a single original (or singly influential) translation from the Hebrew into Greek. The translations, however, display differing translation techniques, and thus each book's translation should be presumed to derive from a different translator.

Though it is often not done, one must carefully consider the relationship of the OG translation to its Hebrew *Vorlage*. Not infrequently, differences from the MT either in individual words or phrases or even in the form of the larger book (e.g., Jeremiah) are due not to theological *Tendenz* but to faithful translation from a different Hebrew parent text.

As far as the evidence indicates, originally the OG would have been a collection of papyrus or leather scrolls, each normally containing one biblical book, each apparently translated by a different translator, and all (or most) attempting to reproduce in Greek the intended meaning of the Hebrew text (Qumran, proto-MT, or other) from which it had been translated.

LEARNINGS FROM THE SCROLLS

Chapter 11

The Absence of "Sectarian Variants" in the Jewish Scriptural Scrolls Found at Qumran

In light of the parade of surprises—the many, varied major intentional variants—exhibited in the scriptural manuscripts reviewed in the preceding chapters, a number of questions naturally arise: Are the scriptural scrolls infected with changes motivated by sectarian *Tendenz*? Are there books that were originally disqualified as "nonbiblical" which in light of post-Qumran thinking should be considered "biblical"? Is it possible to discern the boundaries of the sacred books, in contrast to the pre-scriptural sources that were absorbed into them and the post-scriptural compositions now called "rewritten Scripture"? The following chapters will explore these questions.

There are many reasons to think that the Qumran covenanters would have tailored their texts of the Scriptures to fit their sectarian views, since their scriptural texts display dramatic variants compared to previously known versions, since they composed distinctively sectarian compositions, since the diction expressing their identity through their compositions was so pervasively influenced by scriptural language, and since they clearly applied the Scriptures to their specific situation through the *pesharim*.

The result, however, of the quest to discover sectarian variants in the scrolls was to discover the valuable lesson of the *absence* of sectarian variants.[1] This chapter will retrace that quest through four approaches: (I) some issues and problems involved with the *idea* of "sectarian variants"; (II) some *examples* of sectarian variants in order to clarify what the object of the search would look like if found; (III) a search through the biblical manuscripts in *quest of such variants*; and (IV) some specific probes of selected other manuscripts presumably *copied at Qumran* for clues.

The scope of this chapter must be confined to the more than 200 biblical scrolls, in order to ensure clarity of focus and usefulness of results. A similar, broader study of the quotations and use of the biblical text (both for books that eventually became canonical and for other authoritative books that did not) in biblical commentaries as well as in other nonbiblical, parabiblical, and "rewritten" biblical scrolls, would be highly

[1] 4QJosh[a] highlights a sectarian variant, but that sectarian variant is in the MT, not in the scroll.

desirable.[2] The present analysis of the strictly biblical manuscripts should form a more solid basis for that broader study.

The focus here will be on individual textual variants in the attempt to discover variants that were sectarian in origin or motivation. For this purpose, other levels will not be treated: orthographic differences, variant literary editions, or disputed books. The level of orthographic differences will be ignored insofar as those are almost by definition meaningless. Should orthographic differences or minor variants appear to point to significant variant readings or interpretations, they will of course be examined. On the other hand and perhaps more importantly, the scope of this chapter does not permit discussion either of variant literary editions of books as possibly sectarian in origin or motivation, or of possible variation between Jewish parties with regard to whether disputed books did or did not have authoritative status. Those questions, however, are ripe for detailed investigation.

I. "Sectarian Variants"? Issues and Problems

There are two main issues raised by the question of "sectarian variants": the first centers around the value we should assign to the scriptural scrolls found at Qumran. Are they aberrant or "vulgar"[3] texts and thus of relatively small value for our knowledge of the history of the biblical text, or are they "the oldest, the best, the most authentic"[4] manuscripts of the Bible and thus of highest importance for the history of the biblical text?

The second issue centers around increased knowledge of Judaism in the late Second Temple period. If the variants highlighted by the scrolls are "sectarian"—whether the secondary variants are in the scrolls, in the MT, in the LXX, or in other witnesses—what can this teach us about Judaism in the late Second Temple period and about the history of the biblical text?

There are also two points that cry out for immediate discussion, since many biblical scholars and students will probably begin with predictable assumptions. The first involves texts, the second sects: first, clarification concerning the proper stance for assessing the MT versus the Qumran manuscripts; and second, clarification concerning

---

[2] See two insightful papers in *The Bible as Book*: George Brooke, "The Rewritten Law, Prophets and Psalms: Issues for Understanding the Text of the Bible," 31–40; and James C. VanderKam, "The Wording of Biblical Citations in Some Rewritten Scriptural Works," 41–56. See also Armin Lange and Matthias Weigold, *Biblical Quotations and Allusions in Second Temple Jewish Literature* (Göttingen: Vandenhoeck & Ruprecht, 2011.

[3] Paul Kahle, *Die hebräischen Handschriften aus der Höhle* (Stuttgart: W. Kohlhammer, 1951), 183–84. See also the discussions in Eduard Y. Kutscher, *The Language and Linguistic Background of the Isaiah Scroll (1QIsa^a)* (STDJ 6; Leiden: Brill, 1974), 77–89.

[4] Eugene Ulrich, "The Dead Sea Scrolls and the Hebrew Scriptural Texts," in *The Hebrew Bible and Qumran: The Bible and the Dead Sea Scrolls: Proceedings of the Jubilee Celebration at Princeton Theological Seminary* (ed. James H. Charlesworth; North Richland Hills, Tex.: Bibal Press, 2000), 105–33, esp. 132). See also the conflicting views of Arie van der Kooij ("Preservation and Promulgation: The Dead Sea Scrolls and the Textual History of the Hebrew Bible," in *The Hebrew Bible in Light of the Dead Sea Scrolls* [ed. Nóra Dávid et al.; FRLANT 239; Göttingen: Vandenhoeck & Ruprecht, 2012], 29–40) and Ulrich, "The Fundamental Importance of the Biblical Qumran Scrolls," ibid., 54–59.

the proper stance for assessing the Pharisees or Rabbis versus the Qumranites or Covenanters or Essenes (see Ch. 2).

In the period with which we are dealing, the MT and the Pharisaic party are simply not the principal points for reference or comparison. With regard to texts, the MT was not the "standard text" of "the Bible," nor was it even an identifiable text (in the collective singular) or even an identifiable collection of disparate texts. The text of the various books of Scripture was pluriform, and there is abundant evidence that this pluriformity was widely accepted. The textual form for each book that was later incorporated into the MT was simply one of several forms of the text as they circulated in Judaism during the Second Temple period (see Ch. 2, "Coincidental Nature"). In the late Second Temple period there was no "proto-MT" of the Tanak — or at least it still remains to be demonstrated that there was a "proto-MT" — in the sense of a unified, identifiable collection of texts that together (in conscious contrast to other texts) would move ahead through history and become the Masoretic collection of texts that emerged in the sixth to ninth centuries. There was no standard text. Thus, those texts which differ from the MT are not aberrant; it is only the presuppositions of those who would so claim that are aberrant. The texts were found at Qumran, but they are the scriptures of general Judaism, the texts that Hillel and Jesus would have encountered.[5]

Similarly, with regard to sects or parties within Judaism, the Pharisees did not constitute mainstream "normative Judaism." That is an outdated reconstruction prevalent in the first half of the last century, to be sure, but it has been corrected in many revised descriptions.[6] It is not the case that orthodox belief and practice were represented by the "mainstream" Pharisees, while those who diverged or disagreed with them were unorthodox sects in the modern western sense of that term. "The Pharisees were one group among many, vying for power against others."[7] If the term "sect" is used for the Essenes, one must seek an analogous term appropriate for the Pharisees, Sadducees, and other late Second Temple groups.[8]

So it is a misconception that the Pharisees represented "normative" Judaism, and thus even if there were an identifiable textual collection that could be labeled the "proto-MT," and even if it could in the second or first century B.C.E. be linked to the Pharisees, there is no evidence to substantiate the claim that the proto-MT was to be considered the dominant or standard text.[9]

---

[5] See Ch. 2 for fuller discussion of all these issues.

[6] See, e.g., E. P. Sanders, *Judaism: Practice and Belief 63 B.C.E.–66 C.E.* (London: SCM Press; Philadelphia: Trinity Press International, 1992); Lawrence H. Schiffman, *From Text to Tradition: A History of Second Temple and Rabbinic Judaism* (Hoboken, N.J.: Ktav, 1991); Albert I. Baumgarten, "Pharisees" in *Encyclopedia of the Dead Sea Scrolls*, 2:657–63, esp. 661; and Ulrich, "The Qumran Biblical Scrolls—The Scriptures of Late Second Temple Judaism," 81–87.

[7] Baumgarten, "Pharisees," 661.

[8] For a judicious analysis see Anthony Saldarini, "Sectarianism," in *Encyclopedia of the Dead Sea Scrolls*, 2:853–57, esp. 854. See also Schiffman, *From Text to Tradition*, 98: "The designation of these groups as 'sects' and of this phenomenon as 'sectarianism' is admittedly problematic, since these two terms usually assume a dominant or normative stream from which others have diverged. Rabbinic tradition claimed such a status for Pharisaic Judaism but it is difficult to consider a minority, no matter how influential, to be a mainstream."

[9] See Ulrich, "The Qumran Biblical Scrolls—The Scriptures of Late Second Temple Judaism," 81–87.

With those points made, the focus can return to the main question: whether there are sectarian variants in the MT, the LXX, or the scrolls. The logic itself stumbles. If one group tampered with the text of Scripture in order to promote its views, it would be open to immediate demonstrable refutation. The analogous problem was beginning only a short time later regarding the problem of the differing Hebrew versus Greek texts. In both rabbinic and early Christian circles, the discrepancies between texts eventually became glaringly clear in religious debates, and so began the Greek recension process of "correcting" Greek texts "back" toward the "original" Hebrew text (which from the second century on was assumed to be exclusively the rabbinic text-traditions that developed into the Masoretic texts).[10] All the actors in the Jewish parties had limited viewpoints, but all apparently agreed that the text of the "original" Scriptures should not be altered, and if there were problems, the texts should be corrected toward the "original." Here, it pays to recall the words of Chaim Rabin:

> The conviction of the [Qumran] sect that they were actors in a drama described in the O.T. in all details naturally led them to apply to their own situation those Scripture verses which in their view predicted it. The very fact that there were such verses at hand was a guarantee that their analysis of the situation was right. The place of an event in the divine plan was, so to say, adequately plotted if the verse for it could be found. For this reason, the extensive use of quotation and allusion in the argumentation . . . [is] an intrinsic part of the argument. . . . These allusions were meant to be taken by the reader or listener as proof of the identity of the "prophecy" and the situation to which it was applied.
>
> Now it appears an inescapable conclusion that if one quotes scripture for such purposes, one does—in intent at least—quote it literally. Failure to do so will mean that the reader either misses the point or will be able to raise objections from the correct text.[11]

This does not mean, of course, that no ancient scribe ever made a sectarian variant; but it does mean that such would not be a problem-free action and therefore that a scholar making such a claim today would need clear and thorough-going proof.

II. Examples of Sectarian Variants

A. Sectarian Variants

If the search is for sectarian variants, it is important to know what a sectarian variant looks like. What qualifies, and what does not? Comparison of the SP versus the MT offers clear examples of sectarian variants.

[10] It is interesting to note that those ancient textual scholars, including Origen, made an error analogous to that of modern scholars who presume that the MT was and is the standard text. A valuable witness to the ancient Hebrew text was destroyed when Origen "revised" the OG translation toward the rabbinic text. The OG was generally a faithful translation of one form of the Hebrew text. Such alternate Hebrew texts were eventually lost after the Jewish revolts, and at times their witnesses in Greek were also lost through the "revisions" toward the lone rabbinic form of the texts, in the often mistaken notion that the latter were the "original."

[11] Chaim Rabin, "The Dead Sea Scrolls and the History of the O.T. Text," *JTS* n.s. 6/2 (1955): 174–82, esp. 174–75.

1. The Lord Has Chosen or Will Choose?

In Deuteronomy, where the MT and LXX have the frequent Deuteronomistic formula about "the place where the LORD *will choose*" (יבחר) to have his name dwell (Deut 12:5; 14:23; 16:2; 17:8; 18:6; 26:2; etc.), the SP routinely has "the place where the LORD *has chosen*" (בחר). The polemic here, of course, is that, in the minds of the northerners/ Samari(t)ans, the Lord had at the time of Moses and Joshua chosen Mount Gerizim as true Israel's central shrine, and that should not change; indeed in the Hebrew Bible Shechem retained its status as a revered central shrine during the period of Joshua. For the Judeans, however, Jerusalem would become the central shrine established by David and Solomon, and from Deuteronomy's temporal point of reference, the Lord's choice of Jerusalem still lay in the future. One tradition has clearly made a sectarian revision, and a comprehensive reexamination of the Samari(t)an-Judean problem is a major desideratum.[12] Scholars, oriented from a current MT perspective, generally assume that the MT is original and the SP has introduced the change; but perhaps a reexamination using post-Qumran thinking could lead to better understanding. It is worth exploring whether the changes in the SP are truly sectarian or simply neutral, and whether the variant forms in the MT may be the sectarian replacements (see Ch. 14). But clearly, one tradition or the other has made a sectarian revision.

2. Mount Ebal versus Mount Gerizim

In the SP after Exod 20:17[14] and after Deut 5:21[18] a long commandment is added, stipulating that an altar be built on Mount Gerizim after the Lord has led the people into the land. This commandment, though clearly added by the Samarians/northerners, is not a specifically Samaritan creation; it consists mostly of the stipulations given to Moses in Deut 27:2-7, introduced by 11:29a and followed by 11:30. That is, the SP addition simply repeats text already in the MT and LXX as well as in the SP. The glaring difference is the localization of the altar "on Mount Gerizim" in the SP versus "on Mount Ebal" in the MT at Deut 27:4. Scholars have traditionally concluded that the SP commandment is an addition inspired by Samaritan (or at least northern, Samarian) concerns. But is the addition motivated by sectarian concerns or simply a Samarian explicitation of what they believed based on the shared Samaritan-Jewish Pentateuch? Were this latter the case, Mount Ebal would be the later sectarian variant.

3. The First Altar in Joshua

So it is important to ask: Is "Mount Ebal" at Deut 27:4 in the MT the original reading? 4QJosh^a strongly suggests that it is not (see Ch. 4). That oldest extant manuscript of

[12] See recently Gary N. Knoppers, *Jews and Samaritans: The Origins and History of Their Early Relations* (New York: Oxford University Press, 2013); Magnar Kartveit, *The Origin of the Samaritans* (VTSup 128; Leiden: Brill, 2009); Stefan Schorch, "The Samaritan Version of Deuteronomy and the Origin of Deuteronomy," in *Samaria, Samarians, and Samaritans: Studies on Bible, History and Linguistics* (Studia Samaritana 6; ed. József Zsengellér; Berlin: de Gruyter, 2011), 23–37; idem, "A Critical *editio maior* of the Samaritan Pentateuch: State of Research, Principles, and Problems," *HeBAI* 2 (2013): 100–20. József Zsengellér, *Gerizim as Israel: Northern Tradition of the Old Testament and the Early History of the Samaritans* (Utrechtse Theologische Reeks 38; Utrecht, University of Utrecht, 1998).

Joshua apparently assumes Gilgal as the location of the first altar after Israel had crossed into the land, and this is supported by Josephus and Pseudo-Philo. Thus, Deut 27:2-3a (with no place stipulated) would have been the original reading. At a second level, it is argued, Mount Gerizim was inserted due to northern concerns, and at a third level that insertion was not deleted but was countered by Judeans with the anomalous substitution of "Mount Ebal." Insofar as this interpretation be correct, it should be noted that the variant is not a sectarian variant made at Qumran but a double variant made first by the Samarians/northerners and subsequently by the Judeans/southerners. On this view, it is still an open question whether the addition of Mount Gerizim was a simple explicitation of fact or an assertion motivated by sectarian concerns; in either case, Mount Ebal would be a sectarian variant.

Finally, (regardless of which of the readings was "original" and which secondary) it is to be noted as criteria for a claim of sectarian variants that (1) sectarian readings are clearly *secondary*; (2) they are clearly *intentional*; (3) they are *particular* to the sponsoring group (whether Samari(t)ans/ northerners or Judean/southerners); and (4) the specific theme in the variants is found *repeated*, not a single occurrence.

B. Non-sectarian Variants

In contrast, it is helpful to note that there are numerous variants which are intentionally made in texts transmitted in the MT, the LXX, and the scrolls, but that they should not be considered sectarian. That is, they are characteristic of Jewish authors or scribes more broadly. They are not peculiar to any particular group.

1. 4QJudg^a and the MT

For example, 4QJudg^a highlights a theological insertion into the MT of Judges (Judg 6:7-10), but the MT should not be accused of a sectarian variant (for full discussion see Ch. 5). The text of 4QJudg^a retains the old, uninterrupted folk narrative, continuing from Judg 6:2-6 directly on to Judg 6:11-13. The narrative is about Gideon and repeated raids by the Midianites. Becoming impoverished, the Israelites cried out to the Lord; then the messenger of the Lord came to Gideon (Judg 6:11-12). Just before this last element a short paragraph is inserted into the MT with a nameless prophet repeating the cyclical pattern familiar from Judges 2–3 of apostasy, punishment, cry to the Lord, and deliverance. This paragraph must, however, be considered a general Jewish insertion, based on ancient and widespread Deuteronomistic theology, not a sectarian variant.

2. Hannah's Vow

Similarly, in 1 Sam 1:23, after Hannah's vow about her newborn son Samuel, Elkanah replies:

4QSam^a LXX OL אך יקם יהו]ה היוצא מפיך]

only let the LORD confirm what has come from your mouth.

MT אך יקם יהוה את דברו

only let the LORD confirm his word.

It is probable that 4QSam^a preserves the earlier reading and that the tradition in the MT has been influenced by the Deuteronomistic concern for linking isolated prophetic words with subsequent events and connecting these originally free-standing elements into a prophecy-fulfillment motif (see Ch. 6.II.B). Again, this would be a theologically motivated intentional variant; but it is a general Jewish variant, based on traditional theology, and not a sectarian variant.

III. Sectarian Variants in the Scriptures Found at Qumran?

For this section there is, ironically, both too much to discuss and nothing to report. Since the books of Deuteronomy, Isaiah, Psalms, and (relative to its size) Daniel were among the most widely attested biblical books at Qumran, and since the prophetic books appear the most fertile sources for possible sectarian variants, the discussion will focus on Isaiah, Psalms, and Daniel. But the negative conclusions hold for the other biblical books as well.

A. Isaiah

In 1QIsa^a there are more than 2600 variants from the other Qumran manuscripts, the MT, and the LXX (DJD 32, 2:119–93). In 1QIsa^b, though that manuscript is usually described as virtually identical with the MT, there are more than 183 textual variants against the Masoretic witnesses (DJD 32, 2:208). In the Cave 4 Isaiah manuscripts there are over 460 variants (DJD 15, *passim*).

The most dramatic variants in the book of Isaiah highlighted by the scrolls are the nine large additions of about one to five verses, absent in one tradition but added in another.[13] Some of these appear in 1QIsa^a, some appear in the LXX; interestingly, all these secondary additions are incorporated into the MT, making the received text the latest of our witnesses, at least from this perspective. But none of these dramatic long insertions should be labeled sectarian in nature.

Moreover, of all the thousands of Isaiah variants, in my view none should be classified as sectarian. Two suspicious possibilities, however, may be adduced as examples for consideration, plus one which has in fact been suggested as a sectarian variant.

1. Isaiah 44:25

In Isa 44:25 יסכל ("to render their knowledge *foolish*") occurs in 1QIsa^a, 1QIsa^b, 4QIsa^b, LXX) whereas the MT has ישכל ("to render their knowledge *wise*"). In light of an article by James E. Harding on "The Wordplay between the Roots כשל and שכל in the Literature of the *Yaḥad*,"[14] one is tempted to examine whether one of the Isaiah variants is possibly sectarian. But first, the most plausible explanation is not that the MT has substituted "wise" for "foolish," but that a scribe in the MT tradition simply confused sibilants; confusion of ס/שׂ is not infrequent, and the context and parallelism do not permit "wise."

[13] These occur in the MT and either 1QIsa^a or the LXX at Isa 2:9b-10, 22; 34:17^{fin}–35:2; 36:7; 37:4-7; 38:20; 40:7, 14b-16; 51:6; 63:3^{fin} (see Ch. 7). For brief commentary see *The Dead Sea Scrolls Bible*, 274–75, 322–24, 326, 331–33, 355, 375.

[14] *RevQ* 19/1 (1999): 69–82.

Thus, there is no true variant, only a minor lapse. Much less can it support the claim of a sectarian variant, as is confirmed by the wider support of the third- or early-second-century B.C.E. Greek translation. Harding makes the crucial distinction: important words in scriptural texts are taken and used to develop particular positions by different Second Temple groups within Judaism; but the arguments are developed in the secondary "sectarian" works, while the texts of the Scriptures are left unchanged.[15]

2. Isaiah 53:11

In Isa 53:11 the MT has יראה ("he will see") whereas 1QIsa^a^, 1QIsa^b^, 4QIsa^d^, and LXX have יראה אור ("he will see light"). Considering the sharp contrast drawn in the Rule of the Community between בני אור and בני חושך, one might be tempted to see this addition of אור as sectarian. But again, careful analysis leaves no substance to such a claim (as argued in detail in Ch. 8.). First, the verb is probably from the root רוה ("be filled, saturated; drink one's fill"), not ראה ("see"), as the parallelism with the following שבע ("be sated, satisfied") suggests.[16] Thus, none of our witnesses contains the "original" text. The MT transmits an early erroneous consonantal text, losing the preferable *lectio difficilior*; once it had been understood as "see," a natural complement was added as the direct object, and most of the textual tradition, including even 1QIsa^b^ (which often displays close similarities to the MT but here disagrees), transmits the tertiary reading. The broader attestation by the pre-Qumran LXX deflates claims of sectarian motivation, whereas Judaism generally would immediately resonate with the confession יהוה אורי (as in Ps 27:1).

3. Isaiah 41:22

In Isa 41:22 1QIsa^a^ has או אחרונות או הבאות ("or the last things or the things to come") whereas the MT has אחריתן או הבאות ("their end or the things to come"). Arie van der Kooij sees the author-scribe of 1QIsa^a^ as relating the prophecies of Isaiah to his own time, "actualizing" the prophecies in the same way as the author(s) of the *pesharim*; the suggestion is made that the author-scribe of 1QIsa^a^ is to be compared with the Teacher of Righteousness.[17] The reading of Isa 41:22 and the others adduced to exemplify the actualizing interpretation are not in my view sufficient to support that claim. His book is carefully worked and his claim is important, so it deserves more space than is available here. But I do not agree with it and can offer here only a few points:

---

15 See in agreement George J. Brooke, "*E pluribus unum*: Textual Variety and Definitive Interpretation in the Qumran Scrolls," in *The Dead Sea Scrolls in Their Historical Context*, 107–19.

16 This is also suggested by D. Winton Thomas in *BHS* note 53:11[a].

17 A. van der Kooij, *Die alten Textzeugen des Jesajabuches: Ein Beitrag zur Textgeschichte des Alten Testaments* (Freiburg Schweiz: Universitätsverlag; Göttingen: Vandenhoeck & Ruprecht, 1981), 95–96: "der Verfasser von Q[a] Prophezeiungen des Jesajabuches auf seine eigene Zeit bezog. Das bedeutet, dass er die überlieferten Prophezeiungen auf genau die Weise aktualisierte, wie es auch in den Pescharim geschah. Er und mit ihm andere Mitglieder der Qumrangemeinde waren davon überzeugt, dass die prophetischen Worte von 'den kommenden Ereignissen' auch 'die letzten Ereignisse' darstellten. . . . der Verfasser-Schriftgelehrter von Q[a] ist mit dem (ersten) Lehrer der Gerechtigkeit gleichzusetzen."

(a) The assumption that אחריתן in the MT is the earlier, neutral reading and אחרונות in 1QIsa[a] is the changed, "actualizing" interpretation is questionable. In the previous colon הראשנות is parallel, and when used in pairs in Isaiah, אחרון usually follows ראשון (8:23; 41:4; 44:6; 48:12) and אחרית follows ראשית (46:10). Regarding the "actualization," if such were operative, (הימים) אחרית in the MT could be claimed as potentially as eschatological as אחרונות.

(b) Even if the 1QIsa[a] reading were the secondary one, how can we know that it was the specific scribe of that manuscript who introduced the change—as opposed to a previous scribe of one of its *Vorlagen*, thus clearly pre-Qumran?

(c) In the oracle on the fall of Babylon (Isa 47:7) the same pair of variants recurs (אחרונה in 1QIsa[a], אחריתה in the MT) with no difference in meaning. The text in both 1QIsa[a] and the MT reads:

> 5Sit in silence, . . . daughter Chaldea! . . .
> 7You said: "I will be mistress forever,"
> But you did not take these things to heart,
> nor were you mindful of *their end*.

There is no eschatological significance in these words; this "end" is clearly something in the extended present or imminent future, within the historical process. Babylon's hubris in the past will result in its fall any day now.

(d) Moreover, אחרון is used for both the simple future (8:29[9:1]; 30:8) and the cosmic or eschatological future (41:4; 44:6; 48:12) with both 1QIsa[a] and the MT in agreement.

(e) The claim that a scribe intentionally changed the meaning of the Isaianic prophecies is a serious one, requiring clear and sustained proof. For van der Kooij, part of the broader proof lies in his conviction that the roughly contemporaneous translator of the LXX of Isaiah engaged in the same type of actualizing exegesis. For example, he sees in the Oracle against Tyre (Isaiah 23) a prophecy about the destruction of Carthage instead.[18] But neither do I think that the claim for the LXX translator can be sustained.[19]

---

18 A. van der Kooij, *The Oracle of Tyre: The Septuagint of Isaiah XXIII as Version and Vision* (VTSup 71; Leiden: Brill, 1998): "In contrast to MT which is about a destruction of Tyre, LXX refers to a destruction of Carthage with its serious consequences for Tyre" (p. 186).

19 Briefly: (a) In numerous readings, the Qumran Isaiah manuscripts show that the LXX was not translating from a *Vorlage* like the MT but faithfully attempting to translate a text which was simply a different Hebrew text.

(b) Peter W. Flint ("The Septuagint Version of Isaiah 23:1-14 and the Massoretic Text," *BIOSCS* 21 [1988]: 35–54) has written countering the actualizing interpretation of Isaiah 23, and Ronald L. Troxel ("ἔσχατος and Eschatology in LXX-Isaiah," *BIOSCS* 25 [1992]: 18–27), countering the eschatological use of ἔσχατος by the LXX translator.

(c) Van der Kooij's view is partly influenced by Seeligmann who had earlier proposed this Carthage hypothesis. But Seeligmann's work, written prior to the new knowledge provided by the scrolls, needs a methodological revision, and even van der Kooij objects both to his isolated approach to individual readings rather than the full context, and to his specific understanding of πλοῖα in 23:1 as the subject of ἀπώλετο.

(d) The title of the oracle in 23:1 is משא צר ("Oracle of Tyre") translated faithfully as τὸ ὅραμα Τύρου, and thus the oracle as presented by the Greek translator concerns Tyre, not Carthage.

It is helpful to recall the lifelong experience of Robert Hanhart, the former director of the Septuaginta-Unternehmen in Göttingen:

> With regard to the original form of the Greek translation, [. . .] deviations from the MT must be noticed but should only in the rarest cases be taken as the peculiar expression of the translator by means of which he wants to interpret—let alone reinterpret—his *Vorlage*. The LXX—and this is true for all the books translated— is *interpretation* only insofar as a decision is made between various possibilities of understanding which are already inherent in the formulation of the Hebrew *Vorlage* and thus given to the translator. Furthermore, the LXX is the *actualisation* of the contemporary history of the translator only when the choice of the Greek equivalent is capable of doing justice both to the factuality and history of the original Hebrew witness and also to the contemporary history of the translator. The LXX is essentially *conservation*.[20]

In sum, the first two Isaiah readings that looked suspiciously as though they could have been sectarian turn out not to be so. For the third reading, methodology argues against it. The 1QIsa^a reading may well have been the original, not the changed reading, and even if it were the secondary reading, it is not clear that the change was intentional—it recurs later in the text with no significance attached; it was not specific to the Qumran covenanters; and it was not consistently applied or repeated when the scribe had the opportunity to do so. Thus, for the book of Isaiah no variants adduced to date indicate intentional sectarian change.

B. Psalms

The Psalms scrolls highlight over seven hundred variants in comparison with the MT and the LXX.[21] By far the most instructive variants are at the level of literary editions: Psalters showing the inclusion of additional Psalms beyond the familiar 150 and varia-

---

(e) In 23:5 the Greek "sorrow over Tyre" is a free but faithful translation of the Hebrew "report about Tyre," faithfully but more pointedly and less ambiguously making explicit that the translator understands that it is Tyre, not Carthage, which has suffered.

(f) The immediately following words (23:6) are "Depart to Carthage!" suggesting that Tyre is destroyed and thus they should depart to Carthage which is safe.

(g) Both the Hebrew and the Greek of 23:8 say: "Who has counseled this against Tyre [. . .] whose merchants were princes, rulers of the world?" Thus, presumably it is the formerly mighty Tyre which has fallen, not Carthage.

In short, several places are indeed ambiguous, capable of being interpreted either way. But the Cave 1 and Cave 4 Isaiah manuscripts offer examples of the Hebrew forms such as were seen and faithfully translated by the Greek translator, and other parts of the Greek passage demonstrate that it is Tyre, not Carthage, that has fallen and is to be lamented.

[20] "The Translation of the Septuagint in Light of Earlier Tradition and Subsequent Influences," in *Septuagint, Scrolls, and Cognate Writings: Papers Presented to the International Symposium on the Septuagint and Its Relations to the Dead Sea Scrolls and Other Writings (Manchester, 1990)*, ed. by George J. Brooke and Barnabas Lindars, SBLSCS 33 (Atlanta: Scholars Press, 1992), 339–79, esp. 342–43 (emphasis partly in the original, partly added). See also the responses by Ronald S. Hendel, "On the Text-Critical Value of Septuagint Genesis: A Reply to Rösel," *BIOSCS* 32 (1999): 31–34, and William P. Brown, "Reassessing the Text-Critical Value of Septuagint-Genesis 1: A Response to Rösel," *BIOSCS* 32 (1999): 35–39 to Martin Rösel's excessive claims for "theological intention" by the LXX translator in "The Text-Critical Value of Septuagint-Genesis," *BIOSCS* 31 (1998): 62–70, esp. 63.

[21] DJD 4:19–49; DJD 16:7–170; Peter W. Flint, *The Dead Sea Psalms Scrolls*, 50–116; The *Biblical Qumran Scrolls*, 627–726.

tions in the order in which the Psalms occur. With respect to individual textual variants among the witnesses, however, remarkably few increase our knowledge beyond what intelligent conjectures could have produced. That is, for each Psalm line-by-line, in general only a single text tradition seems to have been transmitted. Thus there emerges a long series of minor isolated individual textual variants or errors, often frustratingly small and meaningless, despite their high number. None of these appears to be sectarian in origin, whether in the MT, in the LXX, or in the scrolls.

There is a notable set of variants in Psalm 145 attested by 11QPs^{a}. It repeats after each verse a refrain drawn from the wording of 145:1-2, just as Psalm 136 is copied in the MT and LXX with a recurring refrain from 136:1. Moreover, 11QPs^{a} preserves, as do one Masoretic manuscript, the LXX, and the Peshitta, the *nun* verse at 145:13 which had been lost from most of the MT tradition.[22] Though otherwise instructive, these variants show no sectarian influence.

The most dramatic variant in all the Psalms, of course, is the variant edition of the entire last third of the Psalter exhibited by 11QPs^{a}, which I and others increasingly view as an edition of the Book of Psalms that was considered scriptural (see Ch. 12). Though the manuscript was *copied* in "the first half of the first century" C.E. (DJD 4:9), it is unknown when this edition, as such, *originated*, but it was probably prior to the beginnings of the Qumran community and was not sectarian (cf. 4QpaleoExod^{m}, quite similar to the SP but not Samaritan). But it does contain a significant variant that could be seen as sectarian. In the section entitled "David's Compositions" a number of claims are made: Davidic authorship of the Psalter, divine inspiration, and prophetic origin of the Psalms (XXVII 2–11). However, none of those is sectarian; all Jews would agree with them. But yet another claim is made: that the year has 364 days (XXVII 6–7). The date of origin of that claim remains to be determined, and so it is uncertain whether the claim was, when *composed*, already polemical or whether it became so only later. But the claim for the solar calendar versus the lunar calendar, which eventually emerged as successful in Judaism, was undoubtedly partisan when this particular manuscript was *copied*.[23]

It is important to analyze the separate aspects of this reading. The place where this scroll was copied is unknown, whether in Jerusalem, in broader Palestine, or at Qumran; a claim for the latter would certainly have to be proved and may not be assumed. The place where this edition was first *composed* is even more difficult to determine. There is good reason to think that it was composed well before the specific manuscript 11QPs^{a} was copied. The composition may well have predated the Qumran period, just as the book of Jubilees, also advocating the 364-day year, was composed prior to the Qumran period but was brought to Qumran and was read and popular there. Thus, though the group at Qumran apparently agreed with the 364-day year, there are no solid grounds for claiming that a specifically Qumran scribe was responsible for composing "David's Compositions."

Moreover, the person responsible for first adding "David's Compositions" into the earlier Psalter of which 11QPs^{a} is a late copy probably thought he was writing, not scripture, but a colophon or appendix to a scriptural manuscript that ended with Psalm

---

[22] See *The Dead Sea Scrolls Bible*, 70–72.

[23] For a clear analysis of calendrical issues, see James C. VanderKam, *Calendars in the Dead Sea Scrolls: Measuring Time* (London: Routledge, 1998).

149, 150, and the "Hymn to the Creator" (cf. col. XXVI) as a fitting climax. At a later time two appendices were added: "David's Last Words" (2 Sam 23:1-7) and "David's Compositions," providing credentials and praise of the author.[24] At a later stage several other Psalms were added, as frequently happens at the end of hymnbooks: Psalms 140, 134, and finally 151 (which was added to the LXX Psalter as well).

Though originally "David's Compositions" was probably was not considered Scripture but an appendix to Scripture, now, however, it should be considered part of a "scriptural" scroll, just as the parallel passage praising Solomon and enumerating his proverbs and songs in 1 Kings 5:9-12 [Eng. 4:29-32], though probably not originally considered Scripture, has now been incorporated into a book that became Scripture. It would still remain a valid principle unviolated by the original author of "David's Compositions" that no change *within* the text of *Scripture* was made for sectarian motives. The variant ends up as a sectarian variant within a scriptural manuscript, but it did not originate as a sectarian variant in Scripture, and there is no evidence that it was introduced by a Qumran scribe. It would not be in the same category with the "Mount Ebal" reading in the MT at Deuteronomy 27:4.

C. Daniel

There are more than a hundred variants in Daniel between the scrolls and the MT (DJD 16:239–89), but none of them is such that it should be considered partisan to any group in Judaism. In fact, there is not a single variant that is even worth mentioning or considering for our present context. That is highly significant for a book whose composition (at least for the twelve-chapter edition) was roughly contemporary with the origins of the Qumran covenanters, which shared the covenanters' intense interest in apocalypticism, and indeed which served as a source for some of their concepts (e.g., "Time of the End") and religious vocabulary (e.g., משכיל, הרבים: "Maskil," "the Many"). If there is not a single variant worth considering as a possible sectarian variant in the Book of Daniel, it would seem all the more dubious that such would be found in other books.

D. Other Books

Both in my working through all the Cave 4 biblical manuscripts for publication in DJD and in a recent review of their variants, I found nothing that I would categorize as a sectarian variant, except for the variant in 4QJosh[a] and Deut 27:2-4 about Gilgal versus Mount Gerizim versus Mount Ebal as the location of the first altar after Israel had crossed into the land. That variant was not a Qumranic sectarian variant but a double Samarian-then-Judean variant in the SP-OG-OL, and in the MT-LXX, respectively.

IV. Manuscripts Copied at Qumran

Thus far, the focus has been on books whose content the covenanters might have found especially fertile for sectarian variants. But since direct evidence that a specific manuscript was copied at Qumran itself is rare, focus on manuscripts that most likely *were* copied at Qumran could prove illuminating.

---

24 Appendices occur at or near the end of several books or major sections thereof, e.g., Judges, Samuel, Isaiah, and perhaps Leviticus and Deuteronomy.

A. 4QSam^c

This manuscript in particular should be examined closely for Qumranic sectarian variants since it has perhaps one of the strongest claims to being a biblical text that was copied at Qumran. It is clearly a biblical manuscript, and it is highly probable that it was copied at Qumran because the same scribe copied the main manuscript of the Rule of the Community from Cave 1 (1QS).[25] Its script is markedly idiosyncratic and is detectable in several other manuscripts, including the Testimonia (4Q175) and a correction in the Great Isaiah Scroll (1QIsa$^{a\,2m}$) at Isa 40:7-8. Moreover, the point could be suggested that this copyist may have been a high-ranking leader in the community: (a) his skill as a scribe or copyist is remarkably low, and thus he may have had some other basis for his role, such as his leadership position; (b) his selection to inscribe the Maskil's Rule and the Testimonia (a meditation on leadership) may be indications of his role as a leader; and (c) he had the authority to correct the scroll of Isaiah.

A review of the variants in 4QSam^c produces interesting results. The extant remains preserve one small scrap from 1 Sam 25:30-32 and multiple fragments from three contiguous columns with text from 2 Sam 14:7–15:15 (see Ch. 6). In the 67 partially surviving lines, the scribe stumbled 21 times (almost one out of every three lines!). Despite his high rate of errors, corrections, and insertions, the text he produced is still superior to the Masoretic *textus receptus*. 4QSam^c has 19 extant readings superior to those in the MT (and 12 more that can be reconstructed), whereas the MT has 13 readings superior to those extant in 4QSam^c (with 4 more that can be reconstructed). Five of the superior readings in 4QSam^c are unique, while a number are also attested in the Greek.[26]

When the focus sharpens to specifically sectarian variants, again the indicator falls to zero. All of the variants in the scroll, the MT, the OG, the later Greek manuscripts, and the OL are virtually meaningless. They consist of minor, routine intentional variants, such as the explicit adding of implicit elements (subject, direct or indirect object, or particles), or minor, routine unintentional variants, such as spelling mistakes, parablepsis, or substitution of more familiar forms or expressions. Not a single variant in the scroll, the MT, or the LXX will sustain the claim that it could be an intentional variant by any of the Jewish parties.

B. The Testimonia

Manuscript 4Q175, copied by the same scribe as 4QSam^c, consists of four quotations selected for the theme of leadership: three positive quotations from Scripture focusing on prophet (Exod 20:21^b[18^b] in the SP, Deut 5:28-29 + 18:18-19 in the MT), king (Num 24:15-17), and priest (Deut 33:8-11), and a negative quotation from the Apocryphon of Joshua focusing on an accursed man who rebuilds Jericho (4Q379; cf. Josh 6:26).

---

[25] For another scribe quite likely to have copied manuscripts at Qumran, see Ulrich, "Identification of a Scribe Active at Qumran: 1QPs^b–4QIsa^c–11QM," in *Meghillot: Studies in the Dead Sea Scrolls* 5–6: *A Festschrift for Devorah Dimant* (2008), *201–*10. This scribe's work is found in three different caves and includes (just as the scribe of 4QSam^c and 1QS) scriptural as well as sectarian works.

[26] See Ch. 6.II.D. For the edition and text-critical analysis of 4QSam^c see DJD 17:247–67, esp. 253–54.

If the text of the four quotations is compared with the MT, numerous variants emerge.

1. Exod 20:21^{b}(18^{b})

For the first, the MT of Exodus does not have the passage at all, whereas the MT of Deuteronomy has variants:

4QTest	וידבר •••• אל מושה לאמור שמעת
MT SP (Deut 5:28[25])	ויאמר יהוה אלי שמעתי

If, however, one avoids the presupposition that the MT is the point of comparison and turns to other available witnesses to the HB, here the SP, 4QTest is seen to quote the SP of Exodus almost verbatim:

4QTest	וידבר •••• אל מושה לאמור שמעת
SP (Exod 20:21^{b})	וידבר יהוה אל משה לאמר שמעתי

And instead of having to claim that 4QTest adapts the wording and excerpts from two different passages in Deuteronomy, it can be seen that the full quotation derives from Exod 20:21^{b} in a Jewish variant literary edition of Exodus in circulation at the time.[27] The quotations also naturally unfold in the established chronological order of the books: Exodus, Numbers, Deuteronomy, Joshua.

Specifically with regard to Exodus: in the early first century B.C.E. when 4QTest was copied, there were at least three forms of the book of Exodus in use in Jewish circles (see Chs. 3 and 13). The earliest form attested in our manuscripts is preserved by the LXX in chapters 35–40.[28] The second variant literary edition is that presented in the MT. The third is that illustrated by 4QpaleoExod^{m}, the text that was used as the basis of the SP. The Christians eventually inherited the early edition, the Rabbis the medial edition, and the Samaritans the late edition; there appears to be no evidence suggesting that any of those parties consciously chose their specific text on either ideological or textual grounds.

2. Num 24:15-17

In the second quotation from Num 24:15-17, the text of 4Q175 is for all practical purposes the same as that in the SP, the MT, and the LXX. Unfortunately, none of the Qumran scrolls of Numbers preserves this passage.

3. Deut 33:8-11

In the third quotation from Deut 33:8-11, 4QTest contains "Give to Levi" which is lacking in the MT and SP. But 4QDeut^{h} and the LXX also attest this reading, again making it virtually certain that the clause was in the text being faithfully quoted by the

---

27 4Q158 frg. 6 also quotes this form of the Exodus text, as Brant James Pitre pointed out in 1999 in an unpublished paper on 4Q175.

28 The LXX edition of Exodus 35–40, however, is not the earliest form of this section but already shows signs of editorial development; see Anneli Aejmelaeus, "Septuagintal Translation Techniques—A Solution to the Problem of the Tabernacle Account?" in *On the Trail of the Septuagint Translators: Collected Essays* (rev. and exp. ed.; Leuven: Peters, 2007), 107–22.

Qumran scribe. Moreover, the clause was either original and lost in the MT-SP tradition or a clarifying explicitation of what was implicit; at any rate there is no change of meaning, and the fact that the third-century B.C.E. LXX had the reading clearly removes it from consideration as an intentional sectarian variant.

4. Josh 6:26

The fourth quotation in 4Q175 appears to be a quotation of Josh 6:26 plus a typical Qumran *pesher*, but it turns out that the entire passage is a quotation of a text also preserved in 4QApocryphon of Joshua^b (4Q379 22 ii 7-15).[29] Not only did this Qumran scribe not alter his source text, in this case it should be noted that the MT exhibits a secondary form of Josh 6:26 with three additions (לפני יהוה, יקום, and את יריחו).

Thus, 4QTestimonia is a composition consisting of three biblical passages plus a fourth biblical passage already amplified in another Qumran text. The four passages were selected and juxtaposed as a quasi-meditation on the theme of leadership, positive and negative. It is not a biblical manuscript, but a free selection of scriptural passages, and thus it might be understandable if the author altered the text of the quotations to suit the community's views. But even here the author or scribe did not. Although 4QTest was possibly composed by, or at least almost certainly copied by an inhabitant of Qumran, there is no reason to suspect that any textual variants were introduced into the scriptural text in order to shape the original text toward the beliefs or views of the Qumran community.

C. A Correction in 1QIsa^a

Finally, this same scribe made a correction inserted into the Great Isaiah Scroll at Isa 40:6-8 (see Ch. 7.III). For that well-known passage the base text of 1QIsa^a reads:

> All flesh is grass,
> and all its beauty like the flowers of the field.
> The grass withers, the flowers fade,
> but the word of our God stands forever.

Subsequently, the scribe of 4QSam^c-1QS-4QTest added, to be inserted after the word "fade," the text in italics:[30]

> All flesh is grass,
> and all its beauty like the flowers of the field.
> The grass withers, the flowers fade,
> *when the breath of •••• blows upon it.*
> *[Surely the people is 'the grass.']*
> *The grass withers, the flowers fade*
> but the word of our God stands forever.

There are two possibilities for this scribal phenomenon. First, the text copied by the scribe of 1QIsa^a was probably the original, with the later insertion by the scribe of 4QSam^c-1QS-4QTest as a secondary amplification; clearly the parenthetical identifi-

[29] See Carol Newsom, DJD 22:278–81.

[30] It need not be mentioned that the scribe of course made several errors in his insertion, misspelling two words and continuing the insertion one or two words beyond where he should have stopped.

cation "Surely the people is 'the grass'" is a secondary amplification. The alternate possibility is that the fuller text was original and the 1QIsa[a] scribe simply committed parablepsis, skipping from the first occurrence of "the flowers fade" to the second, and thus losing a line. In favor of the first alternative, however, is the fact that the OG is a second witness with the same short text, which makes sense as it is, in exact agreement with the text copied by the original scribe (see Ch. 7.III). At any rate, one Hebrew tradition contained the longer text, and the scribe of 4QSam[c] knew that tradition and revised 1QIsa[a] on the basis of it. The main point to be made in the present context is that the Qumran scribe, who also copied 4QSam[c], 1QS, and 4QTest without "sectarian" variants, inserted text into this scriptural manuscript but penned the insertion faithfully, in basic accordance with the text tradition mirrored by the MT and the Hexapla, and without sectarian variants.

Thus, one of the scribes with the strongest claim to being a specifically Qumran scribe copied biblical and excerpted biblical texts without any sign of introducing sectarianly motivated changes.

Before concluding, it can be noted that none of the main proposals concerning the history of the biblical text in light of the scrolls appeals to sectarian variants. Frank Moore Cross argued for a local-text theory, that different text-types had developed in different localities: Palestine, Egypt, and (probably) Babylon.[31] Though it is quite probably true that there were different examples of textual growth that took place in different localities, to my knowledge there is no specific evidence that causally links any particular form of growth with any particular locality. There are no sectarian variants known to be due to the different localities.

Shemaryahu Talmon proposed a theory of many text-forms being reduced to only three. His socio-religious idea of *Gruppentexte* explained why, out of the plethora of textual forms of the books of Scriptures that were generally circulating in the first century C.E., only three textual forms emerged: those saved by the Jews, the Samaritans, and the Christians.[32] It did not, however, explain why each particular community chose its particular text. Why specifically did the Rabbis end up with the collection found in the MT, the Samaritans with the expanded form of the text, and the Christians with the collection found in the LXX? Are there any features that are *group-specific* in any of those texts (other than the three SP features described above)? And if the Qumran community had eventually chosen its own single text form for each book, is there any way to know which of the several available texts for a given book it would have chosen? The challenge for this theory is to discover any evidence that a group changed its form of the text in a manner attributable to the ideology of that group. Finally, neither Emanuel Tov's reconstruction of the history of the biblical text in *Textual Criticism* nor my proposal of variant literary editions appeals to variants due to sectarian motivation.

---

31 "The Evolution of a Theory of Local Texts," in *Qumran and the History*, 306–20.

32 Shemaryahu Talmon, "The Old Testament Text," in *The Cambridge History of the Bible. 1. From the Beginnings to Jerome* (ed. Peter R. Ackroyd and Craig F. Evans; Cambridge: Cambridge University Press, 1970), 159–99, esp. 197–99 [repr. in *Qumran and the History*, 1–41, esp. 40–41]; "Aspects of the Textual Transmission of the Bible in the Light of Qumran Manuscripts," *Textus* 4 (1964): 95–132, esp. 125–32 [repr. in *Qumran and the History*, 226–63, esp. 256–63]; and "The Textual Study of the Bible—A New Outlook," *Qumran and the History*, 321–400.

Conclusion

This chapter, in the attempt to discover textual variants that were "sectarian" in origin or motivation, has focused on individual textual variants highlighted by the Qumran biblical scrolls in contrast with each other and with the Masoretic Text, the Samaritan Pentateuch, and the Septuagint. Its limited scope could not include either variant literary editions as possibly sectarian in origin or the authoritative status of disputed books as possibly promoted or discounted by vying Jewish parties.

Despite the fact that the question regarding sectarian variants seems so obvious, so instinctual, so needing to be asked, both the resulting evidence and the logic of the question point toward a negative answer.

With regard to the textual evidence: no variants emerged to indicate that any sect—whether Pharisaic, Sadducean, Samaritan, Essene, Christian, or other—had tampered with Scripture in order to bolster their particular beliefs, except for the three SP-MT variants: God "had chosen" or "will choose"; Mount Gerizim or Mount Ebal; and the presence or absence of the extra SP commandment. But none of these are Qumran variants.[33]

With regard to the logic: If one group tampered with the text of Scripture in order to promote its views, it would be open to immediate demonstrable refutation. All the groups had limited viewpoints, but all apparently agreed that the text of the "original" Scriptures should not be altered, and if there were problems, the texts should be corrected toward the "original."

The following is what the ancient scribes seem to have done. Almost always, the scribes tried simply to copy faithfully the text that lay before them, or at least the text their eye or mind perceived. Inevitably, they introduced changes into the text, either making inadvertent mistakes (some of which were later corrected, while some remained) or attempting to make the text clearer or smoother; these latter were intended not as changes in content but as minor improvements to bring out the inherent sense more clearly or to make the grammar flow more smoothly.

Rarely, probably less than once per century for any given book, a creative religious leader or theologian produced a new edition of a work—analogous to the revised edition of the Gospel According to Mark produced by the redactor of Matthew or Luke—that transmitted the traditional content faithfully but creatively reshaped it in light of the contemporary historical, theological, or cultural situation. In form, such could be termed a new literary edition of the work; in content and motive, it was a new theological edition. None of the new literary editions show indications of sectarian motivation, with the single exception of the Samaritan focus on Gerizim and the Judean reaction against it.

Rarely did a scribe introduce a theological change,[34] and when this happened, it was not sectarian but in line with general Jewish views or impulses.

---

[33] See in agreement Brooke, "E Pluribus Unum," 108, 110; Tov, *Textual Criticism*, 110; and Timothy H. Lim, *The Formation of the Jewish Canon* (Anchor Yale Bible Reference Library; New Haven: Yale University Press, 2013), 122.

[34] See the cautions and limitations described by Emanuel Tov, "Theologically Motivated Exegesis Embedded in the Septuagint," in *The Greek and Hebrew Bible*, 257–69, and "Theological Tendencies in the Masoretic Text of Samuel," in *After Qumran*, 3–20.

Now it is fully possible, of course, that there are some sectarian variants that I have not noticed or have not correctly understood. It is also true that the biblical variants illuminated by the manuscripts of the Scriptures found at Qumran form a tantalizing collection of data. And we all know that, if there is an attractive mistake waiting to be made, there is probably an eager scholar itching to make that mistake.

So I offer a few criteria that may help future scholars either discover true sectarian variants, if there are such, or not make the mistake of hastily claiming that a variant is "sectarian" if it is not.

First, a sectarian variant must be clearly *secondary* (or later). It cannot be either an original (or earlier) reading or what Shemaryahu Talmon has helpfully categorized as a synonymous variant. It should perhaps be jarring or arresting in the context (as, e.g., כדויד in Amos 6:5).

Second, the variant must be *intentional*. It must be clear that an author or scribe was concerned to change one natural, neutral reading into a reading important to his particular group.

Third, the variant must be *specific* to one group or sect versus another, or supporting a major theme or word peculiar to a specific group as opposed to Jews in general. (It is unlikely, for example, that the presence of אור in Isa 53:11 constitutes a sectarian variant inspired by the motif of בני אור versus בני חושך when virtually all could immediately identify with יהוה אורי in Ps 27:1, and none would consider themselves as among the בני חושך.)

Fourth, the variant ought to be *repeated* or consistently made or accompanied by other similarly sectarian variants in the same manuscript when the opportunity allows, not a single, isolated variant. It should not be easily explainable by simpler, more frequent classes of variants, such as metathesis, confusion of laryngeals or sibilants, confusion of palaeographic forms ד/ר/ו/י, or similar phenomena; these happen so frequently where no meaning is involved that such a variant would be highly implausible without other solid corroboration.

In light of the thousands of biblical variants which involve no significant meaning, no sectarian elements, but are readily assignable to the normal, dull categories of textual variants, there is a ponderous, a Herculean, burden of proof on the person who wishes to claim that a particular variant—especially an isolated variant—is sectarian in nature. In most instances where theological *Tendenz* is claimed for readings in the Septuagint, or where sectarian variants are claimed in the scrolls, the basis for the claim disappears upon analysis. First, sectarian manipulation or theological *Tendenz* is usually only one of several possible explanations of the variant, and usually a maximalist interpretation. Second, the phenomenon is not sustained in other possible occurrences where it would have been expected to be repeated. Third, additional examples of the alternate and usually less exciting explanation often occur, counter-indicating the sectarian or tendential claim. In short, one should rarely be convinced of sectarian motivation or significant theological *Tendenz* in textual variants.[35]

---

[35] See again the quotation from Professor Hanhart in III.A.3.(e) above.

CHAPTER 12

"NONBIBLICAL" SCROLLS NOW RECOGNIZED AS SCRIPTURAL

ARE THERE BOOKS that were originally disqualified as "nonbiblical" which in light of post-Qumran thinking should be considered "biblical," or better "scriptural" (since there was not yet a "Bible")?

The purpose of this chapter is to chart scholars' gradual realization that certain manuscripts originally classified as "nonbiblical" are in fact more accurately seen as "scriptural." The purpose is not to criticize the original editors of these manuscripts, for they provided the necessary foundation: excellent editions that we can now analyze and perhaps see more clearly. Rather, it is to illustrate the epistemological growth: the history of the shift from the commonly shared pre-Qumran mindset—by which we all rendered our judgments about what was "biblical" using the MT-SP-LXX as our limiting model—to post-Qumran thinking (see Ch. 2).

Since there were hundreds of manuscripts found in Cave 4, some proving to be copies of biblical texts while others contained different types of works, the original Cave 4 editorial team, envisioning the many volumes that would be required for the series, quite naturally decided to distinguish "biblical" from "nonbiblical" volumes.[1] The classification of which manuscripts were "biblical" and which were "nonbiblical" was made in the early days, before the current understanding and appreciation of the nature of the biblical text in antiquity was achieved, and the entire forty-volume DJD series continued for consistency with the MT as the criterion for "biblical."

Whereas discussion of all the possibilities, including the excerpted texts, would fill many pages, we must limit discussion here to two examples: 4QPentateuch and 11QPsalms[a].

I. 4QPENTATEUCH

Five manuscripts from Cave 4 presented text that substantially agreed with the traditional text of the Pentateuch but also showed considerable divergence:

4Q158 = 4QPent A or	4QPent[a]	(*olim* 4QRP[a])[2]
4Q364 = 4QPent B	4QPent[b]	(*olim* 4QRP[b])
4Q365 = 4QPent C	4QPent[c]	(*olim* 4QRP[c]) + 4Q365a = 4QPent C (*olim* 4QTemple?)
4Q366 = 4QPent D	4QPent[d]	(*olim* 4QRP[d])
4Q367 = 4QPent E	4QPent[e]	(*olim* 4QRP[e])

[1] The DJD series had made this distinction from the start, but the contents of both Cave 1 and "*les petites grottes*" were limited enough to include both "biblical" and "nonbiblical" scrolls in the same volume.

[2] 4Q158 is the least likely to be the same composition as 4Q364–4Q367 (see n. 5).

These manuscripts departed from the traditional text to such an extent that the original team of Cave 4 editors grouped them with the nonbiblical texts and assigned them to nonbiblical volumes.[3] John Allegro published "Biblical Paraphrase" (4Q158) in DJD 5, and John Strugnell identified and transcribed the fragments of the "Reworked Pentateuch" (4Q364–367), which were eventually fully developed and published by Emanuel Tov and Sidnie White (Crawford) in DJD 13.[4] The editors originally thought that all five scrolls were copies of a single work, though subsequent study eventually separated 4Q158 from the others[5] and raised questions whether all four of the remaining scrolls 4Q364–367 attest a single work or rather are different compositions with similar techniques.[6]

A. The Evidence from the Various Textual Traditions

The editors of the collection in DJD state that the

> text presented here probably contained the complete Pentateuch, reworked by the author of 4QRP.... This composition contained a running text of the Pentateuch interspersed with exegetical additions and omissions. The greater part of the preserved fragments follows the biblical text closely, but many small ... elements are added, while other elements are omitted, or, in other cases, their sequence altered.[7]

It is thus important to study some of the more salient additions, omissions, and altered sequences seen in the texts, in order to judge the proper classification of these manuscripts in light of what the scrolls have taught us in the intervening decades.

Additions

One of the largest additions in 4Q364 (4QPent B) follows the text of Gen 30:26-36, and it demonstrates how the editor worked. Later, in Gen 31:10-13 Jacob tells Rachel and Leah that he had a dream:

> [10]"During the mating of the flock I once had a dream in which I lifted up my eyes and saw that the male goats that leaped upon the flock were striped, speckled, and mottled. [11]Then the angel of God said to me in the dream, 'Jacob,' and I said, 'Here I am!' [12]And he said, 'Lift up your eyes and see that all the goats that leap on the flock are striped, speckled, and mottled; for I have seen all that Laban is doing to you. [13]I am the God of Bethel, where you anointed a pillar and made a vow to

[3] The best recent comprehensive discussion of the character of these manuscripts is Molly M. Zahn, *Rethinking Rewritten Scripture: Composition and Exegesis in the 4QReworked Pentateuch Manuscripts* (STDJ 95; Leiden: Brill, 2011). Sidnie White Crawford has also contributed a very instructive and judicious monograph, *Rewriting Scripture in Second Temple Times* (Grand Rapids, Mich.: Eerdmans, 2008), although I would venture further and claim full scriptural status for 4QPentateuch, *olim* 4QReworked Pentateuch.

[4] Emanuel Tov and Sidnie White, "364–367. 4QReworked Pentateuch[b–e]," in DJD 13:187–351.

[5] Moshe J. Bernstein, "Pentateuch Interpretation at Qumran," in *The Dead Sea Scrolls after Fifty Years*, 1:128–59, esp. 134 n. 7; Michael Segal, "4QReworked Pentateuch or 4QPentateuch?" in *The Dead Sea Scrolls: Fifty Years after Their Discovery* (ed. Lawrence H. Schiffman et al.; Jerusalem: Israel Exploration Society/The Shrine of the Book, Israel Museum, 2000), 391–99, esp. 396; George J. Brooke, "4Q158: Reworked Pentateuch[a] or Reworked Pentateuch A?" *DSD* 8/3 (2001): 219–41.

[6] Segal, "Reworked Pentateuch," 397–98; Brooke, "4Q158: Reworked Pentateuch[a]?" 219–41.

[7] Tov and White, DJD 13:187, 191.

> me. Now arise, get out from this land at once and return to the land of your birth.'" [NRSV adapted]

Fragment 4b–e ii of 4Q364 (4QPent B) contains the common MT-SP-LXX text of Gen 30:26-36, but after 30:36 the fragment continues in lines 21–26 with:

> (Line 21) And [the angel of God sai]d [to Jacob in a dream: 'Jacob,' and he said,] (22) 'He[re I am.' The angel said, 'Lift up] your [eyes and see that all the goats that leap on (23) the flock are striped, spe]ckled, [and mottled; for I have seen all that Laban is doing (24) to you. I am the God of Bethel, wh]ere [you anointed a pillar and made (25) a vow to me. Now arise, get out] fr[om this land and return to the land (26) of your] fa[thers, and I will deal well with you.'][8]

The editor here works as a "supplementer," anticipating Jacob's report of his dream in Gen 31:10-13 by adding after Gen 30:36 the contents (present in 4QPent B and SP, but not in the MT or LXX) of what the messenger of God said to Jacob in that dream, the details of which are drawn from Gen 31:10-13.

In considering whether this addition is biblical, three points should be noted. First, the (biblical) SP in fact contains the passage, which most likely means that the expanded Judean-Samarian edition contained it.[9] Second, this example is similar to other accounts found in the MT-LXX-SP of dreams and the repetition of the details of those dreams. For example, Gen 31:24 contains Laban's dream with a specific command, and 31:29 reports Laban's speech to Jacob using exactly the words of the dream. Again, 41:1-7 contains Pharaoh's dream with specific details, and 41:17-24 reports his recounting the details of the dream to Joseph. Thus, the supplement that occurs in 4Q364 mirrors similar nearby dream reports in MT-SP Genesis. Third, this supplementing is similar to the repeated practice seen in 4QpaleoExod^{m} and the SP (see Ch. 3).

4Q365 (4QPent C) also displays large additions. Fragment 6a col. i contains Exod 14:12-21. The next column on that fragment (frg. 6a ii plus 6c) contains Exod 15:22-26, but that passage is preceded by seven lines on the fragment that are not in the MT-SP-LXX but are best interpreted as the Song of Miriam. Lost between the extant parts of cols. i and ii is presumably the Song of Moses, introduced by 15:1—"Then Moses and the Israelites sang this song to the LORD: 'I will sing to the LORD, for he has triumphed gloriously; horse and rider he has thrown into the sea.'" Note that 15:21 is introduced the same way with virtually identical wording: "Miriam sang to them: 'Sing to the LORD, for he has triumphed gloriously; horse and rider he has thrown into the sea.'" In the MT-SP-LXX, however, the incipit then stops without an ensuing song. The editor of 4Q365 thus apparently supplied, after Exod 15:21 and before 15:22-26, a celebratory song by Miriam that echoes that of Moses. As the DJD editors note, the "Song of Miriam here parallels other songs of triumph by biblical women, e.g., the Song of Deborah in Judges 5."[10] This presumably secondary addition of a song or prayer also parallels other songs or prayers secondarily inserted and subsequently viewed as part of the biblical text,

---

[8] The quotation is based on and adapted from *The Dead Sea Scrolls Reader, Part 3: Parabiblical Texts*, (ed. Donald W. Parry and Emanuel Tov; Leiden: Brill, 2005), 248–49.

[9] Zahn says it well, that several of these texts "preserve major changes also known from the Samaritan Pentateuch, indicating that they . . . used as their base text a version of the Pentateuch that was already pre-Samaritan in type" (*Rethinking Rewritten Scripture*, 97).

[10] DJD 13:271.

e.g., the song of Hannah (1 Sam 2:1-10), the prayer of Daniel (9:4-19), and the prayer of Habakkuk 3.

Another large addition is on frg. 23 of 4Q365. It has text of Lev 23:42-44 plus text identical to 24:1-2aα, followed by at least seven lines which contain directions for various offerings, including "when you come to the land which I am giving you. . . , you will bring wood for a burnt offering" (lines 4–5), and "the [fe]stival of fresh oil. They will bring wood. . ." (line 9). The wood offering is not mentioned in the traditional Pentateuch, but the Temple Scroll[11] sheds light on 4Q365. A small fragment of the second copy (11QT^{b} col. 6 = frg. 10e line 5) mentioning "the wood as a burnt offering" appears to "fit into the lacuna at the top of col. 23 in 11QT^{a}" (the main copy), and "the mention of העצים ("the wood") in line 5 suggests strongly that a feast dedicated to the wood offering is indeed the subject of [11QT^{a}] cols. 23–25."[12]

Although the wood offering is not mentioned in the traditional Pentateuch, Nehemiah, in a rehearsal of obligations regarding various offerings, says

> We have also cast lots among the priests, the Levites, and the people, for the wood offering, to bring it into the house of our God . . . to burn on the altar of the LORD our God, *as it is written in the Torah* (Neh 10:35[34], emphasis added; see also 13:31).

Thus, the legislation regarding the wood offering must have been in one form of the Pentateuch, used by Nehemiah and by the scribes of 4Q365 and the Temple Scroll.

The largest addition in 4Q365 is so strikingly different from known biblical texts that it has been designated in DJD 13 as a different work, 4Q365a ("4QTemple?"). Despite the fact that the five fragments of 4Q365a are "written by the same hand as the main body of 4Q365" and the physical details of the manuscript are identical to those of 4Q365, Yigael Yadin theorized that "frgs. 2 and 3 (as well as frg. 23 of 4Q365)" belonged, not to 4Q365, but to another copy of the Temple Scroll. John Strugnell, however, basing his conclusion on the evidence of the physical details of the manuscript and the script, assigned all the fragments to 4Q365. The DJD editors of 4Q365a tentatively concluded that, because "these five fragments do not include any biblical material," it is very unlikely that they belong to 4QRP."[13]

As with other topics, scholarly discussion over the years has progressed and has now increasingly judged that 4Q365a is part of a Pentateuchal 4Q365 (now 4QPent C) and that the Temple Scroll used this kind of expanded text. For example, Molly Zahn

> begins from the argument that 4QRP C includes the five fragments labeled 4Q365a (4QTemple?) and that 4QRP C should be regarded as an expanded edition of the Pentateuch. Substantial parallels between 4QRP C (both 4Q365 and 4Q365a) and the *Temple Scroll* raise the possibility that an expanded Pentateuch resembling 4QRP C could have constituted the main source with which the *Temple Scroll*'s redactor worked.[14]

---

[11] The Temple Scroll (11QT^{a,b} = 11Q19, 11Q20) is rewritten Torah including parts of Exodus through Deuteronomy.

[12] Zahn, *Rethinking Rewritten Scripture*, 105–6. In addition to the text and discussion in DJD 13:290–96, Zahn offers an in-depth treatment of frg. 23 and the wood offering, 102–8.

[13] DJD 13:319.

[14] Molly M. Zahn, "4QReworked Pentateuch C and the Literary Sources of the *Temple Scroll*: A New (Old) Proposal," *DSD* 19/2 (2012): 133–58, esp. 133. Armin Lange reached the same conclusion in his *Handbuch der Textfunde vom Toten Meer, Band 1* (Tübingen: Mohr Siebeck, 2009), 37, 40.

Analysis of the additions in these manuscripts thus makes it plausible that they are analogous to other additions in the pluriform Scriptures of the Second Temple period.

Omissions

Numbers 33:38 is identified as an omission in 4Q364, since the MT, SP, and LXX have the precise date of Aaron's death "on the first day of the fifth month," whereas 4Q364 lacks the date:

MT, SP, LXX	וימת שם בשנת הארבעים לצאת בני ישראל מארץ מצרים בחדש החמישי באחד לחדש
4Q364	[וי]מ̊]ות שם בשנת הארבעים לצאת בני י]שראל מאר̇ץ מ̊צ̊רים

He died there in the fortieth year after the Israelites had come out of the land of Egypt, *on the first day of the fifth month.*

Moreover, another omission immediately follows: the next verse, Num 33:39, leads directly into 33:41, thus lacking the entire v. 40 found in the MT-SP-LXX:

... he died on Mount Hor. [40]*The Canaanite, the king of Arad, who lived in the Negeb in the land of Canaan, heard of the coming of the Israelites.* [41]They set out from Mount Hor....

These two shorter readings in 4Q364, the second lacking verse 40 which is jarringly out of context, were originally listed as "exegetical shortening of the text."[15]

From the earlier perspective it is understandable that good scholars would view the common MT-SP-LXX as "the biblical text," since all main witnesses agree in the longer text; accordingly, 4Q364 "omits." From the current perspective, however, we can suggest that these are not omissions in 4Q364 but rather intentional insertions in the forerunner of MT-SP-LXX. In both these cases 4Q364 retains the "original" short text. The first reading is an early intentional scribal insertion shared by the MT, SP, and LXX, adding the precise date of Aaron's death. The second is also simply an intentional scribal insertion in the MT, SP, and LXX, adding the intrusive note about the Canaanite king hearing of the Israelites' coming, which is unrelated to what goes before and what comes after (cf. Num 21:1 where the verse does fit).[16]

The DJD editors are to be credited for explicitly mentioning that for the first reading, "It is noteworthy that the exact date of Aaron's death in MT, SP, LXX is not paralleled by traditions about Moses and Miriam, so that it is remotely possible that 4Q364 reflects an ancient textual tradition in which Aaron's death was not mentioned."[17] In a parallel example, the explicit mention of Eli's age at 1 Sam 2:22 in 4QSam[a] but not in the MT was classified as a secondary addition (see Ch. 6.III.A.).

In conclusion, I agree with Zahn that "[l]ike 4Q364, 4Q365 presents several cases of minuses. For none of these is there any compelling evidence that they represent delib-

[15] DJD 13:226. See Zahn's corrective of this excessive term "exegetical," in *Rethinking Rewritten Scripture*, 12–13.

[16] Emanuel Tov, "Biblical Texts as Reworked in Some Qumran Manuscripts with Special Attention to 4QRP and 4QParaGen-Exod," in *The Community of the Renewed Covenant: The Notre Dame Symposium on the Dead Sea Scrolls* (Christianity and Judaism in Antiquity 10; ed. Eugene Ulrich and James VanderKam; Notre Dame, Ind.: University of Notre Dame Press, 1994), 111–34, esp. 130.

[17] DJD 13:226.

erate omissions" but rather they "simply witness to an earlier stage of the text," while the MT-SP-LXX show inserted expansions.[18]

Altered Sequences or Juxtapositions

The tradents occasionally juxtaposed texts from diverse loci that treated the same subject. The DJD editors note this in 4Q364 frg. 23a–b col. i, which contains Num 20:17-18 followed by Deut 2:8-14.

> This represents a long "harmonizing" plus before the text of Deut 2:8. . . , which was intended to bring the account of Deuteronomy into harmony with that of Numbers. Compare with a reverse addition from Deut 2:2-6 after Num 20:13 in SP. The harmonizing addition in 4Q364 in Deuteronomy adds the conversation with the king of Edom from Numbers 20.[19]

Similarly, frg. 36 of 4Q365 contains Num 27:11 followed by Num 36:1-2, clearly to link the two passages which treat the inheritance by the daughters of Zelophahad. The scriptural scroll 4QNum^b also appears to rearrange Num 27:2-11 to fit with Numbers chapter 36; see DJD 12:262–64 (= *BQS* 170–71, 174); this gives a genuinely scriptural analogy to the altered sequence in 4Q365. The manner of juxtaposition in 4QNum^b is somewhat different from that in 4Q365; but the intentional juxtaposition in both is due to the similarity in topic — the inheritance by the daughters of Zelophahad. Tov noted early that these are rearrangements and represent "no real omissions."[20]

B. The Maturing of Analysis

Even prior to the publication of DJD 13 in 1994, scholars were alerted to the surprises of 4Q364–367. With the first DJD volume by the younger generation (DJD 8) published in 1990 and the first biblical volume (DJD 9) already in press, Julio Trebolle Barrera and Luis Vegas Montaner of the Universidad Complutense of Madrid organized the first international conference of Qumran editors in 1991.[21] It was at that ground-breaking conference that Tov and White Crawford offered the first comprehensive announcement and presentation of 4Q364–367, initially labeled 4QPentateuchal Paraphrase.[22]

One of the many reasons the Madrid conference was so important is that it brought together for the first time virtually all the scholars who had been working individually on their editions of various genres of scrolls, in separate cities and countries without the knowledge which others, working on different types of scrolls, were gaining. The conference provided the first global view of the full corpus, and the scholars were able to make valuable connections with the insights of others. They were able to gain illumination from others on the problems that were puzzling in their own texts.

---

[18] Zahn, *Rethinking Rewritten Scripture*, 112.

[19] DJD 13:231.

[20] Tov, "Biblical Texts as Reworked," 128.

[21] For the proceedings of that conference see *The Madrid Qumran Congress: Proceedings of the International Congress on the Dead Sea Scrolls — Madrid, 18–21 March, 1991* (2 vols.; STDJ 11, 1–2; ed. Julio Trebolle Barrera and Luis Vegas Montaner; Leiden: Brill; Madrid: Complutense, 1992).

[22] Emanuel Tov, "The Textual Status of 4Q364–367 (4QPP)," in *The Madrid Qumran Congress*, 1:43–82; Sidnie White, "4Q364 & 365: A Preliminary Report," in *The Madrid Qumran Congress*, 1:217–28.

It was at the Madrid conference, when Tov and White Crawford offered their presentation of the nonbiblical 4QPentateuchal Paraphrase, that Ulrich presented a paper on the pluriformity that characterized the biblical manuscripts.[23] That paper on the scriptural pluriformity appeared juxtaposed to Tov's on the Pentateuchal Paraphrase in the conference publication, though it would take a year or so for the two to blend.

Already by 1993 during a conference at the University of Notre Dame the blend of Ulrich's and Tov's articles began to happen. Ulrich observed that the evidence provided by the larger collection of scriptural scrolls from Qumran demonstrated that moderate additions, omissions, and altered sequences were *characteristic* of the biblical text in its compositional period up to the second century C.E. and that these features were *indicators* of a scriptural text, not features that would disqualify it from scriptural status. He questioned the criteria by which the classification of these texts as "nonbiblical" was made. In light of the pluriform scriptural scrolls, why should "the Pentateuch" and "the biblical text" be understood according to the Masoretic form, or even the MT-SP-LXX form? All the additions and variants encountered in the 4QRP manuscripts are typically biblical, and they seem to be classifiable in the same categories as the variants between the MT, the SP, and the LXX, and as the variants presented in the chapters above. He thus suggested that 4QRP should be reconsidered as possibly a variant edition of the Pentateuch, since the characteristics listed for describing the texts as "reworked" were becoming increasingly recognized as typical characteristics of the scriptural text in the Second Temple period.[24] Then in a 1997 conference in Jerusalem, Michael Segal, a student of Tov's, argued persuasively for the same position.[25]

In 2007 Tov reached the same conclusion, though he arrived at his verdict via a different path of reasoning. Observing the clearly variant MT versus LXX editions of 1 Kings, Daniel, and Esther, plus the fact that various communities considered the different forms as Scripture, he concluded that 4Q364–367 constituted a parallel case and now agrees that 4QRP is "to be reclassified as a biblical text, '4QPentateuch,'" and needs "to be studied as Hebrew Scripture."[26] This accords with the principle articulated below (Ch. 17.II.C.1) that it is the book, not the textual form of the book, that was and is considered Scripture.

Thus, 4Q364–367 preserve yet a third set of copies of a variant literary edition of the Pentateuch, alongside the MT and the second Jewish variant edition that was at home

[23] "Pluriformity in the Biblical Text, Text Groups, and Questions of Canon," in *The Madrid Qumran Congress*, 1:23–41; repr. in *Scrolls and Origins*, 79–98.

[24] Ulrich, "The Bible in the Making: The Scriptures at Qumran," in *The Madrid Qumran Congress*, 77–93 esp. 92 n. 51; repr. in *Scrolls and Origins*, 32.

[25] His lecture was presented in 1997 and published in 2000: Michael Segal, "4QReworked Pentateuch or 4QPentateuch?" 391–99.

[26] Emanuel Tov, "Reflections on the Many Forms of Hebrew Scripture in Light of the LXX and 4QReworked Pentateuch," in *From Qumran to Aleppo: A Discussion with Emanuel Tov about the Textual History of Jewish Scriptures in Honor of His 65th Birthday* (ed. Armin Lange, Matthias Weigold, and József Zsengellér; FRLANT 230; Gottingen: Vandenhoeck & Ruprecht, 2009), 11–28, esp. 27–28; idem, "Three Strange Books of the LXX: 1 Kings, Esther, and Daniel Compared with Similar Rewritten Compositions from Qumran and Elsewhere," in *Hebrew Bible, Greek Bible, and Qumran,* 304–5. I am grateful to Professor Tov for an advance copy of this article. In *Textual Criticism* (323) Tov terms these manuscripts "An Exegetical Edition of the Torah."

in Second Temple Judaism and used by the Samaritans as the textual basis for their form of the Pentateuch.[27] The evidence suggests that they should now be considered "4QPentateuch."[28]

II. 11QPsalms^{A}

Whereas the shift with regard to the Pentateuch evolved over time, the debate regarding the Psalter started immediately upon the publication of Great Psalms Scroll. This beautiful and generously preserved manuscript is an extensive scroll that contains thirty-nine Psalms known from the MT plus ten additional compositions. It was discovered in Cave 11 in 1956 and unrolled in November 1961.[29] James Sanders expeditiously published it in 1965, presenting it as a biblical manuscript, a form of the Psalter (11QPs^{a}). Noting that the order of the psalms differs from the order in the MT and that one passage is in prose, many leading scholars disagreed, arguing that the scroll was a post-biblical, liturgical manuscript.[30]

A. The Debate

Shemaryahu Talmon and Moshe Goshen-Gottstein in successive articles in the same issue of *Textus* confronted Sanders' claim. Both focused on the prose nature of "David's Compositions." Talmon further objected that the non-traditional order and the unaccustomed "interpolations" disqualified it as a Psalter and classified it rather as "an incipient prayer-book."[31] Goshen-Gottstein added that the mention of David's 4050 compositions demonstrated that the intent of the work was not the Psalms as Scripture but rather the enhancement of the "apocryphal hymns" through attribution to David.

This Psalms debate may have constituted the first clash of the pre-Qumran versus post-Qumran mentalities. A poignant example of the attempt to make the leap was provided by the great scholar, Goshen-Gottstein. Surpassing many others, he was able at least to envision the possibility that this scroll was scriptural, and carefully probed both viewpoints:

> The recent publication of what has been termed a 'Psalms Scroll' may change this picture and turn out to be the beginning of a new stage.... the answer to be given may necessitate a reformulation of existing theories.... 11[Q]Ps-a may be a representative of a different collection of psalms which was regarded as 'canonical' by some group somewhere at some time. In that case we are offered a

[27] Indeed it should be noted that many of the readings in 4Q364–367 differing from the traditional MT Pentateuch agree with the Samaritan or, rather, with that other ancient Jewish Pentateuch which was taken up by the Samaritans; see Tov and White, DJD 13:193–94.

[28] See Ulrich, "The Dead Sea Scrolls and the Biblical Text," in *The Dead Sea Scrolls after Fifty Years*, 79–100, esp. 88–89.

[29] James A. Sanders, *The Psalms Scroll of Qumrân Cave 11 (11QPs^{a})* (DJD IV; Oxford: Clarendon, 1965), 3.

[30] Shemaryahu Talmon, "Pisqah Beʾemṣaʿ Pasuq and 11QPs^{a}," *Textus* 5 (1966): 11–21; Moshe H. Goshen-Gottstein, "The Psalms Scroll (11QPs^{a}): A Problem of Canon and Text," *Textus* 5 (1966): 22–33; and Patrick W. Skehan, "A Liturgical Complex in 11QPs^{a}," *CBQ* 34 (1973): 195–205, plus "Qumran and Old Testament Criticism," in *Qumran. Sa piété, sa théologie et son milieu* (ed. M. Delcor; BETL 46; Paris: Duculot; Leuven: Leuven University Press, 1978), 163–82, esp. 168–69.

[31] Talmon, "Pisqah Beʾemṣaʿ Pasuq," 13.

> unique opportunity to cast a glance into the workshop in which Biblical literature, as we know it, grew into a 'canon', and the term 'Psalms Scroll' is appropriate.... At least typologically we are then carried back to a stage in the growth of the canon that we would have never dreamt of reaching.[32]

Thus, he could envision the future clearly, but even a great mind like his could not make the leap. He finally concluded: "To sum up: The theory that 11[Q]Ps-a represents a different 'canon' has little to commend it."[33]

The difficulty in achieving a fully revised mentality can also be seen in Patrick Skehan, himself a DJD editor. Though he readily embraced the notion of the pluriformity of the biblical text in general, he continued to consider 11QPs^a as a secondary, post-biblical composition. He originally viewed 11QPs^a as a collection of the last third of the Psalter though "with liturgical regroupings and 'library edition' expansions"; but he later considered that the prose epilogue "David's Compositions" rendered it unsuitable even as a liturgical work.[34]

Each of the arguments, however, brought against the scriptural status of 11QPs^a has evanesced (just as the arguments against the so-called "4QReworked Pentateuch" disappeared) as our cumulative knowledge about the nature of the biblical text in antiquity has grown.[35]

B. The Objections

The problems raised early against scriptural status should be carefully listed and their resolutions explained. Five principal objections were proposed:

(1) 11QPs^a (11Q5) presents the biblical psalms in an *order* that differs repeatedly from that of the MT.
(2) It includes *additional* psalms not found in the MT.
(3) It is a *liturgical* scroll; for example, within the biblical Psalm 145 an *antiphon* is repeatedly added in contrast to the MT.
(4) The *Tetragrammaton* is written in the Palaeo-Hebrew script, not in the normal Jewish script used for the remainder of the scroll.
(5) It includes a *prose* composition, "David's Compositions," in between psalms.

Before directly addressing the objections, recall that John McKenzie, presumably as yet unaware of the 11QPs^a debate when he wrote, had characterized the fluidity of the psalms:

> There is a special difficulty in handling the Pss because the book was obviously submitted to an *unceasing process of development and adaptation*: individual Pss become collective, private prayers become liturgical, songs of local sanctuaries are adapted to the temple of Jerusalem, royal psalms become messianic, historical psalms become eschatological. Modern interpreters speak of the "rereading" of the Pss; an earlier Ps which has in some way become antiquated (e.g., by the fall of the monarchy, the destruction of Jerusalem and the temple, the loss of political independence) is

---

32 Goshen-Gottstein, "The Psalms Scroll," 23–24 and n. 10.

33 Goshen-Gottstein, "The Psalms Scroll," 31.

34 Skehan, "A Liturgical Complex," 201 n. 24; and "Qumran and Old Testament Criticism," 168–69.

35 See Ulrich, *Scrolls and Origins*, 30, and more fully on 115–20. Emanuel Tov (*Textual Criticism*, 320–21) considers 11QPs^a a "liturgical" scroll that is "Scripture-like."

reworked to fit a contemporary situation and given a direction to the future which was not present in the original composition.[36]

C. The Resolution

Regarding the objections, all of the features listed are contained either in the MT at other places or in different manuscripts which are undeniably biblical. Regarding the individual issues:

(1) Both the LXX (plus 4QJer[b,d]) and the MT (plus 4QJer[a,c]) of Jeremiah are legitimate forms of the biblical book, and the MT is a secondarily revised edition of the book as found in the LXX; the MT presents a major section of the book in a variant order. Similarly, 4QpaleoExod[m]-SP and the MT-LXX have the passage about the golden altar in a variant order (DJD 9:113, 119–20); 4QNum[b] repositions a passage about Zelophahad's daughters (DJD 12:263–64); 4QJosh[a], the MT, and the LXX each position the passage about building the first altar in a variant order; and Greek Papyrus 967 has the chapters in both Ezekiel and Daniel in a variant order. Moreover, it would be naïve to think that the MT order of the Psalms was always the only order.[37] Though there are small groupings of psalms that seem intentionally ordered in the MT, no overall intentional order for the entire MT collection could be substantiated. Indeed, seven manuscripts from Cave 4 each preserve on a single connected fragment one psalm followed by another traditional MT psalm in an order different from the order as in the MT:

4QPs[a]: Psalm 31→33; 38→71
4QPs[b]: Psalm 103→112
4QPs[d]: Psalm 106→147→104
4QPs[e]: Psalm 118(?)→104[+147]→105→146(?)
4QPs[k]: Psalm 135[+ ??]→99
4QPs[n]: Psalm 135:12→136:22
4QPs[q]: Psalm 31→33

(2) With respect to the ten so-called "non-canonical" compositions:

- Four Psalms are in fact found in psalms collections other than the MT Psalter, i.e., Pss 151A and 151B in the LXX and Pss 154 and 155 in Syriac manuscripts. These were clearly originally Hebrew psalms, even if they were not eventually accepted into the MT edition of the Psalter.
- Two poetic passages are included at other loci in the MT or LXX, i.e., 2 Sam 23:1-7 and Sirach 51:13-30.
- Three compositions ("Plea for Deliverance," "Apostrophe to Zion," and "Hymn to the Creator") were no longer preserved or known, but they were written

[36] John L. McKenzie, *Dictionary of the Bible* (New York: Macmillan, 1965), 703, emphasis added. I thank Kevin J. Haley for drawing my attention to McKenzie's insightful observation.

[37] See Goshen-Gottstein, "The Psalms Scroll," 32 n. 42; and Gerald H. Wilson, "The Qumran Psalms Manuscripts and the Consecutive Arrangement of the Psalms in the Hebrew Psalter," *CBA* 45 (1983): 377–88, esp. 385: "We should be careful not to allow ourselves to be persuaded by our own knowledge of the subsequent shape of the canonical Psalter to presume . . . the existence of the fixed, authoritative canonical Psalter."

in the ancient style of the biblical Psalms connected with David, not in the contemporary style of the later Qumran Hodayot with no reference to David.

- "David's Compositions" (below) is paralleled by "Solomon's Compositions" in 1 Kgs 5:9-14 [Eng. 4:29-34].

(3) Of course, 11QPs^a is liturgical, but so is the MT Psalter by its very nature.[38] It is important, however, to distinguish between a *collection* of separate liturgical hymns or prayers (like the Psalter: a hymnbook which contains hymns that were used individually in different liturgies) and a liturgical *composition* (a single connected text prepared to be used as a "liturgy" [Skehan] or a "prayer-book" [Talmon]).[39] The Qumran Psalter, just as the MT Psalter, is a collection. Specifically with regard to the antiphon inserted into Psalm 145, "Blessed be the LORD and blessed be his name forever and ever" is totally derived from verse 1 of Psalm 145 in the identical manner in which the antiphon of Psalm 136, "For his steadfast love endures forever," is derived from verse 1 of that Psalm. And it is systematically repeated in the identical manner in which the antiphon of Psalm 136 in the MT is repeated. It is quite likely that psalms were sometimes sung antiphonally, as in Psalm 136, and so it matters little whether or not the antiphon is repeatedly inserted in the written text, as in Psalms 136 and 145.

(4) The use of the Palaeo-Hebrew script for the Tetragrammaton in a text principally written in the Jewish (square) script had in the early years been considered an indication that the text was not biblical, because at that time the few published manuscripts displaying the phenomenon (e.g., the *pesharim*) happened to be nonbiblical. However, as with the previous points, while that view was understandable in light of the early evidence, it should be laid to rest now that a number of biblical scrolls in the Jewish script have surfaced that present the Tetragrammaton in the Palaeo-Hebrew script.[40]

(5) The prose passage, called "David's Compositions," nestled within a Psalter is strange indeed and needs explanation. The passage enumerates the 4050 types of psalms or songs that David wrote and states that he composed all these "through prophecy that was given to him from before the Most High" (כול אלה דבר בנבואה אשר נתן לו מלפני העליון

[38] See also Timothy H. Lim, *The Formation of the Jewish Canon* (Anchor Yale Bible Reference Library; New Haven: Yale University Press, 2013), 124: "the arguments that the liturgical interests of 11Q5 are incompatible with a canonical psalter seem altogether baffling, for what is a psalter if not a liturgical composition!"

[39] Armin Lange, *Handbuch der Textfunde vom Toten Meer* (Tübingen: Mohr Siebeck, 2009), 1:415–16, also distinguishes between "Psalmenrollen" and "Psalterrollen" (i.e., collections of individual psalms versus a Psalter), the latter often having a "canonical" or theological meaning. That is a helpful distinction, but the latter point does not seem necessary, since "canonical" would be anachronistic in the late Second Temple period, since both the proto-MT and 11QPs^a are parallel literary phenomena ("*books* of psalms"), and since 11QPs^a explicitly claims to be an inspired work ("the spirit of the LORD speaks through me"; David "spoke through prophecy"). That the psalms were authoritative at Qumran is proved by the *pesharim*. Since there is no evidence to rank the proto-MT edition more highly or more authoritative than 11QPs^a, one accurate description may be that the proto-MT collection was a less developed and 11QPs^a a more developed collection with additional psalms, both of which would have been viewed as authoritative (as 11QPs^a XXVII 11 demonstrates for that scroll).

[40] 1QPs^b, 2QExod^b, 4QExod^j, 4QLev^g, 4QDeut^{k2}, and especially 4QIsa^c; see Ulrich, "Multiple Literary Editions," in *Scrolls and Origins*, 117–20 including Plates i–ii.

11QPs^a^ XXVII 11 = DJD 4:48 + Pl. XVI).[41] Two questions thus emerge: How do we explain a prose passage within a Psalter, and can this be a true scriptural Psalter?

First, the order of psalms toward the end of the scroll is Psalms 149, 150, Hymn to the Creator, David's Last Words, David's Compositions.... Thus, it is plausible that at an earlier stage this form of the Psalter concluded with the sequence: Psalms 149, 150 (where the MT ends), plus the Hymn to the Creator (also appropriate as a concluding psalm).[42] Sometime later, two more passages were added—as also happened at the end of other books, such as Samuel, First Isaiah, Amos, etc.—giving the credentials of the author. The first, the poetic Last Words of David (= 2 Sam 23:1-7), panegyrizes "the man God raised up, the anointed of the God of Jacob" (23:1) and then claims, "The spirit of the LORD speaks through me; his word is upon my tongue" (23:2). The second, David's Compositions, strengthening that claim, further asserts that all these psalms "he spoke through prophecy" from God. Thus, the prose composition may well have been, not part of the text, but a sort of colophon at the end of an earlier edition of the collection,[43] staking the claim for the prophetic inspiration by which David composed the Psalms.[44]

At yet a later stage, someone added a few new psalms, as often happens at the end of a hymnbook: Psalms 140, 134, and 151A,B, this last appended as a fitting Davidic finale to the collection in 11QPs^a^, just as a version of the same Psalm provides a finale for the Greek Psalter. Notice that three poetic appendices were similarly added at the end of Sirach: a psalm of thanksgiving (51:1-12), a Hebrew hymn of praise (51:12+; > LXX), and a poem on wisdom (51:13-30, which is also one of the added compositions in 11QPs^a^!).

Second, regarding scriptural status, 11QPs^a^ makes an explicit claim for such status in the Last Words of David and David's Compositions through the words quoted above: "spirit of the LORD," "his word," "spoke through prophecy." In this way it explicitly addresses the question how the humanly composed book of Psalms addressed to God became reclassified as God's word, a divinely inspired book of Scripture for humanity. The book of Psalms began as a collection of human songs written as response either to God's glory or deeds or to the Israelites' troubles or needs. Sometime in the latter part of the Second Temple period it became Scripture, that is, seen as God's word to humanity. 11QPs^a^ explicitly says that it is through "prophecy" that the Psalter makes the transition from being the human hymnbook of the Temple to being God's word as Scripture, an integral part of "the Law and the Prophets."[45]

In a major work in 1997 Peter Flint presented the evidence comprehensively, persuasively arguing for the acceptance of 11QPs^a^ as an alternate edition of the Psalter in

---

41 See the informative article by Vered Noam, "The Origin of the List of David's Songs in 'David's Compositions,'" *DSD* 13/2 (2006): 134–49.

42 Patrick Skehan ("*Jubilees* and the Qumran Psalter," *CBQ* 37 [1975]: 343–47, esp. 343) also thought that David's Last Words and David's Compositions were a later appendix added after the concluding Hymn.

43 This would go against Goshen-Gottstein's comment ("The Psalms Scroll," 28) that "little would be gained by assuming separate origins for [David's Compositions]." Note the brief, prose quasi-colophon both ending Book Two of the MT Psalter ("The prayers of David son of Jesse are ended," 72:20) and indicating that the composition of the Psalter continued to develop.

44 Cf. Acts 2:29-31: "... our ancestor David.... Since he was a prophet.... Foreseeing this, David spoke of the resurrection of the Messiah...."

45 See also James C. VanderKam, *Scrolls and the Bible*, 67–69.

ancient Judaism.[46] Goshen-Gottstein's (not adopted) vision had painted the picture accurately in 1966. What he had seen as "apocryphal hymns" could now be seen as psalms created just as earlier biblical psalms had been, except that they had not been accepted into that sole rabbinic collection that survived the Roman destruction;[47] indeed, the Apostrophe to Zion reads like a biblical psalm which someone like Deutero-Isaiah might have composed.[48] What Talmon had seen as an unorthodox arrangement and as some "unaccustomed 'interpolations'" remained problematic only with respect to the *pre*sumption of a single, orthodox arrangement and the "accustomed" MT Psalter. Those "interpolations" are not "non-canonical"; they are simply non-Masoretic.

Moreover, strengthening the hypothesis for 11QPs^a as a variant edition of the Psalter, a second manuscript (11QPs^b) and perhaps even a third (4QPs^e) attest to the 11QPs^a text tradition, while seven fragmentary scrolls from Cave 4 show Psalms in a sequence different from that transmitted by the MT (see II.C above). In contrast, none of the ancient manuscripts found at Qumran unambiguously supports the MT sequence versus the 11QPs^a sequence of Psalms.[49]

Conclusion

This chapter has offered two specific examples of the quest for more accurate vision discussed in theory in Chapter 2. Originally, the majority of scholars assessed both 4Q(Reworked)Pentateuch and 11QPs^a as nonbiblical compositions. These scrolls seemed to depart too flagrantly from well-known biblical texts to qualify as biblical. Advancing research, however, aided by the publication of many more scrolls and by increasingly clearer vision, produced a gradual paradigmatic shift from pre-Qumran to post-Qumran perception.

Thanks are certainly due to the original editors of these scrolls, on whose shoulders others have been able to climb to gain clearer perspective. The reclassification of biblical scrolls was gained through the increased awareness as the years progressed of the broader limits, wider than formerly known through the MT, of permissible development in additions, omissions, and transpositions within the biblical text. These limits will be discussed in more detail in the next chapter.

---

[46] Peter W. Flint, *The Dead Sea Psalms Scrolls and the Book of Psalms* (STDJ 17; Leiden: Brill, 1997), esp. pp. 202–27. See also idem, "Psalms, Book of," *Encyclopedia of the Dead Sea Scrolls*, 2:702–10; and James A. Sanders, "Psalms Scroll," ibid., 2:715–17.

[47] This view is based on the twin convictions that the hitherto unknown compositions in 11QPs^a are literarily and theologically of the same character as the late biblical psalms (as opposed to, e.g., the more contemporary Hodayot), and that, as Talmon pointed out, the Masoretic collection of texts, the Septuagint collection, and the Samaritan Pentateuch are *Gruppentexte*; i.e., from the previously much richer textual scene they are the three survivors which the Rabbis, the Christians, and the Samaritans happened to have preserved; see Ch. 2 "Coincidental Nature."

[48] Sanders, DJD 4:85–89. See also Conrad E. LeHeureux, "The Biblical Sources of the 'Apostrophe to Zion,'" *CBQ* 29 (1967): 60–74.

[49] See Flint, *The Dead Sea Psalms Scrolls*, 227. Though one Psalms fragment from Masada (MasPs^b; see Ch. 16) does conclude with Psalm 150 in agreement with the MT versus 11QPs^a, no manuscript from Qumran shows that agreement.

Chapter 13

"Pre-Scripture," Scripture (Rewritten), and "Rewritten Scripture": The Borders of Scripture

Recent scholarship recognizes three undisputed facts: First, virtually all the books now recognized as the Hebrew Scriptures did not begin as authoritative "Scripture" but are the late literary results of a complex evolutionary process of composition and were redacted from sources that were national or religious literature, thus "pre-Scripture." Second, the biblical books experienced successive literary growth, even new updated editions, while already recognized as Scripture; thus all of Scripture is rewritten. And third, there were new, interpretive books that were composed using the Scriptures as their basis, but understood by the author as a new, non-scriptural, exegetical work, thus "rewritten Scripture." This last had a double function: (a) to acknowledge and implicitly proclaim that a certain book recognized as scriptural was an important fundamental work to use as a basis for, and lend authority to, updated interpretation on the one hand, and (b) on the other hand to steer current and future interpretive views in a certain direction.

Thus, there were ancient literary traditions that one day would become Scripture; there were books that were clearly considered authoritative Sacred Scripture (though their text could still develop), and there were new compositions based on the scriptural text but understood by the author (and presumably at least originally by the community) as a new non-scriptural work, a work we could categorize as Scripture-based religious literature.[1] This chapter will explore the three types of literature[2] to discern the boundaries between them as well as the criteria for distinguishing them from each other, and to suggest a correlation between "pre-Scripture" and "rewritten Scripture."

Since this chapter attempts to survey all the Law and the Prophets in a short space, it must paint with broad, impressionistic strokes, leaving out many details and nuances addressed in other chapters. But four brief assumptions should articulated:

First, the Torah was recognized as authoritative Scripture by at least the end of the fourth century B.C.E., since it was translated into Greek in the early third century. The

---

[1] A specific example is Ben Sira: more than a half century later, his grandson says in the Prologue (7-12) that "my grandfather Jesus, who had devoted himself especially to the reading of the Law and Prophets [i.e., the Scriptures, ... wrote] something pertaining to instruction and wisdom...." He thus distinguishes Scripture from religious "literature," and his grandfather was composing *literature* (though it would later be seen as Scripture by certain Jews and Christians).

[2] James VanderKam has alerted scholars to study the "spectrum leading from authoritative texts to writings intimately related to them, to works that cite authoritative books, to ones that only allude to scripture or employ scriptural language," in "To What End? Functions of Scriptural Interpretation in Qumran Texts," in *Studies in the Hebrew Bible, Qumran, and the Septuagint Presented to Eugene Ulrich* (ed. Peter W. Flint, Emanuel Tov, and James C. VanderKam; VTSup 101; Leiden: Brill, 2006) 302–20, esp. 304.

Prophets, which included Psalms and eventually Daniel, were similarly recognized during the next century or so.

Second, the forms of the scriptural text that are witnessed in the scrolls, the MT, the SP, and the LXX were circulating and used as authoritative during the last three centuries of the Second Temple period B.C.E. and thus must be considered genuine forms of Scripture.

Third, thus, the types of editorial work observable in those witnesses must be considered legitimate and within the bounds of scriptural transmission. They serve as criteria for acceptable features of revision within the boundaries of legitimate scriptural development.

Fourth, this chapter will focus only on the Law and the Prophets, since, though the books of the Ketuvim were known literature toward the end of the Second Temple period, there is little textual evidence for them and little evidence that they were widely considered Scripture yet.

I. Scripture (Rewritten)

Many if not virtually all books of the Bible are themselves "rewritten Scripture." They have a history of being rewritten; their composition was achieved through a series of developing stages of rewriting. The manuscript evidence retrieved from the latter half of the Second Temple period as well as the evidence of the LXX, the NT, and the writings of Josephus witness to "new and expanded" editions for a number of the books which now comprise the Bible.[3]

The features of the "rewriting" tolerated within the bounds of legitimate revision of the scriptural books can be deduced from the examples of revision within manuscripts generally admitted to be scriptural, that is, the forms of the scriptural texts encountered in the scrolls, in the MT, in the SP, and in the LXX. Those features of rewriting can then be articulated and can help serve to discern the boundaries between Scripture and "rewritten Scripture."

In analyzing the changes in variant forms of scriptural texts it is good to keep in mind the four different and mutually independent levels of variation previously described: orthography, individual textual variants, isolated insertions, and new editions. The first two generally play no part in the discussion, since they are seldom significant enough to demonstrate intentional rewriting of a book; focus should be primarily on new editions and to a certain extent on texts with a number of major isolated insertions.

A. Evidence in the Scrolls of the Rewriting That Produced Revised Editions

The previous chapters have shown that the scrolls, the MT, the SP, and the Hebrew *Vorlagen* of the OG each display rewritten forms of various books, so a brief review here will serve sufficiently. First, five scrolls exhibit evidence of new editions or major insertions:

---

[3] It is important to remember that in antiquity it was the book, not a specific form of the book, that was Scripture or canonical; see Bruce Metzger, *The Canon of the New Testament: Its Origin, Development, and Significance* (Oxford: Clarendon, 1987), 269–70; and Ch. 17.II.C.1.

1–2. Exodus and Numbers (MT → 4QpaleoExod^{m} and 4QNum^{b})

The base text of Exodus and Numbers as preserved in the MT appears in revised, expanded editions in 4QpaleoExod^{m} and 4QNum^{b}. The primary purpose of that revision was to expand the text in two ways: to show Moses' obedience by reporting that he actually carried out the commands of the Lord, the execution of which was merely tacitly assumed in the MT, and to supplement the narrative with details reported in Deuteronomy that were not found in the base text of Exodus and Numbers (see Ch. 3).

3. Samuel (MT → 4QSam^{a})

There are more than ten isolated insertions or longer readings in 4QSam^{a} which are lacking in the MT. But the insertions show no consistent pattern to suggest a revised edition. Rather, the scroll contains a slightly later, but generally superior, textual tradition of the book, with numerous isolated insertions (see Ch. 6).

4. Jeremiah (4QJer^{b,d}-OG → 4QJer^{a,c}-MT)

4QJer^{b}, 4QJer^{d}, and the OG display an early edition of the book, and 4QJer^{a}, 4QJer^{c}, and the MT, display a subsequent, intentionally expanded edition. The new edition of Jeremiah exhibits yet another purpose: to amplify the entire book by routine minor explicitation, clarification, lengthened forms of titles, etc., plus a major rearrangement for the order of the Oracles Against the Nations (see Ch. 9).

5. Psalms (MT → 11QPs^{a})

The Psalms manuscript 11QPs^{a} contains ten compositions beyond those in the MT, which suggests that it is generally a later form than that preserved in the MT. It also shows a different ordering of the last third of the psalms, which indicates that the order of the last part of the collection of psalms was not yet fixed. The purpose of 11QPs^{a} was evidently to include additional psalms composed in the biblical style (as opposed to contemporary hymns such as the Hodayot) and to emphasize both the Davidic composition of the Psalter and his inspiration from the Most High—and thus to stress the status of the Psalter as Scripture (see Ch. 12).

B. Evidence in the MT of the Rewriting That Produced Revised Editions

Similarly, the MT shows evidence of revised editions or major insertions:

1. Genesis (? → MT, SP, LXX)

In Genesis 5 and 11, the ages of the pre-diluvian and post-diluvian ancestors have been revised in the MT, and in the SP and the LXX as well. Each of the three text traditions was revised in a different way from a common source that is no longer preserved (see Ch. 14.II). The point here is that the MT displays intentional revision.

2. Exodus (OG → MT)

Just as 4QpaleoExod^{m} shows development beyond the MT, the MT also shows development beyond the OG *Vorlage*. The account of the construction of the Tabernacle in

Exodus 35–40 appears in two variant editions in the OG and the MT. Though the textual history is complex, in general the OG presents the earlier edition, and the edition transmitted in the MT was probably produced to bring the order and wording of the execution more in line with the order and wording of the commands in Exodus 25–31.[4]

3. Joshua (4QJosh^a → MT)

The order of the narrative in 4QJosh^a, with the building of the first altar in chapter 4 already at Gilgal (not at Mount Gerizim or Mount Ebal) is most plausibly explained as the earliest preserved form. The order of the text in the MT-LXX, with the altar's placement in chapter 8 (though after 9:2 in LXX^B) at Mount Gerizim or Mount Ebal, appears to be a rearrangement of narrative sequence to support a religious claim regarding the chosen sacred site (see Ch. 4).

4. Judges (4QJudg^a → MT)

The short text of 4QJudg^a highlights the large addition in the MT of an episode with a prophetic appearance. The purpose of the insertion about the prophet seems to be to reiterate the book's theology of a cyclic pattern to the history of Israel's rebelliousness versus God's salvation (see Ch. 5).

5. Samuel (OG → MT)

In the David-Goliath story (1 Samuel 17–18) the *Vorlage* of the OG presents an earlier edition of the passage with its own integrity and its own specific viewpoint. The MT has been intentionally expanded beyond the OG account with a narrative containing identifiably different types of material and different David-traditions.[5]

6. Isaiah (1QIsa^a → MT)

Comparison of 1QIsa^a with the MT of Isaiah highlights seven large isolated insertions lacking in 1QIsa^a but added in the MT. Comparison of the LXX with the MT shows two further insertions in the MT.[6] These nine insertions constitute a total of fifteen verses secondarily added in the MT.

7. Ezekiel (P967-OL → MT)

The text of Ezekiel in Greek Papyrus 967 and OL Wirceburgensis exhibits a shorter and differently arranged text (chapters 36–38–39–37–40) in comparison with the MT-LXX. The MT has a longer text in 36, adding about 15 verses (36:23c-38) beyond the OG,

[4] See Anneli Aejmelaeus, "Septuagintal Translation Techniques—A Solution to the Problem of the Tabernacle Account," in *On the Trail of Septuagint Translators: Collected Essays* (rev. ed.; Leuven: Peeters, 2007), 107–22, and Brandon Bruning, "The Making of the Mishkan."

[5] See Ch. 6.IV.D and Dominique Barthélemy, David W. Gooding, Johan Lust, and Emanuel Tov, *The Story of David and Goliath: Textual and Literary Criticism: Papers of a Joint Research Venture* (OBO 73; Fribourg, Suisse: Éditions Universitaires; Göttingen: Vandenhoeck & Ruprecht, 1986).

[6] See Ch. 7 and DJD 32, 2:90–91. For one of these insertions (Isa 40:7aβ-8a) the short LXX agrees with 1QIsa^a, thus providing double attestation that the MT is expanded.

apparently designed to prepare for the new order of chapter 37 before 38–39 as now in the MT (see Ch. 15.III).[7]

8. Daniel (? → MT, LXX)

Chapters 4–6 of Daniel as in the MT and as in the LXX diverge widely. They are both based on an earlier, similar "core" story, but the MT and the LXX each now display different expanded editions (see Ch. 15.IV.B).

C. Evidence of Rewriting in the Samaritan Pentateuch

1. Torah (4QpaleoExod^{m}-4QNum^{b} → SP)

The expanded Jewish textual form of the Pentateuch as witnessed in 4QpaleoExod^{m} and 4QNum^{b} was shared by the Samarians and used as the basis of the SP. On the presumption that the SP is the more developed of the forms, the extra commandment regarding the altar on Mount Gerizim (after Exod 20:17[17a] and Deut 5:21[18]) was added by someone or some group celebrating the north. Similarly, the perfect בחר (whether already in the common tradition or secondarily changed by the Samaritans)[8] was used to refer to Mount Gerizim as the place which Yhwh "has chosen" to have his name dwell there, as opposed to the imperfect יבחר, which was used to refer to Jerusalem as the place to have his name dwell there.

D. Evidence in the LXX of Rewriting in Its Hebrew Vorlagen

The preserved evidence for this section is from Greek manuscripts alone, but it is quite likely that the new editorial work appearing in the LXX was done at the Hebrew stage prior to translation rather than during the Greek transmission see Chs. 10 and 15).

1. Genesis (? → MT, SP, LXX)

See I.B.1 above and Ch. 14.II.

2. Kings (MT ←→ OG?)

There are several large divergences between the MT and the LXX of 1 Kings. A major and sustained divergence regards the chronologies presented, but the divergences extend to a number of varia—meriting the label "Miscellanies"—and the situation is sufficiently complex that scholars still debate whether parts of the LXX precede their MT

[7] See Johan Lust, "Ezekiel 36–40 in the Oldest Greek Manuscript," *CBQ* 43 (1981) 517–33; idem, "Major Divergences between LXX and MT in Ezekiel," in *The Earliest Text of the Hebrew Bible: The Relationship between the Masoretic Text and the Hebrew Base of the Septuagint Reconsidered* (ed. A. Schenker; Atlanta: Society of Biblical Literature, 2003), 83–92; and Emanuel Tov, "Recensional Differences Between the Masoretic Text and the Septuagint of Ezekiel," *The Greek and Hebrew Bible*, 397–410.

[8] See Adrian Schenker, "Le Seigneur choisira-t-il le lieu de son nom ou l'a-t-il choisi?: L'apport de la Bible grecque ancienne à l'histoire du texte samaritain et massorétique," (Ch. 3 n. 15) who argues that the perfect בחר was the earlier form of the tradition, and that the imperfect יבחר was the revised form.

counterparts.[9] However the direction of influence is decided, there is clear editorial intent to revise the text.

3. Daniel (MT → OG)

In addition to the secondarily expanded editions of Daniel 4–6 in both MT and OG mentioned above in I.B.8, the OG further expands the book with the stories of Susanna, Bel and the Dragon, the Prayer of Azariah, and the Prayer of the Three Youths.

4. Esther (MT → OG)

The LXX of Esther contains six large "Additions" (A–F) beyond the form in the MT; most of the Additions (except perhaps B and E) were already in the Hebrew *Vorlage*.[10]

E. The Rewriting Features Visible in Manuscripts of the Books of Scripture

Certain books of early Israel's literature in time reached the general forms we could recognize as the books of Genesis, Exodus, etc.,[11] and they were eventually accepted as Scripture. The preceding sections presented evidence for the features of rewriting by which an early edition of a book became a "new and expanded edition" of that same book:

1. revising chronological problems to avoid inconsistencies (Gen)
2. realigning the order of execution of commands to agree with the original commands (Exod)
3. supplementing one narrative with additional details from another book (Exod, Num)
4. rearranging the sequence of an event to support the claim for a sacred site (Josh)
5. inserting a prophetic appearance to reiterate the book's theology (Judg)
6. inserting an alternate form of the story for completeness (Sam)
7. chronological and miscellaneous other revisions (Kgs)
8. occasionally inserting verses of additional prophetic material (Isa)
9. frequent expansions of phrases, insertion of verses, plus major rearrangement (Jer)
10. rearranging the sequence of one chapter for eschatological view (Ezek)
11. adding more Psalms; emphasizing Davidic authorship and divine inspiration (Pss)
12. inserting repeated examples of narrative embellishment to enhance the story (Dan 4–6)
13. inserting additional stories to a growing cycle (Dan-Additions)

---

[9] See James A. Montgomery, *A Critical and Exegetical Commentary on the Books of Kings* (Edinburgh: T&T Clark, 1951); David W. Gooding, *Relics of Ancient Exegesis: A Study of the Miscellanies in 3 Reigns 2* (Cambridge: Cambridge University Press, 1976); Julio Trebolle Barrera, *Salomón y Jeroboán: Historia de la recensión y redacción de 1 Rey. 2–12; 14* (Bibliotheca Salmanticensis, Dissertationes 3; Salamanca/Jerusalén: Universidad Pontificia/Instituto Español Bíblico y Arqueológico, 1980); Emanuel Tov, "The Septuagint Additions ('Miscellanies') in 1 Kings 2 (3 Reigns 2)," *The Greek and Hebrew Bible*, 549–70; and Jan Joosten's view in Sidnie White Crawford, Jan Joosten, and Eugene Ulrich, "Sample Editions of the Oxford Hebrew Bible: Deut 32:1-9, 1 Kings 11:1-8, and Jeremiah 27:1-10 (34 G)," *Vetus Testamentum* 58 (2008): 352–66, esp. 359.

[10] Lewis B. Paton, *Esther* (ICC; Edinburgh: T&T Clark, 1908); Carey A. Moore, *Daniel, Esther, and Jeremiah: The Additions* (AB 44; Garden City, N.Y.: Doubleday, 1977); Tov, *The Greek and Hebrew Bible*, 538 n. 7.

[11] That is, as the basic form of the full biblical book, as opposed to, e.g., the Yahwist's strand, the plague narratives, the Tabernacle Account, etc.

All these must be considered legitimate features of revising books of Scripture that remain "Scripture." These features serve to enhance, even while expanding, the book being revised; they do not cross the border and produce a different composition.

II. "Pre-Scripture"

Many of the biblical books had a history of literary development prior to their being considered "Scripture." With a few possible minor exceptions, there is no non-rewritten Scripture. It will be helpful to focus for a moment on "pre-Scripture"—the early literary forms of the traditions that eventually became acknowledged as Scripture.

While keeping in mind the difference between the first period of the developing composition of the books prior to the Great Divide and the second period during which the Hebrew text ceased to grow after the Jewish revolts, it is essential to distinguish two phases *within* that first period of development: "pre-Scripture" versus "Scripture." I think it can be safely claimed that generally no ancient author thought he was setting out to write a book of "Scripture."[12] The ancient authors most likely assumed that the works they were composing were (in their early phase) what we should describe as religious *literature*. In a number of such works of religious literature God would be reported as speaking to humans. It was only later, in a second phase, when attribution to that human author may have been forgotten, that sufficiently influential leaders or a significantly large community would have acknowledged and received the work as somehow attributable to God—God's word to the on-going community (see Ch. 18).

Thus, we should differentiate between an early phase of a composition as religious literature (pre-Scripture) and a later phase of that work as Sacred Scripture (even if it was still developing). In the early phase, subsequent scribes would have felt more free to rewrite, reformulate, reinterpret books, since they were anonymous communal, traditional literature. But once the book was considered as Sacred Scripture in the later phase, scribes—as the evidence shows us—still felt free to rewrite, reformulate, and reinterpret, but they did so on a scale that was more circumscribed.

It may prove helpful to present an example. Source critics and redaction critics combined with text critics have identified about a dozen major stages in the development of the Book of Exodus and their presumed purposes:[13]

1. Early memories of escape from Egypt	to recall and pass on the memory of an important event
2. Developed narrative in the *Grundlage*	to combine "Egyptian" with "Canaanite" origins for unity[14]
3. The Yahwist account	national epic, state origins, to celebrate "where we came from"
4. The Elohist account	national epic reformulated in the north after division
5. The redactor of combined J + E	to resume combined "all-Israel" origins after loss of north

[12] See n. 1.

[13] For simplicity and quick recognition I am using (not necessarily endorsing) the well-known Documentary Hypothesis, Martin Noth's *Grundlage* (*A History of Pentateuchal Traditions* [transl. B. W. Anderson; Englewood Cliffs, N.J.: Prentice-Hall, 1972]), and Norman Gottwald's theory of Israel's origins (*The Tribes of Yahweh: A Sociology of the Religion of Liberated Israel, 1250–1050* [Maryknoll, N.Y.: Orbis, 1979]). If anything, the situation was even more complex than described here.

[14] See Noth's five combined themes of G (the *Grundlage*) plus Gottwald's reconstruction of Israel's beginnings, which envisions the uniting of one group who had escaped from Egypt with a second group of dissenting Canaanites to form "all Israel."

6. The P narrative	post-destruction re-theologizing of traditions
7. The P legal material	major block of legal material added
8. The redactor of combined P + JE	to preserve all Israelite major versions; basic book of Exodus
9. Heb. *Vorlage* of OG with 35–40	earliest preserved edition of recognizable book of Exodus[15]
10. MT Exodus	revised edition of 35–40 to match execution with commands
11. 4QpaleoExod^{m}	revised edition adding expansions of "biblical" material
12. Samaritan Pentateuch	"corrected" version of 4QpaleoExod^{m} stressing Mt. Gerizim
13. 4QPentatech[16]	various expansions beyond 4QpaleoExod^{m}

It appears unlikely that any of the early stages (1–7) would have been considered Scripture at the time. Stages 2–5 were probably considered tribal history or national epic, and stages 6–7 may well have been considered authoritative law or even national constitution. But it is only with the redactional combination of P + JE (stage 8) that we get a recognizable form of the full Book of Exodus. During the early phases large-scale changes in the literature were not only possible but evidently successful and welcomed.

A point to stress is that stages 1–8 involved large-scale reformulations of the traditions that were possible because the people welcomed the updating of their communal *literature* to stay abreast of their new socio-historical or socio-religious situations.

In contrast, stages 9–13 were clearly considered Scripture. Each involves only relatively moderate revisions, all within the spirit and the general shape of the Book of Exodus. It is not surprising that the dividing line is approximately the fourth century B.C.E. (after post-exilic P), when the Book of Exodus would probably have been widely seen as part of the Torah, that is, Scripture.

This contrast is important in the discussion of the borders between "Scripture" and "rewritten Scripture." Apparently, broader freedom was used when dealing with "literature," but more moderate freedom when dealing with "Scripture." It will be helpful to compare the features employed in the rewriting involved in "pre-Scripture" with those employed in works of later "rewritten Scripture."

III. "Rewritten Scripture"

A. The Rewriting Features Visible in Works of "Rewritten Scripture"

The four principal compositions usually viewed as parade examples of "rewritten Scripture" are 4QReworked Pentateuch, Jubilees, the Temple Scroll, and the Genesis Apocryphon.[17] The principal features that characterize these works are a combination of large-scale expansions, new speaker, new claim to revelation, new scope or setting, new arrangement or structure, and new theological agenda. The so-called 4QReworked Pentateuch, however, rather than a new work of "rewritten Scripture," is increasingly recognized as Scripture (i.e., "4QPentateuch"; see Ch. 12). It appears intended to supplement, rather than supplant, the earlier form of the Pentateuch. This judgment is corroborated by the contrasts that follow. The salient features visible in these works are:

---

[15] Stage 9 could well be the same as stage 8.

[16] I consider at least 4Q364 and 4Q365 (4QPent B and C, *olim* "4QRP^{b,c}") as developed editions within the boundaries of the Pentateuch; see Ch. 12.

[17] Sidnie White Crawford, *Rewriting Scripture in Second Temple Times* (Grand Rapids, Mich.: Eerdmans, 2008), 57.

4QPentateuch (4Q364, 365)
- moderately large expansions
- no new speaker
- no new claim to divine revelation
- same scope[18] and setting as the Pentateuch
- same arrangement as the Pentateuch (but 4Q365 juxtaposes Numbers 27 and 36)[19]
- same theological agenda as the Pentateuch (but 4Q365a has an expanded festival calendar with new feasts and 364-day calendar)

Jubilees
- large-scale expansions
- new speaker (the angel of the presence quoting God)
- new claim to divine revelation
- new scope (Genesis + parts of Exodus)
- same arrangement as Genesis–Exodus, but major new structure with addition of the Jubilee periods
- new theological agenda (legal interpretation; 364-day calendar; Patriarchs observe Mosaic Torah)

Temple Scroll (11QT^a)
- large-scale expansions (e.g., instructions for the Temple)
- new speaker (God in first person, 45:14)
- new implicit claim to divine revelation (God speaking directly)
- new scope (Exodus 34–Deut 23)
- new arrangement (thorough-going rearrangement and harmonization of legal materials)
- new theological agenda (instructions for the Temple; exegetical interpretation through "conflation, harmonization, and clarification";[20] expanded festival calendar with new feasts and 364-day calendar)

Genesis Apocryphon
- large-scale expansions (e.g., Noah's birth; description of Sarai's beauty and her non-defilement by Pharaoh; plus expansions from Jubilees and 1 Enoch)[21]
- new speakers (first-person Enoch, 5:3; Lamech, 2:3; Noah, 6:6; Abram, 19:14)
- no (preserved) new claim to divine revelation for the entire book, but revelations occur through visions;[22] the Aramaic language may indicate that it is "non-scriptural"
- new scope (Genesis 5 or 6 to 15)
- same general arrangement as Genesis (but a few minor rearrangements)
- new theological agenda ("to combine the equally authoritative traditions of Genesis, Jubilees, and 1 Enoch into a whole")[23]

---

[18] "Scope" refers to the extent of the composition between its beginning and end points: does the new composition share the same beginning and end with either the Pentateuch or one of its books? That would presumably be the case if the new composition were intended as a new edition of the earlier book.

[19] The scriptural 4QNum^b also appears to have the minor rearrangement of Numbers 27:2-11 to fit with chapter 36; see DJD 12:262–64 = *The Biblical Qumran Scrolls*, 170–71, 174. The manner of juxtaposition in 4QNum^b, however, is somewhat different from that in 4Q365; but the juxtaposition in both is due to the similarity in topic, the inheritance by the daughters of Zelophahad.

[20] Crawford, *Rewriting Scripture*, 102.

[21] Crawford, *Rewriting Scripture*, 107.

[22] For example, 1QapGen 6:11, 14.

[23] Crawford, *Rewriting Scripture*, 126–27. See also the analysis by George Nickelsburg, "Patriarchs Who Worry about Their Wives: A Haggadic Tendency in the Genesis Apocryphon," in *George W. E. Nickelsburg in Perspective: An Ongoing Dialogue of Learning* (SJSJ 80; ed. J. Neusner and A. J. Avery-Peck; Leiden: Brill, 2003), vol. 2, 177–99, described in Daniel A. Machiela, *The Dead Sea Genesis Apocryphon: A New Text and Translation with Introduction and Special Treatment of Columns 13–17* (STDJ 79; Leiden: Brill, 2009), 6–7. Machiela singles out four tendencies or techniques noted by Nickelsburg: an Enochic

Thus, there are identifiable features of rewritten Scripture, but 4QPentateuch does not show many of them to a high degree.

B. An Important Distinction

We have been exploring the question of a work's status or identity: that is, whether a new form of a scriptural book is truly "Scripture" (even if a new edition of it), or whether it has crossed the border and is to be considered a new composition. It is important, however, to distinguish between the *identity* of that new form (i.e., whether it should be named a "revised Genesis–Exodus" or rather "Jubilees") and its *scriptural status* (i.e., whether the new form is recognized by the community as endowed with scriptural authority).

For some books it is difficult to determine whether they were accorded scriptural status or not (see Ch. 18), but according to the two criteria distinguished above—did the "rewritten" book remain a copy of the same book upon which it was based, and was it accorded scriptural status?—the compositions appear to align themselves thus:

Composition	*Same Book?*	*Scriptural Status?*
4QPentateuch	yes	apparently, yes[24]
Jubilees	no[25]	apparently, yes[26]
Temple Scroll	no[27]	possibly, but no indicator[28]
Genesis Apocryphon	no	no

perspective (1QapGen 19:25), an "eschatological *Tendenz*," revelation through "Enoch and symbolic dream-visions," and a "psychologizing interest."

[24] 4Q365 is quoted by the Temple Scroll, and Crawford (*Rewriting Scripture*, 47, 56–57) suggests that 4Q364 frg. 3 ii may be a source for Jubilees 27:14, 17; see also Zahn, "Rewritten Scripture," 330. Another indicator of scriptural status is found in Neh 10:35[34 Eng.], which lists "the wood offering . . . , as it is written in the Torah"; see Crawford, *Rewriting Scripture*, 91–92. The wood offering does not appear in the received MT Torah, but it does appear in an expansion in 4Q365, which suggests that Nehemiah's "Torah" agreed with 4Q365 rather than the MT. This suggestion is further strengthened by the parallel phenomenon shown by the Chronicler, whose text of Samuel was not the MT but rather agreed frequently with 4QSam[a] against the MT.

[25] See James C. VanderKam, *The Dead Sea Scrolls and the Bible* (Grand Rapids: Eerdmans, 2012), 77: "It seems more in tune with the evidence to say that the writer of *Jubilees* saw his work as a supplement to the pentateuch narratives. . . . both works were important and both were used."

[26] Jubilees seems to be quoted in 4Q228 1 i 9 (cf. 1 i 2); see James C. VanderKam, "Authoritative Literature in the Dead Sea Scrolls," *DSD* 5/3 (1998): 382–402, esp. 392 and 395. It also appears to be referred to in conjunction with the Law of Moses in CD 16:2–4.

[27] The Temple Scroll appears intended to supersede laws in the Pentateuch; see Zahn, "Rewritten Scripture," 331.

[28] The Temple Scroll makes its own internal claim through divine speech; but there are, to my knowledge, no indicators from external sources that it was accorded scriptural status; see also Crawford, *Rewriting Scripture*, 102.

C. The Features Postulated for "Pre-Scripture" Compared to Those in "Rewritten Scripture"

Many of the features of "Rewritten Scripture" are similar to those seen in "pre-Scripture" (or the compositional or redactional stages that preceded the recognizable forms of the biblical books eventually accepted into the canon).

Some of the features postulated in Israelite literature in its early stages ("pre-Scripture") display a bolder approach to reworking and rewriting than is seen in the preserved manuscripts which were presumably recognized as Scripture. Noted above in section III.A were some of the prominent features of "rewritten Scripture." Those features are listed below with similar examples that scholars have proposed for early phases of what eventually became Scripture, i.e., "pre-Scripture":

Large-scale expansions

- addition of Genesis 1–11 placed before the national epic
- addition of the P legal material within the Pentateuchal narrative
- addition of Second and Third Isaiah and Isaiah 36–39 to Isaiah 1–33
- addition of Ezekiel 40–48 to Ezekiel 1–39
- addition of Daniel 7–12 to Daniel 1–6

New speaker

- God speaking through Moses replaced the anonymous priestly recorder of Lev 1:2b–7:37 once the editorial insertions Lev 1:1-2a and Lev 7:38 were added[29]
- the third-person narration in Daniel 1–6 changed to the first-person in Daniel 7:2–12[30]

New claim to divine revelation

- The personification of Wisdom in Proverbs 1–9 mediates God's revelation
- Daniel 7–12 makes a noticeably stronger claim to revelation than 1–6

New scope

- prefixing Genesis 1–11 to the patriarchal narrative created a new scope
- insofar as an early form of the national epic comprised the story from the promise to the patriarchs to the gaining of the land, the insertion of Deuteronomy constituted a new scope
- the addition of Second and Third Isaiah constituted a new scope to that book
- the addition of Daniel 7–12 constituted a new scope to that book

New arrangement or new structure

- the combination of the Prologue-Epilogue with the Dialogue of Job created a new structure
- prefixing Proverbs 1–9 to the more proverbial 10–31 gave the book a new structure

New theological agenda

- a quite different theological perspective introduced by P
- addition of the P legal material within the Pentateuchal narrative
- addition of Second Isaiah to First Isaiah replaced doom with salvation
- addition of Daniel 7–12 to Daniel 1–6 brought a new apocalyptic perspective

---

[29] See Ch. 18.II.B.

[30] The second half of the book is narrated in the first person, but with occasional switches to third person, as in 10:1. Evidently, the wisdom tales in Daniel 1–6 may not have been regarded as Scripture before the apocalyptic chapters 7–12 were combined with them, since (1) Ben Sira makes no mention of Daniel, and (2) 1 Maccabees mentions, not quoting as Scripture, but alluding as models for martyrdom to "Hananiah, Azariah, and Mishael . . . saved from the flame" and "Daniel . . . delivered from the mouth of the lions" (1 Macc 2:59-60); but it does not refer to the highly charged chapters 7–12; see Ch. 18.II.B.

Conclusion

Virtually all the books of Scripture are rewritten. The process of the composition of the Scriptures was organic, developmental, with successive layers of tradition, revised to meet the needs of the historically and religiously changing community. Thanks to the scrolls, we can now describe and categorize the types of changes as the texts developed and can discern the scribes' motives (or at least their effects) in developing the texts—whether the changes are in the scrolls or in the MT, the SP, or the Hebrew *Vorlage* of the OG. This organic and pluriform character of the texts was the norm throughout Israel's history. The growth can properly be called "evolutionary."

There was no natural conclusion of the process; it did not "achieve completion." There was no indication that the developmental process should stop. No so-called "standardized text" was produced. In contrast, the natural, dynamic, developmental process of textual growth was simply abruptly halted, frozen, by the results of the two Jewish Revolts against Rome, the loss of the Temple, the crisis of the Jesus movement, and the increasing isolation of the Samaritans (Ch. 1 "Uniform Hebrew Text").

The late Shemaryahu Talmon was correct: the three forms of Judaism that survived the catastrophe of the two Revolts—the Israelites of Samaria, the rabbinic Jews, and the Jews who followed Jesus—each simply kept one copy of each scriptural book they endosed in whichever form they happened to have. The MT, the SP, and the LXX are not "text-types" or "recensions." They are mixed collections of *copies* of whichever textual edition of each book each group happened to have in their possession (Ch. 1 "Uniform Hebrew Text").

What are the criteria for legitimate enhancement of scriptural books? What are the criteria which ensure that the revised book remains a true form of the same composition with the same title as the base book, and which prevent its crossing the border and thus constituting a new work that should have a different title?

The principal criteria can be gleaned from the many examples of a new edition of the same scriptural work observable through comparison of the scriptural scrolls, the MT, the SP, and the OG. Although these variant editions (including 4QPent B and C) show a range of re-editing, the size and the amount of revision is relatively moderate, and the revised editions maintain the voice, scope, and function of the original composition. In each case there is no inducement for scholars to seek a new title for the new edition.[31]

In contrast, there were new compositions that we can label "rewritten Scripture." Jubilees, the Temple Scroll, and the Genesis Apocryphon (note the new titles) have crossed the border. Each used parts of the Torah as its base text, and profited and benefited from the authoritativeness of that text. But each has reworked its scriptural text to such a degree—through a combination of large-scale expansions, new speaker, new claim to revelation, new scope or setting, new arrangement or structure, and new theological agenda—that everyone readily recognizes that it is a different composition deserving a different title.

One facet that, to my knowledge, is new to this discussion is that reworkings similar to those in the three "rewritten scriptural books" can be found in the redactional activity that scholars have postulated for the "pre-Scriptures," that is, for Israel's early religious

[31] Except originally regarding the "Reworked Pentateuch" but now "4QPentateuch".

literature before it eventually became its Scriptures. It seems that only moderate types of revision appear in preserved scriptural manuscripts of the late Second Temple period, but this contrasts with the earlier and the later periods. The reworking and rewriting of Israel's post-scriptural literature, with its major types of reworking, mirrors the reworking and rewriting of its pre-scriptural literature.

CHAPTER 14

RISING RECOGNITION OF THE SAMARITAN PENTATEUCH

THE SAMARITAN PENTATEUCH is another area that has benefited from the evidence of the scrolls and from post-Qumran thinking. The scrolls have shed fresh light on the SP, and scholars have been looking at the old evidence without presuming old conclusions. This has sparked a resurgence of Samaritan studies and shown the need for more inclusion of its data in both textual and historical research.[1] Moreover, recent archaeological[2] work and intensified historical[3] and literary-historical[4] study have also contributed in major ways toward clarifying scholarly understanding of Samarian-Judean history and relations from the monarchic period down to the end of the Second Temple period.

---

[1] Recently, e.g., at the 2013 SBL meeting in Baltimore there was a section on "Textual Criticism of the Hebrew Bible" focusing on the SP with papers by Terry Giles, Benyamim Tsedaka, Emanuel Tov, and Stefan Schorch; and a seminar on "Textual Growth: What Variant Editions Tell Us about Scribal Activity" featuring papers by Sidnie Crawford, Stefan Schorch, Molly Zahn, Magnar Kartveit, and Gary Knoppers. In May 2014 David Hamidović and Christophe Nihan organized an international conference at the University of Lausanne on "Samarians-Samaritans in Translation," with papers by Magnar Kartveit, Sarianna Metso, Reinhard Pummer, and Eugene Ulrich.

[2] Yizhak Magen, "The Dating of the First Phase of the Samaritan Temple at Mount Gerizim in Light of the Archaeological Evidence," in *Judah and the Judeans in the Fourth Century B.C.E.* (ed. O. Lipschits, G. N. Knoppers, and R. Albertz; Winona Lake, Ind.: Eisenbrauns, 2007), 157–211; Yizhak Magen, H. Misgav, and L. Tsfania, *Mount Gerizim Excavations. Vol. 1, The Aramaic, Hebrew and Samaritan Inscriptions* (Judea and Samaria Publications 2; Jerusalem: Israel Antiquities Authority, 2004); and Magen, *Mount Gerizim Excavations. Vol. 2, A Temple City* (Judea and Samaria Publications 8; Jerusalem: Israel Antiquities Authority, 2008).

[3] Reinhard Pummer ("ΑΡΓΑΡΙΖΙΝ: A Criterion for Samaritan Provenance?" *JSJ* 18 [1987]: 19–25); idem, "The Samaritans and their Pentateuch," in *The Pentateuch as Torah: New Models for Understanding Its Promulgation and Acceptance* (ed. Gary N. Knoppers and Bernard M. Levinson; Winona Lake, Ind.: Eisenbrauns, 2007), 237–69; Magnar Kartveit, *The Origin of the Samaritans* (VTSup 128; Leiden: Brill, 2009); Gary N. Knoppers, *Jews and Samaritans: The Origins and History of Their Early Relations* (Oxford: Oxford University Press, 2013), with rich bibliography.

[4] Christophe Nihan, "The Torah between Samaria and Judah: Shechem and Gerizim in Deuteronomy and Joshua," in *The Pentateuch as Torah*, 197–223, and literature cited there; Stefan Schorch, "Der Pentateuch der Samaritaner: Seine Erforschung und seine Bedeutung für das Verständis des alttestamentlichen Bibeltextes," in *Die Samaritaner und die Bibel / The Samaritans and the Bible* (ed. Jörg Frey et al.; Studia Samaritana 7; Berlin: de Gruyter, 2012), 5–29; *idem*, "The Construction of Samari(t)an Identity from the Inside and from the Outside," in *Between Cooperation and Hostility: Multiple Identities in Ancient Judaism and the Interaction with Foreign Powers* (ed. Rainer Albertz and Jakob Wöhrle; JAJS 11; Göttingen: Vandenhoeck & Ruprecht, 2013), 135–49.

I. The Samaritan and the Masoretic Pentateuch

A. The Discovery of the Samaritan Pentateuch

Chapter 3 centered on the Pentateuchal scrolls and demonstrated their evidence for recognizing the SP as an important witness to developing forms of the ancient Hebrew text. This chapter, taking the scrolls' preserved evidence as a basis, focuses more directly on the SP and surveys some of the recent advances in the study of the Samaritan and Judean Pentateuch.

The SP was not known in Europe until the seventeenth century and thus was not included in the first biblical polyglot, the Complutensian Polyglot (1514–1517), which included the Masoretic Hebrew, the LXX, a Targum, and the Vulgate.[5]

A century later Pietro della Valle traveled to the Near East and returned in 1616 enriched with a manuscript of the Samaritan Pentateuch, whose text was then included in the Paris Polyglot in 1632. Comparison of the SP with the MT highlighted some six thousand discrepancies; and when about one third of those showed agreement with the LXX, the reputation of the LXX as a faithful witness to an ancient Hebrew text climbed and that of the MT diminished. Through this period and for the next few centuries, however, the religious agenda of the researchers often clouded their textual conclusions. The SP-LXX agreement caused some to suggest that the MT had been secondarily revised by the Rabbis, and thus that the LXX preserved the divine word in purer form. But the Renaissance focus on the original language and the Reformation's concern for translation into the vernacular from the Hebrew rather than from the Vulgate served as a counterbalance in favor of the MT.

In 1815 Wilhelm Gesenius studied the SP and showed that most of its variant readings displayed a secondary reworking of a base text like the MT.[6] Others, such as Zacharias Frankel and Salomon Kohn,[7] added to the devaluation of the SP as a textual witness, due to its errors, its obviously secondary nature as generally dependent on, and later than, the MT, and thus its inability to penetrate behind the MT.[8] Until recently, it has simply been presumed that, because the SP edition is in general secondary to the MT, its variants are inferior to the MT.[9] The arguments below will question the legitimacy of that view.

---

[5] The Complutensian Polyglot celebrated its fifth centennial in 2014.

[6] Wilhelm Gesenius, *De Pentateuchi Samaritani origine, indole, et auctoritate* (Halle: Impensis Librariae Rengerianae, 1815); but see Henry B. Swete, *An Introduction to the Old Testament in Greek* (rev. by Richard R. Ottley; New York: Ktav, 1968), 438.

[7] Zacharias Frankel, *Über den Einfluss der palästinischen Exegese auf die alexandrische Hermeneutik* (Leipzig: J. A. Barth, 1851), 242; Salomon Kohn, "Samaritikon und Septuaginta," *Monatschrift für Geschichte und Wissenshaft des Judentums* 38 (1895): 60 (for the references see Shemaryahu Talmon, "The Old Testament Text," in *Qumran and the History*, 14–15).

[8] Note that the "value" of the witnesses is based on the "originality" of the text form, not on possible richness due to textual, historical, or theological development.

[9] See, e.g., Ernst Würthwein, *The Text of the Old Testament* (2d ed.; trans. Erroll F. Rhodes; Grand Rapids: Eerdmans, 1995), 46.

B. The Shared Samarian-Judean Pentateuch

Patrick Skehan, one of the original team of Qumran Cave 4 editors, in 1955 and 1959 fundamentally revised how we understand the SP with preliminary publications of 4QpaleoExod^{m}.[10] Chapter 3 demonstrated that 4QpaleoExod^{m}, 4QExod-Lev^{f}, and 4QNum^{b} corrected the view that the additions in the SP had been predominantly the work of the Samaritans. Where 4QpaleoExod^{m} is extant or can be confidently reconstructed, it shares with the SP many insertions lacking in the MT.[11] 4QExod-Lev^{f} shows that an insertion in the SP confirming that the Urim and Thummim were made was already in a Qumran manuscript. 4QNum^{b} shares with the SP eight harmonizations from Deuteronomy, five extant and three confidently reconstructed. In addition, at least two further scrolls, 4QPent B (4Q364) and 4QPent C (4Q365), display expanded texts in the SP tradition but expanded yet further. None of these scrolls entails any sectarian readings. Below, two (possibly three) other fragmentary witnesses will be described which argue that the reading "Mount Gerizim" in SP Deut 27:4 is early and that "Mount Ebal" in MT Deut 27:4 and Josh 8:30 is a later, sectarian reading.

With regard to the Palaeo-Hebrew script in 4QpaleoExod^{m}, the fact that it is written in that script is not an indicator that it is a Samaritan manuscript, since six other Judean scrolls are all written in the Palaeo-Hebrew script, but none shows specific affinity with the SP.[12] Some Judean scribes retained the ancient script for certain manuscripts of the books of the premonarchic figures, Moses, Joshua, and Job, just as the Samarians did for the books of Moses.

C. The Chronology of the Texts

It will be helpful to consider the palaeographically assigned dates in the DJD editions for these Pentateuchal and Palaeo-Hebrew manuscripts, plus the edition that each Exodus witness presents. The edition that each manuscript attests, of course, probably precedes by a generation or more the date of the manuscripts.

[Heb. *Vorl.* OG][13]	edn 1	ca. 300 B.C.E.	4QpaleoGenExod^{l}	edn 2	ca. 150–50? B.C.E.
OG translation	edn 1	ca. 280 B.C.E.	4QpaleoExod^{m}	edn 3	"
4QExod-Lev^{f}	edn 3	ca. 250 B.C.E.	4QpaleoDeut^{r}		"
4QpaleoDeut^{s}		ca. 250–200 B.C.E.	4QPent B		ca. 50–25 B.C.E.
4QpaleoJob^{c}		ca. 225–150 B.C.E.	4QPent C	edn 3+	ca. 50–1 B.C.E.
4QpaleoParaJoshua		ca. 150–110 B.C.E.	4QNum^{b}	SP edn	ca. 30 B.C.E. – 20 C.E.

[10] Patrick W. Skehan, "Exodus in the Samaritan Recension from Qumran," in *JBL* 74 (1955): 182–87, and "Qumran and the Present State of Old Testament Text Studies: The Masoretic Text," *JBL* 78 (1959): 21–25, esp. 22–23.

[11] 4QpaleoExod^{m} did not contain the extra Samaritan commandment at 20:17^{b}; see DJD 9:101–2.

[12] 1QpaleoLev-Num^{a}, 4QpaleoGen-Exod^{l}, 4QpaleoDeut^{r}, 4QpaleoJob, 4QpaleoParaJoshua, and 11Q-paleoLev^{a} show no signs of Samaritan influence.

[13] The Hebrew *Vorlage* of the OG must have predated the translation by at least a generation, since it must have been already considered a revered traditional text.

The Exodus texts present three successive editions of the book—the Hebrew *Vorlage* of the OG, the edition inherited by the MT, and that witnessed in the SP, each based upon and expanding beyond the previous edition.[14]

The OG and the witness of 4QExod-Lev^{f} are of high importance historically for understanding the status of the Pentateuch as shared between Samarians and Judeans during the Second Temple period. The OG was translated ca. 280 B.C.E. from a Hebrew text that contained the earliest known edition of the Tabernacle Account in Exodus 35–40.[15] 4QExod-Lev^{f} is dated to ca. 250 B.C.E., and, since it appears already to show the expanded edition beyond the one copied in the MT and the one in the OG, it thus demonstrates that all three editions of Exodus were accepted and circulating in common Jewish circles by at least the early third century B.C.E. and probably by the late fourth century. That is, the Hebrew text which contained the earliest Hebrew edition for Exodus 35–40 and from which the OG was translated must have been available prior to ca. 280 B.C.E., when the OG of the Pentateuch was translated. It must have been at least a generation older (before 300 B.C.E., or earlier), since it was deemed sufficiently authoritative to use for that important translation.

The second edition witnessed by the MT was subsequently based on and developed from that Hebrew *Vorlage* of the OG,[16] and it also must have been available (again, probably at least a generation older, thus 280 B.C.E., or earlier) prior to the third, "pre-Samaritan" edition which is based on it, as 4QExod-Lev^{f} demonstrates.

4QNum^{b} is also, like 4QExod-Lev^{f}, of high importance historically, insofar as it is dated as late as ca. 30 B.C.E. to 20 C.E.,[17] and this "pre-Samaritan" manuscript was still being copied in a deluxe edition with red ink and circulating in a Scripture-focused community in Judea as late as the dawn of the Christian era. It would be difficult to sustain the claim that this "pre-Samaritan" text was not common Jewish Scripture. The only problem for acceptance of a manuscript would be if it specifically included the altar on Mount Gerizim, the past or the future tense of (י)בחר, or the Samaritan tenth commandment. Similarly the LXX texts were available from the first half of the third century B.C.E. until the Christian era. Thus all three text traditions with their various editions, including the Gerizim-Ebal liturgy and a positive attitude toward Shechem, were shared by all Yahwists during the Second Temple period—except eventually for the specifically Samaritan texts of Exodus and Deuteronomy.[18]

---

14 For simplicity, only the three pertinent editions of Exodus are considered here, though there are many stages in its development; see Ch.13.

15 See Ch. 15.II and Bruning, "The Making of the Mishkan."

16 For detailed analysis of the four principles by which the proto-MT editor expanded and rearranged the earlier edition presented in the OG, see Brandon Bruning, "The Making of the Mishkan."

17 DJD 12:211.

18 The SP has an isolated insertion at Gen 31:10-13 and another before Deut 2:8, but 4QPent B (*olim* 4QRP^{b}) also contains both, and so they are not specifically SP but are part of the shared Pentateuch.

D. Crucial Passages

Two crucial passages concerned with the sectarian themes just mentioned shed light on the Samarian-Judean Pentateuch and should be examined: the formula at Deut 12:5 and elsewhere,[19] and insertions in Deuteronomy 27.

1. The Place Which Yhwh Has Chosen/Will Choose

First, in Deut 12:5 and wherever the frequent formula occurs about the place where the Lord's name is to dwell, the SP routinely has "the place where the LORD *has chosen*" (בחר), whereas the MT and LXX have "the place where the LORD *will choose*" (יבחר). The polemic here, of course, is that, in the minds of the northerners or Samarians, the Lord had already in the past, at the time of Moses and Joshua, chosen Mount Gerizim as true Israel's central shrine, and that should not change. For the Judeans, however, Jerusalem would become the central shrine established by David and Solomon, and the Lord's choice of Jerusalem still lay in the future.

Either form, however, could have been original. From the perspective of Deuteronomy, the people had not yet entered the land, and so the future form could be appropriate for either site.[20] Note the future, for example, in Josh 9:27: אל המקום אשר יבחר, where the context is the Gibeonites' service for the altar. This was before either site had been explicitly chosen, but presumably it refers to a northern shrine (Shiloh or Shechem?),[21] since Jerusalem was still in Jebusite hands.

On the other hand, God could also be viewed as having already made the choice—Mount Gerizim or Jerusalem—even before telling Moses, and so the perfect also could be appropriate for either site. Note that the perfect occurs in post-exilic Neh 1:9: אל המקום אשר בחרתי לשכן את שמי, where the context is Nehemiah's prayer quoting God's ancient promise to Moses to bring back the exiles. Adrian Schenker argues that MT Neh 1:9 as well as several manuscripts of the LXX, the OL, and the Bohairic and Sahidic show that the perfect בחר was the earlier form of the tradition, and that the imperfect יבחר was the revised form.[22] Stefan Schorch also reminds us that 4QMMT (4Q394 frg. 8 iv 9–11), ca. 50 B.C.E., "still attests the centralization formula with the perfect reading בחר"[23]:

---

[19] This formula with variations occurs in Deut 12:5, 11, 14, 18, 21, 26; 14:23, 24, 25; 15:20; 16:2, 6, 7, 11, 15, 16; 17:8, 10; 18:6; 26:2; 31:11.

[20] The Qumran scrolls offer little on this problem other than 4QpaleoDeut^{r}, which at Deut 12:4 contains חר[at the edge of frg. 16. The controlled spacing of the adjacent frg. 15 suggests that the *yod* (a very wide letter in the Palaeo-Hebrew script) was necessarily included, thus the Jewish אשר [יב]חר; see DJD 9, Plate XXXIV and pp. 134 and 139.

[21] As the site for Joshua's final address, the LXX names Shiloh at Josh 24:1, 25, whereas the MT, again positively, has Shechem. On Shiloh, see MT Josh 18:1; 19:51, and Hans-Joachim Kraus, *Worship in Israel: A Cultic History of the Old Testament* (trans. Geoffrey Buswell; Richmond, Va.: John Knox, 1965), 152–65.

[22] See Adrian Schenker, "Le Seigneur choisira-t-il le lieu de son nom ou l'a-t-il choisi?" (Ch. 3 n. 15).

[23] Schorch, "The Samaritan Version of Deuteronomy and the Origin of Deuteronomy," in *Samaria, Samarians, Samaritans: Studies on Bible, History and Linguistics* (ed. József Zsengellér; Studia Samaritana 6; Berlin: De Gruyter, 2011), 34; see also Reinhard G. Kratz, " 'The place which He has chosen': The identification of the Cult Place of Deut. 12 and Lev. 17 in 4QMMT," *Meghillot: Studies in the Dead Sea Scrolls* 5–6: *A Festschrift for Devorah Dimant* (2008), *57–*80.

המקום שבחר בו מכל שבטי [ישראל].[24] That is, originally, the formula is ambiguous. It is quite possible that the formula and its variants were in their origin a neutral, non-sectarian expression. Samarian and Judean communities could both read either formula and, because it was ambiguous, interpret it as referring to their own religious center. Eventually, however, one community explicitly specified the site and standardized its formula, causing the other to standardize its formula in sectarian contrast to their rivals.

Finally, Schorch, who is preparing a critical edition of the SP, proposed at the 2013 SBL Meeting, that, for a number of readings where the SP and MT vary, the SP is earlier.[25] He argued that though the SP readings focus on Mount Gerizim, they are neutral, simply affirming a belief in the importance of Mount Gerizim, and they are not tendentious against Jerusalem or the MT reading. It was only subsequently that the sectarian divisions emerged. This significant amount of solid and fruitful inquiry highlights an ongoing exploration that needs to be aggresively pursued in the future.

2. Deuteronomy 27 and Mount Gerizim or Mount Ebal?

Second, from the Judeans' point of view, and from that of most modern scholars accustomed to the MT, the *altar* on Mount Gerizim became the problem. But from the Samaritans' point of view, Jerusalem and its temple became the problem. Both views should be considered, but, since Jerusalem is not mentioned in Deuteronomy, our focus can shift to the place opposed to Mount Gerizim in Deuteronomy, Mount Ebal.

The place name "Gerizim" occurs (other than Judg 9:7, which is not relevant for our purposes) three times in the MT: Deut 11:29; 27:12; and Josh 8:33. "Ebal" occurs five times in the MT: Deut 11:29; 27:4, 13; and Josh 8:30, 33. The three occurrences of "Gerizim" are each paired with "Ebal" in the Gerizim-Ebal liturgy insertions at Deut 11:29; 27:12-13; and Josh 8:33 in the MT, accepted by the Judeans as well as the Samarians for 11:29 and 27:12-13. The two MT occurrences of "Ebal" unmatched by "Gerizim" are both later insertions into the text at 27:4 and Josh 8:30; the SP has "Gerizim" for the former and, if the Samaritans had a Joshua text, presumably it would have had "Gerizim" at Josh 8:30.[26]

All of Deuteronomy chapter 27 is a compilation of disparate passages inserted into, and interrupting, the main Deuteronomic Code 12–26 + 28 (with 11:26-28, 31-32 as the conclusion to the frame of the code).[27] The important verses for our study are 27:2-8 and 12-13.[28] Chapters 3 and 4 have already presented the evidence and the proposed deductions for most of the following conclusions:[29]

---

[24] DJD 10:12.

[25] See Stefan Schorch, *Die Vokale des Gesetzes: Die samaritanische Lesetradition als Textzeugin der Tora;* Band 1: *Das Buch Genesis* (BZAW 339; Berlin: de Gruyter, 2004).

[26] For the Judeans, the commandment of Deut 27:4 was fulfilled in the text at MT Josh 8:30; for the Samaritans, it was fulfilled physically by their altar on Mount Gerizim.

[27] Driver (*Deuteronomy* [ICC; 3d ed.; Edinburgh: T&T Clark, n.d.], 294) notes that "In this chapter the discourse of Moses [12–28] is interrupted, and the writer uses the third person. . . . It contains injunctions relative to *four* ceremonies. . . . Not only are the various parts of which it consists imperfectly connected with each other. . . , but it stands in a most unsuitable place," i.e., between chapters 12–26 and 28.

[28] Two other insertions, Deut 27:9-10 (Moses' announcement that Israel had become God's people that day) and Deut 27:14-28 (a series of curses), do not pertain to our inquiry. The Qumran scrolls again offer little help for Deut 11:29-30 and 27:2-8, 12-13. For 11:29-30, a small fragment of 1QDeut[a] has גריזים

- 4QpaleoExod[m] and 4QNum[b] generally contain the same expansions as the SP in Exodus and Numbers [therefore, the SP did not add them, but they were already in the shared Samarian-Judean Pentateuch].
- For the Book of Joshua the LXX is a shorter text than the MT and 4QJosh[a] is yet shorter than the LXX [therefore, the LXX is probably earlier than the MT in general, and 4QJosh[a] is probably yet earlier].
- One way the MT is longer than the LXX is its frequent addition of place names[30] that are lacking in the LXX [therefore, it is likely that either "Mount Gerizim" or "Mount Ebal" in Deut 27:4 and Josh 8:30 could also be a secondary addition].
- The placement of MT Josh 8:30-35 (the building of the altar and the reading of the Torah) is problematic,[31] while 4QJosh[a] has the Torah reading at the end of Joshua 4, and Noort had astutely judged, even prior to knowing 4QJosh[a], that the end of Joshua 4 was the logical place for the passage [therefore, it is plausible that 4QJosh[a] presents the earlier placement of the building of the altar at the end of Joshua 4].
- Although the fragmentary 4QJosh[a] preserves the report of the Torah reading (MT Josh 8:34-35), the prior setting up of the stones (MT Josh 8:30-33) is not preserved on its extant fragments; however, no text has the Torah reading without the combination of the setting up of the stones [therefore, there is no basis for suggesting that the verses reporting the building of the altar had not originally preceded the Torah reading in the scroll].
- Papyrus Giessen and the OL (plus DSS F.Deut2) have "Mount Gerizim" [therefore, it is not a SP change, but it was already in the shared Samarian-Judean Pentateuch].
- The MT and LXX, as well as the SP, include in a positive manner the liturgy of blessing on Mount Gerizim and curses on Mount Ebal [therefore, these are not Samarian sectarian insertions but commonly shared Jewish texts].
- Both the SP and the MT contain at Deut 27:4 the full sentence with the single-word variant "Mount Gerizim/Mount Ebal" as the place where "these stones" are to be set up [therefore, the sentence was in the commonly shared Judean-Samarian text, and one name was earlier and the other a sectarian variant].

and מ[ו]ל הגלגל, and 1QDeut[b] has [ב]עברה מו[ל, all in agreement with the MT and SP, but note that both scrolls attest the confused portion of the topological gloss in 11:30. For 27:2-8, 4QDeut[f] has a modest amount, again, in insignificant agreement with both the MT and the SP.

29 The preserved evidence is printed in normal type and the proposed deductions in square brackets.

30 Josh 6:26; 8:17; 10:15, and 10:43.

31 The placement of MT Josh 8:30-35 is problematic because (1) Josh 9:1 follows 8:29, not 8:35; (2) the "large stones" (Deut 27:2) from the Jordan must be carried all the way to Shechem; and (3) the army plus the women and children (Josh 8:35) must march twenty miles into a hostile land with no mention of resistance, build the altar, march twenty miles back to Gilgal (9:6), and abandon the altar in enemy territory.

- Deut 27:2-3a and 27:4, 8 exhibit a doublet,[32] vv. 2-3a without a place named [but presumably Gilgal], while v. 4 specifies "Mount Gerizim/Ebal" [therefore, text-critically the shorter, less specified reading in 2-3a is more likely the earlier, while the specified locality is probably an addition made for a specific purpose: to make a religious claim for a changed location for the altar].
- In the MT Mount Gerizim is always viewed positively, and archaeologically there was a shrine there, whereas Mount Ebal, the mountain of the curse, has nothing to recommend it, other than its occurrence in the MT [therefore, the earlier form in Deut 27:4 was Mount Gerizim, and Mount Ebal is a later sectarian variant].[33]
- The SP attests, but the MT-LXX lacks, the additional commandment to build an altar on Mount Gerizim in SP-Exod 20:17^{b} and Deut 5:18^{b} (after MT 5:21) [is this because the SP added it or because the MT-LXX knew but refused to include it?].

The evidence and the plausible deductions listed above provide the basis for the following reconstruction. There were three major stages in the growth of these coordinated passages, plus a number of other sporadic insertions (see the chart). The text there is arranged chronologically by indentations from the left margin. That is, "Deut 12–26, + 28" is the early Deuteronomic Code, and 11:26-28, 31-32 is the conclusion of its introductory frame. As the first stage of growth, the four paragraphs forming most of the left margin constitute the main, early narrative that was inserted into chapter 27. As the second stage, the next set of three coordinated additions about the Gerizim liturgy is indented and marked with a single vertical line. As the third stage, the theme of the *altar* on Mount Gerizim is further indented and marked with a double vertical line. The

[32] Note other Hebrew doublets at 1 Sam 2:24 and 2:31-32, and Greek doublets at Deut 32:43; 1 Sam 1:6; 2 Sam 6:2; 20:8 (see Ch. 6.IV.A.6).

[33] Schenker's view about the priority of the SP is strengthened by the point argued in Chapter 4, that, though Deut 27:2-3a originally mentioned no specific place but presumed the place where the Israelites crossed into the land, Mount Gerizim is the earlier place inserted, and Mount Ebal is the later, reactionary variant. In agreement see Stefan Schorch, "The Samaritan Version of Deuteronomy," 23–37; Magnar Kartveit, *The Origin of the Samaritans*, 300–5, esp. 303 and 305; Timo Veijola, *Das 5. Buch Mose: Deuteronomium, Kapitel 1,1–16,17* (Göttingen: Vandenhoeck & Ruprecht, 2004), 259 n. 807; Gary Knoppers, *Jews and Samaritans*, 202–3; and Christophe Nihan, "The Torah between Samaria and Judah," 213–14. Würthwein, *The Text of the Old Testament*, 46, tentatively favors "Ebal" as the correct reading.

Gerhard von Rad (*Das fünfte Buch Mose: Deuteronomium* [ATD 8; Göttingen: Vandenhoeck & Ruprecht, 1964], 117; = *Deuteronomy* [OTL; Philadelphia: Westminster, 1966], 164) also appears to favor Mount Gerizim. Though the general biblical translation of Deut 27:4 that was used for his volume has "auf dem Berge Ebal" with the MT, von Rad himself in his commentary continues, without explanation: "Das 27. Kapitel beginnt mit einer Aufforderung Mose, nach der Überschreitung des Jordan auf *dem Berge Garzim* 'alle Worte dieses Gesetzes' auf Steinen niederzuschreiben..." (emphasis added). Tov (*Textual Criticism*, 254, n. 96) says that "Ebal" in MT "is probably not anti-Samaritan, but reflects an ancient reading"; but he also says that Gerizim "should probably be considered non-sectarian and possibly original" (88, n. 140). That would mean that Ebal is secondary. Otto Eissfeldt, *The Old Testament: An Introduction* (trans. Peter R. Ackroyd; New York: Harper and Row, 1965), 216–17 and n. 9 concludes: "*Ebal* ... doubtless derives from anti-Samaritan polemic." No one yet has, to my knowledge, offered a rationale for that curious variant other than as a tendentious substitution for Gerizim.

1st add	Gerizim liturgy	*Gerizim stones/altar*	COMMANDMENT (Additions)

||| EXOD 20:17b = DEUT 5:18b CMDMT: GERIZIM ALTAR

11:26-28 See, today I am setting before you a blessing and a curse. . . . [Frame for Deut Code]

| **Deut 11:29 When the Lord your God has brought you into the land that you are entering to occupy, you shall set the blessing on Mount Gerizim and the curse on Mount Ebal.**

(30 Are they not beyond the Jordan, some distance to the west, in the land of the Canaanites ((who live in the Arabah, opposite Gilgal)), near the oak of Moreh?) [cf. Gen 12:6-7 "Shechem, oak of Moreh, Canaanites, land"]

11:31-32 When you cross the Jordan to go in . . . , you must diligently observe. . . . [Frame for Deut Code]

eut 12–26, + 28 These are the statutes. . . . [Deut Code]

Deut 27:2 On the day that you cross over the Jordan into the land that the Lord your God is giving you, you shall set up large stones and cover them with plaster. 3 You shall write on them all the words of this law.

(*when you have crossed over to enter the land that the Lord you God is giving you, a land flowing with milk and honey, as the Lord, the God of your ancestors, promised you*)

|| ***4 When you have crossed over the Jordan, you shall set up these stones about which I am commanding you today on Mount Gerizim and you shall cover them with plaster.***

5 You shall build an altar there to the Lord your God, (an altar of stones on which you have not used an iron tool. 6 You must build the altar of the Lord your God of unhewn stones). Then offer up burnt offerings on it to the Lord your God, 7 make sacrifices of well-being, and eat them there, rejoicing before the Lord your God.

|| ***8 You shall write on the stones all the words of this law very clearly.***

[9-10 today you have become the people of the Lord....]

| **12-13 When you have crossed over the Jordan these shall stand on Mount Gerizim for the blessing of the people: Simeon.... 13 These shall stand on Mount Ebal for the curse: Reuben....**

[14-26 Curses]

|| ***on Mt. Gerizim/Ebal*** ↓ [+ move 4[8]:30-35 from Ch.4 to Ch.8]

Josh 4[8]:30 Then Joshua built an altar to the Lord the God of Israel, 31 just as Moses the servant of the Lord had commanded the Israelites (as it is written in the book of the law of Moses, "an altar of unhewn stones, on which no iron tool has been used"); and they offered on it burnt offerings to the Lord and sacrificed offerings of well-being. 32 And there, in the presence of the Israelites, Joshua wrote on the stones a copy of the law of Moses, which he had written.

| **33 All Israel, alien as well as citizen, with their elders and officers and their judges, stood on opposite sides of the ark in front of the levitical priests who carried the ark of the covenant of the Lord, half of them in front of Mount Gerizim and half of them in front of Mount Ebal, as Moses the servant of the Lord had commanded at the first, that they should bless the people of Israel.**

34 Afterward he read all the words of the law (blessings and curses) according to all that is written in the book of the law. 35 There was not a word of all that Moses commanded that Joshua did not read before all the assembly of Israel, and the women and the little ones, and the aliens who resided among them. 5:X After [the people] had withdrawn [from the Jordan and Joshua had read] to [them] the book of the law, after that, the bearers of the ark [we]nt up and [put the book of the law beside the ark].

insertion of the tenth commandment is noted at the top as closely related, but it is not included in the MT as are all three of the other additions.

Stage 1 presents the basics of the narrative: Just before the crossing into the Promised Land, Moses instructs Joshua to set up large stones, to write the words of the law, to build an altar, offer sacrifices, and rejoice before the Lord. No place is mentioned, but the non-specified wording "On the day that you cross over the Jordan into the land" presumes the immediate region of Gilgal. In the order presented by 4QJosh^{a}, the altar-Torah ritual followed by the rituals of circumcision and Passover in Joshua 5 form a fitting preparation for the conquest of the land, starting in Joshua 6.[34] The detail about the unhewn stones in Deut 27:5b-6a and Josh 8:31 could have been an original part or a later addition, but that is not significant for our purposes.

Stage 2 appears to be the coordinated triple insertion in the shared SP-MT regarding a ritual liturgy of blessings and curses pronounced on Mount Gerizim and Mount Ebal. Note that this is simply a blessing-curse ritual; there is no mention of an altar either on Mount Gerizim or on Mount Ebal. That it is not an original part of the narrative is indicated by the sudden switch within the context of a comprehensive legal parenesis promising covenant blessings and curses depending upon fidelity or infidelity addressed to all Israel, to a minor cultic event of public sayings at a specific locale.

Stage 3 inserts verses 4 and 8 and the corresponding gloss in Josh 8:30. Verses 4 and 8 are a duplicate version of verses 2-3a,[35] with the specification that these stones are to be set up on Mount Gerizim. Note the wording, "these stones," which indicates that verse 4 is later than, and dependent on, verses 2-3a. The gloss in Josh 8:30 specifies that "Joshua built an altar *on Mount Gerizim*" (or *on Mount Ebal*). These insertions were most likely added by northerners, though accepted by the southerners, and they constitute the most logical impetus for the editorial move of the passage about the "altar-Torah" from the end of Joshua 4 to the end of Joshua 8 in the MT tradition, since Gilgal-Jericho is the only region in view before chapter 7.[36] That is, the verses were added by northerners, since it is unlikely that southerners would place the altar in the north. They were accepted by the southerners, since they are retained in the MT. And the editorial move of the altar-Torah passage from chapter 4 at Gilgal to chapter 8 in the north at Gerizim (or Ebal) was made by northern scribes and had already taken place before the finalization of the tradition inherited by the MT.[37]

Two other verses should be mentioned. Deut 11:30 is a later topological gloss with a yet later confusing gloss about the Arabah inserted into it,[38] and Deut 27:3b is an addi-

[34] On the liturgical traditions of Israel centered at Gilgal, see Kraus, *Worship in Israel*, 152–65, and Moshe Weinfeld, *Deuteronomy 1–11* (AB; New York: Doubleday, 1991), 329–30.

[35] For similar duplications see n. 32.

[36] There is close to unanimous agreement that the placement of Josh 8:30-35 in the MT is secondary and difficult (see Ch. 4 note 3 and section I.C).

[37] Just as Dtr used a northern source for much of Deuteronomy (see Schorch, "The Samaritan Version of Deuteronomy," 23), so too did he use the Joshua traditions which are predominantly northern, even if the Samaritans did not accept the book of Joshua as canonical.

[38] Timo Veijola, *Das 5. Buch Mose: Deuteronomium*, 258–59, clearly states: "Ihr Charakter als Nachtrag (bzw. Nachträge) wird allgemein zugestanden," and "Die einzelnen in V. 30 genannten Ortsnamen sind weder unter sich noch mit den in V. 29 genannten Bergen in Einklang zu bringen. . . . Deutlich scheint auf alle Fälle zu sein, dass Geographie hier im Dienste theologischer Polemik steht." See

tional duplicating formulation of "When you have crossed. . . ." That the latter is a late addition is shown by the Samaritan tenth commandment which quotes verses 2-3a but does not include this duplicate insertion of Deut 27:3b.

Deuteronomy 27 as a whole is already an insertion into the Deuteronomic Code of 12–26 + 28, but it accumulated an assortment of other insertions at various times as well:[39]

- Deut 11:30: a topographical gloss on Deut 11:29, locating Mounts Gerizim and Ebal at Shechem
- Deut 11:30: a later confusing insertion "the Arabah opposite Gilgal" into that gloss
- Deut 27:3b: yet another duplicating formulation of "When you have crossed . . ."
- Deut 27:5b-6a and Josh 8:31aβ: the specification of unhewn stones could well be a later insertion, though it could already have been part of the early tradition

In addition, "blessings and curses" in Josh 8:34aβ may be a later insertion, though it could have been in the original.

In conclusion, the study of the SP is benefiting from the scrolls and from fresh post-Qumran thinking, enriched by recent archaeological, textual, literary, and historical work. That the expansions and variants in the SP are not due specifically to the Samaritans is shown by 4QpaleoExod^{m}, 4QExod-Lev^{f}, and 4QNum^{b} which share virtually all the features seen in the SP without any sectarian indications. Moreover, 4QPent B and C in Judah display an expanded edition similar to that used by the Samarians but expanded even further. These last two features demonstrate that the SP, with almost no significant variants, is a form of the text shared in common by both Judeans and Samarians. The book of Exodus, for example, was accepted by all parties, and all three traditions, the OG *Vorlage*, the proto-MT, and the pre-SP, were known already by the early third century B.C.E., and perhaps earlier, and continued to be shared until the turn of the era.

With regard to the יבחר/בחר variants, either could have been original, and both could be accepted and interpreted by Judeans and Samarians as each thought correct. Eventually, one form was specified (perhaps neutrally), and the other group replaced it in its texts, thus now constituting a sectarian variant.

Mount Gerizim is always viewed in a positive light in the MT, except for Deut 27:4 (and perhaps Josh 8:30), where the evidence points to a Judean sectarian replacement with Mount Ebal, with no rationale other than a sectarian denial of Mount Gerizim.

Thus, the texts were shared in both Samaria and Judea throughout the Second Temple period, the only sectarian features being eventually the יבחר/בחר variant, the altar on Mount Gerizim versus on Mount Ebal, and the extra Samari(t)an commandment. Though the original forms of these features may or may not have been inserted or perceived as sectarian, the adoption of the alternate reading would have been a sectarian variant.

---

also Moshe Weinfeld, *Deuteronomy 1–11* (AB; New York: Doubleday, 1991), 452, who notes a similar topological gloss in Judg 21:19, and a similar informational item introduced by הלא in Deut 3:11.

[39] We could say about Deuteronomy 27 what Joseph Blenkinsopp, in *Isaiah 1–39: A New Translation with Introduction and Commentary* (AB 19; New York: Doubleday, 2000), 194, said about Isaiah 2: "Picking our way through the editorial debris that has gradually accumulated in this passage. . . ."

II. The Samaritan and the Greek of Genesis 5 and 11

Although the SP and the MT share the same general edition of Genesis, they do present variant editions of two passages. For the important stories in the formative stages of the book of Genesis, a desire to preserve and transmit each of the differing forms and theologies of the classic stories seems unmistakable. For example, the two creation stories with their different perspectives, the two flood stories with their clashing and irreconcilable details, the two accounts of the covenant with Abraham, and similar doublets almost demand such a explanation. But the redactional combination of those disparate sources entailed the possibility of conflicts.

Examination of the SP, the LXX, and the MT for the chronologies in Genesis 5 and 11 tabulating the ages of the pre-diluvian and post-diluvian ancestors exposes serious conflict between the three witnesses with regard to the ages of the individuals.[40] Closer examination of Gen 5:3-32 reveals that according to the SP Jared, Methuselah, and Lamech were still alive until the year that the flood began; according to the MT Methuselah was still alive; and according to the LXX Methuselah actually lives fourteen years beyond the start of the flood (which Gen 7:23 precludes). Moreover, closer examination of Gen 11:10-32 reveals that similar chronological problems face the post-diluvian ancestors in relation to Abraham's life span.

The problem was well-known to ancient interpreters such as Josephus, Jerome, Augustine, and Eusebius who wrestled with it, as well as to modern scholars as early as Dillmann.[41] Ronald Hendel has recently provided a clear and persuasive exposition of the problem.[42] Agreeing mainly with Ralph Klein's study,[43] he concludes that despite the significant variation in the numbers, "the variant chronologies of [the MT, SP, and LXX] are the result of conscious and systematic revisions of Genesis 5 and 11, motivated by problems implicit in the ages of the individuals at death.... Most remarkably, these problems were solved independently in the textual traditions ancestral to" the MT, SP, and LXX.[44]

The chronological problem resulted from the combination of the *narrative* traditions about the flood (traditional J) with the *list* of the descendants of Adam (ספר תולדות אדם). Each had its distinctive chronological system. The narrative tradition had one set of dates, while the list of the descendants of Adam had a different, much more developed set of dates. At the time of the combination of the two sources the conflicts between the dating schemata were not noticed. But scribes eventually noticed "the scandal that [in the LXX]... Methuselah survives the flood by 14 years" and that after the flood in the MT

---

40 No Qumran Genesis manuscripts are extant for Genesis 5 or 11 except 4QGen^b, which has the single, isolated word קינן for one of the occurrences of the name in 5:9-14.

41 A. Dillmann, *Genesis* (2 vols.; trans. W. B. Stevenson; Edinburgh: T&T Clark, 1987), 1:399; trans. of *Die Genesis* (6th ed. 1892), cited in Ronald S. Hendel, *The Text of Genesis 1–11: Textual Studies and Critical Edition* (New York: Oxford University Press, 1998), 62.

42 Hendel, *The Text of Genesis 1–11*, 61–80.

43 Ralph W. Klein, "Archaic Chronologies and the Textual History of the Old Testament," *HTR* 67 (1974): 255–63.

44 *The Text of Genesis 1–11*, 61.

chronology, "Noah, Shem, and *all* the post-diluvian patriarchs are still alive during Abraham's lifetime, and several survive him."[45]

Once the implications of the conflicts were noticed, various scribal traditions set about solving the problems. Comparison of the numerical calculations of the three text traditions suggests that there had been a common source that has been "corrected" differently in the three versions, forming three variant editions of these two chapters.[46] A common "archetype" behind the three witnesses is no longer extant, but it can be reconstructed with reasonable confidence (though there are a few anomalies).

Accordingly, we can posit five different stages in the development of these sections in the Book of Genesis:

1. an "origins" narrative of the ancestors of Israel (traditional J)
2. a document ספר תולדות אדם which had an elaborate dating schema for the ancestors (traditional P)
3. a combined Genesis story that included the two sources above, with conflicting dates (this would have been an early edition of the text we recognize as Genesis: edition *n*)
4. three independent intentional revisions of the dating schema, to solve the problems (the forerunners of the MT [edition *n* + *1a*], SP [edition *n* + *1b*], and LXX [edition *n* + *1c*])
5. the transmission of the early texts of Genesis, each of which acquired a few textual errors (the few problematic readings now found in the MT, SP, and LXX)

Hendel is also correct to distinguish the two stages listed as the fourth and fifth above:

> Notably, these revised texts were produced some time after the inception of the textual transmission of Genesis, that is, after the "original text" had been produced by the writers and editors of Genesis, and after the time of the textual archetype ancestral to all extant texts of Genesis.... These were not three literary editions that were incorporated successively into one or more scribal traditions ... but three recensions of the book,[47] created synchronically, as it were, in three different streams of textual transmission.... None of these three texts is itself the hyparchetype of the recension; rather, each is a later text, as is shown by the instances of probable scribal error in each version....[48]

In conclusion, instead of seeing a jumble of numerous individual textual variants in the three sources, it is clearer to see in the three text traditions three intelligible macro-variants, or variant editions of chapters 5 and 11. These three traditions had received a common autograph, and each tried to solve the chronological problems in analogous ways. There is no reason to suspect any of the traditions of sectarian manipulation.

---

[45] Hendel, *The Text of Genesis 1–11*, 61–62 (emphasis in the original).

[46] Hendel, *The Text of Genesis 1–11*, 79–80.

[47] For the phrase "recensions of the book" I would substitute "editions of the passages."

[48] Hendel, 79–80.

CHAPTER 15

INSIGHTS INTO THE SEPTUAGINT

THE FINAL SECTION of the previous chapter treating the variant edition of Genesis 5 and 11 in the Samaritan Pentateuch showed that the Septuagint also has a yet different edition of those chapters. Based on the numerous variant editions brought to light by the Hebrew scrolls, this chapter will examine instances in which the Septuagint strongly suggests that it, and quite likely its no-longer-preserved Hebrew *Vorlage*, presents a variant edition from that in the MT.

I. THE OLD GREEK OF ISAIAH

For perspective on LXX editions, the distinction between variant editions and individual variants, and the realization that they operate separately from each other, will prove useful. For this purpose an analysis of the wide variety of different types of LXX correct and incorrect renderings observed in comparison with the Great Isaiah Scroll will hopefully aid clearer understanding of the translation techniques and editions in the LXX.

Chapter 10 showed a variety of Hebrew readings in the scrolls, some correct, some incorrect, documenting plausible sources for variants in the LXX against the MT. Cumulatively, they demonstrate the general fidelity of the translators to their Hebrew source text. Study of the Greek translation of Isaiah in light of 1QIsa^{a} does not reveal a variant edition from the scroll or MT, but it has provided a rich array of instances which illuminate the correctness of some individual variants and the causes behind other readings that are problematic.[1]

The original Greek translator has been both unjustly maligned as a careless translator and excessively credited with visionary imagination. His work was seen as careless by those who compared the translation against the presumed "original text" of the MT and found it unsatisfactory, and it was seen as visionary by others who saw it "actualizing" the ancient prophecies to apply them to events at the time of the translator. But the Hebrew text he translated was not identical to the MT, and the examples of alleged "actualizing exegesis" do not withstand critical scrutiny.

The oft-repeated but mostly overemphasized truism that every translation is an interpretation requires differentiation, especially in light of claims regarding "actualizing exegesis" made about the OG translator of Isaiah. Of course, translators must interpret what they think the source text means; and they must decide on the most appropriate manner of expressing that message so that it is meaningful in the target language. Moreover, translators can provide a translation that is faithful, whether it be a literal

---

[1] See DJD 32, 2:119–93, some examples of which are reprinted here.

translation, that is, noticeably more faithful to the source text, or a free translation, that is, noticeably more faithful to meaning and style for the target audience; both can be "faithful" translations.

But there is an essential difference between what can be termed "simple interpretation" or faithful translation, and "intentional re-interpretation" or actualizing exegesis. "Simple interpretation" (whether literal or free) is the innocent attempt to render into Greek the meaning of the Hebrew parent text as it is understood by the translator. Thus the translator thinks that the Hebrew text means X, and he produces a faithful rendering of X in his Greek translation, even if the Hebrew is incorrect or if certain terms or expressions are adapted to the culture or understanding of the target audience. By "intentional re-interpretation," in contrast, is meant that, although the translator thinks that the Hebrew text means X, nonetheless he produces a rendering Y which he knows differs from the Hebrew; he does so because he wants to make a new point, to make the prophecy relevant to the community's current situation. Although the OG translator of Isaiah tends toward the free, attempting to make the original comprehensible to his Greek community, he does not engage in actualizing exegesis.

Listed below are ten characteristics for help in understanding the OG translation and its procedures. In assessing the original translation it must be remembered that the original Greek has been lost or disturbed or changed at numerous points during the long history of the transmission of the Greek text; such problems should not be attributed to the translator. The *Vorlage* of the OG was similar to, but not identical to either 1QIsa^{a} or the MT. That *Vorlage* did, however, look generally like 1QIsa^{a}: a handwritten scroll in a script mostly clear and legible, but at points damaged, faded, or difficult to decipher. We should envision such a manuscript, not the neat and printed *BHS*.

Many Hebrew biblical manuscripts from Qumran show Hebrew forms which differ from the MT but which had served as the basis for the OG translation; this is also the case in 1QIsa^{a} with the OG of Isaiah. Sometimes it is clear that the OG correctly renders ambiguous or no-longer extant forms, or even misreads or misunderstands forms; but in these cases, though the intended Hebrew is not represented in the Greek, nonetheless the translator was attempting to translate faithfully what he believed he saw in the Hebrew *Vorlage*.

Again, since verse-division was not marked in antiquity, both Hebrew and Greek manuscripts occasionally show different understandings of where the division of the text should be. Moreover, when the Hebrew poetic style uses parallelism or is simply repetitious, the OG often presents only a single expression to represent a pair in the Hebrew, but with no loss of meaning.

Finally, the translator uses understandable equivalents for idiomatic Hebrew expressions and replaces older place names with contemporary ones;[2] the same meaning is conveyed, however, with no sign of "actualizing exegesis." That is, the translator, while understanding the text to mean one thing, does not knowingly present a different meaning in order to show that Isaiah's ancient prophecies are being fulfilled in the present; he is simply using equivalents that were understandable to his contemporary community.

[2] For contemporary names but no "actualizing" see, e.g., Gen 25:20 הארמי MT SP = τοῦ Σύρου LXX.

1. The OG witnesses to an earlier text where 𝔐 inserts:

2:22 om v 22 𝔊] hab v 22 1QIsa^{a} 𝔐 𝔊^{VLC} α′ (add)
40:7 om v 7 1QIsa^{a*} 𝔊] hab 1QIsa$^{a\,2m}$ 𝔐 (add)

2. The OG correctly translates extant Hebrew forms different from 𝔐:

23:10 עבדי 1QIsa^{a} 𝔊(ἐργάζου) 𝔗(גלא)] עברי 𝔐 𝔖 𝔙; עבורי 4QIsa^{c}
41:5 יחדו 1QIsa^{a} 𝔊(ἅμα)] יחרדו 𝔐
45:2 והררים 1QIsa^{a} 1QIsa^{b}(והרורים) 𝔊(καὶ ὄρη)] והדורים 𝔐
45:8 הריעו 1QIsa^{a} 𝔊(εὐφρανθήτω)] הרעיפו 𝔐
50:2 תיבש 1QIsa^{a} 𝔊(καὶ ξηρανθήσονται)] תבאש 𝔐
50:6 הסירותי 1QIsa^{a} 𝔊(ἀπέστρεψα)] הִסְתַּרְתִּי 𝔐^{L}
53:11 אור 1QIsa^{a} 1QIsa^{b} 4QIsa^{d}(אוֹ֯[ר]) 𝔊(φῶς)] > 𝔐 (יראה = err for ירוה || ישבע)

3. Similarly, the OG correctly translates 𝔐 forms which differ from the Qumran form:

6:10 השמ (√שמם) 1QIsa^{a}] השמן 𝔐 𝔊(ἐπαχύνθη) σ′(ελιπανθη)

4. The OG correctly translates ambiguous or alternate forms:

1:27 ושביה 1QIsa^{a}] וְשָׁבֶיהָ 𝔐^{L} α′ σ′; ו֯שביה ושו[ב]י֯ה[4QIsa^{f}; ἡ αἰχμαλωσία αὐτῆς 𝔊(= שְׁבִיָּה)
2:6 ישפיקו 1QIsa^{a} 𝔐 𝔊(πολλὰ ... ἐγενήθη αὐτοῖς) α′ θ′] יספקו 4QIsa^{b} σ′(ἐκρότησαν)
3:8 עיני 1QIsa^{a} α′ σ′] עני 𝔐; διότι νῦν ἐταπεινώθη 𝔊(= √ענה)
55:1 וחלב 1QIsa^{a}] וְחָלָב 𝔐^{L} α′ σ′; καὶ στέαρ (= וְחֵלֶב) 𝔊
56:11 הרועים 1QIsa^{a}] רעים 1QIsa^{b} 𝔐 (= √רעה); πονηροὶ (= √רעע) 𝔊 𝔖 𝔗

5. The OG correctly translates a plausible but non-extant or misread Hebrew text:

16:11 חרש 1QIsa^{a} 𝔐] ὅ ἐνεκαίνισας (= חדש) 𝔊 (cf 41:1)
34:4 יבול כנ(ו)בל ... וכנ(ו)בלת 1QIsa^{a} 𝔐] πεσεῖται ... καὶ ὡς πίπτει 𝔊 (= √נפל)
41:1 החרישו 1QIsa^{a} 𝔐] ἐγκαινίζεσθε (= החדישו) 𝔊 (cf 16:11)
41:2 יוריד 1QIsa^{a} θ′] ירד 𝔐; ἐκστήσει (= יחריד cf v 5 [§2 above] and *BHS* note) 𝔊
44:8 תפחדו 1QIsa^{a} 𝔐] παρακαλύπτεσθε (= תכחדו) 𝔊
44:11 חובריו יבושו 1QIsa^{a} 𝔐^{L}(חֲבֵרָיו יֵבֹשׁוּ)] ὅθεν ἐγένοντο(< ברא?) ἐξηράνθησαν(= חרבו/יָבְשׁוּ) 𝔊
48:9 אאריך (= √ארך) 1QIsa^{a} 𝔐] δείξω σοι (= אראך) 𝔊
59:15 מֵרָע 1QIsa^{a} 𝔐] τὴν διάνοιαν (= מדע?) 𝔊 (cf 16:11; 41:1)

6. The OG misunderstands the Hebrew text:

7:20 בתער השכירה 1QIsa^{a} 𝔐^{L}(הַשְּׂכִירָה) 𝔊^{BO}(τῷ μεμισθωμένῳ = √שׂכר) α′ σ′ θ′] τῷ ξυρῷ τῷ μεγάλῳ
καὶ μεμεθυσμένῳ (= √שׁכר) 𝔊
10:17 וקדושו 1QIsa^{a} 𝔐 σ′(καὶ ὁ ἅγιος αὐτοῦ)] καὶ ἁγιάσει αὐτὸν 𝔊
10:18 וכבוד 1QIsa^{a} 𝔐] ἀποσβεσθήσεται (= יכבה) 𝔊
10:18 כמסס נסס 1QIsa^{a} 𝔐] ὁ φεύγων (= √נוס) ὡς ὁ φεύγων ἀπὸ φλογὸς καιομένης 𝔊
17:11 וכאוב 1QIsa^{a}] וּכְאָב 𝔐^{L}; καὶ ὡς πατὴρ 𝔊

23:3 שחר 1QIsa^{a} 4QIsa^{a} 𝔐^{L}(שִׁחֹר)] μεταβόλων (= *סחר) 𝔊

34:17 להנה(𝔐 לחם) בקו 1QIsa^{a} 𝔐] βόσκεσθαι (= ?לחם בקר) 𝔊

44:11 וחרשים 1QIsa^{a} 𝔐^{L}(וְחָרָשִׁים)] καὶ κωφοὶ (= וְחֵרְשִׁים) 𝔊

55:5 גוי ל(ו)א תדע תקרא 1QIsa^{a} 1QIsa^{b} 𝔐] ἔθνη ἃ οὐκ ᾔδεισάν σε ἐπικαλέσονταί σε 𝔊 (cf v 5aβ)

60:21 נצר 1QIsa^{a} 𝔐^{L}(נֵצֶר)] > 1QIsa^{b} 𝔐^{ms}; φυλάσσων (= נֹצֵר) 𝔊

63:19[64:1] וירדתה 1QIsa^{a}] יָרַדְתָּ 1QIsa^{b} 𝔐; τρόμος (= √רעד cf 33:14) λήμψεται 𝔊 (see 64:2[3])

63:19[64:1] נזלו 1QIsa^{a} 𝔐 (√זלל)] τακήσονται 𝔊 𝔙(*defluerent*) (= √נזל)

7. The OG shows a different division of text:

1:26-27 $^{(27?)}$ציון$^{(27?)}$ 1QIsa^{a}] 27^{init} 𝔐; 26^{fin} 𝔊

3:17-18 ^{18}ביום ההוא יסיר 1QIsa^{a} 𝔐] ἐν τῇ ἡμέρᾳ ἐκείνῃ ^{18}καὶ ἀφελεῖ 𝔊

8:13-14 והוא מערצכם ^{14}ו֯היא(𝔐 4QIsa^{l} והיה) 1QIsa^{a} 4QIsa^{l} 𝔐 α′ σ′ 𝔖] ^{14}καὶ ἐὰν ἐπ’ αὐτῷ πεποιθὼς ᾖς ἔσται σοι 𝔊; ויהי ^{14}ואם לא תקבלון 𝔗

8:22-23[9:1] כ'לו ... ^{23}כעת הרישון 1QIsa^{a} (cf 3:11)] ^{23}כי לא ... כעת הראשון 𝔐; καὶ οὐκ ... ἕως καιροῦ. $^{23[1]}$Τοῦτο πρῶτον ποίει 𝔊

10:5-6 $^{(6?)}$זעמי$^{(6?)}$ 1QIsa^{a}] זעמי ^{6} 𝔐; ^{6}*זעמי 𝔊 (see *BHS* n. 5^{b})

10:17-18 ביום אחד ^{18}וכבוד 1QIsa^{a} 𝔐 σ′] ^{18}τῇ ἡμέρᾳ ἐκείνῃ ἀποσβεσθήσεται (= יכבה) 𝔊

10:29-30 נסה ^{30}צהלי קולך בת 1QIsa^{a} 𝔐 𝔊^{VQmgLC}] ^{30}φεύξεται ἡ θυγάτηρ 𝔊

14:6-7 ^{7}נחה שקטה כ(ו)ל הארץ 1QIsa^{a} 𝔐] ἀνεπαύσατο πεποιθώς ^{7}πᾶσα ἡ γῆ 𝔊

16:1 כרמשל 1QIsa^{a}] כר משל 1QIsa^{b}(כר [) 𝔐; ὡς ἑρπετὰ ἐπὶ 𝔊(= ?כרמשׂ ל-)

16:6-7 לכן ... ^{7}ולכן לוא 1QIsa^{a}] לא כן ... ^{7}לכן 𝔐; οὐχ οὕτως ... οὐχ οὕτως ^{7} 𝔊

22:24-25 הנבלים ^{25}ביום ההוא 1QIsa^{a} 𝔐] ἐπικρεμάμενοι αὐτῷ ἐν τῇ ἡμέρᾳ ἐκείνῃ ^{25} 𝔊

41:16-17 (ו)בקדוש ישראל תתהלל ^{17} 1QIsa^{a} 𝔐] ἐν τοῖς ἁγίοις Ισραηλ ^{17}καὶ ἀγαλλιάσονται 𝔊

8. The OG often gives a single rendering for a pair of parallel words in the Hebrew:

1:11 וכבשים ועתודים 1QIsa^{a} 𝔐] καὶ τράγων 𝔊

2:20 אלילי ... ואת אלילי 1QIsa^{a} 𝔐] τὰ βδελύγματα αὐτοῦ 𝔊

3:15-16 נ(ו)אם אד(ו)ני יהוה צבאות: ^{16}וי(ו)אמר יהוה 1QIsa^{a} 𝔐] ^{16}τάδε λέγει κύριος 𝔊

7:22 יאכל חמאה ... חמאה ודבש יאכל 1QIsa^{a} 𝔐] βούτυρον καὶ μέλι φάγεται 𝔊

8:13 והוא מוראכם והוא מערצכם 1QIsa^{a} 𝔐] καὶ αὐτὸς ἔσται σου φόβος 𝔊

10:5 שבט ... ומטה 1QIsa^{a} 𝔐] ἡ ῥάβδος 𝔊

11:4 בצדק ... במישור 1QIsa^{a} 𝔐] κρίσιν 𝔊

14:22 (ו)נין ונכד 1QIsa^{a} 𝔐] καὶ σπέρμα 𝔊

23:18 ל(ו)א יאצר ול(ו)א יחסן 1QIsa^{a} 𝔐] οὐκ αὐτοῖς συναχθήσεται 𝔊

34:1 לשמ(ו)ע ... הקשיבו 1QIsa^{a} 𝔐] καὶ ἀκούσατε 𝔊

34:4 יבול כנ(ו)בל 1QIsa^{a} 𝔐] πεσεῖται 𝔊 (= √נפל)

40:3 במדבר ... בערבה 1QIsa^{a} 𝔐] ἐν τῇ ἐρήμῳ 𝔊

45:12 עשיתי ... בראתי 1QIsa^{a} 𝔐] ἐποίησα 𝔊

55:7 אל יהוה ... ואל אל(ו)הינו 1QIsa^{a} 𝔐] ἐπὶ κύριον 𝔊

57:15 ואת דכא ושפל רוח 1QIsa^{a} 𝔐] καὶ ὀλιγοψύχοις 𝔊

9. The OG uses contemporary terms for the Hellenistic community (see n. 2):

19:15 כפה ואגמ(ו)ן 1QIsa^a 𝔐] ἀρχὴν καὶ τέλος 𝔊

41:18 למוצאי מים 1QIsa^a 𝔐] ἐν ὑδραγωγοῖς 𝔊

9:11[12] ארם ... ופלשתי(י)ם 1QIsa^a 𝔐] Συρίαν ... καὶ τοὺς Ἕλληνας 𝔊

19:13 צען ... נף ... מצרים 1QIsa^a 𝔐] Τάνεως ... Μέμφεως ... Αἴγυπτον 𝔊

23:1 תרשיש 1QIsa^a 𝔐] Καρχηδόνος 𝔊

23:2 צידון 1QIsa^a 𝔐] Φοινίκης 𝔊

42:11 סלע 1QIsa^a 𝔐] Πέτραν 𝔊

10. Loss or disturbance of the OG in the LXX transmission, as shown by errors or doublets:

20:1 סרגון 1QIsa^a 𝔐] Σαρναν 𝔊^{ed}; Αρνα 𝔊^{ABQSmss}; Σαρνα 𝔊^{L}; Αρνας 𝔊^{ms}; Αρναβα 𝔊^{mss}

46:1 נבו 1QIsa^a 𝔐] Δαγων 𝔊^{ed}; Ναβω 𝔊^{Bmss} α′ θ′

23:13 לציין 1QIsa^a 𝔐(לציים) 𝔊*] + οὐδὲ ἐκεῖ σοι ἀνάπαυσις ἔσται 𝔊^{ASLC} (repeated from 23:12)

29:24 לקח 1QIsa^a 𝔐 𝔊*] + καὶ αἱ γλῶσσαι αἱ ψελλίζουσαι μαθήσονται λαλεῖν εἰρήνην 𝔊^{omn} (cf 32:4)

42:10 ותהלתו 1QIsa^a] תה׳ 4QIsa^h 𝔐; ἡ ἀρχὴ αὐτοῦ (= תחלתו) δοξάζετε τὸ ὄνομα αὐτοῦ 𝔊^{ed}

44:19 ול(ו)א ישיב אל לבו 1QIsa^a 𝔐] καὶ οὐκ ἐλογίσατο τῇ καρδίᾳ αὐτοῦ οὐδὲ ἀνελογίσατο ἐν τῇ ψυχῇ αὐτοῦ 𝔊 (dbl)

48:21 מים 2° 1QIsa^a 1QIsa^b 𝔐 𝔊*] + καὶ πίεται ὁ λαός μοῦ 𝔊^{omn} (cf Exod 17:6)

58:7 ומבשרכ(ה) 1QIsa^a 1QIsa^b 𝔐] καὶ ἀπὸ τῶν οἰκείων σου 𝔊*; καὶ ἀπὸ τῶν οἰκείων τοῦ σπέρματός σου 𝔊$^{ed\ mss}$

Thus, though there are frequently variants in the preserved or no-longer-preserved Hebrew texts, the Greek translator quite consistently attempted to translate faithfully the Hebrew readings he saw, or thought he saw, in the specific manuscript before him.

II. THE OLD GREEK OF JEREMIAH AND EXODUS 35–40

The OG of Jeremiah has long been assessed by most as a faithful Greek translation of a variant Hebrew text that was much shorter than the edition in the MT, and the discovery of 4QJer^{b,d} at Qumran confirmed that assessment.[3] That insight should invite the search for new passages where a similar phenomenon occurs.

One such passage is Exodus 35–40. Though the OG translation is quite close to the MT for Exodus 1–34, and while the character of the Greek itself remains constant throughout 1–40, the translation departs in major ways from the MT in 35–40, both in order and in content. In the past century this departure was judged to be due either to condensation or confusion in the Greek[4] or, as David Gooding proposed, to a later

[3] See Ch. 9 and especially Emanuel Tov, *Textual Criticism*, 286–94; and Pierre-Maurice Bogaert, "Le livre de Jérémie en perspective: Les deux rédactions antiques selon les travaux en course," *RB* 101 (1994): 363–406.

[4] A. H. Finn, "The Tabernacle Chapters," *JTS* 16 (1914–15): 449–82. John W. Wevers (*Text History of the Greek Exodus* [Göttingen: Vandenhoek & Ruprecht, 1992], 118) describes Finn's approach as "written in defense of [the MT], and . . . vitiated by a prejudice against the LXX which makes any conclusions he makes suspect."

revision of the Greek without recourse to any Hebrew text.[5] A principal reason for solutions such as these was "the presupposition that the canonical text being translated was in the main much like the consonantal text of MT."[6] Gooding's work was the fullest treatment of the problem through the remainder of the century.

The perspective gained from the scrolls, however, began to spark a different approach to the problem that gained momentum.[7] Anneli Aejmelaeus, a student of Ilmari Soisalon-Soininen, explored LXX translation technique and concluded that the LXX of Exodus 35–40 was not "troubled" but was a good translation of simply a Hebrew text different from the MT.[8] The investigation culminated in a detailed study by Brandon Bruning, persuasively demonstrating that an alternate Hebrew text retroverted from the Greek had a discernible structure that, though not a report consistently narrating the fulfillment of each of the commands in Exodus 25–31, nonetheless rendered an intelligible account; the study further demonstrated that the form in the MT of 35–40 was a revised edition that used a form of the Hebrew *Vorlage* of the OG as its basis, but regularly augmented it with phraseology from 25–31.[9] Thus, the OG contains an earlier literary edition than the MT for Exodus 35–40, though no Hebrew text that probably served as its basis is preserved.

III. Ezekiel 36–40 and Daniel in Papyrus 967

Similar to the situation for Exodus 35–40, there is preserved evidence for variant editions of Ezekiel 36–40. The Greek Papyrus 967 contains parts of Ezekiel, Daniel, and Esther, and its text of Ezekiel may well display an edition of that book that is earlier than the edition now attested by the MT and the LXX. Pap967, joined by OL Codex Wirceburgensis, exhibits a shorter and differently arranged text (chapters 36–38–39–37–40) in comparison with the MT-LXX, possibly due to differing eschatological views.[10] Either arrangement (with 38–39 before or after 37) could be plausibly argued as earlier versus

[5] David W. Gooding, *The Account of the Tabernacle: Translation and Textual Problems of the Greek Exodus* (Text and Studies 6; Cambridge: Cambridge University Press, 1959).

[6] John W. Wevers, *Notes on the Greek Text of Exodus* (SBLSCS 30; Atlanta: Scholars Press, 1990), xv.

[7] See Judith E. Sanderson, *An Exodus Scroll* (1986); eadem, "The Old Greek of Exodus in the Light of 4QpaleoExod^{m}," *Textus* 14 (1988): 87–104; Ulrich, "Double Literary Editions of Biblical Narratives and Reflections on Determining the Form to be Translated," in *Perspectives on the Hebrew Bible: Essays in Honor of Walter J. Harrelson* (ed. James L. Crenshaw; Macon, Ga.: Mercer University Press, 1988), 101–16; repr., in *Scrolls and Origins,* 34–50, esp. 39.

[8] Anneli Aejmelaeus, "Septuagintal Translation Techniques—A Solution to the Problem of the Tabernacle Account?" in *Septuagint, Scrolls and Cognate Writings* (ed. George J. Brooke and Barnabas Lindars; SBLSCS 33; Atlanta: Scholars Press, 1992), 381–402 [repr.: *On the Trail of the Septuagint Translators* (Kampen: Kok Pharos, 1993; rev. ed.; Leuven: Peeters, 2007), 107–22]. Her paper was first presented in 1990.

[9] See the full analysis by Brandon Bruning, "The Making of the Mishkan."

[10] See Johan Lust, "Ezekiel 36–40 in the Oldest Greek Manuscript," *CBQ* 43 (1981) 517-33; idem, "Major Divergences between LXX and MT in Ezekiel," in *The Earliest Text of the Hebrew Bible: The Relationship between the Masoretic Text and the Hebrew Base of the Septuagint Reconsidered* (ed. Adrian Schenker; Atlanta: SBL, 2003), 83–92; Emanuel Tov, "Recensional Differences between the Masoretic Text and the Septuagint of Ezekiel," *The Greek and Hebrew Bible*, 397–410.

later.[11] But the longer text in the MT adds fifteen verses (36:23c-38) beyond Pap967 and uses a different Hebrew style, while the LXX uses proto-Theodotionic terminology. The likelihood of an earlier variant edition in the OG of Ezekiel has now gained a full and detailed analysis.[12]

Analysis suggests that Pap967 was the early OG form translated from a Hebrew text with that variant order.[13] A later Hebrew editor transposed chapter 37 into its present (MT) position and added the last section of chapter 36 (vv. 23c-38) at the same time as a suitable eschatological introduction to chapter 37. Two further considerations support the conclusion that Pap967 displays the OG and that the remaining LXX manuscripts have been revised toward the MT tradition.

First, a somewhat parallel phenomenon occurred with the OG of Daniel. Prior to the discovery of Pap967 in 1931 there was, as here with the text of Ezekiel, only one solitary Greek manuscript of Daniel (Codex Chisianus = Rahlfs 88, tenth century) that witnessed to the OG; all other Greek manuscripts contained the recension of Theodotion.[14] Pap967 validated Chisianus as the OG.

Second, the likelihood that Ezekiel 40, which begins the vision of the new temple, once directly followed chapter 37 is strengthened by the theme of the concluding verses, 37:26-28:

> I will bless them and multiply them, and will set my sanctuary among them forevermore. My dwelling place shall be with them, and I will be their God, and they will be my people. The nations shall know that I the LORD sanctify Israel, when my sanctuary is among them forevermore.

Pap967 shows a different order in the book of Daniel as well as in Ezekiel. Olivier Munnich has argued with great textual and literary detail that the earlier order in the OG

---

11 The Introduction to the Göttingen edition of Ezekiel (*Ezekiel* [ed. Joseph Ziegler with a Supplement by Detlef Fraenkel; Septuaginta: Vetus Testamentum Graecum 16, 1; Göttingen: Vandenhoeck & Ruprecht, 1952; 3d ed. 2006], 10, n. 1) mentions both possibilities. Floyd V. Filson ("The Omission of Ezek. 12:26-28 and 36:23b-38 in Codex 967," *JBL* 62 [1943]: 27–32) had considered the Pap967 minuses as lost through homoiotelueuton, whereas William A. Irwin (*The Problem of Ezekiel: An Inductive Study* [Chicago: University of Chicago Press 1943, 62 n. 3]) proposed that the OG had not known 36:23-38 because its Hebrew source did not yet have it, and that the transmitted Greek showed a later, possibly θ′-influenced, character.

Ziegler, understandably in 1952 before the pluriformity of the Hebrew was displayed by the scrolls, endorsed Filson's view and thought Irwin's very questionable ("sehr bedenklich"). Detlef contributed an admirable amount of data from Pap967 in his supplement (pp. 332–52), but in the main edition the passage 36:23-38 is included based on the main LXX tradition, and its absence is noted only in the apparatus with simply "ὅτι ἐγώ εἰμι κύριος∩ὅτι ἐγώ εἰμι κύριος (v. 38) 967" (p. 264).

12 Ingrid E. Lilly, *Two Books of Ezekiel: Papyrus 967 and the Masoretic Text as Variant Literary Editions* (VTSup150; Leiden: Brill, 2012).

13 See in agreement Mladen Popović, "Prophet, Books and Texts: Ezekiel, *Pseudo-Ezekiel* and the Authoritativeness of Ezekiel Traditions in Early Judaism," in *Authoritative Scriptures in Ancient Judaism* (ed. idem; JSJS 141; Leiden: Brill, 2010), 227–51, esp. 234–35.

14 Sharon Pace Jeansonne, *The Old Greek Translation of Daniel 7–12* (CBQMS 19; Washington: Catholic Biblical Association, 1988), 10–11.

(i.e., Pap967) was chapters 1–4, 7–8, 5–6, 9–12.[15] Thus, Pap967 exhibits an earlier edition than the MT for both the order in Ezekiel and that in Daniel.[16]

In contrast, the order in the Ezekiel manuscript from Masada (MasEzek; see Ch. 16) clearly agrees with that of the MT, against Pap967. The Ezekiel manuscripts from Cave 4, from the mid first century B.C.E. at the earliest, also show the edition familiar from the MT, thus indicating that that edition was dominant near the end of Second Temple period, probably having widely replaced the earlier edition witnessed by Pap967.

IV. Development and Parallel Versions in Daniel

Chapter 13 explored the developmental spectrum from pre-Scripture to rewritten Scripture. One set of compositions that illustrates such a spectrum is the corpus of Danielic writings.[17] This section will cursorily review the scrolls containing Daniel-related traditions and then focus on the phenomenon of development even *within* scriptural texts: the two parallel editions of Daniel 5 attested in the OG and the MT.

A. Daniel-related Traditions

In addition to the seven fragmentary manuscripts of the full scriptural book of Daniel, the scrolls provide a trajectory of Danielic literature: evidence of possible earlier sources for the book, as well as compositions beyond the book. The tradition seen in the Prayer of Nabonidus (4Q242) is widely accepted as a probable source for chapter 4 of Daniel. The small manuscript 4QDan^{e} (4Q116), which most likely contained only the prayer of Dan 9:4-19,[18] may provide evidence of another source, a separate prayer which was taken and incorporated into chapter 9.[19] Alternatively, it may simply be an "excerpted" manuscript drawn from the completed book. Esther Eshel suggests, in addition to the Prayer of Nabonidus, that Historical Text A [formerly Acts of a Greek King] (4Q248) and column 2 of the Book of Giants (4Q530 EnGiants^{b} ar) may also have served as sources of

---

15 Olivier Munnich, "Texte massorétique et Septante dans le livre de *Daniel*," in *The Earliest Text of the Hebrew Bible*, 93–120.

16 See the discussion by Tov, *Textual Criticism*, 300–1 and 318-19.

17 For the editions of the scriptural scrolls of Daniel see DJD 1:150–52, DJD 3:114–16, DJD 16:239–89, and *The Biblical Qumran Scrolls*, 755–75; for discussion, see Ulrich, "The Text of Daniel in the Qumran Scrolls," in *The Book of Daniel: Composition and Reception* (ed. John J. Collins and Peter W. Flint; Formation and Interpretation of Old Testament Literature 2,2; VTSup 83,2; Leiden: Brill, 2001), 573–85. For editions of the non-scriptural Daniel scrolls see John Collins, DJD 22:83–93, and John Collins and Peter Flint, DJD 22:95–151; for extensive treatment see Collins, *Daniel: A Commentary on the Book of Daniel* (Hermeneia; Minneapolis: Fortress, 1993); and Flint, "The Daniel Tradition at Qumran," in *The Book of Daniel*, 329–67.

18 4QDan^{e} survives in only seven small fragments with parts of 9:12-17; it is the only Qumran attestation of chapter 9. Its small number of lines per column, estimated at only nine, plus the large size of the letters suggest that it contained only the prayer, in five columns. If it were to contain the entire book of Daniel it would require ca. 120 columns; see DJD 16:287 and Pl. XXXVII, and Collins, *Daniel: A Commentary*, 347–48.

19 See the similarly inserted prayer in Daniel 3 (The Prayer of Azariah and the Song of the Three Jews) as well as prayers inserted elsewhere: e.g., Hannah's prayer in 1 Samuel 2, and David's song of thanksgiving in 2 Samuel 22.

the Book of Daniel.[20] Pseudo-Daniel^{a-c} (4Q243–245), and possibly Four Kingdoms^{a-c} (4Q552–553a), represent developments of the wider Danielic traditions, partly similar to the biblical book but also showing differences, especially in the broader scope of Israelite history surveyed.[21]

Though there is a rich Danielic tradition in the centuries leading up to the "Great Divide" (Ch. 2 n. 3), the roots go back much earlier. The approximately fourteenth century B.C.E. Canaanite *Tale of Aqhat* from Ugarit features Dan'el as a just and wise man, father of Aqhat. Ezekiel (14:14, 20; 28:3) also mentions as early as the sixth century such an already legendary and presumably well-known wise and righteous man from earlier times. Especially the latter is commonly seen "as the literary ancestor of the hero" of the biblical book.[22] It is easy to see why stories such as Susanna and Bel and the Dragon also employed the figure of Daniel as their hero.

B. Parallel Editions of Daniel 5

But the spectrum is not simply sources–Scripture–developments; within the scriptural text itself there is "rewritten Scripture," that is, rewritten versions of Daniel 4–6. While preparing the translation of Daniel for the New Revised Standard Version and reflecting on how to establish the text that was to be translated, I noticed the phenomenon of "double literary editions" in Daniel as well as other biblical books.[23] This posed a significant question for producing a single-text Bible. In light of the refinements and additional examples of variant editions gained in the intervening two decades, it seems useful to work out in textual detail here my earlier general impressions of these parallel editions.[24]

In the following texts, the central column lists the words common to both the MT and the OG: that is, words shared by both the MT tradition and the Semitic *Vorlage* of the OG that are faithfully translated in the OG.[25] In the "MT Pluses" column are words

---

[20] Esther Eshel, "Possible Sources of the Book of Daniel," in *The Book of Daniel*, 387–94.

[21] Scholars have suggested that other compositions, such as the Aramaic Apocryphon (4Q246 apocrDan ar), an Apocalypse in Aramaic on papyrus (4Q489 papApocalypse ar), and another entitled Daniel-Susanna? (4Q551 Account ar, *olim* DanSuz? ar), were related to the Book of Daniel, but the suggestions no longer find favor.

[22] See W. Sibley Towner, "Daniel," *NIDB* 2:13.

[23] "Double Literary Editions of Biblical Narratives," in *Scrolls and Origins*, 34–50. See also Dean O. Wenthe, "The Old Greek Translation of Daniel 1–6" (Ph.D. dissertation, University of Notre Dame, 1991).

[24] I must leave to the future the integration of Munnich's analysis in "Texte massorétique et Septante," (n. 15) with that presented here.

[25] The complete text of the MT and OG is printed, but at certain points the text is shortened by omitting unnecessary words. These symbols are used in the columns:

- *italics* denote words that occur in or are presumed by both traditions, with minor changes due to translation technique or narrative adjustment
- ( ) in the Core column denotes a similar expression probably in the original because both MT and OG use it
- ( ) in the MT and OG "Pluses" columns marks words already in the Core
- [ ] refers to occurrences in a different verse
- ... marks the absence of unnecessary words
- ‸ marks the point of insertion for an addition

OG Pluses	Core Narrative	MT Pluses
	1 בלשאצר מלכא	
	עבד לחם רב	
τοῖς ἑταίροις αὐτοῦ		לרברבנוהי אלף
		ולקבל אלפא
	חמרא שתה:	
	2	2 בלשאצר +
	אמר	
	בטעם חמרא	
	להיתיה למאני דהבא וכספא	
	די הנפק נבוכדנצר אבוהי	
τοῦ οἴκου τοῦ θεοῦ … ἀπὸ Ιερουσαλημ	מן היכלא די בירושלם	
	וישתון בהון	
τοῖς ἑταίροις αὐτοῦ		מלכא ורברבנוהי שגלתה ולחנתה:
	3 באדין היתיו	
		מאני דהבא די הנפקו מן היכלא
		די בית אלהא די בירושלם
	ואשתיו בהון	
		מלכא ורברבנוהי
		שגלתה ולחנתה:
	4	4 אשתיו חמרא
	ושבחו לאלהי	
τὰ χειροποίητα αὐτῶν		
		דהבא וכספא נחשא פרזלא
		אעא ואבנא:
καὶ τὸν θεὸν τοῦ αἰῶνος		
οὐκ εὐλόγησαν τὸν ἔχοντα		
τὴν ἐξουσίαν τοῦ πνεύματος αὐτῶν.		
	5 בה שעתה נפקו אצבען	
	די יד אנש וכתבן לקבל נברשתא	
	על גירא די כתל	
τοῦ οἴκου αὐτοῦ		היכלא די מלכא
ἔναντι τοῦ βασιλέως Βαλτασαρ		
	‸חזה פס	ומלכא +
	ידה די כתבה:	
	6 אדין מלכא זיוהי שנוהי	
+ καὶ ὑπόνοιαι	ורעיוני‸ יבהלונה	
		וקטרי חרצה משתרין
		וארכבתה דא לדא נקשן:
ἔσπευσεν οὖν ὁ βασιλεὺς καὶ		
ἐξανέστη καὶ ἑώρα τὴν γραφὴν		
ἐκείνην, καὶ οἱ συνεταῖροι		
κύκλῳ αὐτοῦ ἐκαυχῶντο.		

MT Pluses	**Core Narrative**	**OG Pluses**
	[1]King Belshazzar	
	made a great feast	
for a thousand of his lords,		for his companions,
and before the thousand		
	and he was drinking wine.	
[2]+ Belshazzar	[2]*He* commanded	
	under the influence of the wine	
	that the vessels of gold and silver	
	which Nebuchadnezzar	
	his father had brought from	
	the temple	the house of God
	in Jerusalem be brought in	
the king and his lords,	so *they*	his companions
his consorts & concubines		
	could drink from them.	
	[3]Then they brought *them*	
the gold vessels taken from the		
temple, the house of God in Jer.		
	and they drank from them,	
the king and his lords,		
his consorts and concubines.		
[4]They drank wine	[4]	
	and they praised the*ir* gods	
		made with their hands
of gold, silver, brass, iron,		
wood, and stone;		
		but to the God of the ages
		they did not offer praise,
		the one having power
		over their spirit.
	[5]In that hour fingers of a	
	human hand came out and wrote	
	on the plaster of the wall	
of the royal palace		of his house
	next to the lampstand ‸	+ opposite king Baltasar;
and the king (saw) the palm of	and he saw	
	the hand as it wrote.	
	[6]Then the king's face turned pale	
	and his thoughts ‸ *terrified* him;	+ and fears
the joints of his loins were loosed		
and his knees knocked together.		
		So the king quickly got up and
		was looking the writing,
		and his companions were
		talking loudly around him.

OG Pluses	**Core Narrative**	**MT Pluses**
	7 קרא מלכא בחיל להעלה	
+ καὶ φαρμακοὺς	לאשפיא‸ כשדיא וגזריא	
ἀπαγγεῖλαι τὸ σύγκριμα τῆς		
γραφῆς.		
καὶ εἰσεπορεύοντο		
ἐπὶ θεωρίαν ἰδεῖν τὴν γραφήν,		
καὶ τὸ σύγκριμα τῆς γραφῆς		
οὐκ ἐδύναντο συγκρῖναι τῷ βασιλεῖ.		
	מלכא	ענה
ἐξέθηκε πρόσταγμα λέγων	(אמר)	ואמר
		לחכימי בבל די
	כל אנש די	
ὑποδείξῃ	(יקרא)	יקרה כתבה דנה ופשרה יחונני
τὸ σύγκριμα τῆς γραφῆς,		
	ארגונא ילבש	
	והמונכא די דהבא על צוארה	
	ותלתי במלכותא ישלט:	
	8 אדין עללין	
οἱ ἐπαοιδοὶ καὶ φαρμακοὶ καὶ γαζαρηνοί,	(חכימיא)	כל חכימי מלכא
	ולא כהלין	
τὸ σύγκριμα τῆς γραφῆς ἀπαγγεῖλαι.	(למקרא)	כתבא למקרא ופשרא להודעה
		למלכא:
	9 אדין מלכא	
		בלשאצר שגיא מתבהל
		וזיוהי שנין עלוהי
		ורברבנוהי משתבשין:
ἐκάλεσε τὴν βασίλισσαν περὶ τοῦ	(יקרא ?)	
σημείου καὶ ὑπέδειξεν αὐτῇ,		
ὡς μέγα ἐστί, καὶ ὅτι πᾶς ἄνθρωπος		
οὐ δύναται ἀπαγγεῖλαι τῷ βασιλεῖ		
τὸ σύγκριμα τῆς γραφῆς.		
	10 מלכתא	
		לקבל מלי מלכא ורברבנוהי
		לבית משתיא עללת ענת מלכתא
ἐμνήσθη πρὸς αὐτὸν	(ואמרת)	ואמרת מלכא לעלמין חיי
		אל יבהלוך רעיונך וזיויך אל ישתנו:
περὶ τοῦ Δανιηλ, ὃς ἦν	(דניאל)	[= MT 12]
ἐκ τῆς αἰχμαλωσίας τῆς Ιουδαίας,		
11 καὶ εἶπε τῷ βασιλεῖ	11	
(Ὁ ἄνθρωπος)	גבר	איתי (גבר)
		במלכותך
		די רוח אלהין קדישין בה
[= OG 12]		וביומי אבוך
(ἐπιστήμων ἦν καὶ σοφὸς)	ושכלתנו וחכמה	נהירו (ושכלתנו וחכמה)
		כחכמת אלהין השתכחת בה
(καὶ ὑπερέχων πάντας τοὺς σοφοὺς)	רב חרטמין	ומלכא נבכדנצר אבוך (רב חרטמין)
Βαβυλῶνος,		אשפין כשדאין גזרין הקימה
		אבוך מלכא:

MT Pluses	**Core Narrative**	**OG Pluses**
	7 The king cried aloud to bring	
	the enchanters, ‸	+ magicians,
	Chaldeans, and astrologers,	
		to explain the meaning; they came to see the writing, but the meaning of the writing they were unable to interpret for the king.
	The king	
said	(said)	made a decree, saying:
to the diviners of Babylon:		
	Whoever can	
read this writing	(interpret this)	explain
and tell me its interpretation		the meaning of the writing
	will be clothed in purple, have a gold chain on his neck, and *rule as third* in the kingdom.	
	8 Then came in	
all the king's diviners	(the diviners)	the enchanters, magicians, and astrologers,
	but no one was able	
to read the writing or make known its interpretation to the king.	(to interpret)	to tell the meaning of the writing.
	9 Then *the* king	
Belshazzar feared greatly; his face turned pale, and his lords were perplexed.		
	(called ?)	called the queen about the sign & showed her how large it was and that no one could explain the meaning of the writing to the king.
	10 Then the queen	
because of the king's and his lords' words, came to the banquet hall and said: O king, live forever.	(said)	reminded him
Do not let your thoughts terrify you or your face turn pale. [= MT 12]	(Daniel)	about Daniel, who was from the exiles of Judah.
	11	11 She said to the king:
In your kingdom is a (man)	man	That (man)
in whom is a spirit of the holy gods. In the days of your father	(had)	had [= OG 12]
light, (insight and wisdom)	insight and wisdom	(insight and wisdom),
like the wisdom of the gods was found in him, and Kg.Nebuch.		
your father made him head of	(was head of)	surpassing
the magicians, enchanters, Chaldeans, and astrologers— your father the king.	(the sages)	all the sages of Babylon.

OG Pluses	Core Narrative	MT Pluses
	12 כל קבל די רוח יתירה ... בה	
καὶ ἐν ταῖς ἡμέραις τοῦ πατρός σου τοῦ βασιλέως		[= MT 11]
(συγκρίματα ὑπέρογκα ὑπέδειξε) [= OG 10] Ναβουχοδονοσορ τῷ πατρί σου.	ומשרא קטרין	ומנדע ושכלתנו מפשר חלמין ואחוית אחידן (ומשרא קטרין) השתכחת בה בדניאל די מלכא שם שמה בלטשאצר כען דניאל יתקרי ופשרה יהחוה:
	13 באדין דניאל העל קדם מלכא ענה מלכא ואמר לדניאל	
		אנתה הוא דניאל די מן בני גלותא די יהוד די היתי מלכא אבי מן יהוד:
	14	14 ושמעת עליך די רוח אלהין בך ונהירו ושכלתנו וחכמה יתירה השתכחת בך:
	15	15 וכען העלו קדמי חכימיא אשפיא די כתבה דנה יקרון ופשרה להודעתני ולא כהלין פשר מלתא להחויה:
	16	16 ואנה שמעת עליך די תוכל פשרין למפשר וקטרין למשרא
Ὦ Δανιηλ, (δύνῃ) μοι ὑποδεῖξαι τὸ σύγκριμα τῆς γραφῆς;	תוכל (למקרא)	כען הן (תוכל) כתבא למקרא ופשרה להודעתני
	ארגונא תלבש והמונכא די דהבא על צוארך ותלתא במלכותא תשלט:	
17 (τότε Δανιηλ) ἔστη κατέναντι τῆς γραφῆς καὶ ἀνέγνω καὶ	17 באדין ... דניאל	
(οὕτως ἀπεκρίθη τῷ βασιλεῖ)	ענה (דניאל) ואמר קדם מלכא	(ענה דניאל ואמר קדם מלכא)
		מתנתך לך להוין ונבזביתך לאחרן הב ברם כתבא אקרא למלכא ופשרא אהודענה:
	18	18 אנתה מלכא אלהא עליא מלכותא ורבותא ויקרא והדרה יהב לנבכדנצר אבוך: 19 ומן רבותא די יהב לה כל עממיא אמיא ולשניא הוו זאעין ודחלין מן קדמוהי די הוה צבא הוא קטל ... הוה מחא ... הוה מרים ... הוה משפיל: 20 וכדי רם לבבה ורוחה תקפת להזדה הנחת מן כרסא מלכותה ויקרה העדיו מנה: 21 ומן בני אנשא טריד ולבבה עם חיותא שוי ועם ערדיא מדורה עשבא כתורין יטעמונה ומטל שמיא גשמה יצטבע עד די ידע די שליט אלהא עליא במלכות אנשא ולמן די יצבה יהקים עליה: 22 ואנתה ברה בלשאצר לא השפלת לבבך כל קבל די כל דנה ידעת:

MT Pluses	**Core Narrative**	**OG Pluses**
	12 because an *excellent* spirit was in him.	
[= MT 11] Knowledge, wisdom, interpretation of dreams, explanation of riddles,		In the days of your father the king
and (solutions to problems) were found in him, Daniel, to whom the king gave the name Belteshazzar. Now call Daniel and he will declare its meaning.	solved problems	he (explained difficult meanings) [= OG 10] to Neb. your father.
	13 Then Daniel was brought before the king, who said to *him*:	
Are you Daniel, from the exiles of Judah, whom my father the king brought from Judah?		
14 I have heard that the spirit of the gods is in you and that light, understanding, and surpassing wisdom are found in you.	14	
15 The diviners and enchanters came before me, to read this writing and make known to me its interpretation, but they could not tell the interpretation of the message.	15	
16 But I have heard of you that you can explain riddles and solve	16	
problems. Now if (you are able) to read the writing and make known its interpretation,	Are you able (to interpret)	O Daniel, (Are you able) to explain the meaning of the writing to me?
	you'll be clothed in purple, with a gold chain around your neck, and *rule as third* in the kingdom.	
	17 Then Daniel	(Then Daniel) stood facing the writing, read,
(replied to the king:)	replied to the king:	and (thus replied to the king:)

"Let your gifts be for yourself
and your rewards for another.
Still I will read the writing for the king and make known the interpretation.
18-23 You, O king—God Most High gave your father Neb. kingship,
power, glory, and might. 19 And due to the greatness he gave him, all peoples,
nations, and languages trembled before him. Whomever he wished, he
would execute, ... let live, ... raise up, ... put down. 20 But when
his mind rose high and his spirit hardened to insolence, he was
deposed from his kingly throne and his glory was taken away.
21 He was driven from human company, and his mind was made like that
of wild beasts. He dwelt with wild asses, he was fed grass like oxen, and
his body was wet with the due of heaven until he realized that the
Most High God rules over the kingdom of mortals, and whomever
he wishes he sets over it. 22 And you, Belshazzar his son, have
not humbled your heart, though you knew all this.

OG Pluses	**Core Narrative**	**MT Pluses**
(17)Αὕτη ἡ γραφή	(כתבא)	[= MT 25]
Ἠρίθμηται, κατελογίσθη, ἐξῆρται·		[= MT 25]
καὶ ἔστη ἡ γράψασα χείρ.		
καὶ αὕτη ἡ σύγκρισις αὐτῶν.	(פשרא)	[= MT 26]
23βασιλεῦ, σὺ ἐποιήσω ἑστιατορίαν	23(ואנתה מלכא)	23ועל מרא שמיא התרוממת
τοῖς φίλοις σου καὶ ἔπινες οἶνον,		
	ולמאניא די ביתה	
+ τοῦ θεοῦ τοῦ ζῶντος		
	היתיו קדמיך	
	ואנתה	
καὶ οἱ μεγιστᾶνές σου		ורברבניך שגלתך ולחנתך
	חמרא שתין בהון	
+ πάντα	ולאלהי‸	
τὰ χειροποίητα τῶν ἀνθρώπων·		כספא ודהבא נחשא פרזלא
		אעא ואבנא די לא חזין ולא שמעין
		ולא ידעין
	שבחת	
+ τῷ ζῶντι οὐκ εὐλογήσατε	ולאלהא‸	
	די נשמתך בידה	
		וכל ארחתך לה
καὶ τὸ βασίλειόν σου αὐτὸς ἔδωκέ σοι		
+ οὐδὲ ᾔνεσας αὐτῷ..	לא הדרת‸:	
	24	24באדין מן קדמוהי שליח פסא
		די ידא וכתבא דנה רשים:
[= OG 17]	25(כתבא)	25 ודנה כתבא
		די רשים
[= OG 17]		מנא תקל ופרסין:
	26דנה	
τὸ σύγκριμα τῆς γραφῆς·	(פשרא)	פשר מלתא
		מנא
	מנה‸מלכותך והשלמה:	אלהא +
συντέτμηται καὶ συντετέλεσται	27	27תקל תקילתה במאזניא
		והשתכחת חסיר:
	28	28פרס פריסת
	מלכותך ויהיבת למדי ופרס:	
	29באדין	
		אמר +
+ ὁ βασιλεὺς	בלשאצר‸	
	והלבישו לדניאל ארגונא	
	והמונכא די דהבא על צוארה	
		והכרזו עלוהי +
	די להוא שליט תלתא במלכותא:	
30καὶ τὸ σύγκριμα ἐπῆλθε	30	30בה בליליא קטיל
	בלאשצר מלכא‸	כשדיא: +
καὶ (τὸ βασίλειον) ... ἐδόθη (τοῖς Μήδοις) ...	מלכותא ... למדי	6:1ודריוש (מדיא) קבל (מלכותא) ...

MT Pluses	**Core Narrative**	**OG Pluses**
[= MT 25]	(the writing:)	(17)"This is the writing:
[= MT 25]		"Numbered, counted down, removed."
		The handwriting stopped,
[= MT 26]	(the interpretation:)	and this is its meaning:
23 But you have exalted yourself over the Lord of Heaven.	23 (You, O King,)	23 O King, you made a feast for your friends and drank wine, and
	you brought the vessels	
	of *his* house‸	+ of the living God
	and have been drinking wine from them, you and	
your lords, wives, and concubines		your nobles
	and you praised‸ *your* gods	+ all
of silver, gold, bronze, iron, wood, and stone, which do not see or hear or know,		made by human hands;
	but the‸	+ living
	God‸	+ you did not bless,
	in whose power is your breath	
and to whom belong all your ways,		
		and who gave you your kingdom;
	you did not *honor*‸.	+ or praise him.
24 So from his presence the hand was sent, and this writing was inscribed.	24	
25 And this is the writing that was inscribed:	25 (the writing:)	[= OG 17]
Mene, Tekel, and Parsin		[= OG 17]
	26 This is	
the interpretation of the message:	(the interpretation:)	the meaning of the writing:
Mene: God has		
	numbered and brought	
	to an end‸ your kingdom.	+ is
Tekel: you have been weighed on the scales and found wanting.	27	It has been cut short and is finished.
28 Peres:	28	
+ divided and	Your kingdom is being‸	
	given to the Medes and Persians.	
	29 Then Belshazzar‸	+ the king
+ gave the command and	‸clothed Daniel in purple,	
	put a gold chain around his neck,	
and a proclamation was made	(and made him)	and gave him power to
concerning him that he should	*rule as third* in the kingdom.	
30 That very night was killed	30 (So it happened to)	30 And the meaning came upon
+ of the Chaldeans.	Belshazzar the king‸.	
(6:1) And Darius (the Mede)	And the kingdom ...	(And the kingdom) ... was given
received (the kingdom) ...	to the Medes ...	(to the Medes ...)

distinctive and at variance from (the Semitic *Vorlage* of) the OG, whereas in the "OG Pluses" column are words not found in the MT that the OG translates from its non-Masoretic *Vorlage*.[26] The OG is a translation—closer to free than to literal, but nonetheless faithful—that reflects an Aramaic text that was close to the MT for most of the book but that was simply different from the MT for chapters 4–6.[27] For our purposes here we can pass over in silence considerations of orthography, minor commonplace variants,[28] and *ketiv-qere*;[29] the only emendation of the MT is the excision of the dittography in מנא מנא (5:25), which may or may not have been influenced by the מנא מנה in the following verse.[30] The few rough spots are due to the editors' rewriting.

Whereas most variant editions are successive "new and expanded editions," that is not the situation encountered when comparing the two main witnesses, the MT and the OG, for chapters 4–6.[31] Rather, although for much of chapters 1–2 and 7–12 the MT and OG display the same edition,[32] for chapters 4–6 they display parallel variant editions. It appears that both the MT and the OG are "new and expanded editions" for these chapters, not in comparison with each other, but insofar as they are separate, parallel expansions of a common narrative core which had served as an earlier form of the story.

Thus, the claim is that the central column contains an earlier, no longer extant, complete core form of the story of Belshazzar's feast that served as the basis for the two separate, more developed forms of the story transmitted in the MT and in the OG.[33] To that common narrative core the MT and the OG (*Vorlage*) each added or emphasized distinctive story-telling embellishments to produce their divergent editions.

---

[26] In most cases where it can be determined, the "new and expanded edition" of various books was created at the Hebrew-Aramaic stage, not the Greek stage; see *Scrolls and Origins*, 42–44.

[27] For most of the book the OG shows a faithful translation of a Semitic parent text similar to the MT. The OG also shows no internal difference in chapters 4–6 from its translation style in the rest of the book. Thus, it should be considered a faithful translation of a Semitic parent text that was at variance with the MT for the stories in chapters 4–6. The ubiquitous pluralism visible in virtually all scriptural manuscripts and quotations in the Second Temple period provides a solid basis for suggesting a divergent *Vorlage*.

[28] I have studied the orthography of the two larger scrolls (4QDan^{a,b}) in comparison with the MT in *Scrolls and Origins*, 148–62, and listed the individual textual variants for all eight of the scriptural scrolls vis-à-vis the MT, the OG, and Theodotion in *The Biblical Qumran Scrolls*, 755–75, and in "The Text of Daniel," 575–79.

[29] Both the consistent *qere* המניכא (= OG μανιάκην) and the *ketiv* המונכא (5:7, 16, 29) have much of the word correctly; both should probably be emended to המינכא (< *hamyā(ha)naka*), according to Franz Rosenthal, *A Grammar of Biblical Aramaic* (Wiesbaden: Otto Harrassowitz, 1961), §189, p. 59.

[30] See similar dittographies in the MT at 2 Sam 6:2 (שם שם) and 6:3-4.

[31] For earlier studies of Daniel 4–6 see Rainer Albertz, *Der Gott des Daniel: Untersuchungen zu Daniel 4–6 in der Septuagintafassung sowie zu Komposition und Theologie des aramäischen Danielbuchs* (Stuttgarter Bibelstudien 131; Stuttgart: Verlag Katholisches Bibelwerk, 1988); and Johan Lust, "The Septuagint Version of Daniel 4–5," in *The Book of Daniel* (ed. Adam S. van der Woude; BETL 1086; Leuven: Peeters, 1993), 39–53. I thank Jan Joosten for suggesting these sources.

[32] Chapter 3 is complicated. The edition with Susanna, Bel and the Dragon, and the Prayer of Azariah and the Song of the Three Jews attested by o′ and θ′ should be considered an expanded edition.

[33] The claim is not that these three columns contain the three editions exactly but that they are close approximations. For example, in v. 1 the core narrative may well have contained a word or phrase that was rendered לרברבנוהי אלף in the MT and τοῖς ἑταίροις αὐτοῦ in the OG. Moreover, some of the pluses may have been added later in the transmission processes.

Note in the MT and OG "Pluses" columns the distinguishing story-telling embellishments or favorite quasi-Homeric formulae, many of which are more developed in the MT:

- the king and his lords and concubines in the MT (vv. 1, 2, 3, 9, 10, 23) in contrast to simply his companions in the OG
- the gods of gold and silver in the MT (4, 23) in contrast to the idols made with human hands in the OG
- more emphasis on royal grandeur in the MT ("the royal palace" 5; "O King, live forever" 10; "gave a command" 29; "proclamation was made" 29)
- emphasis in the OG on Daniel's God (2, 4, 23)
- the MT formula: "read the writing and make known the interpretation" vs. the OG "explain the meaning of the writing" (7, 8, 15, 16, 17, 26)
- "the spirit of the holy gods" in the MT, not in the OG (11, 14)
- various formulations for the diviners and enchanters (7, 8, 11)
- the dominant differences: different reactions of the king and expanded speeches.

Different reactions of the king distinguish the two editions. When the king sees the writings (v. 6), in the OG he naturally gets up quickly and watches the writing, and his companions talk excitedly. In the MT, however, his fearfulness is caricatured, with his knees knocking and with a possible euphemism, his hip-joints or loins loosening. Moreover, though the core narrative relates one time that the king's face turned pale (6), the MT repeats that fearful reaction twice more (9, 10).

The largest expansions, however, are the major speeches by the main characters in vv. 10-24, nearly half the chapter. In the OG the queen briefly reminds the king about the wise Daniel. In the MT she gives an extended speech (10-12); the king in turn, summoning Daniel, gives an extended introductory speech (13-16), to which Daniel replies with a rather insolent, extended accusatory speech (17-24).

The OG adds mainly natural story-telling embellishments, whereas the MT is more expanded with stock formulae and especially lengthy rhetorical speeches by the queen, Belshazzar, and finally Daniel.

Thus, subsequent to the one or more scrolls preserved at Qumran that may have served as a source for the book of Daniel, and prior to several more eschatologically developed compositions beyond the scriptural book, there are four variant editions that can be traced within the biblical book itself. We have seen that the MT of chapter 5 is significantly longer than the OG, producing a somewhat different version of the story. Conversely, the OG is longer than the MT in chapters 4 and 6. The least that can be said is that the profile of the three chapters is not consistent. Rather, an analogous process of new and expanded editions produced the different forms of the three chapters. To an earlier core narrative of the three chapters, numerous insertions were added: both minor routine additions and especially larger narrative embellishments that enhanced the stories. Thus, four variant editions of the scriptural Daniel can be distinguished:

1. the edition logically deduced, though no longer preserved, as the necessary basis for the subsequent pair of parallel editions in chapters 4–6;

2–3. the two parallel editions that can be labeled 2α (the expanded edition in [the *Vorlage* of] the OG for 4–6) and 2א (the other expanded edition in the MT for 4–6); and

4. the longer edition of the book with the "Additions" (the Prayer of Azariah and the Song of the Three Jews, Susanna, and Bel and the Dragon).

With regard to chapters 4–6, for edition 1 there is no manuscript attestation that survives. For edition 2α the only attestation is in the OG (preserved only in manuscript 88, Papyrus 967, and the Syro-Hexapla). Edition 2א appears in the MT and, to judge from the few remaining variants, in 4QDan[a], 4QDan[b], and 4QDan[d].[34] The final, longer edition of the book, with the "Additions" in chapter 3 and the extra chapters, appears in the OG and Theodotion (and their non-surviving Semitic *Vorlagen*?); in contrast, 1QDan[b] and 4QDan[d] attest to the shorter edition 2 as opposed to the longer edition, since they both preserve 3:23 followed immediately by 3:24 without the Prayer and Song. The remaining scrolls, 1QDan[a], 4QDan[c], 4QDan[e] and 6QpapDan, are not extant for passages where their affiliation could be determined.

Finally, it should not pass without observation that all the textual copies of the book of Daniel are free of "sectarian variants" (see Ch. 11). Although the final form of the twelve-chapter book was composed in the turbulent period of the Hellenistic crisis—the general time period in which various Jewish parties, such as the Pharisees and the Essenes, were defining themselves and the Qumran experiment eventually began—none of the variants betray "sectarian" tampering. Moreover, our surviving manuscripts were copied during the following couple of centuries, when it must have been tempting to add or revise phrases advantageous to the group producing the copies. But even though clear expansion can be detected at the levels of orthography, individual textual variants (mainly the addition of predictable, neutral words), and literary editions, there is no sign of "sectarian manipulation."[35] The various groups argued and debated vigorously between themselves, and probably even within their own ranks; but the evidence shows that all debate took place outside, not within, the text of the Scriptures.[36]

Insofar as the analysis above be correct, the OG of Daniel 5 and the MT of that chapter represent two separate, parallel editions of the narrative. It seems quite unlikely that either would have been produced by excising the pluses in the other. The most cogent explanation seems to be that there was an earlier version of the narrative that was shorter than the preserved forms, and that the OG (probably the Aramaic *Vorlage* of the OG) expanded the narrative in certain ways, whereas the precursor of the MT expanded it even more fully with different insertions.

In sum, we find editorial and scribal creativity not only in literary forms prior to and subsequent to the biblical book; we find it also within the biblical book.

---

34 These scrolls often have individual variants in agreement with the OG that are minor additions beyond the MT, but for the edition they seem to agree with the MT.

35 In addition to Ch. 11 see George J. Brooke, "*E pluribus unum*: Textual Variety and Definitive Interpretation in the Qumran Scrolls," in *The Dead Sea Scrolls in Their Historical Context* (ed. Timothy H. Lim et al.; Edinburgh: T&T Clark, 2000), 107–119; and Tov, *Textual Criticism*, 110: "no sectarian readings."

36 The single exception noted thus far (in Ch. 4) does not occur in the scrolls but in the SP-OG-OL and the MT: the placement of Joshua's altar. In my view 4QJosh[a] attests the early, neutral, shared Jewish account of an altar at Gilgal, whereas the SP-OG-OL secondarily transfers the altar to Mount Gerizim, and the MT then at a third stage rejects Mount Gerizim, replacing it with the improbable Mount Ebal. The latter two moves would thus be sectarian or at least partisan variants, but they are not in the scrolls.

Conclusion

What is the larger picture gained, when this small study of the Danielic trajectory of traditions—the sources behind the book (e.g., Prayer of Nabonidus), the variant editions of the book itself, and the subsequent compositions (e.g., *Pseudo-Daniel^{a-c}*)—is joined with the results of the other variant editions of biblical books, especially the Greek editions above?

The combined manuscript evidence from preserved Qumran texts and other sources preceding the "Great Divide"[37] (e.g., the Samaritan Pentateuch, the Septuagint, quotations of the Law and the Prophets in the New Testament, the recasting of the biblical narrative in Josephus) sketches a tapestry of developmental composition of the various books of the Bible. As seen in Chapter 13 as well as the Danielic literary trajectory, that tapestry preceded and was developing prior to our preserved sources and continued through the late Second Temple period until the "Great Divide."

The OG of Isaiah and Jeremiah[38] provide solid justification for the starting presumption that the OG is generally a faithful translation, whether free or literal, of a Hebrew or Aramaic text that may or may not have been preserved. This holds for both individual variants and variant editions. Examples from the OG of Isaiah repeatedly showed that the translator intelligently attempted to produce a translation that expressed in Greek what he saw, or thought he saw, in the Hebrew manuscript before him. The Greek readings frequently reflected a Hebrew expression that was actually found in a Hebrew manuscript, or that was an ambiguous or misread form or a plausibly close Hebrew variant.

The clear evidence from the OG of Isaiah and Jeremiah[39] grounds the strong assumption that, though confirming Hebrew evidence is not preserved, the OG of Exodus 35–40 and the order of chapters in both Ezekiel 36–40 and Daniel 5–9 as in the Greek Papyrus 967 witness to an earlier variant Hebrew-Aramaic edition of those sections. The gradual eclipse of those earlier editions resulted from the availability in the late Second Temple period of the newer editions now seen in the MT.

Based on a variety of oral and written literary sources, the early forms of the biblical texts were composed by Israelite leaders reflecting on God's action in human affairs. Due to various historical, social, military, or religious changes, the different sets of traditions were intermittently transformed into what we can loosely term "new and expanded editions" of those compositions. The written forms of those compositions were copied as faithfully as possible for new generations until a newer edition was produced for analogous reasons. The evidence demonstrates that the evolutionary changes, different for each book or group of books, continued sporadically up to the "Great Divide." The evolutionary process continued through the late Second Temple period until it was abruptly frozen (not "standardized") due to the losses in the two Jewish Revolts and the religious challenge of early Christianity.

---

[37] For the term see Ch. 2 n. 3.

[38] See also 4QDeut^{q} in Ch. 10.II.

[39] The numerous examples presented throughout this volume of readings where the Greek agrees with a scroll against the MT offer confirmatory evidence.

CHAPTER 16

THE MASADA SCROLLS

THE PREVAILING VIEW of the scriptural scrolls found at Qumran is that they portray a pluriform text with variant literary editions of several books. The prevailing view of the seven scriptural scrolls found at Masada,[1] in contrast, is that they uniformly display a close relationship to the proto-Masoretic Text.[2] Were this in fact the case, it might offer support to the notion of "stabilization of the proto-MT" outside Qumran possibly before the end of the Second Temple period. I have argued that there was no "stabilization" of the text but rather a "freezing of the development" of the text.[3] Emanuel Tov also rejects the "stabilization" claim, saying "there is no evidence for the assumption of a standard text or stabilization for the biblical text...,"[4] but he goes on to say that "during this period the 𝔐-group remained internally stable...."[5] The purpose of this chapter is to examine the relationship of the Masada scriptural scrolls to the Qumran scrolls, the MT, and the SP, to decide whether that latter view is correct and whether it is the optimal way to describe the situation.[6]

---

[1] Published by Shemaryahu Talmon and Yigael Yadin, *Masada VI: Yigael Yadin Excavations 1963–1965: Final Reports* (Jerusalem: Israel Exploration Society/Hebrew University of Jerusalem, 1999).

[2] See, as representative examples, Shemaryahu Talmon, "Masada: Written Material," *Encyclopedia of the Dead Sea Scrolls*, 1.521–25, esp. 523; Talmon and Yadin, *Masada VI*, 25, 38, 46, 55, 68, 89, 93; Lawrence H. Schiffman, *Reclaiming the Dead Sea Scrolls* (Philadelphia: Jewish Publication Society, 1994), 172; Emanuel Tov, "The Text of the Hebrew/Aramaic and Greek Bible Used in the Ancient Synagogues," in *Hebrew Bible, Greek Bible, and Qumran*, 171–88; idem, "A Qumran Origin for the Masada Non-biblical Texts?" *DSD* 7 (2000): 56–73, esp. 72–73; Ian Young, "The Stabilization of the Biblical Text in the Light of Qumran and Masada: A Challenge for Conventional Qumran Chronology?" *DSD* 9 (2002): 364–90; idem, "The Biblical Scrolls from Qumran and the Masoretic Text: A Statistical Approach," in *Feasts and Fasts: A Festschrift in Honour of Alan David Crown* (ed. Marianne Dacy, Jennifer Downling, and Suzanne Faigan; Sidney: Mandelbaum, 2005), 81–139; and Armin Lange, *Handbuch der Textfunde von Toten Meer* (Tübingen: Mohr Siebeck, 2009), 1:24.

[3] See pp. 10, 212, 249, and 267, and Ulrich, *Scrolls and Origins*, 12.

[4] Tov, *Textual Criticism*, 179.

[5] Tov, *Textual Criticism*, 179; see also Adam van der Woude, "Pluriformity and Uniformity: Reflections on the Transmission of the Text of the Old Testament," in *Sacred History and Sacred Texts in Early Judaism* (ed. Jan N. Brenner and F. García Martínez; Kampen: Kok Pharos, 1992), 151–69, esp. 163.

[6] See Tov's brief listing of the Masada scriptural scrolls in "A Qumran Origin for the Masada Non-biblical Texts?" 72–73. His description is accurate, as always, though our interpretations, conclusions, and articulations differ somewhat.

I. The Masada Scrolls

MasGen

Only one tiny fragment of Genesis, 5.6 × 4.5 cm., was found at Masada. It contains merely eight complete words and six other letters from three broken words, but it can be identified as containing parts of Gen 46:7-11.[7] Talmon offers the following transcription, altered here only by the insertion of the brackets at the end of the first line (since the manuscript is broken off) and by the shift to the left side plus the insertion of brackets at the right to indicate, as Talmon notes, that the words constitute the ends of the lines:

1]]מצרים [ ]
2] מצרי]ם את יעקוב
3]]ו[בנ]י ראובן חנוך
4] ימ]ואל וימין
5]]ובני לוי

Talmon gives the following reconstruction, again altered only by the insertion of the brackets at the end of the first line, the brackets at the beginning of the lines, and the verse numbers:

1]ובנות בניו וכול זרעו הביא אתו] מצרים [*vac*]
2][8]ואלה שמות בני ישראל הבאים מצרי]ם את יעקוב
3]אביהם בכור יעקוב ראובן] [9]ו[בנ]י ראובן חנוך
4]ופלוא וחצרון וכרמי [10]ובני שמעון ימ]ואל וימין
5]ואוהד ויכין וצוחר ושאול בן הכנענית] [11]ובני לוי

There is one orthographic difference from the MT (and on the basis of that fuller spelling Talmon reconstructs fuller spellings for other words where appropriate):

46:8 (line 2) יעקוב MasGen] יעקב MT SP

There are three variants preserved (no Qumran scrolls are extant for Genesis 46):

46:7 (1) מצרים MasGen] מצרימה MT SP
46:8 (2) [מצרי]ם MasGen] מצרימה MT SP
46:8 (2) את יעקוב MasGen] יעקב ובניו MT SP LXX

The first two variants are morphological and do not involve a shift in meaning, but the third variant ("with Jacob") involves a different syntactic pattern and requires Talmon to restore אביהם as the next word, את יעקוב אביהם, in agreement with Jubilees 44:11 (or better, with the variant Genesis text used by Jubilees), as opposed to יעקב ובניו in MT SP LXX.

This means that, of the eight complete and three broken words in MasGen, there are three variants (plus a fourth reconstructed) and an orthographic difference which suggests a pattern of differing orthography—a variation rate of 27%. Though no scrolls from Qumran are extant for this passage, judging from the many other Qumran Genesis

[7] For the edition of MasGen, see Talmon and Yadin, *Masada VI*, 31–35.

scrolls, they too would very likely contain at most minor variants such as those listed above. But meaningless orthographic and morphological differences as well as commonplaces such as ו׳ or את (direct object marker) should not cloud this discussion of general text types. The types of minor variants seen within the MT family of texts should be ignored here.[8] Thus, it is better to conclude that MasGen has one noticeable variant within the eight complete and three broken words—a variation rate of 9%.

Finally, Talmon suggests that "MasGen exhibits an important agreement with MT ... a break [which] dovetails with the masoretic section-divider (*parašah*) after Gen 46:7."[9] One should observe, however, that the blank space is extant for only the width of one letter (or word-division space) after מצרים then breaks off. It is very likely, of course, that the scribe did leave an intentional interval here, but it would have been a short interval of only 1 cm., enough for only three or four letters. Moreover, most scribes or translators would independently start a new section here (see below).

Consideration of how to describe the textual profile of MasGen leads in two directions. On the one hand, since the MT is the center for much of the academic and religious use of the Hebrew Bible, it can be argued that description from the point of view of the traditional MT is a good way to proceed. Moreover, since the MT provides the only complete collection of texts in the original language, it indeed functions in practice as the *textus receptus* of the Hebrew Bible. It has also long been the reference-point for text-critical mapping and has the pedagogical advantage of providing a quick initial textual orientation.

On the other hand, one could make the case that for the Second Temple period the reference-point of textual discussions should be the situation as it existed at that time (see Ch. 2). How would the people who were producing or hearing or reading the texts have described them? What were the operative categories, classifications, and worldview with which they were working? Though the MT preserves faithful copies of texts attested in the late Second Temple period, it represents only one form of the text of many books as Judaism knew them; and it is difficult to find convincing evidence that the collection of individual texts that the Rabbis received and handed on were carefully selected in contradistinction to other forms of the texts used by other Jews (see Ch. 2 "Coincidental Nature").

From the first perspective, one can classify a text under observation primarily by its relationship to the MT, aided by contrast with the SP and the presumed Hebrew behind the LXX or other versions. From the second perspective, the people who penned the texts or lived by them would not have known about the "proto-MT," thought of it as textually or religiously preferable to the "pre-SP" or "LXX(-*Vorlage*)," or thought they should compare their texts to it as a "standard text."[10]

---

[8] For an illustrative list of variants within the MT text family or "MT group" (i.e., MT^{L}, MT^{A}, MT^{q}, MT^{mss}, the Cairo texts, and $1QIsa^{b}$) see Ch. 8 and DJD 32, 2:208–11.

[9] Talmon and Yadin, *Masada VI*, 33.

[10] Were this the case, one would expect that 𝔐 would consistently be a superior form of the text; but, as Tov (*Textual Criticism*, 24) says, "the preference for 𝔐 within Judaism does not necessarily imply that it contains the best (earliest) evidence of the Scripture text; both the Hebrew parent text of 𝔊 and several Qumran manuscripts reflect excellent texts, often better and/or earlier than 𝔐."

Returning specifically to MasGen, is it appropriate to classify this fragment as generally Masoretic? From the first perspective, yes: it agrees with the MT except for five letters in four words, and such small variants are to be expected even within the Masoretic group.

From the second perspective, no. The ancients had no concept or category of "(proto-)MT" and similar labels. More importantly, the SP and the LXX are identical with the MT for all the preserved text of MasGen, so that "agreements with the MT" are equally "agreements with the SP" or "agreements with the LXX." Therefore, classifying MasGen simply as "proto-MT" is open to the charge that it employs solely a narrow MT focus; it is no more acceptable than to claim, without mention of the MT, what is equally true: "MasGen is Samaritan," or "MasGen is Septuagintal."

Similarly, the short interval of 3–4 letters at the end of line 1 before verse 8 is not well characterized as "an important agreement with MT,"[11] since the SP also has a *qiṣṣah*, and Rahlfs' and Wevers' editions of the LXX as well as most translations display a break before the new section. Gen 46:8-27 breaks into the Genesis narrative with a different genre. It is a genealogical list which was inserted into the story, interrupting the narrative that breaks after 46:7 and resumes in 46:28. The majority of ancient scribes would independently place a section break at this point.

In sum, if one's standpoint is the present outcome of history, or the medieval world, or the MT as a cherished religious text, or *BHS* as a practical tool for ease of comparison, one could legitimately conclude that MasGen is quite close to the MT. On the other hand, if one's standpoint is the ancient world represented by Masada and the wider Jewish world of the time, or a modern, academic textual discussion with full context, one would conclude that MasGen appears to be a good representative of the single then-current (and henceforth enduring) edition of Genesis, which nonetheless showed a small number of the minor variants typical of manuscripts of authoritative Scriptures in that period (though one variant agrees with Jubilees against the MT).

MasLev[a]

For MasLev[a] only a pair of contiguous fragments is extant, preserving the left half of eight lines containing Lev 4:3-9.[12] Of Qumran scrolls, 4QLev[c] preserves 4:3-6, and 4QpapLXXLev[b] has 4:3-4, 6-8. When compared with the MT and SP, the only two orthographic differences that emerge are:

4:7 (6) ישפוך MasLev[a]] ישפך MT SP
4:9 (8) היתרת̊ MasLev[a] MT] היותרת SP

[11] Talmon and Yadin, *Masada VI*, 33. Talmon also mentions a break in a Jubilees manuscript, but none appears to be extant for Jubilees 44:11-12; see James C. VanderKam, "The Jubilees Fragments from Qumran Cave 4," *The Madrid Qumran Congress: Proceedings of the International Congress on the Dead Sea Scrolls—Madrid, 18–21 March 1991* (ed. Julio Trebolle Barrera and Luis Vegas Montaner; Studies on the Texts of the Desert of Judah 11/2; Leiden: Brill; Madrid: Editorial Complutense, 1992), 635–48, esp. 642. I thank Professor VanderKam for a recent private communication updating the list in his article.

[12] For the text and edition of MasLev[a], see Talmon and Yadin, *Masada VI*, 36–39. See also the edition of 4QLev[c] by Emanuel Tov in DJD 12:189–92 and pl. XXXV; it has one fragment that overlaps with MasLev[a], but no clear variants are preserved.

When compared with the MT, SP, and LXX, there are three preserved variants (note the meaningless interchangeable wording of the first two):

4:7 (5) מן הדם MasLev^{a} MT SP] *מדם הפר (ἀπὸ τοῦ αἵματος τοῦ μόσχου) LXX
4:7 (6) דם הפר MasLev^{a} MT LXX] הדם SP
4:8 (7) על MasLev^{a} MT^{L}] את MT^{mss} SP LXX (τὰ [ἐνδόσθια])

The extant left half of the lines permits a reasonably confident restoration of the right half which argues for these probable reconstructed variants proposed by Talmon:[13]

4:4 (3) [ראש הפר] MasLev^{a} MT SP] + *לפני יהוה (ἔναντι κυρίου) LXX
4:5 (3-4) [ ]\ המשיח MasLev^{a} MT] + אשר מלא את ידו SP LXX[14]
4:6 (5) [פעמים] MasLev^{a} MT LXX$^{BA\ Rahlfs}$] + באצבעו SP 4QpapLXXLev^{b} 𝔊^{ed} [15]

The preserved text of 4QLev^{c} agrees completely with MasLev^{a} (for the few overlapping extant words) as well as with the MT and the SP.

Again, is it appropriate to summarize the analysis with simply "the text of MasLev^{a} is identical with MT"?[16] From the first perspective, certainly yes, since MasLev^{a} agrees with MT^{L} in all preserved and reconstructable variants (though it disagrees with many MT manuscripts in the third variant at 4:8; see *BHS* n. 8^{b}), differing in only a single orthographic detail. From the second perspective, on the one hand, it is also easy to agree that, when MasLev^{a} is compared specifically with the MT, SP, and LXX, only the MT and 4QLev^{c} consistently agree with it in every textual variant (except MT manuscripts at 4:8). But would it be appropriate to summarize by simply saying "the text of MasLev^{a} is identical with 4QLev^{c}" and not mention the MT? On the other hand, all the orthographic differences and variants are quite minor and routine, involve no change in meaning, and exhibit erratically changing patterns of affiliation. The SP has only two tiny and insignificant variants from MasLev^{a} in the 63 (56 completely and 7 partly) preserved words.[17] Again, would it be appropriate to summarize by simply saying "the text of MasLev^{a} is virtually identical with the SP" and not mention the MT?

---

13 Talmon understandably reconstructs the missing text according to the MT. There are SP variants from some of the recontructed material, but they carry no weight. For example, in Talmon's restored wording prior to the extant text he reconstructs according to the short MT whereas the SP adds במקום הקדש, lacking in the MT; but MasLev^{b} could have read with either the MT or the SP. Also, at Lev 9:2, where the MT has תמימם (plur.), the A. & R. Sadaqa edition prints תמים (sing.); but both the von Gall and the Tal-Florentin editions print תמימם. Finally, his reconstruction of the last word of 11:16 is [למינה]ו (with MT, which would be a variant) but only the top left tip of the final letter is preserved, and it could just as easily be [הנ]ץ (with SP); cf. the *ṣade* of ושקץ five lines above.

14 Note the anomalous interlinear writing of את ידו °°°° above ולקח^{5} הכ֯ה[ן in 4QLev^{c}, which is mentioned in the DJD notes but not entered into the transcription; see DJD 12, pl. XXXV (lower part of frg. 2) and pp. 190–91. For the addition of אשר מלא את ידו in the SP and LXX *Vorlage*, see Lev 8:33; 21:10; and esp. 16:32.

15 This formulation of the variant should replace Talmon's on his p. 38.

16 Talmon and Yadin, 38.

17 The SP also probably disagrees in two reconstructed variants, but compared with the fully reconstructed text of MasLev^{a}, the variant rate would probably not rise significantly.

In the late Second Temple period only one literary edition of the Hebrew Leviticus was in circulation,[18] with minor variants exhibited randomly by the various copies—including the copies at Qumran, the one that served as the *Vorlage* for the LXX, the one that the Rabbis inherited, and the one that the Samaritans adopted.[19] It is plausible to suggest that the Jerusalem priesthood guarded a more or less uniform tradition for the book of Leviticus—not as a "standard text of Scripture" (otherwise, how explain Exodus and Numbers?), but for the correct and consistent praxis in the sacrificial rituals of the Temple. The part of MasLev^{a} that survives displays a copy that was virtually identical with the one that the Rabbis inherited and that formed the consonantal text for what eventually became the MT. Thus, it serves, like 1QIsa^{b} for the most part, to demonstrate the startling fidelity with which the medieval MT preserves a very ancient form of the text. But, as MasGen and other indicators show, that does not mean that the proto-MT had become the standard text.[20] To substantiate a claim for meaningful identity of MasLev^{a} with the MT, clear evidence of their joint disagreement against a variant edition, a set of major isolated insertions, or a series of distinctive errors or secondary variants would be required.

MasLev^{b}

The five columns of MasLev^{b} contain text from Lev 8:31, 33-34; 9:1-10, 12-13, 22-24; 10:1, 9-20; 11:1-13, 15-21; and 23-40.[21] The Qumran fragments have only a few overlaps with MasLev^{b}. There are none for 8:31, 33-34; 9:1-10, 12-13; 10:9-20; or 11:15-21. The following overlaps are preserved:

For 9:22-24; 10:1 — 11QLev^{b} has 9:23-24; 10:1-2, but there is no variant.

For 11:1-13 — 1QpaleoLev-Num^{a} has 11:10-11, and the only variant is:

11:10 (IV 16) ל[כ]ם MasLev^{b} MT SP] > LXX

For 11:23-40 — 2QpaleoLev has 11:22-29, and 11QpaleoLev^{a} has 11:27-32, but, though there are a few orthographic differences, neither has a variant against MasLev^{b}.

Talmon lists six variants against the SP:

11:12 (IV 17) [כ]ל MasLev^{b} MT] וכל SP LXX

11:26 (V 6) [שס]עת MasLev^{b} MT] שסע SP LXX

---

[18] Perhaps the largest variants at Qumran in the book of Leviticus, in addition to the variant at Lev 17:4 (see Ch. 3.IV), are the two complete verses missing from 4QLev-Num^{a}* at Lev 14:24 and 45, but both are probably meaningless, simple omissions by parablepsis (a later hand secondarily inserted the latter verse); see DJD 12:156–57 and pl. XXIII, and *The Biblical Qumran Scrolls,* 117–19.

[19] Once again, one can ask whether the MT, SP, and LXX are the proper and sufficient measuring sticks in the first century C.E. by which to measure MasLev^{a}.

[20] See Tov, *Textual Criticism,* 179; and Ulrich, "The Qumran Biblical Scrolls—The Scriptures of Late Second Temple Judaism," in *The Dead Sea Scrolls in Their Historical Context* (ed. Timothy H. Lim et al.; Edinburgh: T&T Clark, 2000), 67–87. See also the insightful discussion of Julio Trebolle Barrera, "Qumran Evidence for a Biblical Standard Text and for Non-Standard and Parabiblical Texts," ibid., 89–106.

[21] For the text and edition of MasLev^{b}, see Talmon and Yadin, *Masada VI,* 40–50.

11:28 (V 9) את נב]נלתם MasLev^{b} MT] מנבלתם SP

11:28 (V 10) הֹמה MasLev^{b} MT (המה)] הם SP

11:35 (V 19) יתץ̇ MasLev^{b} MT] יתצו SP LXX Targ Pesh

11:36 (V 20) מעין MasLev^{b} MT] + מים SP LXX

Two of these, however, [כ]ל̇ and יתץ̇, must be removed. The area before the *lamed* of [כ]ל is entirely lost, so that it is impossible to know whether MasLev^{b} had [כ]ל with MT, or had [וכ]ל with SP LXX. Again, only the top half of the *ṣade* of יתץ[, is preserved as the leather breaks off, and it is simply unknowable whether the *ṣade* was medial with SP LXX Targ Pesh, or final with MT.

On the other hand, three other variants against the SP, not mentioned by Talmon, can be added for MasLev^{b}:

11:31 (V 12) ב]כל[MasLev^{b} MT] מכל SP LXX

11:32 (V 15) יוב̇א MasLev^{b} MT] יבוא SP

11:38 (V 22) זרע MasLev^{b} MT] הזרע SP; pr כל* LXX

Despite the relatively generous amount of five partial columns of text, there are no variants against the Qumran manuscripts and only a few variants against the SP. All the SP-MasLev^{b} variants are minor, involving no change in meaning; they are of the same type as those encountered within "the MT-group."[22]

Thus, once again, though MasLev^{b} agrees with the MT in all variants, it is insufficient to identify MasLev^{b} as simply MT; it is rather one of the several slightly varying witnesses to the single edition of Leviticus in circulation during the late Second Temple period. There had undoubtedly been earlier forms of the Leviticus traditions, but no variant edition survived or has been preserved from the late Second Temple period.

MasDeut

The two modest and two tiny fragments of MasDeut contain text from Deut 33:17-24 and 34:2-6.[23] Of the Qumran fragments, 1QDeut has four very small fragments with words from 33:12-24, but there is no overlap and thus no variant from MasDeut. Similarly, 4QDeut^{l} has only one small fragment with 34:4-6, and though three letters overlap, there is no variant. 4QDeut^{h} has one large and four small fragments with 33:8-22. It shows one orthographic difference in fragment a, line 1; note that MasDeut agrees with 4QDeut^{h} against the MT and SP:

33:19 (a 3) [ו]ש̇פ̊ני MasDeut 4QDeut^{h}] ושפוני MT SP

MasDeut displays only one variant against 4QDeut^{h} but five against the SP:

---

[22] For the term see Tov, *Textual Criticism*, 24–25.

[23] For the text and edition of MasDeut, see Talmon and Yadin, *Masada VI*, 51–58. See also the edition of 4QDeut^{h} by Julie Duncan in DJD 14:61–70 and pl. XVII–XVIII.

33:17 (a 1) והם 1° MasDeut MT] הם MT^mss SP LXX
33:19 (a 2) הׄר MasDeut MT] הׄדו[ ] 4QDeut^h; הרי SP; ἐξολεθρεύσουσιν LXX
33:19 (a 3) שם MasDeut MT] ושם SP
33:20 (a 5) וטׄרׄף MasDeut MT] טרף SP
33:20 (a 5) אף MasDeut MT] וגם SP

Four of the variants are meaningless and are of the type seen frequently between differing manuscripts of "the MT-group." For the second variant the texts present four unique readings in the cryptic clause עמים הר יקראו. All four readings are difficult though possible, but, following Samuel R. Driver, a decision is not required here.[24] The 4QDeut^h reading הׄדו[ ] ("praise") is virtually certain, and the difference between it and the SP reading could simply be graphic confusion of ד/ר and ו/י by either text. If either הרי in the SP or הר in MasDeut-MT is correct, it could be a sectarian variant in the SP ("They call peoples to *my* mountain") or in the MT (". . . to *a/the* mountain"; note that, since the verse is the blessing of Zebulun and Issachar, the mountain is in the north). The LXX may be reflecting חרם/הרם seen in its *Vorlage* or be attempting to make sense of a difficult reading.

Once again, no claim of textual affiliation is persuasive. In contrast to Exodus and Numbers, for which variant editions were preserved, there was only a single edition of the books of Genesis, Leviticus, and Deuteronomy circulating in the late Second Temple period. The evidence is severely limited for determining meaningful textual affiliation.

MasEzek

The situation changes importantly with MasEzek, providing at last the type of evidence required for major textual affiliation of the Masada scrolls. Large fragments of four contiguous columns contain much of Ezek 35:11–38:14.[25] Chapter 15 discussed a variant edition of Ezekiel 36–40 known only from one Greek and one Latin manuscript, but MasEzek clearly agrees with the edition displayed by the MT and the main LXX text tradition, as opposed to that alternate edition.[26] The scroll has a number of differences from the MT, but given its large amount of preserved text, the differences are relatively few: a few longer and a few shorter orthographic forms, and a few textual variants which should be attributed to scribal dynamics rather than to textual affiliation. These are the types of variants seen routinely within "the MT-group," and Talmon correctly asserts that the "extant text of MasEzek accords with MT, with the exception of some minor deviations."[27] Moreover, the scroll agrees closely with the MT against the LXX in a

[24] Samuel R. Driver (*Deuteronomy* [ICC; 3d ed.; Edinburgh: T&T Clark, n.d. but the 3d ed. Preface is dated 1901)], 409) comments: "The indefiniteness of the expression, coupled with our ignorance of the customs of the time, prevents our interpreting the passage with entire certainty." See also the discussion by John W. Wevers, *Notes on the Greek Text of Deuteronomy* (Atlanta: SBL, 1995), 550.

[25] For the text and edition of MasEzek, see Talmon and Yadin, *Masada VI*, 59–75.

[26] The order of chapters in Pap. 967 and Codex Wirceburgensis (see Ch. 15.III) is 36–38–39–37–40, whereas the MT and LXX have 36–37–38–39–40 plus a large insertion at the end of 36 to prepare for the new placement of 37. The extant parts of MasEzek have 36–37–38 in agreement with the MT.

[27] Talmon and Yadin, *Masada VI*, 68.

number of small pluses, minuses, and other variants. Thus, it may be concluded that MasEzek witnesses to the edition of Ezekiel inherited by the Rabbis and the MT. It should, however, be immediately stated that the six Ezekiel scrolls from Qumran also show close identity with that same edition, and it could be equally accurately affirmed that MasEzek witnesses to the edition of Ezekiel inherited by the Qumranites.

The book of Ezekiel is apparently intermediate between books such as Genesis, Leviticus, and Deuteronomy, for which presumably only a single edition was circulating in the late Second Temple period, and books such as Exodus, Numbers, and Psalms, for which variant editions were circulating. With regard to the chronology and availability of successive variant editions of Ezekiel, the edition seen in the OG (in Pap. 967) from the third or early second century B.C.E. appears to have been waning in the first century B.C.E. It was being replaced by the newer edition which had become predominant near the end of the Second Temple period, the edition seen commonly in the Qumran fragments, the rabbinic tradition, and the main LXX tradition.[28] It is not a major conclusion that MasEzek agrees with the MT; it is rather a more than fifty-fifty probability that it would agree with the dominant edition of the book circulating at that time.

MasPs^{a}

MasPs^{a} consists of two large contiguous fragments containing the full height of the scroll, almost a full central column, and considerable parts of the columns to the right and the left of that column. It has large amounts of text from Pss 81:2b-3, 5-17; 82:1-8; 83:1-19; 84:1-13; 85:1-6a.[29] Unfortunately, the only Qumran manuscripts of Psalms that are extant for those passages are 4QPs^{e} and 11QPs^{d}. 4QPs^{e} has no overlap with MasPs^{a}, and 11QPs^{d} differs only by including the *waw* in יעק(ו)ב at Ps 81:5 (cf. similarly MasGen above). In perhaps the most noticeable variant MasPs^{a} presumably errs at Ps 83:7 with אלהי אדום ("the gods of Edom") for MT אהלי אדום ("the tents of Edom"), but that is probably a simple scribal metathesis (cf. 2 Sam 7:23 in Ch. 6.II.B.), and is not important for textual affiliation. The order of the Psalms is the same as in the MT, but, judging from the available evidence from the Qumran Psalms scrolls for Pss 1–89, there is no reason to suspect that the order differed from that of Qumran. Once again, though MasPs^{a} is close to identical with the MT, that identity is not unique, and there is no reason to believe that it differed significantly from any other copy of the Psalms.

MasPs^{b}

MasPs^{b}, like MasEzek, does offer significant witness. It contains only twenty full and seven partly preserved words from Ps 150:1-6 plus a couple letters from the ends of two

---

[28] The OG of Ezekiel transmitted in Pap. 967 was probably translated in the late third or early second century B.C.E. MasEzek, however, was copied more than a century later, in the latter half of the last century B.C.E., according to Talmon and Yadin, *Masada VI*, 60. 4QEzek^{a} was copied in the middle of the first century B.C.E. (DJD 15:209) and 4QEzek^{b} in the early first century C.E. (DJD 15:216). Thus, the earlier edition attested in the OG may have been waning and being replaced by the newer edition attested in the Hebrew manuscripts; the rabbinic text simply inherited the current edition of Ezekiel at the end of the Second Temple period.

[29] For the text and edition of MasPs^{a}, see Talmon and Yadin, *Masada VI*, 76–90.

words from the previous column.[30] The only Qumran manuscript that preserves Psalm 150 is 11QPs[a], which has extra psalms following Psalm 150. As Talmon notes, the broad left margin of MasPs[b] and the fact that it was unruled, in contrast to the ruled lines in the inscribed area, indicate that the scroll intentionally concluded with Psalm 150 in agreement with the MT, as opposed to 11QPs[a] and the LXX. MasPs[b] thus clearly witnesses to the shorter edition as in the MT.

There are no textual variants between MasPs[b], the MT, and the LXX. The difference in the MT vs. 11QPs[a] editions of the Psalter is not in the line-by-line wording of the individual Psalms but in the extra compositions and the order of the Psalms. Thus, while MasPs[b] does "agree with the MT," just as in the case of Ezekiel, it is not surprising that it agrees with one of the two available editions at the time.

II. Reflections on the Scriptural Manuscripts from Masada

When viewed from the first (i.e., MT-oriented) perspective described above, it is possible to describe the pentateuchal and other scriptural manuscripts, as generally witnessing to the proto-Masoretic tradition. We have seen that this is a legitimate conclusion, especially for MasLev[a], if somewhat less so for MasGen. That conclusion gains in persuasiveness the more one emphasizes the nuance articulated by Tov that the MT "is an abstract unit reflected in various sources that differ from one another in many details,"[31] and the more one insists that it is "an abstract ideal" that includes the modest array of variants exhibited in the collection of Masoretic manuscripts.[32] But since a number of minor variants is to be expected when comparing any manuscripts, for major textual affiliation to be meaningful, clear contrast between variant editions (such as with MasEzek and MasPs[b]), a set of isolated insertions, or agreement in a series of erroneous or indicative readings is required.

But the points made in this and previous chapters invite focus on the second perspective as well. It may have been noticed that three of the short list of scriptural books found at Masada—Genesis, Leviticus, Deuteronomy—have no practical overlap with the list of pentateuchal books found in variant editions at Qumran and in the SP and LXX. That is, for Genesis,[33] Leviticus, and Deuteronomy,[34] the evidence that survives attests only a single edition for each book, and thus the claim of identity with the MT is not particularly meaningful. For Ezekiel, even though the OG shows signs of a variant edition,[35] the small remains of the few Hebrew manuscripts from Qumran offer almost

[30] For the text and edition of MasPs[b], see Talmon and Yadin, *Masada VI*, 91–97.

[31] Tov, *Textual Criticism*, 24–25.

[32] To see the range of variants that occur within the MT text family or "MT-group" see Ch. 8 and DJD 32, 2:208–11.

[33] That is, except for the triple edition or recension in chapters 5 and 11 (see Ch. 14.II), which do not appear in MasGen. See Ralph W. Klein "Archaic Chronologies and the Textual History of the Old Testament," *HTR* 67 (1974) 255–63; and Ronald S. Hendel, *The Text of Genesis 1–11: Textual Studies and Critical Edition* (New York: Oxford University Press, 1998) 61–80.

[34] The agreement of the 4QDeut[q] edition with the LXX is limited to Deuteronomy 32, which is not represented in MasDeut.

[35] See Emanuel Tov, "Recensional Differences Between the MT and LXX of Ezekiel," *ETL* 62 (1986) 89–101; idem, *Textual Criticism*, 333–34, 349–50.

no possibility of comparison where the variation between editions occurs.[36] And for the Psalter, though there are variant editions, the variation is mainly on the macro level (the order and the inclusion or absence of full compositions), not the micro level (individual variant readings); i.e., the wording of individual Psalms of one edition is for the most part identical to that of the other edition.[37]

Thus, from the first perspective, the Masada remains may be described as close to the (proto-)MT. From the second perspective, MasEzek and MasPs^{b} can certainly be classified as agreeing with the MT editions. But the pentateuchal scrolls would be described as preserving only a very limited amount of useful evidence for the history of the biblical text, and they do not meaningfully point to the MT. They have fragments only from books which do not show the pluriform nature typical of the text of Scripture in that period; that is, the *possibility* for significant differentiating information is quite limited. For Ezekiel, though the evidence is slim, it is possible that the earlier, shorter edition that formed the *Vorlage* of the OG in the third or early second century B.C.E. was fading out in the first century in favor of the later edition inherited by the Qumranites, the Rabbis, and the MT.[38]

For the Psalter, though it is argued that "MasPs^{a} corresponds to all intents and purposes to MT," the case is less strong than that claim suggests.[39] Nonetheless, for MasPs^{b}, it should be stated clearly that it unambiguously shows agreement with the edition preserved in the MT against 11QPs^{a} and the LXX, since a blank column follows traditional Psalm 150. On the other hand, the individual wording—as opposed to the edition—is not identical to the MT. Of the 20 complete and 7 partial words preserved, MasPs^{b} has six or seven differences from the MT. It reads הללהו vs. הללוהו MT five times, שפר vs. שופר, and ועוגב (= 11QPs^{a} MT^{L}) vs. ועגב in the Aleppo Codex of the MT. It is possible, but unlikely, that the first represents a textual variant (singular verb; note the collective singular in v. 6); it is more likely, as Talmon suggests, simply orthographic, as are the remaining two instances. But it was argued with respect to MasLev^{b} that the "textual identity of MasLev^{b} with MT is evinced by the meticulous preservation of the defective and plene spellings," and even "the same inconsistency as MT in the employment of defective and plene spellings."[40] By that same criterion, MasPs^{b}, though it would be categorized with regard to edition as sharing the same general text tradition as the proto-MT (in contrast to that of 11QPs^{a} and the LXX), with regard to text, it would be categorized as not especially closely related to the proto-MT.

---

36 4QEzek^{b} at 1:22 does attest the interpolation הנורא = MT, > LXX (see DJD 15.218, and Tov, *Textual Criticism*, 333); however, the small manuscript did not contain the full book, but apparently only chapter 1 and perhaps a few other small passages (see DJD 15:215–16).

37 See Peter W. Flint, *The Dead Sea Psalms Scrolls and the Book of Psalms* (STDJ 17; Leiden: Brill, 1997).

38 This may have been the case also for Joshua and Jeremiah.

39 Some of the examples of variants listed on page 89 in Talmon and Yadin, *Masada VI* should be scrutinized. The variant, e.g., at Psalm 81:13 (singular suffix vs. plural) is not a true variant but simply translation technique on the part of the LXX, as the context shows. The antecedent is the collective עמי/ישראל; therefore the LXX, as commonly happens in many manuscripts, uses the plural form with the singular collective antecedent, as does the MT two words later: לבם. Even the JPS translation of the MT (as well as the NRSV) uses the plural: "My people..., I let *them* go after their willful heart."

40 Talmon and Yadin, *Masada VI*, 46.

Thus, from one perspective the scriptural manuscripts from Masada can be characterized as in agreement with the MT (or proto-MT) to varying degrees. But it seems misleading to say that they agree with the MT without reference to the other text traditions. From a historically preferable perspective, it seems that that description can be enhanced with a more detailed characterization that is first-century oriented and more attuned to the variant-edition status of the Scriptures in the closing centuries of the Second Temple period.

Conclusion

MasGen appears to be a good representative of the single edition of Genesis current at the time, but it nonetheless shows a small number of minor variants, the most significant one being a surprising agreement with Jubilees against the MT.

MasLev^{a} agrees completely with the MT, but it also agrees completely with 4QLev^{c} and the SP, which neutralizes claims for the MT.

MasLev^{b} agrees with the MT but it also agrees with 1QpaleoLev-Num^{a}, 2QpaleoLev, 11QpaleoLev^{a}, and 11QLev^{b}.

MasDeut has regular agreement with the MT against the SP in five very minor variants, four of which are meaningless. The noticeable one (Deut 33:19) is a troubled reading in all witnesses, MasDeut-MT, 4QDeut^{h}, SP, and the LXX, with graphic confusion of ד/ר and ו/י. But this one MasDeut-MT agreement, though small, is noteworthy.

For the pentateuchal scrolls, my suggestion for a description of affiliation would begin by noting that all the remaining evidence indicates that for Genesis, Leviticus, and Deuteronomy, in contrast to Exodus and Numbers, only one literary edition of each was in circulation in the late Second Temple period, with minor variants exhibited randomly by the various copies—including the one that served as the *Vorlage* for the LXX, the copies at Qumran, the one that the Rabbis inherited, and the one that the Samaritans adopted.[41] To substantiate a claim for identity of the Masada scrolls with the MT would require clear evidence of their combined disagreement against a variant edition, a series of major isolated insertions, or a series of *Leitfehler* (distinctive errors or secondary variants). No such evidence is forthcoming.

With regard to editions, MasEzek and MasPs^{b} share the same editions as the MT. MasEzek and the MT share—but so do the six Qumran Ezekiel scrolls and the LXX—the later, newer edition as opposed to the earlier, older edition in Pap967 and OL^{W}; but that older edition from the third or early second century B.C.E. appears to have been waning, replaced by the newer edition by the time MasEzek was copied.

In contrast, MasPs^{b} and the MT share the earlier, shorter edition of the Psalter as opposed to the later, expanded edition in 11QPs^{a}. Without discounting the factual evidence of these agreements, it may still be asked how meaningful is this with relation to the MT? It does not seem surprising that these two scrolls exhibit one or another of the editions available at the time.

For example, if one went to Qumran Cave 4 in search of an Exodus scroll, one might pick up either 4QpaleoGen-Exod^{l} or 4QpaleoExod^{m}. Both were available, both were

[41] Once again, one can ask whether the MT, SP, and LXX are the proper and sufficient measuring sticks in the first century C.E. by which to measure MasLev^{a}.

apparently valued, and there seems to be no evidence that anyone in the Second Temple period differentiated between text types.[42] If one picked up 4QpaleoGen-Exod^{l}, the (anachronistic) judgment would be that 4QpaleoGen-Exod^{l} is virtually identical with the MT; if one picked up 4QpaleoExod^{m}, the judgment would be that 4QpaleoExod^{m} is virtually identical with the SP. The fact that variant editions existed is very important; is the fact that one or other scroll agrees with a specific text, the MT or the SP or the LXX, of equal importance?

[42] That is, anyone other than the comparatively few scribes who produced new editions.

THE ROAD TOWARD CANON: FROM COLLECTION OF SCROLLS TO CANON

CHAPTER 17

THE NOTION AND DEFINITION OF CANON

Socrates: *However, when friendly people . . . want to converse with each other, one's reply must . . . not only be true, but must employ terms with which the questioner admits he is familiar. . . .*

I believe we rejected the type of answer that employs terms which are still in question and not yet agreed upon. . . .

You say this and that about virtue, but what **is** *it?*

. . . to define so-and-so, and thus to make plain whatever may be chosen as the topic for exposition. For example, take the definition given just now. . . , it was that which enabled our discourse to achieve lucidity and consistency.[1]

PLATO MAY NOT SEEM the most apt starting-point for a discussion of the biblical canon, but I suggest that he might be. Though he was not always correct in his views, he did manage to make several rather permanent advances in human civilization. Perhaps one of the most frequently applied — or forgotten with resultant peril — is his insistence that intelligent argument cannot safely proceed without a clear definition of terms. Some scholars think that "canon" is a theological *terminus technicus* with a clear meaning, a specific denotation, and a long history of discussion, while others think that the term may be used more broadly to fit any of several aspects related to the collections of authoritative sacred texts of Judaism or Christianity.

The purpose of this chapter is to consider and attempt to clarify the notion and definition of "canon." It is an understatement to say that confusion currently surrounds the term and permeates recent discussions of the topic. A topic periodically dormant, it has generated a great deal of interest in the current generation due to the new and unexpected light that the discovery of the Dead Sea Scrolls contributes to the rather scant body of evidence otherwise available.

---

[1] Plato, *Meno* 75d and 79d, and *Phaedrus* 265d. The translations are by William K. C. Guthrie and Reginald Hackforth in *The Collected Dialogues of Plato* (ed. Edith Hamilton and Huntington Cairns; Princeton: Princeton University Press, 1961), 358, 362, and 511.

A problem that arises in discussion of topics that are intermittently vigorous and then dormant is that continuity and valuable advances in the discussion get lost. It is quite predictable that the discovery of a cache of ancient manuscripts of books that came to form the Bible of Jews and Christians would excite both popular and scholarly attention, in the hopes of sharpening our knowledge of the history of the Bible's formation. Indeed, great gains have been made in that knowledge, but many recent discussions bemoan the lack of clarity and agreement regarding terminology. Is there a fixed target with a clear bull's-eye that writers must agree to aim at, or is there only a general area within which one may aim at any of a number of spots? Is there "no king in Israel" so that all can do or say what is right in their own eyes? Is there need for a guide to the perplexed?

This chapter will be a sustained attempt at clarifying the definition of "canon" and discussing some of the attendant concepts which partly overlap with that of canon and cause blurring of the picture. The specific histories of the various aspects which make up the Jewish and Christian processes toward the different canons lie beyond the limits of this chapter, but many of those aspects are discussed in *The Canon Debate*.[2] The discussion here will first treat some preliminary considerations and then turn to the definition of "canon," surveying a spectrum of theological dictionaries, isolating the essential elements of the concept of canon, and distinguishing it from other related concepts that tend to cause confusion.

I. Preliminary Considerations

A. Etymology

Although much ink has been spilled discussing the etymology of the "canon" of the Scriptures, the effort produces only mildly interesting and only mildly helpful results, because the word as used in later theology or biblical studies does not coincide with ancient usage for the most part. The word can be traced to the Sumerian *gi*, *gi-na*, meaning "reed" and its extended meaning "standard." Hebrew and other Semitic languages received these meanings, as did Greek, though the last multiplied additional metaphorical uses.[3]

For practical purposes regarding the canon of Scripture, Bruce Metzger is correct that "the word 'canon' is Greek; its use in connection with the Bible belongs to Christian times; the idea of a canon of Scripture originates in Judaism."[4] The term as used in relation to the Bible arose in Christian circles, though it was borrowed from the Hellenistic world. Commonly in Greek the term originally had a concrete meaning and then several metaphorical extensions. It meant a "rod" or "measuring stick" and acquired the figurative senses of "norm" or "ideal": in the realm of sculpture it meant the "perfect form of the human frame"; in philosophy, the "basis ... by which to know what is true

---

2 *The Canon Debate* (ed. Lee M. McDonald and James A. Sanders; Peabody, Mass.: Hendrickson, 2002).

3 See Gerald Sheppard, "Canon," *The Encyclopedia of Religion* (ed. Mircea Eliade; New York: Macmillan, 1987), 3:62–69, esp. 62–63; and H. W. Beyer, "κανών," *TDNT* 3:596–602.

4 Bruce Metzger, *The Canon of the New Testament: Its Origin, Development, and Significance* (Oxford: Clarendon, 1987), v.

and false"; in law, "that which binds us, . . . specific ideals"; and also a "list" or "table."[5] A number of metaphorical uses also pervaded Latin and derivative languages and literatures.

Interestingly, no similar term is attested in Jewish writings, including the LXX, or in the Hebrew language until comparatively late. Although קנה "reed, stalk," is used, principally in Ezekiel (40:3, 5; 41:8; 42:16-19; see also Isa 46:6), in the derived meaning of measuring rod (six cubits), there is no attested biblical use of the word in the extended metaphorical sense of a moral measure, as, for example, אנך "plumb line" in Amos 7:7-8. In the NT the only relevant occurrence of κανών is in Gal 6:16, where it is used in the general sense of "measure of assessment," "norm of one's own action," "norm of true Christianity."[6] But precisely what Paul is referring to in his summary blessing "for those who will follow τῷ κανόνι τούτῳ" is not clear; what is clear is that it does not refer to a set of books of Scripture.[7] Thus, the term and discussion of it are absent from the Hebrew and Greek Bibles, suggesting that the term is post-biblical. If the canon as such had been an important concept or reality in Judaism or nascent Christianity, one would expect that authors would discuss or at least mention it. Though that is admittedly an argument from silence, that silence is possibly significant. A further indication that the term is a post-biblical phenomenon is that it does not occur as an entry in *The Dictionary of Biblical Theology* nor in any meaningful way in the theologies of Walther Eichrodt and Gerhard von Rad.[8]

B. The Canon for Different Faith Communities

Clearly the contents of what is considered the canon are different for different faith communities. But the concept of canon is the same for each. Jews, Catholics, Protestants, and others will list differing numbers of books as their canon, but definition of "the canon of Scripture" remains the same for all (see II.A below).

C. Mentalities

Some of the confusion generated in discussions of the canon arises from the different mentalities or approaches of those addressing the topic. It would seem that the proper stance of one using this book would be that of *the (religious) historian.* That is, one looks at the realities in antiquity as neutrally as possible and describes them as accurately as

[5] Beyer, "κανών," 596–602.

[6] Beyer, "κανών," 598, 600.

[7] That is, unless one could successfully prove—which seems unlikely—both that Paul was referring to his full letter to the Galatians and that he was convinced at the time that his letter was Scripture.

[8] Xavier Léon-Dufour, ed., *Dictionary of Biblical Theology* (trans. P. Joseph Cahill et al.; 2d ed.: New York: Seabury, 1973). Walther Eichrodt has two brief, vague mentions of canon in *Theology of the Old Testament* (trans. J. A. Baker; 2 vols.; Philadelphia: Westminster, 1961, 1967), 2:66, 348. Gerhard von Rad, speaking almost at the end of his second volume of *Old Testament Theology* (trans. D. M. G. Stalker; 2 vols.; New York: Harper & Row, 1962, 1965) about the written publication of Deuteronomy at the time of Josiah, does have the single sentence: "Thus the process of forming a canon began" (2:395). He has another mention of "canonical saving history"; it refers, however, not to the biblical canon but to a tradition used by Ezekiel that ends with the conquest, though it "was apparently not that of any of the source documents which form our Hexateuch" (2:227–28).

possible and with terminology appropriate for the period being described. A contrasting mentality would be that of *the apologist*, who seeks to speak to a modern congregation and thus starts with modern conceptions, categories, views, and conclusions (whether specific to one denomination or not) and explains the evidence from antiquity in light of those views. The stronger this mentality, the more one is tempted to find today's beliefs planted as far back as possible in yesterday's evidence.[9] Yet another mentality is that of *the neophyte or generalist* who comes to the topic without the disciplined training in philosophy or theology required to enter the discussion with sufficient clarity. Though each of these mentalities is justified, I suggest that the discussion here should proceed using the historian's approach, trying to see what antiquity holds, without affirming more than is actually there or minimizing what is there, and describing all in terminology that is accurate and appropriate for the period (see Ch. 2).

D. Historical Shifts

All would agree that at some distant point in the past there was no canon of Scripture and that eventually a canon came to be in the Jewish and Christian communities. Along that trajectory, a number of concomitant developments were taking place, some of which exercised a degree of influence on the canonical process. The following shifts entail important influences on the canon of the Hebrew Bible, but analogous shifts can be highlighted for the canon of the New Testament.

First, there was a shift from the national literature of Israel to the sacred Scripture of Judaism. Just as the Homeric poems had religious significance but were principally seen as national epics, so too the Yahwist's narrative originally would likely have been perceived more as a national epic than as "Scripture." Similarly, an early prophetic booklet would perhaps have been seen as a work which *contained some elements* of revelation, but not as a *revealed book*. The Psalms, probably until quite late, were understood as human hymns to God, and only in the late Second Temple period were they seen as inspired words of God to humanity.[10] In the same way, the collection of Proverbs, starting with chapter 10, would have been seen as precisely a collection of proverbs, until the more theological chapters 1–9 were prefixed to it. Thus, just because the name of a book is mentioned in an ancient source, that does not necessarily mean it was in its final "biblical" edition or that it was even considered a book of Scripture.

Second, after 70 C.E. there was a shift from a Temple-based religion to a text-based religion in Judaism. This shift undoubtedly placed more importance and scrutiny on the Scriptures than had formerly been the case. A reconsideration of the status of the Law and the Prophets and the other ancestral books was undoubtedly required, as well as more highly nuanced reflection and debate about which books would, and which books would not, have been accorded supreme authority.

---

9 For a similar critique of this mentality see Andrew E. Steinmann, *The Oracles of God: The Old Testament Canon* (St. Louis: Concordia Academic Press, 1999), 183.

10 This is explicitly said in 11QPs^a col. 27 line 11, where the text states that David composed all the Psalms through prophecy given to him from the Most High: כול אלה דבר בנבואה אשר נתן לו מלפני העליון. See also 1 Chr 25:1, where "David and the officers of the army also set apart for the service the sons of Asaph, and of Heman, and of Jeduthun, who should prophesy [הנבאים] with lyres, harps, and cymbals."

Third, there was a dramatic shift from the fluidity, pluriformity, and creativeness in composition of the text of the books of Scripture to a "frozen" (not "standardized") single textual form for each book.[11] It is quite likely the case that some books which eventually came to be viewed as Scripture became so only in—and due to the theological thrust of—a late, revised form or edition. An example might be the Book of Esther, insofar as 9:18-32 was added to that book of "historical fiction" as the basis for the celebration of Purim.[12]

Fourth, there was a gradual shift from viewing revelation as dynamic and on-going to viewing it as verbal and recorded from the distant past.[13] This is related (but not necessarily closely related) to the eventual conviction in Judaism that prophecy had ceased sometime in the Second Temple period.

Fifth, the format of the books of the Scriptures shifted from individual scrolls usually containing one or two books to the codex which could contain many books. This shift may have had important ramifications on decisions regarding which books were recognized as belonging to the collection of Scripture or not, inasmuch as it involved a shift from the *mental notion* of what could be termed the table of contents of the Scriptures to a *physical object* which now contained those books included in that table of contents and no others. Critical discussions of whether a book was officially or widely recognized as sacred Scripture were more likely to arise when dealing with a single collection placed between a front and back cover than when dealing with separate scrolls.

II. The Definition of Canon

How has the term been used in the past, how is it used today, and how is it to be used in the future? In this age of the computer, the internet, and rapidly developing communications systems, the imaginative redesignation and use of old words for new realities is common, colorful, and often helpful within those worlds. But in a discussion that deals with ideas and realities which have a history reaching back two millennia and hopefully continuing into the distant future—a discussion that includes writers from antiquity, thinkers from the Middle Ages, and theologians from the Enlightenment to the present and beyond, using many different languages and systems of thought—it is imperative that terminology be understood and employed properly. Haphazard, or convenient, or ideological, or religiously defensive redesignation of terms is sure to bring confusion and muddy the argument—and this is indeed what has happened in the area of canon.

The discussion must proceed along several lines, dictated by (A) guidance from dictionaries; (B) distinctions between the concept of canon and concepts or realities that are closely associated with it but are not identical with it; (C) essential elements of the concept of canon; and (D) some ways that tend to cause confusion in discussions of canon.

---

[11] See pp. 10, 212, 249, and 267, and Ulrich, *Scrolls and Origins*, 12.

[12] See *The Access Bible* (ed. Gail R. O'Day and David Peterson; New York: Oxford University Press, 1999), "Old Testament," 624.

[13] See James A. Sanders, "The Issue of Closure in the Canonical Process," in *The Canon Debate*, 252–63, esp. 257.

A. Guidance from Dictionaries

It will be helpful to begin with the more general definitions of the word in broader areas. In general English usage, the relevant meanings of the word are rather close to the two used in theological discussion and in fact are probably derived from the theological uses: (1) a law, principle, body of law, or set of standards, enacted or endorsed by a competent authority, "accepted as axiomatic and universally binding"; and (2) an officially recognized set of books; "any comprehensive list of books within a field"; "the works of an author which have been accepted as authentic."[14] The *Encyclopaedia Britannica* concurs with these two principal meanings:

> The general applications of the word fall mainly into two groups. . . , rule [and] . . . list or catalogue, *i.e.*, of books containing the rule. Of the first . . . the principal example is of the sum of the laws regulating the ecclesiastical body (see Canon Law). In the second group [is] . . . that of the authoritative body of Scriptures. . . .[15]

It is enlightening to note that the general dictionaries prominently mention the two uses of the term canon when applied to the Scriptures. In his discussion of the topic for world religions, Gerald Sheppard notes that the current uses of the term entail the same two aspects, with the Jewish and Christian Scriptures establishing the patterns of usage for world religions in general.[16] He clearly differentiates "Canon 1" and "Canon 2" to denote the two aspects.

Theological dictionaries — Jewish, Catholic, and Protestant in English, French, German, and Spanish—provide yet more clarity for the definition:

1. "Canon of Scripture: A technical term in theology designating the collection of inspired books that composes Holy Scripture and forms the rule of faith."[17]

2. "The Greek word *kanōn* means both 'rule' and 'list,' and in the second capacity came to be used by the church at a rather late date . . . to designate those Scriptural books which were regarded as inspired. The Protestant canon and the Roman Catholic New Testament canon are identical, but Protestants follow the Old Testament canon of the Hebrew Bible. . . ."[18]

3. "The process by which the various books in the Bible were brought together and their value as sacred Scripture recognized is referred to as the history of the canon. . . . While the OT canon had been formally closed . . . . The rise of heresy . . . was a powerful impulse towards the formation of a definite canon. A sifting process began in which valid Scripture distinguished itself from Christian literature in general on the basis of such criteria. . . . The canon was ultimately certified at the Council of Carthage (397)."[19]

---

[14] *The Random House Dictionary of the English Language* (ed. Jess Stein; New York: Random House, 1969), 217.

[15] *The Encyclopaedia Britannica: A Dictionary of Arts, Sciences, Literature and General Information* (11th ed.; 29 vols.; Cambridge: Cambridge University Press, 1910), 5:190.

[16] Sheppard, "Canon," 3:62–63.

[17] Karl Rahner and Herbert Vorgrimler, *Theological Dictionary* (ed. Cornelius Ernst; trans. Richard Strachan; New York: Herder and Herder, 1965), 65.

[18] *The Westminster Dictionary of Church History* (ed. Jerald C. Brauer; Philadelphia: Westminster, 1971), 156.

[19] *Baker's Dictionary of Theology* (ed. Everett F. Harrison; Grand Rapids, Mich.: Baker, 1960), 94–95.

4. "The term [canon] as applied to the Bible designates specifically the closed nature of the corpus of sacred literature accepted as authoritative because it is believed to be divinely inspired.... In the second century, κανών had come to be used in Christian circles in the sense of "rule of faith." It was the church Fathers of the fourth century C.E. who first applied "canon" to the sacred Scriptures. No exact equivalent of this term is to be found in Jewish sources although the phrase Sefarim Ḥiẓonim ("external books": Sanh. 10:1), that is, noncanonical, is certainly its negative formulation.... The idea enshrined in the "canon" is distinctively and characteristically Jewish.... In short, the development of the canon proved to be a revolutionary step in the history of religion, and the concept was consciously adopted by Christianity and Islam."[20]

5. "Canon ... [is a] term that came to be applied to the list of books that were considered a part of authoritative Scripture. The fixing of the canon of the Hebrew Bible was a long process about which we know little ... it is clear that certain books not in the present list were accepted by some communities; also, some in the present canon were evidently not universally accepted."[21]

6. "The term *canon* ... was first used by the fourth-century Church fathers in reference to the definitive, authoritative nature of the body of sacred Scripture. Both Jews and Christians needed to define, out of the available literature, what should be regarded as divinely inspired and hence authoritative and worthy of preservation; the process was one of rejection rather than selection, a weeding out from among books commonly regarded as sacred.[22]

7. "Canon: En grec: règle. (1) Toute décision solennelle.... (2) Nom donné ... à la grande prière de la messe.... (3) Liste des ouvrages qui font partie du catalogue des livres sacrés, et sont reconnus comme d'inspiration divine et donc canoniques: «canon des Écritures»."[23]

8. "At.licher Kanon ... Vorstufen: Lange bevor die Schriften des AT ... kanonisch wurden..., beanspruchten und erhielten viele ihrer Bestandteile eine Geltung, die der Kanonizität schon verwandt war und den Weg zu ihr hin nachträglich als logisch erscheinen läßt.

"Es ist das Besondere der nt.lichen Kanonbildung, daß die Alte Kirche hist. unter deutlicher Beachtung apostolischer Verfasserschaft der Schriften den Kanon abschloß und begrenzte, [und] daß sie ... in der Korrelation von Norm und Schrift herausstellte.... Die Kanonbildung selbst ist somit nur aus der Geschichte des Urchristentums, aus ihrem Weg in die Alte Kirche und aus den sie bestimmenden Motiven erklärbar."[24]

---

20 *Encyclopaedia Judaica* (Jerusalem: Encyclopaedia Judaica Jerusalem/Macmillan, 1971), 4:817–18.

21 *Dictionary of Judaism in the Biblical Period: 450 B.C.E. to 600 C.E.* (ed. J. Neusner and W. S. Green; New York: Simon & Schuster Macmillan, 1996), 1:112.

22 Norman Solomon, *Historical Dictionary of Judaism* (Lanham, M.D., & London: Scarecrow, 1998), 79.

23 Paul Christophe, *Vocabulaire historique de culture chrétienne* (Paris: Desclée, 1991), 52: "Canon: In Greek: rule. (1) Every solemn decision.... (2) Name given ... to the great prayer of the Mass.... (3) List of works which constitute part of the catalogue of sacred books and are recognized as of divine inspiration and thus canonical: "canon of Scriptures."

24 Rudolf Smend and Otto Merk, "Bibelkanon," *Evangelisches Kirchenlexikon: Internationale theologische Enzyklopädie* (ed. Erwin Fahlbusch et al.; 5 vols.; Göttingen: Vandenhoeck & Ruprecht, 1986–97), 1:468–74: "Old Testament canon ... Preliminary Stages: Long before the writings of the OT ...

9. "Los griegos usan el vocablo *Canon* como sinónimo de *registro* o *catálogo*; y en este sentido lo oímos de los Libros de la Escritura. . . . no es canónico, si está fuera del catálogo. El *Canon Bíblico* es el catálogo de libros inspirados y reconocidos como inspirados."[25]

The sources above are unanimous in their general definition of canon, each including many of the essential aspects, although all do not include all of the aspects important for the complete definition. It is not surprising that all were not attentive to all aspects, since usually there has not been such an acute need to clarify the definition so comprehensively. It should be noticed, however, that, though aspects may be missing, there is no hint of disagreement. From them we learn that:

- canon is a technical term (1; 4?)
- the term is late and Christian (2, 4, 6; 8?), though the idea is Jewish (4)
- it means both "rule" and "list" (1, 2, 4, 8, 9)
- "list" predominates in the discussions (2, 4, 5, 6, 7, 9; 3?, 8?)
- the list involves books (1, 2, 3, 5, 6, 7, 9), not their textual form (not explicit)
- the list is closed or delimited (3, 4, 5, 6, 7, 8, 9; 2?)
- there was a lengthy process whose end was the canon (3, 5, 8; 4?)
- the closed list is the result of a reflexive judgment or series of reflexive judgments, i.e., the books have been recognized and accepted through sifting or debate according to criteria (3, 4, 5, 6, 7, 8, 9)
- the books were authoritative (4, 6) because (4) inspired (2, 4, 6, 7, 9)
- the list of books was accepted or certified by a group or community (6, 8; 3?, 5?)

Thus, when used in biblical or theological discourse among Jews and Christians, the "canon of Scripture" is a technical term with a long-since established meaning in the history of theology. It properly denotes one of two principal meanings:

The canon of Scripture	The canon of Scripture
i.e., the canon which Scripture constitutes	i.e., the canon which constitutes Scripture
the *rule* of faith articulated by the Scriptures	the *list* of books accepted as inspired Scripture
= *norma normans*, the rule that determines faith	= *norma normata*, the list that has been determined
the authoritative principles and guiding spirit	the authoritative list of books
which govern belief and practice.	which have been accepted as Scripture.

Though the adjective "canonical" is used legitimately in both senses, the noun "canon" (meaning the "canon of Scripture") is predominantly used in the second sense,

became canonical. . . , many of their constituent parts laid claim to and received a recognition that was already related to canonicity and that made the path toward [canonization] subsequently appear as logical.

"It is the characteristic of NT canon formation that the early Church historically closed and delimited the canon under the clear consideration of apostolic authorship of the writings, [and] that it . . . presented them in the correlation of rule and writing. . . . The canon formation itself is accordingly explainable only from the history of early Christianity, from its process through the early Church, and from the motives that determined it."

[25] Ricardo Rabanos, *Propedeutica biblica: introducción general a la sagrada escritura* (Madrid: Editorial la Milagrosa, 1960), 110: "The Greeks use the word canon as synonymous with 'register' or 'catalogue'; and in this sense we hear it of the books of Scripture. . . . it is not canonical if it is outside the catalogue. The biblical canon is the catalogue of books that are inspired and recognized as inspired."

less in the first.[26] When the first meaning is being used, thought is seldom given to the distinction between books that are widely accepted as officially recognized Scripture and books that are not; usually the former is simply vaguely assumed. Most religious groups and individuals are seldom influenced by the full range of canonical books while totally excluding noncanonical books, but are guided by a particular part of the canon (a canon-within-a-canon). That is because there are conflicting theologies within the canon, and the discussion usually has a specific focus and therefore envisions a particular thrust or theme within the canonical literature. Thus, the canon as rule of faith is used in theological discussion, but most frequently—especially in relation to the discovery of the scrolls—it is the second sense, the official corpus of books accepted as Scripture, that is intended.

In such cases, the proper meaning of canon is the definitive list of inspired, authoritative books which constitute the recognized and accepted body of sacred Scripture of a major religious group, that definitive list being the result of inclusive and exclusive decisions after serious deliberation.

In light of the definition given above, it is now encouraging to note that *The Access Bible* (1999) offers the following: "Definition: By the *biblical canon* is meant the official list of the books which make up the Scriptures of the Old and New Testaments. Books which appear on this list are called *canonical* and all other books *non-canonical*."[27] Contributors to *The Access Bible* include Protestants, Catholics, and Jews; though it is unknown whether all were consulted on that particular definition and endorsed it, agreement on the concept's definition (if not on the contents) would be plausible in light of the definitions collected from dictionaries and encyclopedias from each tradition.

B. Distinctions Between the Canon and Related Concepts

It is essential to distinguish between a number of terms or realities that are closely associated with, but are not identical with, the concept of canon: an authoritative work, a book of Scripture, the textual form of a book of Scripture, the canonical process, a collection of authoritative Scriptures, and the Bible.

- An *authoritative* work is a composition which a group, secular or religious, recognizes and accepts as determinative for its conduct, and as of a higher order than can

---

[26] The phrase "canonical text," however, is usually used inappropriately; it is often a collapsed way of saying the text of a book that is canonical or the contents of a canonical book. But the phrase should not be used to designate the textual form of a book, because it is not the textual form but the book—regardless of textual form—that is canonical in antiquity (see II.C.1 below). Later, in the case of those whose religious belief includes the canonical status, not only of the books of the canon, but also the wording as in the MT, the MT can be spoken of as "the canonical text"; but does this then imply that readings from other textual traditions should not be used to correct the MT? It would also seem that this is a religious conviction that crystallized after "the Great Divide"—textually (in Talmon's sense, Ch. 2 n. 3), but also religiously. That is, Christianity had already appropriated its Jewish Scriptures, which were neither closed as a collection nor uniform in textual editions, before the Masoretic form of each book became the sole Hebrew form (other than the SP) that survived.

[27] "The Nature of the Biblical Canon," in *The Access Bible*, 26 (and similarly in the "Glossary," 424; emphasis in the original).

be overridden by the power or will of the group or any member. A constitution or law code would be an example.

• A book of *Scripture* is a sacred authoritative work believed to have God as its ultimate author, which the community, as a group and individually, recognizes and accepts as determinative for its belief and practice for all time and in all geographical areas.

• The *textual form* of most books of Scripture was pluriform in antiquity. A book may have been widely and definitively considered Scripture, but it may have been circulating in several textual forms and may have been still developing. It is the book, and not the textual form of the book, that is canonical (see below).

• The *canonical process* is the journey of the many disparate works of literature within the ongoing community of Israel (including eventually both rabbinic Judaism and Christianity, each claiming to be the true Israel) from the early stages when they began to be considered as somehow authoritative for the broader community, through the collection and endorsement process, to the final judgment concerning their inspired character as the unified and defined collection of Scripture—that is, until the judgment of recognition that constituted the canon. The canonical process would not seem to reach back as far as the earliest sources (national religious epic, liturgical and priestly texts, folk wisdom) when they were simply literature and were not yet perceived as authoritative. Canon as such is a static concept, the result of a retrospective conclusion that something has come to be. If the focus is on the collection of books while a historical, developmental trajectory is envisioned or is still in process, then the proper term is "process toward canon" or "canonical process."

• *A collection of authoritative Scriptures* was certainly in existence and taken to be fundamental to the Jewish religion by at least the middle of the Second Temple period. But it is necessary to keep in mind Bruce Metzger's distinction between "a collection of authoritative books" and "an authoritative collection of books."[28] One can designate the growing collection of authoritative books as "canonical" in the first sense of rule, but there is not yet a canon in the second sense of an authoritative list.

• The *Bible*, in the singular, denotes a textual form of the collection of canonical books. Whereas the canon is the normative list of the books, the Bible is the text of that fixed collection of books, conceived of as a single anthology, and usually presented as such. In a sense, the term may seem anachronistic until the format of the collection of scriptural books was the codex (third century C.E.?). "The Scriptures" may be an open collection, but the "Bible" would seem to indicate an already closed collection.

C. Essential Elements in the Concept of Canon

Johann Eichhorn once said that "it would have been desirable if one had never even used the term canon,"[29] but the concept is rich and important, and perhaps it would be better to say that it would be desirable if everyone used the term properly. In fact, many major scholars of the latter twentieth century transmitted discussions concerning the correct

[28] Metzger, *The Canon*, 283.

[29] Johann G. Eichhorn, *Einleitung in das Alte Testament* (5 vols.; 4th ed.; Leipzig, 1820–1824), 1:106, translation cited from Brevard S. Childs, *Introduction to the Old Testament as Scripture* (Philadelphia: Fortress, 1979), 36.

usage. Here I can cite only a few examples for illustration. James Barr maintained that the canon is a later concept and term, and that it is a technical term requiring precise definition and precise usage.[30] Bruce Metzger was strong on the reflexive nature of the decisions regarding canon, pointing out that the process by which the canon was formed "was a task, not only of collecting, but also of sifting and rejecting."[31] Similarly, Julio Trebolle Barrera noted that use of "the Greek term 'canon' comes from New Testament studies . . . [and] belongs to a very late period in the history of the formation of the NT canon . . . [and that in the biblical period to] apply the term 'canon' to the Hebrew Bible, therefore, is quite unsuitable."[32] Sid Leiman provided a definition of a canonical book as "a book accepted by Jews as authoritative for religious practice and/or doctrine, and whose authority is binding upon the Jewish people for all generations. Furthermore, such books are to be studied and expounded in private and in public."[33] It is understandable that not every definition and discussion in the past has explicitly mentioned every essential aspect of the definition of canon. But it is important to note that definitions given above all agree with each other in their explicit elements and show no sign of disagreement due to the elements missing or implicit.

Eichhorn notwithstanding, and in light of the related but distinct terms listed in section B above, there is a need for a definition of "the canon of Scripture." There was and is a need for a term that denotes the final, fixed, and closed list of the books of Scripture that are officially and permanently accepted as supremely authoritative by a faith tradition, in conscious contradistinction from those books that are not accepted. From the fourth century, "canon" is the term employed to denote that list. All the elements of that definition must be present, or the term will be used in a way that may cause confusion.

There are three elements in the definition of canon that perhaps need more discussion due to the new situation occasioned by the discovery of the biblical Dead Sea Scrolls and recent discussions with varying understandings of canon. First, the canon involves books, not the textual form of the books; secondly, it requires reflexive judgment; and thirdly, it denotes a closed list.[34]

1. The book, not its textual form

Prior to the discovery of the scrolls, there was an assumption that the text of the Hebrew Bible was simply more or less equated with the Masoretic Text. The Samaritan Pentateuch and the Septuagint were generally delegated to the sidelines and used primarily to

---

[30] James Barr, *Holy Scripture: Canon, Authority, Criticism* (Philadelphia: Westminster, 1983), 50.

[31] Metzger, *The Canon*, 7. Note Athanasius' directive (cited in Metzger, 212): "Let no one add to these; let nothing be taken away from them."

[32] Julio Trebolle Barrera, *The Jewish Bible and the Christian Bible* (trans. Wilfred G. E. Watson; Leiden: Brill; Grand Rapids, Mich.: Eerdmans, 1998), 148.

[33] Sid Z. Leiman, *The Canonization of Hebrew Scripture: The Talmudic and Midrashic Evidence* (Hamden, Conn.: Archon Books, 1976), 14.

[34] I hasten to say that the evidence from Qumran did not add these aspects to the concept of canon; it merely brings the traditional aspects into sharper view. In fact, a principal thesis of this chapter is that the definition of canon is an ancient and stable technical term that does not and should not change from time to time.

"fix" the MT when there was a problem; the Targums and Peshitta also added overwhelming witness to the form of the text as in the MT. But the scrolls have illuminated an unsuspected stage in the history of the biblical text: a period in which the text of the books of Scripture was pluriform and still creatively developing, prior to the period of a single text for each book.[35] The composition and compilation of each book was a lengthy, diachronic development, from its earliest sources up through its latest literary editions. The process usually involved more than one major author (cf. J, E, D, P for the Pentateuch; the Deuteronomists and their sources for Deuteronomy to Kings; First, Second, and Third Isaiah; the many composers of Psalms and Proverbs; and so forth) in addition to a series of minor authors, redactors, and contributing scribes. Qumran demonstrates that the textual form of most books was still in that state of creative development until at least 70 C.E. and possibly as late as 132.

Now, when considering the books of Scripture in the period of the late Second Temple and the origins of Christianity and rabbinic Judaism, we must distinguish between the book or literary opus and the particular wording or literary edition of that opus which may still have been in the stage of creative development. It was the book, that is, the scroll, not its particular wording or literary edition, which made the hands unclean (i.e., scriptural) according to the Rabbis: "All the Holy Scriptures render the hands unclean."[36] Likewise for Christian theologians:

> Eusebius and Jerome, well aware of such variation in the witnesses, discussed which form of text was to be preferred. It is noteworthy, however, that neither Father suggested that one form was canonical and the other was not. Furthermore, the perception that the canon was basically closed did not lead to a slavish fixing of the text of the canonical books.
>
> Thus, the category of "canonical" appears to have been broad enough to include all variant readings (as well as variant renderings in early versions). . . .
>
> In short, it appears that the question of canonicity pertains to the document *qua* document, and not to one particular form or version of that document.[37]

2. *Reflexive judgment*

The fact of canon represents a conscious, retrospective, official judgment; it confirms that what has gradually come to be will now and must forever be. In philosophical terms this is called a reflexive judgment. It examines what has become the case and ratifies it. It looks back over a process and consciously affirms it as now a static, enduring situation. In this case, it considers the experienced fact that certain books have been functioning as authoritative for the faith community, weighs the situation, recognizes that the necessary

---

[35] The latter period is often labelled the period of "stabilization"; but this seems to be a misnomer, since no evidence surfaces that the Rabbis critically examined the various text forms in circulation and consciously selected a single text for each book. They rather appear simply to have continued to use one of the several editions available for each book. They apparently deliberately chose the Jewish ("square") script against the Palaeo-Hebrew script used by the Samaritans, and they deliberately chose the Hebrew language against the Greek texts increasingly used by the Christian Jews. But it is difficult to find evidence that they systematically compared and selected from among the editions of a book or "stabilized" the text. Insofar as this is accurate, the text was more "frozen" in its development than "stabilized"; though "single form" or "uniform" may be a more neutral term for the resultant texts.

[36] *M. Yad.* 3:5; see also 4:6.

[37] Metzger, *The Canon*, 269–70.

criteria have been met, explicitly accepts and affirms the reality, and decides that this will ever be so:

> Thus, for a long while the community handed down sacred writings that increasingly functioned as authoritative books, but it was not until questions were raised and communal or official agreements made that there existed what we properly call a canon. The simple practice of living with the conviction that certain books are binding for our community is a matter of authoritativeness. The reflexive judgment when a group formally decides that it is a constituent requirement that these books which have been exercising authority are henceforth binding is a judgment concerning canon.[38]

3. Closed list

An essential part of the process toward the canon was the judging and sifting to determine which books were supremely authoritative and which were not. As long as the list was open, there was a collection of authoritative books, a collection of Scriptures, but there was not yet an authoritative collection of books, a canon. We have noted Metzger's insistence, echoing Athanasius, that the process by which the canon was formed "was a task, not only of collecting, but also of sifting and rejecting."[39]

Thus, the requirement of reflexive judgment and an exclusively closed list of books (prescinding from the textual form of the books) are essential elements in the concept of canon. As long as either of those elements is missing, the community indeed has a collection of authoritative books of Scripture, but it does not yet have a canon.

D. Sources of Confusion in Discussions of Canon

One of the most learned and sophisticated books on canon to appear recently is John Barton's *Holy Writings, Sacred Text.* One of the few moments in which I would disagree with him is when he says, "Modern scholars are of course perfectly entitled to use these terms as they wish. . . ." But he immediately exculpates himself when he continues: "but [they] need to recognize the danger of building the conclusions into the premises if they want to use them in discriminating among different historical reconstructions."[40] In fact, his statement results in part from the "sterility of the resulting discussion . . . [g]iven their diverse definitions of 'canon.'"[41]

I would like to make two points. Barton may agree with the first for purely utilitarian reasons, and he would doubtless agree with the second, since I owe the idea to him. First, for future discussion to be useful and to escape from the confusion that now muddies the water, it is imperative to reach consensus on the definition of canon.[42] If the definition

---

38 Ulrich, *Scrolls and Origins*, 57.

39 Metzger, *The Canon*, 7.

40 John Barton, *Holy Writingts, Sacred Text: The Canon in Early Christianity* (Louisville: Westminster John Knox, 1997), 15. The book was originally published as *Spirit and the Letter* (London: SPCK, 1997). See now also Timothy H. Lim's recently published *The Formation of the Jewish Canon* (New Haven: Yale University Press, 2013).

41 Barton, *Holy Writings*, 14.

42 Barton in fact later states that a "lack of agreement about the use of terms bedevils many areas of study. . . ." He defends Sundberg's distinction "between the 'Scripture' which results from the growth of writings perceived as holy, and the 'canon' which represents official decisions to exclude from Scripture

I have presented above is inaccurate or inadequate, appropriate revisions should be made and agreed upon, but continuing confusion has little to recommend itself.

Second, the definition of the canon is a relatively minor matter. Much more important, interesting, and ripe for analysis is the canonical process — the historical development by which the oral and written literature of Israel, Judaism, and the early Church was handed on, revised, and transformed into the Scriptures that we have received, as well as the processes and criteria by which the various decisions were made. *Prophecy and Canon* by Joseph Blenkinsopp constitutes an excellent and promising bellwether in this direction which, unfortunately, few have followed.[43] Barton also has as one of his aims "to open up the question what people did with the 'canon' in the ancient world, and what kinds of meaning they looked for in it."[44]

With regard to the first point, namely, the confusion that results from lack of agreement about definition, there is scope here for only a few reflections.

First, the canon of Scripture, in the sense that that term has been used in the history of Christian theology and within Judaism after it borrowed the term from Christian usage, is the definitive, closed list of the books that constitute the authentic contents of Scripture. It should not be confused either with stages in the canonical process or with single books that are canonical, because books can be, and were, canonical (in Sheppard's sense of Canon 1: i.e., rule) long before there was a canon of Scripture. Although Lee McDonald is correct in general, he indicates a path that can lead toward confusion when he says: "In a very real sense, Israel had a canon when the tradition of Moses receiving the Torah on Sinai was accepted into the community. Whatever functioned in the community of Israel as an authoritative guide was 'canon' in the sense of Sheppard's 'Canon 1.'"[45] That statement is true, but is it helpful for discussions of the canon of the Scriptures? Is the noun "canon" properly used in that sense? Is the term still meaningful when it denotes only a basic authoritative guide toward doing good? Did not Adam and Eve have a canon in this sense when God said "... but of the tree of the knowledge of good and evil you shall not eat" (Gen 2:17)? Neither consistently in antiquity, nor through the history of theological discourse, nor normally today is there use of the noun canon in the sense of Canon 1 (rule). Scripture certainly functioned as authoritative guide, but seldom was it referred to as "a/the canon" in that sense. McDonald himself indicates this when he more prominently says: "Canon, in the general sense that we intend here, denotes a fixed standard or collection of writings that defines the faith and identity of a particular religious community."[46]

Second, if the canon is by definition a closed list of books that have been considered, debated, sifted, and accepted, then talk of an open canon is confusing and counterproductive; it seems more appropriate to speak of a growing collection of books

---

works deemed unsuitable. In my view this distinction can greatly clarify our thinking about both the Old and the New Testament" (157–58).

[43] Joseph Blenkinsopp, *Prophecy and Canon: A Contribution to the Study of Jewish Origins* (Notre Dame, Ind.: University of Notre Dame Press, 1977).

[44] Barton, *Holy Writings*, 159.

[45] Lee M. McDonald, *The Formation of the Christian Biblical Canon* (rev. and expanded ed.; Peabody, Mass.: Hendrickson, 1995), 20.

[46] McDonald, *The Formation*, 13.

considered as sacred Scripture. Andrew Steinmann's *The Oracles of God*, in the midst of many valid and helpful points, asserts that "The canon may be open. . . . The canon may be closed."[47] But this can only perpetuate the confusion in terminology. Steinmann considers the canon "the collection of holy, inspired, authoritative books in the Temple. The canon could be *assumed* to be known and acknowledged by most Jews because of this normative archive."[48] The problem here, however, is that there is no way of knowing which books were normative in that archive beyond the Law and the Prophets, or even knowing which books were included among the Prophets. It would seem likely that there were more books beyond those that eventually formed the Masoretic collection, and unlikely that the *only* books preserved by the Jerusalem priests were those that eventually formed the Masoretic collection. Would it not have been more likely that the priests had Ben Sira and Jubilees and 1 Enoch (if only as sources to confute) than that they had the Song of Songs? Would there have been a clear and agreed-upon understanding of which books were, and which were not "Sacred Scripture"? Steinmann is focusing on the collection of authoritative Scriptures during the canonical process; they were canonical (in the sense of Canon 1), but there was no canon of the Scriptures yet (Canon 2) while the Second Temple stood.

Finally, mere mention of the name of a book or even of a collection of books is occasionally equated with its canonical status, that is, with wide-spread acceptance of that book as Scripture or of that collection as the canon of the Scriptures as we know them.[49] Such maximalist claims must inevitably yield to later, more balanced assessments. Just as it is corrective to reflect that the books of the NT were not in circulation at the time of Jesus and the first Christians, it is corrective to reflect that the books of the Law and the Prophets were not circulating in the form that we know them at the time of Ezra. The books that came to be the Bible did not start off as books of the Bible. For many passages that now constitute those books, their authors did not think that they were writing Scripture. Other than for the book of Daniel, the letters of Paul, and the Gospels, there was usually a lengthy period between the composition of a book and its general acceptance as a book of Scripture.

Thus, with Plato, I urge that we formulate and agree upon a precise definition of the canon of Scripture for the sake of clarity, consistency, and constructive dialogue. If the definition proposed above is inaccurate or insufficient, revisions in harmony with the history of theological discourse will be welcome.

---

47 Steinmann, *Oracles of God*, 19.

48 Steinmann, *Oracles of God*, 185; emphasis in the original.

49 An example would be the interpretation of Luke 24:44 ("the Law of Moses and the Prophets and Psalms") as: "This saying suggests that 'the Law of Moses', 'the Prophets' and '(the) Psalms' are now established names for the three parts of the canon"; see Roger Beckwith, *The Old Testament Canon of the New Testament Church* (Grand Rapids: Eerdmans, 1985), 111. The book is rich in data but tends toward maximalist interpretation; see further the review of Beckwith by Albert C. Sundberg, Jr., "Reexamining the Formation of the Old Testament Canon," *Int* 42 (1988): 78–82, and Andrew Steinmann's critique in *Oracles of God*, 71 n. 113.

CHAPTER 18

FROM LITERATURE TO SCRIPTURE: REFLECTIONS ON THE GROWTH OF A TEXT'S AUTHORITATIVENESS

RIBALD PLAYS FROM BROADWAY are not to be advocated generally as one's primary source for theological insight, but *Beyond the Fringe* may clearly establish the point from which this chapter begins. Alan Bennett delivers a quasi-sermon on one verse from Genesis:

> *But my brother Esau is an hairy man, but I am a smooth man (Gen 27:11)*

which is "paraphrased" by another "from the grand old prophet, Nehemiah":

> *And he said unto me, what seest thou*
> *And I said unto him, lo*
> *I see the children of Bebai,*
> *Numbering six hundred and seventy-three,*
> *And I see the children of Asgad*
> *Numbering one thousand, four hundred and seventy-four (Neh 7:16).*[1]

The reader should be warned that the words which followed were aimed rather at frivolous ears than pious, and that the maximum to be gained from that sermon is therapeutic chuckles, not exegetical insight or spiritual nourishment. A primary source for this humor, of course, is in calling attention to the nature of these specific sentences as, of all things, verses of Holy Scripture. By what process, in fact, did they become Scripture?

In this play a text classified as Sacred Scripture becomes part of a text of (merely) literature. This is not at all uncommon, inasmuch as Scripture is frequently quoted in numerous types of works: most obviously commentaries on Scripture but also religious works seeking authoritative support for ideas or claims, as well as nonreligious works simply quoting scriptural texts as part of the cultural heritage.

In contrast, the present chapter attempts to study the transformation involved when a text properly labeled as (merely) literature becomes acknowledged as Sacred Scripture. It tries to understand some of the factors involved in a text's acquisition of the character of authority along the road toward what will eventually become the canon.[2] Just as there was a lengthy process leading up to the final canon of Scripture, so too there was a

---

[1] Alan Bennett, Peter Cook, Jonathan Miller, and Dudley Moore, *Beyond the Fringe* (New York: Random House, 1963), 78.

[2] For the terminological distinctions regarding canon and related concepts, see Ch. 17. For neither Jews nor Christians was there a clear canon prior to the Roman destruction of the Temple in 70 C.E. This chapter mainly focuses on "the canonical process," or the process toward the canon.

lengthy process by which what we now consider "biblical literature" developed from what should properly be termed "literature" to what we properly call "Scripture." The pages that follow will explore some of the factors at work in transforming the status of a literary work from revered literature to the revealed word of God.

I. The Historical Origins of What Became Scripture

A. Our Image of "Scripture"

Most who will read this book first encountered the Bible as Sacred Scripture, each complete book of which was regarded as recorded verbal revelation. It was a primary element in a text-based religion, and the text was stable and unchangeable, part of a fixed collection in book (codex) form.

B. The Search for a Historical Image

What has long since become Sacred Scripture, however, did not have its origins as Scripture, and inquiry into its origins and its development within the history of the believing community is profitable for intelligent reflection on it. It will be helpful to analyze each of those five factors just mentioned:

- Most of what became Scripture began as small, separate, anonymous oral and written units gradually joined together to form complexes of tradition.[3]
- What became viewed as a complete verbally revealed text for each book began as separate incidents in which an individual claimed, or was understood, to be saying to the people what God wanted said to them; these incidents were editorially attached and encased in nonrevealed prose.
- The texts, later so important for a geographically dispersed faith group, did not exercise such a primary function while the Second Temple stood in Jerusalem and while its sacrificial rituals provided the primary focus of the religion.[4]
- What ended as a stable and unchangeable text for each book had for centuries been pluriform and dynamically growing, in the form of both major new editions and minor expansions or errors, through the repeated creativity of anonymous religious leaders and thinkers, priests and scribes.
- What was encountered as a well-accepted book with known contents, between two covers of a codex, excluding works that did not properly belong, had for a long time

---

[3] Helpful in illustrating the developmental growth of the collected Hebrew Bible is the approach of Otto Eissfeldt, *The Old Testament: An Introduction: The History of the Formation of the Old Testament* (trans. Peter R. Ackroyd; New York: Harper and Row, 1965).

[4] With respect to the text's importance after the loss of the Temple, notice that one of the few mentions of a book of Scripture in Maccabees—that Judas and his warriors "opened the book of the law to inquire" (1 Macc 3:48)—occurs in the context of their exclusion from the Temple. With respect to the dominant focus on ritual and the virtual silence about texts, see, e.g., the account of the cleansing and rededication of the sanctuary in 1 Macc 4:41-58. The first item mentioned is the altar of burnt offering (4:44, 47), and the emphasis throughout is on furnishings of the sanctuary, sacrifices, and celebration. The only mention of texts is in the subordinate clause "as the law directs" (4:53), in the context of describing the *sacrifice* on the new altar. See similarly the description of Aaron and Phinehas in Ben Sira 45:6-25.

been a developing, mostly undefined[5] collection of separate scrolls, valued but not much questioned as regard to relative status.

Insofar as the five views listed above are correct, our received Scriptures had their origins in numerous disparate units, mostly oral, only some of which were viewed as saying what God had revealed or wanted said. The individual books developed organically, each along its own particular trajectory as part of the general Jewish heritage of national literature, but at a level lower than that of the sacrificial rituals of the Temple-focused religion. Our later question—whether a given book was *included* in a special category as once-and-for-all "Sacred Scripture" or was *excluded* from this supreme category—was probably not a question they ever deliberately asked or even thought much about.

It is difficult to think about what we have always regarded as the Bible the way the ancients did, the way that the monarchic Israelites and the early Second Temple period Judeans viewed the literature which would develop into what is for us the Bible. Certainly, toward the end of the Second Temple period, many of the books of Scripture were viewed as God's word. As one of many examples, the Damascus Document cites Isa 24:17 with the introductory formula: ". . . as God spoke through Isaiah the prophet son of Amoz. . . ."[6] But how early was the book of Isaiah regarded as Sacred Scripture? In the monarchic era were the then-extant parts of Isaiah 1–33 viewed *in toto* as God's revelation? Were the poems in Isaiah 40–55, when first composed, viewed as Sacred Scripture? If so, according to what rationale were they supplemented by the composition of other major sections and repeated interpolations? On what basis would the pre-exilic collection of Proverbs be considered Sacred Scripture? When Job was composed, in what ways did it differ from the Greek religious tragedies, composed for the religious festivals in Athens? Both are dramatic sacred meditations searching to understand the relationships between the divine and the human. Did the "author" of Job or his contemporaries think that he was writing "Scripture"?

Certain uses of the traditional texts were what could best be described as simply literary. First Maccabees, for example, offers a number of illustrations of how the sacred traditions were used in the latter part of the Second Temple period as purely literary quotations. In 1 Macc 7:37 the temple priests allude to 1 Kgs 8:29, 43 (Solomon's prayer at the dedication of the temple) in their plea for vindication against Nicanor who had threatened to burn down the temple. Similarly 1 Macc 9:21 quotes the lament over the slain warriors, Saul and Jonathan, from 2 Sam 1:19 (πῶς ἔπεσαν δυνατοί), again not as Scripture, but as an appropriate and glorifying literary tribute to the slain Judas.

[5] Arie van der Kooij ("The Canonization of Ancient Books Kept in the Temple of Jerusalem," in *Canonization and Decanonization* [ed. Arie van der Kooij and Karel van der Toorn; Leiden: Brill, 1998], 17–40, esp. 19, 32, 38) sees a distinction which he terms "a defined, though not necessarily definitive, collection" of Scriptures in the second century B.C.E.; the distinction is not pointedly differentiated, but the "defined" aspect appears to be the tripartite nature (see pp. 32, 38) of the books kept in the Temple which "came to enjoy a more or less canonical status" (p. 36). I, however, find little evidence for a defined collection in that period and much evidence against. Moreover, if clarity be our goal, I would suggest that "authoritative" replace "canonical" in the phrase "more or less canonical status."

[6] CD 4:13–14; cf. 4Q266.

A literary addition in the MT is also highlighted by 4QpaleoExod^{m} at Exod 10:21, the plague of darkness. God commands Moses, "Stretch out your hand toward heaven so that there may be a darkness over the land of Egypt." 4QpaleoExod^{m} and one Greek manuscript end the verse there with [מצ]רים, which was probably the end of the earlier version of the text. But the tradition behind the MT, the SP, and the majority LXX has added וימש חשך ("a darkness that can be felt"; the infrequent verb משש/מוש means "to feel, touch, explore with the fingers, grope"). The added clause in the MT is quite likely a purely literary allusion to, or borrowing from, Job 12:25 ימששו חשך ("They grope in the dark"), that was added to heighten the sensation of darkness experienced by the Egyptians.[7]

It is important for thinking about the origins of Christianity and rabbinic Judaism to work toward clear understanding of the dynamics of the Scriptures in the first century C.E. and in the centuries leading up to that decisive period. One cardinal prohibition would be against the anachronistic imposition of categories such as "canon" and "Scripture" on entities that were not such and were not considered such at the time.

As a preliminary step for simplicity's sake, we can distinguish "literature" from "Scripture" according to authorship: literature is of human authorship, whereas Scripture in some sense has God as author. But this distinction does not bring the full clarity desired. The *Iliad* begins: "Sing, goddess, the wrath of Peleus' son, Achilles. . . ," and the *Odyssey*: "Sing to me, Muse, of the man. . . ." In what sense, or to what degree, is divine authorship being claimed here? Did the Greeks believe that divine inspiration was in some real sense at work, or is it a purely literary device or figure of speech[8]—such as Second Isaiah's "Get you up to a high mountain, O Zion. . ." (Isa 40:9)? And how similar or different would the Israelite authors have considered their situation? Did this ever surface, or when did this eventually surface, as a clear question? That simple distinction also clouds the possibility of intermediate categories. Writings can be considered sacred without necessarily being divinely inspired.

II. The Trajectory from Literature to Scripture

A. Sources of Authoritativeness

There are various factors that enable a work to reach the status of being considered authoritative Scripture. To begin with, it may help to use the Sinai event as a template. God personally comes down onto Mount Sinai and speaks through Moses to the people. Moses relays God's message to the people, and this is affirmed repeatedly. God (Exod 24:12) or Moses writes down the message, and this writing is read to the people, both in the original setting and repeatedly during the course of successive generations. The people collectively and individually accept the writing as having authority over them: "All that the Lord has spoken we will do, and we will be obedient" (Exod 24:7).

Expanding from this example *par excellence* of revelation, we may paint a more generalized picture. A work must normally have an explicit or implicit claim that God is

---

[7] Judith Sanderson and I jointly discovered this as we worked together on the edition of 4QpaleoExod^{m}; see Sanderson, *An Exodus Scroll*, 147–48 and DJD 9:83.

[8] Virgil, modeling the opening of the *Aeneid* on those of the *Iliad* and the *Odyssey*, seems to suppose the figurative understanding for the Homeric poems (and his own): "Of wars and a man *I* sing. . . ."

directly or indirectly the author. There may be a mediator, whether angelic (Jubilees, Daniel 7–12) or human (Ezekiel, Daniel 2; 4–5). Practically the work must be promoted by the priesthood or some other religious authority, institutional or not (e.g., in the liturgy or among prophetic groups), and the promoting group's influence must survive the historical-political-religious conflicts of the future. Finally, the authoritativeness must be recognized and accepted by a majority of the people.

Another dimension that should be noted is the incorporation of elements, passages, or even whole books which on their own may never have merited the status of "Scripture" but which had become part of (or linked with) a work that did acquire that status.[9] It is unlikely (without getting into discussions about authorial intent) that early authors viewed themselves as composing "Scripture," though this may have grown with later redactors, tradents, and scribes.

B. Factors for Individual Books

Each book or subgroup of books had its own particular trajectory toward acquiring the status of Scripture. What were the different factors that affected this development for different types of books? I will offer some suggestions, by no means claiming that the scenarios painted were exactly the forces at work then or that all the factors that played a role in the process are included here.

Genesis

How did the book of Genesis become understood as revelation to Moses? How would Moses have received knowledge about the origins of the world and the human race? One could suggest the following scenario. The received biblical account starts by simply narrating the creation of the cosmos, and neither the identity of the narrator nor the ultimate source of this knowledge is expressed. The complex of traditions in Genesis—which in its earliest stages did not include anything about the origins of the cosmos—developed along a promise-fulfillment theme, with the promise of the land and nation made in the patriarchal sagas finding its fulfillment in the gaining of the land under Joshua.

The primeval stories in Genesis 1–11 were eventually prefixed as an introduction to the patriarchal sagas. Since the books of Exodus to Deuteronomy were viewed as the Books of Moses, and eventually the books written by Moses, and since the book of Genesis had become linked as "part 1" of that story of national origins, the authorship of Genesis—including Genesis 1–11—was also attributed to Moses. Something similar to this scenario had already happened by the early second century B.C.E., since Jubilees paints the scene vividly: "The angel of the presence spoke to Moses according to the word of the LORD, saying: 'Write the complete history of the creation. . .'" (Jub 2:1).[10]

---

[9] Examples might be the opening quotations from *Beyond the Fringe*, the war stories incorporated into the book of Kings, the Samson narratives within the book of Judges, the book of Ruth because coupled with Judges, or the additional non-Masoretic compositions in the expanded Psalter that appear in 11QPs[a]. As parallels to the last, other hymns and prayers, such as Hannah's in 1 Samuel 2 and those in Ezra 9, Nehemiah 9, and Daniel 9, can be mentioned.

[10] See James C. VanderKam, "The Putative Author of the Book of Jubilees," in *From Revelation to Canon: Studies in the Hebrew Bible and Second Temple Literature* (Leiden: Brill, 2000), 439–47, esp. 443;

Leviticus

Large parts of the book of Leviticus read simply like the manual of instructions and regulations for the priests and the ritual and worship life of Israel. It is not difficult to see a late redactional level at work in passages such as 1:1-2a; 4:1-2a; 5:20; 27:1-2a, 34. That which earlier had functioned simply as the priests' ritual handbook, beginning and ending with, e.g.:

> When any of you bring an offering of livestock to the LORD, you shall . . . (1:2b)
>
> . . .
>
> . . . This is the ritual of the burnt offering, the grain offering, the sin offering, the guilt offering, the offering of ordination, and the sacrifice of well-being (7:37).

now through the addition of an introductory verse (1:1-2a) and a concluding verse (7:38) becomes part of the revealed pattern of worship, commanded by God through Moses on Sinai:

> The LORD summoned Moses and spoke to him from the tent of meeting, saying: Speak to the people of Israel and say to them (1:1-2a): (When any of you bring an offering of livestock to the LORD, you shall . . .)
>
> . . .
>
> (. . . This is the ritual of the burnt offering, the grain offering, the sin offering, the guilt offering, the offering of ordination, and the sacrifice of well-being) which the LORD commanded Moses on Mount Sinai, when he commanded the people of Israel to bring their offerings to the LORD, in the wilderness of Sinai" (7:38).

Amos

Just as Amos made it very clear how he viewed the situation in eighth-century B.C.E. Israel, so too the book of Amos provides a reasonably clear example of how a literary collection of his sayings became regarded as Scripture. Amos strongly criticized the northern regime for splitting the people of God in two and drawing worship away from Jerusalem to Bethel, and he excoriated the prosperous northern people for their social injustice, "sell[ing . . .] the needy for a pair of sandals" (Amos 2:6). With his overstated picture of the results they should expect, he threatened—presumably hoping that they would change their ways and avoid the punishment symbolized by his threats—that the Lord would "not revoke the punishment" (2:6) on Israel: "Fallen, no more to rise, is maiden Israel; forsaken on her land" (5:2).

We may assume that Amos' words, not unlike other examples of good advice, evaporated quickly in the northern kingdom, but they were collected into a pamphlet by southern disciples. A few years later, when the north in fact fell to the cruel onslaught of Assyria, some must have reread Amos' words "predicting" the fall of the north and concluded that God had spoken through Amos ("Thus says the LORD," 2:6) and that a prudent move for the future would be to preserve his words and keep them alive in the community's memory. In fact, a later Deuteronomistic edition of the book specifically concluded: "Surely the Lord GOD does nothing without revealing his secret to his servants the prophets" (3:7). In sum, certain sayings of Amos were taken at face value as

---

and Hindy Najman, "Angels at Sinai: Exegesis, Theology and Interpretive Authority," *DSD* 7 (2000): 313–33, esp. 316.

spoken by God, communicated through Amos, as "predictions" of future events, which "came true" (cf. Deut 18:21-22), and were recorded and preserved in a book that continued to grow.[11]

Psalms

There is little opposition to the view that each of the Psalms was originally understood to be not the scriptural word of God but a humanly composed response to Scripture (read in a liturgical setting), or to some aspect of God's nature or activity, or to the plight of the people.[12] How, then, did the Psalter become a book of Scripture? Although reconstructions of the redactional ordering of the Psalter seldom win widespread approval, most can probably endorse Brevard Childs' statement concerning Psalm 1, which presumably was originally a separate psalm:

> The present editing of this original Torah psalm has provided the psalm with a new function as the introduction to the whole Psalter. . . . in its final stage of development, Psalm 1 has assumed a highly significant function as a preface to the psalms which are to be read, studied, and meditated upon.[13]

Childs continues to pursue the question that guides this present chapter:

> The introduction [Psalm 1] points to these prayers as the medium through which Israel now responds to the divine word. Because Israel continues to hear God's word through the voice of the psalmist's response, these prayers now function as the divine word itself. The original cultic role of the psalms has been subsumed under a larger category of the canon.[14]

Insofar as the full strength of Childs' words withstands analysis, he is to be credited with asking the correct question and charting the answer step by step. But I do not follow one step. His statement that "Israel continue[d] to hear God's word through the voice of the psalmist's response" is *quod est demonstrandum*, not an established protasis from which "these prayers now function as the divine word itself" can flow as an apodosis. Consonant with James Sanders' "resignification" as a constitutive element in the making of Scripture,[15] Childs correctly points to the (later?) undeniable fact that Israel repeatedly in new settings "hear[d] God's word through the voice of the psalmist's response." That resignification or adaptability to new circumstances is one important component of the Psalter's status as Scripture. But is that not a factor subsequent to the formation of the Psalter itself, indeed a noticeably later factor?

---

[11] The continuing growth included the substantial seventh-century Deuteronomistic redaction, a number of intermittent small expansions, and the post-exilic (un-Amos-like) section in 9:11-15 promising restoration and prosperity.

[12] Note, e.g., in 1 Macc 4:24, after Judas' defeat of the Seleucid forces, "On their return they sang hymns and praises to Heaven—"For he is good, for his mercy endures forever." These are the responses of the people; there is no hint that the hymns and praises were considered Scripture.

[13] Brevard S. Childs, *Introduction to the Old Testament as Scripture* (Philadelphia: Fortress, 1979), 513.

[14] Ibid. Childs' perspective is later than the one guiding this chapter. Here the focus is on the early factors that transformed Judah's literature into Scripture, whereas Childs is considering the canon as a completed phenomenon and thus the basis for Christian theology.

[15] James A. Sanders, *Canon and Community: A Guide to Canonical Criticism* (Philadelphia: Fortress, 1984), 22.

It appears more likely that the Psalter was accorded the status of Scripture because it was viewed as a prophetic book rather than a wisdom book. Both at Qumran and in the NT it is treated as such. One of the (continuous) *pesharim*, which were composed only for prophetic books, is $4QpPs^a$ (4Q171),[16] which clearly interprets Psalm 37 as concerning the life and times of the Qumran community. The main Psalms scroll, $11QPs^a$, eventually makes it explicit; recounting the large number of psalms and hymns which David composed, it says, "All these he spoke through prophecy which was given to him from the Most High" (27:11). The book of Acts also makes it explicit: "... our ancestor David.... Since he was a prophet.... Foreseeing this, David spoke of the resurrection of the Messiah..." (2:29-31).[17] These indicators—admittedly against the frustrating silence and lack of other sources from antiquity—point to a prophetic view of the Psalter, rather than a wisdom function, as responsible for its becoming Scripture, at least among certain groups.[18] The Rabbis, of course, eventually focused on the wisdom function and classified the Psalter as well as Daniel among the Ketuvim; in this they may have been following a view of the Psalter as a wisdom book, or more strategically have reclassified as "wisdom" the prophetic and apocalyptic aspects, which the Romans may have found dangerous. But the Psalter's transformation to the status of Scripture was evidently due to its prophetic character.

The Psalter helps bring to light another factor. Its use in the liturgy brought an association, an indirect link, with the people's communion with God. Thus the move toward its acceptance as a sacred book was made more natural. The same may possibly have been true for other passages which were originally liturgical but then became part of Scripture: the priestly blessing in Num 6:24-26; perhaps the blessing of Abraham in Gen 12:2-3; and the crossing of the Jordan in Joshua 3–4, in which the miraculous crossing of the Jordan may have functioned as a liturgical reenactment of the delivery at the Sea of Reeds[19] (conveniently closer to Jerusalem than the Sea) and then became part of the "historical" narrative of Israel's entry into the promised land.

Job

It is hazardous to speculate concerning either the date or the pre-MT forms of the book of Job. But one plausible theory is that a principal function that the book served within Israel was as a theological exploration of the divine-human interrelationship as a result of the destruction of Jerusalem and the Temple and the Judean exile. Thus, some form of the dialogue (Job 3:1–42:6) may have been circulating in Judah in the fifth century or not much later. Though the contents of the dialogue draw on ancient Near Eastern wisdom traditions, it is also helpful to note that it was the same fifth century that saw the production of the great tragedies of Aeschylus (ca. 525–456), Sophocles (ca. 496–406), and Euripides (ca. 480–406).

---

[16] See also $1QpPs^a$ (1Q16) and $4QpPs^c$ (4Q173).

[17] See also Matt 13:35; Acts 4:25-26; 13:33-35; Hebrews 1:5, 7-13; and for the prophetic Psalter (not the Hagiographa), Luke 24:44.

[18] 1 Macc 7:17 also quotes Ps 79:2-3 as a prophecy fulfilled by Alcimus' treacherous massacre of sixty men from the peace delegation. It is introduced with the formula, κατὰ τὸν λόγον ὅν ἔγραψεν αυτόν ("in accordance with the word that was written").

[19] See Ps 114:3-5: "When Israel went out of Egypt..., The sea looked and fled; Jordan turned back."

> [These] plays were never, at least while drama flourished at Athens, produced merely for entertainment, but formed a definite part of a religious festival in honour of Dionysos. The principal occasion for the production of new tragedies was the Great Dionysia, in the month Elaphebolion. . . , about equivalent to our March.[20]
>
> One point which must not be passed over in discussing Aeschylus is his theology, for he was one of the poets who are also prophets. . . . so great a master of lyric poetry had abundant opportunities, in the odes sung by his chorus, to set forth his visions concerning God and man. . . . the lofty praises of Zeus . . . form one of the striking features of the *Suppliants*; the chief theme of the *Persians* and of the trilogy to which the *Seven* belonged may be said to be the judgements of God on the sinful and presumptuous. . . . This supreme deity is perfectly wise, beneficent and just; that his ways are past finding out is insisted upon in [the *Suppliants*, lines 1057–58, Aeschylus's] earliest surviving work; "how can I look into the mind of Zeus, that abyss where sight is lost?" ask the Danaids.[21]

That last line, with the name Zeus changed, could well appear in the book of Job. No one would claim that the Greeks understood those religious dramas as divinely inspired Scripture in our sense of that term. Is there any reason to make the same claim for the book of Job when it was first produced? Eventually, yes; originally, probably not.

Proverbs

A large amount of the early elements of the book of Proverbs is obviously human, "armchair" wisdom. No extraordinary revelation is required for the average maxims one encounters, for example, "The lazy person does not plow in season; harvest comes, and there is nothing to be found" (20:4).

The theological introduction provided by the addition of chapters 1–9 and the attribution to Solomon (1:1) may have been the necessary catalyst for classifying it as Scripture. Even within chapters 1–9, many of the proverbs are clearly human *bon mots*, for example, "Listen, children, to a father's instruction. . . . When I was a son with my father. . . , he taught me. . ." (4:1-4; cf. 6:20).

Nonetheless, the prefixing of chapters 1–9 may well have raised the remainder of the book from a collection of human commonplaces to a book of Scripture due to its more elevated theological content. If "the LORD created [Wisdom] at the beginning (8:22), and if "When he established the heavens. . . , when he made firm the skies above. . . , I was beside him" (8:27-30), then Wisdom becomes a conduit of revelation. "The LORD gives wisdom" (2:6) to mortals who seek, and they thereby "find the knowledge of God" (2:5). That is, one can gain insight into the great *raz*, the "mystery" or master plan in the mind of the creator of the universe and Lord of the historical process. It is not difficult to see this as the equivalent of divine revelation concerning nature and the events of history. And it achieves the purpose of revelation: "whoever finds me finds life, and obtains favor from the LORD" (8:35). In sum, it appears that the most persuasive rationale for the book of Proverbs' becoming Scripture is the addition of chapters 1–9 as a theological introduction. Further books possibly raised to the status of Scripture by additions of a theological, pious, or festival nature may be Ecclesiastes, due to its more traditional

---

[20] Herbert Jennings Rose, *A Handbook of Greek Literature* (New York: Dutton, 1960), 145.

[21] Rose, *A Handbook of Greek Literature*, 159.

appendix in Eccl 12:9-14, and Esther, due to the institution of the feast of Purim in Esth 9:18-32.

Ezra

By the time of the return from the exile, the Torah of Moses may well have been recognized as ancient, unquestioned Scripture. The person of Ezra portrayed in the books of Ezra and Nehemiah claimed interpretive authority[22] with respect to that Torah. It is, and probably was, however, unclear whether there was a fixed text that people other than Ezra and his close associates could consult, and, if so, what its contents were. Cautious statements are frequently made, suggesting that Ezra's Torah may not have been "identical" with our present Pentateuch.[23] The focus is usually on specific laws, to which I shall return, but what of the narrative sections of the Pentateuch? Is there any basis, other than the use of the elastic word "Torah," for believing that the major narrative parts of the received Pentateuch were part of "the law of your God which is in your hand" (Ezra 7:14; cf. Neh 8:1)? Why would Genesis or Exodus 1–18 have been included in a law book presented, according to a common hypothesis, to the Persian authority for approval as the law by which the people of Judah would conduct themselves in the province Beyond the River? The law codes as in Exodus–Deuteronomy may have had some narrative framework, but presumably the larger framework of Joshua (the gaining of the land) was not included, and thus one may question the inclusion of Genesis (the promise of the land).[24]

But even laws mentioned in Ezra-Nehemiah do not match the text in the received Pentateuch. Robert North speaks of Ezra's "promulgating his sweeping new codification of Mosaic law,"[25] and we may be sure that Ezra's Torah of Moses was not identical to the earlier texts that had been in the Temple when the Babylonians arrived. But the issue here is whether Ezra's law book was identical to the legal portions of the Torah as subsequently transmitted to us. Hindy Najman makes the key distinction that the "primary function" of the term "Torah of Moses" was not "to *name* this collection of writings" but "to confer authority."[26] She notes two examples of laws, neither of which

[22] See Hindy Najman's insightful article, "Torah of Moses: Pseudonymous Attribution in Second Temple Writings," in *The Interpretation of Scripture in Early Judaism and Christianity: Studies in Language and Tradition* (ed. Craig A. Evans; JSPSup 33; *SSEJC* 7; Sheffield: Sheffield Academic Press, 2000), 206–16, esp. 214. See also her *Seconding Sinai: The Development of Mosaic Discourse in Second Temple Judaism* (JSJS 77; Leiden: Brill, 2003).

[23] To say nothing of the view, difficult to prove, that Ezra's law book was "the final redaction of the whole Pentateuch"; see Robert North, "The Chronicler: 1–2 Chronicles, Ezra, Nehemiah," in *The New Jerome Biblical Commentary* (ed. Raymond E. Brown, Joseph A. Fitzmyer, and Roland E. Murphy; Englewood Cliffs, N.J.: Prentice Hall, 1990), 362–98, esp. 395–96.

[24] We may note that Ezra 7:11 is a bit more precise, suggesting only the legal material: "the priest Ezra, the scribe, *a scholar of the text of the commandments* of the LORD and his *statutes* for Israel" (emphasis added). On the other hand, although one could argue that the confessional prayer in Neh 9:6-37 is clearly built on the narrative strands of the Pentateuch, few would consider it an original part of Ezra-Nehemiah; it is rather a secondarily inserted prayer, similar to that in Dan 9:4-19.

[25] North, "The Chronicler," 395.

[26] Najman, "Torah of Moses," 212 (emphasis in the original).

are in the received Pentateuch:[27] "they set the priests in their divisions and the Levites in their courses. . . , as it is written in the book of Moses" (Ezra 6:18);[28] and "let us . . . send away all these wives and their children. . . ; let it be done according to the law" (10:3).

Najman's main point, of course, is not that this is a deceptive move on Ezra's part but that it is "an early example of inner biblical interpretation."[29] To gain the authority necessary to restore devastated Jerusalem and its community, "the authors of Ezra-Nehemiah identified their history with the history of the authoritative figure, Moses. They associated the Babylonian Exile with enslavement in Egypt, Ezra's public reading of the Torah with the revelation at Sinai. . . ."[30] Ezra sees a need to counter the problem of intermarriage, takes a basis such as Deut 7:3, gives a new interpretation which now includes divorce and expulsion, and claims that the new practice is "according to the law."

The scene of Ezra's public, ceremonial reading of the law book at the festal assembly (Neh 8:1-18), together with the focus on the Temple, priesthood, worship, and devoted adherence to the Torah, may well have been sufficient to gain the status of Scripture for Ezra-Nehemiah. I think Najman has illuminated another of the factors that worked to create a scriptural book: its successful claim for its authentic Mosaic heritage and for its authentic interpretation of the Torah of Moses.

Daniel

The written forms of the book of Daniel fortunately are late enough that we have some reasonably firm material to examine. It is true that the Canaanite texts from Ugarit and the references in Ezek 14:14, 20 (cf. 28:3) attest that the figure of Danʾel is ancient. Moreover, a number of wisdom stories using the name "Daniel" for the protagonist circulated separately in the Persian period. But the written composition of a major section that constitutes part of the biblical book in a form that we would recognize today is relatively late. John Collins argues persuasively that the *collection* of the Aramaic tales in Daniel 1–6 "must be set in the Hellenistic period."[31] He sees a five-stage compositional history:[32]

- Individual court tales (Daniel 2, 3, 4, 5, 6) circulating separately and perhaps primarily orally, presumably during the Persian period, since "Cyrus the Persian is the latest king mentioned in chaps. 1–6" (p. 36);

[27] Najman, "Torah of Moses," 208–9.

[28] With Sara Japhet ("Law and 'The Law' in Ezra–Nehemiah," in *The Proceedings of the Ninth World Congress of Jewish Studies* [ed. David Asaf; Jerusalem: Magnes, 1985], 99–115, esp. 114–15), Najman also notes ("Torah of Moses," 208) that in "2 Chr 35:4-5, the *very same* priestly organization is also attributed to a pre-exilic source, though this time it is *David and Solomon*" (emphasis in the original).

[29] Najman, "Torah of Moses," 210.

[30] Najman, "Torah of Moses," 214.

[31] John J. Collins, *Daniel: A Commentary on the Book of Daniel* (Hermeneia; Minneapolis: Fortress, 1993), 36. See his précis of the history of criticism regarding the composition of the book and his resulting view (24–38).

[32] Collins, *Daniel*, 38.

- An "initial collection of 3:31–6:29, which allowed the development of two textual traditions in these chapters";[33]
- The collection of the Aramaic tales (2–6) which "presupposes the introduction that is provided by chap. 1," (p. 35) collected at the earliest during "the Hellenistic period, because the fourth kingdom of Daniel 2 must be the Greek" (p. 36);
- The vision in Daniel 7, "early in the persecution of Antiochus Epiphanes, before the desecration of the temple";
- The visions in Daniel 8–12, between 167 and 164 B.C.E.

The phenomenon, however, of varied written traditions clustering around the figure of Daniel both precedes and continues past the twelve-chapter edition of the biblical book just described (see Ch. 15.IV.A). In light of the developing collection of the Daniel cycle and the composition of various literary formulations of it, some of which became part of the scriptural book while some did not, it may be asked regarding the twelve-chapter collection (produced ca. 165) when and why it became regarded as Scripture. This edition of the book was clearly viewed as a prophetic book by the time of 4QFlorilegium—"dated to the second half of the first century B.C.E."[34]—which quotes Dan 12:10 with the formula for introducing citations from Scripture: ". . . it is written in the book of the prophet Daniel. . ." (4Q174 1–3 ii 3–4).[35]

But two earlier works add some light. First, Yeshua ben Sira, writing his book ca. 180 B.C.E., composed a hymn in honor of Israel's ancestral heroes (Sirach 44:1–50:24) but makes no mention of Daniel.[36] This silence can be interpreted in various ways,[37] but one plausible explanation is that, though the tales were in existence, they were not yet (or not universally) viewed as Scripture, whereas the visions had not yet even been composed.[38]

The second work does mention Daniel, but it is also inconclusive. First Maccabees, probably written in the last third of the second century B.C.E. (thus approximately contemporary with Ben Sira's grandson), clearly refers to the Daniel cycle: in 1 Macc 2:59-60 Mattathias calls to mind that "Hananiah, Azariah, and Mishael believed and were saved from the flame. Daniel, because of his innocence, was delivered from the mouth of the lions." In contrast to this explicit reference to Daniel 3 and 6, there is no

---

[33] For the variant literary editions of Daniel 4–6 see Ch. 10 and Klaus Koch, *Das Buch Daniel* (Darmstadt: Wissenschaftliche Buchgesellschaft, 1980), 75; Dean O. Wenthe in "The Old Greek Translation of Daniel 1–6" (Ph.D. dissertation, University of Notre Dame, 1991); Ulrich, *Scrolls and Origins*, 69–72, and idem, "The Text of Daniel in the Qumran Scrolls," in *The Book of Daniel: Composition and Reception* (ed. John J. Collins and Peter W. Flint; Leiden: Brill, 2001), 581–83.

[34] George J. Brooke, "Florilegium," in *Encyclopedia of the Dead Sea Scrolls*," 1:297–98.

[35] DJD 5:54. The NT (Matt 24:15 || Mark 13:14) and Josephus (*Ant.* 10.249, 266–67) in the first century C.E. also viewed Daniel as a prophet.

[36] Patrick W. Skehan and Alexander A. Di Lella, *The Wisdom of Ben Sira* (AB 39; New York: Doubleday, 1987), 41.

[37] Especially in light of the fact that Ezra also fails to make the list.

[38] Although his grandson translated Ben Sira into Greek (sometime after 132 B.C.E.) a generation or so after the composition of the twelve-chapter book of Daniel, it remains unclear whether he viewed the six- or twelve-chapter book as Scripture. It remains unmentioned in the translation, and it is difficult to know whether the grandson intended to include it in either category: whether as scriptural ("the Prophets") or not ("the other books of our ancestors").

mention of the persecution by Antiochus, so vividly problematic in Daniel 7–12. Again, various explanations are possible. On the one hand, the context here is a focus on martyrdom; 1 Macc 2:51-60 is an exhortation by Mattathias for his sons to remain courageous and faithful in the face of persecution. He urges that they "Remember the deeds of the ancestors" and he mentions figures such as Abraham, Joseph, and Phinehas, and concludes this parade of examples with the quotation above. Since the focus is on martyrdom, it is quite possible that the author simply selects from the twelve-chapter book a couple of examples of outstanding courage.

But there are two further possibilities. First, the author may have known, or been using, or been thinking about, only the earlier six-chapter edition of the book, which may well have still been circulating though the twelve-chapter edition had already been produced. There are numerous examples attested, of course, of this phenomenon of variant literary editions circulating simultaneously.[39] Second, the author may well have known of both editions but, while accepting the six-chapter book because of its established place in the Jewish literary heritage, scorned the expanded new version, due to its more pacifist stance and its possible snubbing (Dan 11:34) of the Maccabean effort.

Since these two works, written shortly before and after the twelve-chapter edition, do not offer solid clarity, we can analyze Daniel from within. Why and how did parts of this developing collection become regarded as Scripture?

There is nothing in chapters 1, 3, or 6 that would suggest that this book should be considered as Scripture; they are simply edifying tales. The same obtains for the stories of Susanna and Bel and the Dragon. There is no claim that God has spoken or granted any specific revelation.[40]

Chapter 2, however, does present elements that could qualify. Even though parts of the chapter are seen as a secondary set of interpolations of an apocalyptic nature,[41] clear affirmations do occur in the basic stratum of the story: "The thing that the king is asking is too difficult, and no one can reveal it to the king except the gods" (2:11); "There is a God in heaven who reveals mysteries, and he has disclosed..." (2:28). In chapters 4–5 Daniel is professed to be "endowed with a spirit of the holy gods" (4:8, 18; 5:11, 14), and, though it is not narrated that God revealed anything directly to him, Daniel indirectly claims it: "This is the interpretation, O king, and it is a decree of the Most High" (4:24); and "This is the interpretation...: MENE: God has numbered..." (5:26).

But again, the later addition of chapters 7–12 with their stronger claim as revelation may have raised the status of the book from edifying tales to divine revelation. It is not implausible that, on the analogy of Amos—who was later seen as "predicting" the fall of the northern kingdom which in fact happened a few years later—the book of Daniel was also soon considered to be God's revelation. Daniel, who had correctly "predicted" the fall of Babylonian kings, received the later revelation from God assuring the Jews of the

[39] Biblical examples include the variant editions of, e.g., Exodus, Numbers, Joshua, Jeremiah, and the Psalter; the Cave 4 and Cave 1 editions of the Community Rule provide an example of an extrabiblical work.

[40] Dan 1:17, stating that God gave the four youths knowledge and skill in literature and wisdom, is not an exception.

[41] Alexander Di Lella considers 2:14-23, 29-30, 41b-43, 49 secondary; cf. Louis F. Hartman and Alexander A. Di Lella, *The Book of Daniel* (AB 23; Garden City, N.Y.: Doubleday, 1978), 12 and 139–42.

fall of "future" king Antiochus, which "came true" as surely as Amos' threat against Israel. Daniel's interpretation against the Babylonian kings had "come true." The move would have gained momentum especially since the criterion in Deut 18:21-22 (about recognizing a true prophet's word by whether it comes true or not) was itself long since honored as part of Scripture.

Ben Sira

It is difficult to entertain the idea that Yeshua Ben Sira thought of himself as writing Scripture as he composed his book. Nor is it likely that his contemporaries would have thought such. Whereas the books of the Law and the Prophets had ancient holy figures as their authors, he does not claim, as do Daniel, 1 Enoch, and Jubilees, an ancient identity or pseudonym but explicitly identifies himself as the author (Ben Sira 50:27). Even had he not identified himself, his grandson does so in the Prologue. Rather, he wrote the book as a work of instruction (50:27), a meditation on the mind and will of God as expressed in the Law and the Prophets. He was synthesizing the Law and the Prophets and Proverbs (cf. 24:23; 39:1-3) and repackaging them in a contemporary rhetorical teaching style, not authoring new ideas.

Even if he had considered his book as Scripture, there is no hint in the Prologue that his grandson did:

> Now, those who read the scriptures must not only themselves understand them, but must also as lovers of learning be able through the spoken and written word to help the outsiders. So my grandfather Jesus, ... reading the Law and the Prophets and the other books of our ancestors..., was himself also led to write something pertaining to instruction and wisdom....

Ben Sira studied explicitly the Law and the Prophets, but he also traveled abroad and studied "the wisdom of all the ancients" (39:1, 4). The last does not mean Israel's wisdom exclusively, but the literature of other nations as well.[42] It seems clear that he had read and used both Egyptian and Greek literature, including the gnomic work attributed to Phibis and the elegiac poems of Theognis, as well as a possible reminiscence of Homer.[43]

If neither Ben Sira nor his grandson, as late as ca. 125 B.C.E., considered the book Scripture, how did it become a candidate for scriptural status? There are no clear claims of revelation in the book, as there are, for example, in Jubilees. Rather, it would seem that it followed in the path of the book of Proverbs. Not too long after the composition of Ben Sira, Proverbs seems to be regarded by certain groups as having gained the status of Scripture, since Prov 15:8 is quoted in the Damascus Document (CD 11:20-21) with the authoritative formula, "for it is written." Like Proverbs, Ben Sira declares: "All wisdom is from the Lord, and with him it remains forever" (1:1), and it personifies wisdom as the first in creation: "Before the ages, in the beginning, he created me" (24:9). It is quite likely that Ben Sira was an eloquent and popular teacher in Jerusalem, and thus there would probably not have been much resistance to his book's gaining an exalted status.

---

[42] See Skehan and Di Lella, *The Wisdom of Ben Sira*, 46–50. Van der Kooij ("Canonization of Ancient Books," 34) correctly makes the same point.

[43] For details, see Di Lella's judicious discussion in *The Wisdom of Ben Sira*, 47–49.

The Wisdom of his book, as perhaps for Proverbs, may have been seen as "a conduit of revelation."[44]

The New Testament and the early church undoubtedly followed some lines of Jewish tradition in considering Ben Sira Scripture, and it finds a secure place in the LXX:

> The early church (e.g., *Didache*, Clement of Rome, Irenaeus, Tertullian) considered Sir[ach] canonical. There are many allusions to the book in the NT, esp. in James. The fathers of the church attest more frequently to the canonicity of Sir[ach] than to several protocanonical books.[45]

Somewhat earlier, certain Jewish groups must have regarded it as an authoritative book, since—even though eventually the influential Rabbis at the Great Divide (see Ch. 2 n. 3) decided not to classify it as Scripture—

> "[s]ome eighty-two times [it] is quoted with approval in the Talmud and other rabbinical writings. Sometimes its sayings are even introduced by the formula "it is written," which is reserved only for quotations from the canonical Scriptures. . . ."[46]

It is likely that one of the Rabbis' reasons for denying scriptural status[47] was the book's denial of meaningful existence after death (14:16-17; 17:27-28), just as the path toward scriptural status for the book of Daniel was probably enhanced by the promise in Dan 12:2-3.

This and the next example illuminate another factor in the granting of scriptural status, namely, the acceptance of the work by the people as divine truth. If a recent work, despite its claims, did not correspond to beliefs then current, it would be rejected as a scriptural book, even if parts of it continued to be used as a valuable resource.

Jubilees

Jubilees found a fate somewhat similar to that of Ben Sira. On the one hand, in James VanderKam's words, it "blatantly advertises itself as divine revelation,"[48] and some groups accepted it as such. Fifteen or possibly sixteen copies were unearthed at Qumran, rivaling the books of the Torah in frequency, and it was quoted as an authoritative work in CD 16:2–3 (and possibly also in 4Q228). The book was accepted by some probably

---

[44] See the section on Proverbs above.

[45] Alexander Di Lella, "Sirach," in *The New Jerome Biblical Commentary*, 496–509, esp. 497.

[46] Di Lella in Skehan and Di Lella, *The Wisdom of Ben Sira*, 20.

[47] Najman ("Interpretation as Primordial Writing: Jubilees and Its Authority Conferring Strategies," *JSJ* 30 [1999]: 379–410, esp. 405, n. 49) also suggests the lack of claim to be a revelatory text as a factor in the denial. Yet another factor may be the rabbinic "elevation of the Sinai Torah as the preeminent intermediary between God and the phenomenal world. This elevated, or eternal, Torah was the agent of creation, the final judge, the one path to the celestial world. Access to the invisible realms was gained through contemplation of Torah, discovering the secrets hidden in, with and under its letters"; see Stephan K. Davis, *Antithesis of the Ages: Paul's Reconfiguration of Torah* (CBQMS 33; Washington: Catholic Biblical Association, 2002), 215. That is, although Wisdom and Torah are often portrayed as identical, the Rabbis may have wanted to claim specifically for the Torah precisely the role that Ben Sira claimed for the potentially more universal Wisdom, and thus rejected the latter, just as they rejected Paul's "reconfiguration of the Torah image set so that Christ would fill the same theological space as the eternal Torah" (ibid., 216).

[48] James C. VanderKam, *The Dead Sea Scrolls Today* (2d ed.; Grand Rapids, Mich.: Eerdmans, 2010), 191 [1st ed. 1994, 153].

because its claim of "divine revelation" was indeed of the highest order, and because it explained, for those honoring the 364-day calendar, the divine origins of "our calendar."[49] On the other hand, it was rejected by others presumably because it was considered "obviously wrong," since it claimed and promoted a calendar at odds with their current liturgical calendar.

Concluding Reflections

This chapter has offered reflections on some of the factors that helped transform selected works of Judah's national literature into the Jewish Scriptures. It has mainly been an effort to raise questions not frequently asked and to encourage reflections by others on this intriguing topic. It makes no claim that the factors discussed were the principal factors in the process; even less does it claim comprehensiveness or full accuracy in the details of the analyses. In fact, not only are there unanswered questions, there are also unasked questions.

The claim does seem inescapable, however, that what is now considered the Jewish Scriptures did not have its origins as Scripture, and that inquiry into its origins and its development within the cultural history is worthwhile. Small, separate, anonymous oral units gradually joined together to form complexes of tradition which were handed on within various communities and eventually edited to form books which were likely considered as simply the people's literature.[50] This literature served a variety of purposes: as national epic and national history (the early narrative strands of the Pentateuch and the Deuteronomic History), for the liturgy (Leviticus, Psalms, Esther), for religious, moral, and practical education (Jubilees, the Deuteronomic History, Proverbs, Job, Qohelet, Ben Sira), for human love and loyalty (the Song, Tobit, Ruth), and for courage in perilous times (Daniel).

The literature grew as community literature, and numerous mouths and hands contributed to its organic development from sayings, reports, songs, and the like into books sufficiently well known and treasured to keep handing down as important. Just as the community formed the literature, so too the literature formed the ongoing community.[51] One of the functions, whether intended or not, was that it molded the self-identity of the community (Ezra, Ben Sira).

It is not difficult to imagine that in educational or liturgical settings this human literature was proclaimed to be speaking in the name of God. This claim to have God as source took multiple forms: implicit (Who but God could have provided the information on the creation of the world?) or explicit (Jubilees), direct (Exodus, Leviticus, Amos, Ezekiel) or indirect through angelic (Jubilees, Daniel 7–12) or human mediators (Ezekiel, Daniel 2; 4–5), or even through an interpretational mode exterior to the book (Song of Songs).

---

[49] For authorizing strategies in Jubilees, see Florentino García Martínez, "The Heavenly Tablets in the Book of Jubilees," in *Studies in the Book of Jubilees* (ed. Matthias Albani et al.; Mohr Siebeck, 1997), 243–60; VanderKam, "The Putative Author"; and Najman, "Interpretation as Primordial Writing."

[50] The eventual "scripturalization" of the people's tradition(s) invites reconsideration of the old Protestant-Roman Catholic debate about Scripture-Tradition.

[51] In a way, that dynamic is similar to myth in general and to the African-American epic by Alex Haley, *Roots* (New York: Delta, 1997).

One factor that brought the idea of God as author was prophecy, not only in the primary sense that a human was the spokesperson for God, but in the secondary sense that what a prophet had "predicted" for God had then "come true."

Another factor was the theological development of otherwise purely human compositions. For example, the Deuteronomistic History made use of all sorts of sources that may or may not have had religious importance beforehand, but the historian added a theological perspective that could be envisioned as a theological interpretation of history. Thus the boundary lists and city lists of Joshua, war stories, annals of kings, prophetic legends, and so forth became subsumed into a theological work which then became Scripture.

The "resignification" or ready identification of the current community's situation with a situation in past literature (e.g., the association of the Babylonian Exile with the Egyptian captivity and Ezra's public Torah reading with Moses' mediation at Sinai) also functioned in the transformation, as did the contrast of such situations (e.g., Psalm 89:38-51 added to 89:1-37). The same was true for the claim to authentic interpretation of the Mosaic Torah (e.g., Jubilees, Ezra). This function is allied to the socio-political situation in which a group in power makes the claim that a certain book has God as guarantor, which claim must be met with the people's approval.

The antiquity of a work was also a factor. The longer the work had been accepted, the more likely it was to resist dismissal; that would partly explain why Genesis remained established but why Jubilees, which rehearses Genesis and the first half of Exodus and which makes a much stronger claim of divine authorship, could be rejected.

Eventually it did not matter how that claim of divine authorship may have been understood at first, whether literally or with some sort of hermeneutical sophistication. The more the writing became "ancient" and the more the ongoing community continued to hear it and continued to experience some kind of connectedness with God through hearing it, the more they tended to understand it as "the word of God." Eventually, the statement by Brevard Childs (see "Psalms" above), became the reality: "Israel continu[ed] to hear God's word through the voice of the [sacred authors]."[52]

It was human beings sincerely trying to understand, interpret, and articulate the divine who produced the religious classics of the ancient Near East and the religious classics of Israel. In one sense, for Israel the word about God became the word of God. The communities continued to hear it repeated as such, and eventually they described it explicitly as such.

---

[52] Childs, *Introduction*, 513.

Chapter 19

The Scriptures at Qumran and the Road toward Canon

Chapters 3–10 focused on individual scrolls and the new picture that each provided of the developing Scriptures. The last two chapters considered the collection of scrolls, offering a classic definition of the canon of Scripture, an attempt to differentiate between closely related concepts, and reflections on how certain factors may have helped some of Israel's literature develop into Sacred Scripture. Finally, the question now emerges: What evidence does Qumran provide concerning the status of the canon or at least the process of the collection of authoritative Scriptures toward the eventual canon of the Hebrew Bible?

Does it show clearly that there was a canon, and, if so, what were its contents? Or does it show that there was not yet a canon? Is there evidence or at least some clues to mark a milestone along the road toward the eventual canon?

Criteria that would be conclusive for determining whether the writings found at Qumran provide evidence for a canon of Scripture would be the clear mention of a title of the canon or its parts, or a list of the books in the canon. Criteria that would in varying degrees be indicative include: (1) multiple copies of the books; (2) formulae which introduce explicit quotations of Scripture; (3) books explicitly quoted as Scripture; (4) books on which commentaries were written; and (5) books that were translated into the vernacular languages, either Greek or Aramaic.

Let us review the evidence according to these criteria, attempting to judge the evidence appropriately, not granting it too much or too little weight. Unfortunately, for most books it is difficult to demonstrate that they were accorded scriptural status, although there are indicators with various levels of strength.[1] We must be careful to note that there is positive evidence for authoritativeness of certain books, but that, if there is a lack of evidence for canon, it could simply be a *lack* of evidence. That is, it is possible that Qumran had or acknowledged a canon but that the evidence did not survive. Though that is possible, it is unlikely. If we examine the evidence that is preserved, we find that it parallels the evidence of the NT (as we will see below).

[1] Three exemplary articles on the state of the developing canon as seen at Qumran have been published by Julio Trebolle and James VanderKam: Julio Trebolle published the comprehensive and highly insightful article, "A 'Canon within a Canon': Two Series of Old Testament Books Differently Transmitted, Interpreted and Authorized," *RevQ* 19/3 (2000): 383–99; James VanderKam published the carefully worked and nuanced "Authoritative Literature in the Dead Sea Scrolls," *DSD* 5/3 (1998): 382–402, and more recently "Revealed Literature in the Second Temple Period," in his collection *From Revelation to Canon: Studies in the Hebrew Bible and Second Temple Literature* (JSJS 62; Leiden: Brill, 2000), 1–30.

I. The Evidence

A. Conclusive Evidence?

1. Titles or Lists

No list of authoritative books has been preserved in the writings found at Qumran. Titles of subcollections of authoritative books do occur; it is common knowledge that the texts speak of the Law and the Prophets, or Moses and the Prophets, as God's revealed and written word. The very beginning of the Community Rule, for example, directs that the community's initiates are to learn "to seek God with all their heart and with all their soul, to do that which is good and upright before him, just as he commanded through Moses and all his servants the prophets" (1QS 1:1-3). Later, the important self-identity quotation of Isaiah 40:3 ("In the desert, prepare the way of [the Lord]") is interpreted thus: "This is the study of the law wh[i]ch he commanded through the hand of Moses, in order to act in compliance with all that has been revealed from age to age, and according to what the prophets have revealed through his holy spirit" (1QS 8:15-16).[2] The Law and the Prophets is used also in the NT as a title for the Scriptures: for example, Luke 16:16, 29, 31; 24:27; Acts 26:22; 28:23. Thus the books of authoritative Scripture were at times grouped under the quasi-title, the Torah and the Prophets.[3]

But, with one possible exception, just as the NT never offers a more specific title for the Jewish Scriptures, neither do the Qumran texts—either those composed within broader Judaism or those which bear the stamp of the community's particular theology. That one exception is the much-discussed and often inflated testimony of 4QMMT (4Q394–399). The editors translate their composite and partly reconstructed text:[4]

> [And] we have [written] to you so that you may study (carefully) the book of Moses and the books of the Prophets and (the writings of) David [and the] [events of] ages past.[5]

Thus, they interpret "Moses . . . Prophets . . . David" as a tripartite canon. For accuracy, however, and to avoid inflated interpretations, it is important to start by examining the photographs and to note the following points at the palaeographic and textual levels:

---

[2] The translation is from *The Dead Sea Scrolls Study Edition* (ed. Florentino García Martínez and Eibert J. C. Tigchelaar; vol. 1; Leiden: Brill, 1997) 89, 91.

[3] Here we follow the ancient classification that considered Psalms and Daniel among the Prophets, in contrast to the later Masoretic classification in the Ketuvim (see Ulrich, *Scrolls and Origins*, 21–22). It should also be recalled that by the late Second Temple period the Twelve Minor Prophets were viewed as comprising one book.

[4] For fuller treatment of the claim regarding 4QMMT see Ulrich, "The Non-attestation of a Tripartite Canon in 4QMMT," *CBQ* 65 (2002): 202–13. See also the carefully debated discussions of Katell Berthelot, "4QMMT et la question du canon de la Bible hébraïque," in *From 4QMMT to Resurrection: Mélanges qumraniens en hommage à Émile Puech* (ed. Florentino García Martínez, Annette Steudel, and Eibert Tigchelaar; Leiden: Brill, 2006), 1–14; Jonathan G. Campbell, "4QMMT^d and the Tripartite Canon," *JJS* 51 (2000): 181–90, Timothy H. Lim, *The Formation of the Jewish Canon* (New Haven: Yale University Press, 2013), 127–28 and nn. 22–23; Émile Puech, L'epilogue de *4QMMT* revisité," in *A Teacher for All Generations: Essays in Honor of James C. VanderKam* (ed. Eric F. Mason et al.; Leiden: Brill, 2012), 1:309–39; and James C. VanderKam, *Scrolls and the Bible*, 55–60.

[5] Qimron and Strugnell, 4QMMT "Composite Text," C 10–11, DJD 10:58–59.

• For the first word of this line in the "composite text" one of the two overlapping texts, 4Q398, has an anomalous reading that is a variant from 4Q397, and 4Q398 lacks the second word altogether;

• The tiny fragment with [ו]בספר[י] ("[and] in the book[s of]") before [הנ]ביאים ("[the p]rophets" is a separate fragment which is plausibly placed here but which also may not have originally been part of this line;[6] it is even questionable whether a *yod* followed the *resh*, thus leaving the word "book" as singular and out of place here;

• For the word interpreted as "David" only *waw-bet-dalet* -ובד ("and in d[ ]") is clear, followed by two vertical strokes and part of a top horizontal stroke connecting them; "and in David" is a fully plausible suggestion, but several other words are equally possible, including ובדור ("age, generation"; note that דור occurs twice in the next line);

• Just as the spacing (when the two manuscripts are lined up to form a "composite text") causes a problem at the beginning of the sentence, so also it causes a problem between "David" and "ages past." That is, the suggested reading does not fit well the spacing requirements of the manuscripts.

At the level of interpretation we note:

• Whereas "(in) the *book* of" precedes "Moses," it is not certain that "(in) the *book*[*s*] of" precedes "[the p]rophets," and quite importantly "*book*" clearly does not precede "David"; this raises a serious problem for considering the word beginning with *waw-bet-dalet* as a "third section" of a "tripartite canon."

• The absolute ובספר כתוב ("in the book it is written") occurs in the next line (C 11). It appears to presume that the identity of that book (singular) is clear, and perhaps thus that only one book had been named in the previous line.

We are now in a position to watch the escalation from a few possible and plausible restorations to "a significant piece of evidence for the history of the tripartite division of the Canon":[7]

(1) We do not know that "books" of the prophets are mentioned here.

(2) We do not know that "David" is mentioned here.

(3) Even if "David" were mentioned, we do not know whether this is the person or the book. Note that, unlike "the book of Moses," no *book* of David is mentioned; moreover, MMT never otherwise mentions the Psalms but does speak once of the person.[8]

(4) Nonetheless, the DJD translation presents the text in a way that leads the non-specialist reader to think that "the book of Moses and the books of the Prophets and (the writings of) David" is a fully preserved and clear continuous text, except for "the writings

[6] This is an intelligent placement of this fragment, and if I were editing that text I might also place it tentatively here; but it would be essential to have a note to the reader, explicitly saying that the placement is fully conjectural and by no means certain.

[7] Qimron and Strugnell, DJD 10:59 n. 10.

[8] "Remember David, he was a pious man, and indeed he was delivered from many troubles and forgiven" (C 25–26). The translation is by Martin Abegg in Michael Wise, Martin Abegg, Jr., and Edward Cook, *The Dead Sea Scrolls: A New Translation* (San Francisco: HarperSanFrancisco, 1996), 364. Note also: "In the days of Solomon the son of David" (thus again the person, not the book) also occurs in the exhortations regarding blessings and curses (C 18).

of"—and the parentheses might be interpreted as implying that the phrase is a frequent expression readily supplied, whereas in contrast it is a problematic interpretation.

(5) Now that "the books of the Prophets and (the writings of) David" are accepted as in the text, this is then compared to the well-known Lucan phrase "the law of Moses and the prophets and psalms" (Lk 24:44), which is categorized as a "tripartite 'canon' formula."[9]

(6) The DJD edition then stretches further and informs us, in a note on line 10, that "In this context דויד probably refers not only to the Psalms of David, but rather to the Hagiographa. This is a significant piece of evidence for the history of the tripartite division of the Canon."[10]

(7) Finally, a later section on dating, entitled "דויד as Part of the Description of a Tripartite Canon," adopts, though not explaining the rationale, the common view that "a tripartite list is attested in ... the prologue of the grandson of Ben-Sira." It then states that "the title of the third section, whatever it contained, is 'David,'" and a note compares it with "the similar tripartite 'canon' formula in Luke 24:44."[11] Both these examples are questionable. The Prologue to Ben Sira can be interpreted as bipartite, not tripartite (see below), and Luke 24:44 is clearly bipartite, not tripartite: the syntax, ἐν τῷ νόμῳ Μωϋσέως καὶ τοῖς προφήταις καὶ ψαλμοῖς, with two articles, indicates two entities, not three. In this verse the risen Jesus explains that "everything written about me in [1] the law of Moses and [2] the prophets and psalms must be fulfilled." Clearly "psalms" is being viewed as a prophetic source, as in the Qumran *pesharim* and in the NT: "... our ancestor David.... Since he was a prophet.... Foreseeing this, David spoke of the resurrection of the Messiah..." (Acts 2:29-31).

My point in all this is not to criticize the editors. They have done a very good job with a highly challenging set of fragments, and reconstruction is necessary. It is difficult to draw the line between pedantic precision and user-friendly exposition. Also, it is the editor's task or prerogative to suggest interconnections and paths for future research, and I would assent to the plausibility of many of their conclusions (except the tripartite canon). My point is rather that biblical and especially nonbiblical scholars using the "composite text" and translation together with the escalated summary formulations may think they are building on stone rather than a mixture of some stone and some sand, i.e., reconstructions.

Since the Prologue of the grandson of Ben Sira is adduced as a witness to a tripartite canon in the second century B.C.E., it is important to examine that witness as well.

---

[9] Qimron and Strugnell, DJD 10:112, n. 6. The qualification is given that "Phrases of this kind occur in other passages that have, perhaps loosely, been called canon lists." But the remainder of the page gives the appearance of endorsing a tripartite canon.

[10] Ibid., 59 n. 10. A much later summary section (p. 112) does add the qualification: "It is not clear whether 'David' refers just to the Psalter, or denotes a *Ketubim* collection, either one that was open-ended, or one that was closed." But someone studying the text and its explanation would not necessarily see that later qualification.

[11] Ibid., 111–12.

The three lines of the Prologue read as follows:

τοῦ νόμου καὶ τῶν προφητῶν καὶ τῶν ἄλλων τῶν κατ' αὐτοὺς ἠκολουθηκότων
τοῦ νόμου καὶ τῶν προφητῶν καὶ τῶν ἄλλων πατίρων βιβλίων
αὐτὸς ὁ νόμος καὶ αἱ προφητεῖαι καὶ τὰ λοιπὰ τῶν βιβλίων

The NAB translates the three lines as follows:

"the law, the prophets, and the later authors"
"the law, the prophets, and the rest of the books of our ancestors"
"the law itself, the prophets and the rest of the books"

The NRSV translates them as follows:

"the Law and the Prophets and the others that followed them"
"the Law and the Prophets and the other books of our ancestors"
"the Law itself, the Prophecies, and the rest of the books"

These lines are commonly understood as referring to the three divisions of the Hebrew Bible, with the vagueness of and different terms for the third group being due to its relatively new compilation and indeed being mirrored in the equally vague "Ketuvim" (Writings) in current terminology. In fact, the NAB explains in a note on the second line, "The law, the prophets, and the rest of the books [means]: the Sacred Scriptures of the Old Testament written before the time of Sirach, according to the threefold division of the present Hebrew Bible."[12] Similarly, in agreement with many others, Alexander Di Lella notes in his commentary: "Here for the first time mention is made of the threefold division of the OT. . . ."[13]

The wording of the Prologue to Ben Sira can be viewed as providing a foundation for the hypothesis that it attests a tripartite canon, even though I disagree with that hypothesis. The Prologue also provides a foundation for the hypothesis, which I do endorse, of a bipartite grouping of (1) the Scriptures (i.e., the Law and the Prophets) and (2) other important religious literature which is not on the level of Scripture but is helpful toward instruction and wisdom—non-scriptural works, "something . . . in the nature of instruction and wisdom," as the grandson describes Ben Sira's own work.[14] A modern analogy might be a bookstore, with one sign indicating "Bibles" (the bipartite OT and NT), and another sign for "Theology" (books based on Scripture written to help those "who wish to acquire wisdom and are disposed to live their lives according to the standards of the law"). Thus, the Prologue to Ben Sira can be reasonably interpreted as either bipartite or tripartite, but I think that no definitive conclusion about a tripartite canon can be based on 4QMMT C 10.[15]

My assessment of the evidence from Qumran is (1) that there is no reasonably clear mention of a canon or a full list of scriptural books and (2) that "the Law and the Prophets" is the strongest commonly used title of the Scriptures. Even if "David" is the correct reading in 4QMMT C 10, the claim that it refers to the Psalter is problematic

---

[12] *The Catholic Study Bible*, ed. Donald Senior et al. (New York: Oxford University Press, 1990), 822.

[13] Patrick W. Skehan and Alexander A. Di Lella, *The Wisdom of Ben Sira: A New Translation with Notes* (AB 39; New York: Doubleday, 1987), 133.

[14] See the Prologue to Ben Sira.

[15] Note that a few lines later (C 17) neither a book of "David" nor a "third section" occurs in the similarly questionable "[written in the book] of Moses [and in the books of the Prophets]."

without the preceding word "book of," and there is no clear basis for extending the term to the complete Ketuvim. Finally, even if the 4QMMT reference is tripartite, since there is no evidence of a complete third group, it is not a "tripartite canon."

B. Indicative Evidence

1. Multiple Copies of Books

That numerous copies of an individual book were preserved at Qumran is not a conclusive indicator that it was regarded as possessing authoritative scriptural status, but it is one indicator, to be used in concert with others, of the practical importance accorded to a book. A statistical inventory of "Scriptural Scrolls from the Judean Desert" is included among the appendices and lists a recent count of the number of Qumran copies of the books in the received Masoretic Bible.[16] The books of the Torah have double-digit numbers of copies, including Deuteronomy with 36; the Prophets include 21 copies of Isaiah, 9 copies of the XII Prophets, 36 of Psalms, and 8 of the small book of Daniel. The overwhelming impression is that the Torah and the (Latter) Prophets were regarded as Sacred Scripture, and that the historical books (or Former Prophets) and the Ketuvim (with 4 or less) were known but were marginal.

It may be partly due to chance that only one small fragment of the large book of Chronicles was found, whereas many fragments from eight manuscripts of the relatively small book of Daniel were found in three different caves. But one could also argue that that fact is significant and betrays to some extent the relatively high status of Daniel for the community. The latter argument is strengthened when one notes that Daniel is quoted as Scripture and that it exercised a strong influence on the apocalyptic thought and terminology of the community.

2. Citation Formulae

Joseph Fitzmyer wrote a classic study of the formulae introducing quotations of the Scriptures in the Qumran texts.[17] He articulated many of the main points that the formulae provide concerning Jewish beliefs about Scripture during the late Second Temple period. Formulae such as "For thus it is written" (1QS 5:15) and "As for what God said" (CD 8:9) which introduce quotations from Scripture demonstrate that the Qumranites believed certain written texts to have originated as the word of God. Other

---

[16] I realize that the presentation there, based on the categories provided by the received MT, is theoretically problematic, but I list it thus because it is a handy expedient and also because it illustrates the weak case for the "canonicity" of the Ketuvim as a third section in this period. For similar but slightly varying lists see Emanuel Tov, *Revised Lists of the Texts from the Judaean Desert* (Leiden: Brill, 2010), and VanderKam and Flint, *The Meaning of the Scrolls*, 147–50, including discussion of the many minor uncertainties precluding a definitive count. But despite minor differences in the final numbers, the general impression described above is quite clear.

[17] Joseph A. Fitzmyer, "The Use of Explicit Old Testament Quotations in Qumran Literature and in the New Testament," *NTS* 7 (1960–61): 297–333 [repr. in his *Essays on the Semitic Background of the New Testament* (SBLSBS 5; Missoula, Mont.: SBL and Scholars Press, 1974), 3–58]. See also VanderKam, "Authoritative Literature," 391–96.

formulae such as "As God said through Isaiah the prophet" (CD 4:13) and "As you said through Moses" (1QM 10:6) make explicit that writings of Moses and the prophets convey the word of God. This is strong evidence which demonstrates that the writings in the library at Qumran recognized the books so cited as containing the word of God, thus as authoritative Scripture. Only books of the Law and the Prophets receive this endorsement. In this category also the Qumran evidence appears to be representative of Judaism at large, not "sectarian."

3. Books Quoted as Scripture

The next question to ask is which books are quoted with a designation as Scripture at Qumran. This is a vast topic the center of which holds rich data, but the periphery of which is quite difficult to chart precisely. Indeed, for a large percentage of instances it is difficult to prove conclusively that the appeal is to a written authority as Scripture specifically, as opposed to respected national literature. The difficulty in achieving clear criteria for classification is well known from studies of quotations of the OT in the NT, but in general one can say that the quotations in the NT are overwhelmingly from the books of the Pentateuch, Psalms, Isaiah, and the Minor Prophets, with modest representation from Samuel, Kings, Jeremiah, Ezekiel, Daniel, Job, and Proverbs, and virtually no others.[18] If various attempts to catalogue the quotations from Scripture in the Qumran manuscripts[19] are compared, one is satisfied that the broad lines are clear and sufficient for our purposes, giving a reasonable approximation of the truth. One of the most soberly charted recent lists of quotations introduced by citation formulae is presented by James VanderKam.[20] Isaiah and the Minor Prophets are the most frequent, with modest representation from the books of the Pentateuch and Ezekiel; the only others are Psalms, Daniel, Samuel,[21] Jeremiah, Proverbs, and Jubilees.

That the lack of a formal quotation introduced by a citation formula cannot serve as sufficient evidence to disqualify a book from having been considered authoritative Scripture is clear from the fact that Genesis is not so quoted, and Exodus only once. Nonetheless, it can be stated as a general impression that the citation-formula quotations clearly attest the Scriptural status of the Pentateuch and the Latter Prophets, and give indication of the same for Psalms, Daniel, (an oracle in) Samuel, and Proverbs. Note that of the books beyond the Law and Prophets, only Proverbs is so quoted and only once, while Jubilees seems to be quoted once with a formula (in 4Q228 1 i 9; cf. 1 i 2) and

---

[18] See, e.g., *Old Testament Quotations in the New Testament* (ed. Robert G. Bratcher; 3d rev. ed.; London: United Bible Societies, 1987); "Index of Quotations" in *The Greek New Testament* (ed. Kurt Aland et al.; 3d rev. ed.; Stuttgart: United Bible Societies, 1983), 897–98; and Trebolle, "Canon within a Canon," 393–95.

[19] See, e.g., Trebolle, "Canon within a Canon," 389–92; "Index of References" in Wise, Abegg, and Cook, *The Dead Sea Scrolls*, 506–13; and Armin Lange and Matthias Weigold, *Biblical Quotations and Allusions in Second Temple Jewish Literature* (Göttingen: Vandenhoeck & Ruprecht, 2011).

[20] His results are listed in VanderKam, "Authoritative Literature," 394–95, and are accepted by Trebolle, "Canon within a Canon," 389, n. 28. For a more expanded listing extending to various levels of allusions see Lange and Weigold, *Biblical Quotations and Allusions*.

[21] The only quotation from the former prophets is from Nathan's oracle in 2 Samuel 7, thus a small *prophetic* passage.

referred to once importantly in parallel with the Law of Moses (CD 16:2–4).[22] From another perspective, I am not aware that any text quoted as authoritative Scripture by one author is rejected as non-scriptural by another.

Thus, texts that include quotations of Scripture also provide positive evidence to show that certain books were considered authoritative Scripture—again in this case the Law and the Prophets (including Psalms and Daniel), but no Writings except Proverbs—although lack of evidence does not by itself show that a book was not authoritative.

4. Commentaries on Books of Scripture

Continuous commentaries have been identified only on the prophetic books: six on Isaiah,[23] seven (possibly nine?) on the Book of the Minor Prophets,[24] and three on Psalms.[25] It is widely agreed that these commentaries presuppose that the prophetic books are revealed Scripture. The prophets deal with the end time: "as it is written in the book of Isaiah the prophet about the end of days" (4QFlor 1:15), and "who said concerning the end of days by Isaiah the prophet" (11QMelch 15). The well-known passage in the Habakkuk *pesher* shows that God, via the ancient prophetic Scriptures, had in the distant past imparted important revelation and was still offering vital revelation to the chosen through the Teacher of Righteousness (1QpHab 7:1-6). Indeed, "the spirit of prophecy had not ceased at the time of Ezra. . . . [The community] believed that God continued to address his own in order to help them understand the writings of the ancient tradition and to unfold new truths to address the concerns of their times."[26]

Although continuous commentaries appear to be limited to the prophetic books, there are a number of interpretive works on the Torah—more narrative interpretation of Genesis, and more legal interpretation of Exodus to Deuteronomy.[27] These are in addition to the many *ad hoc* references to passages in the Torah concerning halakhic matters, often introduced by introductory formulae.

While the halakhic and continuous commentaries point strongly to the Torah and certain Prophets (Isaiah, the Minor Prophets, and the Psalter) as books of Scripture, Julio Trebolle interestingly highlights a different class of interpretive works widening the prophetic circle: "parabiblical or apocryphal rewritings on the model of Chronicles . . . based on narrative sections of the Pentateuch (particularly Gen 1–11) and on books of the second series," i.e., the Former Prophets, Jeremiah, Ezekiel, and Daniel.[28] Note that the witness of the interpretive works from Qumran again points to the Law and the Prophets, but not the Writings, as Scripture.

---

[22] See VanderKam, "Authoritative Literature," 399.

[23] 3Q4 and 4Q161–165.

[24] Two on Hosea (4Q166–167), one or two on Micah (1Q14; cf. 4Q168?), one on Nahum (4Q169), one on Habakkuk (1QpHab), two on Zephaniah (1Q15; 4Q170), and possibly one on Malachi (cf. 5Q10?)

[25] 1Q16; 4Q171; and 4Q173.

[26] VanderKam, "Authoritative Literature," 401.

[27] For an informative discussion see Moshe J. Bernstein, "Pentateuchal Interpretation at Qumran," in *The Dead Sea Scrolls after Fifty Years*, 128–59; and Julio Trebolle, "Canon within a Canon," 391–93.

[28] Trebolle, "Canon within a Canon," 383, 397–98.

5. *Translations of Books of Scripture*

Translations of a work, in antiquity as today, are some indication of the importance with which a work is regarded, though it is good to consider which type of importance is involved. One Aramaic translation of Leviticus (4Q156) and two of Job (4Q157 and 11Q10) were found at Qumran. The importance of Leviticus would presumably be religious or religio-legal, whereas for Job the importance could as easily be literary as religious, or a blend of both. But the fact that a copy of Job is also preserved in the Palaeo-Hebrew script (4Q101), and that it is the only identified work other than the five books of Moses to be preserved in the Palaeo-Hebrew script, lends more weight to the religious importance accorded that book.

Two Greek translations of Leviticus (4QLXXLev^{a} and 4QLXXLev^{b}) were found in Cave 4, together with one copy each of Numbers (4QLXXNum), and Deuteronomy (4QLXXDeut); a Greek translation of Exodus (7QLXXExod) was found in Cave 7, and a Greek revision of the Septuagint of the Minor Prophets was also found at Naḥal Ḥever (8ḤevXII gr). It is difficult to avoid the two conclusions that Genesis had also been available in Greek and that the purpose for the translations was the religious importance accorded the Torah and the (Minor) Prophets.

II. Authoritative Scriptures but No Canon at Qumran

The single reference in the Qumran literature to a possible tripartite canon is riddled with numerous uncertainties, is not supported by any other references in the Qumran texts, and finds no other clear parallel anywhere else in Jewish Hebrew or Greek literature before the turn of the era. Following the points made in Chapter 2 about post-Qumran thinking, it should be remembered that the current generation began learning our basic biblical knowledge and forming our mental categories, inheriting a tripartite Hebrew Bible canon. Thus, when references to a possible canon arise in ancient literature, our categories are preconditioned to interpret the evidence according to a tripartite schema. But the overwhelming evidence points to "the Law and the Prophets" as the common way of referring to the collection of authoritative books the Jews and the Christians considered Scripture until the end of the Second Temple period.

A similar conclusion results from the various criteria that provide possible indications of scriptural status: the many copies of books, formulae identifying a quote as Scripture, quotations of a book as authoritative, commentaries written on certain books, and translations of books into Aramaic or Greek. The assessment of the evidence might list the relative strength of scriptural status as follows:

Quite strong	*Strong*	*Some*	*Weak*	*Negligible*
Pentateuch	Jubilees	Jeremiah	Joshua	Ecclesiastes
Psalms	1 Enoch	Ezekiel	Judges	Esther
Isaiah	Daniel	Job	Samuel	Ezra
Minor Prophets		Proverbs	Kings	Nehemiah
(Jubilees?)			Ruth	Chronicles
(1 Enoch?)			Canticles	
			Lamentations	

The claims of "quite strong" for Jubilees and 1 Enoch, and "strong" for Daniel, are based on the fact that there are more copies of Jubilees than of Numbers and almost as many as of Leviticus; on whether the nine copies of the Book of Giants were indeed part of 1 Enoch; and that Daniel, relative to its small size, is twice quoted as Scripture and was highly important to the community for its themes and terminology.

Realizing that the indicators above are not proofs but indicators, nonetheless they all point in the same direction. All the evidence points to "the Law and the Prophets" as the clearest, commonly used term for the collection of authoritative Scriptures.

CONCLUSION

Review of the Scrolls

To appreciate the manifold riches in the scriptural Dead Sea Scrolls — the many, varied, major intentional variants exhibited in the manuscripts discussed in the preceding chapters — the Introduction first rehearsed a broad sketch of the complex history of development in the biblical text, and how the scrolls fit into that history. It then offered a reflection on the revised, post-Qumran mindset now possible, and indeed necessary, in light of the new evidence that had not been available prior to the discovery of the scrolls.

The ensuing chapters presented a parade of individual manuscripts of the Scriptures collected at Qumran that took us, in Moshe Goshen-Gottstein words, "back to a stage in the growth of the canon that we would have never dreamt of reaching."

4QpaleoExod^{m} and 4QNum^{b} demonstrate that variant editions of the Torah were circulating, accepted, and used in Palestine during the late Second Temple period. They confirm that the Samaritan Pentateuch is a useful witness to the text of the shared Judean-Samarian Pentateuch.

4QJosh^{a} shows at least a major difference from the *textus receptus*. In my view, it preserves the earlier, preferable report of Joshua's building of the first altar in the newly entered land immediately at Gilgal. Virtually all scholars agree that the report at its present position in the MT is not original, whereas the position in 4QJosh^{a} is natural, neutral, and expected in light of Deut 27:2-3a. A scribe with northern interests moved the passage from the end of chapter 4 to its present position at 8:30-35, closer to Shechem, specifying the locale as Mount Gerizim; later Judeans in opposition to the Samaritan sanctuary curiously substituted Mount Ebal for Mount Gerizim, since (Jebusite) Jerusalem was not yet a possibility historically. Note that Qumran manuscripts of Judges, Isaiah, Jeremiah, and possibly the Song of Songs all show that the Masoretic text tradition made significant later additions or changes in the developing texts.

The Samuel manuscripts displayed Hebrew fragments which confirmed that many readings in the Septuagint were based on ancient Hebrew readings simply different from the Masoretic Text. 4QSam^{a} also proved to be closer than the Masoretic Text of Samuel to the text used as a major source by the Chronicler.

1QIsa^{a} documented more than 2600 textual variants between it, the Masoretic Text, the Septuagint, and other Isaiah scrolls. 1QIsa^{a} and the Old Greek of Isaiah showed that the Masoretic Text tradition had added nine large isolated insertions, totaling fifteen verses, into the earlier text of Isaiah. 1QIsa^{b} confirmed, as the pentateuchal manuscripts did for the Samaritan Pentateuch, that the medieval Masoretic Text of Isaiah very accurately transmits one of the ancient forms of the book, though the 161 orthographic differences and 183 textual variants between them are more numerous than originally reported.

4QJer[b] and fragment 11 of 4QJer[a] (which contains Jer 10:10, not in 4QJer[b]) exhibit in Hebrew the two variant editions of that book, with 4QJer[b,d] solidifying confidence that the short Old Greek text is a faithful translation of an alternate ancient Hebrew edition.

Finally, Greek manuscripts of Exodus, Leviticus, Numbers, and Deuteronomy attest the presence, albeit minimally, of the Septuagint at Qumran, and attest a date as early as the second century B.C.E., in agreement with Septuagint papyri from Egypt. Though closely allied with the main Greek manuscript tradition, they attest some earlier readings than those previously available, readings that are closer to the original translation than the ones from Vaticanus and Alexandrinus that were chosen for the Göttingen critical editions. They also confirm de Lagarde's approach to the Septuagint, that there was a single original translation (or dominant version) that was based on a Hebrew text and that underlies the general Greek manuscript tradition.

An important point to emphasize is that no sectarian variants have been discovered in the scriptural scrolls. Thus, they are the oldest and most authentic witnesses to the ancient text of the Hebrew Bible.

Corollary Learnings

The "never dreamt of" evidence the scrolls now provide, aided by a revised post-Qumran mindset, makes possible new learnings from the old evidence in the Samaritan Pentateuch and Septuagint as well as earlier assessments of certain scrolls. Viewing the broader pluriformity in the scriptural scrolls, it is now possible to see that "4QReworked Pentateuch" represents genuine expanded forms of the Pentateuch, and 11QPs[a] is a genuine psalter.

With regard to the Samaritan Pentateuch, it appears likely that the Samaritans made very few changes in their Torah; many of their variants against the Masoretic Text are due to their use of a shared Judean-Samarian text like 4QpaleoExod[m] and 4QNum[b], which differed from the "proto-MT." A claim might even be suggested that the Samaritans made *no* changes in their Torah. That is, Mount Gerizim is always viewed positively in the Masoretic Text, and it is unknown who inserted the extra commandment about an altar on Mount Gerizim in Exodus and Deuteronomy. The entire text (except the final מול שכם "opposite Shechem," which could have been added at any time) is a mosaic of verses found also in the Masoretic Text, and thus the commandment could have been included in shared Judean-Samarian Torah manuscripts but was excluded from the final Judean version. As unlikely as that suggestion might be, serious questions have also been raised regarding the variant "has chosen" (Mount Gerizim) versus "will choose" (Jerusalem): Which was the original reading? Was it originally neutral, not sectarian? Which group changed the original to the variant reading, thus producing a sectarian variant (compare the explanation of 4QJosh[a] above)?

Now it can be easily recognized that in Genesis 5 and 11 the Samaritan Pentateuch, the Septuagint, and the Masoretic Text contain three variant editions of the date system, each in a different way revised due to the difficulties occasioned by the lifespans of the pre-diluvian and post-diluvian ancestors.

Moreover, the scrolls demonstrate, just as they attest the fidelity of the textual transmission of the Masoretic Text and the Samaritan Pentateuch, that the Septuagint should be credited as a generally faithful translation of an ancient Hebrew text as valuable as, but often not in agreement with, the Masoretic Text. Importantly, in addition to preserving numerous superior individual variants, it preserves variant editions of a number of books, such as Jeremiah, Ezekiel, and Daniel.

With regard to the Masada scrolls, do they witness the pre-Jewish War dominance of the "proto-MT"? Four of the seven manuscripts are from Genesis, Leviticus, and Deuteronomy. But in contrast to Exodus and Numbers, only one literary edition of each of those books was in circulation in the late Second Temple period. For those books all the various preserved copies mostly agree with each other while exhibiting random minor variants. Thus these scrolls do agree with the Masoretic Text, but three of the four also agree just as exactly with the Samaritan Pentateuch, Qumran scrolls, or the Septuagint. MasGen even appears to have an agreement with Jubilees against the Masoretic Text. To substantiate a meaningful claim for identity of the Masada scrolls specifically with the Masoretic Text would require clear evidence of their combined disagreement against a variant edition, or a series of *Leitfehler* (distinctive errors or secondary variants). No such evidence is forthcoming for the four pentateuchal scrolls.

MasEzek and MasPs^{b}, on the other hand, do share the same editions as the Masoretic collection in contrast to other extant editions. Whereas Greek Pap967 and OL^{W} attest an earlier edition of Ezekiel, MasEzek and the Masoretic Text share a later edition. Six Ezekiel scrolls from Qumran, however, as well as the main Septuagint also contain that later edition. It seems that the edition in Pap967 and OL^{W} from the third or early second century B.C.E. was waning, replaced by the newer edition by the time the Qumran Ezekiel scrolls and MasEzek were copied.

MasPs^{b} and the Masoretic Text of Psalms share the earlier, shorter edition of the Psalter as opposed to the later, expanded edition in 11QPs^{a}. Without discounting the factual evidence of these agreements, it may still be asked how meaningful is this with relation to the Masoretic Text? It does not seem surprising, but rather a fifty-fifty probability, that these two scrolls should exhibit one or another of the editions available at the time.

Finally, the combined evidence of the scriptural scrolls and the way they are used indicates that the canon was not yet formed during the Qumran period, though there is solid evidence that there was a widespread conception of a collection of books — "The Law and the Prophets" (the latter term not fully defined) — and that this collection was viewed as authoritative Scripture with God as its inspiration.

POST-QUMRAN THEORIES

With that synopsis of the evidence provided by the scrolls, and since Chapter 1 ended its review with the "Pre-Qumran Theories of the History of the Text," it remains to see how post-Qumran scholars have reconceived that history as the new data accumulated.

The data from the more than two hundred biblical manuscripts from Qumran and neighboring sites eclipsed and transformed the earlier discussions of the history of the biblical text, since for the first time there was authentic manuscript evidence from the Second Temple period, not just learned speculation. Frank Moore Cross and Patrick W. Skehan published in the mid 1950s major fragments of 4QpaleoExod^{m}, 4QDeut^{q}, and 4QSam^{a,b}, showing startling agreements with the Samaritan Pentateuch and the Septuagint against the Masoretic Text. William Foxwell Albright then sparked resumption of inquiry into the larger issue of textual history. Perhaps influenced by then-current New Testament textual criticism, which charted its textual history according to a theory of Alexandrian, Western, and Caesarean local text traditions, Albright quickly by 1955 sketched a theory of Babylonian, Palestinian, and Egyptian recensions for the Hebrew Bible.[1]

During the following years, Cross greatly elaborated that theory of three local texts types, represented by the Masoretic Text, the Samaritan Pentateuch, and the Septuagint, which he explained as developing slowly during the Second Temple period in Palestine, Egypt, and a third locale, presumably Babylon.[2] He retreated from Albright's view of "recensions," since the developments were not so much according to set principles but were more incremental and unsystematic. He amassed a great number of textual readings to illustrate and support this theory and thus set the standards for serious empirical studies of the issue. For years this theory stood alone and unchallenged, since it was based on a large array of textual readings in the scrolls, the Masoretic Text, the Samaritan Pentateuch, and the Septuagint, and since it offered a persuasive explanation of the textual history.

Shemaryahu Talmon, observing the great amount of variants already in the earliest preserved texts, reinvigorated the classic contrast between the theories of de Lagarde and Kahle. In a sense, de Lagarde's thinking along the lines of a single *Urtext* which had developed in three recensions found a parallel in Cross's theory of an original base text developing into three different forms in three different localities. But instead of a "one-to-three" model, Talmon saw the pattern rather as "many-to-three." That is, in light of the great variation in early texts, he concluded that prior to the surviving manuscript evidence there were a number of forms of the texts; then, at the close of the Second Temple period, three main text forms, and only three, survived out of that earlier plethora. Partly from a sociological point of view, he noted that after the two Jewish revolts, only three groups survived and continued to copy their texts: the rabbinic Jews, the Samaritans, and the Christians; and each preserved the form of the Scriptures that they had inherited. Only those three groups survived, and therefore only those three socio-religious *Gruppentexte* survived, while other forms disappeared with the groups that had held them sacred.[3] Thus, just as Cross somewhat paralleled de Lagarde's thinking, Talmon paralleled Kahle's view of a spectrum of vulgar or popular texts which were eventually supplanted by a single official text (one in each surviving community). Talmon also argued for erasing the established line between "higher criticism" and "lower criticism," because he saw the creative scribe functioning as a "minor partner" in the compositional process simultaneously with the transmission process.[4]

Currently, Emanuel Tov and Eugene Ulrich, both of whom were students of both Cross and Talmon, continue to explore ways of envisioning the history of the biblical text in light of the complete publication of all the biblical scrolls. Tov's wide-ranging and

---

[1] William F. Albright, "New Light on Early Recensions of the Hebrew Bible," *BASOR* 140 (1955): 27–33.

[2] Frank Moore Cross, "The Evolution of a Theory of Local Texts," in *Qumran and the History*, 306–20.

[3] Shemaryahu Talmon, "The Old Testament Text," in *Qumran and the History*, 1–41, esp. 40–41; and "The Textual Study of the Bible—A New Outlook," *Qumran and the History*, 321–400.

[4] Talmon, "The Textual Study of the Bible," 381.

detailed analyses of the Masoretic and Septuagint textual traditions have justifiably achieved the current position as the most comprehensive explanation of the state of the art.[5] He is surely correct both that the Masoretic Text, the Samaritan Pentateuch (except for Exodus and Numbers), and the Septuagint are to be seen as simply texts and not recensions or text types, and that many of the Qumran manuscripts do not show consistent agreement with one or other of those three. Noting the difficulty in charting the patterns of variants in the manuscripts, he has called into question both Albright's use of the term "recension" and the neat text types and text families that Cross and others perceived. He posits that they should be regarded as three *texts* rather than *text types*. To be sure, some manuscripts still merit the term text type, that is, texts that consistently agree with one tradition in contrast to another. Thus, he classifies many Qumran manuscripts according to their alignment with the Masoretic Text, the Samaritan Pentateuch, or the Septuagint. But he suggests that many of the texts are to be classified as "non-aligned," insofar as their patterns of agreement and disagreement shift in their allegiance with respect to the Masoretic Text, the Samaritan Pentateuch, or the Septuagint, as well as displaying unique readings.[6] In addition, Tov maintains the traditional distinction between the period of literary growth of a book and that of its textual transmission as important, with textual criticism pertaining only to the latter.[7]

Ulrich, in agreement with Talmon, sees that line between "higher criticism" and "lower criticism" as vanishing.[8] He interprets many instances provided by the scrolls' new evidence as revised literary editions of a previous form of a book, and thus sees the literary process still at work and frequently overlapping with scribal variants typically treated as part of textual criticism. He perceives the accumulated literary results of source and redaction critics as one with the new manuscript evidence of revised literary editions—together they manifest at early and late stages of the same process the developmental nature of the biblical texts from their shadowy beginnings up to their abrupt arrest due to the two Jewish Revolts and the Christian threat. He envisions the successive revised editions as the deliberate activity of a series of creative scribes or authors. They are the result of traditions being handed on to new generations but creatively updated in light of changing religious, social, or historical developments which called for new, insightful relevance of the traditions. Moreover, he sees the pluriformity exhibited by the Qumran scrolls as consistent with the same fluidity of transmission observed among the different books of the Masoretic Text, the Samaritan Pentateuch, and the Septuagint as well as quotations in rabbinic writings, the New Testament, and early authors such as Josephus. That is, the pluriformity and organic growth, seen in the pattern of successive revised literary editions, are characteristic of the biblical text throughout its history up to the second century C.E. There was no "final form" until the organic development of the texts was halted due to extraneous circumstances.

---

[5] Tov, *Textual Criticism*, and *The Text-Critical Use of the Septuagint in Biblical Research* (2d ed.; Jerusalem: Simor, 1997).

[6] Tov, *Textual Criticism*, 107–9.

[7] Tov, *Textual Criticism*, 2, 167, 324–46.

[8] See now also George J. Brooke, "The Qumran Scrolls and the Demise of the Distinction between Higher and Lower Criticism," in his *Reading the Dead Sea Scrolls: Essays in Method* (SBLEJL 39; Atlanta: SBL, 2013), 1–17.

Current Views and Critique

Cross's theory of local texts was foundational, both because its insightfulness stimulated scholars to start thinking about the old issue in new ways and work toward a gradual solution, and because it established the empirical model of presenting a large amount of significant textual readings, keeping theories responsible to the new manuscript evidence.

The advantages of hindsight, however, as well as the results from the subsequent complete publication of the biblical manuscripts brought to light several assumptions that appear to have been operative behind these theories. One assumption behind the local-text theory apparently was that there was an *Urtext*, originally a single pristine text which had developed into many forms through scribal activity and error. But rather than an *Urtext*, there appears to have been "a series of original texts" as each new edition was produced, or as Tov well described it, "a series of subsequent authoritative texts."[9]

A second assumption appears to have been that the Masoretic Text, the Septuagint, and the Samaritan Pentateuch were text types, as opposed to simply texts, and that all or many of the books in each collection shared the same characteristics. Scholars are now increasingly aware that the Masoretic Text and the Septuagint must be discussed not as a whole but book by book, and that they are not text types but simply more or less accurate copies of some edition or other for each book. Another assumption was that a single locality could tolerate only one single text form. Difficulties with this last assumption eventually weakened the local-text theory as it became more and more clear that at Qumran, a single locality, a wide variety of quite diverse texts and text types existed side-by-side among a strongly Scripture-conscious group, and this situation lasted for about one and a half centuries. Moreover, though it is quite likely that texts developed differently in different localities, an explanation of how different localities specifically affected the development of different text types did not emerge.

Talmon's idea of the survival of three socio-religious *Gruppentexte* is and remains a helpful insight, even though the three do not seem to offer evidence of being denominationally chosen. That is, there are no sectarian variants characteristic of any of the groups,[10] and so there appears to be no causal relationship between the religious group and the collection of texts it inherited. There was no deliberate choice of one textual archetype as opposed to another, but rather each group apparently transmitted whichever form for each book that it happened to have. Again, these were not chosen text types, but simply exemplars of one available edition for each book. In contrast, Talmon's idea of earlier multiple pristine texts is not backed by evidence. Though there is clearly pluriformity in our earliest extant manuscripts, the window of visibility starts only ca. 250 B.C.E., not earlier, and analysis shows that all our texts, despite their variety, can be traced genetically back to a single text tradition earlier than the third century.

Tov's four-fold classification of the scrolls according to (1) Proto-Masoretic, (2) Pre-Samaritan, (3) *Vorlage* of the OG, or (4) non-aligned has a constructive function. At the pedagogical level the categories are quite helpful and offer a clear introductory view,

[9] Tov, *Textual Criticism*, 167; Ulrich, *Scrolls and Origins*, 13.

[10] That is, beyond the Samaritans' focus on Mount Gerizim and the subsequent change to "Mount Ebal" at Deut 27:4 and in Josh 8:30-35 in the MT. Recall that the Samaritans used the non-sectarian expanded edition circulating in general Judaism at the time.

since they quickly provide an easily understandable profile of a specific manuscript.

Noting from an epistemological perspective that one begins assessing new evidence according to previously learned categories, Ulrich agrees that those categories are initially useful, even if anachronistic. Then methodologically, he stresses that categories should eventually be scrutinized and reformulated in the most accurate terminology possible to describe the new data. At the close of the Second Temple period the Masoretic Text, the Samaritan Pentateuch, and the Septuagint were not identifiable text types; their texts for each book are simply copies of one edition or other then currently available. Accordingly, they lose their function as standard categories for classifying the biblical scrolls. Furthermore, because they are not text types or standard texts, neither should they serve as standards against which other texts should be, or not be, "aligned."

Rather, surveying many examples of development in the history of the texts, Ulrich proposes classification of manuscripts primarily according to their successive literary editions, earlier and later (see Table 1).[11] He sees four levels of variation that operate independently of each other in manuscripts: (1) different orthographic or morphological

TABLE 1: *Successive Editions*

Edition	*n + 1*	*n + 2*	*n + 3*	*n + 4*	*n + 5*
Clear evidence for successive editions of books					
Exodus	𝔊 35–40	𝔐	4QExod^{m}	SP	4QPent
Numbers	𝔐 𝔊	4QNum^{b}	4QPent?		
Joshua	4QJosh^{a}	(SP)-LXX-𝔐	(𝔐?)		
Jeremiah	4QJer^{b}-𝔊	4QJer^{a}-𝔐			
Psalms	𝔐-Mas^{b}	11Q^{a}, 11Q^{b}, 4Q^{e}			
Partial evidence for variant editions of a book or section					
Judges	4QJudg^{a}	𝔐/𝔊			
Canticles	4QCant^{a}-4QCant^{b}	𝔐/𝔊			
SP and 𝔊 evidence for variant editions of passages					
Gen 5; 11	𝔐 || 𝔊 || SP				
Exod 35–40	𝔊	𝔐/SP			
1 Sam 17–18	𝔊	𝔐			
Ezek 36–39	P967-OL^{W}	𝔐-𝔊			
Daniel 4–6	𝔐 || 𝔊				
Daniel: Addns	𝔐	𝔊			

[11] An initial attempt at sketching the successive variant editions of biblical books might look like Table 1. In the schema, it is presumed that there was a number "*n*" of earlier editions of the books prior to the first edition preserved. The earliest edition preserved is listed as *n + 1*, the second edition as *n + 2*, the third *n + 3*, etc. For further explanation see Ch. 13.I. For Joshua, it is not proposed that the Samaritans accepted the book, but that, in light of Deut 27:4, they would have considered Joshua's fulfillment of Moses' command to have occurred on Mount Gerizim. For discussion of Canticles manuscripts see Ulrich, "The Text of the Hebrew Scriptures at the Time of Hillel and Jesus," in *Congress Volume Basel 2001* (ed. André Lemaire; VTSup 92. Leiden: Brill, 2002), 85–108, esp. 104–5 and n. 44.

forms, (2) individual textual variants, (3) isolated insertions of whole verses, and (4) variant or successive literary editions of a book. Since most variants encountered can be classified in one or another of the four levels above, he thinks that the history of the text should be charted in its primary lines according to the fourth level: successive editions of each book. While the major lines were developing according to variant editions, smaller lines were bifurcating as traditions developed. Influential leaders or scribes occasionally inserted large isolated comments. Meanwhile the inevitable panoply of familiar minor errors, additions, and alternate forms were affecting all texts in each of the branches. The orthographic practices apparently had no relation to the various editions.

Comparison and critiques of Tov's and Ulrich's theories have begun to emerge.[12] The challenge for the near future will be to sift out the permanently useful insights of the pre-Qumran theories and those of Cross, Talmon, Tov, Ulrich, and scholars to come, to lay to rest the less useful, and to move the quest ineluctably forward toward an increasingly accurate view of the history of the biblical text.

[12] Ronald S. Hendel, "Assessing the Text-Critical Theories of the Hebrew Bible after Qumran," in *The Oxford Handbook of the Dead Sea Scrolls* (ed. Timothy H. Lim and John J. Collins; Oxford: Oxford University Press, 2010), 281–302; André Paul, *La Bible avant la Bible: La grande révélation des manuscrits de la mer Morte* (Paris: Cerf, 2005); Hans Debel, "Rewritten Bible, Variant Literary Editions and Original Text(s): Exploring the Implications of a Pluriform Outlook on the Scriptural Tradition," in *Changes in Scripture: Rewriting and Interpreting Authoritative Traditions in the Second Temple Period* (ed. Hanne von Weissenberg, Juha Pakkala, and Marko Martilla; BZAW 419; Berlin: de Gruyter, 2011), 65–91; VanderKam and Flint, *The Meaning of the Scrolls*, 140–47; Al Wolters, "The Text of the Old Testament," in *The Face of Old Testament Studies: A Survey of Contemporary Approaches* (ed. David W. Baker and Bill T. Arnold; Grand Rapids: Baker, 1999), 31; and Paul D. Wegner, *A Student's Guide to Textual Criticism of the Bible* (Downers Grove, Ill.: IVP Academic Press, 2006), 31, 67, 185. Stephen B. Chapman gives a brief discussion, but mainly in relation to canon, in his thoughtful essay, "How the Biblical Canon Began: Working Models and Open Questions," in *Homer, the Bible, and Beyond: Literary and Religious Canons in the Ancient World* (ed. Margalit Finkelberg and Guy G. Stroumsa; Leiden: Brill, 2003), 29–51, esp. 48–49. See now a judicious critique by David Andrew Teeter, *Scribal Laws: Exegetical Variation in the Textual Transmission of Biblical Law in the Late Second Temple Period* (Tübingen: Mohr Siebeck: 2014), which arrived after this volume was sent to press.

ACKNOWLEDGEMENTS AND PERMISSIONS

I am grateful to these presses for permission to use and synthesize many of my publications in revised form.

BRILL BOOKS

"The Evolutionary Growth of the Pentateuch in the Second Temple Period," in *Pentateuchal Traditions in the Late Second Temple Period: Proceedings of the International Workshop in Tokyo, August 28–31, 2007* (ed. Akio Moriya and Gohei Hata; JSJS 158; Leiden: Brill, 2012), 39–56.

"Crossing the Borders from 'Pre-Scripture' to Scripture (Rewritten) to 'Rewritten Scripture,'" in *Rewritten Bible after Fifty Years: Texts, Terms, or Techniques? A Last Dialogue with Geza Vermes* (ed. József Zsengellér; JSJS 166; Leiden: Brill, 2014), 83–105.

"4QJoshua^a and Joshua's First Altar in the Promised Land," in *New Qumran Texts and Studies: Proceedings of the First Meeting of the International Organization for Qumran Studies, Paris 1992* (ed. George J. Brooke with Florentino García Martínez; STDJ 15; Leiden: Brill, 1994), 89–104 and Pls. 4–6.

"The Old Latin, Mount Gerizim, and 4QJosh^a," in *Textual Criticism and Dead Sea Scrolls Studies in Honour of Julio Trebolle Barrera: Florilegium Complutense* (ed. Andrés Piquer Otero and Pablo Torijano Morales; JSJS 157; Leiden: Brill, 2012), 361–75.

"A Qualitative Assessment of the Textual Profile of 4QSam^a," in *Flores Florentino: Dead Sea Scrolls and Other Early Jewish Studies in Honour of Florentino García Martínez* (ed. Anthony Hilhorst, Émile Puech, and Eibert Tigchelaar; JSJS 122; Leiden: Brill, 2007), 147–61.

"The Palaeo-Hebrew Biblical Manuscripts from Qumran Cave 4," in *Time to Prepare the Way in the Wilderness: Papers on the Qumran Scrolls by Fellows of the Institute for Advanced Studies of the Hebrew University, Jerusalem, 1989–1990* (ed. Devorah Dimant and Lawrence H. Schiffman; STDJ 16; Leiden: Brill, 1995), 103–29.

"The Text of Daniel in the Qumran Scrolls," in *The Book of Daniel: Composition and Reception* (ed. John J. Collins and Peter W. Flint; FIOTL 2,2; VTSup 83,2; Leiden: Brill, 2001), 573–85.

"The Evolutionary Production and Transmission of the Scriptural Books," in *The Dead Sea Scrolls: Transmission of Traditions and Production of Texts* (ed. Sarianna Metso, Hindy Najman, and Eileen Schuller; STDJ 92; Leiden: Brill, 2010), 209–25.

"Two Perspectives on Two Pentateuchal Manuscripts from Masada," in *Emanuel: Studies in Hebew Bible, Septuagint, and Dead Sea Scrolls in Honor of Emanuel Tov* (ed. Shalom M. Paul et al.; VTSup 94; Leiden: Brill, 2003), 453–64.

Sarianna Metso and Eugene Ulrich, "The Old Greek Translation of Leviticus," in *The Book of Leviticus: Composition and Reception* (ed. Rolf Rendtorff and Robert A. Kugler; FIOTL 3; VTSup 93; Leiden: Brill, 2003), 247–68.

"Isaiah for the Hellenistic World: The Old Greek Translator of Isaiah," in *Celebrating the Dead Sea Scrolls: A Canadian Collection* (ed. Peter W. Flint, Jean Duhaime, and Kyung S. Baek; SBLEJL; Atlanta: SBL Press; Leiden: Brill, 2011), 119–33.

"The Parallel Editions of the Old Greek and Masoretic Text of Daniel 5," in *A Teacher for All Generations: Essays in Honor of James C. VanderKam*, vol. 1 (ed. Eric F. Mason, Samuel I. Thomas, Alison Schofield, and Eugene Ulrich; JSJS 153/I; Leiden: Brill, 2012), 201–17.

"Biblical Scrolls Scholarship in North America," in *The Dead Sea Scrolls in Scholarly Perspective: A History of Research* (ed. Devorah Dimant; STDJ 99; Leiden: Brill, 2012), 49–74.

Brill Journals

"The Developmental Composition of the Book of Isaiah: Light from 1QIsa[a] on Additions in the MT," *Dead Sea Discoveries* 8/3 (2001): 288–305.

"From Literature to Scripture: The Growth of a Text's Authoritativeness," *Dead Sea Discoveries* 10 (2003): 3–25.

Eerdmans

"The Jewish Scriptures: Texts, Versions, Canons," *The Eerdmans Dictionary of Early Judaism* (ed. John J. Collins and Daniel C. Harlow; Grand Rapids: Eerdmans, 2010), 97–119.

"Methodological Reflections on Determining Scriptural Status in First Century Judaism," in *Rediscovering the Dead Sea Scrolls: An Assessment of Old and New Approaches and Methods* (ed. Maxine Grossman; Grand Rapids: Eerdmans, 2010), 145–61.

Oxford

Discoveries in the Judaean Desert, vols. 9, 12, 14, 15, 16, 32 (Clarendon Press).

"Septuagint," in *Encyclopedia of the Dead Sea Scrolls* (ed. Lawrence H. Schiffman and James C. VanderKam; 2 vols.; New York: Oxford University Press, 2000), 2:863–68.

Peeters

"Intentional Variant Editions or Sporadic Isolated Insertions in 4QSam[a] and the Masoretic Text?" in *In the Footsteps of Sherlock Holmes: Studies in the Biblical Text in Honour of Anneli Aejmelaeus* (ed. Kristin De Troyer, T. Michael Law, and Marketta Liljeström; Leuven: Peeters, 2014), 623–44.

"David, the Plague, and the Angel: 2 Samuel 24 Revisited," in *After Qumran: Old and Modern Editions of the Biblical Texts — The Historical Books* (ed. Hans Ausloos, Bénédicte Lemmelijn, and Julio Trebolle Barrera; BETL, 246; Leuven: Peeters, 2012), 63–79.

"Qumran and the Canon of the Old Testament," *The Biblical Canons* (ed. J.-M. Auwers and H. J. De Jonge; Colloquium Biblicum Lovaniense; BETL 163; Leuven: Leuven University Press and Peeters, 2003), 57–80.

Society of Biblical Literature

"The Evolutionary Composition of the Hebrew Bible," *Editing the Bible: Assessing the Task Past and Present* (ed. John S. Kloppenborg and Judith H. Newman; SBLRBS 69; Atlanta: SBL, 2012), 23–40.

"Isaiah for the Hellenistic World: The Old Greek Translator of Isaiah," in *Celebrating the Dead Sea Scrolls: A Canadian Collection* (ed. Peter W. Flint, Jean Duhaime, and Kyung S. Baek; SBLETL; Atlanta: SBL Press; Leiden: Brill, 2011), 119–33.

Other Presses and Journals

"The Old Testament Text and Its Transmission," in *The New Cambridge History of the Bible,* Vol. 1: *From the Beginnings to 600* (ed. James Carleton Paget and Joachim Schaper; Cambridge: Cambridge University Press, 2013), 83–104.

"Text, Hebrew, History of," *The New Interpreter's Dictionary of the Bible* (5 vols.; Nashville: Abingdon, 2009), 5:534a–540b.

"The Absence of 'Sectarian Variants' in the Jewish Scriptural Scrolls Found at Qumran," in *The Bible as Book: The Hebrew Bible and the Judaean Desert Discoveries* (ed. Edward D. Herbert and Emanuel Tov; London: The British Library and Oak Knoll Press, 2002), 179–195.

"The Fundamental Importance of the Biblical Qumran Scrolls," in *The Hebrew Bible in Light of the Dead Sea Scrolls* (ed. Nóra Dávid, Armin Lange, Kristin De Troyer, and Shani Tzoreff; FRLANT 239; Göttingen: Vandenhoeck & Ruprecht, 2012), 54–59.

"Deuteronomistically Inspired Scribal Insertions into the Developing Biblical Texts: 4QJudg[a] and 4QJer[a]," in *Houses Full of All Good Things: Essays in Memory of Timo Veijola* (ed. Juha Pakkala and Martti Nissinen; Helsinki: Finnish Exegetical Society; Göttingen: Vandenhoeck & Ruprecht, 2008), 489–506.

"Qumran Witness to the Developmental Growth of the Prophetic Books," in *With Wisdom as a Robe: Qumran and Other Jewish Studies in Honour of Ida Fröhlich* (Hebrew Bible Monographs 21; ed. Károly D. Dobos and Miklós Kószeghy; Sheffield: Sheffield Phoenix Press, 2008), 263–274.

"Origen's Old Testament Text: The Transmission History of the Septuagint to the Third Century C.E.," in *Origen of Alexandria: His World and His Legacy* (ed. C. Kannengiesser and W. L. Petersen; Christianity & Judaism in Antiquity 1; Notre Dame: University of Notre Dame, 1988), 3–33.

"Josephus' Biblical Text for the Books of Samuel," in *Josephus, the Bible, and History* (ed. Louis H. Feldman and Gohei Hata; Detroit: Wayne State University, 1989), 81–96.

"The Notion and Definition of Canon," in *The Canon Debate* (ed. Lee M. McDonald and James A. Sanders; Peabody, Mass.: Hendrickson, 2002), 21–35.

"The Non-attestation of a Tripartite Canon in 4QMMT," *Catholic Biblical Quarterly* 65 (2003): 202–14.

SCRIPTURAL SCROLLS FROM THE JUDAEAN DESERT

[number of book copies, not number of MSS]

Book	Cv 1	2	3	Cave 4	5	6	7	8	11	Q Total	Mas	Mur	Hev	HvSe	SDeir	Arug	X?	TOTAL
Genesis	1	1		18 +2p		1p		1		24	1	1			1		2	29
Exodus	1	3		15 + 2p			1g			21+1g		1					2	24 + 1g
Leviticus	2p	1p		9+2g+1t		1p			1+1p	15+2g+1t	2					1	3+1p	22 + 2g + 1t
Numbers	1p	4		5 + 1g						10+1g		1	1	2				14 + 1g
Deuteron	2	3		24+2p+1g	1	2			1	35+1g	1	1		1			4	42 + 1g
Joshua				2						2							1	3
Judges	1			2						3							1	4
Samuel	1			3						4								4
Kings				1	1	1				3								3
Isaiah	2			18	1					21		1					1	23
Jeremiah		1		5						6							1	7
Ezekiel	1		1	3					1	6	1							7
XII Prop				8	1					9		1	1g					10 + 1g
Psalms	3	1	1	23	1	1		1	5	36	2		1					39
Job		1		2+1p+1t					1t	4+2t								4 + 2t
Proverbs				3		1				4								4
Ruth		2		2						4								4
Canticles				3		1				4								4
Qoheleth				2						2								2
Lament			1	1	2					4								4
Esther										0								0
Daniel	2			5		1				8							3	11
Ezra				1						1								1
Nehemia										0							1	1
Chron				1						1								1
Subtotal	17	17	3	163 +4 g +2t	7	9	1g	2	9 + 1t	227 + 5g + 3t	7	6	2+1g	3	1	1	20	269 + 6g + 3t

INDEX OF ANCIENT SOURCES

HEBREW BIBLE

Genesis 3, 5, 8-9, 26, 39, 42, 70, 109, 125, 155, 160, 164-66, 206, 208-211, 254, 258-60, 262, 285, 290, 297, 305-307, 311

1–11 7, 211, 285, 306
2:17 278
5 5, 203, 205, 226-27, 229, 260n, 310
6–8 101, 108
6:16 267
7:23 226
11 203, 205, 226-27, 229, 260n, 310
12:2-3 288
12:7 58
14:19 3
14:22 3
25:20 230n
27:11 281
30:26-36 188-89
31:10-13 188-89, 218n
43:28 93n
46:7-11 252-53
46:20[LXX] 162
46:27[LXX] 162

Exodus 5, 9, 33, 36, 38-39, 41-42, 45, 70, 98, 109, 125, 141, 155, 161, 164-66, 182, 190n, 203-204, 206-210, 217-28, 221, 225, 256, 258-59, 262, 285, 290, 293n, 296-97, 305-307, 310-311, 313

1–18 290
1:5 161
6:9 32
7:15-18 39
7:18-19 30-31, 39
7:19 32
7:21[8:41 LXX] 30
7:29 32
8:1[8:5 LXX] 32
8:19[8:23 LXX] 30, 32
9:5 30, 32
9:19 30, 32
10:2 32
10:21 284
11:3 32
14:12-21 189
14:12 32
15:1, 21, 22-26 189
18:24-25 32-33
20 58
20:1–21:6 34
20:17[14] 34, 37-38, 173, 205, 222
20:19 34
20:21 34, 181-82
24:1 34
24:7, 12 284
25–31 204, 234
26:35 34
27:19 32
28:4-7 156

28:30 34
29:1 156
29:21 32, 34
29:28 32, 34
30:1-10 32, 34
32:10-11 33, 39
32:10 32
35–40 9, 23, 204, 208, 218, 233-34, 249
39:21 32, 34, 43

Leviticus 5, 26, 39, 42, 70, 155, 165-66, 180n, 190n, 256-60, 262, 286, 290, 296, 305, 307-308, 310-311

1–7 6
1:1-2 211, 286
1:11–6:5[5:24 LXX] 153
1:37-38 286
4:3-9 254
7:38 211
8:8 35
8:22-30 34
8:31-39 256-57
9:1-24 256-57
9:2 255n
10:1-20 256-57
10:1-7 34
11:1-40 256-57
11:16 255n
17:3-9 39
17:4 39-40, 43, 256n
19:16 153
20:17 32
20:19 32-33
20:21 32
23:42-44 190
24:1-2 190
24:1 32
24:9 32
26:2-16 152-53
26:35 32

Numbers 5, 9, 26, 39, 41-42, 70, 98, 141, 155, 165-66, 182, 190n, 203, 221, 256, 258-59, 262, 293n, 305, 307-308, 310-311, 313

3:22 34
3:40–4:16 154-55
4:16 34
6:2 81n
6:24-26 288
10:34-36 93n
20:13 36
20:17-18 192
21:1 36n
21:12-13 36-37, 39
21:20-21 36
24:15-17 181-82
27 209
27:11 192
27:23-28:1 38-39
27:23 36
33:38-41 191
36 209
36:1-2 192

Deuteronomy 32-33, 39, 41-42, 70, 98, 109, 145n, 155, 161, 165-66, 175, 180n, 182, 190n, 203, 211, 217-18, 224n, 258-60, 262, 267n, 276, 285, 290, 304-307, 310-311

1:9-18 32-33
2:8-14 192
2:8 218n
2:9 36-37, 39
2:17-19 36-37, 39

2:24-25 36
3:11 63n, 225n
3:21-22 36, 39
3:24-28 36
5 32, 58
5:21[18 SP] 38, 173, 205, 222
5:24-27[21-24 SP] 32-34
5:28-31 33
5:28-29 181-82
7:3 291
7:15 163
9 33
9:20 32-33, 39
11:4 155
11:26-32 48, 58, 61-64, 173, 220-25
12–28 220, 222-23, 225
12 39n
12:4 37n, 219n
12:5 219-20
12:11 81n
12:15 39
18 32
18:18-22 33
18:18-19 181-82
18:21-22 287, 294
20:21 33
27:2-26 47-65 173-74, 217, 220-25, 309, 314n
28:26 145
29:17 145
31:25-26 52
32 260n
32:1-43 159-60
32:8 162
32:43 162
33:8-11 181-83
33:8 161
33:17-24 257-58, 262
34:2-6 257-58

Joshua 5, 9, 47, 54, 59, 70, 141, 161, 182, 204, 221, 261n, 290, 293n, 297, 307
3–4 288
3:15 163
4 47-48, 50-52, 93n, 204, 309
5 47-48, 51-53, 57, 60, 224
5:13-15 105n
6 48, 50-51, 60
6:10 48n
6:26 61, 183
8:17 61
8:29 48, 53, 59
8:30-35 47-65, 93n, 204, 217, 220-25, 309, 314n
9:1 53, 221n
9:2 47-48, 50, 53, 204
9:3-27 59
9:6 53, 61, 221n
9:27 219
10:15 61
10:43 61
13–21 4
14:6 49
18–22 50
18:1 59, 219n
19:51 219n
21:36-37 136
22 47n, 60
23 50
24 50
24:1 219n
24:25 219n

Judges 4, 9, 67n, 69-70, 85n, 174, 180n, 204, 285n, 307, 309
2–3 69, 174
6:2-6 57, 67-69, 174
6:7-10 43, 67-69
6:11-13 57, 67-69, 174
13:7 81
21:19 225n

1-2 Samuel 9, 25, 59, 70, 73, 85, 90, 99-101, 103, 105-108, 159, 180n, 198, 203-204, 210n, 305, 307, 309

1 Samuel
1–2 54, 73
1 85-92, 94-95, 108
1:1 77n
1:11 81, 106
1:22 81, 106
1:23 76, 174
1:24 76-77, 83-84, 106
2 85, 91-100, 108, 236n, 285n
2:9 82
2:22 82, 84, 98-99, 191, 106
2:24 74, 84, 90
2:29-32 85, 90
3:4-8 88
4:15 82, 106n
10:27–11:1 161
11 85, 100, 108
11:9 72, 76, 83-84, 99, 106
14:41 71, 84, 106n, 136
16:4 79
17–18 85, 101, 108, 204
17:4 76
18:17-18 75
20:24 78
20:27 78
20:29 78
20:30 78, 81n
20:32 79, 89
20:38 74
21:3 78
22:12 87
25:30-32 181
25:36 83

2 Samuel
1:19 283
2:11 106
4:1 77
4:2 77
4:12 77, 162
5:4-5 43, 84, 98, 106
6:2 82, 90n, 106
6:7 83
6:13-15 107
7 305n
7:10-14 70n
7:23 77-78, 162, 259
8:7-8 107
8:7 82, 97, 106
10:6 77-78, 82, 97, 106
13:21 83, 97
13:27 83, 97, 106
14:7–15:15 181
14:7 79
14:23 79
14:25 74
14:27 74
14:30 75, 80
15:1 76
15:2 80
20:6-10 75
20:8 75, 90

21 145
21:16-18 75
22 4, 95, 236n
23:1-7 180, 196, 198
23:9-12 75
24 85, 101-107
24:16 100
24:20 100
1-2 Kings 9, 70, 205-206, 276, 285n, 305, 307
1 Kings 193
2:11 84, 106
5:9-14 [4:29-34 Eng.] 197
8:12-13 93n
8:16 71
8:29 283
8:43 283
13 68, 70, 145
14:25-26 82
20–21 93n
2 Kings 134
18:22 120
19 121
20:1-10 122
23 145
23:10 145
Isaiah 3-4, 41, 99, 109, 128-29, 139, 141, 166, 175, 178, 180n, 198, 204, 211, 229-30, 249, 276, 283, 304-307, 309
1–33 113, 211, 283
1:2, 3, 4, 5, 7, 10 111
1:11 111, 232
1:12, 13, 24 111
1:26-27 232
1:26 111
1:27 231
1:29 112
2 225n
2:2-4 4
2:2, 3 111
2:6-22 117
2:6 231
2:7 111-12
2:8 115
2:9-10 43, 115-16
2:19 111, 116
2:20 115, 232
2:21 116
2:22–4:6 117-18
2:22 43, 97n, 115, 117-19, 231
3:3 112
3:7 111
3:8 231
3:10 111
3:11, 12 112
3:15-16 232
3:15 111
3:17-18 232
3:17 114
3:25 111
4:4 111
4:5-6 114
5:5, 9, 14 111
5:18, 19 112
5:20 111
5:25 163
6:2, 3 114
6:9 111
6:10 111, 231
6:13 111
7:2 111-12

7:15 112
7:20 231
7:22 232
8:1, 2 111
8:3 112
8:7 114
8:8 132
8:9 114
8:10, 13-14 232
8:22-23[9:1] 232
9:10 111
9:11[12] 233
9:16[17] 114
10:3 112
10:5-6 232
10:13 111-12
10:14 112
10:16 111-12
10:17-18 231-2
10:29-30 232
10:32 112
11:3 112
11:4 232
13:3 132
13:4, 12 112
13:16 114
13:19 137
13:20 119
13:22 112
14:6-7 232
14:9, 19, 21 112
14:22 232
14:32 112
15:2 112
15:5, 7 132
16:1, 6-7 232
16:8-9 114
16:11 231
17:11 231
19:3 44
19:6 112
19:7, 8 112, 132
19:13, 15 233
20:1 233
20:4 112
21:16 114
22:1, 5 112
22:15 132, 136
22:17, 24-25 232
23:1-2 233
23:3 232
23:4, 8 112
23:10 231
23:13 233
23:18 232
24:17 283
24:19, 20 132
26:1, 2 137
26:5 114
26:7 112
27:13 93n, 112
28:7 112
28:15 132
28:16 114, 132
28:22 114
29:3 137
29:5 132
29:14 112
29:24 233
30:13 145n
33 125
33:21 112

34–66	113	40:11	44, 112
34:1	232	40:14-16	125-26
34:4	231-32	40:15	44, 112
34:5, 7	138	40:21	111
34:13	112	40:26	127
34:17–35:2	34, 118-19	40:28	112
34:17	232	41:1, 2, 5	231
35:10	112	41:7	132
36–39	211	41:11-12	125-26
36:5	111	41:16-17	232
36:7-8	119-20	41:18	233
36:7	97n, 115	41:19	132
37:4-7	120-21	41:22	176-78
37:10	112	41:26	112
37:12	132	42:10-11	233
37:29	112	42:25	112
37:36-38	121	43:1, 2	132
38:1-8	123	43:6	132, 137
38:12-13	136, 139	43:7	132
38:14	112, 136	43:9	132, 137
38:17	111	43:10	137
38:19	122, 132, 136-37	43:24	138
38:20-22	122-23	43:25, 28	112
38:20	132	44:8	231
39:3, 4	132	44:9-20	148
40–66	211	44:11	231-32
40–55	283	44:18-20	148
40:3-4	119	44:19	233
40:3	109, 200, 232	44:24	132
40:4	78	44:25	132, 136, 175
40:6-8	127, 181, 183-84, 204n	44:26	112, 132
40:6	44	44:27, 28	132
40:7-8	123-24, 154n, 162	45:2	112, 231
40:7	110n, 115, 128, 231	45:3	132
40:9-11	119	45:8	231
40:9	284	45:8, 10	133

45:11 112, 133
45:12 232
45:13 133
45:14 93n
46:1 233
46:4 133
46:6 93n, 112
46:7 133
46:8 131, 133
46:11 137
46:12 133
47:11 112, 133
47:13 112
48:9 231
48:17 133, 136
48:18 133
48:21 133, 232
48:22 129
49:3 136
49:4, 5 133
49:6 136
49:7 133, 136
49:8, 10 133
49:21 111
49:26 112
50:2 112, 231
50:6 231
50:11 112
51:4 133, 136
51:6 127-29, 133
51:7 133
51:9 112
51:11 112, 133
51:20 112
52:2 112
52:8 133
52:9 133, 136
52:11 136
52:12 133
52:13 137
52:14 133
53:3 133, 137
53:4 136
53:5, 7 133
53:8 137
53:9 112
53:10 139
53:11 114, 133, 136, 138, 176, 231
53:12 112, 137
54:2 133
54:3 137
54:4 133
54:5 112, 133, 136
54:15 112
55:1 231
55:3 133
55:4 131, 133
55:5 112, 137, 232
55:7 232
55:8 134, 137
55:10 138
55:12 112
56:2, 4, 5, 7 134
56:8 134, 136
56:10 134
56:11 134, 231
56:12 112, 134
57:2 134, 137
57:13 112
57:15 232
57:18 134
57:19 112

57:20 137
57:21 136
58:2 112, 134
58:3 134, 137
58:4, 5 137
58:6 134
58:7 134, 233
58:8, 9 134
58:10 136
58:11 112, 134, 137
58:12, 13 134
58:14 112, 134, 136
59:2 134, 136-37
59:3 134
59:4 112, 134, 136
59:5, 7 134
59:15 231
59:21 137
60:2 134
60:4 136
60:5 134-37
60:6 135
60:7 136
60:8, 10, 12, 13 135
60:14 136
60:16, 18 135
60:19-20 136, 139
60:21 112, 135, 137, 232
61:1 135-36
62:3 135
62:6 135, 137
62:7 137
62:8 136-37
62:9 135
62:10 137
63:1 112
63:3 126
63:5 135-36
63:6, 7 135
63:19[64:1] 232
65:9 112
65:20 137
65:23-24 131
65:23 112, 135
65:24 135
65:25 112
66:1, 2, 3 135
66:4 135, 137
66:12 135
66:17 137
66:19 112, 137
Jeremiah 6, 9, 26, 41, 85n, 97, 141, 146, 150, 159, 166-67, 196, 203, 249, 261n, 293n, 305-307, 309, 311
7:1 6, 150
7:28–9:2 142
7:30–8:3 43, 70n, 115n, 141-46
9:22–10:21 158
9:22–10:11 146-48
9:22-23 96
10:6-8 43
10:10 310
16:1 150
16:4 145
17:6 145n
19 145
19:7 145
25 159
25:9 150
26 150
27[34 LXX]:1-10 149-50
31:14 138

34:20 145
36:4-26, 32 141
43:10 150
45:1 141
46–51 93n
46:10 138
50:39 119
Ezekiel 9, 196, 211, 235-36, 259-62, 296, 305-307, 311
1–39 211
1:22 261n
14:14, 20 237, 291
28:3 237
35:11–38:14 258-59
36–40 204, 234-36, 249, 258-59
36:23-28 146, 204
40–48 211
The Twelve 9, 41, 157, 166, 300n, 304-307
Hosea 25, 306n
Amos 4-5, 198, 286-87, 293, 296
2:6 286
3:7 286
5:2 286
9:11-15 287n
Micah 306n
4:1-3 4
Nahum 306n
Habakkuk 306
Zephaniah 306n
Malachi 306n
Psalms 2, 5, 9, 41, 109, 175, 179, 198-99, 202-203, 206, 259, 261, 268, 276, 279n, 285n, 287-88, 293n, 296, 300-307, 311
1–89 259
14 95
18 4, 95
29 3
37 288
53 95
68:13 89n
72:20 198
79:2-3 288n
79:2 145
81:2-17 259
81:13 261n
82:1-8 259
83:1-19 259
83:7 78, 162
83:10 145
84:1-13 259
85:1-6 259
89 297
91:16 138n
96:12 160n
104 3
114:3-5 288n
134 180, 198
136 197
140 180, 198
145 179, 197
145:13 179
149 198
149:5 160n
150 198, 259
151 180 , 198
154 196
155 196
Plea for Deliverance 196
Apostrophe to Zion 196, 199
Hymn to the Creator 196, 198
David's Last Words 198
David's Compositions 194-95, 197-98

Job 3, 5, 9, 211, 283, 288-89, 296, 305, 307
1–2 103n
3:1–42:6 288
10:15 138n
12:25 284
44:11 252, 254n
Proverbs 3, 5, 9, 41, 211, 268, 276, 283, 289-90, 294-96, 305-307
1–9 211, 268, 289, 307
1:1 289, 294
2:5-6 289
2:8 95n
4:1-4 289
6:20 289
8:22, 27-30, 35 289
10–31 211, 268, 307
15:8 294
20:4 289
24:9 294
Ruth 5, 89n, 285n, 296, 307
1:11 89n
Song of Songs 2-5, 9, 279, 296, 307, 309
Ecclesiastes/Qoheleth 5, 289-90, 296, 307
12:9-14 290
Lamentations 9, 307
3:15 138
Esther 5, 193, 206, 234, 269, 290, 296, 307
9:18-32 269, 290
Daniel 5, 9, 26, 56n, 158-59, 166, 175, 180, 193, 196, 202, 205-206, 211, 234-37, 247-49, 279, 285, 288, 291-96, 300n, 304-308, 311
1–6 211, 291-93
1 246, 293
1:17 293n
2 246, 285, 293, 296
2:11, 28 293
3 246n, 292-93
3:23-24 248
4–6 205-206, 237, 246-48, 292n
4 236, 285, 296
4:8, 19, 24 293
5–9 249
5 285, 296
5:1-30 237-48
5:7 246n
5:11, 14 293
5:16 246n
5:26 293
5:29 246n
6 292-93
7–12 211, 246, 285, 292-93, 296
7:2-12 211
9 285n
9:4-19 236, 290n
9:12-17 236n
11:34 293
12:2-3 295
12:10 292
Ezra 290-91, 292n, 296-97, 307
6:18 291
7:11 290n
7:14 290
9 285n
10:3 291
Nehemiah 290-91, 307
1:9 38n, 219
7:16 281
8:1-18 291
8:1 290
8:8 7-8

9 285n
9:6-37 290n
10:35[34 Eng.] 43, 190, 210n
1-2 Chronicles 8-9, 47-48n, 74, 105-108, 159, 210n, 304, 306-307, 309
1 Chronicles
11:3-4 84
13:6 82
15:26-28 107
18:7-8 107
18:8 82
19:1 100
19:6-7 82
21 101-107
25:1 268n
2 Chronicles
6:5-6 71
15:8 145

APOCRYPHA, PSEUDEPIGRAPHA
Tobit 5, 296
Ben Sira 5, 8, 211n, 279, 292n, 295-96
Prologue 7-12 201, 302-303
14:16-17 295
17:27-28 295
39:1, 4 294
44:1–50:24 292
45:6-25 282n
50:27 294
51:1-12 198
51:13-30 196, 198
Letter of Jeremiah 156, 166
Additions to Daniel
Prayer of Azariah 206, 236n, 246-47
Song of the Three Jews 206, 236n, 246-47
Susanna 206, 237, 246-47, 293
Bel and the Dragon 206, 237, 246-47, 293
1 Maccabees
2:51-60 293
2:59-60 211n, 292
3:48 282n
4:24 287n
4:41-58 282n
7:17 288n
7:37 283
9:21 283
2 Maccabees
5:23 55
6:2 55
Jubilees 5, 7, 26, 42, 179, 208-10, 212, 262, 279, 285, 294-97, 305, 307-308, 311

DEAD SEA SCROLLS
CD (Damascus Document) 210n, 283, 294-95, 304-306
1QS (Community Rule) 73-74, 99, 109-110, 118-19, 123, 154n, 176, 181, 293n, 300, 304
1QM (War Scroll) 305
1QpHab 306
1QpaleoLev-Num[a] 217n, 256, 262
1QDeut[a] 220-21n
1QDeut[b] 220-21n, 257
1QSam 75-76, 101
1QIsa[a] 9, 18, 43-44, 73n, 93n, 97, 109-129, 131, 136-39, 141, 154n, 161-62, 175-76, 181, 183-84, 204, 229-30
1QIsa[b] 9, 73n, 109, 113, 131-39, 161n, 175-76, 253, 256, 309
1QPs[b] 309

1QDan[a] 248
1QDan[b] 248
1QpPs[a] (1Q16) 288n
1QapGen 208-210, 212
2QExod[b] 197n
2QpaleoLev 256, 262
3QpIsa (3Qp4) 306n
4QGen-Exod[a] 161
4QGen[b] 226n
4QpaleoGen-Exod[l] 125, 217, 262-63
4QExod[b] 161
4QExod[j] 197n
4QpaleoExod[m] 9, 30-39, 41-42, 55-56, 58, 92, 97-99, 129, 179, 196, 203, 205, 208, 217, 221, 225, 262-63, 284, 309-311
4QExod-Lev[f] 33-37, 43, 217-18, 225
4QpapParaExodus gr (4Q127) 157, 166
4QLev-Num[a] 256n
4QLev[c] 254-55, 262
4QLev[d] 39-40, 43
4QLev[g] 197n
4QtgLev 307
4QLXXLev[a] (4Q119) 152-55, 164-65, 307
4QpapLXXLev[b] (4Q120) 153-54, 157, 164-65, 254, 307
4QNum[b] 9, 36-39, 41-42, 55-56, 97-98, 129, 192, 196, 203, 205, 209n, 217-18, 221, 225, 309-310
4QLXXNum (4Q121) 153-55, 157, 307
4QDeut[f] 221n
4QDeut[h] 95n, 161, 182, 257-58, 262
4QDeut[j] 162
4QDeut[k2] 197n
4QDeut[l] 257
4QDeut[q] 9, 159-62, 249n, 260n, 311
4QpaleoDeut[r] 37n, 217, 219n
4QpaleoDeut[s] 217
4QLXXDeut (4Q122) 155, 164, 307
4QPent 27, 56n, 187-94, 208-10
4QPentA (4Q158 *olim* 4QRP[a]) 187-88, 192-94
4QPent B (4Q364 *olim* 4QRP[b]) 187-89, 192-94, 208-210, 212, 217-18, 225
4QPent C (4Q365 *olim* 4QRP[c]) 43, 187-94, 208-10, 212, 217-18, 225
4QPent C (4Q365a *olim* 4QTemple?) 187-88, 190, 192-94
4QPent D (4Q366 *olim* 4QRP[d]) 187-88, 192-94
4QPent E (4Q367 *olim* 4QRP[e]) 187-88, 192-94
4QJosh[a] 9, 47-65, 70, 93n, 169n, 173, 196, 204, 221, 224, 248n, 309-310
4QJosh[b] 161, 163
4QpaleoParaJoshua (4Q123) 58, 217
4QJudg[a] 43, 57, 67-70, 72, 85n, 174, 204
4QSam[a] 9, 43, 54, 59, 70-71, 73-78, 80-86, 88-108, 159-62, 165, 174-75, 191, 203, 210n, 309, 311
4QSam[b] 73-75, 78-81, 159-60, 311
4QSam[c] 73-76, 79-81, 123, 154n, 181
4QKgs 70-72
4QIsa[a] 43
4QIsa[b] 43, 116, 163, 175
4QIsa[c] 136-37
4QIsa[d] 136-38, 176
4QIsa[m] 136-37
4QIsa[n] 136
4QJer[a] 43, 70n, 115n, 141-46, 196, 203, 310

4QJer[b] 9, 43, 69, 85n, 146-49, 151, 158-60, 196, 203, 233-34, 310
4QJer[c] 196, 203
4QJer[d] 9, 85n, 196, 203, 233-34, 310
4QEzek[a] 259n
4QEzek[b] 259n, 261n
4QPs[a] 196
4QPs[b] 196
4QPs[d] 196
4QPs[e] 196, 199, 259
4QPs[k] 196
4QPs[n] 196
4QPs[q] 196
4QpPs[a] (4Q171) 288, 306n
4QpPs[c] (4Q173) 288n, 306n
4QpaleoJob[c] 217
4QtgJob (4Q157) 8, 307
4QRuth[a] 89n
4QDan[a-e] 236, 248
4QUnid gr (4Q126) 157, 166
4Qp Isa[a-e] (4Q161-165) 306n
4QFlorilegium (4Q174) 70n, 292, 306
4QTestimonia (4Q175) 25, 61, 74, 123, 154n
4QWork with a citation of Jubilees (4Q228) 210n, 295
4QPrayer of Nabonidus (4Q242) 236-37, 249
4QPseudo-Daniel[a,b,c] (4Q243-245) 237, 249
4QAramaic Apocryphon (4Q246) 237n
4QHistorical Text A (4Q248) 236-37
4QS[b,d] (Community Rule 4Q256, 258) 118-19, 293n
4QapocrJoshua[b] (4Q379) 25, 61, 181, 183
4QMMT[a-f] (4Q394-99) 70n, 219, 300-304
4QFour Kingdoms[a-c] (4Q552-553a) 237
5QDeut 163
6QpapDan 248
7QpapLXXExod (7Q1) 156, 307
7QpapEpJer (7Q2) 156
7QpapEnoch (7Q4) 156-57, 166
11QpaleoLev[a] 39-40, 43, 217n, 256, 262
11QLev[b] 256, 262
11QPs[a] 27, 42, 70n, 179, 194-99, 203, 260-62, 268n, 285n, 288, 310-311
11QPs[b] 199
11QtgJob (11Q10) 8
11QT[a] (11Q19) 7, 43, 208-10, 212
11QT[b] (11Q20) 190
11QMelch 306
MasGen 252-54, 256, 259-60, 262, 311
MasLev[a] 254-56, 260, 262
MasLev[b] 255-57, 261-62
MasDeut 257-58, 260n, 262
MasEzek 236, 258-62, 311
MasPs[a] 162, 259, 261
MasPs[b] 199n, 259-62, 311
8ḤevXII gr 154, 157-58, 163-64, 307
MurXII 73n
F.Deut2 221

RABBINIC LITERATURE

m. Soṭah 60n, 64-65
m. Yad. 276
Sanh. 271
t. Soṭah 50n, 60n, 64-65
y. Soṭah 50n, 64n
y. Ta'ana 25n

NEW TESTAMENT

Matthew

6:9-13 99, 115n
13:35 288n
24:15 166, 292n

Mark

13:14 292n

Luke

24:44 279n, 288n, 302

Acts

2:29-31 302
4:25-26 288n
7:14 162
13:33-35 288n

Romans

15:10 160

1 Timothy

3:16–4:3 156

Hebrews

1:5-13 288n
1:6 160

Jude **157**

14-16 160

Revelation

16:16 54

OTHER SOURCES

1 Enoch 26, 156, 166, 279, 294, 307-308
Aeschylus 288
Ahikar proverbs 3
Aqhat 237
Aristeas, Letter of 8, 151, 166
Codex Chisianus 235, 248
Demetrius the Chronographer 164
Elephantine Papyri 154n
Euripides 288
Eusebius 63
Gilgamesh 8
Homer, *Iliad, Odyssey* 6, 8, 284, 294
Josephus 9, 48-49, 52, 59-61, 63-65, 76, 78, 80-84, 100, 106-108, 159, 174, 226, 292n
Nash Papyrus 95n
Old Latin Codex Wirceburgensis (OL^{W}) 234, 258n, 262, 311
Old Latin Codex 100 54, 57, 60, 64-65
Origen, *Hexapla* (LXX^{O}) 53, 76, 79, 84
Papyrus 967 9, 56n, 146, 196, 204, 234-36, 248-49, 258-59, 262, 311
Papyrus Fouad 266 153, 164
Papyrus Giessen 53-55, 57-58, 60-62, 64-65, 221
Peshitta 10, 60, 77-80, 93, 179, 276
Phibis 294
Philo 155n
Plato, *Meno* 265, 279
Plato, *Phaedrus* 265, 279
Pseudo-Philo 48-49, 59-60, 63-65, 174
Rylands Papyrus 458 152-53, 155, 164
Sophocles 288
Sumerian "Innocent Sufferer" 3
Syro-Hexapla 55-56, 248
Theognis 294
Virgil, *Aeneid* 4, 284n

INDEX OF AUTHORS

Abegg, Martin, Jr. 13, 73, 113, 301, 305
Aejmelaeus, Anneli 92, 94-102, 106, 108, 152, 161, 182, 204, 234
Albertz, Rainer 246
Albrektson, Bertil 16
Albright, William Foxwell 92, 311-13
Allegro, John 3, 88, 99, 188
Auld, Graeme 102
Auwers, Jean-Marie 13
Baillet, Maurice 58, 156
Baltzer, Klaus 123, 138
Barr, James 275
Barthélemy, Dominique 101, 131, 138, 157-58, 164, 204
Barton, John 277-78
Baumgarten, Albert I. 171
Bearman, Gregory 50
Beckwith, Roger 279
Begg, Christopher 59
Bernstein, Moshe J. 188, 306
Berthelot, Katell 300
Beyer, H. W. 266-67
Blenkinsopp, Joseph 115-117, 119, 129, 138, 225, 278
Bogaert, Pierre-Maurice 106, 146, 233
Bowersock, Glen W. 63
Bratcher, Robert G. 305
Brooke, George 170, 176, 185, 188, 248, 292, 313
Brown, William P. 178
Bruning, Brandon 13, 204, 218, 234
Butler, Trent 47
Campbell, Jonathan G. 300
Carr, David M. 13
Chapman, Stephen B. 315
Charlesworth, James H. 57
Childs, Brevard 117, 122-23, 287, 297
Christophe, Paul 271
Collins, John J. 236, 291-92
Cook, Edward 301, 305
Crawford, Sidnie White 21, 161, 188, 192-94, 208-210, 215
Crenshaw, James L. 20
Cross, Frank Moore 13, 34-35, 47, 54, 59, 71, 73-75, 80, 85, 92, 100-101, 108, 141, 158-59, 161-62, 165, 184, 311-15
Davila, James 30, 160
Davis, Stephan K. 295
Debel, Hans 315
De Troyer, Kristin 49-49
Di Lella, Alexander 292-95, 303
Dillmann, August 226
Dimant, Devorah 92, 157
Dion, Paul E. 102
Dorival, Gilles 13
Driver, Samuel R. 62-63, 101, 220, 258
Duhm, Bernhard 129
Duncan, Julie 161, 257
Eichhorn, Johann G. 274-75
Eichrodt, Walther 267
Eissfeldt, Otto 29, 222, 282

Eshel, Esther 236-37
Fabry, Heinz-Josef 48
Fernández Marcos, Natalio 13, 69
Fields, Weston W. 131
Filson, Floyd V. 235
Finn, A. H. 233
Fishbane, Michael 48
Fitzmyer, Joseph 304
Flint, Peter 13-14, 25, 70, 153, 177-78, 198-99, 236, 261, 304, 315
Fraenkel, Detlef 152, 235
Frankel, Zacharias 12, 216
Freedman, David Noel 39
García Martínez, Florentino 18, 296, 300
Geiger, Abraham 39
Gesenius, Wilhelm 12, 20, 216
Giles, Terry 215
Gooding, David W. 101, 204, 206, 233-34
Goshen-Gottstein, Moshe 12-13, 194, 198-99, 309
Gottwald, Norman 207
Greenspoon, Leonard 47, 153, 164
Grossman, Maxine 15
Guthrie, William K. C. 265
Hackforth, Reginald 265
Haley, Alex 296
Hamidović David 215
Hanhart, Robert 178, 186
Hanson, J. 164
Harding, James E. 165, 175
Harl, Marguerite 13
Harrison, Everett F. 270
Hartman, Louis F. 293
Hatch, Edwin 155
Hawkins, Ralph K. 62
Hendel, Ronald S. 21, 178, 226-27, 260, 315
Hengel, Martin 165
Herbert, Edward D. 13
Hess, Richard S. 69
Hiltunen, Chelica 34
Holladay, William L. 129, 141, 144, 164
Holmes, Samuel 49
Irwin, William A. 235
Jastram, Nathan 36
Jellicoe, Sidney 151, 164, 166
Jonge, H. J. de 13
Joosten, Jan 21, 206, 246
Jull, A. J. Timothy 47
Kahle, Paul E. 12, 56, 166, 170, 312
Kartveit, Magnar 58, 60-62, 173, 215, 222
Kempinski, Aharon 61
Kennicott, Benjamin 12
Klein, Ralph W. 226, 260
Knoppers, Gary N. 23, 38, 47-48, 58, 61-63, 173, 215, 222
Koch, Klaus 292
Kohn, Salomon 12, 216
Kooij, Arie van der 21, 23, 170, 176-77, 283
Kraft, Robert A. 157
Kratz, Reinhard G. 219
Kraus, Hans-Joachim 95, 219, 224
Kugler, Robert 76
Kutscher, Edward Yechezkel 109-110, 113, 128-29, 170
Lagarde, Paul de 12, 166, 310
Lange, Armin 170, 190, 197, 251, 305
Lange, Nicholas de 165
Law, T. Michael 107
LeHeureux, Conrad E. 199
Leiman, Sid Z. 275
Léon-Dufour, Xavier 267
Lewis, Jack P. 29

Lilly, Ingrid E. 235
Lim, Timothy H. 25, 186, 197, 277, 300
Lundblom, Jack R. 141
Lust, Johan 101, 204-205, 234, 246
Machiela, Daniel A. 209-210
Magen, Yizhak 61-62, 215
Mathews, Kenneth A. 39
Mazar, Amihai 61
Mazor, Lea 49
McCarter, P. Kyle 75, 80, 90, 94, 102
McDonald, Lee M. 13, 29, 266, 278
McKane, William 141, 144-46
McKenzie, John 195-96
McKenzie, Steven L. 69
Meer, Michaël van der 49
Menocal, María Rosa 13
Merk, Otto 271
Metso, Sarianna 21, 118-19, 215
Metzger, Bruce 20, 202, 266, 274-77
Milgrom, Jacob 39
Miller, Robert D., II 62
Misgav, H. 215
Montgomery, James 206
Moore, Carey A. 206
Mroczek, Eva 102
Munnich, Olivier 13, 235-37
Muraoka, Takamitsu 155
Murphy, Catherine 141-42
Najman, Hindy 21, 286, 290-91, 295
Nebe, G.-Wilhelm 156
Nelson, Richard 61-62
Neusner, Jacob 271
Newsom, Carol 69, 183
Nickelsburg, George 209
Niehoff, Maren R. 13
Nihan, Christophe 215, 222
Noam, Vered 198
Noeldeke, T. 12
Noja, S. 54
Noort, Ed 47-48, 52-53, 61-64, 221
North, Robert 290
Noth, Martin 62, 207
O'Connell, Kevin G. 164
Olshausen, J. 12
Orlinsky, Harry M. 18
Pace Jeansonne, Sharon 235
Parker, D. C. 55
Parry, Donald W. 73
Parsons, Peter 152, 157
Paul, André 315
Paul, Shalom M. 44, 138
Paton, Lewis B. 206
Person, Raymond E. 13
Peters, Melvin K. H. 165
Pietersma, Albert 154
Pisano, Stephen 102
Pitre, Brant James 182
Popović, Mladen 235
Porton, Bezalel 154
Pritchard, James B. 13
Puech, Émile 21, 57, 106, 156, 300
Pummer, Reinhard 54-55, 215
Qimron, Elisha 300-302
Rabanos, Ricardo 272
Rabin, Chaim 172
Rabinowitz, Isaac 53
Rad, Gerhard von 58, 62, 76, 222, 267
Rahlfs, Alfred 152, 254
Rahner, Karl 270
Rajak, Tessa 13
Redpath, Henry A. 155
Rieder, Joseph 164

Riordan, Joseph 145
Roberts, C. H. 153, 157
Rofé, Alexander 49, 60, 64, 85, 102, 104, 160
Rose, Herbert Jennings 289
Rösel, Martin 178
Rosenmüller, Ernst F. C. 12
Rosenthal, Franz 246
Rossi, Giovanni de 12
Saldarini, Anthony 171
Saley, Richard 73, 80, 100, 108, 165
Sanders, E. P. 22, 24, 171
Sanders, James 12-13, 22, 24, 29, 194, 199, 266, 269, 287
Sanderson, Judith 30, 34, 161, 234, 284
Schenker, Adrian 38, 205, 219, 222
Schiffman, Lawrence H. 13, 22-23, 171, 251
Schorch, Stefan 173, 215, 219-20, 222, 224
Seeligmann, Isac 177
Segal, Michael 188, 193
Seitz, Christopher 123
Sheppard, Gerald 266, 270, 278
Skehan, Patrick 30, 34, 37, 58, 152, 154-55, 161, 194-95, 197-98, 217, 292, 294-95, 303, 311
Smend, Rudolf 271
Smith, Henry Preserved 90
Soisalon-Soininen, Ilmari 234
Solomon, Norman 271
Sommer, J. G. 12
Steinmann, Andrew E. 268, 279
Strugnell, John 160, 188, 190, 300-302
Sukenik, Eleazar 113, 128, 131
Sundberg, Albert C., Jr. 277-79
Stern, Ephraim 61
Sweeney, Marvin A. 117
Swete, Henry B. 155, 216
Talmon, Shemaryahu 13, 15, 22-25, 56, 184, 186, 194, 197, 199, 212, 216, 251-61, 273, 312-15
Teeter, David Andrew 39, 315
Thenius, Otto 85-86
Thomas, D. Winton 176
Tigchelaar, Eibert J. C. 300
Toorn, Karel van der 13
Tov, Emanuel 13-14, 16, 20-21, 23-26, 39, 42-43, 45, 49, 51-56, 62, 91-99, 101, 108-109, 113, 141, 143-44, 146, 152, 154, 157, 159, 161, 164-65, 184-85, 188, 191-94, 204-206, 215, 222, 233-34, 236, 248, 251, 253-54, 256-57, 260-61, 304, 312-15
Towner, W. Sibley 237
Trebolle Barerra, Julio 14, 18, 49, 56-57, 67, 69-71, 101, 106, 192, 206, 256, 275, 299, 305-306
Troxel, Ronald L. 177
Tsedaka, Benyamim 215
Tsfania, L. 215
Turner, Nigel 164
Valle, Pietro della 11, 216
Van Seters, John 25
VanderKam, James 13-14, 25-27, 70, 87, 153, 170, 179, 198, 201, 210, 254, 285, 295-96, 299-300, 304-306, 315
Van-Deventer, H. J. M. 69-70
Vegas Montaner, Luis 59, 192
Veijola, Timo 222, 224
Vorgrimler, Herbert 270
Waddell, William G. 154
Walters, Stanley 85-91, 96, 108
Wegner, Paul D. 315
Weigold, Matthais 170, 305

Weinfeld, Moshe 63, 224-25
Weissenberg, Hanne von 70
Wellhausen, Julius 67, 85-86, 93, 101
Wenthe, Dean O. 237, 292
Wevers, John W. 54-55, 151, 153-55, 164, 233-34, 258
White, Sidnie (*see Crawford*)
Williamson, Hugh G. H. 21
Wise, Michael 301, 305
Wolters, Al 315
Woude, Adam van der 251
Würthwein, Ernst 216
Yadin, Yigael 113, 131, 190, 251-61
Yardeni, Ada 141, 154
Young, Ian 251
Zahn, Molly M. 188-91, 210, 215
Zertal, Adam 61
Ziegler, Joseph 235
Zsengellér, József 173
Zuckerman, Bruce 50, 57
Zuckerman, Kenneth 50, 57

INDEX OF SUBJECTS

4QReworked Pentatuch 26-27, 187-94, 310
Alexandrinus, Codex 152, 310
Aquila 10, 138n, 158, 164-66
Complutensian Polyglot 11, 216
Cairo Geniza 12
Canon, canonical process 17, 25, 27, 157, 265-79, 281, 283-84, 287, 299-308, 309, 311
Covenanters (*see Qumranites*)
Deuteronomistic History 3, 5, 41, 53n, 67-70, 76, 86, 141, 144-45, 173-75, 276, 286-87, 296-97
Divine name 109n, 153-55, 157, 195, 197
Documentary Hypothesis 3, 276, 296-97
Ebal, Mount 47-49, 52-53, 57-65, 173-74, 185, 204, 217-27, 248n, 309, 314n
Editions 3, 9-10, 18, 20, 24, 26, 29, 36, 38-45, 49, 56, 59, 69, 73-74, 85, 92, 94-103, 107-108, 115, 129, 139, 141, 146, 149-50, 158-59, 185, 193, 201-207, 210, 229, 249, 251, 282, 309, 313-15
Essenes (*see Qumranites*)
Frozen text (*see Standard text*)
General Judaism, shared texts 9-10, 15-16, 38, 48-49, 55-56, 58, 109-110, 113, 170-71, 174-76, 179, 218, 283, 305, 314n
Gerizim, Mount 10, 26, 34, 37-38, 47-49, 54, 56-65, 98, 173-74, 185, 204-205, 208, 217-27, 248n, 309-10, 314n
Gilgal 47-49, 53, 59-65, 174, 204, 221-222, 224-25, 248n, 309
Greek recension (LXX^R) 11-12, 92, 103n, 106n, 151-52, 154-55, 157-58, 163-66, 172, 212, 235, 312-13
Gruppentexte 184, 199n, 312, 314
Hesychius 12
Hexapla (LXX^O) 10, 12, 53, 55-56, 76, 79, 98n, 108, 165, 184
Hillel 171
Hodayot 197, 199n, 203
Homer 4, 6, 8, 247, 268
Individual textual variants 39-40, 43-45, 73-81, 113-14, 169-70, 174, 185-86, 229, 315
Inspiration 5-7, 268, 270-74, 279, 284, 289, 296-97, 311
Isolated insertions 40, 42-43, 73-74, 81-85, 92, 97-98, 115-27, 139, 141
Jesus 10, 109, 171
Josephus 18, 23, 25, 202, 249, 313
Kaige 10, 79, 108, 158
Leningradensis, Codex 20
Local-text theory 184, 312, 314
Lucian (LXX^L) 12, 79-80, 93n, 156, 165
Madaba Map 63
Masada 15, 21n, 42n, 251-63
Masoretes 9, 11, 20-21, 43-44, 163
Masoretic Text, MT-group 9-12, 16-26, 29-30, 40-45, 151-52, 160, 163-65, 167, 199n, 253-54, 260-62, 273n, 275-76, 279, 309-15

National literature 3-6, 44, 70, 201, 207-208, 211, 268, 274, 283, 296, 305
Old Greek (OG, G_2) 11, 42, 80-81, 106-108, 151-52, 158, 164-67, 172n, 229-30, 233-37, 309-310
Old Latin (OL) 11, 54, 56-57, 59-61, 65
Orality 2-7, 29, 44-45, 99-100, 115, 146
Origen (Hexapla) 10, 12, 55-56n, 98n, 108, 165, 172n, 184
Original text 1-4, 10-12, 20, 29, 45, 80, 123, 138, 149, 158, 165, 172, 176, 312, 314
Orthography 17, 40, 43-45
Palaeo-Hebrew 38n, 58, 126, 154, 157, 217, 276n, 307
Paris Polyglot 11, 216
Pentateuch 3, 5-6, 8, 23, 29-45, 151, 164
Pesharim 99, 166, 169, 176, 197, 288, 302, 306
Peshitta 10-11, 60, 77-79, 93n, 276
Pharisees 21-23, 60, 171, 185, 248
Pluriformity 1-2, 9, 18, 21, 23-25, 30, 39, 41, 59, 163, 171, 191, 193, 212, 251, 261, 269, 274, 276, 282, 310, 313-14
Priestly source 6, 101, 108, 211, 274, 288
Proto-MT 10, 12, 19, 21, 23, 25n-26, 49n, 93n, 145-46, 158, 167, 171, 251, 253-54, 260-61, 311, 314
Qumranites 23, 37-38, 49n, 123, 128, 169, 171, 178-80, 184-85, 248, 261
Rabbis 9-11, 16n, 20-21, 23, 38, 42, 56n, 64, 139, 151, 163-65, 171-72, 184, 199, 216, 253, 256, 259, 261-62, 276, 288, 295, 312
Rewritten Scripture 169, 201-213
Sadducees 22-23, 171, 185
Samaritan Pentateuch (SP) 9-11, 18, 20-21, 23, 25-26, 29-30, 40-43, 45, 54-56, 97-98, 129, 172-74, 184, 199n, 215-27, 248, 275-76, 309-15
Scripture 2-11, 15-19, 23, 25-27, 41, 44, 58-59, 70, 109, 128, 156-57, 163, 165-66, 169-70, 172, 179, 187-99, 201-212, 216, 248, 261-62, 266-79, 281-97, 299-308, 310
Sectarian variant 16, 23, 25, 37n, 49n, 55, 62, 169-86, 248, 305, 310, 314
Septuagint (LXX) 6, 9-12, 18, 20-27, 29-30, 41, 43, 45, 53-55, 151-52, 158, 160, 163-67, 172, 199n, 248, 275-76, 309-15
Septuaginta Unternehmen 12, 152n, 178
Shechem 50, 53, 58-59, 63, 173, 218-19, 309-10
Sinaiticus, Codex 152
Standard text, standardization 1, 10, 12, 14-15, 18-25, 171, 212, 249, 251, 253, 256, 269, 276n, 315
Successive editions (*see Editions*)
Symmachus 10, 164-66
Synonymous variant 2-3, 78-79
Syro-Hexapla (Syh) 55-56
Targum 8, 10-11, 60, 80, 113, 166, 216, 276
Tetragrammaton (*see Divine name*)
Text type, text family 23-26, 30, 44, 56n, 109-110, 128, 131, 139, 184, 212, 253, 260n, 263, 312-15
Textus receptus 9, 20, 29, 43, 47, 56, 77, 81, 128, 159, 253, 309
Theodotian 10, 56n, 138n, 158, 164-66, 235
Urtext (*see Original text*)
Variant editions (*see Editions*)
Vulgate 11, 216